4. Use a workshop approach. Just as students benefit from varied exercises, they profit from varied approaches to a skill. One way to cover a skill is to work through a chapter page by page, alternating between putting some of the material on the board and explaining or reading some of it aloud. When you get to a practice in a chapter, give students a couple of minutes to do the practice. When a majority of the class has finished the practice, call on someone to read the first question and answer it. If the answer is right, say "Good job," and call on someone else to read the next question. If the answer is wrong, say something like "Does anyone have a different answer?" This can lead to a discussion where you can see if students are catching on, and you can find a way to move them in the right direction.

You should feel confident about having students read a sentence or so out loud. Even if they have limited reading skills, a sentence or two will not cause them undue anxiety or embarrassment. On the other hand, reading an entire paragraph may be too much for some students. It is best to call on volunteers for paragraphs or to read them aloud yourself. Or, if there are time constraints, have students read the paragraph silently and then ask them to read aloud the questions that follow the paragraph.

5. Use a small-group approach at times. When you get to a review test, you may want to divide the class into groups of four and ask them to work together to do the answers for the test. Tell them that when they are done and everyone in the group agrees on the answers, a representative from the group should go to the board and write down the group's answers. Say, "Let's see which group is first to answer all the questions correctly."

Put a grid such as this one on the board:

	1	2	3	4	5
Kim's Group					
Robert's Group					
Nelson's Group					
Nina's Group					

Students will enjoy the competition, and peer pressure will keep everyone attentive and involved. When all of the groups have finished, you and the class can look at the board together to see just where the groups agree and disagree. You can then focus discussion on answers where there is disagreement.

6. Use a pairs approach at times. Having two students work together on questions is another way to energize students and help them teach one another. When an exercise has been completed by the majority of the class, one way to go over the material is to have one student in each pair read a question and the other student read the answer.

7. Use a one-on-one approach at times. If your class is small, have students work on their own on a given chapter, reading the explanations and doing the activities. Call students up to your desk individually to check their answers and to confer on the skill. Make the conference short—five minutes per student is enough time. Students really benefit from the individualized, personal contact.

8. Evaluate frequently. Students have been conditioned to work hard on tests. Take advantage of this conditioning by giving a lot of tests. The mastery tests in Part One and the combined-skills tests in Part Three will give students a chance to see that they are learning the material and will show them that they are capable of success. The tests are also clear signals to students who are not learning the skills. Note that there are eighty of these tests in the book as well as twenty-two more tests available online.

When you grade a test, try to include some praise or encouragement for each student. A personal comment such as "Good job, Elena" or "Well done, Hakim" can do wonders for a student's self-esteem.

9. For variety, make some tests count and some not. When it is time to do a test, have students put their names on it and tell them that you may or may not count the test. The fact that you may count the test will ensure that students give their full effort. At times, don't collect the test, but simply go over it in class. Doing so will help to provide immediate feedback to students. Afterward, you can give another mastery test that will count as a grade.

When tests do count, have students exchange papers. The best way to do this is to collect the papers and distribute them to students in other parts of the room. (Some students resist marking an answer as wrong on a paper that belongs to the person sitting right next to them.) Have class members read and answer the questions as well as grade the papers.

10. Require some writing at the end of each class. To help students integrate what they have learned in a given class, have them do a writing assignment in the last part of the class. One good summarizing activity is to have students write a "Dear _____" letter to a missing classmate, telling him or her what was learned in the class that day. Have students give you the letters before they leave, and explain you will read the letters and then pass them on to the missing student.

Another exercise is to have students write about a reading selection discussed in class. Pages 588–600 contain two writing assignments for each of the twenty readings in the book. Ask students to choose one of the two and to turn in a paper to you before they leave. In some cases, you may want to make the paper an overnight assignment instead.

These activities will help make your classroom lively and will turn learning into an active process. I think you will find them rewarding, and I encourage you to try them out. I wish you luck!

John Langan

— FIFTH EDITION —

TEN STEPS
to
BUILDING
COLLEGE
READING SKILLS

John Langan

ATLANTIC CAPE COMMUNITY COLLEGE

INSTRUCTOR'S EDITION

Books in the Townsend Press Reading Series:

Groundwork for College Reading with Phonics
Groundwork for College Reading
Ten Steps to Building College Reading Skills
Ten Steps to Improving College Reading Skills
Ten Steps to Advancing College Reading Skills
Ten Steps to Advanced Reading

Books in the Townsend Press Vocabulary Series:

Vocabulary Basics
Groundwork for a Better Vocabulary
Building Vocabulary Skills
Building Vocabulary Skills, Short Version
Improving Vocabulary Skills
Improving Vocabulary Skills, Short Version
Advancing Vocabulary Skills
Advancing Vocabulary Skills, Short Version
Advanced Word Power

Supplements Available for Most Books:

Instructor's Edition
Instructor's Manual and Test Bank
Online Exercises
PowerPoint Slides

Copyright © 2011 by Townsend Press, Inc.
Printed in the United States of America
9 8 7 6 5 4 3 2 1

ISBN-13 (Student Edition): 978-1-59194-243-6
ISBN-10 (Student Edition): 1-59194-243-8
ISBN-13 (Instructor's Edition): 978-1-59194-244-3
ISBN-10 (Instructor's Edition): 1-59194-244-6

Send book orders and requests for desk copies or supplements to:

Townsend Press Book Center
439 Kelley Drive
West Berlin, New Jersey 08091

For even faster service, contact us in any of the following ways:

By telephone: 1-800-772-6410
By fax: 1-800-225-8894
By e-mail: cs@townsendpress.com
Through our website: www.townsendpress.com

Contents

Part Two

Part Three

Appendixes

Preface: To the Instructor

We all know that many students entering college today do not have the reading skills needed to do effective work in their courses. A related problem, apparent even in class discussions, is that students often lack the skills required to think in a clear and logical way.

The purpose of *Ten Steps to Building College Reading Skills, Fifth Edition*, is to develop effective reading and clear thinking. To do so, **Part One** presents a sequence of reading skills that are widely recognized as essential for sound comprehension:

- Knowing how to use the dictionary
- Understanding vocabulary in context
- Recognizing main ideas
- Identifying supporting details
- Locating main ideas in different parts of a passage
- Understanding relationships that involve addition and time
- Understanding relationships that involve examples, comparison and/or contrast, and cause and effect
- Making inferences
- Determining implied main ideas
- Evaluating arguments

In every chapter in Part One, the key aspects of a skill are explained and illustrated clearly and simply. Explanations are accompanied by a series of practices, and each chapter ends with four review tests. The last review test consists of a reading selection so that students can apply the skill just learned to real-world reading materials, including newspaper and magazine articles and textbook selections. Together, the ten chapters provide students with the skills needed for a solid understanding of reading materials.

Following each chapter in Part One are **at least six mastery tests for the skill in question.** The tests progress in difficulty, giving students the additional practice and challenge they may need to learn a skill. While designed for quick grading, the tests also require students to think carefully before answering each question.

Part Two is made up of ten additional readings that will improve both reading and thinking skills. Each reading is followed by *Vocabulary Questions* and *Reading Comprehension Questions* so that students can practice all of the skills presented in Part One. In addition, an *Outlining, Mapping,* or *Summarizing* activity after each reading helps students think carefully about the basic content and organization of a selection. *Discussion Questions* then afford instructors one more opportunity to engage students in a variety of reading and thinking skills and to deepen their understanding of a selection.

Part Three consists of a section on active reading followed by eighteen combined-skills tests. The tests provide a review of the skills in Part One and help prepare students for the standardized reading exam that is often a requirement at the end of a semester.

Finally, the **Appendixes** contain new chapters on separating fact from opinion and identifying an author's purpose and tone, writing assignments for all twenty readings in the text, and a limited answer key.

Important Features of the Book

- **Focus on the basics.** The book seeks to explain, in an extremely clear, step-by-step way, the essential elements of each skill. Many examples are provided to ensure that students understand each point. In general, the focus is on teaching the skills—not just on explaining or testing them.

- **Frequent practice and feedback.** Because abundant practice and careful feedback are essential to learning, this book includes numerous activities. Students can get immediate feedback on the practice exercises in Part One by turning to the limited answer key at the back of the book. The answers to the review and mastery tests in Part One, the reading questions in Part Two, and the combined-skills tests in Part Three are in the *Instructor's Manual.*

The limited answer key increases the active role that students take in their own learning. They are likely to use the answer key in an honest and positive way if they know they will be tested on the many activities and selections for which answers are not provided. (Answers not in the book can be easily copied from the *Instructor's Edition* or the *Instructor's Manual* and passed out at the teacher's discretion.)

● **High interest level.** Dull and unvaried readings and exercises work against learning. Students need to experience genuine interest and enjoyment in what they read. Teachers as well should be able to take pleasure in the selections, for their own good feeling about them can carry over favorably into class work. The readings in the book, then, have been chosen not only for the appropriateness of their reading level but also for their compelling content. They should engage teachers and students alike.

● **Ease of use.** The logical sequence in each chapter—from explanation to example to practice to review test to mastery test—helps make the skills easy to teach. The book's organization into distinct parts also makes for ease of use. Within a single class, for instance, teachers can work on a new skill in Part One, review other skills with one or more mastery tests, and provide variety by having students read one of the selections in Part Two. The limited answer key at the back of the text also makes for versatility: it means that the teacher can assign some chapters for self-teaching. Finally, the mastery tests—each on its own tear-out page—and the combined-skills tests make it a simple matter for teachers to test and evaluate student progress.

● **Integration of skills.** Students do more than learn the skills individually in Part One. They also learn to apply the skills together through the reading selections in Parts One and Two and the material on active reading in Part Three. They become effective readers and thinkers by means of a good deal of practice in applying a combination of skills.

● **Online exercises.** As they complete each of the ten chapters, students are invited to go online to the Townsend Press website to work on two additional practice exercises for each skill—exercises that reinforce the skill taught in the chapter.

● **Thinking activities.** Thinking activities—in the form of outlining, mapping, and summarizing—are a distinctive feature of the book. While educators agree that such organizational abilities are important, these skills are all too seldom taught. From a practical standpoint, it is almost impossible for a teacher to respond in detail to entire collections of class outlines or maps. This book then, presents activities that truly involve students in outlining, mapping, and summarizing—in other words, that truly make students *think*—and yet enable a teacher to give feedback. Again, it is through continued practice *and* feedback on challenging material that a student becomes a more effective reader and thinker.

In addition, the final chapter in Part One, "The Basics of Argument," provides extensive explanation and practice in the concepts of point and support that are central to critical thinking.

● **Supplementary materials.**

Print Supplements

The two helpful supplements listed below are available at no charge to instructors using the text. Any or all can be obtained quickly by writing or calling Townsend Press (439 Kelley Drive, West Berlin, NJ 08091; 1-800-772-6410), by sending a fax to 1-800-225-8894, or by e-mailing Customer Service at cs@townsendpress.com.

1 An *Instructor's Edition*—chances are that you are holding it in your hand—is identical to the student book except that it also provides hints for teachers (see the front of the book), answers to all the practices and tests, and comments on most answers. *No other book on the market has such detailed and helpful annotations.*

2 A combined *Instructor's Manual and Test Bank* includes suggestions for teaching the course, a model syllabus, and readability levels for the text and the reading selections; as well as a complete answer key and a series of three short textbook selections that instructors can use to give students practice in taking notes. The test bank contains **four** additional mastery tests for each of the ten skills and **four** additional combined-skills tests—all on letter-sized sheets so they can be copied easily for use with students.

Online Supplements

Three online supplements are available through the TP website by going to the "Supplements" area for instructors at www.townsendpress.com.

1 PowerPoint presentations.

2 Online exercises.

3 Blackboard cartridges.

- **One of a sequence of books.** This text is the third in a series of six books.

    Groundwork for College Reading with Phonics and *Groundwork for College Reading* are the basic texts in the series. They are suitable for ESL students and basic adult learners.

    Ten Steps to Building College Reading Skills is often the choice for a first college reading course.

    Ten Steps to Improving College Reading Skills is an intermediate text appropriate for the core developmental reading course offered at most colleges.

    Ten Steps to Advancing College Reading Skills is a higher-level developmental text than the *Improving* book. It can be used as the core text for a more advanced class, as a sequel to the intermediate book, or as a second-semester alternative to it.

    Finally, *Ten Steps to Advanced Reading* is the most advanced text in the series. It can also be used as a sequel (or a second-semester alternative) to either the *Improving* or the *Advancing* text.

    A companion set of vocabulary books, listed on the copyright page, has been designed to go with the *Ten Steps* books. Recommended to accompany this book is *Building Vocabulary Skills* (300 words and word parts) or *Building Vocabulary Skills, Short Version* (200 words).

    Together, the books and all their supplements form a sequence that should be ideal for any college reading program.

    To summarize, *Ten Steps to Building College Reading Skills, Fifth Edition,* provides ten key reading skills to help developmental college students become independent readers and thinkers. Through an appealing collection of readings and a carefully designed series of activities and tests, students receive extensive guided practice in the skills. The result is an integrated approach to learning that will, by the end of a course, produce better readers and stronger thinkers.

Changes in the Fifth Edition

Following are changes in this edition of the book:

- **A full-color design.** Color has been carefully used throughout, not as window dressing but to add clarity and readability to the different parts of the book.

- **Numerous cartoons and other graphics.** Because so many students today are visual learners, over fifty illustrations have been added to help introduce or reinforce points made in the book.

- **New sections on fact–opinion and purpose–tone.** Located in the Appendixes, these chapters explain skills now included in the basic developmental reading courses at many colleges. Additional practice materials and tests are available at the Online Learning Center.

● **Many new models and practice materials and five new readings.** For example, the popular combined-skills tests in the previous edition have been expanded now to eighteen passages. The five new readings include a true story of how one couple adopted its newest pet, essays explaining the importance of touching and eye contact in human relationships, and a moving account of a young woman's discovery, at age 15, that life is not fair.

Acknowledgments

I am grateful for the many helpful suggestions provided by the following reviewers: Barbara A. Cartwright, Bunker Hill Community College; Ronald Covil, Burlington County Community College; Nancy Deutsch, Cypress College; Mary Ellmann, Long Beach City College; Nora R. Garza, Laredo Community College; Allan Hill, West Chester University; Iris Hill, Wake Technical Community College; Judith B. Isonhood, Hinds Community College; Karen Johnsen, Salt Lake Community College; William McNeill, Robeson Community College; Spencer Olesen, Mountain View College; Therese Parr, Essex Community College; Betty Patton, Eastern New Mexico University; Patricia L. Rottmund, Harrisburg Area Community College; Diane Schellack, Burlington County College; Carol G. Shier, Fullerton College; Julie Z. Uslan, Santa Monica College; and Phyllis West, El Camino College. For this new edition, instructive reviews were provided by Pam Franke, Blinn College; Sherry Lindquist, Northland Community and Technical College; Barbara Nixon, Salem Community College; Betty Payne, Montgomery College; Florinda Rodriguez, South Texas College; Michael Vensel, Miami Dade College; and, in particular, Joanne Nelson, Hillsborough Community College.

At Townsend Press, I thank Kathryn Bernstein, Bill Blauvelt, Denton Cairnes, Beth Johnson, and Ruth A. Rouff for the help they provided along the way. And I owe special thanks to two TP editors who brought their exceptional talents to this revision. Barbara Solot is responsible for a layout and full-color text design that are as clear as they are inviting. The result of her artistry is a strikingly attractive book that both students and teachers will appreciate. Janet Goldstein has provided design input along with her usual superb editorial skills. Her insights, coupled with her many years of classroom teaching, have strengthened the clarity and pedagogy of the book.

It is always a special pleasure to work with people who aspire toward excellence. With help from my colleagues in the teaching profession and at Townsend Press, I have been able to create a much better book than I could have managed on my own.

John Langan

Introduction

1 Getting Off to a Strong Start

Hello, and welcome to this book. You're going to be using the book to learn reading skills that will help in your courses and on tests. But in addition to the reading skills, there are three other essentials to your success: your attitude about learning, your use of study skills, and your involvement with reading. Each will be discussed in turn.

Your Attitude about Learning

Several years ago, my wife and I were vacationing in New Mexico. As we drove into one small town, we suddenly came upon a huge billboard. I was so struck by what it said that I stopped our car and wrote down the words.

> **If you never have a dream,**
>
> **you'll never have a**
> **dream come *true*.**

I think your starting point must be a dream inside you—a belief and resolve in your heart that you will use this book as a step on your road to success. If you don't have the right attitude, you might as well throw this book in the trash.

I'm not kidding. Some students are just pretenders: they talk the talk, but they're not ready to walk the walk. This book will help you "walk the walk"; it will help you master the basic reading and thinking skills you need to succeed. But you must first have a dream and a resolve inside you.

Respecting Yourself

Consider this basic truth about human nature: **we all want to respect ourselves.** We all want to live our lives in such a way that we think well of our behavior and others think well of us. We do not want to be disrespected or seen as bad people. An equally basic truth is that the only way we can get respect is to earn it. At a certain point in growing up, we realize that life doesn't give us something for nothing. What is important and meaningful is what we earn through trying hard and working hard.

- Take a minute to think about the following question: Imagine two people. One person has drifted unhappily through life, putting in a minimal effort at a series of jobs and maybe even at times living off others. One morning the telephone rings and someone says to this person, "Congratulations. You have just won a million dollars in the state lottery." The other person works hard and eventually earns a million dollars; that person is well regarded by others and has a strong sense of accomplishment and self-worth. Which person would you rather be— the one who *won* a million dollars or the one who *earned* a million dollars?

Chances are you would choose to be the person who worked hard, overcame obstacles, and achieved success. If you relate to that person, your attitude may be something like this: "I want to respect myself and have others respect me. To get this respect, I'm going to work hard to succeed. At this stage in my life, that means doing well in school because education is clearly a key to success." And if you've made mistakes in the past (and many of us have), your attitude should be: "I can change my behavior. I'm going to learn to work hard so I can get somewhere and be someone."

Doing the Work

You need to believe in the saying, "No pain, no gain." The only way to get self-respect and success is to work for them. When I was teaching full-time, I found that among the two hundred or so students I met each year, there was no way of telling at first which students had this attitude and which did not. Some time had to pass for people to reveal their attitude by what they did or did not do. What happened was that, as the semester unfolded and classes had to be attended and work had to be done, some people took on the work and persisted even if they hit all kinds of snags and problems. Others didn't take on the work or didn't persist when things got rough. It became clear which students had determined inside themselves, "I will do the work," and which had not.

The heart of the matter is not the *speed* at which a person learns; the heart of the matter is his or her determination—"I *will* learn." I have seen people who had this quality of determination or persistence do poorly in a course (often because of out-of-class problems or events), come back and repeat it, and finally succeed.

Through knowing such determined people, I've come to feel that the single most important factor for school survival and success is an inner commitment to doing the work. When the crunch comes—and the crunch is the plain hard work that school requires—the person with the commitment meets it head-on; the person without the commitment avoids it in a hundred different ways.

● If you have not yet taken charge of your life, the above paragraphs are the most important ones in the book for you. On the following scale of *Passive* to *Determined*, where would you rate yourself?

● Take several minutes to think about, or to discuss with others, why you rated yourself as you did. What are some of your strengths? What are some of the personal challenges you must overcome?

Key Study Skills

While it's not the purpose of this book to teach study skills, I do want to give you four important tips that can make you a better student. The tips are based on my thirty years of experience working with first-year college students and teaching both reading and study skills.

 TIP 1:   Take Lots of Notes in Class

The most important steps you can take to succeed in school are to go to every class and take a lot of notes. If you don't go to class, or you go but just sit there without taking notes, chances are you're heading for a heap of trouble. The most important steps you can take to succeed in school are to go to every class and take a lot of notes. If you don't go to class, or you go but just sit there without taking notes, chances are you're heading for a heap of trouble.

Yes—I have deliberately repeated the above sentences. That's how essential the steps are. If I had only thirty seconds to speak to a student and offer advice, the above is the advice I would give.

I have interviewed hundreds of today's students who have said the same thing. Let me quote just two of them:

Ryan: "Attendance is as important as studying itself. So is taking notes. I take notes even in classes where they say you don't have to take notes. It's very easy to forget material otherwise."

Jhoselyn: "You definitely have to take a lot of notes. When the teacher is talking and you're just listening, everything is very clear. But you're just not going to remember it all. You have to get it down on paper."

● You may not realize just how quickly new information can be forgotten. For example, how much class material do you think most people forget in just two weeks? Check (✓) the answer you think is correct.

_____   20 percent is forgotten within two weeks

_____   40 percent is forgotten within two weeks

_____   60 percent is forgotten within two weeks

✓   80 percent is forgotten within two weeks

The truth is that within two weeks most people forget almost 80% of what they have heard! Given that fact, you need to get to class and take notes!

 TIP 2:   Know Which Comes First—the Textbook or the Instructor

Let me ask you a question: Which is more important—learning how to read a textbook or learning how to read your instructor? Write your answer here:

Learning how to read your instructor.

You may be surprised at the answer: What is far more important is *learning how to read your instructor*—to understand what he or she expects you to learn in the course.

I remember becoming a good student in college only after I learned the truth of this statement. And I have interviewed hundreds of students over the years who have said the same thing. Let me quote just one of them:

> "You absolutely have to be in class. Then you learn how to read the teacher and to know what he or she is going to want on tests. You could read an entire textbook, but that wouldn't be as good as being in class and writing down a teacher's understanding of ideas."

 ## TIP 3:   Have a Textbook Study Method

When I first began to teach study skills, I visited my students' classes to get a good sense of what skills they really needed. I was not too surprised to find out that very often students did not have to read their textbooks to do well on tests. I had had the same experience in school: If I took good notes in class, I seldom had to read or study the textbook. The bottom line is that teachers will test you on the ideas they feel are most important—and most of the time those are the ideas they cover in class.

For those times when you do have to read and learn a textbook chapter, do the following.

1   First, read the first and last few paragraphs of the chapter; they may give you a good overview of what the chapter is about.

2   Second, as you read the chapter, look for and mark off definitions of key terms and examples of those definitions. You'll learn about definition and examples in "Relationships II" (pages 261–294) of this book.

3   Third, as you read the chapter, number major lists of items. If there is a series of points and you number the points 1, 2, 3, and so on, it will be easier to understand and remember them. You'll learn about numbering lists of items in "Supporting Details" (pages 155–178) and "Relationships I" (pages 221–248) of this book.

4   Fourth, after you've read the chapter, take notes on the most important material, and test yourself on those notes until you can say them to yourself without looking at them.

TIP TIP 4: Organize Your Time   *Answers will vary.*

Are you an organized person? Answer these questions:

● Do you get out of bed on time, and do you get to places on time?

___ Yes   ___ No

● Do you have any trouble keeping up with schoolwork?

___ Yes   ___ No

● Do you allow enough time to study for tests and write papers?

___ Yes   ___ No

If you are not an organized person, you're going to have trouble in school. Here are three steps to take to control your time:

1   First, pay close attention to the course outline, or **syllabus**, that your instructors will probably pass out at the start of a semester. Chances are that syllabus will give you the dates of exams and tell you when papers or reports are due.

2   Second, move all those dates onto a **large monthly calendar**—a calendar that has a good-sized block of white space for each date. Hang the calendar in a place where you'll be sure to see it every day—perhaps above your desk or on a bedroom wall.

OCTOBER

Sun	Mon	Tues	Wed	Thurs	Fri	Sat
			1	2	3	4
5	6 English paper	7	8	9 Math test	10	11
12	13	14	15 History test	16	17	18
19	20	21 Math test	22	23	24	25
26	27	28	29	30 Speech report	31	

3   Third, buy a small notebook and write down every day a **"to do" list** of things that need to get done that day. Decide which items are most important and focus on them first. (If you have classes that day, going to those classes will be "A" priority items. Other items may be a "B" or a "C" in importance.) Carry your list with you during the day, referring to it every so often and checking off items as you complete them.

● Look over the following "to do" list for one day. Label each of the items *A, B,* or *C* depending on what seems to be its level of importance.

Answers will vary.

> To Do – Monday
> 1. Go to History and English class.
> 2. Study for math test tomorrow.
> 3. Cash check at bank.
> 4. Meet Ben for lunch.
> 5. Check e-mail.
> 6. Pick up drinks and snacks for later.

● Finally, answer these questions:

1. Of the three steps for organizing time, which is the most important one for you, and why?

Answers will vary.

_____

_____

2. Which step is the second most important for you, and why?

_____

_____

Your Involvement with Reading

I can make my point here by asking you two questions:

1. What is the best way to learn how to become a good driver?

_____   A. Study the driver's manual.

_____   B. Take a lecture class on how to drive a car.

_____   C. Watch films of good drivers.

_____   D. Sit in the passenger's seat with a good driver.

✓   E. Drive the car.

You know the answer. The best way to learn how to be a good driver is to *drive the car*. In other words, the way to become good at a skill is to practice the skill.

2. What, then, is the best way to become a better reader?

    Based on question 1, you can probably guess. Write your answer here:

    <u>Do a lot of reading.</u>

The best way to become a better reader is to do a lot of reading. In this book, you will do a fair amount of reading at the same time you learn and practice key reading skills. All the reading and practice are sure to make you a better reader.

At the same time, I strongly recommend that you not limit your reading to what is in this book. I know from my many years of working with students that you should **read even more**. It's like becoming a better driver: the more you drive, the better you become. The more you read, the better you become.

My Own Experience

In my experience, a lot of students come to college without having done much reading in their lives. I was lucky. Up until the end of my sophomore year in high school, I was not a reader. If I had to do a book report, I got a plot summary and slipped by. Then one idle summer day I saw a sign on a bus that said, "Open your mind. Read a book." I decided to read a book just to disprove the sign. I resented the suggestion that my mind was closed just because I did not read.

But here's what happened: When I read a book—*The Swiss Family Robinson,* about a family stranded on an island and having to survive until rescuers arrived—I knew in my bones that there was both pleasure and power in reading. I sensed that the more I read, the better off I would be, so I began to read a lot. I became an active learner, and it made all the difference. It is why I am now here writing to you.

A Question, and a Challenge

But enough about me. Let's get back to you.   *Answers will vary.*

● How many books would you guess you have read in your life? _____

I have had many students say they have never read a single book from cover to cover in their lives. At most they read a book or two in school, but their memories of such books are seldom pleasant ones. They often describe that reading as a kind of forced death march—a chapter at a time with lots of worksheets and quizzes. Such experiences are not true reading experiences.

A true reading experience would be to read an appealing story from cover to cover. To find a good story, you may want to do one of the following:

● Take advantage of the special offer on page 12 of this book.

● Or you may want to get book suggestions from friends, family, or your instructor.

The important thing is that you give yourself a chance to develop a reading habit— for all the reasons shown below.

● Are you willing to take on this challenge: To read at least one outside book at the same time you are using this textbook?

___ Yes   ___ No   ___ Maybe

The Heart of the Matter: Regular Reading

Many people (and I am one of them) believe that regular reading is the very heart of education. Here is what they say:

1   **Reading provides language power.** Research has shown *beyond any question* that frequent reading improves vocabulary, spelling, and reading speed and comprehension, as well as grammar and writing style. If you become a regular reader, all of these language and thinking abilities develop almost automatically!

2   **Reading increases job power.** In today's world more than ever before, jobs involve the processing of information, with words being the tools of the trade. Studies have found that the better your command of words, the more success you are likely to have. *Nothing will give you a command of words like regular reading.*

3   **Reading creates human power.** Reading enlarges the mind and the heart. It frees us from the narrow confines of our own experience. Knowing how other people view important matters helps us decide what we ourselves think and feel. Reading also helps us connect with others and realize our shared humanity. Someone once wrote, "We read in order to know that we are not alone." We become less isolated as we share the common experiences, emotions, and thoughts that make us human. We grow more sympathetic and understanding because we realize that others are like us.

To the Instructor: If you have adopted *Ten Steps to Building College Reading Skills*, you are entitled to one free Townsend Library book for each student in your class. Details and guidelines for this special offer are described on the Townsend Press website: **www.townsendpress.com**.

Regular reading can, in short, change your life. It can open the door to a lifetime of pleasure as well as learning. But you must be the one to decide whether to walk through that door.

A Special Offer

To promote your reading growth, Townsend Press will send you three books at no charge except for postage and handling. Here are the three books:

Reading Changed My Life!   Letters My Mother Never Read   Everyday Heroes

Use the order form on the next page, enclosing five dollars to cover the cost of shipping and handling. You'll then be sent these three very readable books.

ORDER FORM

YES! Please send me copies of *Reading Changed My Life!, Letters My Mother Never Read,* and *Everyday Heroes.* Enclosed is five dollars to cover the shipping and handling of the books.

Please PRINT the following very clearly. It will be your shipping label.

Name _____

Address _____

City _____ *State* _____ *Zip* _____

MAIL TO: TP Book Center, 439 Kelley Drive, West Berlin, NJ 08091.

2 One Reader's Story

Preview

Ryan Klootwyk's childhood was torn apart by drugs, alcohol, and violence. He had no one to turn to for help. But as a little boy, he discovered a safe place he could always go when times were hard. That place was the world of books. Ryan's story shows how a love of reading can carry a person through painful experiences.

1   "Drink it. It will make a man out of you."

2   Ryan Klootwyk jerked his head away from the cup of beer that his stepfather Larry was shoving in his face. "But I don't like how it smells," he pleaded. For a moment, Larry just glared drunkenly at the eight-year-old boy, his bloodshot eyes like two cracked windows. Then he raised the cup high in the air and poured the contents on Ryan's head. As Larry stormed out of the room, Ryan sat quietly at the table, drenched in the stinking fluid. He was relieved. Larry could have done much worse; he usually did.

3   Nearly twenty years later, Ryan remembers that moment as if it were yesterday. He tells the story, sitting at another table—his own—with his wife and two young sons. Watching his kids play, Ryan thinks how different their childhood is from his own. "My children will never have to go through what I went through," he says, shaking his head. "Never."

4   Ryan's childhood home was shattered by heroin. Both his parents were addicts. When Ryan was six years old, his father died, an apparent drug-related suicide. Alone and vulnerable, his mother soon brought a new man into their home. This was Larry.

5   When Larry first entered Ryan's life, he seemed friendly. He took Ryan and his brother Frank fishing. He bought new furniture for the house, and Ryan's mother told the kids to call him "Dad." The two lonely young boys started to accept Larry in his new role. But Larry was keeping a secret from the family. Underneath his pleasant exterior, Larry was a monster.

6   Ryan's first glimpse into Larry's true nature occurred a few months after he had moved in with the family. Ryan's

dog—one that had belonged to Ryan's father—had an accident on the carpet. High and drunk, Larry announced he was going to kill the dog. Horrified, Frank shouted for him to stop. "That's my dad's dog! That's my dad's dog!" he screamed.

7   Larry ignored Frank's screams, but when their mother heard the commotion and yelled, "Larry, what are you doing?" he snapped. Seven-year-old Ryan watched in helpless horror as Larry beat her, hitting her face with his fists. "My childhood ended that night," Ryan says today. "I hid behind the table and watched him. I had no idea why he acted that way. I only knew I was scared that he would kill one of us." Ryan, Frank and their mother fled into the boys' bedroom. Immediately, Larry cornered them there and issued a stern warning. "Don't you ever, *ever* mention your father to me again," he hissed. Terrified, the little boys could only stare.

8   As Larry wandered away, Ryan felt emptiness and terror threaten to overwhelm him. There was nowhere to go; there was no one to turn to. But a comforting thought broke through his despair. Reaching under his bed, he pulled out a battered copy of his favorite book, *The Five Chinese Brothers*. Crawling into bed, he quickly lost himself in the familiar pages. Thoughts of Larry's brutality, of fear, of pain, of humiliation faded as he read the story of the brave, clever little brother who saved everyone. Ryan was only seven, but he had already found the lifeline that would keep him

Ryan Klootwyk today.

afloat through the horrifying years ahead. He had discovered books.

9   Larry supported himself by robbing nearby households and businesses. With the police constantly trailing him, he had to keep moving. The moves would often occur without notice. "I would come home from school, and we'd be out the door," Ryan remembers. Traveling from motels to shelters, from friends' houses to apartments, Ryan lived in six different states and passed through fifteen separate schools, never staying in one place more than a year and a half. The constant moving took its toll. "I wanted to be a normal kid," he says, "but transferring from school to school made that impossible. The only people that were constant in my life

were my mother and my brother. They were the only ones who knew how bad things were. My biggest fear as a child was that I would lose them, that I would be totally alone."

10   When Ryan was eight years old, that fear almost came true. This time, the family was in Texas. Even drunker and angrier than usual, Larry began kicking and stomping on Ryan's mother. Frank, now nine years old, made a desperate effort to protect her. When he stepped between Larry and his mother, shouting "Don't hit her!" Larry turned on the boy. He kicked him in the face with his heavy black boots. Frank crumpled to the floor.

11   For the rest of that evening, little Ryan watched over his brother and tried to comfort him. "I could see that his eye was swollen shut, and pus and fluid were oozing out of it," he recalls. "Nothing Larry ever did hurt me inside more than when he hurt my brother like that," says Ryan, his voice wavering. Alone in the darkness with his silent, wounded brother, Ryan quietly sobbed through the night.

12   The next day Frank was a little better, and his mother took him to the hospital. Ryan went along. Larry instructed the boys to lie about what had happened. "Tell them you were playing baseball and Frank got hit in the head with the bat," Larry said. The boys and their mother obediently lied, but the injury still made people at the hospital suspicious. A police officer questioned the kids, but they stuck to Larry's story.

13   "I wanted to tell the truth, but we were so afraid of Larry," says Ryan. He still feels the frustration of those days. "We knew what would happen if we told the truth. They would take him away, he would be in jail for a short time, and then he would come out and get us, and he would kill Mom." Without the boys' cooperation, the police could do nothing. And a few weeks later, Larry, aware of the watchful eye of the police, decided to move the family again. In yet another state and another school, the beatings continued.

14   Amazingly, amidst the constant abuse at home, Ryan did well in school. "School was the one safe place in my life. When I was in school, I was away from Larry. I was free from threats to my family. I could pretend to be a normal kid," recounts Ryan.

15   As a third-grader, Ryan won a school reading contest. The prize was a copy of *Charlotte's Web*. The book quickly became a new favorite. In it, a little runt pig, Wilbur, has his life saved twice: first by a kind little girl, and then by a clever and loving spider, Charlotte. Charlotte's first word to Wilbur is "Salutations!" Like Wilbur, Ryan had no idea what the word meant. He appreciated Charlotte's explanation to Wilbur: "Salutations are greetings," she said. "When I say 'salutations,' it's just my fancy way of saying hello." Ryan loved Charlotte for her friendship and kindness to lonely little Wilbur.

16   Charlotte and Wilbur joined the five Chinese brothers and Ryan's other

favorite characters as pieces in a shield between him and the horrors of his home life. "Reading was a way I could forget about everything," he says. "It was the only thing that was completely in my control. I am not sure if I would have survived without it." He looked for things to read the way a hungry child might look for food that others had overlooked. "Once I even found some old history textbooks in the school trash can. To someone, those old books were trash, but to me they were a treasure. I took them home and read them cover to cover."

17   Ryan's success at school had no effect on his troubled home. Each time he transferred to a new school, he concealed the painful truth of his home, of his mother's addiction, of the constant moves, and of Larry. Ryan's strong grades and good adjustment to school were all his teachers saw. Outwardly he seemed to be doing well. Inwardly, he was begging for help. "Sitting in all those classrooms, I remember thinking, 'Why doesn't anyone do something about what is happening?' I desperately wanted someone to ask about us, to investigate, to care. I was incapable of asking for help. I was ashamed about what was happening to us, ashamed at what Mom allowed to go on, ashamed that I couldn't do anything about it. And, on top of all that, I was afraid that if someone found out about our family, they might separate my mother and brother and me. I was so scared, I just kept it all inside," he explains. In silence,

Ryan endured years of abuse, violence, and intimidation at the hands of Larry. "I just hoped that we would run away from Larry one day. That is what kept me going."

When Ryan was ten years old, his 18 dream almost came true. His mother took the two boys and fled to Michigan, not letting Larry know where they were going. For three months, Ryan was free of the constant threat of violence. But the freedom did not last. Ryan returned from school one day to find Larry sitting on the couch with a smile on his face. "Hi," he said smugly.

Ryan could barely speak. "My soul 19 dropped. I just wanted to cry. It was as if something inside me died." Again the cycle of terror began. This time, Ryan's mother sought legal help. A judge granted her a restraining order that barred Larry from being near her home. Larry's response was to stalk the family. Lying in bed one night soon after the order had been issued, Ryan heard a window break. When he went to investigate, he found Larry punching his mother. She managed to call the police, but Larry ran away before they arrived. For three more years the family ran from Larry, moving from town to town and from school to school.

As Ryan grew up, so did his tastes in 20 reading. Instead of make-believe heroes like Charlotte and the clever Chinese brother, Ryan was drawn to real-life stories of brave men and women. He read biographies of Abraham Lincoln, once a poor boy who would walk miles to borrow a book. He read about Frederick Douglass, a former slave who became a fiery speaker for human rights. Larry's stalking continued until Ryan's mother became involved with a new boyfriend. The two men got into a fight in the street outside Larry's house, and Larry was almost killed. At last, he disappeared from Ryan's life.

21   At the age of 13, Ryan felt that life was starting at last. Ryan's mother overcame her drug addiction and moved into a nicer apartment. For the first time in his life, Ryan was able to attend the same school for more than a year. He began to put down roots, make friends, feel at home. The future looked bright—briefly. Then Ryan's mother announced she could no longer afford the apartment they were living in. They were going to move again.

22   The news that he would have to uproot his life once again shocked Ryan. This time, he rebelled. "I was 13, and I had *had* it," he remembers. "I did not want to move any more. For the first time in my life, I had gotten a chance to have a normal, healthy life, and now someone was going to take it away again." Ryan begged and pleaded for his mother to stay, but she refused. "When we moved, something inside me snapped. It is sad to say, but in ninth grade I just stopped caring. I figured no one ever seemed to care about me, so why should I?"

23   Ryan's grades reflected his changing attitude. In just months he went from a B+ student to a student who got D's and

F's. "I started skipping school, hanging out with the wrong crowd, and then using drugs. I just gave up. All the anger that had built up inside all those years was coming out, and nobody could do anything to stop me." A low point occurred when a cousin called, asking Ryan if he knew someone who would buy stolen jewelry. Ryan arranged the sale. After he and his cousin spent the eighty dollars they'd made on drugs and whiskey, Ryan asked who owned the jewelry. The cousin had stolen it from his own parents, Ryan's aunt and uncle.

Because of Ryan's poor perfor- 24 mance in school, he was sent to a high school for troubled young people. There he was surrounded by students who spent much of their time trying to find a way to smoke marijuana in class. Fights were common. Far more attention was given to discipline than to learning. Once again, overwhelmed by the surrounding violence, Ryan retreated to the one safe place he knew—the world of books.

"I cut school to go to the public 25 library and read," he remembers. "At school, it was clear that the teachers had given up on the students. They were more like babysitters than anything else. But at the library—away from the dangers of school—I could read and learn about anything I wanted." By this time, he was drawn to stories from the pages of military history books. He read about prisoners of war who survived long years of unspeakable torture. One book in particular, *The Forgotten Soldier,* moved him. It told the story of a man fighting his own personal war against himself as World War II rages around him. The author had been a prisoner. Ryan thought of himself as a kind of prisoner, too. But unlike Ryan, the author had pulled himself out of his prison and into a better life. Ryan was still locked inside his own private jail.

26   Somehow, despite poor grades and a complete lack of direction, Ryan managed to graduate from high school. He went to work as an industrial painter. While working long hours at manual labor, Ryan had time to think about his life since Larry disappeared. "I realized that I had lost control of my life. I asked myself, 'Is this what I want? Is this all there is?'" In order to cope with his own dissatisfaction, Ryan continued reading. "I worked all day and read all night," says Ryan. "I read true stories about people who overcame incredible obstacles, about people who survived wars and concentration camps.

I would get depressed because I'd read about people doing amazing things, and I wasn't doing anything except complaining."

Ryan's constant reading and the drudgery of his work forced him to rethink the choices he had made. "I said to myself, 'How did I get here? What am I doing? Where am I taking my life?'" His self-examination was painful. "I became aware of how I had hurt myself, how I had wasted time and made poor choices. But I could not see anything in my future except more of the same. It all seemed like a big nothing. I grew very depressed." 27

Then things got worse. On the job one day, Ryan slipped off a pedestal and shattered his wrist. He couldn't work. His wife was pregnant, and now she had to work more hours to support their household. Feeling scared and sorry for himself, Ryan went to see his brother Frank. 28

Ryan works on a project in his home office.

29   "I was looking for sympathy when I went over there," Ryan admits. "I told him I had no income, no food, no money to buy food, no way to support my wife." But Frank didn't want to listen to Ryan's complaints. Instead, Frank gave Ryan the best advice he could think of. With disgust in his voice, Frank said, "Why don't you go back to school and get an education so you can be somebody when you *do* grow up?"

30   "I wanted to punch his lights out," Ryan says. "I had come over to find a friendly, supportive brother, and instead I found someone telling me what to do." Angry and frustrated, Ryan barged out of his brother's home. Yet Frank's words lingered with him. "The more I thought about it, the more I realized that what Frank said was right. I needed to take charge of my life, and I needed to hear someone say it. Today I thank Frank for telling me the truth."

31   One of the next books to make an impression on Ryan was *Embattled Courage.* In that book, soldiers who fought the long-ago American Civil War spoke of what the war had done to them and their innocent dreams. "Once again, I realized that people who go through hell *can* learn to cope with life."

32   These long-dead soldiers were in Ryan's mind a year later when he enrolled in Muskegon Community College in Michigan. He was the first one in his family to go to college. The transition was not easy.

33   "The first day I set foot on campus, I was terrified," he says. "I looked around and saw that I was ten years older than most of my fellow students, and I thought, 'What am I doing here?' I was sure that everyone in the school was looking at me, thinking I was stupid for being so old. Sometimes I still feel that way," he admits.

34   "But worse than anything was my fear of failure. I was afraid that I wasn't prepared for the demands of college, since my high school years had been such a waste. I thought if I failed, then I would be a complete failure in life, that I wouldn't amount to anything, that everything that happened years earlier would have beaten me."

35   But over the course of his first semester, Ryan's fear faded. His constant reading over so many years had done more than help him to survive: it had helped prepare him for college. Ryan quickly became one of the strongest students in his classes. His love of learning had been buried under the years of abuse and poor choices, but it had not died. "I had given up on school for so long, but when I stepped into college, my mind woke up again," Ryan says. "It was like being reborn." After two years in community college, Ryan was a solid A student.

36   His college work inspired Ryan to decide on a direction for his life. "For years, I survived because I read books about people who kept on fighting, who kept on struggling in the face of horror. At college, I realized that I could teach these same stories to others. It became clear to me that what I wanted to do

with my life was to be a history teacher."

37   Ryan has made his goal a reality. He went on to Grand Valley State University, where he earned a degree in secondary education. He is now teaching history at the same high school where he had once been a student.

38   "When I read books about extraordinary people, when Larry was hurting us or when I was depressed, I would say to myself, 'If they can survive, so can I,'" says Ryan. "Today, there are people everywhere—kids and adults—who are fighting to survive, just as I was. Abuse, drugs, violence—the problems are still out there; they aren't going away. But if just one person can learn to make it, either by my story or the ones I teach, then all that I have been through is worthwhile," he says. "You have to learn from the past to build your future. That is the lesson of history."

39   "I have another mission too," he says, watching his two sons playing nearby. His older boy, Ryan Richard, is five years old; Reid, his second son, is three. "It is to be something for them that I never had. . . ." He pauses for a moment, picks up Ryan Richard, and gives him a warm hug. "A dad," he says, cradling his son. His eyes are moist when he puts Ryan Richard down. Reid doesn't notice his father coming over to hug him. He is engrossed in his favorite book—*Goodnight Moon*—one which has been read to him so many times that he can recite the words by memory. Ryan puts his big hand gently on Reid's small shoulder and embraces him. "They

are what I live for most," Ryan says, drying his eyes. "When I look in their faces, when I see them looking back at me—safe, secure, and loved—I know why I am here. And despite all my anger and resentment for so many years, I feel thankful."

40   He sits on the floor with Reid. "Can we read, Daddy?" Reid asks hopefully.

41   "Yeah, but you have to start," Ryan replies.

42   Reid's childish voice carefully recites the book's first line: *In the great green room there was a telephone and a red balloon . . .*

43   Ryan smiles. He is writing his own kind of book, the book of his life. A painful chapter has ended, and a new one filled with promise and possibilities has begun.

An Update

44   "One Reader's Story" was written in 1997, when Ryan Klootwyk was 31. Before reprinting the story, we checked in with Ryan to ask for an update on his life. This is what we learned:

45   Ryan, who is now 44, spent two and a half years teaching high-school social studies. But as the last-hired "low man on the totem pole," he was laid off when the school reduced its staffing. He was offered another teaching job near Grand Rapids, Michigan, but he and Ronda chose to stay in their hometown. "Ronda loves her job at the hospital, where she maintains surgical supplies," Ryan explained. "And as the boys got older,

we were determined to keep them in one school district, rather than make them go through the sort of uprooting that I experienced so much of." He went to work part-time for an educational publishing company. Contacts he made on that job led him to be hired by a company that provides online programs for long-distance learning. "I'm in sales, which is the last thing I'd ever thought I'd do," Ryan says, "but I love it. It makes all the difference if you're selling a product you truly believe in."

46   In the meantime, Ryan and Ronda's sons have grown up. Ryan Richard has just graduated from high school and will go to the same community college his father attended. Ryan describes his older son as "a great kid; very smart; not *always* as good a student as his dad would like, but with a personality that draws people to him." He is interested in studying journalism, with hopes of becoming a sportscaster. Reid will be starting his junior year in high school. "He's more of the bookworm type," his dad says, adding that Reid pays close attention to his grades, and wants to study to become a pharmacist. Both boys play tennis and the tuba. Ryan takes special pleasure in the fact that both boys have "a great group of friends" who are constantly in and out of the Klootwyk house. "They've got their hideaway in the basement, with a TV and video games, and Ronda cooks for them and generally mothers them all."

47   Ryan's brother Frank still works as a machinist in the area, and the brothers see each other often. Frank's three children are grown and have children of their own now. Ryan speaks with regret of one much loved nephew who has been in prison since he was 17. The boy had been breaking into houses to steal items. "We love and miss him so much," Ryan says sadly. He adds, "I never think of him without reminding myself, 'That could so easily have been me.'"

48   He gives great credit for his own stable life to Ronda. "We dated for six years and have been married for 21, and through every day of it, she's kept me on the straight and narrow. When I was young and could have so easily gone wrong—more wrong than I did—she was the one who kept me focused on a different kind of life. I love her a lot and owe her everything."

49   Ryan's mom spent some years living in the state of Washington, but has recently returned to live near Ryan and his family. "It's great to have her here and more involved in the boys' lives," he said. "Everyone's happy to be closer together."

50   One thing that has not changed in Ryan's life is his passion for reading. "Oh, that'll never change!" he says with a laugh. "Right now I'm on a self-help book tear. And I read lots of magazines and journals related to my job. But military history will always be my first love. I've got my own little library, and whenever I have time to just read for the fun of it, that's where I go."

*Ryan enjoys a late-summer day at home with his wife, Ronda,
and their sons, Ryan Richard and Reid.*

Questions for Discussion

1. As a child, Ryan used books as a "lifeline" to escape his troubled home life. When you are troubled or stressed, what do you like to do to make yourself feel better? Does your "lifeline" work as well for you as books worked for Ryan? Explain.

2. Ryan's favorite book was *The Five Chinese Brothers*. Later, he found a new favorite: *Charlotte's Web*. Judging from his story, why do you think these two books appealed so much to Ryan? If you also had a favorite book when you were younger, why did you like it so much? What did it teach you or make you think about?

3. Ryan tells about a "low point" in his life when he helped a cousin sell stolen jewelry and then spent the proceeds on drugs and liquor. Yet he managed to reject such behavior and eventually turned his life around. Have you or has anyone you've known come back from a similar low point in life? Describe the experience and its lessons.

4. "You have to learn from the past to build your future," Ryan says. What lessons has Ryan learned from his past? How, according to the update to Ryan's story, have these lessons helped build his future? What lessons from your past do you think can help you build *your* future?

3 How to Become a Better Reader and Thinker

The chances are that you are not as good a reader as you should be to do well in college. If so, it's not surprising. You live in a culture where people watch an average of *over seven hours of television every day!!!* All that passive viewing does not allow much time for reading. Reading is a skill that must be actively practiced. The simple fact is that people who do not read very often are not likely to be strong readers.

Answers will vary.

- How much TV do you guess you watch on an average day? _____

Another reason besides TV for not reading much is that you may have a lot of responsibilities. You may be going to school and working at the same time, and you may have a lot of family duties as well. Given a hectic schedule, you're not going to have much time to read. When you have free time, you're exhausted, and it's easier to turn on the TV than to open up a book.

- Do you do any regular reading (for example, a daily newspaper, weekly magazines, occasional novels)? _____

- When are you most likely to do your reading? _____

A third reason for not reading is that school may have caused you to associate reading with worksheets and drills and book reports and test scores. Experts agree that many schools have not done a good job of helping students discover the pleasures and rewards of reading. If reading was an unpleasant experience in school, you may have concluded that reading in general is not for you.

- Do you think that school made you dislike reading, rather than enjoy it?

  _____

Here are three final questions to ask yourself:

- Do you feel that perhaps you don't need a reading course, since you "already know how to read"? _____

● If you had a choice, would you be taking a reading course? (It's okay to be honest.) _____

● Do you think that a bit of speed reading may be all you need? _____

Chances are that you don't need to read *faster* as much as you need to read *smarter*. And it's a safe bet that if you don't read much, you can benefit enormously from the reading course in which you are using this book.

One goal of the book is to help you become a better reader. You will learn and practice ten key reading comprehension skills. As a result, you'll be better able to read and understand the many materials in your other college courses. The skills in this book have direct and practical value: they can help you perform better and more quickly—giving you an edge for success—in all of your college work.

The book is also concerned with helping you become a stronger thinker, a person able not just to understand what is read but to analyze and evaluate it as well. In fact, reading and thinking are closely related skills, and practice in thoughtful reading will also strengthen your ability to think clearly and logically. To find out just how the book will help you achieve these goals, read the next several pages and do the brief activities as well. The activities are easily completed and will give you a quick, helpful overview of the book.

How the Book is Organized

The book is organized into four main parts:

Introduction (pages 1–31)

In addition to this chapter, which will give you a good sense of the book, there are two other parts to the introduction, "Getting Off to a Strong Start" and "One Reader's Story." "Getting Off to a Strong Start" describes several essentials for success in school. In the space provided below, write the essential that is presented on pages 3–5.

Your Attitude about Learning
_____

The next essential for success, "Key Study Skills," presents four tips that can make you a better student. If I had time to give just four tips to incoming college students, based on my thirty years of teaching experience, these are the things I would say. In the space below, write in the first and second of these tips, described on pages 5–7.

Take lots of notes in class.
_____
Learn how to read your instructor.
_____
OR: Know which comes first—the textbook or the instructor.

The last essential for school success is to increase your involvement with reading. Regular reading is seen as the very heart of education for three reasons. Turn to page 11 to complete the list of reasons:

1. Reading provides language power.
2. Reading increases job power.
3. Reading creates human power.

Part One: Ten Steps to Building College Reading Skills (pages 33–428)

To help you become a more effective reader and thinker, this book presents a series of ten key reading skills. They are listed in the table of contents on pages v and vi. Turn to those pages to fill in the skills missing below:

1 Dictionary Use
2 Vocabulary in Context
3 Main Ideas
4 Supporting Details
5 Locations of Main Ideas
6 Relationships I
7 Relationships II
8 Inferences
9 Implied Main Ideas
10 The Basics of Argument

Each chapter is developed in the same way.

First of all, clear **explanations** and **examples** help you *understand* each skill. **Practices** then give you the "hands-on" experience needed to *learn* the skill.

● How many practices are there for the third chapter, "Main Ideas" (pages 113–142)? Seven

Closing each chapter are **four review tests**. The first review test provides a check of the information presented in the chapter.

● On which page is the first review test for "Main Ideas"? 132

The second and third review tests consist of activities that help you practice the skill learned in the chapter.

● On which pages are Review Tests 2 and 3 for "Main Ideas"? 132–136

The fourth review test consists of a story, essay, or textbook selection that both gets you reading and gives you practice in the skill learned in the chapter as well as skills learned in previous chapters.

● What is the title of the reading selection in the "Main Ideas" chapter?

"Group Pressure"

Following each chapter are **six mastery tests** that gradually increase in difficulty.

● On what pages are the mastery tests for the "Main Ideas" chapter? *143–154*

The tests are on tear-out pages and so can be easily removed and handed in to your instructor. So that you can track your progress, there is a score box at the top of each test. Your score can also be entered into the "Reading Performance Chart" on the inside back cover of the book.

Part Two: Ten Reading Selections (pages 429–526)

The ten reading selections that make up Part Two are followed by activities that give you practice in all of the skills studied in Part One. Each reading begins in the same way. Look, for example, at "Winners, Losers, or Just Kids?" which starts on page 431. What are the headings of the two sections that come before the reading itself?

● *"Preview" and "Words to Watch"*

Note that the vocabulary words in "Words to Watch" are followed by the numbers of the paragraphs in which the words appear. Look at the first page of "Winners, Losers, or Just Kids" and explain how each vocabulary word is marked in the reading itself.

● *It has a small circle after it.*

Activities Following Each Reading Selection

After each selection, there are four kinds of activities to improve the reading and thinking skills you learned in Part One of the book.

1 The first activity consists of **vocabulary questions**—questions involving vocabulary in context as well as "Words to Watch."

● Look at the vocabulary questions for "Winners, Losers, or Just Kids?" on pages 433–434. The first five questions deal with understanding vocabulary in context. How many questions then help you learn words taken from "Words to Watch"? *Five*

2   The second activity consists of **reading comprehension questions**—questions involving vocabulary in context, main ideas (including the central point and implied main ideas), supporting details, relationships, and inferences.

● Look at the questions for "Winners, Losers, or Just Kids?" on pages 435–436. Note that the questions are labeled so you know what skill you are practicing in each case. How many questions deal with the central point and main ideas? __Two__

3   The third activity involves **outlining, mapping,** or **summarizing**. Each of these activities will sharpen your ability to get to the heart of a piece and to think logically and clearly about what you read.

● What kind of activity is provided for "Winners, Losers, or Just Kids?" on page 437? ____Summarizing____

● What kind of activity is provided for the reading titled "Owen, the Stray Cat" on pages 446–447? ____Outlining____

● What kind of activity is provided for the reading titled "Disaster and Friendship" on page 464? ____Mapping____

Note that a **map**, or diagram, is a highly visual way of organizing material. Like an outline, it shows at a glance the main parts of a selection.

4   The fourth activity consists of **discussion questions**. These questions provide a chance for you to deepen your understanding of each selection.

● How many discussion questions are there for "Winners, Losers, or Just Kids?" (page 438)—and indeed for every other reading? __Four__

Part Three: Active Reading and Combined-Skills Tests (pages 527–574)

This part of the book gives you tips on becoming an active reader and then provides a series of combined-skills tests that help you practice a number of the skills in the book.

● How many tips are provided on page 530 for becoming an active rather than a passive reader? __Six__

● How many "Combined-Skills Tests" are there on pages 537–573? __18__

These tests are made up of short passages that closely resemble the ones typically found in standardized tests.

Appendixes (pages 575–606)

At the beginning of the "Appendixes" are two short chapters that your instructor may assign for additional skills practice.

- What is the topic of the first chapter (pages 577–580)?
  <u>Separating Fact from Opinion</u>

Another section, "Writing Assignments," presents writing assignments for all twenty of the reading selections in the book. Reading and writing are closely connected skills, and writing practice will improve your ability to read closely and to think carefully.

- How many assignments are offered for each reading? <u>Two</u>

  Also included in the appendixes is a limited answer key.

Helpful Features of the Book

1 The book centers on *what you really need to know* to become a better reader and thinker. It presents key comprehension skills and explains the most important points about each one.

2 The book gives you *lots of practice*. We seldom learn a skill only by hearing or reading about it; we make it part of ourselves by repeated practice. There are, then, numerous activities in the text. They are not "busywork," but carefully designed materials that should help you truly learn each skill.

   Notice that after you learn each skill in Part One, you progress to review tests and mastery tests that enable you to apply the skill. And as you move from one skill to the next, the reading selections help you practice and reinforce the skills already learned.

3 The selections throughout the book are *lively and appealing*. Dull and unvaried readings work against learning, so subjects have been carefully chosen for their high interest level. Almost all of the selections here are good examples of how what we read can capture our attention. For instance, begin "All the Good Things" on page 96 and try not to be moved by the conclusion. Or read Emily Carlin's engaging story about a stray cat on pages 439–442. Or look at the textbook selection on pages 505–509, which is full of helpful information about understanding and controlling one's feelings.

4   The readings include *selections from college textbooks*. Therefore, you will be practicing on materials very much like those in your other courses. Doing so will increase your chances of transferring what you learn in your reading class to your other college courses.

How to Use the Book

1   A good way to proceed is to read and review the explanations and examples in a given chapter in Part One until you feel you understand the ideas presented. Then carefully work through the practices. As you finish each one, check your answers with the "Limited Answer Key" that starts on page 601.

For your own sake, *don't just copy in the answers without trying to do the practices!* The only way to learn a skill is to practice it first and then use the answer key to give yourself feedback. Also, take whatever time is needed to figure out just why you got some answers wrong. By using the answer key to help teach yourself the skills, you will prepare yourself for the review and mastery tests at the end of each chapter as well as the other reading tests in the book. Your instructor can supply you with answers to those tests.

If you have trouble catching on to a particular skill, stick with it. In time, you will learn each of the ten skills.

2   Read the selections first with the intent of simply enjoying them. There will be time afterward for rereading each selection and using it to develop your comprehension skills.

3   Keep track of your progress. Fill in the charts at the end of each chapter in Part One and each reading in Part Two. And in the "Reading Performance Chart" on the inside back cover, enter your scores for all the review and mastery tests as well as the reading selections. These scores can give you a good view of your overall performance as you work through the book.

In summary, *Ten Steps to Building College Reading Skills, Fifth Edition,* has been designed to interest and benefit you as much as possible. Its format is straightforward, its explanations are clear, its readings are appealing, and its many practices will help you learn through doing. *It is a book that has been created to reward effort,* and if you provide that effort, you will make yourself a better reader and a stronger thinker. I wish you success.

John Langan

Part One

Ten Steps to Building College Reading Skills

1 Dictionary Use

To the Instructor: Any material in this smaller type appears only in the *Instructor's Edition.*

This Chapter in a Nutshell

- You should own both a paperback and a hardbound dictionary.

- Your computer (if you have one) may have a built-in dictionary; also, you can easily visit an online dictionary.

- Use spelling hints to help you look up in the dictionary a word you cannot spell.

- A dictionary entry will tell you how a word is spelled and pronounced and give you the various meanings of the word. It will also provide other helpful information about words.

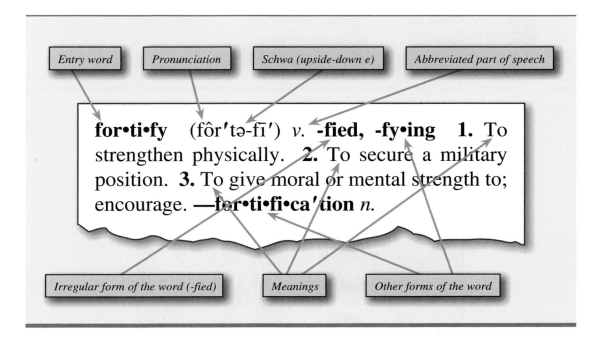

The dictionary is a valuable tool. To help you use it, this chapter explains in a clear and detailed way what you need to know about dictionaries and the information they provide.

Owning Your Own Dictionaries

You can benefit greatly by owning two dictionaries. The first dictionary you should own is a paperback edition you can carry with you. Any of the following would be a good choice:

The American Heritage Dictionary, Paperback Edition
The Merriam-Webster Dictionary, Paperback Edition
New American Webster Handy College Dictionary

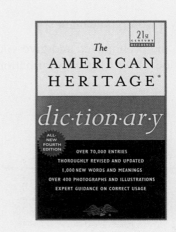 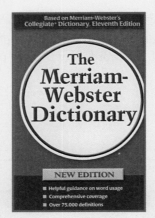 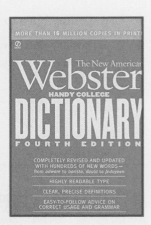

The second dictionary you should own is a desk-sized, hardcover edition, which should be kept in the room where you study. Here are two good hardbound dictionaries:

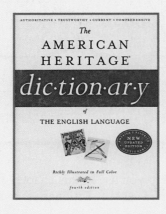 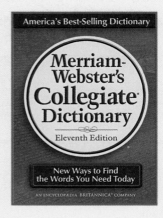

Hardbound dictionaries contain a good deal more information than the paperback editions. For instance, a hardbound dictionary defines far more words than a paperback dictionary. And there are more definitions per word, as well. Although they cost more, they are worth the investment, because they are valuable study aids.

Dictionaries are often updated to reflect changes that occur in the language. New words come into use, and old words take on new meanings. So you should not use a dictionary that has been lying around the house for a number of years. Instead, buy yourself a new dictionary. It is easily among the best investments you will ever make.

Online Dictionary

Copyright © by Randy Glasbergen.
www.glasbergen.com

GLASBERGEN

"How did you look up words before there were online dictionaries, Dad?"

If your computer is connected to the Internet, you may find it easy to check words online. Here is one dictionary site you can go to:

www.merriam-webster.com

For example, if you go online to **www.merriam-webster.com** and type in the word *fortify*, you will see something like this:

for·ti·fy 🔊 *verb*

for·ti·fied | for·ti·fy·ing

Definition of FORTIFY

transitive verb

: to make strong: as

a : to strengthen and secure (as a town) by forts or batteries

b : to give physical strength, courage, or endurance to <*fortified* by a hearty meal>

c : to add mental or moral strength to : ENCOURAGE <*fortified* by prayer>

d : to add material to for strengthening or enriching <*fortified* milk>

intransitive verb

: to erect fortifications
— **for·ti·fi·er** 🔊 *noun*
↗ See fortify defined for English-language learners »

Examples of FORTIFY

- *fortify* a city against attack
- a city *fortified* by high walls
- Support for his theories has been *fortified* by the results of these experiments.

(continued)

- He took a deep breath to *fortify* himself before stepping onto the stage.
- milk *fortified* with vitamin D

Origin of FORTIFY

Middle English *fortifien,* from Anglo-French *fortifier,* from Late Latin *fortificare,* from Latin *fortis* strong
First Known Use: 15th century

Synonyms: brace, forearm, nerve, poise, psych (up), ready, steel, strengthen

Antonyms: debilitate, enervate, enfeeble, weaken
[+]more

Rhymes with FORTIFY

abide by, Adonai, alibi, alkali, amplify, apple-pie, argufy, assegai, azo dye, basify, beautify, butterfly, by-and-by, caddis fly, calcify...
[+]more

Browse

- Next Word in the Dictionary: fortis
- Previous Word in the Dictionary: fortified wine
- All Words Near: fortify

Notice the speaker icon next to the word *fortify*. **If you click on this icon, the word will be pronounced for you.**

These sites also give you information on **synonyms** (words with similar meanings to the word you have looked up) and **antonyms** (words with opposite meanings to the word you have looked up). Synonyms and antonyms are explained further on pages 51, 80, and 83.

Note: Some computer programs come with a built-in dictionary. For example, if you use Microsoft Word on a Macintosh, click on "Tools" and then choose "Dictionary." If you are using Word for Windows, highlight a word in your document, scroll down to "Look Up," and then click on one of the dictionaries listed.

Finding Words in the Dictionary

Using Guidewords to Find a Word

One way to find a given word in a dictionary is to use **guidewords**—the pair of words at the very top of each dictionary page. Shown below are the top and bottom parts of a page in one paperback dictionary.

armful | arsenic   38

arm•ful (ärm′fŏŏl′) *n., pl.* **-fuls.** As much as an arm can hold.
arm•hole (ärm′hōl′) *n.* An opening for the arm in a garment.
ar•mi•stice (är′mĭ-stĭs) *n.* A temporary suspension of hostilities by mutual consent; truce. [<NLat. *armistitium.*]
arm•let (ärm′lĭt) *n.* A band worn around the upper arm for ornament or identification.

playing or singing of the notes of a chord in rapid succession rather than all at once [Ital.]
ar•raign (ə-rān′) *v.* **1.** To summon before a court to answer to an indictment. **2.** To accuse; denounce. [<OFr. *araisnier.*] **–ar•raign′ment** *n.*
ar•range (ə-rānj′) *v.* **-ranged, -rang•ing. 1.** To put into a specific order or relation; dispose.

a•rouse (ə-rouz′) *v.* **a-roused, a-rous-ing. 1.** To awaken from or as if from sleep. **2.** To stir up; stimulate; excite. [*a-* (intensive) + ROUSE.] **–a-rous′al** *n.*
ar•peg•gi•o (är-pĕj′ē-ō, -pĕj′ō) *n.,pl.* **-os.** The

munition. **2.** A stock or supply, esp. of weapons [< Ar. dār-as-sinā′ah.]
ar•se•nic (är′sə-nĭk) *n. Symbol* **As** A highly poisonous metallic element used in insecticides, weed killers, solid-state doping agents, and various

The first guideword tells what the first word is on that page; the second guideword tells what the last word is on the page. All the word entries on the page fall alphabetically between the two guidewords.

Check Your Understanding

Now see if you understand how to use guidewords. Underline the three words below that would appear on the page with the guidewords *armful / arsenic*:

art   <u>aroma</u>   <u>army</u>   <u>arrest</u>   ax   allow

Explanation

The guidewords **armful / arsenic** tell us right away that every word on the page will begin with *ar*. That immediately eliminates *ax* and *allow*. The words that would fall on the page with those guidewords are *aroma, army*, and *arrest*. The word *art* also begins with *ar*, but alphabetically it comes after *arsenic*, the last word on the page.

Helpful hint: Students might write out the alphabet on a piece of paper in order to remind them of alphabetical order and speed up the word-search process.

PRACTICE 1

Below are five pairs of dictionary guidewords followed by other words. Underline the **three** words in each series that would be found on the page with the guidewords.

1. **peer / pendant**

   <u>pelican</u>   peephole   <u>Peking</u>   penknife   <u>penalty kick</u>

   Peephole is incorrect because "peep-" comes before "peer."
2. **every / exalt**   *Penknife* is incorrect because "penk-" comes after "pend-."

   evergreen   <u>exact</u>   <u>evil</u>   <u>ewe</u>   example

   Evergreen is incorrect because "everg-" comes before "every."
3. **kidney / kindhearted**   *Example* is incorrect because "exam-" comes after "exal-."

   <u>kindergarten</u>   <u>killing</u>   kickback   kingdom   <u>kilowatt</u>

   Kickback is incorrect because "kic-" comes before "kid-."
4. **dumbbell / dustpan**   *Kingdom* is incorrect because "king-" comes after "kind-."

   <u>during</u>   <u>duplicate</u>   dye   <u>dunk</u>   dull

   Dye is incorrect because "dy-" comes after "du-."
5. **stuffed shirt / subconscious**   *Dull* is incorrect because "dul-" comes before "dum-."

   <u>stumble</u>   sunstroke   <u>subcompact</u>   straw   <u>style</u>

   Sunstroke is incorrect because "sun-" comes after "sub-."
   Straw is incorrect because "str-" comes before "stu-."

Finding a Word You Can't Spell

"If I can't spell a word," you might ask, "how can I find it in the dictionary?" The answer is that you have to guess what the letters might be.

Guessing is not too difficult with certain sounds, such as the sounds of *b* and *p*. But other sounds are more difficult to pin down because they can belong to more than one letter. And that's where the guessing comes in. Here are three hints to help in such cases:

Hints for Finding Words

Hint 1: If you're not sure about the vowels in a word, you will simply have to experiment. Vowels often sound the same. So try an *i* in place of an *a*, an *i* in place of an *e*, and so on. If, for example, you don't find a word that sounds as if it begins with *pa*, try looking under *pe*, *pi*, *po*, *pu* or *py*.

Hint 2: Following are groups of letters or letter combinations that often sound alike. If your word isn't spelled with one of the letters in a pair or group shown below, it might be spelled with another in the same pair or group. For example, if it isn't spelled with a *k*, it may be spelled with a *c*.

c / k	c / s	f / v / ph	g / j	qu / kw / k	s / c / z
sch / sc / sk	sh / ch	shun / tion / sion		w / wh	able / ible
ai / ay	al / el / le	ancy / ency	ate / ite	au / aw	ea / ee
er / or	ie / ei	ou / ow	oo / u	y / i / e	

Hint 3: Consonants are sometimes doubled in a word. If you can't find your word with a single consonant, try doubling it.

PRACTICE 2

For this practice you will need a dictionary. Try using your ear, the hints on this page, and guidewords to help you find the correct spelling of the following words. Write each correct spelling in the answer space.

1. occazion _____occasion_____

2. dooty _____duty_____

3. dicided _____decided_____

4. aksident _____accident_____

5. nieghbor _____neighbor_____

6. awtumn _____autumn_____

7. rimember _____remember_____

8. atenshun _____attention_____

9. experament _____experiment_____

10. fotocopy _____photocopy_____

Learning from a Dictionary Entry

Each entry word in a dictionary is in **boldface type**. Here is a sample entry:

Sample Dictionary Entry

> **dis•re•spect** (dĭs′rĭ-spĕkt′) *n.* Lack of respect or regard; rudeness; discourtesy. —*tr .v.* **-spect•ed, -spect•ing, -spects.** To show a lack of respect for: *disrespect one's elders; disrespect the law.*

All of the following information may be provided in a dictionary entry:

   1   Spelling and Syllables

   2   Pronunciation Symbols and Accent Marks

   3   Parts of Speech

   4   Irregular Forms of Words

   5   Definitions

   6   Synonyms

   7   Usage Labels

Note: Some but not all dictionaries will also include notes on word origins, often too brief to be of practical help to students.

The rest of the chapter will look at each kind of information above.

1   Spelling and Syllables

The dictionary first gives the correct spelling and syllable breakdown of a word. Dots separate the words into syllables. Each syllable is a separate sound, and each sound includes a vowel. In the entry shown above, *disrespect* is divided into three syllables.

How many syllables are in each of the following words?

   do•nate   com•pen•sate   o•be•di•ent

If you answered two for *donate*, three for *compensate*, and four for *obedient*, you were right.

PRACTICE 3

Use your dictionary to separate the following words into syllables. Put a large dot (•) between the syllables. Then write down the number of syllables in each word. The first one is done for you as an example.

1. b i r t h • p l a c e   <u> 2 </u> syllables

2. d i s c l o s e   <u> 2 </u> syllables   *dis • close*

3. h u r r i c a n e   <u> 3 </u> syllables   *hur • ri • cane*

4. u n d e r t a k e r   <u> 4 </u> syllables   *un• der • tak • er*

5. i n h u m a n i t y   <u> 5 </u> syllables   *in • hu • man • i • ty*

2   Pronunciation Symbols and Accent Marks

A dictionary entry word is followed by information in parentheses, as in the entry for *disrespect*:

dis•re•spect (dĭs′rĭ-spĕkt′)

The information in parentheses shows you how to pronounce the word. It includes two kinds of symbols: pronunciation symbols and accent marks. Following are explanations of each.

Pronunciation Symbols

The **pronunciation symbols** tell the sounds of the consonants and the vowels in a word. The sounds of the consonants are probably familiar to you, but you may find it helpful to review the vowel sounds. Vowels are the letters *a, e, i, o,* and *u*. (Sometimes *y* is also a vowel, as in *myself* and *copy*.) To know how to pronounce the vowel sounds, use the pronunciation key in your dictionary. Here is a sample pronunciation key:

Pronunciation Key

ă hat	ā pay	âr care	ä card	ĕ ten	ē she	ĭ sit
ī hi	îr here	ŏ lot	ō go	ô all	oi oil	ou out
ŏŏ look	yŏŏ cure	ōō cool	yōō use	ŭ up	ûr fur	th thick
th then	ə ago, item, easily, gallop, circus					

To use the pronunciation key, match the symbol (ă, ā, and so on) with the letter or letters in **bold print** in the short word that follows the symbol. For instance, ă (also called "short *a*") sounds like the *a* in *hat*.

You can pronounce the *i* and the first *e* in *disrespect* by first finding the matching symbol within the parentheses. Note that the matching symbol for both vowels is ĭ. Then look for that symbol in the Pronunciation Key. It shows you that ĭ has the sound of *i* in the short word *sit*. You can also use the Pronunciation Key to pronounce the second *e* in *disrespect* (ĕ). It shows you that ĕ is pronounced like the *e* in *ten*.

A long vowel (a vowel with a line over it) has the sound of its own name. Long *a* (ā) sounds like the *a* in *pay*; long *e* (ē) sounds like the *e* in *she*; etc.

Finally, note that the last pronunciation symbol in the key looks like an upside-down e: ə. This symbol is known as the **schwa**. As you can see by the words that follow it, the schwa has a very short sound that sounds much like "uh" (as in *ago, gallop,* and *circus*) or "ih" (as in *item* and *easily*).

 PRACTICE 4

Refer to the pronunciation key to answer the questions about the following ten words. In the space provided, write the letter of each of your answers.

___A___   1. **kit•ten** (kĭt′n)
    The *i* in *kitten* sounds like the *i* in
    A. *sit.*   B. *hi.*

___A___   2. **blos•som** (blŏs′əm)
    The first *o* in *blossom* sounds like the *o* in
    A. *lot.*   B. *go.*

___B___   3. **live•ly** (līv′lē)
    The *i* in *lively* sounds like the *i* in
    A. *sit.*   B. *hi.*

___A___   4. **thun•der** (thŭn′dər)
    The *u* in *thunder* sounds like the *u* in
    A. *up.*   B. *fur.*

Item 1: The *i* in *kitten* has the short-vowel marking, meaning that it is pronounced like the *i* in the word *sit* in the pronunciation key on the previous page. (Similar explanations apply to items 2–10.)

_A_   5. **gam•ble** (găm′bəl)
     The *a* in *gamble* sounds like the *a* in
     A. *hat.*   B. *pay.*

_B_   6. **bla•tant** (blāt′nt)
     The first *a* in *blatant* sounds like the *a* in
     A. *hat.*   B. *pay.*

_B_   7. **boast** (bōst)
     The *oa* in *boast* sounds like the *o* in
     A. *lot.*   B. *go.*

_B_   8. **fu•ture** (fyo͞o′chər)
     The first *u* in *future* sounds like the *oo* in
     A. *look.*   B. *cool.*

_B_   9. **ve•hi•cle** (vē′ĭ-kəl)
     The first *e* in *vehicle* sounds like the *e* in
     A. *ten.*   B. *she.*

_B_   10. **hyp•o•crite** (hĭp′ə-krĭt′)
     The *o* in *hypocrite* sounds like the
     A. *a* in *hat.*   B. schwa in the word *gallop.*

PRACTICE 5

A. Below are pronunciation symbols for five common words. Write in the word in each case and also the number of schwa sounds in each word. The first item has been done for you as an example.

Pronunciation symbols	*Word itself*	*Number of schwas*
1. (dĭs′ə-plĭn)	discipline	1
2. (mə-jôr′ĭ-tē)	majority	1
3. (ī′sə-lāt′)	isolate	1
4. (är′tə-fĭsh′əl)	artificial	2
5. (năch′ər-əl)	natural	2

B. Use your dictionary to find and write in the pronunciation symbols for the following words. Make sure you can pronounce each word. The first word has been done for you as an example.

6. cynic   _____sĭn′ĭk_____

7. advocate   _____ăd′və-kāt′_____

8. optimist   _____ŏp′tə-mĭst_____

9. arrogant   _____ăr′ə-gənt_____

10. hypothesis   _____hī-pŏth′ĭ-sĭs_____

Accent Marks

Notice the black marks in the pronunciation guide (the information shown in parentheses) for the noun form of *disrespect*. The marks look a little like apostrophes.

dis•re•spect (dĭs′rĭ-spĕkt′)

The darker line (′) is a bold accent mark, and it shows which syllable has the strongest stress. That means the third syllable in *disrespect* is pronounced a little louder than the other two. Syllables without an accent mark are unstressed. Some syllables—like the first syllable in *disrespect*—are in between, and they are marked with a lighter accent mark (′).

The word *interview* is accented like this:

in•ter•view (ĭn′tər-vyo͞o′)

Say *interview* to yourself. Can you hear that the strongest accent is on *in*, the first syllable? Can you hear that the last syllable, *view,* is also accented, but not as strongly? If not, say the word to yourself again until you hear the differences in accent sounds.

Here are some familiar words with syllable divisions and accent marks shown in parentheses. Use those guides to help you pronounce the words to yourself.

● ma•chine (mə-shēn′)

● de•ter•gent (dĭ-tûr′jənt)

● in•for•ma•tion (ĭn′fər-mā′shən)

● val•en•tine (văl′ən-tīn′)

● al•pha•bet•i•cal (ăl′fə-bĕt′ĭ-kəl)

Think for a moment of how each of these words would sound if you accented the wrong syllable.

PRACTICE 6

Answer the questions following each of the five words below.

1. **pro•cras•ti•nate** (prō-krăs′tə-nāt′)

   A. How many syllables are in *procrastinate?* ___Four___

   B. Which syllable is most strongly accented? ___Second___

2. **mag•nif•i•cent** (măg-nĭf′ĭ-sənt)

   A. How many syllables are in *magnificent?* ___Four___

   B. Which syllable is most strongly accented? ___Second___

3. **un•der•dog** (ŭn′dər-dôg′)

   A. How many syllables are in *underdog?* ___Three___

   B. Which syllable is most strongly accented? ___First___

4. **so•phis•ti•ca•ted** (sə-fĭs′tĭ-kā′tĭd)

   A. How many syllables are in *sophisticated?* ___Five___

   B. Which syllable is most strongly accented? ___Second___

5. **ter•mi•nate** (tûr′mə-nāt′)

   A. How many syllables are in *terminate?* ___Three___

   B. Which syllable is **least** strongly accented? ___Second___

3   Parts of Speech

Every word in the dictionary is either a noun, a verb, an adjective, or another part
of speech. In dictionary entries, the parts of speech are shown by letters in italics.
In the entry for *disrespect*, for example, the abbreviations *v.* and *n.* tell us that
disrespect is both a verb and a noun. The entry below for *insult* tells us that this
word is both a verb and a noun.

> **in•sult** (ĭn-sŭlt′) *v.* To speak to or treat with disrespect or contempt. —*n.*
> (ĭn′sŭlt′). An offensive or disrespectful action or remark.

When a word is more than one part of speech, the dictionary gives the definitions for each part of speech separately. In the above entry for *insult*, the abbreviation telling us that *insult* is a verb comes right after the pronunciation symbols; the verb definition follows. When the verb meaning ends, the abbreviation *n.* tells us that the noun definition will follow.

Parts of speech are abbreviated in order to save space. Following are the most common abbreviations for parts of speech:

n. — noun	*v.* — verb
pron. — pronoun	*conj.* — conjunction
adj. — adjective	*prep.* — preposition
adv. — adverb	*interj.* — interjection

Note: Many dictionaries use the abbreviations *tr.* and *intr.* (or *vt* and *vi)* to indicate two types of verbs, not other parts of speech. The abbreviations *tr.* and *vt* stand for a transitive verb (one that has a direct object); the abbreviations *intr.* and *vi* stand for an intransitive verb (one that does not have a direct object).

PRACTICE 7

Use your dictionary to list the parts of speech for each of the following words. Each word has more than one part of speech.   *Answers may vary slightly.*

Parts of speech

1. praise   noun, verb

2. bridge   noun, verb

3. panic   noun, verb, adjective

4. around   preposition, adverb

5. level   noun, verb, adjective, adverb

4   Irregular Forms of Words

Look at the following two words and the forms that follow them in most dictionaries.

know (nō) *v.* **knew** (no͞o, nyo͞o), **known, know•ing.**

fun•ny (fŭn′ē) *adj.* **-ni•er, -ni•est.**

When other forms of a word are spelled in an irregular way, those forms are shown. As you can see in the examples on the previous page, those forms are given after the part of speech in an entry. With irregular verbs, the dictionary gives the past tense (*knew*), and the past participle (*known*), as well as the present participle (*knowing*). With adjectives, the dictionary gives the comparative (*funnier*) and superlative (*funniest*) forms.

Plural forms with irregular spellings are also included in this spot in an entry. For example, the entry for *country* begins:

coun•try (kŭn′trē) *n., pl.* **-tries.**

After the part of speech of *country* (*n.* for noun), the entry gives the irregular form of the plural (*pl.*) of *country*.

Finally, comparative forms of adjectives and adverbs are also given at this point in the entry. Here are two examples:

good (go͝od) *adj.* **bet•ter** (bĕt′ər), **best** (bĕst)

wide (wīd) *adj.* **-er, -est**

PRACTICE 8

Below are the beginnings of three dictionary entries. In the blanks, write in the part of speech and irregular or other troublesome spellings in full (not abbreviated).

1. **write** (rīt) *v.* **wrote** (rōt), **writ•ten** (rĭt′n), **writ•ing**

   Part of speech: _____ verb _____

   Spelling of past tense: _____ wrote _____

   Spelling of past participle: _____ written _____

   Spelling of present participle: _____ writing _____

2. **cra•zy** (krā′zē) *adj.* **-zi•er, -zi•est**

   Part of speech: _____ adjective _____

   Spelling of form that means *most crazy* (with *-est* ending):

   _____ craziest _____

3. **qual•i•ty** (kwŏl′ĭ-tē) *n.* **-ties**

   Part of speech: _____ noun _____

   Spelling of plural: _____ qualities _____

5 Definitions

Words often have more than one meaning. When they do, their definitions may be numbered in the dictionary. You can tell which definition of a word fits a given sentence by the meaning of the sentence. For example, the following are three of the definitions of the verb form of *revive* given in most dictionaries:

1. To bring back to life or consciousness.
2. To impart or regain health or vigor.
3. To restore to use.

Which of these definitions best fits the sentence below?

Modern technology can revive patients who have actually been considered medically dead.

The answer is definition 1: Modern technology can bring a patient back to life.

PRACTICE 9

Below are three words and their dictionary definitions. A sentence using each word is also given. Choose the dictionary meaning that best fits each sentence.

1. **idle: 1.** Not working; inactive. **2.** Avoiding work; lazy.

    Which definition best fits the sentence below? _____1_____

    The streetcar tracks in our city have been *idle* since 1960, when the city switched from streetcars to buses.   Streetcar tracks cannot be lazy.

2. **suspicion: 1.** The act of suspecting the existence of something, esp. of something wrong, with little evidence or proof. **2.** A faint trace; hint.

    Which definition fits the following sentence? _____2_____

    There was a *suspicion* of rum in the chocolate cake.   The cake contains a trace of rum, not an act.

3. **sterile: 1.** Incapable of reproducing sexually. **2.** Producing little or no vegetation. **3.** Free from microorganisms.

    Which definition fits the following sentence? _____2_____

    The real estate agent had cheated young farmers by selling them *sterile* land.

    Farmers would be cheated if they bought land that could produce no vegetation.

6   Synonyms

"This online dictionary is great! It gives me synonyms I can use to write a more impressive paper."

A **synonym** is a word whose meaning is similar to that of another word. For instance, two synonyms for the word *fast* are *quick* and *speedy*.

Dictionary entries sometimes end with synonyms. For example, the word *foreign* in some dictionaries ends with several synonyms: *alien, exotic, strange.* A hardbound dictionary in particular will provide synonyms for a word and explain the differences in meaning among the various synonyms.

More information on synonyms as well as **antonyms** (words with opposite meanings) can be found in a **thesaurus** (thĭ-sôr′əs), which is a collection of synonyms and antonyms. A thesaurus can improve your writing by helping you to find the precise word needed to express your thoughts. A thesaurus works much like a dictionary. You look up a word and, instead of definitions, you get a list of synonyms and perhaps an antonym of the word. To help you find the right word when writing, a thesaurus goes along well with your dictionary. If you have access to the Internet, you can find a free thesaurus online by going to

www.merriam-webster.com or **www.thesaurus.com**

Or, if you are using a recent word-processing program, see if it has a built-in thesaurus. For example, if you use Microsoft Word on a Macintosh computer, click on "Tools" and then choose "Thesaurus." (If you are using Word for Windows, highlight a word in your document, then scroll down to "Synonyms.")

Or you may want to own a paperback thesaurus such as one of the following:

7   Usage Labels

Besides listing definitions, a dictionary often includes **usage labels**: terms that tell us if a meaning is considered something other than "Standard English." For example, the dictionary labels one meaning of the verb *crash*, "to go to sleep," as "*Slang*." Other common labels include "*Informal*" (the phrase *hang in,* meaning "to persist," is labeled as informal) and "*Nonstandard*" (the word *ain't* is labeled nonstandard). Such labels indicate language not considered appropriate in formal speech and writing.

In addition to usage labels, the dictionary provides **field labels**—special meanings of a word within a certain field. For instance, one dictionary definition of the word *mouse* is labeled "Computer Science" and is followed by a meaning that applies to the field of computers: "A hand-held input device used to move about a computer screen and operate programs."

CHAPTER REVIEW

In this chapter, you learned the following:

- It is helpful to own two dictionaries. One should be a small paperback edition you can carry with you. The other should be a large hardbound version for use at home.

- If you have a computer, you can easily use a dictionary site online. You may also have a dictionary that comes with the word-processing software on your computer.

- You can find a word in the dictionary with the help of guidewords, the two words at the top of each dictionary page.

- You can use the spelling hints on page 41 to help you find a word you cannot spell.

- A dictionary entry will tell you 1) how a word is spelled and broken into syllables; 2) how a word is pronounced; 3) a word's part (or parts) of speech; 4) irregular forms of the word; 5) definitions of the word; 6) in some cases, synonyms; 7) any usage labels for the word.

The next chapter—Chapter 2—will show you how you can use context, rather than a dictionary, to figure out the meaning of a word.

On the Web: If you are using this book in class, you can visit our website for additional practice in using the dictionary. Go to **www.townsendpress.com** and click on "Online Learning Center."

REVIEW TEST 1

To review what you've learned in this chapter, answer the following questions by writing the letter of the correct answer.

  _B_   1. Guidewords can help you
       A. pronounce a word in a dictionary.
       B. find a word in a dictionary.
       C. define a word in a dictionary.

See page 39.

_C_   2. You can learn how to pronounce a word by using the pronunciation
symbols and
A. the part of speech.
B. usage labels.   See page 43.
C. the pronunciation key.

_A_   3. A dark accent mark shows
A. which syllable has the strongest stress.
B. which syllable has the weakest stress.   See page 46.
C. that the word has only one syllable.

_A_   4. A schwa is an unaccented syllable that sounds like the *a* in the word
A. *ago*.
B. *cake*.   See page 43.
C. *cat*.

_E_   5. Dictionary entries will show you all of the following *except*
A. how to spell a word.
B. how to pronounce a word.   See page 42.
C. the meaning or meanings of a word.
D. whether a word is a noun, verb, adjective or other part of speech.
E. common spelling errors of a word.

REVIEW TEST 2

A. Where would you find the numbered words below—before, on, or following the
page with the guidewords? Fill in each blank with a **B** (for *before*), an **O** (for *on*),
or an **F** (for *following*). →A (after) would work

Guidewords: **mace / magazine**

1. machine	_O_	**Item 1:** "Mach-" comes after "mace" and before "mag-."
2. macaroni	_B_	**Item 2:** "Maca-" comes before "mace."
3. moody	_F_	**Item 3:** "Mo-" comes after "ma-."
4. mailman	_F_	**Item 4:** "Mai-" comes after "mag-."
5. Mafia	_O_	**Item 5:** "Maf-" comes after "mac-" and before "mag-."

B. Use your dictionary to find the correct spellings of the following words:

    6. kabinit   _cabinet_

    7. sircus   _circus_

    8. dezign   _design_

    9. jinjerbread   _gingerbread_

    10. dinamite   _dynamite_

C. Answer the questions about the five words below. The pronunciation key on page 43 will help you answer some of the questions.

> **de•ter•mi•na•tion** (dĭ-tûr′mə-nā′shən)   **pro•file** (prō′fīl′)
>
> **hu•man•ize** (hyōō′mə-nīz′)   **sa•vor** (sā′vər)
>
> **lu•na•tic** (lōō′nə-tĭk)

11–12. Which two words have the sound of the long *a*, as in *pay*?

     determination   _savor_

13–14. Which two words have the sound of the long *i*, as in *hi*?

     humanize   _profile_

15. Which word has the long oo sound, as in *cool*? _lunatic_

16. Which word has the long *yoo* sound, as in *use*? _humanize_

17. In the word *savor*, a schwa sound appears in which syllable? _Second_

18. Which syllable is more strongly accented in the word *profile*? _First_

19. Which syllable is most strongly accented in the word *determination?*

     Fourth

20. How many syllables are in the word *determination*? _Five_

REVIEW TEST 3

Use your dictionary to do all of the following.

A. Place dots between the syllables in the following words. Then write the correct pronunciation symbols, including the accent marks.

1. s c a p e g o a t _____scape • goat_____   skāp′gōt′

2. e x h a u s t _____ex • haust_____   ĭg-zôst′

3. d e c i s i o n _____de • ci • sion_____   dĭ-sĭzh′ən

4. c e l e b r a t e _____cel • e • brate_____   sĕl′ə-brāt′

5. r e c i p r o c a t e _____re • cip • ro • cate_____   rĭ-sĭp′rə-kāt′

B. List the parts of speech for each of the following words.

6. before   *Parts of speech:* _____preposition, adverb_____

7. desire   *Parts of speech:* _____noun, verb_____

C. Write the irregular form or forms of the following words.

8. memory   *Irregular form:*_____memories_____

9. lively   *Irregular forms:* _____livelier, liveliest_____

D. What dictionary definition of *drown* fits the following sentence?

10. Elsie drowned her strawberry pancakes in strawberry syrup.

_____To drench thoroughly or cover with or as if with a liquid_____

Wording of answer may vary.

REVIEW TEST 4

Here is a chance to apply your understanding of dictionary use to an excerpt from the longtime popular book *The Road Less Traveled.* The author, M. Scott Peck, a psychiatrist, explains a key first step in dealing with personal problems. He does so by offering examples of two people who fail to think clearly about their own problems.

Words to Watch

Below are some words in the reading that do not have strong context support. Each word is followed by the number of the paragraph in which it appears and its meaning there. These words are indicated in the selection by a small circle (°).

self-evident (1): not requiring any explanation
ludicrous (2): laughable because of being obviously ridiculous
clarified (19): made clear
amenable (23): agreeable
whining (29): childish complaining
glared (37): stared angrily

RESPONSIBILITY

M. Scott Peck

1   We cannot solve life's problems except by solving them. This statement may seem idiotically self-evident°, yet it is seemingly beyond the comprehension of much of the human race. This is because we must accept responsibility for a problem before we can solve it. We cannot solve a problem by saying, "It's not my problem." We cannot solve a problem by hoping that someone else will solve it for us. I can solve a problem only when I say, "This is my problem and it's up to me to solve it." But many, so many, seek to avoid the pain of their problems by saying to themselves: "This problem was caused by other people, or by social circumstances beyond my control, and therefore it is up to other people or society to solve this problem for me. It is not really my personal problem."

2   The extent to which people will go psychologically to avoid assuming responsibility for personal problems, while always sad, is sometimes almost ludicrous°. A career sergeant in the army, stationed in Okinawa and in serious trouble because of his excessive drinking, was referred for psychiatric evaluation and, if possible, assistance. He denied that he was an alcoholic, or even that his use of alcohol was a personal problem, saying, "There's nothing else to do in the evenings in Okinawa except drink."

3   "Do you like to read?" I asked.

4   "Oh yes, I like to read, sure."

5   "Then why don't you read in the evening instead of drinking?"

6   "It's too noisy to read in the barracks."

7   "Well, then, why don't you go to the library?"

8   "The library is too far away."

9   "Is the library farther away than the bar you go to?"

10   "Well, I'm not much of a reader. That's not where my interests lie."

11   "Do you like to fish?" I then inquired.

12   "Sure, I love to fish."

13   "Why not go fishing instead of drinking?"

14   "Because I have to work all day long."

15   "Can't you go fishing at night?"

16   "No, there isn't any night fishing in Okinawa."

17   "But there is," I said. "I know several organizations that fish at night here. Would you like me to put you in touch with them?"

18   "Well, I really don't like to fish."

19   "What I hear you saying," I clarified°, "is that there are other things to do in Okinawa except drink, but the thing you like to do most in Okinawa is drink."

20   "Yeah, I guess so."

21   "But your drinking is getting you in trouble, so you're faced with a real problem, aren't you?"

22   "This damn island would drive anyone to drink."

23   I kept trying for a while, but the sergeant was not the least bit interested in seeing his drinking as a personal problem which he could solve either with or without help, and I regretfully told his commander that he was not amenable° to assistance. His drinking continued, and he was separated from the service in mid-career.

24   A young wife, also in Okinawa, cut her wrist lightly with a razor blade and was brought to the emergency room, where I saw her. I asked her why she had done this to herself.

25   "To kill myself, of course."

26   "Why do you want to kill yourself?"

27   "Because I can't stand it on this dumb island. You have to send me back to the States. I'm going to kill myself if I have to stay here any longer."

28   "What is it about living on Okinawa that's so painful for you?" I asked.

29   She began to cry in a whining° sort of way. "I don't have any friends here, and I'm alone all the time."

30   "That's too bad. How come you haven't been able to make any friends?"

31   "Because I have to live in a stupid Okinawan housing area, and none of my neighbors speak English."

32   "Why don't you drive over to the American housing area or to the wives' club during the day so you can make some friends?"

33   "Because my husband has to drive the car to work."

34   "Can't you drive him to work, since you're alone and bored all day?" I asked.

35   "No. It's a stick-shift car, and I don't know how to drive a stick-shift car, only an automatic."

36   "Why don't you learn how to drive a stick-shift car?"

37   She glared° at me. "On these roads? You must be crazy."

Dictionary Questions

Use your dictionary to answer the questions that follow. Each question is about a word taken from the selection.

1. What pronunciation does your dictionary give for *amenable?*

   ə-mē′nə-bəl (*also* ə-měn′əbəl)

2. Which syllable in *amenable* is accented?

   Second

3. What part of speech is the word *amenable?*

   Adjective

4. What pronunciation does your dictionary give for *ludicrous?*

   lōō′dĭ-krəs

5. Which syllable in *circumstances* is most strongly accented?

   First

6. What part of speech is the word *clarified?*

   Verb

7. Use your dictionary to determine the number of syllables in the word *responsibility.* Write the word, with dots between the syllables, below:

   re • spon • si • bil • i • ty (6 syllables)

8. Use your dictionary to determine the number of syllables in the word *idiotically.* Write the word, with dots between the syllables, below:

   id • i • ot • i • cal • ly (6 syllables)

 A   9. Below are dictionary definitions of *assume.* Choose the meaning that best fits *assuming* as used in the first sentence of paragraph 2 of the reading:
   A. To take upon oneself
   B. To put on
   C. To take for granted

   "The extent to which people will go psychologically to avoid assuming responsibility for personal problems, while always sad, is sometimes almost ludicrous."

   As the entire selection indicates, people do not want to take the responsibility for personal problems upon themselves.

    A   10. Below are dictionary definitions of *glare*. Choose the meaning that best fits *glared* as used in paragraph 37 of the selection:

    A. To stare angrily
    B. To shine intensely
    C. To stand out in an obvious way

The speaker's words indicate anger.

"She glared at me. 'On these roads? You must be crazy.'"

Questions about the Reading

For each question, write the letter of your answer in the space provided.

    B   1. In the excerpt below, the word *comprehension* probably means
    A. meaning.
    B. understanding.
    C. confusion.
    D. absence.

A statement like this one is something people would try to understand.

"We cannot solve life's problems except by solving them. This statement . . . is seemingly beyond the comprehension of much of the human race." (Paragraph 1)

    D   2. In the sentence below, the word *excessive* probably means
    A. good-natured.
    B. unwilling.
    C. moderate.
    D. more than normal.

Drinking more than normal can cause a person serious trouble.

"A career sergeant . . . in serious trouble because of his excessive drinking, was referred for psychiatric evaluation and, if possible, assistance." (Paragraph 2)

    C   3. Which sentence best expresses the central point of the entire selection?
    A. In Okinawa, Peck met two people who refused to take responsibility for their own problems.
    B. Some people find ways to come up with creative excuses for their irresponsibility.
    C. Many people, like the sergeant and the young wife, won't solve their problems because they refuse to take responsibility for them.
    D. The sergeant and the young wife would rather see their careers and lives ruined than take responsibility for their problems.

See the title of the selection and the first paragraph. Answers A, B, and D are too narrow. Each covers only the two examples Peck gives and ignores the idea presented in the title and the first paragraph.

_____D_____ 4. Which sentence best expresses the main idea of paragraphs 2–22?
    A. A career sergeant was in trouble because of his drinking.
    B. The sergeant denied that he had a problem with alcohol.
    C. Peck was expected to evaluate the sergeant and, if possible, help him.
    D. People will go to ridiculous lengths to avoid responsibility for their problems.   Answers A, B, and C are facts presented in paragraphs 2–22. Answer D states the main idea illustrated by these paragraphs.

_____D_____ 5. What seems to be the main idea of paragraph 23?
    A. Peck tried for some time to help the sergeant.
    B. Drinking has destroyed the lives of many people.
    C. Peck told the commander that he could not help the sergeant.
    D. The sergeant, whom Peck was unable to help, had to leave the service.   Answers A and C cover only part of the first sentence of the paragraph. Answer B is not mentioned. Answer D summarizes the whole paragraph.

_____C_____ 6. Peck states that the sergeant was not willing to be helped. What evidence does he give for that statement?
    A. The sergeant did not like to fish.   See paragraphs 5–22.
    B. The sergeant did not like to read.
    C. The sergeant refused every one of Peck's suggestions.
    D. All of the above

_____B_____ 7. The young wife first saw Peck because she
    A. was drinking too much.   See paragraph 24.
    B. had cut her wrist.
    C. had tried to return to the States.
    D. wanted to learn to drive.

_____A_____ 8. The young wife said she could not drive to the wives' club because
    A. she could not drive a stick-shift car.
    B. she had to be away at work all day.   See paragraph 35.
    C. none of the other wives spoke English.
    D. she and her husband did not own a car.

_____B_____ 9. Which statement would Peck be most likely to make to the young wife?
    A. "No one in your situation could be expected to be happy."
    B. "Since you're not willing to learn to drive a stick-shift car, you don't really want to help yourself."
    C. "Your neighbors really should learn English so that they can talk to you."
    D. "The military should make better arrangements for spouses who are living far away from home."

  Answers A, C, and D are incorrect because they would help the wife avoid taking responsibility for her own problems, and Peck's point is that people need to take responsibility.

_B_ 10. The sergeant and the young wife probably
   A. knew each other.
   B. wanted someone else to solve their problems.
   C. could have solved their problems if they were back in the United States.
   D. became happier and stronger after their meetings with Peck.

   Answers A, C, and D are not supported. Answer B states the point
   Peck is making by choosing these two people as examples.

Discussion Questions

1. Peck says that some people will go to ridiculous lengths to avoid assuming responsibility for their personal problems. What is ridiculous about the sergeant's behavior? About the young wife's behavior?

2. What details might Peck have included in this selection if he had chosen students as examples? What responsibilities do students typically avoid? What excuses do they make?

3. Peck states that "we must accept responsibility for a problem before we can solve it." What does he mean by this statement? Do you agree? Use examples from your own life or someone else's to support your view.

4. Why do you think it's so difficult for people to take responsibility for their problems?

Note: Writing assignments for this selection appear on page 588.

Check Your Performance   DICTIONARY USE

Activity	Number Right	Points	Score
Review Test 1 (5 items)	_____	× 2 =	_____
Review Test 2 (20 items)	_____	× 1.5 =	_____
Review Test 3 (10 items)	_____	× 3 =	_____
Review Test 4 (10 items)	_____	× 3 =	_____
		TOTAL SCORE =	_____%

Enter your total score into the **Reading Performance Chart: Review Tests** on the inside back cover.

DICTIONARY USE: Mastery Test 1

A. Answer the following questions about the dictionary entries for *avert* and *emerge*. Use the pronunciation key below for help as needed.

Pronunciation Key

ă hat	ā pay	âr care	ä card	ĕ ten	ē she	ĭ sit
ī hi	îr here	ŏ lot	ō go	ô all	oi oil	ou out
oŏ look	yoŏ cure	ōō cool	yōō use	ŭ up	ûr fur	th thick
th then	ə ago, item, easily, gallop, circus					

a•vert (ə-vûrt′) *v.* **1.** To turn away: *avert one's eyes.* **2.** To ward off; prevent. **—a•vert′i•ble** or **a•vert′a•ble** *adj.*

___B___ 1. Which syllable in *avert* is accented?
    A. The first   B. The second

___B___ 2. The *e* in *avert* is pronounced like the
    A. *u* in *up*.   B. *u* in *fur*.

___B___ 3. What part of speech is *avert*?
    A. Noun   B. Verb   C. Adjective

___2___ 4. Which definition of *avert* best fits the sentence below—1 or 2?

Gene saw the other car swerve, but too late to avert a collision.

___1___ 5. Which definition of *avert* best fits the sentence below—1 or 2?

The chef averted her face to avoid the heat from the oven.

Item 4: It is too late for Gene to prevent a collision.
Item 5: The chef turned her face away to avoid the heat.

(Continues on next page)

e•merge (ĭ-mûrj′) *v.* **e•merged, e•merg•ing. 1.** To rise up or come forth into view; appear. **2.** To become known or evident. **3.** To come into existence. **—e•mer′gence** *n.* **—e•mer′gent** *adj.*

_B_   6. The first *e* in *emerge* sounds like the
       A. *e* in *ten.*   B. *i* in *sit.*

_2_   7. How many syllables are in the word *emerged*?

_A_   8. What part of speech is *emergence*?
       A. Noun   B. Verb   C. Adjective

_1_   9. Which definition of *emerge* best fits the sentence below—1, 2, or 3?
       The sun emerged from behind the clouds.   The sun appeared from behind the clouds.

_2_ 10. Which definition of *emerge* best fits the sentence below—1, 2, or 3?
       The fact that the defendant was once a prison guard emerged in court last week.   The fact about the defendant became known in court.

B. Use your dictionary to find the correct spelling of the following words. (Feel free to use the spelling hints on page 41.)

11. toona   tuna

12. freaze   freeze

13. tendancy   tendency

14. paralel   parallel

15. accelarate   accelerate

C. Use your dictionary to put dots between the syllables in each word. Then write out the word with the correct pronunciation symbols, including the accent marks.

16. i m p a i r   im • pair   ĭm-pâr′

17. s a d i s t i c   sa • dis • tic   sə-dĭs′tĭk

18. i n e v i t a b l e   in • ev • i • ta • ble   ĭn-ĕv′ĭ-tə-bəl

19. a p p r e h e n s i v e   ap • pre • hen • sive   ăp′rĭ-hĕn′sĭv

20. s t e r e o t y p e   ster • e • o • type   stĕr′ē-ə-tīp′

DICTIONARY USE: Mastery Test 2

A. Answer the following questions about the dictionary entries for *notable* and *undermine*. Use the pronunciation key below for help as needed.

Pronunciation Key

ă hat	ā pay	âr care	ä card	ĕ ten	ē she	ĭ sit
ī hi	îr here	ŏ lot	ō go	ô all	oi oil	ou out
ŏŏ look	yŏŏ cure	ōō cool	yōō use	ŭ up	ûr fur	th thick
th then	ə ago, item, easily, gallop, circus					

no•ta•ble (nō′tə-bəl) *adj.* **1.** Worthy of note or notice; remarkable. **2.** Widely known and celebrated. —**no′ta•ble•ness** *n.* —**no′ta•bly** *adv.*

___A___ 1. *Notable* would be found on the dictionary page with which guidewords?
    A. **nostalgia / notation**   C. **notary / notify**
    B. **northwest / nostril**   D. **novice / noxious**

___3___ 2. How many syllables are in the word *notable*?

___A___ 3. Which syllable is accented?
    A. The first   B. The second   C. The third

___B___ 4. The *o* in *notable* is pronounced like
    A. the *o* in *lot*.   B. the *o* in *go*.   C. the *a* in *hat*.

___C___ 5. The *a* in *notable* is pronounced like
    A. the *a* in *hat*.   B. the *a* in *pay*.   C. the *a* in *ago*.

> **Item 1:** Answer B is incorrect because "not-" comes after "nos-."
> Answer C is incorrect because "notab-" comes before "notar-."
> Answer D is incorrect because "not-" comes before "nov-."

(Continues on next page)

un•der•mine (ŭn′dər-mīn′) *v.* **-mined, -min•ing, -mines. 1.** To weaken by wearing away a base or foundation. **2.** To ruin in an underhand way. **3.** To dig a mine or tunnel under.

_____A_____ 6. *Undermine* would be found on the dictionary page with which guidewords?
  A. **underling / undershirt** C. **understand / underworld**
  B. **under / undercover**   D. **underground / underhand**

_____3_____ 7. How many syllables are in the word *undermine*?

_____C_____ 8. The stronger accent is on the
  A. first syllable. B. second syllable. C. last syllable.

_____B_____ 9. The *u* in *undermine* is pronounced like
  A. the *u* in *use*. B. the *u* in *up*. C. the *u* in *circus*.

_____B_____ 10. What part of speech is *undermine*?
  A. Noun   B. Verb   C. Adjective

B. Use your dictionary to find the correct spelling of the following words. (Feel free to use the spelling hints on page 41.)

11. consede   concede

12. retreave   retrieve

13. pessemist   pessimist

14. iluminate   illuminate

15. inevitible   inevitable

C. Use your dictionary to put dots between the syllables in each word. Then write out the word with the correct pronunciation symbols, including the accent marks.

16. a s p i r e   as • pire   ə-spīr′

17. r e p r i m a n d   rep • ri • mand   rĕp′rə-mănd′

18. p r i n c i p a l   prin • ci • pal   prĭn′sə-pəl

19. t e r m i n a t e   ter • mi • nate   tûr′mə-nāt′

20. i m a g i n a t i o n   i • mag • i • na • tion   ĭ-măj′ə-nā′shən

  Item 6: Answer B is incorrect because "underm-" comes after "underc-."
     Answer C is incorrect because "underm-" comes before "unders–."
     Answer D is incorrect because "underm-" comes after "underh-."

DICTIONARY USE: Mastery Test 3

A. Answer the following questions about the dictionary entries for *destiny* and *tentative*. Use the pronunciation key below for help as needed.

Pronunciation Key

ă hat	ā pay	âr care	ä card	ĕ ten	ē she	ĭ sit
ī hi	îr here	ŏ lot	ō go	ô all	oi oil	ou out
ŏŏ look	yŏŏ cure	ōō cool	yōō use	ŭ up	ûr fur	th thick
th then	ə ago, item, easily, gallop, circus					

des•ti•ny (dĕs′tə-nē) *n.* A fixed order of things that will inevitably happen in the future; fate.

___B___ 1. *Destiny* would be found on the dictionary page with which guidewords?
   A. **designate / desperate**   C. **detach / determine**
   B. **despise / destructive**   D. **descent / design**

___3___ 2. How many syllables are in the word *destiny*?

___A___ 3. Which syllable is accented?
   A. The first   B. The second   C. The third

___B___ 4. The *e* in *destiny* is pronounced like
   A. the *e* in *she*.   B. the *e* in *ten*.   C. the *a* in *hat*.

___A___ 5. What part of speech is *destiny*?
   A. Noun   B. Verb   C. Adjective

Item 1: Answer A is incorrect because "dest-" comes after "desp-."
Answer C is incorrect because "des-" comes before "det-."
Answer D is incorrect because "dest-" comes after "desi-."

(Continues on next page)

ten•ta•tive (tĕn′tə-tĭv) *adj.* **1.** Not definite; not final. **2.** Uncertain or unsure; hesitant. —**ten′ta•tive•ly** *adv.* —**ten′ta•tive•ness** *n.*

___C___ 6. *Tentative* would be found on the dictionary page with which guidewords?
    A. **tennis / tentacle**   C. **tent / term**
    B. **tender / tension**   D. **tepid / terminate**

___3___ 7. How many syllables are in the word *tentative*?

___A___ 8. Which syllable is accented?
    A. The first   B. The second   C. The third

___C___ 9. The *a* in *tentative* is pronounced like
    A. the *a* in *hat*.   B. the *a* in *pay*.   C. the *a* in *ago*.

___C___ 10. What part of speech is *tentative*?
    A. Noun   B. Verb   C. Adjective

B. Use your dictionary to find the correct spelling of the following words. (Feel free to use the spelling hints on page 41.)

11. exersize   *exercise*

12. decieve   *deceive*

13. finaly   *finally*

14. gullable   *gullible*

15. persitant   *persistent*

C. Use your dictionary to put dots between the syllables in each word. Then write out the word with the correct pronunciation symbols, including the accent marks.

16. e l a p s e   *e • lapse*   ĭ-lăps′

17. d u b i o u s   *du • bi • ous*   do͞o′bē-əs

18. a n t i d o t e   *an • ti • dote*   ăn′tĭ-dōt′

19. i n g e n i o u s   *in • gen • ious*   ĭn-jēn′yəs

20. p e r s e v e r a n c e   *per • se • ver • ance*   pûr′sə-vîr′əns

Item 6: Answer A is incorrect because "tentat-" comes after "tentac-."
           Answer B is incorrect because "tent-" comes after "tens-."
           Answer D is incorrect because "ten-" comes before "tep-."

DICTIONARY USE: Mastery Test 4

A. Answer the following questions about the dictionary entries for *suspend* and *universal*. Use the pronunciation key below for help as needed.

Pronunciation Key

ă hat	ā pay	âr care	ä card	ĕ ten	ē she	ĭ sit
ī hi	îr here	ŏ lot	ō go	ô all	oi oil	ou out
ŏŏ look	yŏŏ cure	ōō cool	yōō use	ŭ up	ûr fur	th thick
th then	ə ago, item, easily, gallop, circus					

sus•pend (sə-spĕnd′) *v.* **1.** To bar for a period from a privilege, office, or position. **2.** To cause to stop for a period; interrupt. **3.** To put off; defer: *suspend judgment.* **4.** To render ineffective temporarily: *suspend parking regulations.* **5.** To hang so as to allow free movement.

__B__ 1. Which syllable in *suspend* is accented?
   A. The first   B. The second

__B__ 2. The *u* in *suspend* sounds like
   A. the *u* in *up.*   B. the *u* in *circus.*

__A__ 3. The *e* in *suspend* sounds like
   A. the *e* in *ten.*   B. the *e* in *she.*

__2__ 4. Which definition of *suspend* best fits the sentence below—1, 2, 3, 4, or 5?

   The parade was suspended for a while on Broad Street while the police pushed back the crowds.

__1__ 5. Which definition of *suspend* best fits the sentence below—1, 2, 3, 4, or 5?

   The bus driver was suspended until it could be determined if he had used marijuana.

   Item 4: The parade was stopped until the police pushed back the crowds.
   Item 5: The driver was barred from his position (driving the bus).

(Continues on next page)

u•ni•ver•sal (yoo′nə-vûr′səl) *adj.* **1.** Extending to or affecting the entire world; worldwide. **2.** Including or affecting all members of a class or group. **3.** Of or pertaining to the universe; cosmic.

___B___ 6. The stronger accent in *universal* is on the
   A. first syllable.   B. third syllable.

___A___ 7. The *u* in *universal* is pronounced like
   A. the *u* in *use*.   B. the *u* in *up*.

___A___ 8. The *a* in *universal* is pronounced like
   A. the *a* in *ago*.   B. the *a* in *hat*.

___1___ 9. Which definition of *universal* best fits the sentence below—1, 2, or 3?
   Clean air and pure drinking water are a universal goal in our world today.

___2___ 10. Which definition of *universal* best fits the sentence below—1, 2, or 3?
   The universal opinion of weekend moviegoers was disappointment in the new action film.

B. Use your dictionary to list the parts of speech given for the following words.

11. muzzle ___verb, noun___

12. moderate ___verb, noun, adjective___

13. stray ___verb, noun, adjective___

14. sedate ___verb, adjective___

15. compliment ___noun, verb___

C. Use your dictionary to write the irregular plural forms for the following words.

16. strategy ___strategies___

17. alumnus ___alumni___

18. mother-in-law ___mothers-in-law___

19. crisis ___crises___

20. passerby ___passers-by or passersby___

Item 9: Clean air and pure drinking water are a worldwide goal.
Item 10: All the members of the group of moviegoers were disappointed in the film.

DICTIONARY USE: Mastery Test 5

Using your dictionary, write the pronunciation and meaning of the boldfaced word in each sentence. Make sure that you choose the definition that best fits the sentence.

Wording of definitions may vary.

1. My sister, a kindergarten teacher, makes me laugh with every funny **anecdote** she tells about her young students.

   A. Pronunciation: _____ ăn′ĭk-dōt′ _____

   B. Definition: _____ An entertaining short story about an event _____

2. Suzanne is looking for a small used car—a Nissan Versa or something **comparable** in size and price.

   A. Pronunciation: _____ kŏm′pər-ə-bəl _____

   B. Definition: _____ Similar; able to be compared _____

3. Ken is too **skeptical** to believe in UFOs visiting from other worlds. He would have to see the proof with his own eyes.

   A. Pronunciation: _____ skĕp′tĭ-kəl _____

   B. Definition: _____ Doubting; questioning _____

4. My mother **imposes** on my brother's good nature by always asking him to run errands for her.

   A. Pronunciation: _____ ĭm-pōz′ĭs _____

   B. Definition: _____ Takes unfair advantage _____

5. I have asked my brother to **delete** an embarrassing photo of me that he posted on his Facebook page.

   A. Pronunciation: _____ dĭ-lēt′ _____

   B. Definition: _____ To cross out or erase; remove _____

6. A zoo is a place to see **exotic** animals, such as tigers from Asia and elephants from Africa.

   A. Pronunciation: _____ ĭg-zŏt′ĭk _____

   B. Definition: _____ Foreign; from a different part of the world; _____
   strange or different in an appealing way

(Continues on next page)

7. Jesse is **susceptible** to headaches whenever her life becomes too stressful.

   A. Pronunciation: _____ sə-sĕp'tə-bəl _____

   B. Definition: _____ Likely to be affected (with) _____

8. I could not offer the teacher a **plausible** excuse for not handing in the paper.

   A. Pronunciation: _____ plô'zə-bəl _____

   B. Definition: _____ Seemingly or apparently valid, likely, or acceptable _____

9. Some divorced parents who want to see more of their children use an illegal **strategy**: kidnapping.

   A. Pronunciation: _____ străt'ə-jē _____

   B. Definition: _____ A plan of action intended to accomplish a specific goal _____

10. Many people are afraid of spiders and snakes, but some have a more unusual **phobia**, such as a fear of bridges or stoplights.

    A. Pronunciation: _____ fō'bē-ə _____

    B. Definition: _____ A continuing, abnormal extreme fear of a particular thing or situation _____

DICTIONARY USE: Mastery Test 6

Using your dictionary, write the pronunciation and meaning of the boldfaced word in each sentence. Make sure that you choose the definition that best fits the sentence.

Wording of definitions may vary.

1. The staff at the drug store gave out the wrong medicine because they could not read the doctor's **illegible** handwriting.

    A. Pronunciation: _____ ĭ-lĕj′ə-bəl _____

    B. Definition: _____ Not able to be read or deciphered _____

2. As the sprinkle turned into a downpour, the crowd at the baseball game began to **disperse**.

    A. Pronunciation: _____ dĭ-spûrs′ _____

    B. Definition: _____ To move in different directions; scatter _____

3. In the court case, the decision of the jury was **unanimous**; everyone believed the defendant was innocent.

    A. Pronunciation: _____ yōō-năn′ə-məs _____

    B. Definition: _____ Based on complete agreement _____

4. The air escaping from the balloon **propelled** it across the table and into the punch bowl.

    A. Pronunciation: _____ prə-pĕld′ _____

    B. Definition: _____ Caused to move forward _____

5. It's important to keep household cleaners locked up safely away from children, as many of these products can be **lethal** if swallowed.

    A. Pronunciation: _____ lē′thəl _____

    B. Definition: _____ Able to cause death; deadly _____

6. A large part of war is **propaganda**: spreading information—which is often untrue—that makes the enemy look bad.

    A. Pronunciation: _____ prŏp′ə-găn′də _____

    B. Definition: _____ Ideas spread to support or oppose a cause _____

(Continues on next page)

7. Although twins Jon and Ron look very much alike, there are a few **subtle** differences that help their friends tell them apart.

   A. Pronunciation: _____ sŭt′l _____

   B. Definition: _____ Hardly noticeable; not obvious _____

8. Police officers used flashlights to **illuminate** the basement as they searched for the missing girl.

   A. Pronunciation: _____ ĭ-lo͞o′mə-nāt′ _____

   B. Definition: _____ To provide or brighten with light _____

9. The drug was pulled off the market when it was learned that researchers had **altered** test results to hide the fact that the drug was dangerous.

   A. Pronunciation: _____ ôl′tərd _____

   B. Definition: _____ Changed or made different; modified _____

10. Scholars believe the practice of drinking tea **originated** in China thousands of years ago when some leaves accidentally blew into a pot of boiling water.

    A. Pronunciation: _____ ə-rĭj′ə-nāt′ĭd _____

    B. Definition: _____ Came into being; started _____

2 Vocabulary in Context

To the Instructor: Pronunciations are provided for the words in this chapter and for vocabulary questions that follow the readings in Parts One and Two. You may want to review with students the material about pronunciation symbols and accent marks on pages 43–46.

This Chapter in a Nutshell

● You don't always have to use a dictionary to learn the meanings of new words in your reading. You can often use *context* to figure out the meaning of a word:

— *Examples* may provide clues to what a word means.

— *Synonyms*—words that mean the same as an unknown word—may provide clues to a meaning.

— *Antonyms*—words that mean the opposite of an unknown word—may help you figure out a meaning.

— The *entire sentence* may provide clues to a meaning.

● Textbook authors often tell you a word's meaning; they *italicize* or **boldface** terms you may not know and give definitions and examples of those terms.

Do you know the meaning of the word *savor*? Look at the following cartoon and see if the sentences underneath (spoken by the older brother) help you choose the correct answer.

___A___   *Savor* (sā′vər) means

    A. enjoy.

    B. wonder about.

    C. forget.

The older brother is advising his younger brother to take enough time to appreciate the taste of the candy. The **context**—the words surrounding the unfamiliar word—tells us that *savor* means "appreciate" or "enjoy." In this chapter, you will learn how to use the context to figure out the meanings of words.

Understanding Vocabulary in Context

Do you know the meaning of the word *vital*? How about the word *appropriate*? Or the word *passive*?

You may not know the meaning of one or more of these words. However, if you saw these words in sentences, chances are you could come up with fairly accurate definitions. For example, read each sentence below and see if you can understand the meaning of the word in *italics*. In the space provided, write the letter of the meaning you think is correct. Then read the explanation.

Do not use a dictionary for this work. Instead, in each sentence, try the word you think is the answer. For example, put *unimportant* or *necessary* or *surprising* into the sentence in place of *vital* to see which one makes the best sense.

___B___ 1. All animals share the same *vital* needs, such as food, water, and shelter.

        Vital (vīt′l) means
        A. unimportant.   B. necessary.   C. surprising.

___A___ 2. In the United States, shaking hands is the *appropriate* way to greet someone; in China, bowing is the right way.

        Appropriate (ə-prō′prē-ĭt) means
        A. proper.   B. artificial.   C. insulting.

___B___ 3. Winners in life take an active role in making things happen, instead of being *passive* and waiting for good luck.

        Passive (păs′ĭv) means
        A. insincere.   B. inactive.   C. flexible.

In each sentence above, the context surrounding the unfamiliar word provides clues to the word's meaning. You may have guessed from the context that *vital* means "necessary," that *appropriate* means "proper," and that *passive* means "inactive."

Using context clues to understand the meaning of unfamiliar words will help you in three ways:

1 It will save you time when reading. You will not have to stop to look up words in the dictionary. (Of course, you won't always be able to understand a word from its context, so you should have a dictionary nearby as you read.)

2 It will improve your "working vocabulary"—words you recognize as you read and will eventually be able to use when you speak and write. You will therefore add to your vocabulary simply by reading thoughtfully.

3 It will give you a good sense of how a word is actually used, including any shades of meaning it might have.

Types of Context Clues

There are four common types of context clues:

1 Examples
2 Synonyms
3 Antonyms
4 General sense of the sentence or passage

In the following sections, you will read about and practice each type. The practices will sharpen your skills in recognizing and using context clues. They will also help you add new words to your vocabulary.

Remember *not* to use a dictionary for these practices. Their purpose is to help you develop the skill of figuring out what words mean *without* using a dictionary. Pronunciations are provided in parentheses for the words, and a guide to pronunciation is on page 43.

1   Examples

An unfamiliar word may appear with **examples** that reveal what the word means. For instance, note the examples in this sentence from the previous page: "All animals share the same vital needs, such as food, water, and shelter." The examples—food, water, and shelter—helped you figure out that the word *vital* means "necessary."

Look at the cartoon below and see if the example helps you choose the correct meaning of the word *vague*.

Copyright 2002 by Randy Glasbergen.
www.glasbergen.com

GLASBERGEN

"When my folks ask when I'm going to get a job, I always give some vague answer such as 'Oh, sooner or later.'"

_C_   *Vague* (vāg) means

      A. angry.   B. humorous.   C. unclear.

Notice that the example of a vague answer—"Oh, sooner or later"—helps you understand that *vague* means "unclear."

 ## Check Your Understanding

Now read the items that follow. An *italicized* word in each sentence is followed by examples that serve as context clues for that word. These examples, which are **boldfaced**, will help you figure out the meaning of each word. On each line, write the letter of the answer you think is correct. Then read the explanation that follows.

    Note that examples are often introduced with signal words and phrases like *for example, for instance, including,* and *such as.*

_C_   1. In our house, clothes hangers have various odd *functions*. For instance, we use them to **scratch backs** and **hold up plants in the garden**.

      Functions (fŭngk′shənz) are
      A. shapes.   B. problems.   C. uses.

      Hint: Remember that in the exercises in this chapter, you can insert into each sentence the word you think is the answer. For example, substitute *shapes, problems,* or *uses* in sentence 1 in place of *functions* to see which one fits.

_B_   2. Our baseball team's pitcher has a few *eccentric* habits, such as **throwing exactly thirteen pitches when warming up** and **never wearing socks**.

      Eccentric (ĭk-sĕn′trĭk) means
      A. normal.   B. strange.   C. messy.

_A_   3. Throughout history, humans have built a wide variety of *dwellings*, including **simple mud huts, stone castles,** and **marble mansions**.

      Dwellings (dwĕl′ĭngs) are
      A. homes.   B. stores.   C. churches.

Explanation

In each sentence, the examples probably helped you to figure out the meanings of the words in italics:

    1. The correct answer is C. In sentence 1, the examples of the odd functions of hangers—scratching backs and holding up plants—may have helped you to guess that *functions* are "uses."

    2. The correct answer is B. In sentence 2, the examples of strange habits show that *eccentric* means "strange."

3. The correct answer is A. The examples in sentence 3 indicate that *dwellings* are homes.

Note that the examples in the sentences are introduced by the signal words *for instance*, *such as*, and *including*.

in class

PRACTICE 1: Examples

Read each item below and then do two things:

1. Underline the examples that suggest the meaning of the word in italics.
2. Then write the letter of the word's meaning on the answer line.

Note that the last five sentences have been taken from college textbooks.

___C___ 1. The *debris* in the stadium stands included numerous paper cups, ticket stubs, sandwich wrappings, and cigarette butts.   Signal word: *included.*
The examples given are of trash.
Debris (də-brē′) means
A. products.   B. papers.   C. trash.

___C___ 2. For his weak stomach, Mario ate a *bland* diet of white bread, rice, and mashed potatoes.   The examples given are of mild foods.
Bland (blănd) means
A. spicy.   B. varied.   C. mild.

___B___ 3. New York, Boston, and Philadelphia are three of the oldest *urban* areas in the United States.   The examples given are of cities.
Urban (ûr′bən) means
A. empty.   B. city.   C. country.

___A___ 4. Many people take dietary *supplements*—for example, extra calcium or large doses of vitamin C—in the belief that they will cure or prevent disease.   Signal words: *for example.* The examples given are of additions to people's diets.
Supplements (sŭp′lə-mənts) means
A. additions.   B. losses.   C. suggestions.

___B___ 5. My uncle often has embarrassing *mishaps*, such as backing his car into the side of his boss's Cadillac and trying to walk through a glass door.
Mishaps (mĭs′hăps′) means   Signal words: *such as.*
The examples given are of accidents.
A. clever moves.   B. accidents.   C. projects.

B   6. The death of a child and the death of a spouse are two of life's most
         traumatic experiences.   The examples given are of painful experiences.
         Traumatic (trou-măt′ĭk) means
         A. rare.   B. painful.   C. interesting.

C   7. A *transaction*, such as buying or selling a product, is the most basic part
         of an economy.   Signal words: *such as*. The examples
                                           given are of business deals.
         Transaction (trăn-săk′shən) means
         A. profit.   B. loss.   C. business deal.

B   8. Religious *rituals* like baptisms, church weddings, and funeral services
         give many people a sense of peace and comfort.   Signal word: *like*.
                                           The examples given are of ceremonies.
         Rituals (rĭch′oō-əls) means
         A. lessons.   B. ceremonies.   C. prayers.

A   9. When discussing the Internet, professionals often use such *jargon* as
         "adware," "clickthrough rate," and "spambot," which others may not
         understand.   Signal words: *such . . . as*. The examples are
                                        words that belong to a special language.
         Jargon (jär′gən) means
         A. special language.   B. clear instructions.   C. mean insults.

B   10. There are hundreds of different kinds of *retailers*, ranging from car
         dealerships and department stores to frozen-yogurt stands and online
         drugstores.   The examples given are of businesses that sell directly to users.
         Retailers (rē′tāl′ərs) means
         A. customers.   B. businesses that sell   C. businesses that
                                    directly to users.   make products.

2 Synonyms

Context clues are often found in the form of **synonyms**: one or more words that
mean the same or almost the same as the unknown word. Look again at the sentence
on page 76: "In the United States, shaking hands is the *appropriate* way to greet
someone; in China, bowing is the right way." Here the synonym "right" tells you
the meaning of *appropriate*. A synonym may appear anywhere in a sentence as a
restatement of the meaning of the unknown word.

Now look at the cartoon on the following page.

"I try to refrain from overeating, but I can't stop myself!"

Notice that the synonym for *refrain*—expressed in the dog's words "stop myself"—helps you understand that *refrain* (rĭ-frān′) means "to hold oneself back."

 ## Check Your Understanding

Each item below includes a word or phrase that is a synonym of the *italicized* word. Underline that synonym in each sentence. Then read the explanation that follows.

1. The cat soon found it <u>useless</u> to smack her paws against the front of the fish tank; her effort to catch a fish was a *futile* (fyo͞ot′l) one.

2. My best friend *squandered* (skwŏn′dərd) all his money; his drinking and gambling <u>wasted</u> his earnings.

3. Because my boss runs the toy store like a *tyrant* (tī′rənt), all of the employees call her "the little <u>dictator</u>."

Explanation

In each sentence, the synonym given probably helped you understand the meaning of the word in italics:

1. In the first sentence, the synonym of *futile* is "useless."

2. In sentence 2, the synonym of *squandered* is "wasted."

3. In sentence 3, the synonym of *tyrant* is "dictator."

in class

PRACTICE 2: Synonyms

Each item below includes a synonym of the *italicized* word. Write each synonym in the space provided.

Note that the last five items have been taken from college textbooks.

____self-important____   1. Everyone turned to look at the *arrogant* (ăr′ə-gənt) customer who spoke to the manager in a self-important voice.

   Hint: What does the voice reveal about the customer?

____powerful____   2. The medicine that Nina is taking is very *potent* (pōt′nt). It is so powerful that she must not take it for more than a week. What must the medicine be if Nina has to stop taking it after only one week?

____cloudy____   3. After the heavy rains, the stream became *murky* (mûr′kē); in fact, the water was so cloudy you couldn't see the bottom. What kind of water would you be unable to see through?

____secret____   4. Some overweight people are called *furtive* (fûr′tĭv) eaters because they eat large quantities of food in secret. In what way do these people eat their food?

____believable____   5. A con artist was apparently very believable as he went door to door telling a *plausible* (plô′zə-bəl) story about having his wallet stolen and needing twenty dollars to get home. What kind of story would a con artist have to tell to make people give him money?

____discussion____   6. The first step in reaching a peace agreement was to set up a *dialog* (dī′ə-lôg′) between the two sides. Without discussion, peace was impossible. What would have to be set up in order to reach a peace agreement?

____force____   7. You cannot *coerce* (kō-ûrs′) people into learning. If they are not interested, it is impossible to force them. If people aren't interested in learning, what can't be done to them?

____rich____   8. While Ved may not be *affluent* (ăf′lōō-ənt) by American standards, he is rich compared with most people in his homeland of India. Although Ved is rich by Indian standards, what might he not be by American standards?

____prove____   9. Several tests are necessary to *verify* (vĕr′ə-fī′) that a virus is present. One is never enough to prove a virus exists. What will several tests do that one test cannot do?

____variety____   10. The *diversity* (dĭ-vûr′sĭ-tē) of the population of the United States is the result of accepting immigrants from a wide variety of cultures and nations. If the United States accepts people from many different cultures and nations, what would its population have?

3   Antonyms

Antonyms—words and phrases that mean the opposite of a word—are also useful as context clues. Antonyms are sometimes signaled by words and phrases such as *however, but, yet, on the other hand, instead of,* and *in contrast.*

Look again at the sentence on page 76: "Winners in life take an active role in making things happen, instead of being passive and waiting for good luck." Here the words *instead of* indicate that *passive* must be the opposite of *active.*

Now look at the cartoon below.

"What do you mean 'unreasonable,' Miss Jones? I think this is a perfectly rational way to keep myself organized."

Notice that the antonym "unreasonable" helps you figure out that *rational* (răsh′ə-nəl) must mean "reasonable."

✓ *Check Your Understanding*

In each of the following sentences, underline the word or phrase that means the opposite of the *italicized* word. Then, on the answer line, write the letter of the meaning of the italicized word. Finally, read the explanation that follows.

____B____ 1. The coach takes every opportunity to *reprimand* his players, yet he ignores every chance to <u>praise</u> them.

  Reprimand (rĕp′rə-mănd) means

  A. approve of.   B. criticize.   C. choose.

____A____ 2. "I am having *acute* pains in my chest now," said the patient, "but an hour ago, all I felt was a <u>dull</u> ache."

  Acute (ə-kyo͞ot′) means

  A. sharp.   B. weak.   C. no.

___B___ 3. Some teachers are too *lenient*. I'd rather have <u>strict</u> teachers who take the class seriously.

Lenient (lē′nē-ənt) means
A. hard.   B. easygoing.   C. busy.

Explanation

In each sentence, the antonym given probably helped you understand the meaning of the word in italics:

1. The correct answer is B. *Reprimand* is the opposite of *praise*, so the answer to sentence 1 is *criticize*.

2. The correct answer is A. In sentence 2, the opposite of *acute* is *dull*, so *acute* must mean "sharp."

3. The correct answer is B. In sentence 3, "lenient" teachers are the opposite of "strict" teachers, so *lenient* means "easygoing."

Note that *reprimand* and *acute* are indicated by signal words: *yet* and *but*.

PRACTICE 3: Antonyms

Each item below includes a word or phrase that is an antonym of the *italicized* word. Underline each of those antonyms. Then, on the line, write the letter of the meaning of the italicized word.

Note that the last five items have been taken from college textbooks.

___A___ 1. After his accident, Brad expected an <u>in-depth</u> examination at the hospital. Instead, a doctor gave him a quick, *superficial* checkup and said, "You're fine."

Hint: What would be the opposite of an in-depth examination?

Superficial (sōō′pər-físh′əl) means
A. lacking depth.   B. complicated.   C. satisfactory.

___A___ 2. A <u>temporary</u> cough is nothing to worry about, but a *chronic* one can be a sign of a serious illness.   What would be the opposite of a *temporary* cough?

Chronic (krŏn′ĭk) means
A. continuing.   B. brief.   C. mild.

___C___ 3. When drinking was *prohibited* by the Nineteenth Amendment, alcohol became more popular with some people than it had been when it was <u>allowed.</u>   What would be the opposite of *allowing* alcohol?

Prohibited (prō-hĭb′ĭt-ĭd) means
A. permitted.   B. defined.   C. forbidden.

_____A_____ 4. "What we need is an *innovative* idea!" cried the chairman. "All I've heard so far are the same old ones."   What would be the opposite of *old* ideas?

      Innovative (ĭn′ə-vā′tĭv) means

      A. new.   B. traditional.   C. loud.

_____B_____ 5. The class was in *turmoil* when only the substitute teacher was there, but it quickly came to order once the principal entered the room.

      Turmoil (tûr′moil′) means   In a classroom, what would be the opposite of *order*?

      A. peace.   B. confusion.   C. attendance.

_____B_____ 6. In ordinary life, people's facial expressions are *spontaneous*. However, actors must learn to use planned ways of showing emotion.

      Spontaneous (spŏn-tā′nē-əs) means   What would be the opposite of *planned*?

      A. varied.   B. unplanned.   C. hidden.

_____C_____ 7. A computer *novice* is lucky if he or she knows someone who is an expert and is willing to offer advice.   What kind of person would need an expert's help?

      Novice (nŏv′ĭs) means

      A. a child.   B. a friend.   C. a beginner.

_____C_____ 8. Some patients drop out of drug therapy before it is completed. Instead of making progress, they may then *revert* to previous bad habits.

      Revert (rĭ-vûrt′) means   What would be the opposite of *making progress*?

      A. say no.   B. improve.   C. go back.

_____C_____ 9. Our Constitution would be in danger if all Americans were *indifferent to* it. However, history has shown that concerned citizens will always come forward to defend it.   What kind of person would be the opposite of a *concerned* citizen?

      Indifferent to (ĭn-dĭf′ər-ənt tōō) means

      A. insulted by.   B. aware of.   C. uninterested in.

_____B_____ 10. In warfare, as in chess, *impulsive* actions will fail. To win in either case, carefully thought-out moves are needed.   What kind of action is not *carefully thought out*?

      Impulsive (ĭm-pŭl′sĭv) means

      A. fearful.   B. unplanned.   C. strong.

4   General Sense of the Sentence or Passage

Often, the context of a new word contains no examples, synonyms, or antonyms. In such cases, you must do a bit more detective work; you'll need to look at any clues provided in the information surrounding the word. Asking yourself questions about the passage may help you make a fairly accurate guess about the meaning of the unfamiliar word.

Look at the cartoon below about a job interview.

There are no examples, synonyms, or antonyms in the woman's statement. However, the applicant's costume—that of an executioner—and the huge axe he carries suggest that *ruthless* (rōōth′lĭs) means "showing no mercy."

 ## *Check Your Understanding*

Each sentence below is followed by a question. Think about each question; then write the letter of the answer you feel is the meaning of the italicized word.

___A___ 1. The newlyweds agreed to be very *frugal* in their shopping because they wanted to save enough money to buy a home.

(How would people shop if they wanted to save money?)

Frugal (frōō′gəl) means
A. thrifty.   B. wasteful.   C. interested.

___B___ 2. So many customers have complained about the noise in the restaurant that the owners are trying to find ways to *mute* the noise.

(What would the restaurant owners probably want to do about noise?)

Mute (myōōt) means
A. increase.   B. quiet.   C. create.

___C___ 3. Friends tried to *dissuade* ninety-year-old Mrs. Kellen from attending her son's trial, but she went anyway, to show her support.

(What would the elderly woman's friends have tried to do to her if they didn't want her to go to her son's trial?)

Dissuade (dĭ-swād′) means

A. question.   B. describe.   C. discourage.

Explanation

In each sentence, your answer to the question should have helped you figure out the meaning of the word in italics:

1. The correct answer is A. The first sentence provides enough evidence for you to guess that *frugal* means "thrifty." The newlyweds had to be thrifty if they wanted to save money.

2. The correct answer is B. *Mute* in the second sentence means "quiet"; a restaurant owner would probably want to reduce the noise.

3. The correct answer is C. *Dissuade* means "discourage"—Mrs. Kellen went to the trial despite her friends' attempts to discourage her.

If you use context clues, you may not get the exact dictionary definition of a word, but you will often be accurate enough to make good sense of what you are reading.

PRACTICE 4: General Sense of the Sentence or Passage

Figure out the meaning of the word in *italics* by looking at clues in the rest of the sentence. First, try to answer the question in parentheses that follows each item below. Then, on the basis of your answer, write the letter of the meaning you think is correct.

Note that the last five items have been taken from college textbooks.

___C___ 1. To reach a *sound* conclusion about an issue, you must carefully consider all the facts involved.

(What kind of conclusion would you reach by carefully considering all the facts?)

Sound (sound) means

A. early.   B. obvious.   C. reasonable.

___A___ 2. My mother refuses to *divulge* the secret ingredients she uses in her fried chicken recipe.

(What would someone refuse to do with ingredients that are secret?)

Divulge (dĭ-vŭlj′) means
  A. reveal.   B. hide.   C. invent.

___A___ 3. Because the nicotine in cigarettes is harmful, many people favor *stringent* laws against their sale.

(What type of laws would be favored by people concerned about the harm of nicotine?)

Stringent (strĭn′jənt) means
  A. strict.   B. weak.   C. confusing.

___C___ 4. Taking the expression "raining cats and dogs" *literally*, the child looked for little animals on the ground after the storm.

(In what way did the child interpret the phrase "raining cats and dogs"?)

Literally (lĭt′ər-ə-lē) means
  A. symbolically.   B. musically.   C. as the real facts.

___A___ 5. It's too late to *alter* the plans for the party. The restaurant and band have been reserved, and all the invitations have been sent out.

(If the plans have all been made, what is it too late to do to the plans?)

Alter (ôl′tər) means
  A. change.   B. surprise.   C. repeat.

___B___ 6. Organ transplants will not succeed unless the *donor* has the same blood type as the person receiving the organ.

(Who would need to have the same kind of blood as the person receiving the transplant?)

Donor (dō′nər) means
  A. one who receives.   B. one who gives.   C. one who doubts.

___C___ 7. Few American officials in Iraq were *fluent* in the Iraqi language, so all communication had to be in English.

(What would an American have to be in order to communicate in the Iraqi language?)

Fluent (flōō′ənt) means
  A. able to remember.   B. able to teach.   C. able to speak well.

B   8. The placing of a huge cable on the floor of the Atlantic Ocean in 1866 made it possible to *transmit* telegraph signals from Europe to North America.

(What did the cable allow us to do with signals between Europe and North America?)

Transmit (trăns-mĭt′) means

A. check.   B. send.   C. lose.

A   9. Over years, the movement of water in a stream will *erode* the surrounding soil and rock. As a result, the stream will be wider and deeper.

(What does water do to soil and rock to enlarge a stream?)

Erode (ĭ-rōd′) means

A. wear away.   B. escape.   C. build up.

C   10. In the 1950s, Americans felt that the Soviet Union was a *menace* threatening their national security. As a result, Senator Joseph McCarthy was able to persuade millions of people that the Soviets had secret agents in the United States government.

(What would a country that threatened our national security be regarded as?)

Menace (měn′ĭs) means

A. puzzle.   B. friend.   C. danger.

An Important Point about Textbook Definitions

You don't always have to use context clues or the dictionary to find definitions. Very often, textbook authors provide definitions of important terms. They usually follow a definition with one or more examples to make sure that you understand the word being defined.

Here is a short textbook passage that includes a definition and an example. Note that the term to be defined is set off in **boldface** type, and the definition then follows.

> [1]The changing work force has changed lifestyles and needs. [2]No wonder many workers have found **flextime** a desirable choice. [3]Instead of working the standard nine-to-five day, five days a week, they choose their own hours. [4]For instance, they may decide to work four days at ten hours a day rather than five days at eight hours.

Textbook authors, then, often do more than provide context clues: they set off the terms they are defining in *italic* or **boldface** type, as above. When they take the time to define and illustrate a word, you should assume that the material is important enough to learn.

More about textbook definitions and examples appears on pages 264–265 in the "Relationships II" chapter.

CHAPTER REVIEW

In this chapter, you learned the following:

- To save time when reading, you should try to figure out the meanings of unfamiliar words. You can do so by looking at their **context**—the words surrounding them.

- There are four kinds of context clues: **examples** (marked by words like *for example, for instance, including,* and *such as*); **synonyms** (words that mean the same as unknown words); **antonyms** (words that mean the opposite of unknown words); and **general sense of the sentence** (clues in the sentence or surrounding sentences about what words might mean).

- Textbook authors typically set off important words in *italic* or **boldface** and define those words for you, often providing examples as well.

The next chapter—Chapter 3—will introduce you to the most important of all comprehension skills, finding the main idea.

 On the Web: If you are using this book in class, you can visit our website for additional practice in understanding vocabulary in context. Go to **www.townsendpress.com** and click on "Online Learning Center."

 REVIEW TEST 1

To review what you've learned in this chapter, answer the following questions by writing the letter of each correct answer.

___C___ 1. The context of a word is   See page 76.
A. its meaning.   B. its opposite.   C. the words around it.

___A___ 2. Which type of context clue often follows signal words like *including, such as,* and *for instance*?
A. Example
B. Synonym   See page 78.
C. Antonym

___B___ 3. In the sentence below, which type of context clue is provided for the italicized word?
  A. Example
  B. Synonym
  C. Antonym

  Synonym clue: unusual.

  I'm looking for a *unique* (yōō-nēk′) gift for my boyfriend; he appreciates unusual things.

___C___ 4. In the sentence below, which type of context clue is provided for the italicized word?
  A. Example
  B. Synonym
  C. Antonym

  Instead signals that there is an antonym: *renewed.*

  Expecting that his license would be renewed, the pilot was surprised when it was *revoked* (rĭ-vōkt′) instead.

___A___ 5. Often, when textbook authors introduce a new word, they provide a definition and help make the meaning of the word clear by including one or more
  A. examples.   B. synonyms.   C. antonyms.

  See page 89.

REVIEW TEST 2

A. Look at the cartoon below about cavemen painting over drawings in their cave, and notice the caption, "First Graffiti Eradication Program." Then answer the question that follows.

in class *homework*

FIRST GRAFFITI ERADICATION PROGRAM

___B___ 1. Using the context clues in the cartoon, write the letter of the best meaning of *eradication* (ĭ-răd′ĭ-kā′shən) in the space provided.
  A. writing   B. removal   C. contest

  If the graffiti are painted over, what has been done to them?

B. Using context clues for help, write the letter of the best meaning for each italicized word. Use the space provided.

____C____ 2. Though people who work nonstop can accomplish a great deal, they may also *forfeit* (fôr′fĭt) their health.   What might working nonstop do to a person's health?
    A. strengthen   C. give up
    B. remember   D. talk about

____C____ 3. The principal was known to *intimidate* (ĭn-tĭm′ĭ-dāt′) students by walking through the halls with a baseball bat and shouting through a bullhorn.   What would the principal's behavior do to kids?
    A. encourage   C. frighten
    B. entertain   D. fail

____D____ 4. My aunt has no *empathy* (ĕm′pə-thē) when it comes to other people's problems. She thinks only one person really has troubles, and that's herself.   What does the aunt lack?
    A. pleasure   C. pride
    B. fear   D. understanding

____B____ 5. The crowd of protesters *dispersed* (dĭ-spûrst′) quickly when the police arrived with growling German shepherds.   What would police and growling dogs cause a crowd to do?
    A. cheered   C. questioned
    B. scattered   D. paid

C. Using context clues for help, write the definition for each italicized word. Then write the letter of the definition in the space provided. Choose from the definitions in the box below. Each definition will be used once.

A. clear and brief	B. lazy	C. messy
D. violations	E. warning	

____D____ 6. Paula was suspended from school because of several *infractions* of the rules, including smoking in the washroom and dressing improperly.

    Infractions (ĭn-frăk′shəns) means _____ violations _____.
                    Examples of violations are given. Signal word: *including*.

____E____ 7. We began the picnic in spite of such *ominous* signs as dark clouds and a falling temperature.

    Ominous (ŏm′ə-nəs) means _____ warning _____.
                    Examples are of weather warning signs.

_B_   8. While Luis is hardworking, his *indolent* brother spends most of his time watching TV or sitting around with friends.

    Indolent (ĭn′də-lənt) means _____ lazy _____ .

        Antonym clue: Luis is hardworking; his brother is the opposite.

_C_   9. Although Alex usually looks *unkempt*, he had a very neat appearance at his job interview.

    Unkempt (ŭn-kĕmpt′) means _____ messy _____ .

       Antonym clue: At the interview, Alex looked neat; he usually looks the opposite.

_A_ 10. When you write a report, your statement of purpose should be *concise*. State your point clearly in as few words as possible.

    Concise (kən-sīs′) means _____ clear and brief _____ .

        Synonym clues: *clearly* and *few words*.

REVIEW TEST 3

A. Look at the cartoon below, and then answer the questions that follow.

in class

© Randy Glasbergen.
www.glasbergen.com

GLASBERGEN

"My appearance is deceptive. I may look fierce, but that's untrue—I'm really a gentle, sensitive guy."

_C_   1. Using the context clues in the cartoon, write the letter of the best meaning of *fierce* (fîrs) in the space provided.

    A. false   B. unhappy   C. scary

        A businessman who looks like a crocodile is scary.

_C_   2. Which kind of context clue helps you understand the meaning of the cartoon?

    A. Examples clue   B. Synonym clue   C. Antonym clue

        Antonym clues: *gentle* and *sensitive*.

B. Four words are **boldfaced** in the textbook passage below. Write the definition for each boldfaced word, choosing from the definitions in the box. Then write the letter of the definition in the space provided.

Be sure to read the entire passage before making your choices. Note that six definitions will be left over.

A. disliked	B. encourage	C. expensive	D. explanation
E. fearful	F. punishment	G. reward	H. small
I. warning	J. well-known		

¹Suppose someone asked you to sit on top of a flagpole for twelve hours and promised you a prize. ²After you returned to earth, you learned the prize was a stick of gum. ³Would you be likely to repeat the flagpole-sitting behavior? ⁴Chances are you would not unless there was a severe gum shortage and you were dying for gum. ⁵Although the gum was a prize, it was a **paltry** one. ⁶It would not serve as a **positive reinforcement** that would lead to more of the same behavior. ⁷What would it take to **induce** you to climb up and sit on top of the flagpole again? ⁸Perhaps a good positive reinforcement for you would be a more **lavish** prize, such as a new car, a screen test from a movie studio, or a free vacation to Hawaii. ⁹For such a reinforcement to be effective enough to shape behavior, it must be suitable.

Items 3–5:
General sense of the sentence.

Item 3: A stick of gum is a small prize.

Item 4: What might make you want to repeat a task?

Item 5: Someone who wants you to climb would encourage you.

Item 6: Example clues: *new car, screen test, free vacation.*

___H___ 3. *Paltry* (pôl′trē) means _____small_____.

___G___ 4. *Positive reinforcement* (pŏz′ĭ-tĭv rē′ĭn-fôrs′mənt) means _____ _____reward_____.

___B___ 5. *Induce* (ĭn-do͞os′) means _____encourage_____.

___C___ 6. *Lavish* (lăv′ĭsh) means _____expensive_____.

C. Four words are **boldfaced** in the textbook passage on the following page. Write the definition for each boldfaced word, choosing from the definitions in the box. Then write the letter of the definition in the space provided.

Be sure to read the entire passage before making your choices. Note that six definitions will be left over.

A. attracts	B. benefit	C. catch and eat	D. closes
E. danger	F. empties	G. explore	H. loosens
I. play with	J. rush away from		

Items 7–10:
General sense of the sentence.

Item 7: *While* signals an antonym-like clue: some plants provide food; others do what?

Item 8: What would "sweet perfume" do to small insects?

Item 9: What must the jaws do to hold the insect?

[1]While plants often provide food for animals, some plants turn the tables and **prey on** smaller members of the animal kingdom. [2]One, the Venus's-fly-trap, uses its leaves like a steel trap. [3]It **lures** small insects with its sweet perfume and then **clamps** its "jaws" so it can digest the insects at its leisure. [4]Another leafy hunter is the pitcher plant, whose sweet juices tempt insects to explore the plant. [5]Once deep within the plant, the insect meets a watery death. [6]Plants are essential for animal life, but for inhabitants of the insect community, they can also be a **hazard** that may end life.

__C__ 7. *Prey on* (prā ŏn) means _____ *catch and eat* _____.

__A__ 8. *Lures* (loŏrs) means _____ *attracts* _____.

__D__ 9. *Clamps* (klămps) means _____ *closes* _____.

__E__ 10. *Hazard* (hăz'ərd) means _____ *danger* _____.

Item 10: To insects, what are these hungry plants?

REVIEW TEST 4

Here is a chance to apply the skill of understanding vocabulary in context to a full-length selection. This story describes a moment in a teacher's life when she learned how important a single act of hers had been. Its author, Sister Helen Mrosla, was a Franciscan nun from Little Falls, Minnesota. Since 1991, when she wrote this account of a true incident in her life, the story has been reprinted many times and even circulated on the Internet. Read the selection, and then answer the questions on vocabulary that follow.

Words to Watch

Below are some words in the reading that do not have strong context support. Each word is followed by the number of the paragraph in which it appears and its meaning there. These words are indicated in the selection by a small circle (°).

mischievousness (1): minor misbehavior
novice (3): new
deliberately (5): slowly and on purpose
concept (8): idea
crankiness (8): grouchy mood
lull (13): brief silence
taps (16): a bugle call sounded at night and at a military funeral
sheepishly (20): with embarrassment
frazzled (20): worn-out; ragged

ALL THE GOOD THINGS

Sister Helen P. Mrosla

1   He was in the first third-grade class I taught at Saint Mary's School in Morris, Minnesota. All thirty-four of my students were dear to me, but Mark Eklund was one in a million. He was very neat in appearance, but had that happy-to-be-alive attitude that made even his occasional mischievousness° delightful.

2   Mark talked incessantly. I had to remind him again and again that talking without permission was not acceptable. What impressed me so much, though, was his sincere response every time I had to correct him for misbehaving—"Thank you for correcting me, Sister!" I didn't know what to make of it at first, but before long I became accustomed to hearing it many times a day.

3   One morning my patience was growing thin when Mark talked once too often, and then I made a novice° teacher's mistake. I looked at him and said, "If you say one more word, I am going to tape your mouth shut!"

4   It wasn't ten seconds later when Chuck blurted out, "Mark is talking again." I hadn't asked any of the students to help me watch Mark, but since I had stated the punishment in front of the class, I had to act on it.

5   I remember the scene as if it had occurred this morning. I walked to my desk, very deliberately° opened my drawer, and took out a roll of masking tape. Without saying a word, I proceeded to Mark's desk, tore off two pieces of tape, and made a big X with them over his mouth. I then returned to the front of the room. As I glanced at Mark to see how he was doing, he winked at me.

6   That did it! I started laughing. The class cheered as I walked back to Mark's desk, removed the tape, and shrugged my shoulders. His first words were, "Thank you for correcting me, Sister."

7   At the end of the year I was asked to teach junior-high math. The years flew by, and before I knew it Mark was in my classroom again. He was more handsome than ever and just as polite. Since he had to listen carefully to my instruction in the "new math," he did not talk as much in ninth grade as he had talked in the third.

8   One Friday, things just didn't feel right. We had worked hard on a new concept° all week, and I sensed that the students were frowning, frustrated with themselves—and edgy with one another. I had to stop this crankiness° before it got out of hand. So I asked them to list the names of the other students in the room on two sheets of paper, leaving a space after each name. Then I told them to think of the nicest thing they could say about each of their classmates and write it down.

9   It took the remainder of the class period to finish the assignment, and as the students left the room, each one handed me the papers. Charlie smiled. Mark said, "Thank you for teaching me, Sister. Have a good weekend."

10   That Saturday, I wrote down the

name of each student on a separate sheet of paper, and I listed what everyone else had said about that individual.

11   On Monday I gave each student his or her list. Before long, the entire class was smiling. "Really?" I heard whispered. "I never knew that meant anything to anyone!" "I didn't know others liked me so much!"

12   No one ever mentioned those papers in class again. I never knew if the students discussed them after class or with their parents, but it didn't matter. The exercise had accomplished its purpose. The students were happy with themselves and one another again.

13   That group of students moved on. Several years later, after I returned from a vacation, my parents met me at the airport. As we were driving home, Mother asked me the usual questions about the trip—the weather, my experiences in general. There was a slight lull° in the conversation. Mother gave Dad a sideways glance and simply said, "Dad?" My father cleared his throat as he usually did before something important. "The Eklunds called last night," he began. "Really?" I said. "I haven't heard from them in years. I wonder how Mark is."

14   Dad responded quietly. "Mark was killed in Vietnam," he said. "The funeral is tomorrow, and his parents would like it if you could attend." To this day I can still point to the exact spot on I-494 where Dad told me about Mark.

15   I had never seen a serviceman in a military coffin before. Mark looked so handsome, so mature. All I could think at that moment was, Mark, I would give all the masking tape in the world if only you would talk to me.

16   The church was packed with Mark's friends. Chuck's sister sang "The Battle Hymn of the Republic." Why did it have to rain on the day of the funeral? It was difficult enough at the graveside. The pastor said the usual prayers, and the bugler played taps°. One by one those who loved Mark took a last walk by the coffin and sprinkled it with holy water.

17   I was the last one to bless the coffin. As I stood there, one of the soldiers who had acted as pallbearer came up to me. "Were you Mark's math teacher?" he asked. I nodded as I continued to stare at the coffin. "Mark talked about you a lot," he said.

18   After the funeral, most of Mark's former classmates headed to Chuck's farmhouse for lunch. Mark's mother and father were there, obviously waiting for me. "We want to show you something," his father said, taking a wallet out of his pocket. "They found this on Mark when he was killed. We thought you might recognize it."

19   Opening the billfold, he carefully removed two worn pieces of notebook paper that had obviously been taped,

folded and refolded many times. I knew without looking that the papers were the ones on which I had listed all the good things each of Mark's classmates had said about him. "Thank you so much for doing that," Mark's mother said. "As you can see, Mark treasured it."

20   Mark's classmates started to gather around us. Charlie smiled rather sheepishly° and said, "I still have my list. It's in the top drawer of my desk at home." Chuck's wife said, "Chuck asked me to put his list in our wedding album." "I have mine too," Marilyn said. "It's in my diary." Then Vicki, another classmate, reached into her pocketbook, took out her wallet, and showed her worn and frazzled° list to the group. "I carry this with me at all times," Vicki said without batting an eyelash. "I think we all saved our lists."

That's when I finally sat down and 21 cried. I cried for Mark and for all his friends who would never see him again.

To the Instructor: Most of the context clues in the following items are general sense of the sentence. To help students understand the correct answers, you might ask the question or give the explanation that appears in red next to each item.

Vocabulary Questions

Use context clues to help you decide on the best definition for each italicized word. Then, in the space provided, write the letter of each choice.

___B___ 1. In the excerpt below, the word *incessantly* (ĭn-sĕs′ənt-lē) means
    A. slowly.
    B. constantly.
    C. quietly.
    D. pleasantly.

    "Mark talked incessantly. I had to remind him again and again that talking without permission was not acceptable." (Paragraph 2)   If Mark had to be reminded over and over again to stop talking, how did he talk?

___D___ 2. In the excerpt below, the words *accustomed to* (ə-kŭs′təmd tōō) mean
    A. afraid of.
    B. confused by.
    C. warned about.
    D. used to.

    "What impressed me so much, though, was [Mark's] sincere response every time I had to correct him for misbehaving—'Thank you for correcting me, Sister!' I didn't know what to make of it at first, but before long I became accustomed to hearing it many times a day." (Paragraph 2)
    What happens if you hear something over and over again?

___A___ 3. In the sentence below, the words *blurted out* (blûrt′ĭd out) mean
    A. said suddenly.
    B. watched for.
    C. ran away.
    D. looked at.

    "It wasn't ten seconds later when Chuck blurted out, 'Mark is talking again.'" (Paragraph 4)   How did Chuck tell Sister Helen about Mark?

___B___   4. In the excerpt below, the word *proceeded* (prō-sēd'ĭd) means
    A. stayed.   C. wrote.
    B. went.   D. threw.

> "I walked to my desk, very deliberately opened my drawer, and took out a roll of masking tape. Without saying a word, I proceeded to Mark's desk, tore off two pieces of tape, and made a big X with them over his mouth." (Paragraph 5)   Sister Helen went to Mark's desk with the tape.

___C___   5. In the sentence below, the word *edgy* (ĕj'ē) means
    A. funny.   C. easily annoyed.
    B. calm.   D. happy.

> "We had worked hard on a new concept all week, and I sensed that the students were frowning, frustrated with themselves—and edgy with one another." (Paragraph 8)   What describes frustrated and frowning students?

___A___   6. In the sentence below, the word *remainder* (rĭ-mān'dər) means
    A. what was left.   C. smallest part.   How much of the
    B. beginning.   D. memo.   class period was used to finish the assignment?

> "It took the remainder of the class period to finish the assignment, and as the students left the room, each one handed me the papers." (Paragraph 9)

___B___   7. In the sentence below, the word *individual* (ĭn'də-vĭj'oo-əl) means
    A. day.   C. paper.   Synonym clue:
    B. person.   D. teacher.   *each student.*

> "That Saturday, I wrote down the name of each student on a separate sheet of paper, and I listed what everyone else had said about that individual." (Paragraph 10)

___C___   8. In the excerpt below, the word *accomplished* (ə-kŏm'plĭsht) means
    A. forgotten.   C. been successful for.
    B. liked.   D. missed.

> "The exercise had accomplished its purpose. The students were happy with themselves and one another again." (Paragraph 12)
>   If the students were happy, the assignment must have been successful.

___A___   9. In the excerpt below, the word *responded* (rĭ-spŏnd'ĭd) means
    A. answered.   C. asked.
    B. interrupted.   D. left.

> "'The Eklunds called last night,' he began. 'Really?' I said. 'I haven't heard from them in years. I wonder how Mark is.'
> "Dad responded quietly. 'Mark was killed in Vietnam,' he said." (Paragraphs 13–14)   What did Dad quietly do after he heard Sister Helen's question?

___B___ 10. In the sentence below, the word *treasured* (trĕzh'ərd) means
      A. hid.   C. sold.
      B. valued.   D. lost.

> "I knew without looking that the papers were the ones on which I had listed all the good things each of Mark's classmates had said about him. 'Thank you so much for doing that,' Mark's mother said. 'As you can see, Mark treasured it.'" (Paragraph 19)
>
> How did Mark feel about the comments his classmates made?

Discussion Questions

1. In this story, we read of two classroom incidents involving Sister Helen and her students. In one, she briefly taped a third-grader's mouth closed. In another, she encouraged junior-high students to think of things they liked about one another. In your opinion, what do these two incidents tell about Sister Helen? What kind of teacher was she? What kind of person?

2. Why do you think so many of Sister Helen's students kept their lists for so long? Why were the lists so important to them? What souvenir of the past have you kept for a long time? What does it mean to you?

3. At the end of the story, Sister Helen tells us that she "cried for Mark and for all his friends who would never see him again." Do you think she might have been crying for other reasons, too? Explain what they might be.

4. "All the Good Things" has literally traveled around the world. Not only has it been reprinted in numerous publications; many readers have sent it out over the Internet for others to enjoy. Why do you think so many people love this story? Why do they want to share it with others?

Note: Writing assignments for this selection appear on page 589.

Check Your Performance   VOCABULARY IN CONTEXT

Activity	Number Right	Points	Score
Review Test 1 (5 items)	_____	× 2 =	_____
Review Test 2 (10 items)	_____	× 3 =	_____
Review Test 3 (10 items)	_____	× 3 =	_____
Review Test 4 (10 items)	_____	× 3 =	_____
		TOTAL SCORE =	_____%

Enter your total score into the **Reading Performance Chart: Review Tests** on the inside back cover.

VOCABULARY IN CONTEXT: Mastery Test 1

A. Look at the cartoon below, and then answer the questions that follow.

© 1998 Randy Glasbergen.

GLASBERGEN

"I'm a little apprehensive about the new boss.
His snoopiness makes me uneasy."

___C___ 1. Using the context clues in the cartoon, write the letter of the best meaning of *apprehensive* (ăp′rĭ-hĕn′sĭv) in the space provided.
  A. pleased B. forgetful C. worried

___B___ 2. Which kind of context clue helps you understand the meaning of the cartoon?
  A. Examples clue B. Synonym clue C. Antonym clue

Items 1 and 2: Synonym clue: *uneasy.*

B. For each item below, underline the **examples** that suggest the meaning of the italicized word. Then, on the answer line, write the letter of the meaning of that word.

___A___ 3. Carol survived her freshman year despite various *adverse* (ăd-vûrs′) events. For instance, she missed two weeks of class because of a strep throat and had all her books stolen just before finals.
  A. unfavorable C. fortunate
  B. evil D. pleasant

Signal words: *For instance.*

___D___ 4. The new principal took *drastic* (drăs′tĭk) steps to deal with school funding cuts, including firing teachers and doing away with sports.
  A. funny C. approving
  B. small D. extreme

Signal word: *including.*

(Continues on next page)

C. Each item below includes a word or words that are a **synonym** of the italicized word. Write the synonym of the italicized word in the space provided.

_____show off_____ 5. The old saying "If you've got it, *flaunt* (flônt) it" means that you should show off your good qualities.
The word means signals the synonym for flaunt: show off.

_____signal_____ 6. The company president made a brief *gesture* (jĕs′chər) with her hand. It was a clear signal that the interview was over.
The second sentence presents the synonym of gesture: signal.

D. Each item below includes a word or words that are an **antonym** of the italicized word. Underline the antonym of each italicized word. Then, on the answer line, write the letter of the meaning of the italicized word

__D__ 7. The chef hates a <u>dirty</u> kitchen. If the kitchen isn't *immaculate* (ĭ-măk′yə-lĭt) at the end of a day, he insists that somebody stay late to finish cleaning.
The chef hates dirty kitchens. He wants the opposite of dirty: spotless.
 A. large   C. crowded
 B. messy   D. spotless

__D__ 8. If parents show *apathy* (ăp′ə-thē) toward their children's education, how can we expect the students to show <u>interest</u>?
If parents show no interest, how can we expect students to show interest?
 A. attention   C. teaching
 B. knowledge   D. lack of interest

E. Use the **general sense of each sentence** to figure out the meaning of each italicized word. Then, on the answer line, write the letter of the meaning of the italicized word.

__A__ 9. My aunt is so *obstinate* (ŏb′stə-nĭt) that once she makes up her mind, nothing any member of her family says can change it.
A person who does not change her mind is stubborn.
 A. stubborn   C. easy-going
 B. clever   D. cooperative

__D__ 10. Building the Brooklyn Bridge was a huge struggle involving men, materials, and nature. Numerous *obstacles* (ŏb′stə-kəls) had to be overcome in order to complete the structure in 1883.
 A. buildings   C. places
 B. causes   D. difficulties
A "huge struggle" is likely to involve difficulties.

VOCABULARY IN CONTEXT: Mastery Test 2

A. Look at the cartoon below, and then answer the question that follows.

Copyright 2006 by Randy Glasbergen.
www.glasbergen.com

SALES TRAINING

GLASBERGEN

"There are several crucial things to remember before you go on a sales call, Jones. One of them is to get dressed."

___A___ 1. Using the context clues in the cartoon, write the letter of the best meaning of *crucial* (kroo′shəl) in the space provided.
   A. very important   B. expensive   C. unusual

   Getting dressed is an example of a very important thing to remember.

B. For each item below, underline the **examples** that suggest the meaning of the italicized term. Then, on the answer line, write the letter of the meaning of that word.

___D___ 2. The employees showed the *contempt* (kən-tĕmpt′) they felt for their boss by ignoring his memos and making fun of him behind his back.
   A. admiration   C. fear   Examples of insulting
   B. envy   D. disrespect   acts are given.

___A___ 3. The apples were on sale because many of them had *defects* (dē′fĕkts′), such as brown spots, soft places, or small holes in the skin.
   A. imperfections   C. prizes   Examples of imperfections
   B. peelings   D. leaves   are given.

(Continues on next page)

C. Each item below includes a word or words that are a **synonym** of the italicized word. Write the synonym of the italicized word in the space provided.

_____make clear_____   4. Textbook authors often *clarify* (klăr′ə-fī′) general statements with specific examples; the illustrations make clear what the general point is saying. The second part of the sentence presents a synonym for *clarify: make clear.*

_____never happened_____
_____before_____   5. The event was *unprecedented* (ŭn-prĕs′ĭ-dĕn′tĭd)—the election of a pig to the student council is something that had never happened before.   The phrase after the dash presents a synonym for *unprecedented: never happened before.*

_____die down_____   6. The comedian waited for the laughter to *subside* (səb-sīd′) before going on with his next joke. The audience's reaction did not die down for two whole minutes.   The second sentence presents a synonym for *subside: die down.*

D. Each item below includes a word or words that are an **antonym** of the italicized word. Underline the antonym of each italicized word. Then, on the answer line, write the letter of the meaning of the italicized word.

__A__   7. Before the game, the locker room had been cheerful; but now, after losing the game, the players were *morose* (mə-rōs′). *But* signals opposite
   A. sad and gloomy   C. pleased   moods in the locker
   B. tired   D. happy and excited   room: cheerful
                                                               and morose.

__D__   8. "It is better to *retreat* (rĭ-trēt′) to safety," said the general, "than to go forward foolishly."   *Retreat* is the opposite of *go forward.*
   A. attack   C. look
   B. investigate   D. move back

E. Use the **general sense of each sentence** to figure out the meaning of each italicized word. Then, on the answer line, write the letter of the meaning of the italicized word.

__C__   9. When I couldn't fall asleep last night, I realized I had been *imprudent* (ĭm-prōōd′nt) to drink so much coffee after dinner.   If drinking coffee
   A. pleased   C. unwise   prevents sleep, it is
   B. clever   D. fortunate   unwise to do
                                                            it after dinner.

__D__ 10. How you interpret the *ambiguous* (ăm-bĭg′yōō-əs) sentence "Visiting relatives can be boring" may depend on which you find annoying—relatives who visit or visits to relatives.
   A. long and boring   C. having a clear meaning
   B. difficult to say   D. having more than one meaning
            If a sentence can be interpreted differently, it has more than one meaning.

VOCABULARY IN CONTEXT: Mastery Test 3

Using context clues for help, write the letter of the best meaning for each italicized word.

___A___ 1. Greg wanted to become *proficient* (prə-fĭsh′ənt) on the saxophone, so he practiced every day for several hours.
   A. highly skilled
   B. very loud
   C. dependent
   D. tired

   What would someone become by practicing for several hours a day?

___C___ 2. Otis was faced with the *dilemma* (dĭ-lĕm′ə) of putting more money into his ancient Chevy or doing without a car.
   A. happy situation
   B. bad mood
   C. unpleasant choice
   D. victory

   Example clue: The sentence gives an example of a dilemma.

___D___ 3. Our children are so afraid of snakes that even a toy rubber snake *provokes* (prə-vōks′) panic in them.
   A. amuses
   B. closes
   C. prevents
   D. causes

   A toy snake would cause panic among kids afraid of snakes.

___B___ 4. Janice often asks *impertinent* (ĭm-pûr′tn-ənt) questions such as "Where did you get that ugly shirt?" or "Did you cut your own hair?"
   A. clever
   B. rude
   C. important
   D. friendly

   Examples of rude questions are given.

___C___ 5. At the family reunion, the older relatives sat together and *reminisced* (rĕm′ə-nĭst′) for hours about events of fifty years ago.
   A. forgot
   B. were irritated
   C. discussed past events
   D. argued

   What were the older relatives doing about events of fifty years ago?

___B___ 6. The wolf was *wary* (wâr′ē), circling around the camp until he felt sure that all the hikers were asleep.
   A. hungry
   B. cautious
   C. brave
   D. tired

   What does the wolf's behavior indicate about him?

___C___ 7. Don't be *naïve* (nä-ēv′) enough to believe commercials and e-mail ads that promise instant riches, effortless weight loss, and valuable free prizes.
   A. dishonest
   B. absent-minded
   C. unsuspecting
   D. critical

   What kind of person would believe in instant wealth, easy weight loss, and free prizes?

(Continues on next page)

_____A_____ 8. A fight between the two brothers seemed *inevitable* (ĭn-ĕv′ĭ-tə-bəl) that rainy Saturday; they had been teasing each other all morning.
  A. unavoidable
  B. welcome
  C. impossible
  D. unwanted

_____C_____ 9. The teacher decided that the test results were not *valid* (văl′ĭd) because some students had gotten hold of the questions before the test.
  A. high
  B. interesting
  C. reliable
  D. unusual

_____D_____ 10. Because Mac had left out a *vital* (vīt′l) ingredient, the apple cake came out looking like a pancake.
  A. bad-tasting
  B. unnecessary
  C. small
  D. very important

Item 8: A fight becomes unavoidable for two brothers who teased each other all morning.
Item 9: What would the test results *not* be if students had seen the test beforehand?
Item 10: Only an important ingredient could change the cake's shape.

VOCABULARY IN CONTEXT: Mastery Test 4

Using context clues for help, write the letter of the best meaning for each italicized word. Note that all of the sentences have been taken from college textbooks.

__B__ 1. After a baby is born, an older child may become jealous. Wanting the attention the newborn is receiving, the child may *regress* (rĭ-grĕs′) to such behavior as sucking a thumb or crying.
  A. look   C. talk
  B. go back   D. advance   If an older child
                                    begins to suck a thumb or cry, what has the child done?

__D__ 2. Certain marine bacteria contain chemicals that produce light. Passengers sailing at night in the Indian Ocean often pass through "glowing seas" *illuminated* (ĭ-lōō′mə-nāt′ĭd) by countless bacteria.   Synonym-like
  A. polluted   C. made dangerous   clues: *produce*
  B. cleaned   D. lit up   *light; glowing.*

__A__ 3. Nobody needs proof to know that conflict is part of life—it is *self-evident* (sĕlf′ ĕv′ĭ-dənt).
  A. obvious   C. unclear   What sorts of things do
  B. possible   D. unlikely   not need to be proved?

__B__ 4. In historical novels, the main events that occur, such as the Civil War, are factual, but many of the characters are *fictitious* (fĭk-tĭsh′əs).
  A. old   C. unimportant
  B. not real   D. active   *But* signals that
                                    fictitious means the opposite of *factual.*

__D__ 5. Teenagers are often *gregarious* (grĭ-gâr′ē-əs), finding status and a sense of identity by spending all their leisure time with a particular circle of friends.
  A. quiet and reserved   C. wanting their own way
  B. independent   D. seeking the company of others
                  What kind of people spend so much time with friends?

__B__ 6. It is a *fallacy* (făl′ə-sē) to assume that if one event happens before another, then the first event is the cause of the second one. Actually, the two events may be completely unrelated.
  A. promise   C. good idea
  B. mistake   D. truth

                  If the two events may be completely unrelated,
                  it is a mistake to assume one caused the other.

(Continues on next page)

_C_ 7. Throughout history, governments have attempted to justify their actions through *propaganda* (prŏp'ə-găn'də), including political speeches, books and pamphlets, and media campaigns.

A. spending money   C. information spread to support a

B. noise   cause   *The examples given*

                            D. good behavior   *are of information*
spread to support a cause. Signal word: including.

_D_ 8. Patients suffering from tuberculosis used to be placed in *seclusion* (sĭ-klōō'zhən), away from anyone who was in danger of catching the disease.   *Synonym-like clue: away from anyone who was in danger*

A. hospitals   C. groups   *of catching the disease.*

B. bed   D. away from others

_C_ 9. Certain mental disorders can cause *delusions* (dĭ-lōō'zhəns), such as the false belief that one is being spied on by the police.   *The false belief*

A. sudden actions   C. mistaken ideas   *that one is*

B. good feelings   D. strong objections   *being spied on*

                 is an example of a mistaken idea. Signal words: such as.

_D_ 10. The increasing popularity of online social networking sites has led to new legal and ethical problems, such as what should be done about people who use those networks to bully and *harass* (hə-răs') one another.

A. support   C. agree with

B. ignore   D. attack

                               Synonym clue: bully.

VOCABULARY IN CONTEXT: Mastery Test 5

do only Part B

A. Using context clues for help, write the letter of the best meaning for each italicized word.

_D_   1. The story the former drug addict told was so *engrossing* (ĕn-grō′sĭng) to the students that they didn't move even when the bell rang.

     A. pleasing   C. confusing   A story that keeps
     B. boring   D. fascinating   students from leaving
                                            must be fascinating.

_B_   2. Everyone *evacuating* (ĭ-văk′yoo-ā′tĭng) the burning hotel, including those as far up as the twentieth floor, had to use the stairs.

     A. staying in   C. paying for   People use stairs
     B. leaving   D. arriving at   to leave a building.

_A_   3. Some members of organizations are good only at thinking up ideas. So although they are able to *initiate* (ĭ-nĭsh′ē-āt′) a project, they need others to complete it.

                                     Antonym clue: *complete.*
     A. start   C. try out   One group completes
     B. name   D. work on   a project; the other does
                        the opposite and *initiates*, or begins, the project.

_C_   4. During high tide, waves advance, covering most or all of the beach, but during low tide, the water *recedes* (rĭ-sēds′), leaving behind seaweed and shells and occasionally leaving fish behind on the sand.

     A. appears   C. goes back   Antonym clue: *advance.*
                                      At low tide, waves
     B. comes forward   D. becomes dangerous   advance; at
                high tide, they do the opposite and *recede*, or go back.

_D_   5. Colleges have several resources to aid students in determining which *vocations* (vō-kā′shəns) would be best for them. These include preference tests, a job placement center offering information about opportunities in various fields, and the services of career counselors.

     A. classes   C. study skills   Synonym clues:
     B. living arrangements   D. jobs   *job, fields, career.*

(Continues on next page)

B. Five words are **boldfaced** in the textbook passage below. Write the definition for each boldfaced word, choosing from the definitions in the box. Then write the letter of the definition in the space provided.

Be sure to read the entire passage before making your choices. Note that three definitions will be left over.

A. coating	B. drops off	C. enjoyable
D. enormous	E. increases	F. lie down
G. small	H. step forth	

¹One of the most unusual bodies of water in the world is the Dead Sea. ²Surrounded by desert, this "sea" is actually 26 percent dissolved minerals, 99 percent of which are salts. ³Over 45 miles long and 11 miles wide, the Dead Sea is so salty that its water actually feels oily and leaves a chalky **residue** on the skin. ⁴Bathers brave enough to **venture** just a few feet into the Dead Sea will discover that the human body floats in the salty mixture. ⁵Because of the **vast** amount of salt in the water, a person can actually **recline** on the surface of the Dead Sea as if it was a giant waterbed. ⁶While clear, the sea's water is so thick that ripples and waves are visible even beneath its surface. ⁷Unfortunately, this natural marvel is shrinking. ⁸Each year, the water level **diminishes** by three feet. ⁹At this rate, the Dead Sea will become a salty desert in a few centuries.

___A___ 6. In sentence 3, *residue* (rĕz′ĭ-do͞o′) means _____coating_____.

___H___ 7. In sentence 4, *venture* (vĕn′chər) means _____step forth_____.

___D___ 8. In sentence 5, *vast* (văst) means _____enormous_____.

___F___ 9. In sentence 5, *recline* (rĭ-klīn′) means _____lie down_____.

___B___ 10. In sentence 8, *diminishes* (dĭ-mĭn′ĭsh-ĭs) means _____drops off_____.

Item 6: What is left on the skin?
Item 7: In order to discover that the human body floats, bathers would have to step forth into the water.
Item 8: Sentences 1–3 discuss the large amount of salt in the Dead Sea.
Item 9: If the surface is like a giant waterbed, people can lie down on it.
Item 10: Synonym clue: *is shrinking*.

VOCABULARY IN CONTEXT: Mastery Test 6

A. Using context clues for help, write the letter of the best meaning for each italicized word. Note that all of the sentences have been taken from college textbooks.

_A_ 1. In deciding on a sentence, the judge often considers whether or not the criminal has shown *remorse* (rĭ-môrs′). If there is evidence that the convicted person is sorry for what he or she has done, the punishment tends to be less severe. *Synonym-like clue: sorry for what he or she has done.*
   A. regret and guilt   C. innocence
   B. evidence   D. pleasure and satisfaction

_C_ 2. In the third stage of its life cycle, the caterpillar shuts itself into a cocoon. When it *emerges* (ĭ-mûrj′ĭs) months later, it will be a beautiful butterfly. *Antonym-like clue: shuts itself into [a cocoon].*
   A. folds up   C. comes out
   B. goes inside   D. cries out

_B_ 3. The male woodpecker can be quite *persistent* (pər-sĭs′tənt) in his attempts to attract a female. He is usually not discouraged by her refusal and will continue to court her for several hours. *An animal that continues for hours and is "not discouraged" is steady.*
   A. late   C. afraid
   B. steady   D. uncaring

_B_ 4. According to research, a majority of U.S. teenagers hold part-time jobs during the school year. Most teens consider their work *tedious* (tē′dē-əs), but some find their jobs to be an enjoyable social experience. *Signal word: but. Antonym clue: enjoyable.*
   A. exciting   C. helpful
   B. boring   D. educational

_A_ 5. New employees should be reminded that it is *prudent* (proōd′nt) to accept assignments and carry out orders without objecting. Workers who seem unwilling to go along with company policy will probably soon find themselves looking for new jobs. *Accepting assignments and carrying out orders are wise steps for new employees.*
   A. wise   C. risky
   B. friendly   D. unhelpful

(Continues on next page)

B. Five words are **boldfaced** in the textbook passage below. Write the definition for each boldfaced word, choosing from the definitions in the box. Then write the letter of the definition in the space provided.

Be sure to read the entire passage before making your choices. Note that three definitions will be left over.

A. dangerous	B. discouragement	C. done together
D. force	E. get involved	F. imitate
G. insincere	H. stand up to	

¹Studies of school violence suggest that as many as 80 percent of students who witness bullying do nothing to stop it. ²Why? ³According to sociologists, there are four main reasons students refuse to **intervene** and help their peers. ⁴First of all, most bystanders are simply afraid of getting hurt. ⁵Jumping into a fight is **treacherous**—it may lead to injury all too quickly. ⁶A second reason students don't stand up for their peers is that they are afraid bullies will turn on them. ⁷Fear of becoming a new target is such a powerful **deterrent** that most students choose to do nothing—even when their classmates are suffering. ⁸A third reason students don't **compel** bullies to stop is that most bystanders believe their actions can make a situation worse. ⁹In reality, however, doing nothing helps no one and can actually encourage bullies to attack. ¹⁰Last, bystanders do not **confront** bullies because they don't know what to do or how to do it. ¹¹Clearly schools need to teach students how to respond to bullying so that schools—and students—are safer.

___E___ 6. In sentence 3, *intervene* (ĭn′tər-vēn′) means _____get involved_____.

___A___ 7. In sentence 5, *treacherous* (trĕch′ər-əs) means _____dangerous_____.

___B___ 8. In sentence 7, *deterrent* (dĭ-tûr′ənt) means _____discouragement_____.

___D___ 9. In sentence 8, *compel* (kəm-pĕl′) means _____force_____.

___H___ 10. In sentence 10, *confront* (kən-frŭnt′) means _____stand up to_____.

Item 6:   Antonym clue: *do nothing to stop it.*
Item 7:   Behavior that can lead to injury is dangerous.
Item 8:   What would fear of becoming a target do to students?
Item 9:   The entire passage is about why bystanders don't force bullies to stop.
Item 10: What are bystanders afraid to do to bullies?

3 Main Ideas

This Chapter in a Nutshell

- Recognizing an author's **main idea**, or point, is the most important reading skill.
- The main idea is a general idea supported by specific ideas and details.
- Learn to think as you read by asking yourself, "What is the author's point?"

What Is the Main Idea?

Copyright 2006 by Randy Glasbergen.
www.glasbergen.com

"Things were good at work today. The boss was out sick. The computer network was working for a change. And the vending machine was giving everyone free cups of coffee."

"What's the point?" People ask this question when they want to know what main idea is being presented. Sometimes a main idea is clear right away, as in the cartoon above. What would you say is the speaker's point in the cartoon?

Explanation

The main idea is that the speaker had a good day at work. He then supports his point with three specific reasons: the boss was out, the computer network was working, and the vending machine was dispensing free coffee.

When you read, get in the habit of asking, "What is the main point the writer is trying to make?" Recognizing the **main idea**, or point, is the most important key to better reading.

Check Your Understanding

For instance, read the following paragraph, asking yourself as you do, "What is the author's point?"

> ¹Poor grades in school can have various causes. ²For one thing, students may have financial problems. ³If they need to work long hours to make money, they will have little study time. ⁴Another cause of poor grades may be trouble with relationships. ⁵A student may be unhappy over family problems or a lack of friends. ⁶That unhappiness can harm schoolwork. ⁷A final cause of poor grades may be bad study habits. ⁸Some students have never learned how to take good notes in class, how to manage their time effectively, or how to study a textbook. ⁹Without such study skills, their grades are likely to suffer.

Here is a good two-step way to find an author's point, or main idea:

1   Look for a general statement.

2   Decide if that statement is supported by most of the other material in the paragraph. If it is, you have found the main idea.

Below are four statements from the passage about poor grades. Pick out the general statement that is supported by the other material in the passage. Write the letter of that statement in the space provided. Then read the explanation that follows.

Four statements from the passage

   A. Poor grades in school can have various causes.

   B. For one thing, students may have financial problems.

   C. A final cause of poor grades may be bad study habits.

   D. Some students have never learned how to take good notes in class, how to manage their time effectively, or how to study a textbook.

The general statement that expresses the main idea of the passage is: ___A___

Explanation

Sentence A: The phrase "various causes" in sentence A is a general one. It is broad enough to include all of the specific causes mentioned in the other sentences—financial problems, trouble with relationships, and bad study habits. Sentence A, then, is the sentence that expresses the main idea of the passage.

Sentence B: This sentence is about only one type of problem, financial problems. "Financial problems" is not general enough to include the other two listed causes of poor grades: trouble with relationships and bad study habits.

Sentence C: This sentence also mentions only one specific cause: bad study habits. "Bad study habits" is not general enough to include the other two causes presented in the paragraph.

Sentence D: This sentence lists three specific study problems. It does not cover the other material in the paragraph.

The Main Idea as an "Umbrella" Idea

Think of the main idea as an "umbrella" idea. The main idea is the author's general point. The other material of the paragraph fits under it. That other material is made up of specific supporting details—evidence such as examples, reasons, or facts. The diagram below shows the relationship:

The explanations and activities on the following pages will deepen your understanding of the main idea.

How Do You Recognize a Main Idea?

To recognize the main idea of a passage, you must **become an active reader**. Active readers *think* as they read. Instead of merely taking in words, an active reader constantly asks, "What's the point?" In addition, active readers use a variety of other strategies to determine an author's main idea. Below are three active reading strategies you can use to help find the main idea in a passage.

    1 Look for general versus specific ideas.
    2 Use the topic to lead you to the main idea.
    3 Use key words to lead you to the main idea.

Each strategy is explained on the following pages.

1   Look for General versus Specific Ideas

You saw in the paragraph on the causes of poor grades that the main idea is a *general* idea that is supported by *specific* ideas. To improve your skill at finding main ideas, then, it will be helpful to practice separating general from specific ideas.

✓ Check Your Understanding

See if you can do the following brief exercises. Then read the explanations that follow.   *Answers will vary; below are some possibilities.*

    1. You often use general and specific ideas without even realizing it. Consider the following:

      ● *Animal* is a general term. Write the names of three specific animals:

            _____dog_____   _____raccoon_____   _____bear_____

      ● *Vegetables* is a general term. Write the names of three specific vegetables:

            _____carrot_____   _____onion_____   _____celery_____

      ● *Emotion* is a general term. Write the names of three specific emotions:

            _____anger_____   _____sadness_____   _____happiness_____

Explanation

In answering the above items, you might have chosen such specific animals as a dog, raccoon, or bear; such specific vegetables as carrots, onions, or celery; such specific emotions as anger, sadness, or happiness.

2. Let's say that a new year is starting, and you decide to make some New Year's resolutions. Your general idea might be as follows:

General idea: Starting in January, I want to make some changes in my life.

● Now write three *specific* ideas—three resolutions that you might make:

Get to bed earlier

Eat less junk food

Spend at least a half hour reading each day

Explanation

Three examples of specific resolutions might be to get to bed earlier, to eat less junk food, and to spend at least a half hour reading each day.

3. In thinking about your teachers, you might decide that one of your high-school English teachers was your best teacher. Your general idea might be as follows:

General idea: _____Mrs. Hill_____ is the best teacher I ever had.

● Now write three *specific* reasons you thought so highly of this teacher:

She explained ideas clearly.

She was friendly.

She spent individual time with each student.

Explanation

You might, for instance, have liked a given teacher because he or she gave clear explanations of ideas, had a friendly manner, and spent individual time with each student.

4. Finally, suppose you have found a good part-time job. Your general idea might be as follows:

General idea: ___Working at the diner___ has been a good part-time job for me.

● Now write three *specific* supporting reasons for liking the job:

Pay of $10.00 per hour

Convenient work hours after school each day

Travel time of only fifteen minutes to the job

Explanation

Three particular reasons for liking a job might include pay of ten dollars an hour, convenient work hours after school each day, and a short travel time of only fifteen minutes to the job.

Now do the practices that follow, which will give you more experience in telling the difference between general and specific ideas.

PRACTICE 1

Each cluster of words below consists of one general idea and three specific ideas. The general idea includes all the specific ideas. Identify each general idea with a **G** and the specific ideas with an **S.** Look first at the example.

Example

_S_ frying

_S_ baking

_G_ cooking

_S_ steaming

To the Instructor: You might want to ask questions such as the following:

Item 1: Which of the ideas are actual *liquids?*
Item 2: Which of the ideas are specific *snacks?*
Item 3: Which of the ideas are kinds of *fabrics?*
Item 4: Which of the ideas are actual *forms of entertainment?*
Similar questions can be asked for items 5 through 10.

(*Cooking* is the general idea. It includes three specific types of cooking: frying, baking, and steaming.)

1. _S_ soup
   _S_ water
   _G_ liquid
   _S_ coffee

2. _S_ potato chips
   _S_ pretzels
   _S_ salted nuts
   _G_ snacks

3. _S_ cotton
   _G_ fabric
   _S_ silk
   _S_ wool

4. _G_ entertainment
   _S_ movies
   _S_ concerts
   _S_ card games

5. _S_ cans
   _S_ boxes
   _S_ bags
   _G_ containers

6. _S_ rock
   _S_ classical
   _S_ country
   _G_ music

7. _S_ necklace
   _G_ jewelry
   _S_ ring
   _S_ bracelet

8. _G_ fish
   _S_ tuna
   _S_ salmon
   _S_ flounder

9. _S_ coughing
   _S_ sneezing
   _G_ symptom
   _S_ sore throat

10. _S_ speaking
    _S_ listening
    _S_ writing
    _G_ communicating

PRACTICE 2

In each item below, one idea is general and the others are specific. The general idea includes the specific ideas. In the spaces provided, write two more specific ideas that are covered by the general idea.

Example   *General:* school subjects
             Specific: biology, Spanish, ___history___ , ___math___

             (School subjects is the general idea; *biology* and *Spanish* are specific subjects, as are *history* and *math.)*

                                                Answers will vary; below are some possibilities.

1. *General:* beverages
   Specific: iced tea, water, ___milk___ , ___coffee___

2. *General:* sport
   Specific: baseball, soccer, ___football___ , ___basketball___

3. *General:* relatives
   Specific: cousin, mother ___father___ , ___nephew___

4. *General:* sandwich
   Specific: ham, grilled cheese, ___tuna___ , ___egg salad___

5. *General:* reading material
   Specific: textbook, comic book, ___newspaper___ , ___magazine___

6. *General:* seafood
   Specific: clams, lobster, ___shrimp___ , ___crabmeat___

7. *General:* tone of voice
   Specific: excited, surprised, ___angry___ , ___pleading___

8. *General:* negative personal quality
   Specific: greed, cowardice, _____selfishness_____, _____dishonesty_____

9. *General:* positive personal quality
   Specific: reliability, determination, _____loyalty_____, _____honesty_____

10. *General:* greeting
    Specific: "How are you," "Hello," _____"Hi there"_____, _____"Good morning"_____

PRACTICE 3

In the following groups, one statement is the general point (and main idea), and the other statements are specific support for the point. Identify each point with a **P** and each statement of support with an **S**.

1. _S_ A. A mosquito can find you in the dark.
   _S_ B. A mosquito can keep you awake all night.
   _P_ C. Though a mosquito is small, it has a lot of power.
   _S_ D. A mosquito can make you scratch yourself until you bleed.

   Three examples of a mosquito's power are listed.

2. _S_ A. The bread the waiter brought us is stale.
   _S_ B. We've been waiting for our main course for over an hour.
   _S_ C. The people at the next table are awfully loud.
   _P_ D. It is time to speak to the restaurant manager.

   Three reasons to speak to the restaurant manager are listed.

3. _S_ A. The apartment has no closets.
   _S_ B. The kitchen is so small only one person can be there.
   _S_ C. Each morning the apartment fills with exhaust fumes from a nearby bus station.
   _P_ D. The apartment has some real drawbacks.

   Three drawbacks to the apartment are listed.

4. _P_ A. That teacher is very demanding.
   _S_ B. She calls on students who don't make eye contact with her.
   _S_ C. Students must e-mail her if they intend to miss a class.
   _S_ D. A paper handed in late is reduced a whole grade for each day it's late.

   Three ways in which the teacher is demanding are listed.

PRACTICE 4

In the following groups—all based on textbook selections—one statement is the general point (and main idea), and the other statements are specific support for the point. Identify each point with a **P** and each statement of support with an **S.**

1. __S__ A. Only one in three adults engages in regular physical activity.

   __S__ B. The percentage of obese adults has more than doubled in the past 40 years.

   __S__ C. About one in five adults still smokes cigarettes.   Statements A, B, and C give examples of ways

   __P__ D. Americans are not as healthy as they should be.   Americans are not healthy.

2. __S__ A. Couples committed to each other gain strength from their mutual support.

   __S__ B. Committed couples are financially more successful than singles.

   __P__ C. Committed relationships offer many benefits.

   __S__ D. Happily married adults live longer and have fewer emotional problems.
   Three benefits of committed relationships are listed.

3. __S__ A. Finding safety in numbers, bats live in large colonies numbering from several thousand to a million or more.

   __P__ B. Bats are creatures with a strong instinct to protect their own kind.

   __S__ C. Mother bats, who usually have one offspring per year, leave their young only to get food.

   __S__ D. When colonies containing mother bats are disturbed, the mothers will try to move their young to a safer location.   Three examples of bats' protective instinct are listed.

4. __P__ A. In 17th-century Europe, people went through a lot of trouble to wear makeup.

   __S__ B. To wear makeup at that time, men and women had to put an unpleasant mixture of lead, egg whites, and vinegar on their faces.

   __S__ C. Once a person's makeup was applied, he or she had to be careful not to laugh, or the new "face" would crack.

   __S__ D. The lead in the makeup caused scars and blemishes, which had to be covered with patches of cloth.   Statements B, C, and D give examples of the trouble people went through to wear makeup.

2   Use the Topic to Lead You to the Main Idea

You already know that to find the main idea of a selection, you look first for a general statement. You then check to see if that statement is supported by all or most of the other material in the paragraph. If it is, you've found the main idea. Another approach that can help you find the main idea of a selection is to look for its topic.

The **topic** is the general subject of a selection. It is not a complete sentence, but can be simply expressed in several words. Knowing the topic can help you find a writer's main point about that topic.

Textbook authors use the title of each chapter to state the overall topic of that chapter. They also provide many topics and subtopics in boldface headings within the chapter. For example, here is the title of a section in a psychology textbook:

Why We Communicate

And here are the subtopics:

Physical Needs

Identity Needs

Social Needs

Practical Goals

If you were studying the above chapter, you could use the topics to help find the main ideas. (Pages 5–9 explain just how to do so, as well as providing other textbook study tips.)

But there are many times when you are not given topics—with standardized reading tests, for example, or with individual paragraphs in articles or textbooks. To find the topic of a selection when the topic is not given, ask this simple question:

Who or what is the selection about?

For example, look again at the beginning of the paragraph that started this chapter:

Poor grades in school can have various causes.

What, in just a few words, is the above paragraph about? On the line below, write what you think is the topic.

Topic: _____ *Poor grades in school* _____

You probably answered that the topic is "poor grades in school." As you reread the paragraph, you saw that, in fact, every sentence in it is about poor grades.

The next step after finding the topic is to decide what main point the author is making about the topic. Authors often present their main idea in a single sentence. (This sentence is also known as the **main idea sentence** or the **topic sentence**.) As we have already seen, the main point about poor grades is "Poor grades in school can have various causes."

Check Your Understanding

Let's look now at another paragraph. Read it and then see if you can answer the questions that follow.

> ¹Phobias are continuing fears of things that are not likely to be harmful. ²For example, some people have a phobia about elevators. ³They worry that if they enter an elevator, the cable will break and they will fall hundreds of feet to their death. ⁴While such an accident can happen, it is extremely rare. ⁵Another instance of a phobia is a fear of medical needles. ⁶Some people will refuse to receive an injection, even if they are seriously ill. ⁷They may faint if given a needle; so great is their fear that they are about to die. ⁸Perhaps the most common phobia is fear of public speaking. ⁹Some people will not go to school or take jobs if they have to speak before a group. ¹⁰Their fear—that they will embarrass themselves and that people will pity or reject them—has little basis in reality. ¹¹These and other phobias can usually be overcome, often fairly quickly, with the right direction and treatment.

__B__ 1. Write the letter of the *topic* of the paragraph. To find the topic, ask yourself what the paragraph is about. (It often helps as you read to look for and even circle a word, term, or idea that is repeated in the paragraph.)

    A. dangers
    B. phobias
    C. worry about elevators

__1__ 2. Write the number of the sentence that states the *main idea* of the paragraph. In other words, what point is the author making about the topic? (Remember that the main idea will be supported by the other material in the paragraph.)

Explanation

As the first sentence of the paragraph suggests, the topic is "phobias." Continuing to read the paragraph, you see that, in fact, everything in it is about phobias. And the main idea is clearly sentence 1: "Phobias are continuing fears of things that are not likely to be harmful." This idea is a general one that sums up what the entire paragraph is about. It is an "umbrella" statement under which all the other material in the paragraph fits. The parts of the paragraph could be shown as follows:

Topic: Phobias

Main idea: Phobias are continuing fears of things that are not likely to be harmful.

Supporting details:
1. Fear that an elevator ride will end in a fall to death.
2. Fear that an injection will cause death.
3. Fear that speaking in public will lead to pity or rejection.

The following practices will sharpen your sense of the difference between a topic, the point about the topic (the main idea), and the supporting details.

 PRACTICE 5

Below are groups of four items. In each case, one item is the topic, one is the main idea, and two are details that support and develop the main idea. Label each item with one of the following:

T   — for the **topic** of the paragraph
MI — for the **main idea**
SD — for the **supporting details**

Note that an explanation is provided for the first group; reading it will help you do this practice.

Group 1

_SD_ A. One pitcher smoothes the dirt on the pitcher's mound before he throws each pitch.

_SD_ B. One infielder sits in the same spot on the dugout bench during every game.

_MI_ C. Some baseball players think that certain superstitious habits help them win games.

_T_ D. Superstitious baseball players.

Explanation

All of the statements in Group 1 involve superstitious baseball players, so item D must be the topic. (A topic is expressed in a single word or short phrase and is not a complete sentence.) Statements A and B each describe specific superstitious habits of individual baseball players. Statement C, however, is more general—it states that some players think certain superstitious habits help them win games. Statement C thus gives the main idea, and statements A and B are supporting details that explain that main idea.

Group 2

_SD_ A. Houdini learned to pop his shoulder out of its socket in order to escape from straight jackets.

_MI_ B. Harry Houdini, the famous escape artist, worked hard at his career.

_T_ C. Harry Houdini.

_SD_ D. Houdini trained to hold his breath for over five minutes in order to pull off underwater escapes.   All of the statements involve Harry Houdini, so item C is the topic. (Note that C is not a complete sentence.) Statements A and D provide details that show how hard Houdini worked at his career.

Group 3

_MI_ A. Some body fat is essential.

_T_ B. Body fat.   All the statements involve body fat, so item B is the topic. (Note that B is not a complete sentence.) Statements C and D explain specific ways in which fat is essential.

_SD_ C. Body fat insulates against the cold.

_SD_ D. Body fat protects organs from injury.

Group 4

_SD_ A. At dinnertime, instead of cooking, many people simply go to a fast-food restaurant or order take-out.

_SD_ B. More and more families rely on prepared meals from the frozen-foods section or the "deli" counter.

_MI_ C. Home cooking is becoming a lost art.

_T_ D. Home cooking.   Statements A and B provide specific reasons why home cooking (the topic) is becoming a lost art.

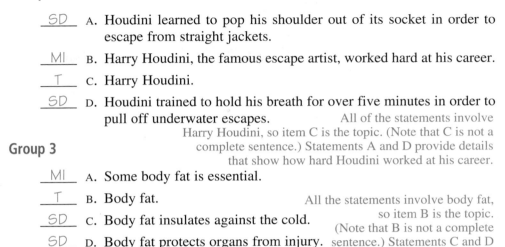

PRACTICE 6   *Homework*

Following are four paragraphs. Read each paragraph and write the letter of the item you think is the topic of the paragraph. Then write the number of the sentence you think states the main idea of the paragraph.

Here is how to proceed:

1 Ask yourself, "What seems to be the topic of the paragraph?" (It often helps to look for and even circle a word or idea that is repeated in the paragraph.)

> *Hint*: When looking for the topic, make sure you do not pick one that is either **too broad** (covering a great deal more than is in the selection) or **too narrow** (covering only part of the selection). The topic and the main idea of a selection must include everything in that selection—no more and no less.

2 Next, ask yourself, "What point is the writer making about this topic?" This will be the main idea. In this practice, it is stated in one of the sentences in the paragraph.

3 Then test what you think is the main idea by asking, "Is this statement supported by all or most of the other material in the paragraph?"

Paragraph 1

¹The influence of sports reaches far and wide. ²Most of us have had some experiences with athletics, either as players or as spectators. ³Schools, from kindergarten to college, provide many chances to participate in sports. ⁴Newspapers and the Internet carry more news about sports than about politics, crime, or the economy. ⁵Radio and television newscasts seldom go on the air without a sports report. ⁶Football, basketball, baseball, and other games are often broadcast in full, even in place of regular programming. ⁷Sports have so much influence on our lives that our everyday speech is full of sports expressions: "struck out," "touch base," "ballpark figure," "game plan," "teamwork," "cheap shot," and so on.

_B_ 1. The topic of the paragraph is
    A. athletics.
    B. influence of sports.
    C. sports expressions.

The word *sports* is mentioned six times in the paragraph. Answer A is too broad, and answer C is too narrow.

_1_ 2. Write the number of the sentence that states the main idea of the paragraph. Sentence 1 states that sports' influence reaches far and wide. The remaining sentences provide examples of the influence of sports.

Paragraph 2

¹The female black widow spider is not as terrible a killer as is generally believed. ²While the creature is certainly poisonous, she is also very shy and will bite humans only when she feels cornered. ³Also, the idea that the black widow always kills the male after mating is untrue. ⁴The male is often spared—if he remembers to tap out a special signal as he ventures onto his mate's web. ⁵The vibrations on the web let her know he is one of her own kind, not an insect to be rushed at and killed.

_A_ 3. The topic of the paragraph is
    A. the female black widow spider.
    B. poisonous spiders.
    C. the unlucky male black widow spider.

Answer B is too broad; answer C is too narrow.

_1_ 4. Write the number of the sentence that states the main idea of the paragraph. Sentence 1 states the female black widow is not as terrible a killer as many believe. Sentences 2–5 provide specific examples to support this idea.

Paragraph 3

¹Potato chips got their start because of a hard-to-please restaurant customer in 1853. ²In that year, George Crum was working as a chef at an elegant resort in Saratoga Springs, New York. ³He prepared thick-cut French-fried potatoes for diners there. ⁴But one diner kept sending his potatoes back to the kitchen, complaining that they were too thick for his taste. ⁵Crum cut the potatoes thinner and thinner and finally, very annoyed, made a serving of potatoes too thin and crisp to eat with a fork. ⁶To his surprise, the guest loved them. ⁷Other guests demanded a taste. ⁸Soon "Saratoga Chips" were the most popular item on the menu.

___C___ 5. The topic of the paragraph is
　　　　　　A. a hard-to-please customer.
　　　　　　B. the origins of foods.
　　　　　　C. potato chips.

Answer A is too narrow; answer B is too broad.

___1___ 6. Write the number of the sentence that states the main idea of the paragraph. *Sentence 1 states potato chips began with a hard-to-please restaurant customer. The remaining sentences provide details to support this idea.*

Paragraph 4

¹People have always loved bike riding. ²Biking, however, can be a dangerous activity. ³One danger is "getting doored"—having a car driver open his or her door directly into the path of an oncoming bike. ⁴Another risk is aggressive drivers who feel they have more right to the roads than bikes do. ⁵Such drivers will scream, honk, or gesture wildly. ⁶They may block off bikers without a signal or a look, giving the biker no time to avoid running off the road or into the car. ⁷An added source of danger for bikers is poor road design, which in many cases allows just enough room for a car on either side of the road, but no extra room for a biker to be on the same road. ⁸Recently, the U.S. Department of Transportation noted that bicycling is now more dangerous than flying in planes or riding in buses, boats, or trains.

___A___ 7. The topic of the paragraph is
　　　　　　A. biking.
　　　　　　B. transportation.
　　　　　　C. getting "doored."

Answer B is too broad; answer C is too narrow.

___2___ 8. Write the number of the sentence that states the main idea of the paragraph. *Sentence 1 is introductory material. Sentence 2 states that biking can be dangerous. The remaining sentences provide specific examples of the dangers of biking.*

3   Find and Use Key Words to Lead You to the Main Idea

Sometimes authors make it fairly easy to find their main idea. They announce it by using **key words**—words or phrases that are easy to recognize. These key words are clues to the main idea.

One type of key word is a **list word** or words, which tell you a list of items is to follow. For example, the main idea in the paragraph about poor grades was stated like this: *Poor grades in school can have various causes.* The expression *various causes* helps you zero in on the main idea. You realize that the paragraph will be about the causes of poor grades. As you read on and see the series of causes, you know your guess about the main idea was correct.

Below are some common words that often announce a main idea. Note that nearly all of them contain a word that ends in **s**—a plural that suggests the supporting details will be a list of items.

List Words

several kinds of	various causes	a few reasons
a number of	a series of	three factors
four steps	among the results	several advantages

When expressions like these appear in a sentence, look carefully to see if that sentence might be the main idea. Chances are a sentence with these words will be followed by a list of major supporting details.

Check Your Understanding: List Words

Underline the list words in the following sentences.

> *Hint:* Remember that list words usually end in *s*.

Example   Being a middle child in a large family has <u>several drawbacks</u>.

1. The rising rate of diabetes among young people seems to have <u>three causes</u>.

2. <u>Several symptoms</u> may indicate that a person is having a heart attack.

3. The Pilgrims faced <u>a number of challenges</u> during their first winter in America.

4. Community colleges have <u>some real advantages</u> over four-year colleges.

5. Students offer <u>a variety of excuses</u> for their homework being late.

Explanation

In the first sentence, you should have underlined the phrase *three causes.* Those words suggest that a list of the three causes of the rising rate of diabetes among young people may follow. In sentences 2–5, you should have underlined these groups of words: *several symptoms, a number of challenges, some real advantages,* and *a variety of excuses.* Each of those phrases also tells you that a list of supporting details may follow.

There is another type of key word that can alert you to the main idea. This type of key word, called an **addition word**, is generally used right before a supporting detail. Below is a box of words that often introduce major supporting details and help you discover the main idea.

Addition Words

one	to begin with	in addition	last
first	another	next	last of all
first of all	second	moreover	final
for one thing	also	furthermore	finally

Check Your Understanding: Addition Words

Reread the paragraph about causes of poor grades and underline the addition words that alert you to supporting details. Also, see if you can circle the list words that suggest the main idea.

[1]Poor grades in school can have various causes. [2]For one thing, students may have financial problems. [3]If they need to work long hours to make money, they will have little study time. [4]Another cause of poor grades may be trouble with relationships. [5]A student may be unhappy over family problems or a lack of friends. [6]That unhappiness can harm schoolwork. [7]A final cause of poor grades may be bad study habits. [8]Some students have never learned how to take good notes in class, how to manage their time effectively, or how to study a textbook. [9]Without such study skills, their grades are likely to suffer.

Explanation

The words that introduce each new supporting detail for the main idea are *For one thing, Another,* and *final.* These addition words help you realize that all the details in the paragraph are supporting the idea that poor grades in school can have various causes. You should have underlined these three words.

Since *various causes* are list words, you should have circled them. Even before you saw the addition words, those list words could have suggested to you that the paragraph may list the different causes of poor grades. As you can see, in this paragraph (as in many others), list words and addition words work hand in hand.

PRACTICE 7

The chapters that follow will offer a good deal of practice in key words. For now, do the activity below.

A. Underline the list words in each of the following sentences.

1. Living alone has a number of advantages.

2. Physical punishment can be harmful to a child in several ways.

3. The Industrial Revolution came about quickly because of three major inventions.

4. A series of mistakes led to the arrest and imprisonment of the wrong person.

5. To memorize materials effectively, there are two important steps to follow.

6. The National Board of Medical Examiners has released some alarming facts about doctors.

B. (7–10.) Underline the four addition words or phrases in the following passage.

List words:
*several
reasons*

¹Women don't hold more political power in the United States for several reasons. ²First of all, women are still a minority in law and business. ³Those are the fields from which most politicians come. ⁴In addition, political careers usually require a great deal of time spent away from home, and such hours don't tie in well with motherhood. ⁵Also, women are less likely to have a supportive spouse at home, ready to help out with child care, housework, and the like. ⁶Finally, men have not been eager to open up the "boys' club" of political power to women. ⁷They tend to support and encourage upcoming male candidates, not female ones.

A Note on the Central Point

In selections made up of many paragraphs, the overall main idea is called the **central point**, also known as the **central idea** or **thesis**. You can find a central point in the same way that you find a main idea. First, identify the topic (which is often suggested by the title of the selection). Then look at the supporting material. The paragraphs within the longer reading will provide supporting details for the central point.

The following chapter, "Supporting Details," provides more information about (and practice in) the list and addition words that help signal main ideas and the details that support them.

CHAPTER REVIEW

In this chapter, you learned the following:

- Recognizing the main idea is the most important key to good comprehension. The main idea is a general "umbrella" idea; the specific supporting material of the paragraph fits under it.
- Three strategies that will help you find the main idea are to 1) look for general versus specific ideas; 2) use the topic (the general subject of a selection) to lead you to the main idea; 3) use key words to lead you to the main idea.

The next chapter—Chapter 4—will increase your understanding of the specific details that authors use to support and develop their main ideas.

On the Web: If you are using this book in class, you can visit our website for additional practice in recognizing main ideas. Go to **www.townsendpress.com** and click on "Online Learning Center."

REVIEW TEST 1

To review what you've learned in this chapter, answer each of the following questions by filling in the blank or writing the letter of the correct answer.

1. The umbrella statement that covers the material in a paragraph is the *(topic or main idea?)*_____ main idea _____.

   See page 115.

2. The supporting details are always more *(general or specific?)* _____ specific _____ than the main idea.

   See page 116.

3. To help yourself find the *(topic or main idea?)* _____ topic _____ of a paragraph, ask yourself, "Who or what is this paragraph about?"

   See page 122.

4. To help you decide if a certain sentence is the main idea of a paragraph, ask yourself, "Is this sentence _____ supported _____ by all or most of the other material in the paragraph?"

   See page 126.

5. One way to help find the main idea is to look for **addition words** like *first, second, also,* and *finally.* Such words often introduce the supporting _____ detail _____s for a main idea.

   See page 129.

REVIEW TEST 2

A. Each cluster of words below consists of one general idea and three specific ideas. The general idea includes all the specific ideas. Underline the general idea in each group.

1. kneeling	<u>position</u>	standing	sitting
2. water	electricity	gas	<u>utility</u>
3. <u>housing</u>	condominium	palace	apartment
4. hearing	touch	<u>sense</u>	sight
5. nicotine	alcohol	<u>drug</u>	aspirin
6. flour	<u>ingredient</u>	yeast	eggs
7. tinsel	colored lights	<u>decoration</u>	wreath
8. car payment	credit-card bill	personal loan	<u>debt</u>

B. In each item below, one idea is general and the others are specific. The general idea includes the specific ideas. In the spaces provided, write two more specific ideas that are covered by the general idea. *Answers will vary; below are some possibilities.*

9–10. *General:*   pet
        Specific: parakeet, hamster,   *cat*   ,   *dog*

11–12. *General:*   sharp object
        Specific: razor, broken glass,   *knife*   ,   *needle*

13–14. *General:*   footwear
        Specific: boots, slippers   *sandals*   ,   *shoes*

15–16. *General:*   breakfast item
        Specific: orange juice, oatmeal,   *toast*   ,   *coffee*

C. (17–20.) In the following group, one statement is the general point, and the other statements are specific support for the point. Identify the point with a **P** and each statement of support with an **S**.

    _S_   A. When you're speaking to Doug, he is often looking around the room.

    _S_   B. He never asks questions of the other person.

    _P_   C. Doug is not skilled at conversation.

    _S_   D. He interrupts when he thinks of something he wants to say.

Statements A, B, and D give specific examples of how Doug is not skilled at conversation.

REVIEW TEST 3

A. (1–12.) Each group of four items includes one topic, one main idea, and two supporting details. In the space provided, label each item with one of the following:

     T — for the **topic** of the paragraph
     MI — for the **main idea**
     SD — for the **supporting details**

Group 1

    _MI_   A. The human skeleton has certain important functions.

    _SD_   B. The skeleton gives the body support and shape.

    _SD_   C. The skeleton protects internal organs.

    _T_   D. The human skeleton.   Item D is the topic (a phrase).
Items B and C are examples of the important functions of the human skeleton, the main idea is expressed in item A.

Group 2

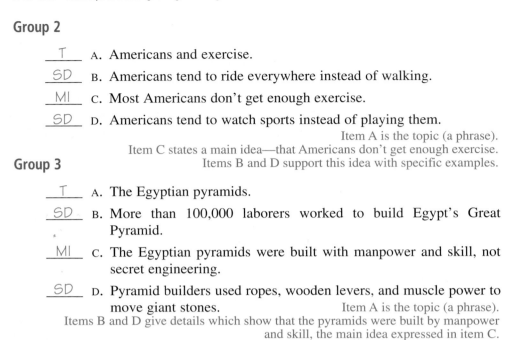

__T__   A. Americans and exercise.

__SD__ B. Americans tend to ride everywhere instead of walking.

__MI__ C. Most Americans don't get enough exercise.

__SD__ D. Americans tend to watch sports instead of playing them.

Item A is the topic (a phrase).
Item C states a main idea—that Americans don't get enough exercise.
Items B and D support this idea with specific examples.

Group 3

__T__   A. The Egyptian pyramids.

__SD__ B. More than 100,000 laborers worked to build Egypt's Great Pyramid.

__MI__ C. The Egyptian pyramids were built with manpower and skill, not secret engineering.

__SD__ D. Pyramid builders used ropes, wooden levers, and muscle power to move giant stones.

Item A is the topic (a phrase).
Items B and D give details which show that the pyramids were built by manpower and skill, the main idea expressed in item C.

B. Read each paragraph below and write the letter of the item you think is the topic of the paragraph. Then write the number of the sentence that states the main idea of the paragraph.

Paragraph 1

[1]The hedgehog, a spiny animal that lives in much of Europe and Africa, is a very effective snake-killer. [2]First, the hedgehog sneaks up on the snake and bites its tail firmly. [3]The hedgehog immediately curls up into a tight ball, still holding the snake's tail in its mouth. [4]The snake then strikes the hedgehog again and again, but all it does is injure itself against the hedgehog's pointed spines. [5]As the snake strikes, the hedgehog continues chewing until the snake is dead. [6]Finally, the hedgehog uncurls and enjoys its meal.

__B__ 13. The topic is
  A. snake-killers.
  B. the hedgehog.
  C. the hedgehog's spines.

Answer A is too broad; answer C is too narrow.

__1__ 14. What is the number of the sentence that states the main idea?

Sentence 1 states the main idea—that the hedgehog is an effective snake-killer. The remaining sentences support this idea.

Paragraph 2

¹Almost every week you're likely to see a TV commercial or an ad for a new health product. ²It might promise better sleep, more energy, clearer skin, firmer muscles, lower weight, brighter moods, longer life—or all of these combined. ³The product is often endorsed by ordinary-looking people who have been carefully rehearsed. ⁴However, if a health product sounds too good to be true, it probably is. ⁵If, for example, a magic pill really *could* trim off excess pounds or remove wrinkles, the world would be filled with thin people with unlined skin. ⁶Look around, and you'll realize that's not the case.

_B_ 15. The topic is
   A. TV commericals and ads.
   B. new health products.
   C. magic pills.

Answer A is too broad; answer C is too narrow.

_4_ 16. What is the number of the sentence that states the main idea?

Sentences 1–3 introduce the topic of new health products. Sentence 4 states the main idea—that health products that sound too good to be true probably are. Sentences 5–6 support this idea.

C. In the space provided, write the letter of the list words in each sentence.

_C_ 17. A teenager in serious emotional trouble is likely to display certain kinds of behavior.
   A. *serious emotional trouble*
   B. *likely to display*
   C. *certain kinds of behavior*

The word *kinds* is often a list signal.

_C_ 18. The widespread pollution of the lakes in the region has a number of causes.
   A. *widespread pollution*
   B. *lakes in the region*
   C. *a number of causes*

The expression *a number of,* one of the words in the box on page 128, often signals a main idea.

D. In the space provided, write the letter of the addition word in each sentence.

_A_ 19. The best single way to become a better student is to attend every class; another important step is to take good notes in class.
   A. *another*
   B. *important*
   C. *better*

See page 129.

____B____ 20. Extreme stress can lead some people to escape through drug abuse; stress may also lead to such severe depression that a person attempts suicide.

A. *stress*

B. *also*

C. *depression*

See page 129. Students should note that the addition word does not always come at the beginning of a sentence.

REVIEW TEST 4

Here is a chance to apply your understanding of main ideas to a full-length reading. First read the following selection from the college textbook *Sociology, Third Edition*, by Rodney Stark—it will give you a fascinating view of the type of behavior we all witness every day. Then answer the questions that follow about topics, main ideas, and the central point. There are also vocabulary questions to help you continue practicing the skill of understanding vocabulary in context.

Words to Watch

Below are some words in the reading that do not have strong context support. Each word is followed by the number of the paragraph in which it appears and its meaning there. These words are indicated in the selection by a small circle (°).

> *conformity* (2): behavior in accordance with group ideas and customs
> *confirming* (2): proving true
> *perception* (3): observation
> *at odds* (8): in disagreement
> *stakes* (10): something to be gained or lost

GROUP PRESSURE

Rodney Stark

1   It is self-evident that people tend to conform to the expectations and reactions of others around them. But what are the limits of group pressure? Can group pressure cause us to deny the obvious, even physical evidence?

2   Over thirty-five years ago, Solomon Asch performed the most famous experimental test of the power of group pressure to produce conformity°. Since then his study has been repeated many times, with many variations confirming° his original results. Perhaps the best way to understand what Asch discovered is to pretend that you are a subject in his experiment.

3   You have agreed to take part in an experiment on visual perception°. Upon arriving at the laboratory, you are given the seventh in a line of eight chairs. Other students taking part in the experiment sit in each of the other chairs. At the front of the room the experimenter stands by a covered easel. He explains that he wants you to judge the length of lines in a series of comparisons. He will place two decks of large cards upon the easel. One card will display a single vertical line. The other card will display three vertical lines, each of a different length. He wants each of you to decide which of the three lines on one card is the same length as the single line on the other card. To prepare you for the task, he displays a practice card. You see the correct line easily, for the other lines are noticeably different from the comparison line.

4   The experiment begins. The first comparison is just as easy as the practice comparison. One of the three lines is obviously the same length as the comparison line, while the other two are very different. Each of the eight persons answers in turn, with you answering seventh. Everyone answers correctly. On the second pair of cards, the right answer is just as easy to spot, and again all eight subjects are correct. You begin to suspect that the experiment is going to be a big bore.

5   Then comes the third pair. The judgment is just as easy as before. But the first person somehow picks a line that is obviously wrong. You smile. Then the second person also picks the same obviously wrong line. What's going on? Then the third, fourth, fifth, and sixth subjects answer the same way. It's your turn. You know without doubt that you are right, yet six people have confidently given the wrong answer. You are no longer bored. Instead, you are a bit confused, but you go ahead and choose the line you are sure is right. Then the last person picks the same wrong line everyone else has chosen.

6   A new pair is unveiled, and the same thing happens again. All the others pick an obviously wrong line. The experimenter remains matter-of-fact, not commenting on right or wrong answers but just marking down what people pick. Should you stick it out? Should you go along? Maybe something's wrong with the light or with your angle of vision. Your difficulty lasts for eighteen pairs of cards. On twelve of them, all the others picked a line you knew was incorrect.

7   When the experiment is over, the experimenter turns to you with a smile

and begins to explain. You were the only subject in the experiment. The other seven people were stooges paid by Professor Asch to answer exactly the way they did. The aim of the experiment was to see if social pressure could cause you to reject the evidence of your own eyes and conform.

8   In his first experiment, Asch tested fifty people in this situation. Almost a third of them went along with the group and gave the wrong answer at least half of the time. Another 40 percent yielded to the group some of the time, but less than half of the time. Only 25 percent refused to yield at all. Those who yielded to group pressure were more likely to do so as the experiment progressed. Nearly everyone withstood the group the first several times, but as they continued to find themselves at odds° with the group, most subjects began to weaken. Many shifted in their chairs, trying to get a different line of vision. Some blushed. Finally, 75 percent of them began to go along at least a few times.

9   The effects of group pressure were also revealed in the behavior of those who steadfastly refused to accept the group's misjudgments. Some of these people became increasingly uneasy and apologetic. One subject began to whisper to his neighbor, "Can't help it, that's the one," and later, "I always disagree—darn it!" Other subjects who refused to yield dealt with the stress of the situation by giving each nonconforming response in a progressively louder voice and by casting challenging looks at the others. In a recent replication of the Asch study, one subject loudly insulted the other seven students whenever they made a wrong choice. One retort was "What funny farm did you turkeys grow up on, huh?"

10   The Asch experiment shows that a high number of people will conform even in a weak group situation. They were required merely to disagree with strangers, not with their friends, and the costs of deviance were limited to about half an hour of disapproval from people they hardly knew. Furthermore, subjects were not faced with a difficult judgment—they could easily see the correct response. Little wonder, then, that we are inclined to go along with our friends when the stakes° are much higher and we cannot even be certain that we are right.

would be more pressure among friends/family

Reading Comprehension Questions

Vocabulary in Context

__B__   1. In the sentence below, the word *stooges* (stoōj′s) means
   A. comedians.
   B. people who played a role.
   C. true subjects in an experiment.
   D. educators.

   What best describes people who were paid to answer in a certain way?

   "The other seven people were stooges paid by Professor Asch to answer exactly the way they did." (Paragraph 7)

__C__   2. In the sentence below, the word *withstood* (wĭth-stood′) means
   A. recognized.
   B. agreed with.
   C. resisted.
   D. understood.

   Signal word: but.
   Antonym clue: weaken.

   "Nearly everyone withstood the group the first several times, but as they continued to find themselves at odds with the group, most subjects began to weaken." (Paragraph 8)

__A__   3. In the excerpt below, the word *steadfastly* (stĕd′făst′lē) means
   A. constantly.
   B. wrongly.
   C. helpfully.
   D. comfortably.

   What kind of refusal would make the students uneasy and apologetic?

   "The effects of group pressure were also revealed in the behavior of those who steadfastly refused to accept the group's misjudgments. Some of these people became increasingly uneasy and apologetic." (Paragraph 9)

__B__   4. In the excerpt below, the word *replication* (rĕp′lĭ-kā′shən) means
   A. memory.
   B. repeat.
   C. image.
   D. prediction.

   What was done recently with the Asch study?

   "In a recent replication of the Asch study, one subject loudly insulted the other seven students . . . ." (Paragraph 9)

_D_   5. In the excerpt below, the word *retort* (rĭ-tôrt′) means
      A. genuine question.
      B. form of praise.
      C. choice.
      D. quick, sharp reply.

        If the subject is insulting others, what sort of statement is he/she likely to make?

> "... one subject loudly insulted the other seven students whenever they made a wrong choice. One retort was 'What funny farm did you turkeys grow up on, huh?'" (Paragraph 9)

_C_   6. In the sentence below, the word *deviance* (dē′vē-əns) means
      A. going along with the crowd.
      B. an experimental test.
      C. differing from the normal group behavior.
      D. being a stranger.

        Synonym-like clue: required to disagree.

> "They were required merely to disagree with strangers, not with their friends, and the costs of deviance were limited to about half an hour of disapproval from people they hardly knew." (Paragraph 10)

Central Point

_C_   7. Which of the following is the topic of the whole selection?
      A. Visual perception
      B. Solomon Asch
      C. Asch's experiment on group pressure
      D. Stooges in an experiment

        Answers A, B, and D are too narrow.

_D_   8. Which sentence from the reading comes closest to expressing the central point of the whole selection?
      A. "Upon arriving at the laboratory, you are given the seventh in a line of eight chairs."
      B. "The experimenter remains matter-of-fact, not commenting on right or wrong answers but just marking down what people pick."
      C. "In his first experiment, Asch tested fifty people in this situation."
      D. "The Asch experiment shows that a high number of people will conform even in a weak group situation."

        Answers A, B, and C are too narrow.

Main Ideas

__A__ 9. The topic of paragraph 9 is
    A. the behavior of subjects who refused to accept the group's misjudgments.
    B. subjects who became uneasy and apologetic.
    C. a duplication of the Asch study.
    D. subjects who insulted others.

Answers B, C, and D are too narrow.

__A__ 10. The main idea of paragraph 9 is expressed in its
    A. first sentence.
    B. second sentence.
    C. next-to-the-last sentence.
    D. last sentence.

Sentence 1 states that the effects of group pressure were revealed in people's behavior. Sentences 2–6 give specific examples of how people's behavior was affected.

Discussion Questions

1. Were you at all surprised by the results of Solomon Asch's experiment? If you had been one of the subjects, do you think you would have stuck to your answers, or would you have gone along with the group? Why?

2. What reasons might the subjects in the Asch experiment have had for eventually giving in and accepting the group's wrong answers?

3. Stark refers to the Asch experiment as a "weak group situation," one in which the group is made up of strangers and the stakes are not very high. What might a "strong group situation" be? Give examples.

4. Have you ever been in a situation when you wanted to resist group pressure? What was the situation, and why did you want to resist? What could you have done to resist?

Note: Writing assignments for this selection appear on pages 589–590.

Check Your Performance   MAIN IDEAS

Activity	Number Right	Points	Score
Review Test 1 (5 items)	_____	× 2 =	_____
Review Test 2 (20 items)	_____	× 1.5 =	_____
Review Test 3 (20 items)	_____	× 1.5 =	_____
Review Test 4 (10 items)	_____	× 3 =	_____
		TOTAL SCORE =	_____%

Enter your total score into the **Reading Performance Chart: Review Tests** on the inside back cover.

MAIN IDEAS: Mastery Test 1

A. Each cluster of words below consists of one general idea and three specific ideas. The general idea includes all the specific ideas. Underline the general idea in each group.

1. oak   <u>tree</u>   maple   pine

2. iron   tin   <u>metal</u>   aluminum

3. <u>insect</u>   ant   roach   fly

4. basketball   hockey   tennis   <u>sport</u>

B. In each item below, one idea is general, and the other two are specific. The general idea includes the specific ideas. In the spaces provided, write **two** more specific ideas that are covered by the general idea.

Answers will vary; below are some possibilities.

5–6. *General:* fruit
      Specific: orange, pineapple, ____banana____ , ____grape____

7–8. *General:* country
      Specific: Canada, Greece, ____Mexico____ , ____Egypt____

9–10. *General:* holiday
      Specific: Independence Day, Labor Day, ____Thanksgiving____ , ____Christmas____

11–12. *General:* criminal
      Specific: kidnapper, arsonist, ____murderer____ , ____robber____

C. (13–20.) In each group below, one statement is the general point, and the other statements are specific support for the point. Identify the point with a **P** and each statement of support with an **S**.

Group 1

__S__ A. Pet owners survive longer after a major illness than people who don't own pets.

__S__ B. Daily time with pets aids relaxation and decreases stress.

__P__ C. Pet ownership has positive effects on people's health.

__S__ D. Petting an animal lowers blood pressure in humans.

List signal: *positive effects.* Statements A, B, and D are three of these effects.

(Continues on next page)

Group 2

S A. Certain harmless snakes eat poisonous ones.

S B. Snakes help control the rodent population by eating mice and rats.

S C. Medicines for humans have been developed from snake venom.

P D. Despite their poor public image, snakes have their good points.

List signal: *good points.*
Statements A, B, and C are three examples of good points about snakes.

MAIN IDEAS: Mastery Test 2

A. Each cluster of words below consists of one general idea and three specific ideas. The general idea includes all the specific ideas. Underline the general idea in each group.

1. rose	daisy	tulip	<u>flower</u>
2. sofa	<u>furniture</u>	table	chair
3. <u>illness</u>	flu	measles	pneumonia
4. socks	jacket	<u>clothes</u>	shirt

B. In each item below, one idea is general, and the other two are specific. The general idea includes the specific ideas. In the spaces provided, write **two** more specific ideas that are covered by the general idea.

Answers will vary; below are some possibilities.

5–6. *General:* beverages
Specific: water, milk, _____coffee_____ , _____tea_____

7–8. *General:* bird
Specific: parrot, turkey, _____canary_____ , _____pigeon_____

9–10. *General:* natural disaster
Specific: earthquake, hurricane, _____flood_____ , _____forest fire_____

11–12. *General:* happy event
Specific: birth of a child,
getting an A, _____getting married_____, _____graduation_____

C. (13–20.) In each group below, one statement is the general point, and the other statements are specific support for the point. Identify the point with a **P** and each statement of support with an **S**.

Group 1
List signal: *several simple steps.*
Statements A, B, and D are three of these steps.

_S_ A. Bringing homemade popcorn to the movies is cheaper than buying expensive theater popcorn.

_S_ B. Buying candy at a grocery store, not a theater, cuts candy costs in half.

_P_ C. Moviegoers can take several simple steps to save money at the movie theater.

_S_ D. Going to movies early in the day can reduce ticket prices by several dollars.

(Continues on next page)

145

Group 2

_S_ A. Naps improve people's moods and alertness.

_S_ B. Taking a nap boosts energy and increases work productivity.

_S_ C. After a nap, it is easier to concentrate and make decisions.

_P_ D. People should take a nap every day.

Statements A, B, and C are specific reasons
people should take a nap every day.

MAIN IDEAS: Mastery Test 3

A. (1–12.) In each group below, one statement is the general point, and the other statements are specific support for the point. Identify each point with a **P** and each statement of support with an **S**.

Group 1

_S_ A. Tall buildings in the United States often have twelfth and fourteenth floors— but not a thirteenth floor.

_S_ B. Houses in France are never numbered thirteen.

_P_ C. Throughout the world, the number thirteen is viewed as unlucky.

_S_ D. Many global airlines have removed seat number thirteen from airplane seating charts.

Statements A, B, and D give specific examples that show the number thirteen is viewed as unlucky— the main idea expressed in statement C.

Group 2

_P_ A. Restaurant ratings are based on more than just food.

_S_ B. A restaurant's service can be almost as significant as the meal itself.

_S_ C. For many restaurant critics, the comfort of the surroundings will be a part of their evaluation.

_S_ D. Menu prices are always taken into consideration.

Statements B, C, and D give examples of things other than food that determine a restaurant's ratings.

Group 3

_S_ A. The average American child is exposed to 12,000 violent acts—including rape and murder—on TV each year.

_S_ B. Adults who watch TV two hours a day increase their chances of obesity by 25 percent and diabetes by 14 percent.

_S_ C. Toddlers who watch TV for an hour each day increase their risk of having attention problems by 10 percent.

_P_ D. TV watching can be an unhealthy activity.

Statements A, B, and C give specific reasons why watching TV is unhealthy.

(Continues on next page)

B. (13–20.) Each group of four items includes one topic, one main idea, and two supporting ideas. In the space provided, label each item with one of the following:

    T — for the **topic** of the paragraph
   MI — for the **main idea**
   SD — for the **supporting details**

Group 1

  _SD_   A. Researchers believe one quarter of "mysterious" fires in dwellings in the United States are caused by rats.

  _T_   B. Problems caused by rats.

  _SD_   C. Studies show that rats are to blame for 26 percent of electrical cable failures in houses and apartments.

  _MI_   D. Rats cause serious problems to homeowners and apartment dwellers.
                  Item B is the topic (a phrase).
       Items A and C present specific problems caused by rats, the main idea expressed in item D.

Group 2

  _SD_   A. Young Americans are more likely to eat fast food, avoid exercise, be obese, and smoke cigarettes.

  _SD_   B. Many do not have health insurance or get regular physical or dental exams and do not receive health care when they need it.

  _MI_   C. Young Americans moving into adulthood face significant health risks.

  _T_   D. Health risks for young Americans.

       Item D is the topic (a phrase). Items A and B name specific reasons young Americans face health risks, the main idea expressed in item C.

MAIN IDEAS: Mastery Test 4

A. (1–12.) In each group below, one statement is the general point, and the other statements are specific support for the point. Identify each point with a **P** and each statement of support with an **S**.

Group 1

___P___ A. Some people find it difficult to live without technology.

___S___ B. You never see them sitting quietly reading a book.

___S___ C. When they are out during the day, they do a lot of text-messaging or talking on their cell phones.

___S___ D. At home they watch TV, read e-mail, and spend time on Facebook and other social networks.   Statements B, C, and D describe activities that illustrate how involved some people are with technology. These support the main idea in statement A—that some people find it difficult to live without technology.

Group 2

___S___ A. Most teens who work do so to develop responsibility and gain independence from their parents.

___S___ B. Almost all teens who work are motivated by a desire to earn spending money.

___S___ C. For a majority of teens, work offers an opportunity to spend time with peers.

___P___ D. Teenagers choose to work during the school year for a variety of reasons.

Statement D has a list clue: *a variety of reasons*. Statements A, B, and C give specific reasons teenagers work during the school year.

Group 3

___S___ A. Panic disorder, a type of anxiety in which people experience feelings of panic, affects eight out of every thousand people.

___P___ B. Anxiety is a widespread disorder that many people deal with each day.

___S___ C. Five to 10 percent of Americans suffer from phobias, a type of anxiety in which people experience intense fear of things such as spiders, dogs, or bridges.

___S___ D. About 12 million Americans experience strong fear in social situations—social anxiety—each year.

Statements A, C, and D present statistics that support the idea that anxiety is a widespread disorder, the main point expressed in answer B.

(Continues on next page)

B. (13–20.) Each group of four items includes one topic, one main idea, and two supporting ideas. In the space provided, label each item with one of the following:

T — for the **topic** of the paragraph
MI — for the **main idea**
SD — for the **supporting details**

Group 1

<u>SD</u>   A. Women have 15–20 percent more "gray matter" in their brains than men.

<u>SD</u>   B. A man's brain is larger and has more "white matter" than a woman's.

<u>MI</u>   C. When it comes to their brains, men and women are not equal.

<u>T</u>   D. Men's and women's brains.   Item D is the topic (a phrase). Items A and B provide specific examples of how men's and women's brains are not equal, the main idea expressed in item C.

Group 2

<u>MI</u>   A. Crocodiles have shown a remarkable ability to survive.

<u>SD</u>   B. Crocodile-like creatures have existed for around 200 million years.

<u>T</u>   C. The survival of crocodiles.

<u>SD</u>   D. Crocodiles have been known to survive an entire year without food.   Item C is the topic (a phrase). Items B and D provide specific details that show crocodiles have remarkable survival ability, the main idea expressed in item A.

MAIN IDEAS: Mastery Test 5

A. (1–4.) In the group below, one statement is the general point, and the other statements are specific support for the point. Identify the point with a **P** and each statement of support with an **S**.

<u>S</u> A. On each square inch of your skin, there are millions of live bacteria.

<u>S</u> B. Your mouth is home to the "tooth amoeba," a tiny organism that feeds on food and dead cells.   Statements A, B, and D provide examples of organisms that live on the human body.

<u>P</u> C. Your body, like those of all humans, is home to many organisms.

<u>S</u> D. Tiny mites live in the roots of your eyelashes and feed on dead tissue.

B. (5–12.) Each group of four items includes one topic, one main idea, and two supporting details. In the space provided, label each item with one of the following:

T — for the **topic** of the paragraph
MI — for the **main idea**
SD — for the **supporting details**

Group 1

<u>SD</u> A. One or two cups of coffee a day relieve drowsiness and can increase concentration.

<u>SD</u> B. Drinking a cup of coffee before a workout boosts strength and fights muscle fatigue.

<u>T</u> C. The effects of drinking coffee.

<u>MI</u> D. Coffee, when consumed in reasonable amounts, can produce positive effects on the body.   Item C is the topic (a phrase).
Item D contains list words (*positive effects*)
to suggest the main idea. Items A and B list those effects.

Group 2

<u>SD</u> A. Sunglasses that block harmful ultraviolet light were first developed by the space program.

<u>MI</u> B. Surprisingly, the U.S. space program has led to some useful items in everyday life.

<u>SD</u> C. The material in football helmets and protective padding was first made to protect astronauts in space.

<u>T</u> D. Some unexpected benefits of the U.S. space program.

Item D is the topic (a phrase).
Item B contains list words (*some useful items*) to suggest the main idea.
Items A and C present examples of those useful items.

(Continues on next page)

C. In the space provided, write the letter of the list words in each sentence. (List words are a clue to what supporting details to look for in a paragraph.)

Items 13–16:
See page 128.
The words *a number of, several key factors, effects,* and *reasons* often signal main ideas.

___A___ 13. People who do not vote in national elections give a number of excuses.
        A. *a number of excuses*   C. *people who do not vote*
        B. *national elections*

___C___ 14. To decide whether or not to take a job, consider several key factors.
        A. *To decide*   B. *whether or not*   C. *several key factors*

___C___ 15. One study after another has found that cigarette smoking has long-term effects on the body.
        A. *One study after another*   C. *long-term effects on the body*
        B. *cigarette smoking*

___C___ 16. Advertising should not be permitted on children's television shows for a variety of reasons.
        A. *Advertising should not be permitted*   C. *a variety of reasons*
        B. *children's television shows*

D. Read the following passage. Then, in the space provided, write the letter of the addition words that introduce each supporting detail.

Items 17–20:
See page 129.
Addition words such as *For one thing, In addition, Another,* and *Finally* are commonly used to signal details that support the main idea.

[1]Illiterate people face great problems in our society. [2]For one thing, people who cannot read or write are limited in a world full of print. [3]They can't read stories in the newspaper or the menu in a restaurant. [4]In a supermarket, they must depend on packages with familiar pictures and colors. [5]In addition, illiterate people do not vote. [6]As a result, they are "half-citizens" who cannot exercise their democratic rights. [7]Another problem is in pursuing an education. [8]Illiterate people find it difficult to take courses that might help them advance in their job or get a better job. [9]Finally, they have trouble helping their children learn. [10]They are not able to help with homework and often do not visit a school for fear of embarrassing their child or themselves.

___B___ 17. The addition words that signal the first problem of illiterate people are
        A. *limited in a world full of print.*
        B. *For one thing.*
        C. *familiar pictures and colors.*

___C___ 18. The addition words that signal the second problem of illiterate people are
        A. *"half-citizens."*   B. *democratic rights.*   C. *In addition.*

___A___ 19. The addition word that signals the third problem of illiterate people is
        A. *Another.*   B. *education.*   C. *courses.*

___C___ 20. The addition word that signals the fourth problem of illiterate people is
        A. *trouble.*   B. *embarrassing.*   C. *Finally.*

MAIN IDEAS: Mastery Test 6

A. (1–4.) In the group below, one statement is the general point, and the other statements are specific support for the point. Identify the point with a **P** and each statement of support with an **S**.

   <u>S</u>   A. In 1908, a meteor struck a remote region in Russia, destroying thousands of square miles of forest.

   <u>S</u>   B. In March 2004, an asteroid just missed the Earth, passing inside the moon's orbit.

   <u>P</u>   C. There is a real chance that an asteroid will collide with the Earth.

   <u>S</u>   D. In 2028, a mile-wide asteroid—big enough to destroy a continent—is expected to come dangerously close to Earth.   Statements A, B, and D list examples of past and future collisions and near-collisions of asteroids with the Earth.

B. (5–12.) Each group of four items includes one topic, one main idea, and two supporting details. In the space provided, label each item with one of the following:

    T — for the **topic** of the paragraph
    MI — for the **main idea**
    SD — for the **supporting details**

Group 1

   <u>SD</u>   A. Those exposed to secondhand smoke for 30 years or more are 23 percent more likely to get lung cancer.

   <u>MI</u>   B. Exposure to secondhand smoke presents a number of serious health hazards to nonsmokers.

   <u>T</u>   C. Exposure to secondhand smoke.

   <u>SD</u>   D. Nonsmokers exposed to secondhand smoke at home have a 15 percent higher death rate than those exposed to clean air.

    Item C is the topic (a phrase). Item B contains list words (*a number of serious health hazards*) to suggest the main idea. Items A and D list those hazards.

Group 2

   <u>T</u>   A. Advances in computer technology.

   <u>SD</u>   B. E-mail is now used to steal people's identification and credit card information.

   <u>SD</u>   C. High-speed Internet connections are used to send harmful viruses around the world.

   <u>MI</u>   D. Advances in computer technology have created new tools for criminals.   Item A is the topic (a phrase). Item D, the main idea, states that computer technology has given criminals new tools. Items B and C are examples of those tools.

(Continues on next page)

C. In the space provided, write the letter of the list words in each sentence.

Items
13–16:
See page
128. The
words *for
several
reasons, a
number of,*
and *some*
often
signal
main ideas.

_C_ 13. Most mothers cradle their babies in their left arms for several reasons.
A. *Most mothers* C. *for several reasons*
B. *cradle their babies*

_B_ 14. Marriage has undergone a number of changes in recent years.
A. *Marriage* C. *in recent years*
B. *a number of changes*

_C_ 15. The original versions of famous fairy tales have some shocking outcomes.
A. *original versions* C. *some shocking outcomes*
B. *famous fairy tales*

_C_ 16. Although most celebrities would probably not choose different lives, they would agree that fame has some real drawbacks.
A. *most celebrities* C. *some real drawbacks*
B. *different lives*

D. Read the following passage. Then, in the space provided, write the letter of the addition words that introduce each supporting detail.

Items 17–20:
See page
129. Addition
words such
as *first, also,
next,* and *final*
are commonly
used to signal
details that
support the
main idea.

[1]There are several parenting styles. [2]The first is the authoritarian style. [3]Authoritarian parents give orders and punish their children if those orders are not quickly obeyed. [4]There is also the authoritative style. [5]Authoritative parents make it clear they are in charge, but they are open to seeing their children's point of view. [6]The next style is that of permissive parents, who avoid ever saying "no" and give the children a good deal of power. [7]The final parenting style is uninvolved. [8]An uninvolved parent does not ask much of children, and does not give much attention either. [9]Most child-raising experts feel that children's needs are best met by authoritative parents.

_B_ 17. The addition word that signals the first parenting style is
A. *several.* B. *first.* C. *punish.*

_A_ 18. The addition word that signals the second parenting style is
A. *also.* B. *but.* C. *point.*

_C_ 19. The addition word that signals the third parenting style is
A. *permissive.* B. *avoid.* C. *next.*

_B_ 20. The addition word that signals the fourth parenting style is
A. *uninvolved.* B. *final.* C. *best.*

4 Supporting Details

This Chapter in a Nutshell

- Supporting details are the evidence—such as reasons or examples—that backs up main ideas. Those details help you understand main ideas.

- Outlines and maps (diagrams) can show you a main idea and its supporting details at a glance.

- There are often two levels of supporting details—major and minor.

- List words and addition words can help you find major and minor supporting details.

Look at the following cartoon and see if you can answer the questions that follow.

- What is the frog's *main idea*, or point?
- What is his *support* for his point?

Explanation

The frog's main idea, or point, is that he does not need any insurance. He supports his point by providing four reasons he doesn't need health insurance: no house, no car, no possessions, no health worries.

Chapter 3 introduced you to the most important reading skill—the ability to find the main idea. A closely related reading skill is the ability to locate supporting details. Supporting details provide the added information that is needed for you to make sense of a main idea.

What Are Supporting Details?

Supporting details are reasons, examples, steps, or other kinds of evidence that explain a main idea, or point.

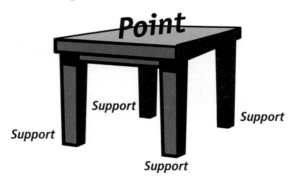

In the model paragraph in Chapter 3, the supporting details appear as a series of reasons:

> [1]Poor grades in school can have various causes. [2]For one thing, students may have financial problems. [3]If they need to work long hours to make money, they will have little study time. [4]Another cause of poor grades may be trouble with relationships. [5]A student may be unhappy over family problems or a lack of friends. [6]That unhappiness can harm schoolwork. [7]A final cause of poor grades may be bad study habits. [8]Some students have never learned how to take good notes in class, how to manage their time effectively, or how to study a textbook. [9]Without such study skills, their grades are likely to suffer.

Check Your Understanding

See if you can complete the basic outline below that shows the three reasons that support the main idea. The first one has been added for you. Then read the explanation that follows.

> **Main idea: Poor grades in school can have various causes.**
>
> Supporting detail 1: Financial problems
> Supporting detail 2: *Trouble with relationships*
> Supporting detail 3: *Bad study habits*

Explanation

You should have added "Trouble with relationships" and "Bad study habits" as the two other supporting details. Notice that the supporting details provide the added information—the specific causes of poor grades—that is needed for you to fully understand the main idea. To read effectively, then, you must recognize both main ideas and the details that support those ideas.

In the paragraph on the previous page, about poor grades, the supporting details are *reasons*. Now look at the paragraph below, in which the main idea is explained by *examples*. In the outline provided, write in the main idea and the words that serve as examples.

> [1]Some everyday words are actually based on people's names. [2]For example, the word *sandwich* originated when the Earl of Sandwich, a British nobleman who loved to play cards, became hungry during a game in 1762. [3]Not wanting to stop playing, he asked a servant to bring him some roast beef between two pieces of toasted bread. [4]The quick portable snack was soon called a *sandwich*. [5]Another person whose name became a word is a Frenchman named Dr. Guillotin. [6]During the French Revolution, he pleaded for a quicker, kinder way than hanging to execute criminals. [7]The result was the *guillotine*, a machine with a heavy blade used to behead people. [8]A third example comes from a 19th-century Irish landlord named Mr. Boycott. [9]When he refused to lower the high rents he was charging, his tenants stopped speaking to him. [10]Today, to *boycott* means to refuse to do business with a person or company.

> **Main idea:** *Some everyday words are actually based on people's names.*
>
> Supporting detail 1: *Sandwich*
> Supporting detail 2: *Guillotine*
> Supporting detail 3: *Boycott*

Explanation
The main idea is the first sentence of the paragraph, and the supporting details are the three examples given: *sandwich, guillotine,* and *boycott.*

Outlining

Preparing an outline of a passage will help you see clearly the relationship between a main idea and its supporting details. Notice how the outlines on this page and the next page help you see and understand material at a glance.

   Outlines are lists that show the important parts of a piece of writing. They begin with a main idea, with supporting details placed, in order, underneath the main idea. There may be two levels of supporting details—major and minor. The **major details** explain and develop the main idea. In turn, the **minor details** under them help fill out and make clear the major details.

   Once you know how to outline, you can use the skill to prepare very useful study notes. Instead of studying fact after fact in sentence after sentence, you can organize the material into outlines. Good outlines clearly tie ideas together, making them easier to understand and remember.

   Below is a more detailed outline of the paragraph on poor grades. This outline shows both major and minor details:

Main idea: Poor grades in school can have various causes.

Major detail:	1.	Financial problems
Minor details:		a. Need to work long hours after school
		b. No time left to study
Major detail:	2.	Trouble with relationships
Minor details:		a. Unhappiness over family problems
		b. Unhappiness over a lack of friends
Major detail:	3.	Bad study habits
Minor details:		a. No skill in taking class notes
		b. No skill in time management
		c. No skill in studying a textbook

   The main idea is supported and explained by the major details, and in turn the major details are supported and explained by the minor details. For example, the major detail of "bad study habits" is supported by three details: no skill in notetaking, time management, or textbook studying.

Check Your Understanding

See if you can fill in the missing major and minor supporting details in the outline of the following paragraph.

> ¹To motivate workers, managers should practice several methods of building self-esteem. ²One way to build self-esteem is to show a genuine interest in what workers have to say. ³Ask for their opinions, and really listen to their responses. ⁴A second method of improving self-esteem is to practice good conversational habits. ⁵Do so in three ways: by looking a worker in the eye, by smiling frequently, and by calling workers by their first name—the most important word in the language to every person. ⁶Last of all, managers can build esteem by admitting mistakes. ⁷Doing so, they show that it is simply human to do the wrong thing at times.

Main idea: **To motivate workers, managers should practice several methods of building self-esteem.**

1. Show genuine interest in what workers have to say.
   a. Ask for their opinions.
   b. Really listen to their responses.

2. Practice good conversational habits.
   a. Look a worker in the eye.
   b. Smile frequently.
   c. Call workers by first name.

3. Admit mistakes.

Wording of answers may vary.

Explanation

You should have added two major details: (2) practice good conversational habits; (3) admit mistakes. And below the second major supporting detail, you should have added three minor details: (a) look a worker in the eye; (b) smile frequently; (c) call workers by first name.

Notice that just as the main idea is more general than its supporting details, major details are more general than minor ones. For instance, the major detail "to practice good conversational habits" is more general than the three minor supporting details: looking a worker in the eye, smiling, and using first names.

Outlining Tips

The following tips will help you prepare outlines:

 TIP 1   Look for words that tell you a list of details is coming. List words were introduced in Chapter 3 on page 128. Here are some common list words:

List Words

several kinds of	various causes	a few reasons
a number of	a series of	three factors
four steps	among the results	several advantages

For example, look again at the main ideas in two of the paragraphs already discussed, and circle the list words:

- Poor grades in school can have (various causes.)
- To motivate workers, managers should practice (several methods) of building self-esteem.

Explanation

In the main ideas above, the words *various causes* and *several methods* tell us that a list of major details is coming. You will not always be given such helpful signals that a list of details will follow. However, be ready to take advantage of them when they are present. Such list words can help you understand quickly the basic organization of a passage.

 TIP 2   Look for words that signal major details. Such words are called **addition words**, and they were also introduced in Chapter 3 on pages 129–130. Here are some common addition words:

Addition Words

one	to begin with	in addition	last
first	another	next	last of all
first of all	second	moreover	final
for one thing	also	furthermore	finally

Check Your Understanding

Now look again at the selection on poor grades, shown below, and answer the questions that follow.

> [1]Poor grades in school can have various causes. [2]For one thing, students may have financial problems. [3]If they need to work long hours to make money, they will have little study time. [4]Another cause of poor grades may be trouble with relationships. [5]A student may be unhappy over family problems or a lack of friends. [6]That unhappiness can harm schoolwork. [7]A final cause of poor grades may be bad study habits. [8]Some students have never learned how to take good notes in class, how to manage their time effectively, or how to study a textbook. [9]Without such study skills, their grades are likely to suffer.

- Which words signal the first major detail? _____*For one thing*_____
- Which word signals the second major detail? _____*Another*_____
- Which word signals the third major detail? _____*final*_____

Look also at the selection on motivating workers, shown below, and answer the questions that follow.

> [1]To motivate workers, managers should practice several methods of building self-esteem. [2]One way to build self-esteem is to show a genuine interest in what workers have to say. [3]Ask for their opinions and really listen to their responses. [4]A second method of improving self-esteem is to practice good conversational habits. [5]Do so in three ways: by looking a worker in the eye, by smiling frequently, and by calling workers by their first name—the most important word in the language to every person. [6]Last of all, managers can build esteem by admitting mistakes. [7]Doing so, they show that it is simply human to do the wrong thing at times.

- Which word signals the first major detail? _____*One*_____
- Which word signals the second major detail? _____*second*_____
- Which words signal the third major detail? _____*Last of all*_____

Explanation

In the first selection, on poor grades, the addition word signals are *For one thing, Another,* and *final*. In the second selection, on motivating workers, the word signals are *One, second*, and *Last of all*.

TIP 3   **In your outline, put all supporting details of equal importance at the same distance from the margin.** In the outline of the paragraph on poor grades (page 158), the three major supporting details all begin at the margin. Likewise, the minor supporting details are all indented at the same distance from the margin. You can therefore see at a glance the main idea, the major details, and the minor details.

 ## Check Your Understanding: List Words

Put appropriate numbers (*1, 2, 3*) and letters (*a, b, c*) in front of the major and minor details in the following outline.

>   **Main idea**
>   _1_ **Major detail**
>   _a_ Minor detail
>   _b_ Minor detail
>   _2_ **Major detail**
>   _a_ Minor detail
>   _b_ Minor detail
>   _3_ **Major detail**

Explanation

You should have put a *1, 2,* and *3* in front of the major details and an *a* and *b* in front of the minor details. Note that an outline proceeds from the most general to the most specific, from main idea to major details to minor details.

The practice that follows will give you experience in finding major details, in separating major details from minor details, and in preparing outlines.

> *Hint:* As you read each passage in this practice and those that follow, circle the list words and underline the addition words. Another helpful technique is to number the major details in each passage *1, 2, 3,* etc.

 PRACTICE 1

Read each passage. Then complete the outline that follows by filling in the missing major and minor details. (Some details have been added for you.) Finally, answer the questions that follow each outline.

To the Instructor: You may want to remind students to circle list words, underline addition words, and put numbers before major details. These markings have been inserted for you in the practices in this *Instructor's Edition.*

Passage 1

List words *(signs of addiction to shopping)* suggest the main idea in sentence 2. Addition words *(One . . . second . . . Another . . . Last of all)* signal the major supporting details.

¹We all enjoy buying a new shirt or book or DVD. ²According to experts, though, some people show ⟨signs of addiction to shopping.⟩ ³One such sign is that a shopper develops¹ serious money problems. ⁴Checks are bounced, or credit card debt becomes so great that the minimal payment cannot be made each month. ⁵A <u>second</u> sign of a shopping addict is a²distinct mood pattern. ⁶Before shopping, tension builds up in the addict as he or she looks forward to a "fix." ⁷After shopping, there is a pleasant release from that tension, and for a time the shopper will feel happy and at rest. ⁸<u>Another</u> sign of a shopping addict is³shoplifting, especially if this has not been a behavior of the person in the past. ⁹<u>Last of all</u>, a shopping addict often suffers from⁴other addictive behaviors, such as overeating, overdrinking, or frequent gambling.

Main idea: Some people show signs of addiction to shopping.

Wording of answers may vary.

1. Serious money problems

    a. Checks that bounce

    b. Minimal monthly payment on credit card cannot be made

2. Distinct mood pattern

    a. Tension before shopping

    b. After shopping, a pleasant release from tension

3. Shoplifting

4. Other addictive behaviors

Questions about the passage

- Which words in the main idea tell you that a list is coming?

  signs of addiction to shopping

- Which word signals the first major detail?   One

- Which word signals the second major detail?   second

- Which word signals the third major detail?   Another

- Which words signal the fourth major detail?   Last of all

Passage 2

List words
*(several
advantages)*
suggest the
main idea in
sentence 1.
Addition words
*(One . . .
Moreover . . .
Finally)* signal
the major
supporting
details.

¹There are several advantages to watching a football game or other sports event on television instead of going to the game itself. ²One advantage is that it's ¹cheaper to watch a game at home. ³Going to a sports event can cost at least $50 for parking and an admission ticket. ⁴Then it's all too easy to spend an added $30 for drinks and snacks. ⁵Moreover, it's ²more comfortable at home. ⁶There is no bumper-to-bumper traffic to and from a sports arena or stadium. ⁷There are no noisy, pushy crowds of people to deal with while trying to get to one's seat, which is made out of uncomfortably hard plastic or wood. ⁸Finally, watching a game on television is ³more informative. ⁹Camera coverage is so good that every play is seen close up, and many plays are shown on instant replay. ¹⁰At the same time, the game is explained in great detail by very informed commentators. ¹¹The fan at home always enjoys an insider's view about what is happening in the game at every minute.

Main idea: There are several advantages to watching a football game or other sports event on television instead of going to the game itself.

1. Cheaper _____.

 a. $50 for parking and admission to event

 b. Additional $30 for drinks and snacks _____

2. More comfortable _____.

 a. No bumper-to-bumper traffic _____

 b. No noisy, pushy crowds or hard seats

3. More informative _____.

 a. Close-ups and instant replays _____

 b. Detailed explanations by commentators _____

Questions about the passage

- Which words in the main idea tell you that a list of details is coming?

  _____ several advantages _____

- Which word signals the first major detail? _____ One _____

- Which word signals the second major detail? _____ Moreover _____

- Which word signals the third major detail? _____ Finally _____

Preparing Maps

Students sometimes find it helpful to use maps rather than outlines. **Maps**, or diagrams, are highly visual outlines in which circles, boxes, or other shapes show the relationship between main ideas and supporting details. Each major detail is connected to the main idea. If minor details are included, each is connected to the major detail it explains.

 ### *Check Your Understanding*

Read the following passage, and then see if you can complete the map and answer the questions that follow.

[1]People daydream for a variety of reasons. [2]One cause of daydreaming is [1]boredom, at school or on the job. [3]To make life more interesting, people imagine being somewhere else. [4]For example, a student might dream of lying on the beach and flirting with an attractive person on a nearby blanket. [5]A production worker might dream about winning the lottery or becoming the big boss at the company. [6]Another cause of daydreaming is [2]a lack of something. [7]For instance, a starving person might dream about food, or a poor person might dream about owning a house or a car. [8]A third cause of daydreaming is [3]angry feelings. [9]An angry student might dream about getting a hated math instructor fired.

Questions about the passage

● Which words in the main idea tell you that a list of details is coming?

  a variety of reasons

● Which word signals the first major detail? _____ *One* _____

● Which word signals the second major detail? _____ *Another* _____

● Which word signals the third major detail? _____ *third* _____

Explanation

In the main idea above, the words *a variety of reasons* tell us that a list of major details is coming.

The word signals for the three major reasons are *One, Another,* and *third.* The map also includes minor details in the form of examples.

To the Instructor: Again, you may want to remind students to circle list words, underline addition words, and put numbers before major details.

PRACTICE 2

Read each passage. Then complete the map that follows by filling in the missing major details. Finally, answer the questions that follow each map.

Wording of answers in the maps may vary.

Passage 1

¹To complain to people and still keep them as friends, follow (several sensible) (guidelines) for criticism. ²First, be specific. Don't say, "Your behavior at the dinner was awful!" ³Instead, say, "You embarrassed me by getting drunk and loud and telling off-color jokes to my parents." ⁴Second, stick to the present. ⁵Hauling up old offenses from last month or last year just takes away attention from the problem at hand. ⁶In addition, don't use insults. ⁷Calling someone names like "idiot" or "animal" will only create anger and hurt any chance of getting the person to listen to you. ⁸The last guideline is to complain privately. ⁹Never criticize a person in front of friends, parents, children, or anyone else, for that matter. ¹⁰Criticizing in front of others has the same effect as insults. ¹¹It shames the person being criticized and makes it likely that he or she will want to put you down rather than listen to you.

List words (*several sensible guidelines*) suggest the main idea in sentence 1. Addition words (*First . . . Second . . . In addition . . . last*) signal the major supporting details.

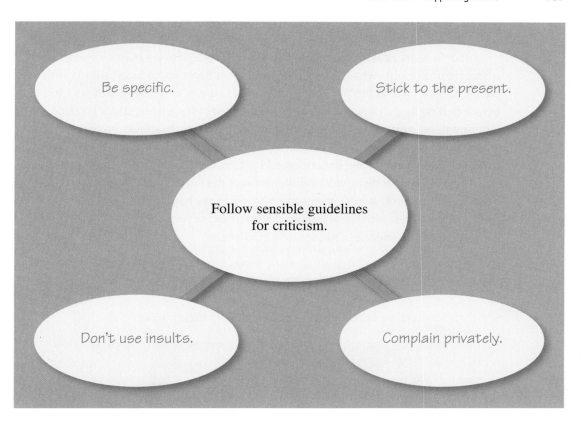

Questions about the passage

● Which words in the main idea tell you that a list of details is coming?

several sensible guidelines

● Which word signals the first major detail? _First_

● Which word signals the second major detail? _Second_

● Which words signal the third major detail? _In addition_

● Which word signals the fourth major detail? _last_

Passage 2

¹Some heart attacks are sudden and intense—like ones we might see in a movie—where no one doubts what's happening. ²But most heart attacks start slowly, with mild pain or discomfort. ³Often people affected aren't sure what's wrong and wait too long before getting help. ⁴Here are various signs that can mean a heart attack is taking place. ⁵For one thing, you may have¹ chest discomfort. ⁶Most heart attacks involve discomfort in the center of the chest that lasts more than a few minutes, or that goes away but then comes back. ⁷It can feel like uncomfortable pressure, squeezing, fullness or pain. ⁸Next, you may have² pain or discomfort in other areas of the upper body, including one or both arms, the back, neck, jaw, or stomach. ⁹Also, you may have³ shortness of breath. ¹⁰This feeling often comes with chest discomfort, but it can occur without it. ¹¹Finally, you may experience⁴ lightheadedness, nausea, or a cold sweat.

List words (various signs) suggest the main idea in sentence 4.
Addition words (For one thing . . . Next . . . Also . . . Finally) signal the major supporting details.

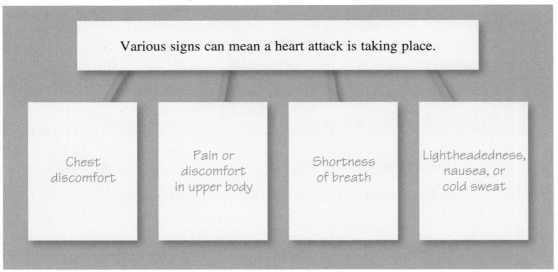

Questions about the passage

- Which words in the main idea tell you that a list of details is coming?

  various signs

- Which words signal the first major detail?   *For one thing*

- Which word signals the second major detail?   *Next*

- Which word signals the third major detail?   *Also*

- Which word signals the final major details?   *Finally*

A Final Note

This chapter has centered on supporting details as they appear in well-organized paragraphs. But keep in mind that supporting details are part of readings of any length, including selections that may not have an easy-to-follow list of one major detail after another. Starting with the reading at the end of this chapter (page 173), you will be given practice in answering all kinds of questions about key supporting details. These questions will develop your ability to pay close, careful attention to what you are reading.

CHAPTER REVIEW

In this chapter, you learned the following:

● Supporting details go hand in hand with main ideas. They provide the added information you need to make sense of a main idea.

● There are often two levels of supporting details—major and minor.

● List words and addition words can help you to find major and minor supporting details.

● Outlining and mapping are useful note-taking strategies.

● Outlines and maps, or diagrams, show the relationship between the main idea, major details, and minor details of a passage.

The next chapter—Chapter 5—will deepen your understanding of the relationship between main ideas and supporting details.

 On the Web: If you are using this book in class, you can visit our website for additional practice in identifying supporting details. Go to **www.townsendpress. com** and click on "Online Learning Center."

 REVIEW TEST 1

To review what you've learned in this chapter, fill in the blank or write the letter of your answer.

1. Two closely related skills are finding the main idea and identifying the

   major and minor _____*details*_____ that support the main idea.
   See page 156.

2. Supporting details are reasons, examples, facts, steps, or other kinds of evidence that explain a _____main idea (or point)_____.   See page 156.

3. A _____map_____ is a highly visual outline; it shows at a glance the relationship between a main idea and its supporting details.
See page 165.

__B__ 4. Words such as *several reasons, a number of factors,* and *three advantages* tell you that a series of details is coming. Such words are known as
   A. addition words.   B. list words.   See page 160.

__A__ 5. Words such as *first, also, another,* and *finally* often tell you that a new supporting detail is being introduced. Such words are known as
   A. addition words.   B. list words.   See page 160.

REVIEW TEST 2

A. Complete the outline below by filling in the missing major details. Then answer the questions that follow the outline.   *Wording of answers may vary.*

[1]Researchers have learned that people lie for (five main reasons.) [2]The primary reason is to prevent discomfort. [3]For example, if a coworker asked, "Do you like my new haircut?" you might say yes even if you hate it, to avoid hurting his or her feelings. [4]Another common reason for lying is to avoid conflict. [5]If a friend angers you and asks, "Are you upset with me?" you might answer "No" to avoid a scene. [6]People also lie as a way of being socially acceptable. [7]For instance, they might say "That's interesting" when they actually find another person's conversation boring. [8]In addition, people lie to increase or decrease interaction with someone. [9]Many people rid themselves of undesired company with the lie "I have to go now." [10]Finally, people lie to have greater control over a situation. [11]For example, if someone asks you out at the last minute and you have nothing planned, you might still say "I have other plans" in order to be the one "in charge."

Main idea: People lie for five main reasons.

1. ___To prevent discomfort_____.

2. ___To avoid conflict_____.

3. ___To be socially acceptable_____.

4. ___To increase or decrease interaction with someone_____.

5. ___To have greater control over a situation_____.

    List words (*five main reasons*) suggest the main idea in sentence 1.
    Addition words (*Another . . . also . . . In addition . . . Finally*) signal four
    of the five major details.

B. Now answer the following questions about the passage you have outlined.

6. Which words tell you that a list of details is coming? _____
_____ *five main reasons*

7. Which word introduces the second major detail? ___ *Another* ___

8. Which word introduces the third major detail? ___ *also* ___

9. Which words introduce the fourth major detail? ___ *In addition* ___

10. Which word introduces the last major detail? ___ *Finally* ___

REVIEW TEST 3

A. (1–4.) Fill in the major details and one minor detail needed to complete the map below.   *Wording of answers may vary.*

¹Colonial Americans experienced (a number of dangerous medical treatments.) ²One of the most popular was bloodletting. ³This involved cutting a patient's skin and allowing him or her to bleed enough to remove the cause of the disease. ⁴Sometimes so much blood was lost that patients died. ⁵Another harmful treatment used in colonial America was "sweating." ⁶A patient would be kept in a small, hot room covered in the heaviest clothing and blankets available. ⁷The result was extreme weakness, heat exhaustion, and sometimes death. ⁸A third harmful colonial treatment was purging. ⁹Patients would be forced to swallow syrup that made them vomit in order to remove poison believed to be in the body. ¹⁰With all these treatments, the "cure" was usually worse than the disease.

The addition words (*One, Another, third*) signal the major supporting details. The words *a number of* are often used as part of a list signal.

Colonial Americans experienced dangerous medical treatments.		
Bloodletting	Sweating	Purging
Cutting a patient's skin and letting the patient bleed	Keeping a patient in a small hot room, heavily covered	Forcing patients to swallow syrup that made them vomit

B. (5.) What are the list words that tell you a series of details is coming?

a number of dangerous medical treatments

REVIEW TEST 4

Here is a chance to apply your understanding of supporting details to an excerpt from a recent autobiography. The author, Roxanne Black, describes her reactions when, as a teenager, she learned she had an incurable disease. Read the selection, and then answer the questions that follow about its supporting details.

To help you continue to strengthen your work on skills taught in previous chapters, there are also questions on vocabulary in context and main ideas.

Words to Watch

Below are some words in the reading that do not have strong context support. Each word is followed by the number of the paragraph in which it appears and its meaning there. These words are indicated in the selection by a small circle (°).

foreboding (15): a feeling that something bad is going to happen
chronic (18): lasting for a long time; continuing to occur
remission (21): lessening of the symptoms of a disease
terse (30): brief and to the point
biopsy (32): the removal of sample tissue for laboratory examination
intoned (37): said something in a slow and serious way
muster (39): gather

A DOOR SWINGS OPEN

Roxanne Black

1   I sat at my bedroom window in my wheelchair, watching my high-school rowing team pull away from the shore, eight friends smiling and waving as they moved into the choppy water. Not long ago, I'd been one of them.

2   I loved everything about rowing, the feeling of freedom, the teamwork, the sense of strength and accomplishment. When I rowed, I was at peace and forgot about my problems. Not that I'd had many then. In most ways, I was a typical New Jersey teenager, a shy high-school freshman who lived with her mother in a small row house that overlooked Lake's Bay. My mother and I didn't have two dimes to rub together, but with that view from our windows, we considered ourselves rich.

3   It was after rowing one afternoon that I had the first warning that something might be wrong with me—a sharp stab of back pain that took my breath away.

4   "What's the matter?" my mother asked when she saw me wincing.

5   "I don't know," I said, stretching. "I guess I strained a muscle."

6   By evening, the pain was almost too painful to bear. My mother filled a hot bath with Epsom salts, and later gave me a heating pad. I took a couple of Tylenol and decided I'd stay away from crew practice for a few days. In my young life, this had been the antidote for any ailment. Eventually everything passed, given time and a little rest.

7   But not this time. Instead of decreasing, the pain grew so intense that I could barely sit up in bed the next morning.

8   My mother took one look at me and said, "I'm taking you to the doctor."

9   But by the time we arrived at the office, the pain had subsided; and the doctor advised that we simply continue with the heating pad and baths.

10   Two days later, I developed chest pains that by evening were so acute I could barely breathe. Now I was beginning to worry.

11   This time the doctor prescribed antibiotics, thinking I might have an infection. The pains intensified over the next few days; then they too vanished.

12   This pattern of new symptoms that appeared, intensified, then vanished continued with an itchy red rash, which covered my body. After it mysteriously disappeared, my ankles swelled so severely that I was unable to fit into any of my shoes.

13   Although the doctor tracked my reports, took bloodwork, and examined me closely, he couldn't figure out what was wrong. My symptoms were elusive; it was hard to pin them down.

14   Finally he referred me to a specialist. By the day of my appointment, all my symptoms had subsided except for my swollen ankles. My mother and I arrived at his office, expecting this new doctor would prescribe another medication for what was probably an allergic reaction.

15   Although I'd never seen this

how can you figure out word from context?

doctor's face before, his cool, sober expression as we walked in gave me a sense of foreboding°.

16   After a routine examination, he studied my bloodwork, then touched my ankles, which were so full of fluid they could be molded like lumps of clay.

17   Then he looked up and a strange word floated from his mouth. <u>Lupus</u>. I saw it, like in a cartoon caption, odd and ominous, hanging in the air.

18   The word meant nothing to me, but my mother's reaction did; she covered her face with her hands. In her work as a nurse, she'd spent years caring for patients with chronic° illness. As I watched her sniff and take out a Kleenex, it hit me that this must be serious, something that Tylenol and bed rest weren't going to solve.

19   My health had always been part of my identity, something I was as certain of as my strong legs and pumping heart. Now I was being told baffling facts about kidney function, inflammation, and antibodies.

20   But when the doctor said I was to be admitted to a children's hospital in Philadelphia the following day for testing, I realized a chapter of my life was suddenly ending and a new one was about to start.

21   When I returned home, I looked up lupus in our medical dictionary: a chronic autoimmune disease, potentially weakening and sometimes fatal, that was first discovered in the Middle Ages. The illness follows an unpredictable course, with episodes of activity, called flares, alternating with periods of remission°. During a flare, the immune system attacks the body's cells

and tissue, resulting in inflammation and tissue damage.

22   The words "sometimes fatal" stood out to me, as if they were written in blood. Just as alarming were the lists of possible signs: dermatological, musculoskeletal, hematological, renal, hepatic, pulmonary. What else was there?

23   How had this ancient disease—that only affected one in many hundreds in the United States—ended up in Atlantic City, residing in a teenager like me?

24   For that, there was no answer.

25   "There's always one moment in childhood when the door opens and lets the future in," Graham Greene wrote. I don't know if most people remember that moment, but I do.

26   At the children's hospital, I shared a room with a three-year-old girl with a charming face and shiny black hair cut in a bob. She was so energetic and lively, I assumed she was someone's daughter

or sister, until I glimpsed a tiny hospital ID bracelet on her wrist.

27 Her name was Michelle, and we bonded from the moment we met. She brought a herd of plastic ponies to my bedside, and we brushed their manes and made up stories.

28 "Why's she here?" I asked when her parents arrived, looking drawn and worried.

29 "She has a hole in her heart," her mother told me. "She's having open-heart surgery tomorrow."

30 A steady stream of doctors arrived to talk to Michelle's parents. I heard the terse° murmur of their voices behind the curtain that separated our room. Through it all, Michelle dashed between the beds, oblivious to the drama around her. She was so vital and energetic, it was hard to believe that anything serious was wrong with her.

31 I'd never known a sick child before, and now I was in a hospital full of them. It seemed unnatural seeing toddlers on IV's, babies on ventilators, adolescents with leg braces, struggling to walk. A parade of pediatric malfunction passed my door, children smashed in motor accidents, suffering from muscular dystrophy and leukemia. This alternate world had existed all along, behind my formerly sunny, innocent life.

32 The next day I was to find out the results of my kidney biopsy°, and Michelle was headed to surgery. Before she left, she walked over and hugged me so tightly that I could smell the baby shampoo in her hair. Then she solemnly handed me a drawing she'd made of a house, a girl, and a tree.

main idea

33 "This is you, isn't it?"

34 She nodded.

35 "Well it's beautiful, thanks. I'll see you later."

36 I waited all day for them to bring Michelle back, trying to distract myself by reading and crocheting, but it was no use. Breakfast came and went, then lunch, and still there was no sign of her.

37 Early in the evening, I was talking on the pay phone in the hallway when an alarm sounded, and doctors began running down the hall from all directions. A woman's voice intoned° a code over the loudspeakers, a foreign babble.

38 As I hung up, I saw two new figures running down the hallway. Their features grew terribly familiar as they approached. It was Michelle's parents, their faces smeared with tears, heading in the same direction as the doctors.

39 My mother came out and hurried me back into the room. When she shut the door, I stood there, looking at Michelle's bed, at the picture on the table she had drawn for me. I took out a little prayer book I'd brought along and began a prayer, filling it with all the love and intention I could muster°. A long, terrible female scream pierced the silence.

40 A young floor nurse walked in a short while later. Her sad face was statement enough, but then she told us. Michelle hadn't made it. She'd suffered a heart attack and died.

41 So there it was, and I had to face it: Life wasn't fair. Prayers weren't always answered. The young and innocent could be lost. The door had swung open, and I had been pushed through to the other side.

Reading Comprehension Questions

Vocabulary in Context

____B____ 1. In the excerpt below, the word *antidote* (ăn′tĭ-dōt′) means
   A. explanation.
   B. cure.
   C. cause.
   D. symptom.

   Tylenol and rest would be a cure for an ailment.

   "I took a couple of Tylenol and decided I'd stay away from crew practice for a few days. In my young life, this had been the antidote for any ailment." (Paragraph 6)

____A____ 2. In the excerpt below, the word *subsided* (səb-sīd′-əd) means
   A. became less.
   B. gotten worse.
   C. returned.
   D. stayed the same.

   If the doctor suggests continuing the same treatment, it must have had the desired result—the pain became less.

   "My mother took one look at me and said, 'I'm taking you to the doctor.' But by the time we arrived at the office, the pain had subsided; and the doctor advised that we simply continue with the heating pad and baths." (Paragraphs 8–9)

____B____ 3. In the sentence below, the word *acute* (ə-kyōōt′) means
   A. effortless.
   B. sharp.
   C. mild.
   D. predictable.

   If she could barely breathe, the pain must have been sharp.

   "Two days later, I developed chest pains that by evening were so acute I could barely breathe." (Paragraph 10)

____D____ 4. In the excerpt below, the word *elusive* (ə-lōō′sĭv) means
   A. difficult to treat.
   B. difficult to see.
   C. difficult to forget.
   D. difficult to define.

   The synonym-like clue hard to pin . . . down *suggests that* elusive *means "difficult to define."*

   "Although the doctor tracked my reports, took bloodwork, and examined me closely, he couldn't figure out what was wrong. My symptoms were elusive; it was hard to pin them down." (Paragraph 13)

___A___   5. In the excerpt below, the words *oblivious to* (ə-blĭv′ē-əs tōō) mean
   A. unaware of.
   B. saddened by.   If Michelle is dashing back and forth in the room,
   C. confused by.   she is unaware of the drama around her.
   D. conscious of.

   "A steady stream of doctors arrived to talk to Michelle's parents. I heard
   the terse murmur of their voices behind the curtain that separated our
   room. Through it all, Michelle dashed between the beds, oblivious to the
   drama around her." (Paragraph 30)

Central Point

___D___   6. The central idea of the selection is that
   A. Black was shocked to learn that she had a chronic disease.
   B. Black was saddened when a little girl she met in the hospital died.
   C. before becoming ill with lupus, Black had been in excellent health.
   D. as the result of her own chronic illness and the death of a child, Black
      realized that life isn't fair.   Answer A covers only paragraphs 19–24.
                                 Answer B is suggested by paragraphs 39–40.
                                     Answer C covers part of paragraph 19.
Main Ideas   Answer D, the central point, is suggested in the concluding paragraph.

___C___   7. Which sentence best expresses the main idea of paragraph 2?
   A. When Black rowed, she forgot about her problems.
   B. Black lived with her mother in a small row house overlooking Lake's
      Bay.
   C. In most ways, Black, who loved rowing, was a typical teenager.
   D. Although Black and her mother didn't have much money, they
      considered themselves rich.   Answers A, B, and D each cover
                                   only one sentence of the paragraph.

Supporting Details

___D___   8. Black first thought the intense pain she was experiencing was
   A. an insect bite.
   B. an allergic reaction.
   C. an infection.   See paragraph 5.
   D. a muscle strain.

___C___   9. When the doctor tells Black she has lupus, her mother
   A. tells the doctor he's wrong.
   B. screams and then breaks out into loud sobs.   See paragraph 18.
   C. covers her face with her hands and takes out a Kleenex.
   D. says she knew it all along.

___B___ 10. Michelle was in the hospital because she had
      A. leukemia.
      B. a hole in her heart.   See paragraph 29.
      C. a brain tumor.
      D. been injured in an auto accident.

Discussion Questions

1. When Black enters the hospital, she becomes aware of an "alternate world" that "had existed all along, behind my formerly sunny, innocent life." What is this "alternate world"? What, in particular, does she find surprising about it?

2. Black quotes Graham Greene, who wrote, "There's always one moment in childhood when the door opens and lets the future in." What might this statement mean? According to Black's story, when did this experience happen to her? Why do you think she was so upset afterward?

3. Have you ever known anyone who, like Black, suffers from chronic illness? If so, how does it affect his or her life? What adjustments has the person made in order to live with this condition?

4. Do you remember a moment in *your* life when "the door opened and let the future in"? Describe the event, and explain what it made you realize.

Note: Writing assignments for this selection appear on page 590.

Check Your Performance   **SUPPORTING DETAILS**

Activity	Number Right	Points	Score
Review Test 1 (5 items)	_____	× 2 =	_____
Review Test 2 (10 items)	_____	× 3 =	_____
Review Test 3 (5 items)	_____	× 6 =	_____
Review Test 4 (10 items)	_____	× 3 =	_____
		TOTAL SCORE =	_____%

Enter your total score into the **Reading Performance Chart: Review Tests** on the inside back cover.

SUPPORTING DETAILS: Mastery Test 1

A. (1–6.) Complete the outline below by filling in the missing major details. Then answer the questions that follow the outline. *Wording of details may vary.*

[1]If you are like most people, you feel that writing is not one of your talents and there's nothing you can do about it. [2]The truth is that some common-sense tips can help you become a better writer. [3]First of all, write often. [4]Like other crafts, writing improves with practice. [5]Also, organize your material with an outline. [6]An outline will provide you with a good guideline without limiting you, as you can change it at any time. [7]Next, write in a plain style. [8]Don't try to use overly fancy language. [9]Instead, just say what you mean simply and clearly. [10]Finally, tighten your writing. [11]Nothing improves writing more than eliminating unnecessary words.

Main idea: Some common-sense tips can help you become a better writer.

1. Write often. _____
2. Organize your material with an outline. _____
3. Write in a plain style. _____
4. Tighten your writing. _____

Questions about the passage

5. Which addition words introduce the first major detail?

_____ First of all _____

6. Which addition word introduces the second major detail?

_____ Also _____

    List words (*some common-sense tips*) suggest the main idea in sentence 2. Addition words (*First of all, Also, Next, Finally*) signal the major supporting details.

To the Instructor:
The addition words in the test passages are underlined in red in this *Instructor's Edition.*

(Continues on next page)

B. (7–10.) Fill in the major details needed to complete the map below.

¹The 14th-century Italian poet Dante is probably best known for a work called *The Inferno*. ²In it, he writes of visiting the nine circles of Hell. ³As he goes down from each level to an even deeper one, he sees the worst of all evildoers. ⁴Here are candidates for the people Dante might put in the lowest levels of Hell if he were writing today. ⁵I think that child molesters would be suitable for the seventh circle of Hell. ⁶Any person who would coldly rob a child of his or her innocence, trust, and physical and emotional well-being deserves no better. ⁷Next, to the eighth circle, I would send selfish politicians who sit in comfortable offices and make decisions that send young men and women off to die in needless wars. ⁸Politicians must be willing to fight those wars themselves—and send their own sons and daughters into battle—before they declare war. ⁹Last, in the lowest circle of Hell, I would place terrorists of every nationality, faith, or cause. ¹⁰There is no moral justification for spreading fear, death, and suffering as the bodies of the innocent are blown apart. ¹¹The lowest circle of Hell is the only place fit for terrorists.

Wording of details may vary.

Here are candidates for the lowest circles of Hell.

Child molesters	Selfish politicians	Terrorists

10. Which two addition words introduce the people in the eighth and ninth circles?

            Next   Last

Sentences 1–3 provide introductory details.
Sentence 4 uses key words to signal the main idea: Here are candidates.

SUPPORTING DETAILS: Mastery Test 2

A. (1–6.) Complete the outline below by filling in the missing major details.

¹There are a number of ways to tell if a person has a drug problem. ²First, a drug abuser cannot stop using or drinking. ³Secondly, the person turns into a "different" person when she or he is using the drug, acting in unusual ways. ⁴Another signal is that the user makes excuses for using drugs. ⁵He or she will say that it was an especially bad day at school or work, or that a relationship has become very stressful. ⁶Fourth, an abuser will try to cover up drug use, or will pretend that it "isn't that bad." ⁷Yet another signal is that the abuser will forget things that happen while he or she is high or drunk. ⁸Finally, the abuser will be the last to recognize that he or she has a problem.

Wording of answers may vary.

Main idea: There are ways to tell if a person has a drug problem.

1. Drug abuser cannot stop using or drinking.

2. Drug abuser turns into a different person when using.

3. User makes excuses for using drugs.

4. User will try to cover up drug use or will pretend it isn't that bad.

5. User will forget what happens while he or she is high or drunk.

6. Abuser will be the last to recognize he or she has a problem.

List words: *a number of ways.*
Addition words (underlined) signal the major supporting details.

(Continues on next page)

B. (7–10.) Fill in the major details needed to complete the map below. Then answer the question that follows the map.   *Wording of details may vary.*

[1]Experts have several theories to explain why people yawn. [2]One explanation is that yawns help boost oxygen levels in the blood. [3]By forcing the body to breathe deeply, yawns increase airflow to the lungs and rush oxygen to the bloodstream. [4]A second theory is that yawns help the body change its level of alertness. [5]It is for this reason yawns happen whether a person is waking up or getting sleepy. [6]Yet another explanation is that yawns, like stretches, give the body exercise. [7]When a person yawns, blood pressure and heart rate gently increase and muscles flex. [8]No matter what the cause for yawning, one thing is clear. [9]Fifty-five percent of the people who read this paragraph will yawn in less than five minutes.

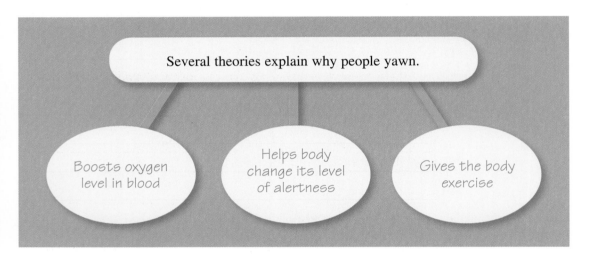

Several theories explain why people yawn.

Boosts oxygen level in blood

Helps body change its level of alertness

Gives the body exercise

10. What are **two** of the addition words used to set off the major details in the passage?

_____   _____
Any two of the following: One, second, another

List words: *several theories.*
Addition words (underlined) signal the major supporting details.

SUPPORTING DETAILS: Mastery Test 3

A. (1–6.) Complete the outline below by filling in the missing major and minor details. Some details have been added for you. *Wording of answers may vary.*

¹There are several guidelines you can follow to avoid being bitten by a dog. ²First of all, don't trust appearances. ³A dog with a wagging tail isn't always friendly. ⁴Even small dogs that look harmless can deliver a painful bite. ⁵Secondly, be cautious. ⁶Allow a dog to see and sniff you before you pet it. ⁷Be especially careful around a dog when it's eating, sleeping, or caring for puppies. ⁸Next, watch for warning signs. ⁹Dogs that stare at you with their heads lowered are probably unfriendly. ¹⁰Likewise, a dog that growls or shows its teeth should be avoided. ¹¹Fourth, learn defensive strategies to prevent a dog from biting you. ¹²For example, stand still with arms at your sides if you find yourself facing an angry dog. ¹³Also avoid eye contact with the dangerous animal so that it knows you are not challenging it.

Main idea: **There are several guidelines you can follow to avoid being bitten by a dog.**

1. Don't trust appearances.

   a. A dog wagging its tail isn't always friendly.

   b. Small harmless-looking dogs can deliver a painful bite.

2. Be cautious.

   a. Let a dog see and sniff you before petting it.

   b. Be especially careful around a dog that's eating, sleeping, or caring for puppies.

3. Watch for warning signs.

   a. Dogs that stare with lowered heads are probably not friendly.

   b. Dogs that growl or show their teeth should be avoided.

4. Learn defensive strategies.

   a. Stand still with arms at your sides if you face an angry dog.

   b. Avoid eye contact with a dangerous dog.

List words: *several guidelines.*
Addition words (underlined) signal the major supporting details.

(Continues on next page)

183

B. (7–10.) Fill in the major details needed to complete the map below. Then answer the question that follows the map.

¹Practically everyone needs to complain at times about a product or service that has been unsatisfactory. ²It is helpful, then, to keep in mind some steps for effective written complaints. ³<u>First</u>, always address your complaint to a person in charge, such as a manager or the head of the company. ⁴You can get the person's name by calling the company's switchboard. ⁵<u>Next</u>, write your complaint in a clear and matter-of-fact way. ⁶You will be taken less seriously if you sound emotional or threatening. ⁷<u>Finally</u>, explain exactly what action you want taken. ⁸If, for example, you want a company to replace a defective microwave, say, "Please give me the go-ahead to return this microwave. ⁹Then arrange for a new one to be sent to me." ¹⁰Don't leave it up to the company to figure out what you would consider a satisfactory response.

Wording of details may vary.

Here are steps for effective written complaints.

Address complaint to person in charge.

Write complaint in a clear, matter-of-fact way.

Explain exactly what action you want taken.

10. What are the **three** addition words used to set off the major details in the passage?

    First   Next   Finally

List words: *steps for effective written complaints.*
Addition words (underlined) announce the major supporting details.

SUPPORTING DETAILS: Mastery Test 4

A. (1–6.) Complete the outline below by filling in the missing major and minor details. Some details have been added for you. *Wording of answers may vary.*

¹High schools should require all students to wear uniforms. ²One reason for doing so is that uniforms would save money for parents and children. ³Families could simply buy two or three inexpensive uniforms. ⁴They would not have to constantly put out money for designer jeans, fancy sneakers, and other high-priced clothing. ⁵A second advantage of uniforms is that students would not have to spend time worrying about clothes. ⁶They could get up every day knowing what they were wearing to school. ⁷Their attention, then, could be focused on schoolwork and learning and not on making a fashion statement. ⁸Last, uniforms would help all students get along better. ⁹Well-off students would not be able to act superior by wearing expensive clothes, and students from modest backgrounds would not have to feel inferior because of lower-cost wardrobes.

Main idea: High schools should require all students to wear uniforms.

1. Uniforms would save money for parents and children.

   a. Families could just buy two or three inexpensive uniforms.

   b. They wouldn't have to buy designer jeans, fancy sneakers, and other high-priced clothing.

2. Students would not have to spend time worrying about clothes.

   a. Students would know what they were going to wear every day.

   b. They could concentrate on schoolwork and learning, not on making a fashion statement.

3. Uniforms would help all students get along better.

   a. Well-off students would not be able to act superior.

   b. Students from modest backgrounds would not have to feel inferior because of lower-cost clothes.

Implied list words: *several reasons.*
A "should" statement usually suggests that details will explain "why."
Addition words (underlined) announce the major supporting details.

(Continues on next page)

B. (7–10.) Fill in the major details and the one minor detail needed to complete the map below. *Wording of answers may vary.*

> [1]A number of factors influence the pace at which people age. [2]First of all, genes—traits inherited from parents—play a major role in how people age. [3]Genes play a role in how much hair loss we have or how much weight we gain. [4]Genes also help explain why some people at 75 years old look 60, while others who are 60 appear to be 75. [5]A <u>second</u> factor that influences aging is a person's lifestyle. [6]Older-looking skin and wrinkles can be caused by too much sun exposure in youth—part of an outdoor, active lifestyle. [7]On the other hand, a person who does not exercise is more likely to look and feel older than one who is physically active. [8]Social forces are a <u>third</u> factor that influence aging. [9]Older people who feel isolated or lonely often age faster than those who don't report having those feelings. [10]But older people who are involved with others—their families, religious groups, or peer groups—age more slowly and live longer than those who don't.

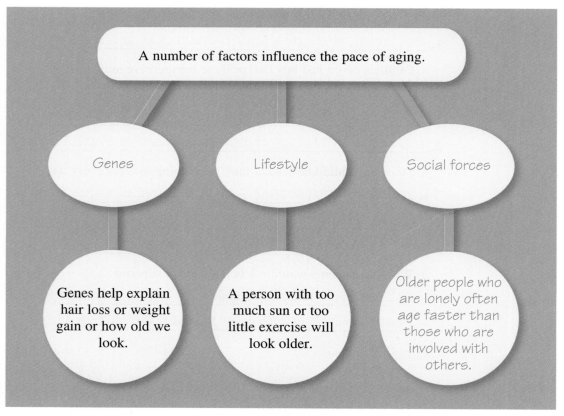

List words: *a number of factors*.
Addition words (underlined) signal the three major supporting details.

SUPPORTING DETAILS: Mastery Test 5

A. (1–6.) Complete the outline below by filling in the missing major and minor details. Some details have been added for you.   *Wording of answers may vary.*

¹Certain physical conditions affect how well people perform their work. ²Temperature is one factor that has been shown to greatly influence workers. ³If a workspace is too warm, people become cranky and uncomfortable. ⁴On the other hand, workers who are cold are more likely to pursue nonwork activities, such as chatting or making warm drinks. ⁵Color is another factor that affects worker performance. ⁶A workspace that has lots of red tends to stimulate and excite workers. ⁷Blue, on the other hand, usually soothes workers, making them feel relaxed and comfortable. ⁸Finally, lighting has a powerful effect on employees. ⁹Bright, direct light encourages good listening, close concentration, and comfortable reading. ¹⁰Low light, however, promotes relaxation and personal conversation—rather than getting work done.

Main idea: Physical conditions affect work performance.

1. Temperature
   a. If a workspace is too warm, workers become cranky and uncomfortable.
   b. Cold workers are more likely to pursue nonwork activities.

2. Color
   a. Reds tend to stimulate and excite workers.
   b. Blue soothes workers.

3. Lighting
   a. Bright, direct light encourages good listening, close concentration, and comfortable reading.
   b. Low light promotes relaxation and personal conversation.

List words: *Certain physical conditions.*
Addition words (underlined) signal the major supporting details.

(Continues on next page)

B. (7–10.) Fill in the major details and one minor detail needed to complete the map below.   *Wording of answers may vary.*

¹Nearly every family has members who don't get along. ²But for some, these disagreements grow into painful feuds that can last for years. ³Fortunately, there are certain strategies that can help heal even the most difficult family feuds. ⁴The <u>first</u> step is to get people to share the blame for their disagreement. ⁵Family rifts are rarely caused by a single person. ⁶For healing to take place, then, everyone involved must accept responsibility for his or her part in the conflict. ⁷The <u>second</u> step is to increase the communication between family members. ⁸Writing a note, making a phone call, or attending a family event allows people to express their feelings to each other. ⁹Such actions show care and help rebuild damaged relationships. ¹⁰A <u>third</u> step is to set realistic goals. ¹¹A family feud that has lasted for thirty years will not be solved by a single talk. ¹²However, that talk may lead to a truce and help build a foundation for healing.

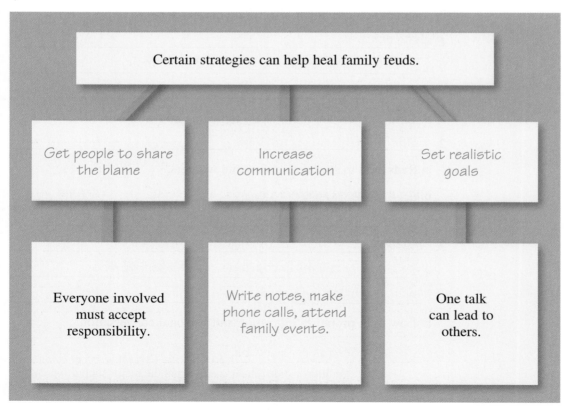

The first two sentences are introductory details.
List words: *certain strategies*.
Addition words (underlined) introduce the major supporting details.

SUPPORTING DETAILS: Mastery Test 6

A. (1–6.) Complete the outline below by filling in the missing major and minor details. Some details have been added for you. *Wording of answers may vary.*

¹People sometimes express their thoughts not by speaking, but by using their bodies in various ways. ²<u>One</u> way people use the body to communicate is through the eyes. ³By glaring, people can send the message that they are angry without saying a word. ⁴Likewise, people can show interest in what another person is saying by just looking at the person, using direct eye contact to send the message. ⁵<u>Another</u> way that people use their bodies to communicate is through facial expressions. ⁶Studies show that people all over the world use the same facial expressions to show emotions. ⁷Just by looking at a face, it is possible to tell if a person is sad, happy, afraid, or surprised. ⁸Body posture is a <u>third</u> way that people send messages to each other without speaking. ⁹For example, sitting upright or leaning forward shows great interest and attention. ¹⁰On the other hand, if a person has arms crossed at the chest, it is a sign that he or she dislikes or disagrees with the speaker.

Main idea: People can communicate by using their bodies.

1. Through the eyes
   a. By glaring, people can show they are angry without saying a word.
   b. People can show interest in a speaker through direct eye contact.
2. Through facial expressions
   a. All over the world, people use the same facial expressions to show emotions.
   b. By looking at a face, one can tell if a person is sad, happy, afraid, or surprised.
3. Through body posture
   a. A person who is sitting upright or leaning forward shows great interest and attention.
   b. A person with arms crossed dislikes or disagrees with the speaker.

List words: *various ways.*
Addition words (underlined) signal the major supporting details.

(Continues on next page)

B. (7–10.) Fill in the major details and one minor detail needed to complete the map below.   *Wording of answers may vary.*

¹Mysteries are questions in life without satisfying answers. ²One mystery is why there is so much hatred on the planet. ³We are all mortal and here on Earth for only a little while. ⁴Yet instead of being kind to one another, we continue to start wars—the main effect of which is to kill each other. ⁵A <u>second</u> mystery is how good and evil can exist together in the same person. ⁶For example, we have all heard of a person who is liked and even admired in the community. ⁷We then learn that the person has been abusing his wife or children. ⁸A <u>third</u> mystery is why some wealthy Christians do little to help the poor. ⁹They go to church on Sunday but act as if the lives of the poor are none of their concern. ¹⁰Yet the Bible says that it's easier for a rich man to pass through the eye of a needle than to enter the kingdom of Heaven.

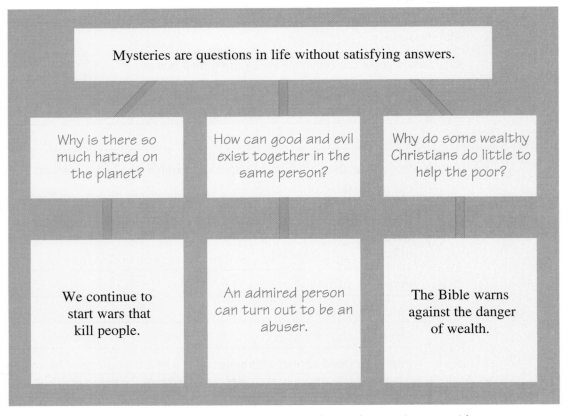

List words: *questions . . . without . . . answers.*
Addition words (underlined) signal the major details.

5 Locations of Main Ideas

This Chapter in a Nutshell

- The main idea most often appears in the first sentence of a paragraph.

- The main idea may include such list words as *various kinds* and *a number of.* Supporting details may be introduced with such addition words as *first of all, next,* and *finally.*

- Sometimes the first sentence or two of a paragraph act only as an introduction to the main idea. The main idea then appears in the second or third sentence. Often a word like *but* or *however* signals such a main idea.

- The main idea may also appear in the middle or at the end of a paragraph.

Like the freight train pictured above, a paragraph has a beginning, a middle, and an end. In the previous chapters, most of the main ideas were at the beginning: the first sentence of each paragraph. But the main idea "engine" may appear in the middle or at the end of the paragraph as well.

This chapter describes common locations of the main idea and gives you practice in finding the main idea in a series of paragraphs.

As you work through this chapter, remember what you have already learned about finding main ideas:

1   Look for a **general idea** and ask yourself, "Is this idea supported by all or most of the other material in the paragraph?"

2   See if you can decide on the **topic**—the general subject of the paragraph— and then ask, "What point is the paragraph making about the subject?"

3   Look for **list words** such as *several reasons* or *various factors* or *three steps*; such words often appear in the main idea sentence. (See page 128.) Also, look for **addition words** such as *first, another, also*, and *finally*; such words may introduce details that support the main idea. (See page 129.)

Main Idea at the Beginning

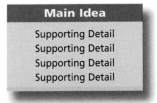

Authors often begin a paragraph with the main idea. The rest of the paragraph then supports the main idea with details.

 Check Your Understanding

See if you can underline the main idea in the following paragraph.

> [1]Pain can cause aggression. [2]When two rats in the same cage were given foot shocks, they attacked each other immediately. [3]In addition, stronger shocks resulted in more violent aggression. [4]Pairs of various other animals reacted similarly. [5]A stubbed toe or a headache has been known to cause similar responses in humans. [6]A parent with a bad headache, for instance, is more likely to shout at or even slap children.

Explanation

The author's main idea is presented in the *first* sentence. The following sentences support the main idea with examples of pain that causes aggression.

But a main idea does not necessarily appear in the very first sentence of a passage. See if you can underline the main idea in this paragraph:

> [1]College is supposed to be a place of discovery. [2]But for some students, college can be a place of fear. [3]In the classroom, for example, many students are afraid of appearing stupid in front of their classmates or professors. [4]Such students often try to hide in class by sitting in the back of the room and avoiding eye contact with instructors. [5]Fear prevents them from raising their hands, answering questions, or being part of class discussions. [6]Fear also leads to problems outside the classroom. [7]Worried their peers won't like them, many college students smoke or drink heavily to blend in with the crowd. [8]They also try drugs, join in hurtful pranks, or practice unsafe sex—all out of fear. [9]And sadly, after getting in trouble, students are often too scared to seek the help they need to solve their problems.

Explanation

In the above paragraph, the main idea is stated in the *second* sentence. The first sentence introduces the topic (college), but it is the idea in the second sentence—college can be a place of fear—that is supported in the rest of the paragraph. So keep in mind that the first sentence may simply introduce or lead into the main idea of a paragraph.

> *Note:* In paragraphs beginning with one or more introductory sentences, very often a word like *but, however,* or *yet* then signals the main idea. In the above paragraph, the word *but* helps mark the main idea.

Main Idea in the Middle

The main idea at times appears in the middle of a paragraph.

Check Your Understanding

Here is an example of a paragraph in which the main idea is somewhere in the middle. Try to find and underline it. Then read the explanation that follows.

> [1]Exercise thickens the bones and can slow the loss of calcium that normally occurs with age. [2]Physical activity increases flexibility in the joints and improves digestion and elimination. [3]It builds lean body mass, so the body burns more calories and body fat decreases. [4]<u>If exercise could be packed into a pill, it would be the single most widely used medicine in the world.</u> [5]Exercise also lowers the risk of developing diabetes. [6]It helps to prevent strokes and heart attacks, and it lowers the risk of certain cancers. [7]It can actually extend your lifespan and sharpen your memory and mind.

Explanation

If you thought the fourth sentence contains the main idea, you were correct. The first three sentences give some of the benefits of exercise. Then the writer presents the main idea, which is that if exercise were a pill, everyone would take it. The rest of the paragraph goes on to support this idea with even more benefits of exercise.

Main Idea at the End

Sometimes all the sentences in a paragraph will lead up to the main idea, which is stated at the end.

Check Your Understanding

See if you can underline the main idea in the following paragraph.

> [1]A woman's son had just graduated from college. [2]So when a florist's truck pulled in front of her house, she was not surprised, thinking that a relative or friend was congratulating her son. [3]However, she was surprised when she saw that the dozen red

roses were addressed to her. ⁴The card read, "Thanks, Mom, for making this day possible. ⁵I could not have done it without your love and support." ⁶In an unusual switch, the graduate had given his mother a graduation gift.

Explanation

Here the supporting details appear first, and the point of the supporting details—that a son had surprised his mother with a gift—appears at the end.

> *Note:* At times, the main idea will appear at the beginning of a paragraph and also, in different words, at the end. Writers may repeat the main idea if they want to emphasize it.

 PRACTICE 1

The main idea may appear at any place within each of the four paragraphs that follow. Write the number of each main idea sentence in the space provided.

Hints: Remember the three ways to find main ideas:

1 Look for a general idea and ask yourself, "Is this idea supported by all or most of the other material in the paragraph?"

2 See if you can decide on the topic—the general subject of the paragraph—and then ask, "What point is the paragraph making about the subject?"

3 Look for list words such as *several reasons* or *various factors* or *three steps*; such words often appear in the main idea sentence. Also, look for addition words such as *first, another, also*, and *finally*; such words may introduce details that support the main idea.

____1____   1. ¹One of the most important secrets of good communication is knowing how to ask return questions. ²For example, if someone asks, "Did you have a good weekend?" you should offer a reply and then ask a question in return. ³You might say something like "What did you do this weekend?" or "Is today going to be busy for you?" or "Do you think the weather is going to get better soon?" ⁴What you ask is not as important as the fact that you respond with a question of your own. ⁵Many adults are not good at conversation because they have not mastered this skill. ⁶All of us enjoy talking more with people who show interest in us.

Sentences 2–6 give examples of return questions and explain their importance. These support the main idea in sentence 1—that knowing how to ask return questions is important to good communication.

_____2_____ 2. ¹Americans tend to say directly what is on their minds. ²However, people in Asian cultures are more likely to speak indirectly. ³In Asia, if you visit a friend on a hot day and feel thirsty, you would not ask point-blank, "May I have a glass of water?" ⁴Instead, you would state your request indirectly by saying, "Isn't it hot today?" ⁵In Japan, at the end of a long business meeting, if you ask, "So will you do business with us?" the Japanese will always say "yes" even if they mean "no." ⁶They will not say "no" directly because they do not want to embarrass you.

Sentence 1 is an introductory detail. Sentence 2 states the main idea—that people in Asian cultures speak indirectly. Sentences 3–6 provide examples of and details about indirect speaking.

_____9_____ 3. ¹The set of cooking knives is offered at an unbeatable price. ²You hurry to the department store. ³There, the sympathetic clerk tells you he is so sorry, but he's all sold out. ⁴But, he adds, the quality of the knives wasn't that good, anyway. ⁵If you want a real value, he suggests that you purchase another set. ⁶True, it costs more, but the knives are certainly worth the extra money. ⁷So you buy the more expensive knife set. ⁸Later, you notice that the super-low-priced set of knives you had originally wanted is still being advertised. ⁹The store ran an illegal operation called a "bait-and-switch": you were "baited" with an inexpensive item, then "switched" to something more expensive.

Sentence 9 states the main idea—that the store runs an illegal bait-and-switch operation. Sentences 1–8 explain the operation.

_____5_____ 4. ¹Everyone has heard a few "Your mama is ugly" jokes. ²"Your mama is so ugly that when she entered an ugly contest, the judge said, 'Sorry, no professionals.'" ³"Your mama is so ugly that when she went to a haunted house, she came out with a paycheck." ⁴"In the dictionary, your mother's picture is next to the word 'ugly.'" ⁵There are several reasons why "your mama" jokes are popular. ⁶First of all, humor usually contains something surprising or even shocking. ⁷We aren't expected to make fun of someone's mom, so a "your mama" joke has the element of surprise. ⁸Secondly, humor is a way we deal with taboos, or things that are forbidden. ⁹Insulting anybody is bad enough, but insulting somebody's mother is really out of line. ¹⁰Finally, "your mama" jokes are generally told between close friends as a way to express friendship and affection. ¹¹Mothers aren't really being insulted. ¹²Instead of getting angry, the friend on the receiving end of the joke usually laughs.

Sentences 1–4 are introductory details. The list words *several reasons* signal the main idea in sentence 5. Addition words—*First of all, Secondly, Finally*—signal the three specific reasons.

PRACTICE 2

The main idea may appear at any place within each of the four paragraphs that follow. Write the number of each main idea sentence in the space provided.

_____8_____   1. ¹One way poor spellers can improve their spelling is to keep a list of words they are constantly looking up in the dictionary. ²They can review and test themselves on a few of these words each day. ³Breaking up a word into its parts also makes spelling a less forbidding task. ⁴For example, the word *formidable* can be broken into three parts: *for*, *mid*, and *able*. ⁵Third, learning little verbal tricks is helpful. ⁶One such trick is "There's *a rat* in *separate*." ⁷Another is "*Iron* is found in the *environment*." ⁸Using these methods, poor spellers can become more reliable spellers.

The list words *these methods* signal the main idea in sentence 8. Addition words— *One, also, Third, Another*—signal the four specific methods.

_____1_____   2. ¹When a company "downsizes"—that is, reduces its workforce—there are both positive and negative results. ²On the one hand, as labor costs are reduced, the company usually becomes more profitable. ³It makes more money for its shareholders, and the price of its stock is likely to rise. ⁴On the other hand, the remaining employees at a company must usually work harder and longer. ⁵Both managers and workers may have to deal with more stress and burnout. ⁶And morale often falls because employees feel that the company has no loyalty to them and cares only about the bottom line.

The list words *positive and negative results* signal the main idea in sentence 1. Sentences 2–3 detail the positive results referred to in sentence 1. Sentences 4–6 detail negative results.

_____2_____   3. ¹Today, we take for granted many of the comforts of our everyday lives. ²However, people living before 1900 had relatively few modern conveniences. ³Running water, bathtubs, and indoor toilets were luxuries of the rich. ⁴Most people washed with basins in their rooms and used outdoor privies. ⁵A metal bathtub might be hauled out once a week, but the water had to be carried from a well. ⁶The kitchen stove, which used coal or wood, did double duty for cooking and heating. ⁷Refrigerators were not yet made, but some people had iceboxes, which required regular supplies of ice. ⁸A few homes were lit by electricity, but most still used kerosene or gas.

Sentence 1 is an introductory detail. The word *However* in sentence 2 introduces the main idea, which is then supported by all of the details that follow.

_____3_____   4. ¹Some people believe the superstition that cats have nine lives because they can fall from high places with few, if any, injuries. ²They may have minor injuries, such as a bloody nose or cracked teeth or ribs, but they recover. ³Cats are able to survive long falls because they possess several advantages. ⁴For one thing, their small size and low body weight soften the impact as they make contact with the ground. ⁵Also, their highly developed inner ears give them a keen sense of balance, so they can quickly adjust themselves in the air to ensure a landing on all fours. ⁶As a result, the impact is absorbed by all their legs. ⁷Additionally, cats bend their legs when they land, which cushions and spreads the impact, not only through bones that might break otherwise, but through the joints and muscles as well.

Sentences 1 and 2 are introductory details. The list words *several advantages.* signal the main idea in sentence 3. Addition words— *For one thing, Also, Additionally*—signal the three advantages.

PRACTICE 3

The main idea may appear at any place within each of the four paragraphs that follow. Write the number of each main idea sentence in the space provided.

___2___ 1. [1]Vocabulary is a major part of almost every standardized test, including college placement exams. [2]But there are reasons for building a strong vocabulary other than to prepare for standardized tests. [3]Common sense tells us that the more words we know, the better we will be able to understand what we read. [4]If our vocabulary is not large enough, our reading comprehension will suffer. [5]Another reason for building vocabulary is that words are the tools not just of better reading, but also of better writing, speaking, and thinking. [6]In addition, studies have shown that a good vocabulary, more than any other factor, is common to people enjoying successful careers.

Sentence 1 is an introductory detail. The word *But* in sentence 2 introduces the main idea, which uses a list signal: *reasons*. Addition words: *Another, In addition*.

___1___ 2. [1]People with higher status are generally given more space and privacy. [2]For instance, we knock before entering our boss's office, but we walk into the office work area without hesitating. [3]In many schools, teachers have offices, dining rooms, and even toilets that are private, but students do not have such special places. [4]In the world of show business, stars receive their own dressing rooms or private trailers. [5]Among the military, greater space and privacy usually come with rank: privates sleep forty to a barrack, sergeants have their own rooms, and generals have government-provided houses.

Sentence 1 states the main idea—that people with higher status are given more space and privacy. Sentences 2–5 support this idea with specific examples.

___7___ 3. [1]Have you ever seen a fast-food ad that shows the factories where French fries are made? [2]Or a fast-food ad that shows the slaughterhouse where cattle are turned into ground beef? [3]Or an ad that tells you what's really in your fast-food milkshake and why some strange-sounding chemicals make it taste so good? [4]Or an ad that shows overweight, unhealthy kids stuffing their faces with greasy fries at a fast-food restaurant? [5]You probably haven't. [6]But you've probably seen a lot of fast-food commercials that show thin, happy children having a lot of fun. [7]The fact is that companies that sell fast food don't want you to know where it comes from or how it's made or what eating too much of it might do to you.

Sentences 1–6 present evidence for the main idea— that fast-food restaurants don't want you to know the facts about their food—stated in sentence 7.

___2___ 4. [1]Many English people sailed to Jamestown, Virginia, in 1607 in order to get away from problems in England. [2]But a number of problems awaited the English settlers in the New World. [3]Of the first 10,000 who landed in Virginia, only 2,000 survived. [4]They died of disease, Indian attack, and hunger. [5]In a land of plenty, not all of them learned quickly enough how to hunt, or fish, or raise crops, or gather food. [6]Nor were they all ready to cope with the heat, which in August could reach 100 degrees. [7]Some of the English gentlemen felt they needed to wear sixty-pound suits of metal armor to be safe from

Sentence 1 is an introductory detail. The list words *a number of problems* signal the main idea in sentence 2. Sentences 3–10 support this idea with specific details.

Indian arrows. [8]Under the armor they wore wool clothing because that is what they would have done in England. [9]It was impossible to hunt animals in such hot, heavy, noisy outfits. [10]And the firearms that the settlers carried were not as accurate as rifles (which had not been invented yet) or even bows and arrows (which few settlers knew how to use).

CHAPTER REVIEW

In this chapter, you learned the following:

- The first place to check for the main idea is the first sentence. But the main idea can appear anywhere within a paragraph.

- At times the first sentence or two serve as an introduction to the main idea, which then appears in the second or third sentence. In such cases, a word like *but* or *however* often signals the main idea.

The next two chapters—Chapter 6 and Chapter 7—explain common connections between ideas and the ways authors organize supporting details.

On the Web: If you are using this book in class, you can visit our website for additional practice in locating main ideas. Go to **www.townsendpress.com** and click on "Online Learning Center."

REVIEW TEST 1

To review what you've learned in this chapter, complete each of the following sentences.

1. The main idea appears most often in the (*first, second, final*)
   _____ first _____ sentence of a paragraph.   See page 191.

2. Sometimes the first sentence or so of a paragraph may simply introduce
   or lead into the _____ main idea _____, which may appear in the second
   or third sentence.   See page 191.

3. The main idea may occur at the beginning, in the middle, or at the
   _____ end _____ of a paragraph.   See page 191.

4. _____List_____ words such as *several reasons* or *various factors* or *three steps* often appear as part of the main idea sentence.

See page 192.

5. Addition words such as *first, another, also,* and *finally* often introduce _____details_____ that support the main idea.   See page 192.

REVIEW TEST 2

The main idea may appear at any place within each of the four paragraphs that follow. Write the number of each main idea sentence in the space provided.

___1___ 1. ¹Soup has become more popular than ever, for good reasons. ²For one thing, it can help you lose and maintain weight. ³Since you can't eat soup on the run, you're forced to eat slowly. ⁴And slow eating usually means a lower calorie intake. ⁵Soup can also help you feel better when you've got a cold or bronchitis. ⁶Hot chicken soup, especially if it's spiced with pepper or garlic, helps to break up the congestion in your throat and chest. ⁷As a result, you can breathe more easily. ⁸In addition to being healthful, soup is available everywhere, it's inexpensive, and it's easy to prepare.

The list words good reasons *signal the main idea in sentence 1. Note the addition words—* For one thing, also, In addition*—that signal the three specific reasons.*

___5___ 2. ¹In the past, workers didn't worry about losing a good job if they went on strike. ²They knew the factory would shut down during the stoppage and that a job would be waiting when the strike was over. ³In the present, though, many U.S. companies keep up production during strikes by hiring replacement workers or persuading workers to cross the picket line. ⁴Many strikers fear that if they strike too long, the company will no longer need or want them. ⁵Clearly, today's striking workers face a much more difficult choice than union strikers faced in times past.

Sentences 1–4 provide details about the difficulties faced by today's striking workers—the main idea expressed in sentence 5.

___2___ 3. ¹Speaking before a group is more frightening to many people than almost anything else. ²But there are ways to overcome the fear of speaking and become an effective speaker. ³The first step to take is to think positively. ⁴Replace thoughts of failure with statements such as, "I am interested in my topic, and I will make my listeners interested, too." ⁵It also helps to plan a speech with only two or three major points and to develop each of those points with examples. ⁶Moreover, visualize yourself standing in front of your audience, feeling comfortable and relaxed. ⁷Finally, rehearse your speech a number of times, speaking naturally, almost the way you would in everyday conversation, rather than speaking in a formal way.

Sentence 1 is an introductory detail. The list words ways to overcome fear *signal the main idea in sentence 2. Sentences 3–7 support this idea by detailing specific ways to overcome fear.*

___1___ 4. ¹Roads of the nineteenth century were much different from roads of today. ²The average street in the 1800s was a dirt path between six and eight feet wide. ³In the fall and spring, these roads were often muddy and marked by holes and puddles caused by stagecoaches. [4]In the summer, dry dirt roads would create huge clouds of dust whenever anyone traveled on them. [5]Slightly better roads during this period were made with wood. [6]Workers would get round logs and lay them on the ground next to each other. [7]Roads made from logs lacked the dust and holes of dirt roads, but had other problems. [8]Often the logs rolled under the weight of coaches, causing horses to slip. [9]Sometimes, ankles would get caught in the gaps between the logs, resulting in broken bones. [10]Even the best roads of the time—those made with wooden planks—were not without trouble. [11]Plank roads were smoother, but their wooden surfaces would quickly rot away. [12]Only later in the century did workers use crushed stones, clay, and gravel to build roads.

Sentence 1 states the main idea— that nineteenth-century roads were different from today's roads. Sentences 2–12 provide specific details to explain the differences.

REVIEW TEST 3

The main idea may appear at any place within each of the four paragraphs that follow. Write the number of each main idea sentence in the space provided.

____2____ 1. [1]Feeling chilly? [2]To fight the cold, you should understand how to use clothing to stay warm. [3]Because heat rises, one of the best ways to keep your whole body warm is to wear a hat or cap. [4]Dressing in layers is another useful tip, since air trapped between layers stays warm. [5]This principle also applies when choosing gloves. [6]Loose-fitting gloves trap warm air near your skin. [7]On the other hand, tight gloves are not as warm because they lack this layer of air.

Sentence 1 (a question) is an attention-getter. Sentences 3–7 explain how clothing can help fight the cold.

____1____ 2. [1]A lack of social connections is dangerous to people's health. [2]Individuals without strong bonds of friendship, family, or community get colds at four times the rate of people who have such bonds. [3]According to research, a lack of relationships poses as great a health risk as smoking, obesity, high blood pressure, or lack of exercise. [4]Divorced people are five times more likely to get cancer than married people of the same age. [5]Loners are two to three times more likely to die prematurely than people with social ties.

Sentence 1 states the main idea—that a lack of social connections is dangerous to people's health. Sentences 2–5 provide specific details which support this idea.

____1____ 3. [1]Television ads urge you to buy products by scaring you, appealing to your desire for the comforts of home, or promising popularity. [2]You can probably think of some mildly fearful ads: commercials for deodorants, soaps, mouthwash, denture adhesive, or diarrhea usually begin with someone suffering rejection or facing a problem. [3]Other ads are more pleasant, with products associated with a warm, loving, old-fashioned atmosphere. [4]For example, you may be told about cookies, breads, or spaghetti sauce such as Grandmother used to make. [5]And some ads appeal to your desire for popularity. [6]They imply, for instance, that if you wear the right brand of jeans or use the right perfume or drink the right kind of beer, you will have more friends.

Sentence 1 states the main idea—that TV ads urge people to buy products in three ways. Sentences 2–6 present details about the three ways.

____9____   4. ¹Near the end of the Civil War, the Confederate and Union forces met at
Gettysburg, Pennsylvania. ²The Confederate general, Robert E. Lee, had his
forces bombard the Union soldiers, who were camped on high ground at
a site called Cemetery Hill. ³After two hours of nonstop cannon fire, Lee felt
that most of the Union line had been destroyed. ⁴He did not realize that most
of the poorly aimed cannons had done little damage to the Union soldiers.
⁵Lee then ordered his soldiers out of the protective woods and across a wide
stretch of open field toward the Union forces. ⁶The sight was impressive:
fifteen thousand men in gray uniforms, the bright sun reflecting off their
silver bayonets and red flags. ⁷Elbow to elbow, as if in a parade, they marched
forward in an orderly line almost a mile wide and half a mile deep. ⁸Protected
by a low stone wall, the Union forces opened fire and mowed down row after
row of the advancing Rebel soldiers. ⁹General Lee's ill-advised battle plan
resulted in a shockingly bloody defeat for the Confederate Army.

*Sentences 1–8
present details that
support the main
idea mentioned in
sentence 9—that
General Lee's
battle plan resulted
in defeat.*

REVIEW TEST 4

Here is a chance to apply your understanding of main ideas to a full-length
selection. Read the following article, and then answer the questions that follow on
the central point and main ideas. For review purposes, there are also questions on
vocabulary in context and supporting details.

This selection tells what it might mean when your boss pats you on the back,
when men and women run their hands through their hair, and more. The selection
may convince you that no matter how quiet you are, your body has been speaking
loudly and clearly.

Words to Watch

Below are some words in the reading that do not have strong context support.
Each word is followed by the number of the paragraph in which it appears and its
meaning there. These words are indicated in the selection by a small circle (°).

> *gestures* (2): motions made that express thought or emphasize speech
> *context* (2): overall situation
> *seductive* (6): tempting, often in a sexual way
> *abrupt* (10): rudely sudden
> *staging* (11): performing
> *preening* (14): grooming
> *meek* (15): willing to yield to the power of another

BODY LANGUAGE

Beth Johnson

1   Imagine yourself in the following situation: You're a young woman interviewing for a new job. You have been talking for about half an hour with the interviewer, a pleasant man slightly older than yourself. You feel the interview has gone well, but you're not sure what he's thinking. Suddenly the mood in the room changes. Your interviewer sits back in his chair, crosses one ankle over his knee and begins tapping his pen against his shoe. Should you:

(a) Forget about the job?
(b) Congratulate yourself?
(c) Tell him you're not that kind of girl?

The answer is *b*—you're probably going to be hired, says Dr. Robert Rosenthal of Harvard University. Dr. Rosenthal, a clinical psychologist, is a pioneer in the study of how people send and receive nonverbal messages—in other words, "body language."

2   Researchers say that body language sends out messages far more powerful than we're generally aware of. At the same time, they warn that nonverbal communication—which involves gestures°, posture, tone of voice, and eye contact—is more complicated than the drugstore-type books on the subject suggest. Body language can be explained only within its context°, they say; you shouldn't expect to find a "dictionary" for reliable definitions of crossed arms, sideways glances, and tapping toes.

3   Still, those that study the field agree that a better awareness of nonverbal communication makes you a more sensitive observer of any situation. Such awareness can also help you understand how people perceive you.

4   Let's take an example: How would a student of body language explain the interview described above? What in the world does touching a shoe have to do with making a favorable hiring decision? Dr. Rosenthal admits he doesn't know for sure. But after watching many job interviews, he is certain that the foot-touching gesture means the interview subject has made a good impression. This is his theory: an interview is likely to make both persons involved feel uneasy. Both will probably sit stiffly in their chairs. But once the interviewer decides, "Yes, I'm going to hire this person," he relaxes. At that point, he's apt to shift into a more comfortable position, often bringing his foot within easy touching distance.

5   Status differences on the job offer other interesting examples, points out Allan Mazur, a professor of sociology at Syracuse University. When a respected executive talks with a lower-ranking employee, for example, the employee usually keeps his or her eyes glued to the boss's face. But when the employee is talking, the executive feels free to

glance around the room. Another example is the manager who shows his or her superiority by patting a worker on the back—something the employee would never do to the manager. In an office, the person with the most status even establishes how a conversation will take place: If the higher-status person stands, the lower-ranking person remains standing as well. If lower-status people violate any of these rules, they risk looking disrespectful.

6   Of course, the working world is not the only place where body language is used. Every would-be Romeo or Juliet knows that the language of courtship goes far beyond words. Much of our flirtatious behavior is instinctive, not consciously thought out. But if you can get them to admit it, many expert flirts are aware of their seductive° use of body language.

7   "I've got my tricks," admits Patti, 22, a college student who spends many evenings out dancing with a group of friends. Patti is not a beauty, but she always attracts men at the clubs she goes to.

8   "I don't know why some things work the way they do, but certain gestures make men feel more confident about coming up to me," she says. When asked to describe those gestures, she laughs nervously. "That's kind of embarrassing. . . . It's just little things like glancing sideways at a guy with a little smile. Then you look away as if you didn't do it. But a minute later you sort of let your eyes slide back to meet his while you're talking to someone else. After that, he'll usually get up and come over."

9   When you spend an hour observing Patti in action, you see other "tricks" she uses while talking to men she's attracted to. She lightly draws her finger across her lip as she listens to a man. She plays with her hair. She tilts her head and gazes upward into his eyes. She lazily shrugs her shoulders. It's no wonder Patti gains all the attention she can handle, according to Dr. David Givens, an anthropologist at the University of Washington. Her "vocabulary" of body language sends out a strong signal: "I'm friendly. I'm approachable."

10   Taken a step further, the message becomes "I'm sexually available." Patti admits that the men she enjoys flirting and dancing with often read that message in her behavior. So she has become equally expert at "freezing" a too-insistent man with a nonverbal vocabulary of rejection: a stiff posture, expressionless face, and abrupt° gestures. Patti is a pro with body language, and as she says, "You can say about anything you want without words."

11   Where does nonverbal communication come from? Researchers trace

[handwritten annotation: would be called a "tease"]

various kinds of body language back to our roots in the animal world. Courtship practices such as marking out one's territory, staging° battles before the object of one's affection, or grooming oneself in front of a would-be mate are all common animal behaviors that humans use as well.

12   An evening of observation at a singles bar demonstrates the links between animal and human body language. Si and Mark are a couple of factory workers in their early twenties out for an evening at Lights, their favorite hangout. As they settle at the bar, they automatically scatter their jackets, Si's car keys, and a cigarette lighter across the bar in front of them. They're marking out their territory—warning other men to stay away.

13   Before long they have spotted several women that they particularly like. As those women move into hearing range, Si and Mark's casual, low-volume conversation changes noticeably. Their voices rise and take on a challenging, though still good-humored, quality. They begin to argue: "You're crazy!" "You're outta your mind!" "I can't believe this guy." They are laughing, but their voices are loud and rough. They glance around, hoping to include the women in their conversation. But they are passed by, and Si and Mark's conversation quickly returns to a lower tone.

14   Later in the evening, however, Si has better luck with a second target. As she approaches, he and Mark go into their "arguing" routine. She pauses. Catching Si's eye, she leans against the wall and begins running her fingers through her already well-combed hair. Si slowly makes his way across the room to speak to her. The message of her preening° in response to his masculine display is one he quickly recognizes—as would any animal scientist.

15   Animal behavior, however, is not the only source of nonverbal communication. As Dr. Givens points out, another rich source of nonverbal vocabulary is our childhood. When we want to seem meek° and friendly—which in the case of women often translates into "romantically available"—we may borrow gestures from as far back as babyhood. An infant scared by a loud noise will respond with the "startle reflex": a combination of lifting the shoulders, lowering the head and pulling in the chin. An older child will use the same gestures when being scolded, making the child seem cute and meek. But when used by Patti upon meeting new dance partners, the same moves seem less childish than seductive and feminine.

16   Dr. Givens further demonstrates this point by putting together photographs of children looking adorable and adult female fashion models looking sexy: the poses are identical.

17   Everyone uses body language. Because nonverbal communication, based in our animal roots and childhoods, is universal, it is useful to become more aware of it. What we and others "say" when we're not saying anything can enrich and entertain us as we spend each day in the human "laboratory."

Reading Comprehension Questions

Vocabulary in Context

___B___ 1. In the excerpt below, the word *apt* (ăpt) means
   A. unlikely.   C. unable.
   B. likely.   D. not ready.

   > A person who relaxes is likely to shift into a comfortable position.

   "But once the interviewer decides, 'Yes, I'm going to hire this person,' he relaxes. At that point, he's apt to shift into a more comfortable position. . . ." (Paragraph 4)

___B___ 2. In the sentence below, the word *instinctive* (ĭn-stĭngk'tĭv) means
   A. planned.
   B. natural.
   C. strange.
   D. poor.

   > Antonym-like clue: *thought out.* (Instinctive behavior is the opposite of "thought-out" behavior.)

   "Much of our flirtatious behavior is instinctive, not consciously thought out." (Paragraph 6)

___D___ 3. In the excerpt below, the word *links* (lĭngks) means
   A. differences.
   B. questions.
   C. friendship.
   D. connections.

   > If humans have "roots in the animal world," what must exist between animal and human body language?

   "Researchers trace various kinds of body language back to our roots in the animal world. . . . An evening of observation at a singles bar demonstrates the links between animal and human body language." (Paragraphs 11–12)

Central Point

___D___ 4. Which of the following sentences from the reading best expresses the central point of the selection?
   A. "Dr. Rosenthal, a clinical psychologist, is a pioneer in the study of how people send and receive nonverbal messages—in other words, 'body language.'"
   B. "Every would-be Romeo or Juliet knows that the language of courtship goes far beyond words."
   C. "Researchers trace various kinds of body language back to our roots in the animal world."
   D. "Because nonverbal communication, based in our animal roots and childhoods, is universal, it is useful to become more aware of it."

   Answers A, B, and C are too narrow.

Main Ideas

___A___ 5. The main idea sentence of paragraph 5 is its
  A. first sentence.
  B. second sentence.
  C. third sentence.
  D. last sentence.

> The rest of paragraph 5 discusses the "other interesting examples" mentioned in sentence 1.

___A___ 6. The main idea of paragraph 9 is expressed in its
  A. first sentence.
  B. second sentence.
  C. third sentence.
  D. fourth sentence.

> The rest of the paragraph discusses the "other tricks" mentioned in sentence 1.

___D___ 7. A main idea sentence sometimes provides the main idea for more than one paragraph. The first sentence of paragraph 12 expresses the main idea for paragraphs
  A. 10–12.
  B. 11–13.
  C. 12–13.
  D. 12–14.

> Paragraphs 12–14 describe the "evening of observation" mentioned in the first sentence.

___B___ 8. The main idea of paragraph 15 is expressed in its
  A. first sentence.
  B. second sentence.
  C. next-to-last sentence.
  D. last sentence.

> The rest of the paragraph discusses how "childhood" is a "source of nonverbal vocabulary"—the idea mentioned in sentence 2.

Supporting Details

___A___ 9. When people are having a talk with their boss, they
  A. usually look continuously at the boss.
  B. may glance around while the boss is talking.
  C. may sit while the boss is standing.
  D. may show approval by patting the boss on the back.

> See paragraph 5.

___D___ 10. Animal courtship practices that influence human body language include
  A. marking of territory.
  B. staging battles in front of a desirable female.
  C. grooming in front of a desired mate.
  D. all of the above.

> See paragraph 11.

Discussion Questions

1. How aware of body language were you before you read this article? After reading it, might you behave any differently in situations where you are meeting people for the first time? Explain.

2. What is some of the "vocabulary" of classroom body language? Consider both students' and teachers' nonverbal communication.

3. Johnson gives several examples of ritual and body language in courtship. What others could you add?

4. Johnson writes, "Body language can be explained only within its context . . . you shouldn't expect to find a 'dictionary' for reliable definitions of . . . tapping toes." Give some examples in which certain body language has different meanings in different situations. For example, what are some different meanings that tapping toes might have?

Note: Writing assignments for this selection appear on page 591.

Check Your Performance   **LOCATIONS OF MAIN IDEAS**

Activity		Number Right	Points	Score
Review Test 1	(5 items)	_____	× 2 =	_____
Review Test 2	(4 items)	_____	× 7.5 =	_____
Review Test 3	(4 items)	_____	× 7.5 =	_____
Review Test 4	(10 items)	_____	× 3 =	_____
		TOTAL SCORE	=	_____%

Enter your total score into the **Reading Performance Chart: Review Tests** on the inside back cover.

LOCATIONS OF MAIN IDEAS: Mastery Test 1

The main idea may appear at any place within each of the five paragraphs that follow. Write the number of each main idea sentence in the space provided.

___5___ 1. ¹"Ladies and gentlemen of the jury," said the prosecuting attorney, "two reliable witnesses—both respectable citizens—have testified that they saw the defendant commit the robbery at the jewelry store. ²Three more witnesses have testified that they saw him fleeing the store just after the crime was committed. ³In addition, his fingerprints were found in several places in the store. ⁴What is more, he was caught just several blocks from the store, just minutes after the robbery, and arrested with the stolen jewelry still in his possession. ⁵All the evidence proves that the defendant is guilty beyond a reasonable doubt, and you should convict him."

Sentence 5 states the main idea—that all the evidence proves the defendant guilty. Sentences 1–4 list the evidence that supports this idea.

___2___ 2. ¹Someone once said, "Seeing yourself as you want to be is the key to personal growth." ²You can help yourself grow in self-knowledge through the following exercises. ³First of all, take the tombstone test. ⁴What would you like to have written on your tombstone? ⁵In other words, how would you like to be remembered? ⁶Your honest answer should reveal, in a few words, what you value most. ⁷Next, see if you can describe yourself, as you are today, in a brief sentence. ⁸You might want to ask friends or family members how they would describe you in a few words. ⁹Then decide how you would have to change to become the person you want to be remembered as. ¹⁰Finally, try the adjective test. ¹¹Choose three adjectives that you'd like to see connected with your name. ¹²Then list what you've done or can do to earn such a reputation.

Sentence 1 introduces the topic of personal growth. Sentence 2 states the main idea— certain exercises can help you grow as a person. Sentences 3–12 list and describe three such exercises.

___1___ 3. ¹In Europe, in the Middle Ages, children were regarded as miniature adults. ²At the age of seven, boys began training for a career. ³They often left home for good at this age to become an assistant to the butcher, jewelry-maker, blacksmith, shopkeeper, farmer, or whoever would employ them. ⁴Girls generally stayed home until they married, but after age seven they too were expected to do a full day's work around the house. ⁵They sewed, spun, cooked, cleaned, tended farm animals, helped raise younger children, and generally took on the duties of full-grown women.

Sentence 1 states the main idea—that children in the Middle Ages were viewed as adults. Sentences 2–5 support this idea with specific details.

(Continues on next page)

_____2_____   4.   ¹Most people think the mind functions like a simple file cabinet—with all memories being stored in the same way. ²Research, however, has proven that the human brain has three different types of memory. ³Sensory memory records anything that comes in through the senses. ⁴It can hold data from the eyes, ears, and so on, but just for a few seconds. ⁵Short-term memory, the next type, holds memories longer—up to about twenty seconds. ⁶It helps us in daily life, reminding us, for example, that we put sugar in our coffee or grabbed our books before heading to class. ⁷Long-term memory, the most powerful memory type, can store information indefinitely, perhaps for life.

Sentence 1 introduces the topic. Sentence 2 states the main idea—that there are "three different types of memory." Sentences 3–7 provide details to support this point.

_____1_____   5.   ¹Eating habits differ widely from one culture to another. ²Many Japanese relish toasted grasshoppers, and members of some Brazilian tribes enjoy eating ants. ³If you find such fare disgusting, keep in mind that many Europeans consider corn on the cob fit only for nonhuman animals, and many Asians and Africans reject cheese because they find it too smelly. ⁴It's socially acceptable to eat dog flesh in Korea and horseflesh in France. ⁵The thought of eating either dogs or horses offends most Westerners. ⁶Orthodox Jews and Muslims avoid eating pork, which they consider sinful and unclean. And orthodox Hindus—vegetarians who regard cows as sacred—find beef particularly offensive.

Sentence 1 states the main idea—that eating habits differ from one culture to another. Sentences 2–6 give examples of those differences.

LOCATIONS OF MAIN IDEAS: Mastery Test 2

The main idea may appear at any place within each of the five paragraphs that follow. Write the number of each main idea sentence in the space provided.

____1____ 1. [1]Storage facilities have become part of our culture. [2]You see them everywhere—under overpasses, in industrial parks, and along busy highways. [3]In the past, most people rented these climate-controlled, garage-like rooms only for brief periods. [4]Perhaps they were moving from one state to another and needed to store their belongings while they looked for a new house. [5]But today, people rent storage facilities year-round. [6]Self-storage units are stuffed with unused clothes, bicycles, Grandma's old furniture, duplicate toasters and food processors, boxes of books, unwanted Christmas gifts, televisions, pool tables, model trains, cars, motorcycles, boats, sets of dishes, oriental rugs, pots and pans, and virtually anything else you can think of. [7]Items that were once sold at yard sales, given to friends, or donated to charity now sit untouched for years at a time.

Sentence 1 states the main idea—that "storage facilities have become part of our culture." Sentences 2–7 support this idea with specific details.

____2____ 2. [1]They're moist, wiggly creatures, and many people don't like to touch them. [2]Nevertheless, earthworms are very useful. [3]People who like to fish, of course, know that worms make great bait. [4]They also help improve the condition of the soil. [5]As they dig under the ground, earthworms constantly take soil into their bodies. [6]Their bodies use part of the soil and pass out the rest in the form of fine powder. [7]That powder, called cast, makes the earth richer. [8]In addition, the tunnels that worms create make the earth better able to absorb water and air.

Sentence 1 introduces the topic. Sentence 2 states the main idea—that earthworms are useful. Sentences 3–8 support this idea with specific details.

____6____ 3. [1]A dermatologist brought together sixty-five young people who were prone to acne. [2]Every day for four weeks, he fed each of them either a super-chocolate bar, containing ten times the chocolate of an ordinary candy bar, or a look-alike candy bar that tasted like chocolate but contained none. [3]None of the subjects knew whether or not they were eating real chocolate. [4]Halfway through the experiment, the dermatologist switched bars on the subjects. [5]The subjects' acne was not affected by including chocolate in their diets. [6]The dermatologist's experiment suggests that chocolate is not to blame for complexion problems.

Sentences 1–5 present details about an experiment which shows chocolate does not cause complexion problems—the main idea expressed in sentence 6.

(Continues on next page)

___3___ 4. ¹Congratulations: your tire is as flat as the road, you're supposed to be at an important meeting in an hour, and there's no help to be found anywhere. ²What should you do? ³You can change your own tire by following several safe, effective steps. ⁴Park on level ground away from traffic, put the car in park, and put on the emergency brake. ⁵Next, block the wheels at the opposite end from the flattened tire to prevent the car from rolling. ⁶Take out the spare tire and the jack, and take off the hubcap. ⁷Jack the flat tire up at least two or three inches above the ground, remove the lug nuts, and put them inside the hubcap, where you won't lose them. ⁸Then pull off the flat tire and put on the spare tire. ⁹Replace the lug nuts, but don't tighten them all the way. ¹⁰Jack down the car most of the way, and then finish tightening the lug nuts. ¹¹Finally, lower the car all the way, clean yourself up, and continue on your way.

Sentences 1–2 introduce the topic. Sentence 3 states the main idea—that there are "several safe, effective steps" to changing a tire. Sentences 4–11 explain those steps.

___1___ 5. ¹Preventing, not treating, social problems is the goal of an increasing number of programs. ²By teaching teenagers to resist peer pressure, for example, one program helped them avoid serious problems with drinking and drugs. ³In another program, nurses taught poor, young, pregnant women all the basics of good child care. ⁴These young mothers then gave better care to their babies than mothers who did not receive such training. ⁵A third program paired at-risk teenagers with adults from the community. ⁶Each adult agreed to meet with the teenager on a regular basis through all four years of high school. ⁷The result was that none of the teenagers dropped out of high schools in which the average dropout rate was close to 50 percent. ⁸Instead, almost all of the teenagers went on to college.

Sentence 1 states the main idea—that preventing social problems is the goal of a "number of programs." Sentences 2–8 provide specific examples of those programs.

LOCATIONS OF MAIN IDEAS: Mastery Test 3

The main idea may appear at any place within each of the five paragraphs that follow. Write the number of each main idea sentence in the space provided.

___2___ 1.

Sentence 1 is an introductory detail. Sentence 2 states the main idea—that the Middle Ages was a difficult time to stay alive. Sentences 3–8 support this idea with specific details.

[1]According to Hollywood movies, the Middle Ages was a wonderful time of romantic castles and unbeatable knights. [2]In reality, ho,wever, the Middle Ages was a difficult time to stay alive. [3]Recent studies indicate that the average life span for English and Scottish kings between 1000 and 1600 A.D. was just 50 years. [4]Nobles, including knights and other important people, had even shorter lives. [5]In one study of a group of 23 noblemen, only one lived into his 70s. [6]The rest died in their 20s, 30s and 40s. [7]Common people had the shortest lives. [8]For them, middle age began after adolescence, and death usually occurred in the mid- to late 30s.

___10___ 2.

Sentences 1–9 describe ways in which "the polar bear is very skillful at moving around its . . . environment"—the main idea expressed in sentence 10.

[1]Polar bears are excellent swimmers. [2]They slip through the water at speeds up to six miles an hour, using their front legs to move them forward. [3]With their nostrils closed and their eyes open, they can also dive underwater, staying there for as long as two minutes. [4]When they emerge, they immediately shake the water off their fur before the water freezes. [5]Polar bears are equally able to move well over the icy landscape. [6]On very smooth, slippery slopes, a polar bear may move by sliding on its belly. [7]With its legs stretched outward, it will descend in a spray of powdery snow. [8]When walking over ice, the polar bear walks bow-legged with toes inward. [9]This posture enables the huge animal to move along without slipping. [10]Clearly, the polar bear is very skillful at moving around its watery and icy environment.

___2___ 3.

Sentence 1 is an introductory detail. Sentence 2 states the main idea—that a liar's body language gives clues that he or she is lying. Sentences 3–10 list those clues.

[1]We believe one man because he has an "honest face," but we do not trust another person who, we notice, has "shifty eyes." [2]In fact, a liar's body and voice do give clues that he or she is not telling the truth. [3]When people are lying, they tend to speak in a higher voice than usual. [4]They stumble over their words, saying "uh" and "er" a lot. [5]People smile less when they are lying. [6]When they do smile, the smile tends to look forced. [7]Many people, when they lie, don't use their hands much. [8]They keep them still or out of sight. [9]And yes, "shifty" eyes can indicate that a person is lying. [10]People telling a lie tend to look away from the person they are speaking to.

(Continues on next page)

_____1_____ 4. ¹Studies have shown that people believed to have a high status tend to have more influence on others' actions. ²Researchers demonstrated the effect of status by first having a poorly dressed man violate the "wait" signal at street corners in Austin, Texas. ³His action triggered little jaywalking from other pedestrians. ⁴Then the same man dressed like a bank president. ⁵After his change in wardrobe, his going against the "wait" prompted many more pedestrians to jaywalk with him. ⁶A separate experiment in Sydney, Australia, had similar results. ⁷Pedestrians in Sydney were more cooperative when approached by a well-dressed survey taker than they were when approached by one who was poorly dressed.

Sentence 1 states the main idea— that high-status people have greater influence on others' behavior. Sentences 2–7 support this idea with examples from two experiments.

_____1_____ 5. ¹Sundays aren't what they used to be—a day for reading and rest. ²In the past, most stores and businesses were closed on Sunday. ³Liquor was unavailable by law. ⁴Worship and family time helped recharge people's energy for the week ahead. ⁵Today, religious services and family meals may still be on the agenda. ⁶Nevertheless, people use Sundays to catch up on errands, watch sports on TV, or work around the house or at their job. ⁷At present, more than thirty-one states permit sales of alcohol on Sunday. ⁸Stores stay open because Sunday shopping offers additional profit. ⁹There's even a bank with an advertising campaign based on doing business on Sundays. ¹⁰And circulation of the Sunday newspaper has dropped dramatically, with people saying they no longer have time to read.

Sentence 1 states the main idea— that Sundays are different today from in the past. The rest of the paragraph provides details supporting this idea.

LOCATIONS OF MAIN IDEAS: Mastery Test 4

The main idea may appear at any place within each of the five paragraphs that follow. Write the number of each main idea sentence in the space provided.

___2___ 1. [1]Have you ever heard a kid in public pleading with a parent, saying over and over something like "Please? Please? Please?" or "Mom, Mom, Mom"? [2]Kids have a number of successful ways to nag their parents. [3]The riskiest type is the acting-out nag, in which kids throw an all-out tantrum in a public place— holding their breath, crying, and refusing to leave a store until they get what they want. [4]Sugar-coated nags promise love in return for a purchase and may rely on sweet, adorable comments like "You're the best dad in the world." [5]Pity nags claim that a kid will be heartbroken or humiliated or teased by friends if a parent refuses to buy something. [6]Threatening nags are the nastiest, with kids vowing to hate their parents forever or to run away from home if what they want isn't bought at once. [7]Kids may even use a number of nags at the same time.

Sentence 1 introduces the topic. The list words a number of . . . ways *in sentence 2 signal the main idea. Sentences 3–7 list and describe four types of nags.*

___5___ 2. [1]The dandelion, widely known as an annoying weed, is also a nutritious vegetable that can be eaten raw or cooked. [2]Acorns, though bitter-tasting, are found everywhere and can be ground up into a paste that is safe to eat. [3]Grasshoppers, crickets, and beetles are also a widespread and healthy food source. [4]Even the common earthworms and some caterpillars can be eaten by humans. [5]As these examples suggest, there are many sources of food available in the outdoors—for those brave enough to eat them.

Sentences 1–4 present examples of foods available in the outdoors— the main idea expressed in sentence 5.

___5___ 3. [1]"Take some chicken soup for your cold." [2]"Eating carrots will help you see better." [3]Just about everyone can cite old wives' tales like the ones above. [4]They've been around as long as mothers have, probably because they offer comforting advice about experiences we all share and worry about. [5]The amazing thing is that in our modern scientific world, some old wives' tales have actually been proven true. [6]For example, eating chicken soup really *does* help a cold. [7]Although it can't cure it, the soup opens the sinuses and helps fight head congestion. [8]In addition, chicken contains natural chemicals which thin the mucus in the lungs that causes coughing. [9]The carrots in the old wives' tale won't actually improve vision, but the beta carotene they contain helps fight against an eye disease that can eventually cause blindness. [10]Finally, Mom was also right about fish being brain food. [11]It contains zinc, which affects brain function, including memory, and it's healthy in other ways as well.

Sentences 1–4 are introductory details. Sentence 5 states the main idea—some old wives' tales have been proven to be true. Sentences 6–11 support this idea with specific examples.

(Continues on next page)

215

___2___ 4. ¹No one likes a bully. ²So if your child has been terrorizing other children, you'll be glad to know you can redirect that antisocial behavior in several ways. ³Bullies need a physical outlet for their aggressive feelings. ⁴Encourage the child to join a sports team or get regular physical exercise. ⁵Also, reward the bully for cooperative social behavior, even if you have to arrange a situation where he or she can be pleasant to others. ⁶Point out those good qualities the bully does have, and say that those very qualities can get a person the attention he or she so much wants. ⁷Last, help the bully find a positive role model. ⁸Children often behave like their parents in social situations. ⁹Be prepared to change your behavior if you yourself use aggression to accomplish goals.

Sentence 1 is an introductory detail. Sentence 2 states the main idea— that children's antisocial behavior can be redirected in several ways. Sentences 3–9 list those ways.

___1___ 5. ¹Aside from its enormous population—there are 4,000 different species of this insect worldwide—the lowly cockroach has some amazing characteristics. ²In the first place, the bug is fast. ³Even the smallest roach can run up to three miles an hour. ⁴What's more, cockroaches can change course as often as twenty-five times in a second, making them the most nimble animals known. ⁵Roaches are tough to catch. ⁶With sense organs located front and back, they can start to flee from predators within 0.054 seconds of detecting potential danger. ⁷Second, they are ideally adapted to living with people. ⁸They eat almost anything and are comfortable anywhere as long as the temperature is above freezing. ⁹Most species can fit through a crevice no wider than the thickness of a quarter, so any building gives them endless places to rest and breed. ¹⁰And they're perfect travelers, hitching a ride in pant cuffs or grocery bags. ¹¹Finally, the cockroach has an astonishing capacity for survival. ¹²It can hold its breath for nearly forty minutes under water. ¹³Because its brain is spread throughout its body, the roach can survive for several weeks if its head is removed carefully enough to prevent it from bleeding to death. ¹⁴And because roaches sample food before it enters their mouths, they have learned to avoid foul-tasting poisons. ¹⁵This makes them hard to kill with insecticides.

Sentence 1 states the main idea— that cockroaches have "amazing characteristics." The rest of the paragraph provides details to explain these characteristics.

LOCATIONS OF MAIN IDEAS: Mastery Test 5

The main idea may appear at any place within each of the five paragraphs that follow. Write the number of each main idea sentence in the space provided.

__6__ 1. [1]Studies of men's speech show that it is typically direct and positive. [2]Women's speech, on the other hand, tends to be less bold and more hesitant. [3]While a man is likely to state, "It's cold in here," a woman is more likely to ask, "Is it cold in here, or is it just me?" [4]Similar studies show that men interrupt women far more often than women interrupt men. [5]And in listening to couples' conversations, researchers have found that topics that succeed (those that are pursued in the conversation) are usually introduced by the man. [6]Apparently, men's greater social power influences how men and women speak.

Sentence 6 states the main idea—that "men's greater social power" influences how men and women speak. Sentences 1–5 support this idea with specific examples.

__3__ 2. [1]"Fatso!" "Goof-off!" "Jerk!" [2]Most people realize that such name-calling shows disrespect. [3]But verbal disrespect also comes in less obvious forms. [4]One such form is criticism that reduces a person to some undesirable behavior: [5]"All you ever do is sit around"; "You've always been a lousy cook." [6]Repeatedly interrupting someone also shows disrespect. [7]Such interruptions often indicate that what the person is about to say is unimportant to you. [8]Using someone's remark as a way of changing the subject to yourself also is disrespectful. [9]For instance, if someone says, "I can't find my car keys" and your only response is "I've been looking all day for my math book," you're suggesting that *your* concerns matter, but theirs don't.

Sentences 1–2 are introductory details. The word *But* in sentence 3 introduces the main idea. Note the list words *less obvious forms.* Sentences 4–9 give examples of these less obvious forms.

__3__ 3. [1]Leadership style is the way a manager uses authority to lead others. [2]Every manager has a definite style. [3]Still, three broad categories of leadership have been identified. [4]First is the ruling style. [5]Rulers centralize leadership. [6]They do not involve others in decision-making. [7]Next is the democratic style. [8]Democratic leaders transfer authority. [9]They involve employees in decision-making and encourage open communication. [10]Yet they make it clear that the leader has the final say. [11]The third style of leadership is the hands-off approach. [12]Hands-off leaders take the role of consultants. [13]They provide encouragement for employees' ideas and offer opinions when asked. [14]Their goal is to assist but not to direct.

Sentences 1–2 are introductory details. The list words *three broad categories* in sentence 3 signal the main idea. Sentences 4–14 present details about these categories.

(Continues on next page)

___1___ 4. ¹Government agencies that collect information on crime divide illegal acts into three categories. ²The first type is crimes against people. ³These involve physical violence or the threat of it. ⁴Murder, assault, and rape fall into this category. ⁵So does robbery, which is theft by force, violence, or threat. ⁶The second group, crimes against property, involves taking something belonging to another. ⁷Burglary, which is unlawful entry for the purpose of theft, is an example. ⁸Stealing cars and setting fires are other types of property crimes. ⁹Unlike crimes against people, the victims of crimes against property generally do not fear for their lives or safety. ¹⁰Victimless crimes are the third group of unlawful acts. ¹¹They are harder to define than the other categories because there is no specific victim to make a complaint and no specific criminal to arrest and bring to trial. ¹²Instead, prostitution, gambling, and illegal drug use have an effect on society as a whole.

Sentence 1 states the main idea—that government agencies divide illegal acts into three categories. Sentences 2–12 provide details about these three categories.

___9___ 5. ¹One man robs a gas station of $250 and is sent to prison for six months. ²Another man makes millions through illegal securities trading on Wall Street and is required only to pay a fine that he can easily afford. ³A man feuding with another man plants a bomb in his car. ⁴When caught, he is charged with conspiracy and murder. ⁵Ford Motor Company sold millions of a car called the Pinto, even though its own tests had shown that the rear-mounted gas tank might explode if the car was hit in the back. ⁶Over the next eight years, five hundred people were burned to death in accidents involving Pintos. ⁷Ford paid millions of dollars in damages, but was found not guilty of criminal charges. ⁸No one went to jail. ⁹As these cases suggest, the social response to corporate and white-collar crime is quite different from the treatment of "common criminals."

Sentence 9 states the main idea—that the social response to white collar crimes and "common criminals" is different. Sentences 1–8 list specific examples of these differences.

LOCATIONS OF MAIN IDEAS: Mastery Test 6

The main idea may appear at any place within each of the five paragraphs that follow. Write the number of each main idea sentence in the space provided.

___2___ 1. [1]Thousands of children are sent home from school each year because tiny, blood-sucking lice have made their home on the children's little heads. [2]Because of their behavior and size, children are much more likely to get head lice than adults. [3]Children are very likely to spread lice to others through playing. [4]They are often touching each other and roughhousing. [5]Girls and boys commonly share hats and hooded sweatshirts at school. [6]They also borrow each other's combs and brushes. [7]Because children are short, their heads often rest against the tops of seats as they sit in classes, buses, airplanes, theaters, and restaurants. [8]Lice can then transfer easily from one child to the next child who sits in that place. [9]A single child may spread the condition to dozens of other children before receiving treatment.

Sentence 1 is an introductory detail. Sentence 2 states the main idea—that, because of their behavior and size, children are more likely to get head lice than adults. Sentences 3–6 describe behaviors that spread head lice. Sentences 7–9 explain the relationship between children's size and head lice.

___1___ 2. [1]People's sense of what is morally right and wrong develops as they age. [2]In childhood, people use rules to make moral choices. [3]External factors such as punishments or rewards become the basis of a person's sense of right and wrong at this stage. [4]Later, in adolescence, people begin to look to others in their social group to determine morality. [5]At this stage, peer groups and social expectations are used to judge whether something is right or wrong. [6]In adulthood, people develop their own standards of morality. [7]At this stage, they may view "the rules" or "the crowd" as morally incorrect. [8]While not everyone reaches this stage, those that do look to themselves—not others—to determine what is morally good and bad.

Sentence 1 states the main idea—that people's sense of right and wrong develops as they age. Sentences 2–8 support this claim with details about childhood, adolescence, and adulthood.

___7___ 3. [1]Half of all the plant and animal species in the world live in rain forests. [2]Many of the medicinal drugs used in the United States contain ingredients that originate in rain forests. [3]For instance, 73 percent of the 3,000 plants identified as having cancer-fighting properties come from the world's rain forests. [4]Rain forests also help regulate the flow of water on Earth. [5]They soak up the water from heavy tropical rains like enormous sponges. [6]They then release the water slowly, providing a supply for people living hundreds and even thousands of miles away. [7]For all these reasons, it is essential that nations around the world work together to protect the rain forests.

Sentences 1–6 support the main idea stated in sentence 7—that nations should work together to protect rain forests.

(Continues on next page)

_____3_____ 4. ¹As the weekend rolls to a conclusion, many people experience a downward mood swing around three o'clock on Sunday. ²No matter how much fun the weekend has been, they describe a sense of depression, sadness, or even loneliness late in the day. ³Scientists offer various explanations for the Sunday blues. ⁴The first three theories are physical. ⁵One says that feeling out of sorts is a result of too much eating and drinking the night before. ⁶A second explanation places the blame on caffeine withdrawal by students and workers who taper their coffee intake on the weekends. ⁷The third says that the internal body clock gets out of whack when people stay up later and sleep in. ⁸Other theories about Sunday's unhappy mood are much more psychological. ⁹After two days off, people with stressful jobs may actually desire the daily adrenaline rush by late Sunday. ¹⁰Then there are those folks who are so used to structure in their lives that they feel lost because of the free time they have later on Sunday. ¹¹And then there are those people who hate school, hate their job, or just plain hate Monday. ¹²From their perspective, the Sunday blues are a result of having nothing but a long, hard week to look forward to after the promise of the weekend.

Sentences 1–2 are introductory details. The list words *various explanations* in sentence 3 signal the main idea. Sentences 4–12 present and discuss these explanations.

_____2_____ 5. ¹Scientists wondered why certain tiny, colorful frogs found in Central and South America are so poisonous. ²An American scientist then argued in convincing fashion that the poison results from the ants in the frogs' diet. ³Tests showed that the frogs were harmless when born. ⁴Only mature frogs produced a deadly coating of poisons. ⁵The poison is so deadly, in fact, that one single frog has enough poison on it to kill a hundred people. ⁶The American scientist then examined the stomach contents of various types of these frogs. ⁷("Imagine looking into a stomach the size of a speck," she said.) ⁸In those stomachs, she found 135 species of ants, with the ants containing 15 to 20 poisonous substances. ⁹The ants, she discovered, provide 70 percent of the diet of the most deadly of the frogs.

Sentence 1 is an introductory detail. Sentence 2 states the main idea— that ants are the reason certain frogs are poisonous. Sentences 3–9 present details which explain how ants make frogs poisonous.

6 Relationships I

This Chapter in a Nutshell

- To help make their ideas clear, authors use **transitions**—signal words that carry the reader from one sentence or idea to the next.
  - Typical addition transitions are *for one thing, in addition, also,* and *finally.*
  - Typical time transitions are *first, next, then, after,* and *last.*
- In addition to transitions, authors also use **patterns of organization** to show relationships between ideas and to make their ideas clear.
  - The **list of items pattern** presents a series of reasons, examples, or other points.
  - The **time order pattern** presents steps or events in the order in which they happen.

Ideas in a reading selection are almost always connected to each other. Learning to recognize these connections, or **relationships**, will help you become a better reader.

As you will see, authors use two common methods to show relationships and make their ideas clear. These two methods—**transitions** and **patterns of organization**—are explained in turn in this chapter.

Transitions

Look at the following two items. Then check (✓) the one that is easier to read and understand:

____   Paperback books cost less than hardback books. They are easier to carry.

✓   Paperback books cost less than hardback books. Also, they are easier to carry.

You probably found the second item a bit easier to read and follow. The word *also* makes it clear that the writer is discussing the advantages of paperback books. One advantage is that the books are less expensive. An *additional* advantage is that they are easier to carry.

Transitions are words or phrases (such as *also*) that show the relationship between ideas. They are "bridge" words, carrying the reader across from one idea to the next.

Paperback books cost less than hardback books.  , they are easier to carry.

Two major types of transitions are described in this chapter: words that show addition and words that show time.

Words That Show Addition

Once again, put a check (✓) beside the item that is easier to read and understand:

____   Climbing stairs is good exercise for your muscles. It burns a lot of calories.

✓   Climbing stairs is good exercise for your muscles. In addition, it burns a lot of calories.

The words *In addition* in the second item helps make the relationship between the two sentences clear. The author is listing the benefits of climbing stairs. The first benefit is good exercise for the muscles. In addition, climbing stairs burns a lot of calories. *In addition* and words like it are known as addition words.

Addition words signal added ideas. These words tell you a writer is presenting one or more ideas that continue along the same line of thought as a previous idea. Like all transitions, addition words help writers organize their information and present it clearly to readers. In the cartoon on the next page, the words *To begin with* introduce a list, and the words *Second* and *Also* add to the list of reasons why the dog should be hired.

Below are some common words that show addition:

Addition Words

one	to begin with	in addition	last
first	another	next	last of all
first of all	second	moreover	final
for one thing	also	furthermore	finally

Examples

The following items contain addition words. Notice how these words introduce ideas that *add to* what has already been said.

● Hippos give birth under water. They *also* nurse their young there.

● One reason people have dogs is for companionship; *another* reason is for protection.

● The human body has six pounds of skin. *Furthermore,* it contains sixty thousand miles of blood vessels.

PRACTICE 1

Complete each sentence with a [...] box. Try to use each transition once. Then, in the s[...] of the transition you have chosen.

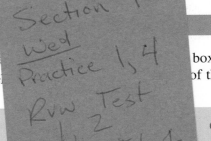

Section 1
Wed
Practice 1, 4
Rvw Test
1, 2
Mastery Tst 1

A. also	**C. for one thing**
D. in addition	

Hint: Make sure that each addition word or phrase that you choose fits smoothly into the flow of the sentence. Test each choice by reading the sentence aloud.

_B_ 1. One good way to be friendly is to ask people questions about themselves. _____Another_____ way is to listen carefully when they answer.

_A_ 2. Employers today say they want college graduates to have good writing and speaking skills. They _____also_____ want them to be able to think critically and solve problems.

_D_ 3. Almost 80 percent of college students drink alcohol. _____In addition_____, about 40 percent either binge drink or drink to get drunk.

_C_ 4. I find your attitude insulting. _____For one thing_____, you pull out your phone and begin to text-message when I try to talk with you.

_E_ 5. There are different ways to solve problems. One way is simple trial and error. A _____second_____ way to proceed is to break a problem into smaller, more manageable pieces. Each piece is easier to solve than the problem as a whole.

Words That Show Time

Check (✓) the item that is easier to read and understand:

____ I had blood work done. I went to the doctor.

_✓_ I had blood work done. Then I went to the doctor.

The word *Then* in the second item clarifies the relationship between the sentences. After having blood work done, the speaker goes to the doctor. *Then* and words like it are time words.

Time words indicate a time relationship. These transitions tell us *when* something happened in relation to when something else happened. They help writers organize and make clear the order of events, stages, and steps in a process. In the cartoon below, the words *First, Then,* and *Finally* mark different stages in "growing up."

"Growing up isn't easy. First, in preschool, you have to learn to tie your shoes. Then in kindergarten, it's the alphabet. Finally, in first grade, they hit you with addition and subtraction."

Here are some common time words:

Time Words

before	next	while	later
previously	soon	during	after
first	often	until	eventually
second	as	now	finally
third	when	then	last

Note: Additional ways of showing time are dates ("In 1850 . . ."; "Throughout the 20th century . . ."; "By 2018 . . .") and other time references ("Within a week . . ."; "by the end of the month . . ."; "in two years . . .").

Examples

The following items contain time words. Notice how these words show us *when* something takes place.

- *After* our kids take their morning showers, there is usually no hot water left.

- It used to take me thirty-five minutes to get to school. *Now*, because of road construction, that time has nearly tripled.

- I begin my "Things To Do" list by writing down everything I need to do the next day. *Then* I label each item A (very important), B (important), or C (not important).

Helpful Tips about Transitions

Here are two points to keep in mind about transitions:

 TIP 1 **Some transition words have the same meaning.** For example, *also, moreover*, and *furthermore* all mean "in addition." Authors typically use a variety of transitions to avoid repetition.

 TIP 2 **Certain words can serve as two different types of transitions, depending on how they are used.** For example, the word *first* may be used as an addition word to show that the author is presenting a series of points, as in the following sentences:

- My mother has some strange kitchen habits. *First*, she loves to cook with the television on full blast. *Moreover*, she . . .

First may also be used to signal a time sequence, as in this sentence:

- The paramedics raced to the man who had collapsed on the sidewalk. *First*, they checked his pulse and breathing. *Then* . . .

PRACTICE 2

Complete each sentence with a suitable time word from the box. Try to use each transition once. Then, in the spaces provided, write the letter of the transition you have chosen.   *Answers may vary.*

A. after	**B. before**	**C. during**
D. then	**E. when**	

> *Hint:* Make sure that each time word that you choose fits smoothly into the flow of the sentence. Test each choice by reading the sentence aloud.

___A___ 1. ____After____ playing outside most of the day, the children fell asleep quickly that night.

___E___ 2. ____When____ I was in the shower, a hairy spider crept out of the drain.

___D___ 3. First, my uncle studies the food ads to see which stores have the best specials. ____Then____ he clips all the cents-off coupons.

___B___ 4. ____Before____ the school lays off any teachers, it should reduce the size of its office staff.

___C___ 5. Some people rudely talk with each other and use their cell phones ____during____ a movie.

Patterns of Organization

You have learned that transitions show the relationships between ideas in sentences. In the same way, **patterns of organization** show the relationships between supporting details in paragraphs, essays, and chapters. It helps to recognize the patterns in which authors arrange information. You will then be better able to understand and remember what you read.

The rest of this chapter discusses two major patterns of organization:

● The **list of items pattern**
(Addition words are often used in this pattern of organization.)

● The **time order pattern**
(Time words are often used in this pattern of organization.)

Noticing the transitions in a passage often can help you become aware of its pattern of organization. Transitions can also help you find the major supporting details.

1   The List of Items Pattern

List of Items
Item 1
Item 2
Item 3

To understand the list of items pattern, try to arrange the following group of sentences in an order that makes sense. Put a *1* in front of the sentence that should come first, a *2* in front of the sentence that comes next, a *3* in front of the third sentence, and a *4* in front of the sentence that should come last. The result will be a short paragraph. Use the addition words as a guide.

___3___   Also, when you're on foot, you are more likely to meet neighbors and make new friends.

___4___   Finally, a brisk walk is an excellent and inexpensive form of exercise.

___1___   Walking can be a rewarding experience.

___2___   For one thing, walking lets you see firsthand what's going on in your neighborhood.

This paragraph should begin with the main idea: "Walking can be a rewarding experience." The next three sentences go on to list three reasons, resulting in the pattern of organization known as a list of items. The transitions *For one thing, Also,* and *Finally* introduce the points being listed and indicate their order. The sentences should read as follows:

> [1]Walking can be a rewarding experience. [2]For one thing, walking lets you see firsthand what's going on in your neighborhood. [3]Also, when you're on foot, you are more likely to meet neighbors and make new friends. [4]Finally, a brisk walk is an excellent and inexpensive form of exercise.

A **list of items** is a series of reasons, examples, or other points that support an idea. The items are listed in the order the author prefers. Addition words are often used in a list of items to tell us that another supporting point is being added to one or more points already mentioned. Textbook authors frequently organize material into lists of items, such as a list of the steps in the writing process, the results of stress, or the reasons why some people never vote.

Addition Words Used in the List of Items Pattern

one	to begin with	in addition	last
first	another	next	last of all
first of all	second	moreover	final
for one thing	also	furthermore	finally

Check Your Understanding

The paragraph below is organized as a list of items. Complete the outline of the paragraph by adding the three major details listed in the paragraph. Then read the explanation that follows.

To help you find the major details, do two things to the paragraph:

- Underline the addition words that introduce the major details in the list;
- Number (*1, 2, . . .*) each item in the list.

¹A number of different theories attempt to explain crime. ²One theory says that crime is caused by¹biology. ³This explanation says that people inherit the tendency to commit crime much as they inherit eye color. ⁴Another theory suggests that crime is caused by²psychological factors. ⁵According to this view, anger caused in childhood—by such painful events as abuse and neglect—drives people to commit crimes. ⁶A third, more recent view is that crime is caused by ³social forces. ⁷According to this theory, economic, social, and political inequalities create an environment in which crime is likely to happen.

Main idea: A number of different theories attempt to explain crime.

Wording of answers may vary.

1. Biology

2. Psychological factors

3. Social forces

Explanation

The main idea is that a number of different theories attempt to explain crime. Note the list words: "a number of different theories." (At times you may also express the main idea in a short heading that describes what's being listed; the heading here could be "Theories to Explain Crime.") Following are the three theories you should have added to the outline:

1. Crime is caused by biology. (This item is signaled by the addition word *One*.)

2. Crime is caused by psychological factors. (This item is signaled by the addition word *Another*.)

3. Crime is caused by social forces. (This item is signaled by the addition word *third*.)

PRACTICE 3 *Homework*

A. The following passage uses a listing pattern. Outline the passage by filling in the major details.

> *Hint:* Underline the addition words that introduce the items in the list, and number the items.

The phrase *three different types of kindness* suggests a list of items.

Item 1: Natural kindness (introduced with the addition words *First of all*).

Item 2: Rule-guided kindness (introduced with the addition word *second*).

¹Research has revealed three different types of kindness. ²<u>First of all</u>, there is ¹natural kindness, based on our ability to identify with others and sense what they're feeling. ³This kindness shows up at a very early age. ⁴A grade-school child who says that a caged gorilla looks sad or who gets upset when another child is bullied has this natural kindness. ⁵The <u>second</u> type of kindness is ²rule-guided. ⁶Rule-guided people have learned "It's wrong to do that." ⁷For example, rule-guided children do not hit other children because they have been taught that hitting is wrong. ⁸The <u>last</u> type of kindness is ³imitative. ⁹We imitate the behavior of people we admire. ¹⁰For instance, imitative children who admire their parents will avoid behavior that their parents disapprove of—because they want to be like their parents.

Main idea: Research has revealed three different types of kindness.

Wording of answers may vary.

1. Natural _____

2. Rule-guided _____

3. Imitative _____

Item 3: Imitative kindness (introduced with the addition word *last*).

B. The following passage uses a listing pattern. Complete the map of the passage by filling in the missing major details.

¹Opossums use a few defense methods to cope with danger. ²The best-known defense is ¹"playing dead." ³An opossum using this defense goes into a coma. ⁴In that state, it appears dead and can be dropped, kicked, or even cut without responding. ⁵This may seem to be a foolish method of defense, for it leaves the animal open to attack. ⁶But many predators will not eat what they haven't killed, and others won't attack something that doesn't run away from them. ⁷However, most opossums—over 90 percent—never use this method. ⁸Instead, their defense is simply to ²run away from danger immediately. ⁹<u>Finally</u>, others use the method of trying to ³scare off enemies—they hiss, salivate, bare their teeth, excrete wastes, or release a terrible odor.

To the Instructor:
In this *Instructor's Edition*, throughout this chapter and the tests that follow, transitions relevant to the patterns of organization are underlined.

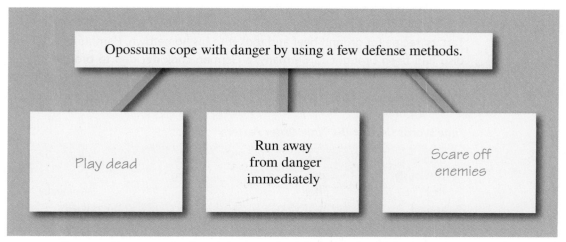

Sentence 2 presents the first defense method: "playing dead." Sentence 8 presents the second method: "run away." Sentence 9 presents the third method: "scare away enemies."

2   The Time Order Pattern

To understand the time order pattern, try to arrange the following group of sentences in an order that makes sense. Put a *1* in front of the sentence that should come first, a *2* in front of the sentence that comes next, a *3* in front of the third sentence, and a *4* in front of the sentence that should come last. The result will be a short paragraph. Use the time words as a guide.

  _3_ **After** the dish had been brought to Germany, a German cook decided to broil the meat, calling it Hamburg steak.

  _4_ **Finally,** German immigrants took the dish to the United States, where it became known as "hamburger."

  _1_ For centuries, a dish made of raw ground beef was eaten by the Tartars, a group living in central Asia.

  _2_ **Then** a merchant from Germany discovered the Tartars' recipe for ground beef and took it to his hometown, Hamburg.

Authors usually present events in the order in which they happen, resulting in a pattern of organization known as **time order**. Clues to the pattern of the above sentences are time words (*Then, After, Finally*). The sentences should read as follows:

¹For centuries, a dish made of raw ground beef was eaten by the Tartars, a group living in central Asia. ²Then a merchant from Germany discovered the Tartars' recipe for ground beef and took it to his hometown, Hamburg. ³After the dish had been brought to Germany, a German cook decided to broil the meat, calling it Hamburg steak. ⁴Finally, German immigrants took the dish to the United States, where it became known as "hamburger."

Time Words Used in the Time Order Pattern

before	next	while	later
previously	soon	during	after
first	often	until	eventually
second	as	now	finally
third	when	then	last

As a student, you will see time order used frequently. Textbooks in all fields describe events and processes, such as the events leading to the uprisings in Egypt in 2011, the steps involved in writing a paper, the growth of Henry Ford's auto empire, or the stages in the development of a tadpole into a frog.

In addition to time transitions, signals for the time order pattern include dates, times, and such words as *stages, series, steps,* and *process.*

The two most common kinds of time order are 1) a series of events or stages and 2) a series of steps (directions for how to do something). Each is discussed below and on the pages that follow.

Series of Events or Stages

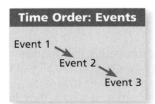

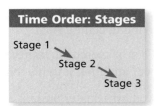

Authors sometimes describe a series of events—for example, the financial mistakes that led to the major recession that began in 2008 in the United States. Or authors may explain a series of stages, such as those that turn a caterpillar into a butterfly. In both cases, they use time order. They discuss the first event or stage, then the second, and so on until the final event or stage in the series is reached.

Check Your Understanding

Here is a paragraph that is organized according to time order. Complete the outline of the paragraph by listing the missing stages in the order in which they happen.
  To help you find the stages, do two things to the paragraph:

● Underline the time words that introduce each stage in the process;

● Number (*1, 2, . . .*) each stage in the process.

¹Very young children in a hospital often go through three stages of separation anxiety. ²In the <u>first</u> stage,¹ "protest," these children try actively to get the parent (especially the mother) back. ³For instance, they may shake their cribs and hurl themselves about. ⁴In the <u>second</u> stage,² "despair," the babies and children become inactive and withdrawn. ⁵They may cry, but generally they are so quiet that they are mistakenly assumed to have accepted the hospital. ⁶In the <u>final</u> stage, ³"detachment," they respond to hospital workers—they eat, play with toys, and are friendly. ⁷But they fail to respond to a visiting parent.

Main idea: Very young children in a hospital often go through three stages of separation anxiety.

1. *Protest*

2. *Despair*

3. *Detachment*

Explanation

You should have added the following stages to the outline:

1. Protest. (The author signals this stage with the time transition *first*.)

2. Despair. (The author signals this stage with the time word *second*.)

3. Detachment. (The author signals this stage with the time word *final*.)

As you can see by the transitions used, the relationship between the points is one of time: the second stage happens *after* the first, and the third stage *after* the second.

PRACTICE 4

The following passage describes a sequence of events. Outline the paragraph by filling in the major details. Note that the major details are signaled by time words.

Hint: Underline the time word or words that introduce each major detail, and number each major detail.

[1]All of us have certain fears at different points in our lives. [2]When we are young children, we worry that something bad will happen to our parents. [3]We are afraid of being alone if our parents die or go away. [4]Then, as teenagers, we fear that we will be socially rejected or seen as "uncool" nobodies. [5]We often act against our better instincts in order to be accepted as one of the crowd. [6]Later, if we become parents, our greatest fear is that someone or something will harm our children. [7]Our sense of love and responsibility for our kids makes the thought of our children being hurt our greatest nightmare. [8]Last, when elderly, we fear poor health and death. [9]We worry about losing our independence, being a burden to other people, and, of course, the end of our lives.   *Wording of answers may vary.*

The phrase *different points in our lives* suggests a time order.

Item 1: Childhood fear of parents being harmed (introduced with the time word *When*)

Item 2: Teenage fear of social rejection (introduced with the time word *Then*)

Main idea: **All of us have certain fears at different points in our lives.**

1. Young children worry about something bad happening to their parents.

2. Teenagers fear social rejection.

3. Parents fear that their children will be harmed.

4. Elderly people are afraid of poor health and death.

Item 3: Parents' fear of children being harmed (introduced with the time word *Later*)

Item 4: Elderly fear of poor health and death (introduced with the time word *Last*)

Series of Steps (Directions)

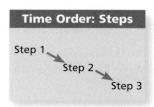

Time Order: Steps

Step 1

Step 2

Step 3

When authors give directions, they use time order. They explain step 1, then step 2, and so on through the entire series of steps that must be taken toward a specific goal.

Check Your Understanding

Here is a paragraph that gives directions. Complete the outline of the paragraph that follows by adding the missing steps in the correct sequence. Then read the explanation that follows.

To help yourself identify each step, do two things to the paragraph:

- Underline the time words that introduce each item in the sequence;
- Number (*1, 2, . . .*) each step in the sequence.

¹To improve your memory for names, follow this procedure. ²<u>First</u>, when you are introduced to someone, make sure you hear the person's name clearly. ³<u>Next</u>, repeat the name with your greeting: "Nice to meet you, Ms. Baron." ⁴<u>Then</u> take a good look at the person and concentrate on matching the face with the name. ⁵<u>Last</u>, repeat the name again when you are leaving the person: "Good meeting you, Ms. Baron."

Main idea: To improve your memory for names, follow this procedure.

1. Make sure you hear the person's name clearly during an introduction.

2. Repeat the name as you greet the person.

3. Concentrate on matching the name with the face.

4. When you leave the person, repeat his or her name.

Explanation

You should have added these steps to the outline:

1. Make sure you hear the person's name clearly during an introduction. (The author signals this step with the time word *First*.)

2. Repeat the name as you greet the person. (The author signals this step with the time word *Next*.)

3. Concentrate on matching the name with the face. (The author's signal is the time word *Then*.)

4. When you leave the person, repeat his or her name. (The author signals this final step with the time word *Last*.)

The following passage gives directions involving several steps that must be done in order. Complete the map below by filling in the three missing steps. To help yourself identify each step, do two things:

● Underline the time words that introduce each item in the sequence;

● Number (*1, 2, . . .*) each step in the sequence.

> The four steps are introduced with the time words *First, After, next,* and *last.*

¹To study a textbook effectively, follow a few helpful steps. ²First, preview the reading. ³This means a quick reading of the first and last paragraphs and of the headings in the chapter. ⁴Previewing will help you understand the selection better once you do begin reading. ⁵After previewing, you are ready to read and mark the selection. ⁶Mark key definitions with "Def"; useful examples with "Ex"; important lists of items with "1, 2, 3"; and key points with underlines. ⁷Your next step is to write study notes for the selection. ⁸By selecting and writing down the important parts of the chapter, you will have already begun to learn them. ⁹The last step of this process is to study the ideas in your notes. ¹⁰Do so by repeating the material over and over to yourself. ¹¹When you can recite it without looking at your notes, you'll really know the material.

Wording of answers may vary.

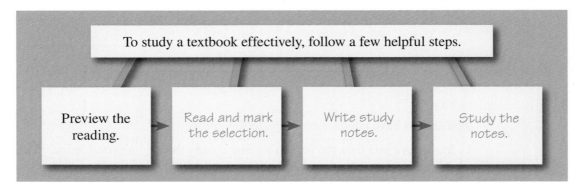

To study a textbook effectively, follow a few helpful steps.

| Preview the reading. | Read and mark the selection. | Write study notes. | Study the notes. |

A Note on Main Ideas and Patterns of Organization

A paragraph's main idea may indicate its pattern of organization. For example, here's the main idea of the paragraph you just read: "To study a textbook effectively, follow a few helpful steps." The words *a few helpful steps* suggest that this paragraph will be organized according to time order. Another good example is the main idea of the earlier paragraph on the causes of crime: "People have come up with different theories to explain crime." The words *different theories* suggest that this paragraph will be a list of items.

Paying close attention to the main idea, then, can give you a quick sense of a paragraph's pattern of organization. Try, for instance, to guess the pattern of the paragraph with this main idea:

While there are hundreds of opportunities for volunteering, most fall into four basic categories.

The statement that volunteer opportunities "fall into four basic categories" is a strong indication that the paragraph will list those categories. The main idea helps us guess that the paragraph will be a list of four items.

Homework

PRACTICE 6

Most of the main ideas below have been taken from college textbooks. In the space provided, write the letter of the pattern of organization that each main idea suggests.

__B__ 1. April 12, 1861, marked the beginning of the four years of bloodshed and bitterness called the Civil War.   Time signals: *April 12, 1861,*
   A. List of items   B. Time order   *beginning, four years.*

__A__ 2. America's highways would be safer if drivers followed three simple rules.   List signal: *three simple rules.*
   A. List of items   B. Time order

__A__ 3. The widespread use of the Internet has changed American society in a number of ways.   List signal: *a number of ways.*
   A. List of items   B. Time order

__B__ 4. A series of important world events led to the creation of the United Nations in 1945.   Time signal:
   A. List of items   B. Time order   *series of . . . events.*

__A__ 5. There are several guidelines that every person needs to follow for good health.   List signal:
   A. List of items   B. Time order   *several guidelines.*

__B__ 6. Children pass through various stages on their way to becoming adults.
   A. List of items   B. Time order   Time signal: *stages.*

__A__ 7. The students who are most likely to drop out of school often share a few characteristics.   List signal:
   A. List of items   B. Time order   *a few characteristics.*

__B__ 8. In order to create a mummy, ancient Egyptians followed a sequence of unusual steps.   Time signal:
   A. List of items   B. Time order   *sequence of unusual steps.*

__A__ 9. Therapists use a broad variety of methods to help individuals cope with their lives.   List signal:
   A. List of items   B. Time order   *variety of methods.*

___B___ 10. Income taxes have been part of society throughout history, from the time
of the Bible to the present day.
A. List of items   B. Time order

Time signals:
throughout history,
from the time of the Bible
to the present day.

Two Final Points

1 While many passages have just one pattern of organization, often the patterns
are mixed. You may find that part of a passage uses a list of items pattern, and
another part of the same passage uses a time order pattern. (For example, in
the paragraph on page 236 about studying a textbook, the steps are given in
time order, but the second step contains a list of four kinds of items to mark.)

2 Remember that not all relationships between ideas are signaled by transitions.
An author may present a list of items, for example, without using addition
words. So as you read, watch for the relationships themselves, not just the
transitions.

CHAPTER REVIEW

In this chapter, you learned how authors use transitions and patterns of
organization to make their ideas clear. Just as transitions show relationships
between ideas in sentences, patterns of organization show relationships
between supporting details in paragraphs and longer pieces of writing.

You also learned two common kinds of relationships that authors use to
make their ideas clear:

● **Addition relationships**

— Authors often present a list or series of reasons, examples, or
other details that support an idea. The items have no time order,
but are listed in whatever order the author prefers.
— Transition words that signal such addition relationships include
for one thing, in addition, also, and *finally.*

● **Time relationships**

— Authors usually discuss a series of events or steps in the order in
which they happen, resulting in a time order.
— Words that signal such time relationships include *first, next, then,
after,* and *last.*

The next chapter—Chapter 7—will help you learn three other important
kinds of relationships: definition-example, comparison and/or contrast, and
cause-effect.

On the Web: If you are using this book in class, you can visit our website for additional practice in understanding relationships that involve addition and time. Go to **www.townsendpress.com** and click on "Online Learning Center."

REVIEW TEST 1   *Homework*

To review what you've learned in this chapter, complete each item by filling in the blank.

1. _____*Transitions*_____ are words or phrases (like *also* or *another* or *then* or *last of all*) that show the relationships between ideas. They are bridges that connect one idea with another.   See page 222.

2. Patterns of _____*organization*_____ show the relationships between supporting details in a paragraph or longer passage.   See page 227.

3. Typical_____*addition*_____ words are *for one thing, also, moreover,* and *another.* Such words tell us the writer is presenting one or more ideas that add to the same line of thought as a previous idea.
          See pages 222–223.

4. Typical _____*time*_____ words are *then, next, later,* and *after.* They tell us when something happened in relation to when something else happened.   See page 225.

5. Sometimes the _____*main idea*_____ of a paragraph may suggest the pattern of organization in the paragraph.   See page 236.

REVIEW TEST 2

A. (1–2.) Name the type of transition used in each of the following cartoons.

___A___ 1. A. addition B. time

List clue: *three ways.*
Addition words: *First, Second, third.*

___B___ 2. A. addition B. time

A series of steps, each introduced by a time
word: *First, Then, Finally.*

B. Fill in each blank with one of the transitions in the box. Use each word once. Then write the letter of the word in the space provided.

A. also	B. another	C. before	D. then

___C___ 3. _____*Before*_____ the thunderstorm struck, the air was strangely quiet, and the sky was an odd yellow color.

___B___ 4. One good thing about my apartment's location is that it is close to school. _____*Another*_____ benefit is that it's in a safe area.

___D___ 5. Break six eggs, separating the whites from the yolks. _____*Then*_____ beat the whites at high speed until they are light and fluffy.

___A___ 6. I've found that a short nap before dinner relaxes me after the stresses of the day. The nap _____*also*_____ gives me the energy I'll need to do homework in the evening.

C. Fill in each blank with an appropriate transition from the box. Use each transition once.

first	then	while

¹Few people are able to resist the following directions. ²They will keep trying over and over again to see if they can outsmart their foot, but they won't succeed. ³(7)_____ *First* _____ sit down in a chair, preferably a straight chair. ⁴(8)_____ *Then* _____ lift your right foot off the floor and make clockwise circles with it. ⁵(9)_____ *While* _____ doing so, draw the number "6" in the air with your right hand. ⁶You will not be able to stop your foot from moving in the opposite direction. ⁷You and I both know how stupid this is, but before the day is done, you are going to try it again—if you've not already done so!

___*B*___ 10. The pattern of organization of the above selection is

      A. list of items.   B. time order.   The word *directions* suggests a series of steps. The time transitions further show that the selection has a time order pattern.

REVIEW TEST 3

A. Fill in each blank with one of the transitions in the box. Use each transition once.

finally	first of all	second
then	when	

The words *certain things* suggest a list pattern. The three items in the list are signaled by the addition words *First of all, Second,* and *Finally.* Within two of the items in the list, there is a time pattern, signaled by the time words *Then* and *When.*

¹If I were the king (or queen) of America and had total power, there are certain things I would do in Washington. ²(1)_____ *First of all* _____, I would see that every person in our country has the same high level of health care that our politicians do. ³Our elected officials should not get better medical treatment than ordinary American citizens. ⁴(2)_____ *Second* _____, I would make Washington provide a maternal leave policy. ⁵A working mother should get at least ten weeks of time off, with pay, to be with her newborn baby. ⁶(3)_____ *Then* _____ she will really have time to bond with her child and learn to be a caring parent. ⁷Most countries in North and South America provide a paid leave of at least ten weeks, and Canada provides up to fifty weeks. ⁸(4)_____ *Finally* _____, I would limit the power of lobbyists in Washington. ⁹Right now there are hundreds of thousands of well-paid lobbyists working full-time in Washington. ¹⁰They make sure that our politicians pass laws that are good for the companies they represent. ¹¹(5)_____ *When* _____ companies benefit, the best interests of ordinary Americans often suffer. ¹²All Americans—not just the wealthy and powerful—should be the ones who matter most in Washington.

B. Below are the beginnings of five passages. Label each one with the letter of its pattern of organization. (You may find it helpful to underline the transition or transitions in each item.)

     A List of items
     B Time order

  _B_ 6. ¹Eskimos begin building an igloo by cutting blocks of ice from well-packed snow. ²The tops are cut at a slight angle, so <u>when</u> they are piled in a circle, they curve inward and form a dome. ³<u>When</u> the igloo is completed, a door is carved out. . . .   The passage presents the series of steps in building an igloo.

  _A_ 7. ¹Homeless people may resist being taken to city shelters, where they could get a hot meal and a bed for the night. ²<u>For one thing</u>, they may feel safer on their own than crowded together with others, some of whom may be mentally unstable. ³There is <u>also</u> the matter of simple pride. . . .   The passage lists reasons the homeless resist shelters.

  _B_ 8. ¹The <u>first</u> printed ad appeared in about 1440. ²Hung on church doors, it advertised a prayerbook. ³The <u>next</u> big event for advertising came soon <u>after</u> the newspaper was born <u>in the early 1600s</u>. ⁴An ad in a London newspaper offered a reward for the return of some stolen horses. . . .   The passage presents a sequence of important events in advertising.

  _B_ 9. ¹In Edgar Allan Poe's story "The Tell-Tale Heart," the insane narrator describes his murder of an old man who had been a tenant in his house. ²<u>First</u> he tells how he treated the old man kindly during the week before the murder. ³<u>Then</u> he explains how, <u>on the eighth night</u>, he . . .   The passage presents the sequence of events in Poe's story.

  _A_ 10. ¹Effective treatment of diabetes depends on early detection. ²Various symptoms suggest the presence of diabetes. ³<u>Some</u> are excessive thirst, hunger, weight loss, and blurry vision. ⁴<u>Additional</u> symptoms are frequent bouts of fatigue and frequent urination. . . .   The passage lists the symptoms of diabetes.

REVIEW TEST 4

Here is a chance to apply your understanding of addition and time relationships to a full-length reading. The following selection from the college textbook *Sociology: An Introduction*, Third Edition, deals with a troubling aspect of family life.

To help you continue to strengthen your work on the skills taught in previous chapters, there are also questions on vocabulary in context, the central point and main ideas, and supporting details.

Words to Watch

Below are some words in the reading that do not have strong context support. Each word is followed by the number of the paragraph in which it appears and its meaning there. These words are indicated in the selection by a small circle (°).

unique (2): unusual
resolved (3): settled
virtually (3): almost entirely
brutalizes (5): treats cruelly
stakes (6): benefits that can be gained and lost
appalled (6) : horrified
intensity (6): great strength of feeling
restraints (7): controls
intercede (7): become involved in order to bring about agreement
constitute (8): make up, form

BEHIND CLOSED DOORS: VIOLENCE IN THE FAMILY

Michael S. Bassis
Richard J. Gelles
Ann Levine

1   "And they lived happily ever after." Hundreds of stories about marriages and families end with this line. Typically, loved ones are reunited; obstacles to marriage overcome; problems with children resolved. Indeed, the very idea of living happily ever after is linked, in our minds, with the special warmth of the family. Yet if we look behind the closed doors of many American households, we discover that all is not peace and harmony.

Some Myths and Realities

2   With the exception of the police and the military, the family is the most violent social group in our society. The home is a more dangerous place than a dark alley. A person is more likely to be murdered in his or her home, by a member of the family, than by anyone else, anywhere else, in society. One in every four murders in the United States is committed by a member of the victim's family. Our country is not unique° in this respect.

3   In an earlier time, few Americans would have believed these statements. Then the sociologists Murray Straus, Richard Gelles, and Barbara Steinmetz conducted a national survey on family violence. Rather than relying on official statistics (incidents of physical abuse known to the police and other social agencies), the researchers asked a representative sample of Americans how they resolved° family conflicts, whether they had hit, spanked, punched, or otherwise assaulted a family member,

and how often. The results of this survey exploded a number of myths about violence in the home. The first myth was that incidents of family violence are rare. They are not. In a year-long study, nearly two million children had been punched, kicked, beaten up, or injured with a knife or gun by a member of their own family. Sixteen percent of couples reported at least one incident of violence in the year of the survey, and nearly a third had experienced violence at some point in their marriage. Two-thirds reported that they had hit a child at least once. In most cases, child abuse was not an isolated incident: if a child was assaulted once, he or she was usually assaulted several times. A second myth suggested that violence occurs only in poor, uneducated families. This, too, proved false. Economic stress does make family violence more likely. But someone had been slapped (or worse) in virtually° every household in the United States, regardless of family income. One reason for the belief that only poor families are violent is that the wealthy take their injuries to private doctors, who were more likely to treat the problem as a private matter than to report family violence to authorities.

4   As for educational level and family violence, 16 percent of college students in one survey knew of at least one physical fight between their parents during the preceding year. Nearly 50 percent of the students had been hit by their parents during their senior year of high school, and 8 percent had been injured severely enough to require first aid or medical attention.

5   Most of us assume that anyone who brutalizes° a loved one is "sick"— mentally ill. This is also a myth. The proportion of violent family members who are psychologically disturbed, in the clinical sense, is no higher than the proportion in the population as a whole.

Sociological Explanations

6   How do sociologists explain the high levels of violence in the family? A number of factors seem to be at work. The first is *intimacy*. Family members are intensely involved with one another. They have deep emotional investments in one another. When quarrels break out or problems arise, the stakes° are higher than in other social groups. A man who is amused by the behavior of a female colleague who is drunk may become enraged if his wife has a little too much to drink. A politician who has been an active supporter of gay rights, at some risk to her career, may be appalled° to discover that her own child is homosexual. Why? Because the behavior of a member of our family is a direct reflection on ourselves. The intensity° of family relationships tends to magnify the most trivial things, such as a burned dinner or a whining child. When did you last hear of someone beating up the cook in a restaurant for preparing an unacceptable meal? But such minor offenses and small oversights often spark violent family fights.

7   A second factor contributing to violence in the home is *privacy*: because family affairs are regarded as private, there are few outside restraints° on violence. When a family quarrel threatens to become a fight, there

are no bystanders to break it up, as there might be on the street or in some other public place. Police are reluctant to intercede° in family quarrels—for good reason. More police are killed responding to calls about domestic disturbances than are killed chasing armed robbers. Neighbors may know that a parent is abusing a child but resist "getting involved." The family, after all, has a right to privacy. Victims may be too ashamed to report family violence to the police. Indeed, a small child may not know something is wrong or unusual when Mother holds his or her hand in a flame as punishment.

8   Third, and perhaps most disturbing, there is a good deal of *social and cultural support* for the use of physical force in the family. Parents are allowed—indeed, encouraged—to spank their children. "Spare the rod and spoil the child," the old saying goes. Most people do not think of spanking a child as violence. But suppose a total stranger in the supermarket smacked your daughter because he disapproved of something she said? Suppose a teacher hit her across the face? Either would constitute° assault and battery in a court of law. What makes parents different? In effect, parenthood confers a "license for hitting" in our society. So, according to some, does marriage. In one survey, one out of four people agreed that it is sometimes justifiable for a husband to hit his wife. Battered wives often say (and believe), "I asked for it" or "I had it coming." (Imagine if the attacker had been her boss, another "authority"

figure, but one whose authority is limited. Because it was her husband who beat her, the situation is viewed quite differently.)

9   Finally, in the process of *socialization,* we learn to associate violence with the family. Our first experience of force nearly always takes place at home. Most of our parents use physical punishment on occasion—for our own good, of course, and because they love us. (The child is told, "This hurts me more than it hurts you.") From here it is only a small step to the conclusion that the use of violence is legitimate whenever something is really important. And the things that are most important to us are often family matters. In addition, we learn how to be violent from our families. (It takes observation and practice, perhaps with siblings, to learn how to beat up another person.) Study after study has shown that the more violence an individual experiences as a child, the more violent he or she will be as a parent. Brutality breeds brutality.

Reading Comprehension Questions

Vocabulary in Context

<u>D</u>   1. In the sentence below, the word *trivial* (trĭv′ē-əl) means
   A. rare.
   B. colorful.
   C. pleasant.
   D. unimportant.

   A burned dinner and a whining child are examples of trivial things.

   "The intensity of family relationships tends to magnify the most trivial things, such as a burned dinner or a whining child." (Paragraph 6)

<u>B</u>   2. In the excerpt below, the word *confers* (kən-fûrs′) means
   A. denies.
   B. gives.
   C. repeats.
   D. destroys.

   Because parents are "encouraged" to spank, parenthood practically "gives" them the right (a license) to do so.

   "Parents are allowed—indeed, encouraged—to spank their children. . . . In effect, parenthood confers a 'license for hitting' in our society." (Paragraph 8)

Central Point and Main Ideas

The reading lists and explains two things: (1) myths that lead to understating the amount of family violence, and (2) factors that encourage family violence. Answer B gives an overview of these two things. Answers A, C, and D are too narrow.

<u>B</u>   3. Which sentence best expresses the central point of the selection?
   A. Numerous murders take place at home.
   B. The American family is more violent than previously thought, a situation for which several causes have been identified.
   C. According to sociologists, there are a number of factors that explain family violence.
   D. Because family affairs are considered private, there are few outside controls on violence in the home.

<u>A</u>   4. The main idea of paragraph 7 is best expressed in its
   A. first sentence.
   B. second sentence.
   C. third sentence.
   D. last sentence.

   The rest of the paragraph explains the impact of privacy on family violence.

Supporting Details

__C__ 5. The major details of paragraphs 6–9 are
    A. myths about family violence.
    B. steps to take to counteract family violence.
    C. factors that explain the high levels of violence in the family.
    D. the effects of family intimacy.

In the reading, the factors are highlighted with italics; they are intimacy, privacy, social and cultural support, and socialization.

__F__ 6. TRUE OR FALSE? People who experience violence as children are more likely to avoid using violence with their own children.

See the last two sentences of the reading.

Transitions

__B__ 7. The sentences below express a relationship of
    A. addition.
    B. time.

"In an <u>earlier</u> time, few Americans would have believed these statements. <u>Then</u> the sociologists Murray Straus, Richard Gelles, and Barbara Steinmetz conducted a national survey on family violence." (Paragraph 3)

The words *earlier* and *Then* suggest the time relationship.

8. Find the addition transition in the sentences below and write it here:

    _____also_____

"Most of us assume that anyone who brutalizes a loved one is 'sick'—mentally ill. This is also a myth." (Paragraph 5)   See page 223.

Patterns of Organization

__A__ 9. Just as paragraphs are organized according to patterns, so are groups of paragraphs. What is the main pattern of organization of paragraphs 3–5?
    A. List of items
    B. Time order

The paragraphs list myths about violence in the home.

__C__ 10. Which words signal the pattern of organization of paragraphs 6–9?
    A. *Intimacy, privacy, social and cultural support, socialization*
    B. *Number, factor, force, process*
    C. *First, second, third, finally*
    D. *Family, home, parents, legitimate*

Paragraph 6 states that "a number of factors" explain family violence. List words—*first* (paragraph 6), *second* (paragraph 7), *Third* (paragraph 8), and *Finally* (paragraph 9)—introduce these factors.

Discussion Questions

1. Why do you think the researchers "asked a representative sample of Americans how they resolved family conflicts" instead of using official statistics such as police reports? What did their method accomplish that relying on official statistics would not have accomplished?

2. What myths about family violence did the survey disprove? Why might these myths have existed in the first place?

3. Were you or was someone you know ever punished with physical force as a child? If so, what do you think have been the effects of this use of force?

4. What can society—for instance, schools, religious institutions, government, the media—do to prevent further violence in families?

Note: Writing assignments for this selection appear on pages 591–592.

Check Your Performance   RELATIONSHIPS I

Activity	Number Right	Points	Score
Review Test 1 (5 items)	_____	× 2 =	_____
Review Test 2 (10 items)	_____	× 3 =	_____
Review Test 3 (10 items)	_____	× 3 =	_____
Review Test 4 (10 items)	_____	× 3 =	_____
		TOTAL SCORE =	_____%

Enter your total score into the **Reading Performance Chart: Review Tests** on the inside back cover.

RELATIONSHIPS I: Mastery Test 1

A. Fill in each blank with an appropriate transition from the box. Use each transition once. Then, in the space provided, write the letter of the transition you have chosen.

A. after	**B. another**	**C. before**
D. second	**E. then**	

Hint: Make sure that each word or phrase that you choose fits smoothly into the flow of the sentence. Test your choices by reading each sentence to yourself.

___A___ 1. ¹_____After_____ a bad nightmare awakened me in the middle of the night, I decided to turn on the bedroom lights for a while.

> First, the speaker had a nightmare; *after* that, the lights were turned on.

___E___ 2. ¹Blinking helps to keep your eyes healthy. ²When you close your eyes, your eyelids sweep away dirt and other harmful particles. ³Fluids _____then_____ moisten and bathe the surface of your eyes.

> *Then* introduces the second step in the process of blinking.

Item 3:
The sentences list reasons why today's parents are busy. One reason is that they must raise their children. *Second* introduces another responsibility of busy parents.

___D___ 3. ¹Many parents today are busier than ever. First of all, they must raise their own children. ²And often their _____second_____ responsibility is to care for aging parents, even to the point of having the parents live with them.

___B___ 4. ¹A major trend in education has been the return of adults to the classroom. ²One type of nontraditional student is the adult worker seeking to advance in a job or retrain for a new career. ³_____Another_____ type is the homemaker preparing to enter the job market in middle age. ⁴A third type is the retired person now pursuing interests there was no time for in earlier years.

> *Another* introduces the second item in a list of three major trends in education.

___C___ 5. ¹The American custom of dating has changed. ²_____Before_____ the 1970s, dating was more formal. ³Males usually had to ask for a date at least several days in advance. ⁴These days, dating has become more casual. ⁵In fact, the word "date" now sounds a bit old-fashioned to many young people. ⁶"Getting together" and "hanging out" are more likely ways of referring to dating today.

> The sentences describe a series of events in the history of dating, the earliest of which took place *before* the 1970s. Note the other time transitions: *These days, now,* and *today.*

(Continues on next page)

B. Fill in each blank with an appropriate transition from the box. Use each transition once.

after	before	then	when

¹(6)_____ When _____ President Theodore "Teddy" Roosevelt visited the South in 1902, he was invited to a hunting party. ²The organizers staked a bear cub to the ground so that the President could not miss. ³(7)_____ After _____ he realized that the bear was pinned down, Roosevelt refused to fire. ⁴A political cartoon based on the incident appeared in a number of newspapers. ⁵The cartoon, with a drawing of the small bear, was seen by a shop owner in Brooklyn. ⁶The shop owner (8)_____ then _____ made up a window display version of the little bear in a soft, plush material. ⁷(9)_____ Before _____ offering the bear to customers, the shop owner asked Roosevelt for permission to sell the new toy as "Teddy's Bear." ⁸The President gave his approval but wrote, "I don't think my name is worth much to the toy bear cub business." ⁹He was clearly wrong, for a bear-buying frenzy swept the country, and the teddy bear has been popular ever since.

___B___ 10. The pattern of organization of the above selection is
  A. list of items.
  B. time order.   The paragraph presents a series of events showing how the teddy bear originated and became popular. (Note that all the missing transitions are time words.)

RELATIONSHIPS I: Mastery Test 2

A. Fill in each blank with an appropriate transition from the box. Use each transition once. Then, in the spaces provided, write the letter of the transition you have chosen.

A. also	**B. another**	**C. before**
D. during	**E. second**	

___A___ 1. ¹Ice is the safest and most effective immediate treatment for athletic injuries. ²It can be used, for example, on torn ligaments, strained muscles, and bruises. ³Ice relieves pain while slowing the blood flow. ⁴Ice _____ also _____ helps reduce internal bleeding and promotes faster healing.

___E___ 2. ¹There are excellent reasons for taking a night class. ²One is that it is a good way to develop a new interest or hobby. ³A _____ second _____ reason is that it's a great way to meet people with similar interests.

___D___ 3. ¹Only a little over a century ago, guns were considered a necessity for American pioneers. ²People hunted with guns to provide food for their families. ³Guns were used for protection against threats from the wilderness. ⁴_____ During _____ the 1800s and into the early 1900s, a gun was as common as a coffeepot in most American homes.

___C___ 4. ¹Some simple methods can improve your ability to relax. ²One method, called progressive relaxation, involves tensing a muscle group and then slowly relaxing the muscles in that group. ³Your whole body feels relaxed after you repeat this process for all the major muscles. ⁴Another simple relaxation method is to stop what you are doing and take a few deep breaths. ⁵Next time you watch a basketball game, notice how a player will use this technique just _____ before _____ shooting a free throw.

___B___ 5. ¹Hispanic Americans, also called Latinos, are the largest minority group in the United States. ²The group includes Mexican Americans, Puerto Ricans, and immigrants from Cuba and other Central and South American countries. ³The Spanish language is the unifying force among Hispanic Americans. ⁴_____ Another _____ source of common identification is religion: at least 85 percent are Roman Catholic.

(Continues on next page)

B. Fill in each blank with an appropriate transition from the box. Use each transition once.

finally	first of all	moreover	secondly

¹United States schools are not entirely to blame for the lower achievements of their students compared with the achievements of Japanese students. ²(6)_____ First of all _____, our schools deal not just with learning (the only concern of Japanese schools) but also with such social problems as alcohol and drug abuse and teenage pregnancy. ³(7)_____ Secondly _____, American parents are often too stressed, tired, or self-absorbed to do what Japanese mothers do—help with their children's homework and make sure they study three or four hours a night. ⁴(8)_____ Moreover _____, many American teenagers hold part-time jobs, reducing their ability to hit the books after school. ⁵Working after school is almost unheard of in Japan. ⁶(9)_____ Finally _____, American teenagers are under great pressure from their peers to look good, drink, date, or even have sex. ⁷With Japanese teenagers, the pressure instead is to study hard.

___A___ 10. The pattern of organization of the above selection is
      A. list of items.
      B. time order.   The paragraph lists reasons why American schools are not to blame for the lower achievements of their students compared to those of Japanese students. (Note that all the missing transitions are addition words.)

To the Instructor:
In the paragraphs in Tests 2–6, the main ideas and transitions relevant to the pattern of organization are underlined.

RELATIONSHIPS I: Mastery Test 3

A. (1–4.) Arrange the scrambled sentences below into a logical paragraph by numbering them *1, 2, 3,* and *4* in an order that makes sense. Then, in the space provided, write the letter of the main pattern of organization used.

Note that transitions will help you by making clear the relationships between sentences.

____3____ Another method is acupuncture, in which a tiny needle is placed in a smoker's earlobe to remove the craving for a cigarette.

____4____ Finally, many feel that being strongly motivated and quitting "cold turkey" is the best way to conquer the habit.

____2____ One method involves chewing a special nicotine gum whose nicotine content decreases at regular intervals.

____1____ Several ways have been suggested to help long-time smokers stop smoking.

List transitions dictate the order of these items: One,

____A____ 5. The pattern of organization of the above selection is *Another, Finally.*
   A. list of items.
   B. time order.
                                        List signal: Several ways.

B. Read the passage and answer the question that follows. You may find it helpful to underline transitions as you read.

   ¹There is a false idea that lemmings, small mouselike creatures that live in northern regions, often commit suicide. ²The truth is, however, that lemmings end their lives by accident. ³Normally they live quietly in underground nests, feeding on roots and moss. ⁴But every few years, the lemming population grows so large that the food supply becomes too small to feed them all. ⁵Then all the lemmings leave their nests and go in search of food. ⁶As they travel, the lemmings eat everything in their path. ⁷After traveling for weeks, they reach the shore—but they don't stop there. ⁸Still searching for food, the tiny rodents plunge into the ocean and begin swimming. ⁹In a short time, the little creatures become exhausted and drown.

____B____ 6. The pattern of organization of the above selection is
   A. list of items.
   B. time order.   *The paragraph presents the sequence of events in*
                              which lemmings end their lives. The time transitions
                              include Then, As, After, In a short time.

(Continues on next page)

C. Fill in each blank with an appropriate transition from the box. Use each transition once.

after	then	when

[1]Gary began stealing liquor from his parents at the age of fourteen, and within two years, he regularly came to school drunk. [2](7)_____When_____ he was in his early twenties, he realized that he was completely dependent on alcohol, but he continued to drink. [3]Gary's moment of truth came at age twenty-five. [4]He narrowly escaped death in a drunk-driving accident, and he was responsible for injuring someone else. [5]He soon committed himself to the local alcohol-recovery center. [6](8)_____After_____ an intensive four-week treatment and a ninety-day follow-up program, Gary was free of alcohol for the first time in over ten years. [7]He (9)_____then_____ returned to college and received a degree. [8]Today Gary works as a counselor in the same treatment center that gave him his second chance. [9]Gary's story should inspire many of his own clients at the alcohol-recovery center.

___B___ 10. The pattern of organization of the above selection is
   A. list of items.
   B. time order.   The paragraph narrates a series of events in Gary's life.
                      (Note that all the missing transitions are time words.)

RELATIONSHIPS I: Mastery Test 4

A. (1–4.) Arrange the scrambled sentences below into a logical paragraph by numbering them *1, 2, 3,* and *4* in an order that makes sense. Then, in the space provided, write the letter of the main pattern of organization used.

Note that transitions will help you by making clear the relationships between sentences.

___4___ Then, often quite suddenly, a chimp would grab the stick, poke it through the bars of the cage, and drag the banana within reach.

___1___ A series of experiments showed how chimps solved the problem of reaching a banana placed on the ground outside their cage.

___3___ After a while, the chimps would start looking at what was lying around the cage, including a stick left there by the experimenters.

___2___ The chimps almost always tried <u>first</u> to reach the food with their hands.

___B___ 5. The pattern of organization of the above selection is

    A. list of items.   Solving a problem involves following certain steps.

    B. time order.   The words *solved the problem* suggest a sequence of steps.
The time order pattern is further supported by the time transitions (*first, After, Then*).

B. Read the passage and answer the question that follows. You may find it helpful to underline transitions as you read.

                    [1]Every year, about 35,000 Americans commit suicide. [2]Sadly, research shows that many of these deaths can be avoided. [3]In order to prevent this needless loss of life, people must learn to recognize the warning signs of a potential suicide. [4]Such signs include, <u>first of all</u>, severe depression and withdrawal, often combined with the inability to sleep or eat. [5]Extreme mood swings, from joy to deep depression, are <u>also</u> danger signs. [6]<u>In addition</u>, suicidal people may begin giving away valued belongings. [7]<u>Last</u>, any life crisis, such as the death of a loved one or the loss of a job, may make a potentially suicidal person feel that he or she can't go on.

___A___ 6. The pattern of organization of the above selection is

    A. list of items.   List signal: *warning signs.*

    B. time order.   Addition words: *first of all, also, In addition, Last.*
The passage lists four warning signs of a potential suicide.

(Continues on next page)

C. Fill in each blank with an appropriate transition from the box. Use each transition once.

later	now	then	when

¹Popcorn has long been a favorite food. ²An early Spanish explorer in the Americas wrote of toasted corn that burst and looked very much like white flowers. ³In 1621, Indians brought corn to the first Thanksgiving. ⁴They taught the colonists to hold oiled ears on sticks over the fire and chew the popped kernels off. ⁵Two centuries (7)_____*later*_____, in 1846, the first cookbook to mention popcorn was published. ⁶The recipe directed the cook to pour corn kernels into a kettle of hot fat. ⁷When the corn popped, it was skimmed off the top. ⁸Popcorn appeared, too, in recipes for soup and beer. ⁹Popcorn balls became a holiday treat, and candied popcorn was flavored with lemon, rose, peppermint, honey, vanilla, or molasses. ¹⁰(8)_____*When*_____ the first corn poppers were invented in the 1890s, boys in large cities and small towns sold popcorn on street corners. ¹¹It was a good way to make a profit since vendors could buy twenty-five pounds of popping corn for a nickel and sell multiple individual bags for the same price. ¹²Movie theaters (9)_____*then*_____ brought the taste treat indoors. ¹³During World War II, when sugar was rationed, Americans ate three times as much popcorn as they had before. ¹⁴(10)_____*Now*_____ we nibble approximately seventy quarts of the snack food per person a year.

The passage presents a sequence of events in the history of popcorn. The events are in time order from past to present.

RELATIONSHIPS I: Mastery Test 5

Read each textbook passage, and then answer the questions or follow the directions provided.

A. [1]People have differing feelings about their work. [2]First of all, for some it can be just a job, something done only for the paycheck, with a limited emotional reward. [3]For a second type of worker, work is a career and a part of the person's self-image. [4]A career person is challenged by the work and cares about the power and prestige that the job offers, not just the money. [5]Last, work can be a calling. [6]A person with a calling is passionately committed to the work itself, apart from the money or status that it may bring. [7]In general, people with callings are happier than those with mere jobs or careers.

___A___ 1. The pattern of organization of the above selection is
    A. list of items.
    B. time order.
                      List signal: differing feeings.

2–3. Two of the transitions that signal major details of the paragraph are
                  Any two of the following: First of all, second, Last

B. [1]In 1814, a military victory was won—not with soldiers or guns, but with animals! [2]The battle took place in Chile when a Chilean leader named O'Higgins was fighting to win his country's independence from Spain. [3]The Chilean patriots were surrounded by a larger, well-armed Spanish army. [4]Wounded and seemingly without any options, O'Higgins came up with an idea. [5]He ordered his soldiers to gather together as many cows, mules, sheep, and dogs as possible. [6]Then, using gunshots to frighten the herd, O'Higgins got the animals to stampede toward the Spanish camp. [7]In a short time, the Spanish forces were being attacked by a frightened crowd of charging beasts. [8]While the Spanish were busy trying to protect themselves from the animals, O'Higgins and his men escaped into the nearby mountains. [9]Three years later, O'Higgins and an army of four thousand men returned from the mountains and defeated the Spanish once and for all.

___B___ 4. The pattern of organization of the above selection is
    A. list of items.   *The paragraph presents a sequence of events*
    B. time order.   *leading to O'Higgins's victory.*

5–6. Two of the transitions that signal major details of the paragraph are
         Any two of the following: In 1814, when, Then, In a short time, While, Three years later

(Continues on next page)

C. [1]A good conclusion should tie a speech together and give the audience the feeling that the speech is complete. [2]It should not introduce any new ideas. [3]There are several kinds of conclusions to speeches that have proved their value time and time again. [4]One is a summary of the main ideas of your speech. [5]This type of conclusion is especially useful if you want your audience to remember your main points. [6]Another common and useful type of conclusion is a quotation. [7]If you can find a quotation that fits your subject, the conclusion is one good place to use it. [8]For example, if your speech was about the importance of reading aloud to little children, you could end with this quotation by Dr. Ruth Love: [9]"If we could get our parents to read to their preschool children fifteen minutes a day, we could revolutionize the schools." [10]A quotation such as this gives added authority to what you have said. [11]A third useful conclusion is one that inspires the audience to action. [12]When you give a speech, especially a persuasive speech, your goal is often to inspire the audience to some course of action. [13]If this has been your goal, conclude by telling audience members precisely what they should do.

___A___ 7. The pattern of organization of the above selection is
      A. list of items.   The paragraph lists several kinds of
      B. time order.   conclusions to speeches.

8–10. The paragraph is about three kinds of conclusions to speeches.

    ● Which transition word signals the first kind of conclusion?

                          One

    ● Which transition word signals the second kind of conclusion?

                          Another

    ● Which transition word signals the last kind of conclusion?

                          third

The three conclusions—all major details—are signaled
by the addition words *One*, *Another*, and *third*.

RELATIONSHIPS I: Mastery Test 6

Read each textbook passage, and then answer the questions or follow the directions provided.

A. ¹The history of books is marked by many important milestones. ²Among the earliest of these would have to be the establishment of the first public library. ³This event took place in Athens, Greece, in 540 B.C. ⁴Books then had to be copied by hand until 1456, when another important milestone was reached. ⁵The German inventor Johann Gutenberg built a printing press capable of producing multiple copies of one book. ⁶After printing presses were established, books spread everywhere. ⁷By the 1800s, American publishing houses were pumping out works to satisfy a reading-hungry public. ⁸An example of a best-selling book was *Uncle Tom's Cabin*, which was published in 1852 and sold seven million copies. ⁹The next chapter in the history of books began in the 1980s, with the publishing of books on audiotape. ¹⁰Today, we even have electronic books that can be downloaded from the Internet.

The passage presents a sequence of important events in the history of books. Time transitions are used throughout.

___B___ 1. The pattern of organization of the above selection is
    A. list of items.   B. time order.

2–3. Two of the transitions that signal major details of the paragraph are
Any two of the following: earliest, in 540 B.C., then, until 1456,
After, By the 1800s, in 1852, next, in the 1980s, Today

B. ¹There's no foolproof way to keep a burglar out, but there are precautions you can take. ²First of all, the best defense against a break-in is lights. ³Keep an inside and an outside light on at night. ⁴Second, if you are going to be home late or away, use timers to turn the lights, radio, and television on and off to give the appearance that someone is home. ⁵Also, think of your house as a fort. ⁶In many burglaries, thieves simply breeze in through unlocked doors or windows. ⁷Keep doors locked even when you are home. ⁸A final step is to deprive burglars of what they need. ⁹Keep bushes and trees trimmed, if they are near windows and doors, to eliminate places for burglars to lurk. ¹⁰Put away ladders, rakes, brooms, and other equipment that thieves might use to help them break in. ¹¹These steps won't guarantee that your house will be safe, but they will help minimize the risk.

The passage lists precautions to prevent burglary. Addition transitions are used throughout.

___A___ 4. The pattern of organization of the above selection is
    A. list of items.   B. time order.

5–6. Two of the transitions that signal major details of the paragraph are
Any two of the following: First of all, Second, Also, final

(Continues on next page)

259

C. ¹For several reasons, some people find it hard to show appreciation or give praise to others. ²One reason is that they may have received little praise or appreciation themselves. ³Not having received it, they don't know how to give it. ⁴Another reason for not making positive remarks about others is insecurity. ⁵Insecure persons often have a need to put others down. ⁶If they can make someone else feel bad, they feel better by comparison. ⁷A final reason for not complimenting others is fear. ⁸Showing affection or appreciation is a way of opening oneself up to someone else, of offering friendship. ⁹But people are afraid they may be rejected, so they decide it is safer not to try.

___A___ 7. The pattern of organization of the above selection is
        A. list of items.
        B. time order.

> The passage lists several reasons why people find it hard to give praise. The reasons are signaled by addition words: *One, Another,* and *final.*

8–10. Complete the map of the selection.

Wording of answers may vary.

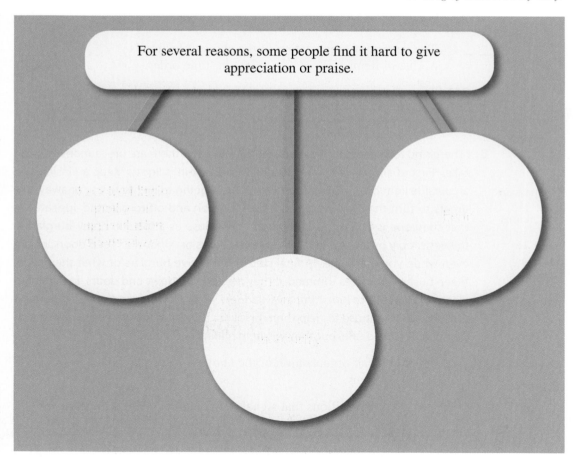

For several reasons, some people find it hard to give appreciation or praise.

7 Relationships II

This Chapter in a Nutshell

In this chapter, you will learn about three other types of relationships:

- Relationships that involve **illustration**
    - Typical illustration transitions are *for example* and *for instance.*
- Relationships that involve **comparison and/or contrast**
    - Typical comparison transitions are *alike* and *similar.*
    - Typical contrast transitions are *but* and *however.*
- Relationships that involve **cause and effect**
    - Typical cause-effect transitions are *reasons, because,* and *therefore.*

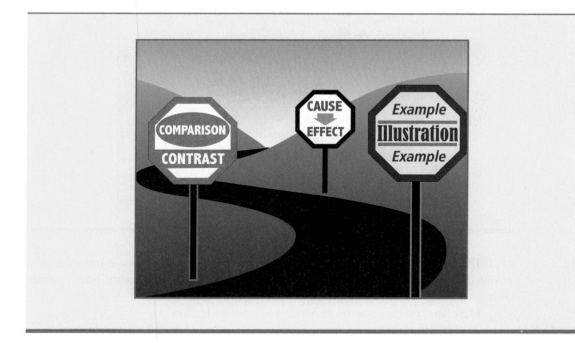

In Chapter 6, you learned about two common types of relationships: ones that involve addition and ones that involve time. In this chapter, you will learn about relationships involving **illustration**, **comparison**, **contrast**, and **cause and effect**.

1 Illustration

Words That Show Illustration

Check (✓) the item that is easier to understand:

____ Anyone can become a safer driver. Do not talk or send text messages on your cellphone.

✓ Anyone can become a safer driver. For instance, do not talk or send text messages on your cellphone.

The second item is easier to understand. The words *For instance* make it clear that not talking or sending text messages on a cellphone is one way to be a safer driver. *For instance* and other words and phrases like it are illustration words.

"I try to limit how much I eat. For example, I allow myself to have only one dessert after a big meal."

Illustration words tell us that an author will provide one or more *examples* to clarify a given idea. In the cartoon above, the man gives his doctor one example of how he tries to limit what he eats—having only one dessert!

Here are some common words that show illustration:

Illustration Words

(for) example	(for) instance	to illustrate
including	such as	once

Examples

The following items contain illustration words. Notice how these words signal that one or more *examples* are coming.

● Some birds, *such as* the penguin and the ostrich, cannot fly.

● People came to America for many reasons. The Puritans, *for example*, arrived in 1620 seeking religious freedom.

● My mother's love of chocolate has led to some pretty weird combinations. *Once* she put Hershey's syrup on a cheese sandwich.

To the Instructor: Remind students that transitions are **bridges** that connect ideas. For one or more of the example sentences in this chapter, you might wish to put a bridge diagram (similar to the one on page 222) on the board.

PRACTICE 1   *Assigned for homework*

Complete each item with a suitable illustration word or phrase from the box on the previous page. Try to use a variety of transitions.   *Answers may vary.*

Hint: Make sure that each word or phrase that you choose fits smoothly into the flow of the sentence. Test each choice by reading the sentence aloud.

1. A large part of what seems to be taste is really smell. _____*For example*_____, try eating some bread while holding a banana or piece of onion near your nose.

2. When we were young, my older brother liked to tease me. _____*Once*_____ he put raisins in my cereal and told me they were roaches.

3. The Italian restaurant offers pizza with unusual toppings, _____*such as*_____ sweet corn, sunflower seeds, and carrots.

4. Some children are very caring. _____*For instance*_____, they will want to share their toys with others, or they will reach out to comfort a crying friend.

5. Power is the ability to control the behavior of others, even against their will. If a robber forces us to hand over our wallets, that is an _____*example*_____ of power.

Illustration words are common in all types of writing. One way they are used in textbooks is in the definition and example pattern of organization.

The Definition and Example Pattern

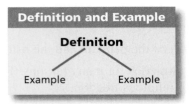

To understand the definition and example pattern, try to arrange the following sentences in an order that makes sense. Put a *1* in front of the sentence that should come first, a *2* in front of the sentence that comes next, and a *3* in front of the sentence that should be last. The result will be a short paragraph. Then read the explanation that follows.

_2_   When acupuncture is used to kill pain, needles are inserted far from the area of pain.

_1_   Acupuncture is a Chinese medical technique that involves inserting special needles in certain places in the body.

_3_   In one stomach operation, for instance, four needles in the patient's outer ears eliminated pain.

This paragraph begins with a definition: "Acupuncture is a Chinese medical technique that involves inserting special needles in certain places in the body." The second sentence further explains acupuncture by discussing a special use: "When acupuncture is used to kill pain, needles are inserted far from the area of pain." Finally, an example of the use of acupuncture for pain is given: "In one stomach operation, for instance, four needles in the patient's outer ears eliminated pain." The third sentence includes the illustration words *for instance*. As you can see, the **definition and example pattern of organization** includes just what its name suggests: a definition and one or more examples.

An Important Study Hint: Good textbook authors want to help readers understand the important ideas and terms in a subject—whether it is psychology, sociology, business, biology, or any other field. Such authors often take time, then, to include key definitions. These ideas and terms are usually set off in *italic* or **boldface** type, and the definitions are signaled by such words as *is, are, is called, termed,* and *refers to*. Here are some definitions from a variety of textbooks:

● A **placebo** is a "sugar pill" without any significant medical properties.

● **Hypotheses** are predictions stated in a way that allows them to be tested.

● A low sense of personal worth is what psychologists call **negative self-esteem.**

- The chemical change in which a solid turns into a liquid is termed **melting**.

- **Narcolepsy** refers to an uncontrollable need to sleep for short periods during the day.

- Many critics argue that tests like the SAT are **culturally biased—** favoring one ethnic or racial group over others.

(***Note:*** Sometimes a dash is used to signal a definition.)

If an author defines a term, you can assume that it is important enough to learn. So when reading and taking notes on a textbook, always do two things:

1) Write down key definitions.

2) Write down a helpful example for each definition. When a definition is general and abstract, authors often provide examples to help make a meaning clear.

Check Your Understanding: List Words

The paragraph below defines a term, explains it a bit, and then gives an example of it. After reading the paragraph, see if you can answer the questions below. Then read the explanation that follows.

> [1]Self-fulfilling prophecies are predictions that come true because we predict them. [2]For example, Tyrone may tell himself, "I bet I can get a good grade in this history class." [3]This thought makes Tyrone likely to work hard, making his prediction come true. [4]Children get their self-fulfilling prophecies from others. [5]For instance, if someone tells a child that he or she will "never amount to much," there is a good chance that is what will happen. [6]But if someone keeps saying to a child, "You can be one of the stars of your class," that child is likely to do well.

1. What term is being defined?   _Self-fulfilling prophecies_

2. Which sentence contains the definition?   _1_

3. In which sentence does the first example begin?   _2_

4. How many examples are given in all?   _Three_

Explanation

The term *self-fulfilling prophecies* is defined in sentence 1: "predictions that come true because we predict them." (Note that the definition is signaled by the word *are*.) The first example, about Tyrone's self-fulfilling prophecy, begins in sentence 2. A second example, about a child, appears in sentence 5, and a third example begins in sentence 6. Note that the author introduces two of the examples with the

To the Instructor: The terms being defined are double-underlined in this *Instructor's Edition*. Also, throughout this chapter and the tests that follow, transitions relevant to the patterns of organization are underlined.

transition words *for example* and *for instance*. By providing clear examples, the author helps the reader understand the new term.

PRACTICE 2

Each of the following passages includes a definition and one or more examples. Underline the term being defined. Then, in the spaces provided, write the number of the definition sentence and the number of the sentence where each example begins.

A. [1]Have you ever been up at one o'clock in the morning, trying to finish the last chapter of the text on which you are being tested in the morning? [2]If so, you may have turned to a stimulant to keep you awake. [3]A <u>stimulant</u> is a substance that temporarily increases one's activity or alertness. [4]One common stimulant is caffeine, which is found in coffee, tea, soft drinks, and chocolate. [5]Another <u>example</u> of a common stimulant is nicotine, which is found in cigarettes. [6]Both caffeine and nicotine cause a rise in your heart rate and blood pressure, making you feel more wide-awake.

Definition ____3____   Example 1 ____4____   Example 2 ____5____

B. [1]Frequently, members of a group will develop a <u>jargon</u>, or specialized language, which distinguishes the group from the wider society. [2]The police are well known for their use of distinctive jargons. [3]<u>For instance</u>, members of New York City's police department refer to a suspect as a "perp" (short for "perpetrator"), to a gun as a "piece," and to the police shield as the "tin." [4]Chicago police also have their own terms, <u>such as</u> calling a suspect an "offender"; they call a gun a "biscuit" and the police shield the "button."

Definition ____1____   Example 1 ____3____   Example 2 ____4____

2 Comparison and Contrast

Words That Show Comparison

Check (✓) the item that is easier to understand:

____ Human infants suck their thumbs; baby elephants suck their trunks.

__✓__ Just as human infants suck their thumbs, baby elephants suck their trunks.

The first item makes us wonder what the author is focusing on—how human infants and baby elephants are alike or how they are different. The words *just as* in the second version show the author is focusing on the similarity. *Just as* and words like them are comparison words.

"Do you realize how much we resemble each other? We'll both eat anything. We both like to sleep on the furniture. And we're both overweight."

Comparison words signal similarities. Authors use a comparison transition to show that a second idea is *like* the first one in some way. In the above cartoon, the words *resemble* and *both* show the dog is making a comparison between himself and the man. The dog names three ways he and the man are similar: both of them eat anything, sleep on the furniture, and are overweight.

Here are some common words that show comparison:

Comparison Words

(just) as	in like (similar) manner	same
(just) like	similar(ly)	in the same way
alike	similarity	resemble
likewise	both	equally

Examples

The sentences below contain comparison words. Notice how these words show that things are *alike* in some way.

● The carpet was so old and faded it looked *like* a gray shadow.

● Parents today often dislike the music their children listen to, *just as* their own parents disliked the Beatles or the Rolling Stones.

● Tattoos, which used to be seen as lower class, are part of our culture today. *Likewise*, many middle-class people now have body piercings.

> *To the Instructor:* Remind students to use the hint on
> page 263 as they complete these sentences.

PRACTICE 3

Complete each sentence with a suitable comparison word or phrase from the box on the previous page. Try to use a variety of transitions.   *Answers may vary.*

1. Bats and frogs hibernate during the winter, _____just as_____ bears do.

2. Many Hispanic girls have a special party for their fifteenth birthday. _____Similarly_____, Anglo girls often celebrate their sixteenth birthday in a special way.

3. Good teachers are _____as_____ skilled in praising what students have accomplished as they are in challenging them to do more.

4. We are often attracted to people who have a social and religious background _____similar_____ to our own.

5. As we turned onto the country road, the view in front of us—a bright rainbow rising over a gentle hill—looked _____just like_____ a scene in a fairy tale.

Words That Show Contrast

Check (✓) the item that is easier to understand:

✓ The weather in Florida is usually wonderful, but the summers are hot and humid.

____ The weather in Florida is usually wonderful. The summers are hot and humid.

In the second item, we're not sure if the author feels that the weather in Florida is wonderful *because of* or *in spite of* the hot and humid summers. The transition *but* in the first item makes the relationship clear: the weather in Florida is wonderful in spite of the summer heat and humidity. *But* and words like it are known as contrast words.

"That's the difference between us.
You like to read at meals, and I like to talk."

Contrast words signal differences. A contrast word shows that two things *differ* in one or more ways. Contrast words also inform us that something is going to *differ from* what we might expect. In the cartoon above, the woman uses the word *difference* to contrast what her husband likes to do at meals (read) with what she likes to do (talk).

Here are some common words that show contrast:

Contrast Words

but	instead	still	difference
yet	in contrast	as opposed to	different(ly)
however	on the other hand	in spite of	differs from
although	on the contrary	despite	unlike
nevertheless	even though	rather than	while

Examples

The sentences below contain contrast words. Notice how these words signal that one idea is *different from* another idea.

● *Although* the movie had an exciting plot, the actors in the lead roles were not very convincing.

● A laptop computer is convenient and portable; *on the other hand*, a desktop computer is usually less expensive.

● Only 10 percent of the population is left-handed. *In contrast*, of babies that are born more than two months prematurely, 54 percent are left-handed.

PRACTICE 4   *Assigned for homework*

Complete each sentence with a suitable contrast word or phrase from the box on the previous page. Try to use a variety of transitions.   *Answers may vary.*

1. Our Toyota is ten years old, _____ but _____ it still runs perfectly.

2. _____ Although _____ many people own running shoes, most of these people are not runners.

3. American women have been dyeing their hair for years. American men, _____ on the other hand _____, only recently started coloring theirs.

4. _____ Despite _____ the fact that the sign in the corner market window said "Open," the door was locked and no one was in sight.

5. Fast-food chains sell French fries for prices much higher than what they paid for them. The farmer who planted and grew the potatoes, _____ however _____, doesn't get such a good deal. Out of every $1.50 that you spend on a large order of French fries, maybe 2¢ goes to the farmer.

Comparison and contrast transitions often signal the pattern of organization known as the comparison-contrast pattern.

The Comparison-Contrast Pattern

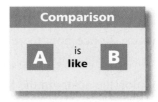

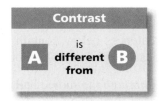

To understand the comparison-contrast pattern, arrange the following group of sentences in an order that makes sense. Put a *1* in front of the sentence that should come first, a *2* in front of the sentence that comes next, and a *3* in front of the sentence that should be last. The result will be a short paragraph. Then read the explanation that follows.

  2   The snakes have <u>similar</u> markings: red, yellow, and black bands.

  1   The coral snake and the milk snake may look <u>alike,</u> <u>but</u> there's an important <u>difference</u> between them.

  3   <u>However</u>, the milk snake is harmless, <u>while</u> the coral snake is very poisonous.

The first sentence of this paragraph is the general one, the one with the main idea: "The coral snake and the milk snake may look alike, but there's an important difference between them." The words *alike, but*, and *difference* suggest a comparison-contrast pattern. As the comparison word *similar* and the contrast words *however* and *while* suggest, the other two sentences do in fact compare and contrast two things: "The snakes have similar markings: red, yellow, and black bands. However, the milk snake is harmless, while the coral snake is very poisonous."

The **comparison-contrast pattern** shows how two things are alike or how they are different, or both. When things are compared, their similarities are pointed out. When things are contrasted, their differences are discussed.

Authors often find it useful to compare and/or contrast. Here are two examples.

Comparison

[1]House cats and their larger relatives, jungle cats, have traits in common. [2]Both have eyes suited for night vision, and both prefer to sleep by day and move about at night. [3]Also, just as pet cats use their tails to keep their balance and show emotions, so do lions and other large cats. [4]In addition, both kinds of cats can leap great distances. [5]Finally, cats at home are not the only ones that purr: cats in the wild also purr when content.

Contrast

[1]Times have changed, and I know this because I have children, two of them, one born in the old days and one in modern times. [2]One was born back before seat belts, when a child might ride standing up in the front seat next to Daddy as he drove 75 mph across North Dakota, and nobody said boo, though nowadays Daddy would do jail time for that. [3]In contrast, my younger child rides in a podlike car seat, belted in like a little test pilot. [4]She likes it. [5]Another difference is that the older child grew up inhaling clouds of secondary smoke, while the younger one lives in a house in which nobody even thinks about smoking.

Check Your Understanding

In the following paragraph, the main idea is stated in the first sentence. As is often the case, the main idea suggests a paragraph's pattern of organization. Here the transition *differ* is a hint that the paragraph may be organized in a comparison-contrast pattern. Read the paragraph, and answer the questions below. Then read the explanation that follows.

[1]Humans differ from other primates, but not as much as one might think. [2]It's true that there are important differences in size and shape between humans and other primates. [3]And, of course, humans are by far the more intelligent. [4]It is also true that there are striking similarities between the two. [5]To use chimpanzees as an example, both they and humans have the same muscles and bones, located in almost the same places and working in nearly the same ways. [6]The internal organs of both animals are also very much alike, as are their blood and other body fluids. [7]Seen under a microscope, even their genes are strikingly similar.

1. Is this paragraph comparing, contrasting, or both? _____Both_____

2. What two things are being compared and/or contrasted? _____
    Humans and other primates
    _____

3. Write out four of the comparison and/or contrast words that are used in the
    paragraph. _____Any four of the following: differ, but, differences,_____
    similarities, both, same, alike, similar
    _____

Explanation

The paragraph both compares and contrasts—it discusses both similarities and differences. First, it contrasts humans and other primates in terms of size, shape, and intelligence. The words used to indicate that contrast are *differ, but*, and *differences*. The paragraph also discusses similarities between humans and other primates—in their muscles, bones, internal organs, body fluids, and genes. The words used to indicate comparison are *similarities*, *both, same, alike*, and *similar*.

To the Instructor: In the paragraphs in the practices and tests that follow, the main ideas and transitions relevant to the pattern of organization are underlined in this *Instructor's Edition*.

PRACTICE 5

The following passages use the pattern of comparison or contrast. Read each passage and answer the questions which follow.   *Wording of answers may vary.*

A. ¹The lives and deaths of two assassinated Presidents, Abraham Lincoln and John F. Kennedy, contain a number of odd <u>similarities</u>. ²Lincoln was elected to Congress in 1846; Kennedy was elected to Congress in 1946. ³Lincoln was elected President in 1860, and Kennedy in 1960. ⁴<u>Both</u> presidents were shot on a Friday, and <u>both</u> were shot in the head. ⁵After their deaths, they were succeeded by men with the <u>same</u> name: Johnson. ⁶Lincoln's assassin, John Wilkes Booth, was born in 1839, while Kennedy's killer, Lee Harvey Oswald, was born in 1939. ⁷<u>Both</u> presidents' assassins were themselves murdered before they could stand trial.

Check (✓) the pattern used in this paragraph:

__✓__ Comparison   ____ Contrast

The passage compares the lives and deaths of Presidents Lincoln and Kennedy. Comparison words: similarities, both, and same.

What two things are being compared or contrasted?

1. _____Abraham Lincoln_____   2. _____John F. Kennedy_____

B. ¹High school and college offer very <u>different</u> educational experiences for students. ²In high school, teachers often treat students like children. ³For instance, teachers may call parents if a student skips class or fails to hand in an assignment. ⁴<u>On the other hand</u>, college teachers treat students like adults. ⁵Students are expected to take full responsibility for their attendance and their work. ⁶Also, in high school, students typically live at home and depend on their parents. ⁷In college, <u>however</u>, students live in apartments (or dorms) and have no one to depend on but themselves.

Check (✓) the pattern used in this paragraph:

____ Comparison   __✓__ Contrast

What two things are being compared or contrasted?

1. _____High school_____   2. _____College_____

The passage contrasts students' experiences in high school and college. Contrast words: different, On the other hand, and however.

3 Cause and Effect

Words That Show Cause and Effect

Check (✓) the item that is easier to understand:

_____ Nina cares for her elderly parents. She has very little free time.

__✓__ Because Nina cares for her elderly parents, she has very little free time.

In the first item, we are not sure of the relationship between the two sentences. Does Nina have little free time *with which* to care for her parents? Or does she have little free time *because* she cares for her parents? The word *because* in the second item shows the connection between the two ideas. *Because* and words like it are known as cause and effect words.

"The reason I got the promotion is that I always dress for success."

Copyright © by Randy Glasbergen.
www.glasbergen.com

Cause and effect words signal that the author is explaining *the reason why* something happened or *the result* of something happening. In the cartoon above, the dog explains that dressing for success (the *cause*) has led to his promotion (the *effect*).

Here are some common cause and effect words:

Cause and Effect Words

therefore	so	because (of)	thus
(as a) result	effect	as a consequence	results in
cause	explanation	consequently	led to
affect	due to	since	reason

Examples

The following items contain cause and effect words. Notice how these words introduce a *reason* for something or a *result* of something.

- People eat fewer hamburgers today than they did in the past. *Therefore*, fast-food restaurants have developed new items for their menus.

- *Because* roses are considered the flowers of romance, many people give them for Valentine's Day.

- Digital cameras do not require the use of film; *as a result*, they have become more popular than conventional cameras.

To the Instructor: Remind students to use the hint on page 263 as they complete these sentences.

PRACTICE 6

Complete each sentence with a suitable cause and effect word or phrase from the box on the previous page. Try to use a variety of transitions. *Answers may vary.*

1. _____Because_____ there's no room in your mouth for your wisdom teeth, they will have to be removed.

2. Gail wanted a large wedding reception. _____Therefore_____, her parents had to rent a hall.

3. The construction of a Home Depot and a Wal-Mart right outside of the town _____resulted in_____ the closing of a number of small businesses in the area.

4. Elephants were killed for many years for the valuable ivory in their tusks. ___As a result___, the elephant population declined significantly.

5. The _____reason_____ our skin wrinkles when we're in the water a long time is that the top layer of skin absorbs much more water than the bottom one.

Cause and effect transitions often signal the cause and effect pattern of organization.

The Cause and Effect Pattern

Arrange the following group of sentences in an order that makes sense. Put a *1* in front of the sentence that should come first, a *2* in front of the sentence that comes next, and a *3* in front of the sentence that should be last. The result will be a short paragraph. Then read the explanation that follows.

  _3_   Accidents are also <u>caused</u> by speeding, as drivers try to get home as quickly as possible.

  _1_   Traffic accidents are more likely to <u>result</u> during evening rush hour.

  _2_   <u>Because</u> drivers are tired at the end of the day, they are not able to respond quickly enough to changes in traffic.

As the words *result*, *Because*, and *caused* suggest, this paragraph is organized in a cause and effect pattern. In paragraph form, the sentences would read as follows:

> [1]Traffic accidents are more likely to result during evening rush hour. [2]Because drivers are tired at the end of the day, they are not able to respond quickly enough to changes in traffic. [3]Accidents are also caused by speeding, as drivers try to get home as quickly as possible.

The paragraph begins with an effect—that more accidents occur during rush hour—and then follows with two causes.

Information in a **cause and effect pattern** addresses the questions "Why does a behavior or event happen?" and/or "What are the results of a behavior or event?" An author may then discuss causes, or effects, or both causes and effects.

Authors usually don't just tell *what* happened. They both describe what has happened and try to explain *why*. For example, a sociology textbook would not just say that the test scores of American students have declined for most of the last thirty years. The book would also explain the likely *causes* of this decline. Or a health textbook would not just describe the ways that medical care has changed in the last few years. It would also examine the *reasons* for such changes.

Check Your Understanding

Read the paragraph below and see if you can answer the questions about cause and effect. Then read the explanation to see how you did.

¹Experts point out four reasons why the divorce rate has increased in the United States. ²One explanation is a lack of time for many couples to work at their marriage. ³With husband and wife often holding down jobs outside the home, there may be little energy for everything else that goes into a partnership. ⁴Another cause is the "me-first" attitude in today's society. ⁵Some people put their own personal happiness ahead of the well-being of a spouse and family. ⁶In addition, women now have more freedom of choice. ⁷Their ability to support themselves means that they can more easily leave an unhappy marriage. ⁸Finally, because divorce is so much more common, it has also become more socially acceptable. ⁹People are no longer embarrassed to say they are divorced.

Wording of answers may vary.

1. What are the four *causes* described in this paragraph?

   a. Lack of time to work at marriage

   b. "Me-first" attitude

   c. Women's greater freedom of choice

   d. Divorce now more socially acceptable

2. What is the *effect* of these causes?

   Higher divorce rate in the United States.

3. What three cause-effect transitions are used?

   a. explanation

   b. cause

   c. because

Explanation

The paragraph presents four causes: lack of time to work at the marriage, the "me-first" attitude in today's society, more freedom of choice for women, and divorce becoming more socially acceptable. The four causes lead to one effect: the increased divorce rate. The cause-effect transitions used are *explanation, cause,* and *because.*

PRACTICE 7

A. Read the paragraph below, looking for the **one** effect and the **two** causes. Then complete the map that follows. (The effect has been added for you.)

The *effect:* increase in numbers of overweight Japanese adults (sentences 2–3). The *causes:* lifestyle change (sentence 5) and diet changes (sentences 6–7).

¹For centuries, Japan had one of the lowest rates of obesity in the world. ²But that is changing. ³About a quarter of adult Japanese are now considered significantly overweight. ⁴Two reasons in particular explain this weight gain among the Japanese. ⁵For one thing, lifestyles have become less active as more and more rural Japanese move into cities. ⁶More importantly, many Japanese are turning away from their traditional low-fat diet emphasizing rice, fish, and vegetables. ⁷They are instead adopting a more Western diet that features lots of processed food that is high in fat. *Wording of answers may vary.*

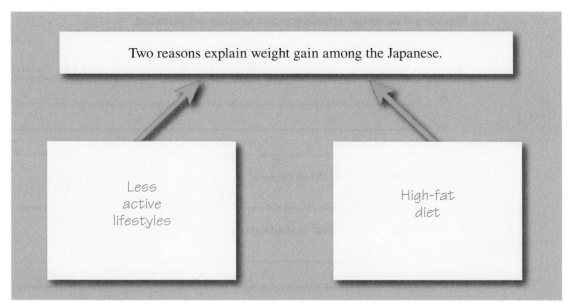

Two reasons explain weight gain among the Japanese.

Less active lifestyles

High-fat diet

B. Read the paragraph below, looking for the **one** cause and the **three** effects. Then complete the outline that follows. *Wording of answers may vary.*

¹Increases in the numbers of elderly people will have a major impact in Europe, Canada, and the United States. ²One effect of the aging of these populations is that the number of working-age people will go sharply down, leaving fewer people available to fill jobs. ³Also, as the number of retired people increases, there will be a bigger demand on the countries' pension systems. ⁴A third effect will be an immense strain on national medical services. ⁵Elderly people draw upon far more of a society's health-care services than do young people.

Main idea (*the cause*):___Increases in the numbers of elderly people will have a major impact in Europe, Canada, and the United States.___

      Major supporting details (*the effects*):

        1. ___Fewer people available to fill jobs___.

        2. ___Bigger demand on pension systems___.

        3. ___Great strain on national medical services___.

        Sentence 1 states the *cause:* increases in the numbers of elderly people. The three *effects* are stated in sentences 2, 3, and 4.

A Note on Main Ideas and Patterns of Organization

As mentioned on page 236, a paragraph's main idea often indicates its pattern of organization. Try, for instance, to guess the pattern of the paragraph with this main idea:

> For various reasons, as many as half of all battered women do not leave their abusive husbands.

The word *reasons* suggests that the author is using a cause-effect pattern. The paragraph will go on to explain the reasons why many abused women stay with their husbands.

    Recognizing a main idea, and the pattern of organization that may be implied in a main idea, are both helpful steps in understanding the material in a paragraph.

 PRACTICE 8

Most of the main ideas below have been taken from college textbooks. In the space provided, write the letter of the pattern of organization that each suggests.

__B__ 1. One of the major <u>differences</u> between men and women is their degree of aggression.

       A. Definition and   B. Comparison-   C. Cause and effect
          example   contrast

__A__ 2. A <u>stereotype</u> is an oversimplified, inaccurate mental picture of others, such as the idea that the poor are lazy.

       A. Definition and   B. Comparison-   C. Cause and effect
          example   contrast

___C___ 3. People often form strong first impressions of others for unusual <u>reasons</u>.
   A. Definition and   B. Comparison-   C. Cause and effect
      example   contrast

___B___ 4. The eyes of newborns are both <u>similar</u> to and <u>different</u> from those of adults.
   A. Definition and   B. Comparison-   C. Cause and effect
      example   contrast

___C___ 5. Strong emotions tend to <u>affect</u> the flow of digestive juices and upset digestion.
   A. Definition and   B. Comparison-   C. Cause and effect
      example   contrast

___A___ 6. <u>Self-esteem</u> refers to how one feels about oneself; people with low self-esteem, <u>for instance</u>, do not like themselves.
   A. Definition and   B. Comparison-   C. Cause and effect
      example   contrast

___C___ 7. Viruses that <u>cause</u> colds and flu are often spread through sneezing, coughing, and unsanitary habits.
   A. Definition and   B. Comparison-   C. Cause and effect
      example   contrast

___B___ 8. Irish-Americans were once harshly discriminated against in the United States, <u>just as</u> Italian immigrants were.
   A. Definition and   B. Comparison-   C. Cause and effect
      example   contrast

___A___ 9. A <u>closed shop</u> is a business with an employment agreement that requires the company to hire only union workers.
   A. Definition and   B. Comparison-   C. Cause and effect
      example   contrast

___C___ 10. Childhood dental problems in the United States have decreased significantly <u>because of</u> the widespread use of fluoride in drinking water and toothpaste.
   A. Definition and   B. Comparison-   C. Cause and effect
      example   contrast

A Final Point

Keep in mind that a paragraph or a longer passage sometimes contains more than one pattern of organization. For instance, the paragraph in this chapter about the reasons for the increased divorce rate in the United States uses a cause-effect pattern. But the reasons themselves—lack of time to work at the marriage, a "me-first" attitude, more freedom of choice for women, and the greater social acceptability of divorce—are presented as a list of items. In other words, the paragraph combines two patterns.

Or consider the following passage:

cause/effect ¹People with more wealth tend to have more power. ²This fact is apparent in the domination of top government positions by the wealthy. ³Higher-income persons are also more likely to feel a strong sense of power. ⁴<u>As a result</u>, they are more likely to be politically active, working to keep or increase their power. ⁵<u>In *compare/ contrast* contrast</u>, lower-income people are more likely to feel powerless to influence major political decisions. ⁶Therefore, they are more indifferent to politics and less likely to be involved in political activity.

The paragraph partly uses a contrast pattern, noting the *difference* between higher-income people and lower-income people with regard to political activity. But it also uses a cause-effect pattern: it describes the *effect* of feeling a sense of power or feeling no sense of power.

CHAPTER REVIEW

In this chapter, you learned about three kinds of relationships that authors use to make their ideas clear:

● **Definitions and examples**

— To help readers understand the important ideas and terms in a subject, textbook authors often take time to include key definitions (often setting them off in *italic* or **boldface**) and examples of those definitions. When reading a textbook, it is usually a good idea to mark off both definitions and examples.

— Transition words that signal the definition and example pattern include *for example* and *for instance*.

(Continues on next page)

- ● **Comparison and/or contrast**

    — Authors often discuss how two things are alike or how they are different, or both.

    — Transition words that signal comparisons include *alike* and *similar*.

    — Transition words that signal contrasts include *but* and *however*.

- ● **Cause and effect**

    — Authors often discuss the reasons why something happens or the effects of something that has happened.

    — Transition words that signal causes and effects include *reason*, *because*, and *therefore*.

Note that pages 307–312 list and offer practice in all the transitions and patterns of organization you have studied in "Relationships I" and "Relationships II."

The next chapter—Chapter 8—will develop your skill in making inferences about what you read.

On the Web: If you are using this book in class, you can visit our website for additional practice in understanding relationships that involve examples, comparison or contrast, and cause and effect. Go to **www.townsendpress.com** and click on "Online Learning Center."

Homework

REVIEW TEST 1

To review what you've learned in this chapter, write the letter of each correct answer in the space provided.

___C___ 1. Words such as *but, although*, and *however* are known as
- A. cause and effect words.
- B. illustration words.   See page 269.
- C. contrast words.

___B___ 2. Words such as *for example, for instance*, and *including* are known as
- A. definition words.
- B. illustration words.   See page 262.
- C. cause and effect words.

___C___ 3. Words such as *reason, because,* and *therefore* are known as
   A. comparison words.
   B. definition words.   See page 274.
   C. cause and effect words.

___A___ 4. Words such as *likewise, in the same way,* and *just as* are known as
   A. comparison words.
   B. definition words.   See page 267.
   C. cause and effect words.

___C___ 5. When textbook authors provide a definition of a term, they often help
   make that definition clear by providing one or more
   A. comparisons.
   B. causes.   See pages 264–265.
   C. examples.

REVIEW TEST 2

A. (1–2.) Name the type of transition used in each of the following cartoons.

"The reason you should hire me is that I can really bring home the bacon."

"The trouble is my wife and I are exactly the same. We both like to spend more money than we earn."

___C___ 1. A. Example
           B. Comparison
           C. Cause and effect

___B___ 2. A. Example
           B. Comparison
           C. Cause and effect

Item 1: *Cause:* I can bring home the bacon.
Effect: You should hire me.
Cause-effect word: *reason.*

Item 2: The statement compares
the wife with the husband.
Comparison words: *same, both.*

B. Complete each sentence by filling in the blank with one of the transitions in the box. Use each word once. Then write the letter of the word in the space provided.

A. for example	B. however	C. like	D. therefore

___C___ 3. Transitions are _____like_____ bridges—they carry the reader across from one thought to another.

___D___ 4. Sports injuries can keep even a champion on the sidelines. _____Therefore_____, experts urge every athlete to do warm-up exercises, which help prevent injuries.

___A___ 5. Clothes reflect society's values. _____For example_____, in Victorian times, when women were expected to be inactive, they wore clothing that limited their movements.

___B___ 6. Research shows that married people are healthier than people who have never been married. Marriage does pose one health hazard, _____however_____: weight gain. Married men are more likely to be overweight.

C. Below are the beginnings of four passages. Label each one with the letter of its pattern of organization. (You may find it helpful to underline the transition or transitions in each item.)

    A Definition and example
    B Comparison-contrast
    C Cause and effect

___C___ 7. [1]<u>Because</u> there are so few parking spaces downtown, people have had to change their shopping habits. [2]One <u>effect</u> of the lack of parking is that shoppers are going to suburban malls instead of downtown stores. [3]Another <u>consequence</u> has been significant growth in online shopping. . . .

___B___ 8. [1]There have always been homeless people in the United States. [2]But the homeless today <u>differ</u> in some ways from their counterparts of thirty years ago. . . .

___A___ 9. [1]<u>Snap judgments</u> are opinions formed on the spot, often on little evidence. [2]One <u>instance</u> of such a judgment is deciding that someone is a no-good after meeting him or her briefly at a party. . . .

_C_ 10. ¹There are several <u>reasons</u> why travelers so often become ill. ²The unfamiliar foods and water in foreign countries cause digestive upsets. ³Fatigue—from jet lag and the strain and exertion of traveling—lowers travelers' resistance. ⁴Finally, travelers may be exposed to infectious diseases to which their bodies have never developed any natural immunity. . . .

REVIEW TEST 3

Read each paragraph and answer the questions that follow.

A. ¹Recent studies indicate that male and female babies act very <u>differently</u> after only a few <u>months of life</u>. ²Baby girls seem to be more interested in people. ³They can recognize individual faces and voices at four months, well before baby boys can. ⁴In addition, they begin to smile and speak earlier than boys, and their vocabularies are larger. ⁵<u>In contrast</u>, baby boys react to objects with as much interest as they react to human beings. ⁶They will try to talk to the brightly colored toys that hang over their cribs just as often as they will try to talk to a parent. ⁷And before long, they will attempt to take these objects apart.

_C_ 1. The main pattern of organization of the selection is
   A. definition-example.
   B. cause-effect.
   C. comparison-contrast.

   The paragraph contrasts male and female babies.

2. One transition that signals the paragraph's pattern of organization is
   differently or In contrast .

B. ¹Events <u>leading to</u> alcohol abuse in the United States took place in the eighteenth century. ²At that time, developments in agriculture had <u>caused</u> a surplus of grain. ³Farmers in the Midwest wanted to sell their surplus grain on the East Coast, which was more heavily populated. ⁴The most profitable way to do this was to convert the extra grain into something Easterners would buy: whiskey. ⁵<u>As a result</u>, whiskey production rose. ⁶And the increase in whiskey <u>led to</u> an increase in its use. ⁷Before long, alcohol consumption in the country rose to alarming proportions.

_B_ 3. The main pattern of organization of the selection is
   A. definition-example.
   B. cause-effect.
   C. comparison-contrast.

   The paragraph discusses the causes of alcohol abuse in the United States during the eighteenth century.

4. One transition that signals the paragraph's pattern of organization is
   leading to or caused or As a result or led to .

C. ¹An altruistic person is someone who will help others even when he or she expects no benefits in return. ²Consider the example of one of the passengers on a plane that crashed into the Potomac River one cold January day in 1982. ³Most of the passengers died under the ice, but six passengers escaped into the icy waters. ⁴Every time a life preserver was lowered by a helicopter, one man passed it on to one of the other five. ⁵When the helicopter had lifted out all five, it returned to pick up that last survivor. ⁶But he had disappeared under the ice.

___A___ 5. The main pattern of organization of the paragraph is
   A. definition and example.
   B. contrast.
   C. cause and effect.

> The paragraph defines and provides an example of the term *altruistic person.*

6. One transition that signals the paragraph's pattern of organization is
   _____ *example* _____.

D. ¹As news sources, websites have several advantages over newspapers. ²Online news sources can publish a story within minutes of an event happening, or continually update an existing story. ³On the other hand, a daily newspaper is published just once a day. ⁴Websites are more friendly to the environment; they require no raw material, while newspapers mean the destruction of many trees. ⁵And the search feature on most news websites lets readers find the story they want quickly, as opposed to wading through many pages looking for it.

___B___ 7. The main pattern of organization of the paragraph is
   A. definition and example.
   B. comparison-contrast.
   C. cause and effect.

> The passage contrasts news websites and newspapers.

8. One transition that signals the paragraph's pattern of organization is
   _____ *On the other hand or while or as opposed to* _____.

E. ¹Although caffeine is the world's most widely consumed drug, few of its users realize how powerful it is. ²Caffeine is a drug that acts fast. ³In less than five minutes after you've drunk a cup of coffee, caffeine is racing to every part of your body. ⁴Its effects are many, including increasing the flow of urine and stomach acid, relaxing involuntary muscles, and stepping up the intake of oxygen. ⁵Caffeine also boosts the pumping strength of the heart, and too much caffeine can cause an irregular heartbeat. ⁶A small dose of caffeine can improve your performance as you type or drive, but the effect of too much caffeine is that you'll feel shaky and unsteady.

___C___ 9. The main pattern of organization of the paragraph is
      A. definition and example.
      B. contrast.
      C. cause and effect.

> The paragraph discusses the effects of caffeine on the body.

    10. One transition that signals the paragraph's pattern of organization is

effects or cause or effect
_____.

REVIEW TEST 4

Here is a chance to apply your understanding of transitions and patterns of organization to a selection about the power of touching. Human beings can be very strong. We can come back from serious disease and injury and can survive terrible loss. But as strong as we are, we still need physical contact—as the following selection points out.

To help you continue to strengthen your skills, the reading is followed by questions not only on what you've learned in this chapter but also on what you've learned in previous chapters.

Words to Watch

Below are some words in the reading that do not have strong context support. Each word is followed by the number of the paragraph in which it appears and its meaning there. These words are indicated in the selection by a small circle (°).

> *grafts* (2): transplants
> *hesitant* (4): uncertain
> *unconditional* (7): total, absolute
> *regressed* (9): went backward
> *untouchables* (13): in India, persons of lowest status in society
> *dignity* (13): sense of self-worth
> *conceivably* (17): possibly
> *embedded* (19): set into
> *recoil* (20): shrink back
> *lavish* (24): give plentifully

WIRED FOR TOUCH

Deborah Grandinetti

1   He had been a good-looking kid. Nice face. Good bone structure. A well-built, muscular body.

2   That was before the fire. Afterward, his back, neck, and arms were never the same. He went through a long and painful series of skin grafts°. Once he was released from the hospital, he never again left the house without wearing a long-sleeved, collared shirt, even on the hottest of days.

3   For years, he lived with his mother. She provided him with the tender, loving care only a mother could. In her eyes, he was still the same beautiful young man.

4   He was 28 when she died. The loss must have been unbearable. And he must have said as much to those who cared about him, because someone urged him to visit a massage therapist. I can only imagine how hesitant° he was at first, how scary it must have been to consider the reaction he might get when he took his shirt off for a complete stranger.

5   But he was in pain and barely hanging on. So he pushed past the fear and asked for referrals. One name kept coming up, and he called this massage therapist even though her office was more than 90 minutes away. He liked what she said and how she sounded, so he made an appointment.

6   The therapist who met with him said later, "When I saw his terrible scars, I had to go very deep within myself to draw strength."

7   She did. She opened her heart wide, letting go of any feelings of shock and disgust at his appearance. She also said a silent prayer, asking that she be guided to give this client just what he needed. As she did, the energy of loving, unconditional° regard for this young man began to flow through her. And this is what her touch communicated as she massaged his damaged skin.

8   The quality of her touch seemed to relax him. He let down his guard. And then, about halfway through the massage, he wept—tears of loss and release.

9   "What I felt, under my hands, is that emotionally he had regressed° since his mother's death," she said. "I got the sense that he didn't know how to be in the world without her." Part of him feared that he wouldn't be able to survive this second loss.

10   Slowly, but surely, the massage helped him know—at a level deeper than words—that he was seen and fully accepted by a woman other than his mother. It told him that he was still worthy of love and goodness. That knowledge helped give him the strength to go on.

11   He returned twice after that. Each time he left, he looked a little more relaxed, a little more alive.

12   Such is the power of touch. Sometimes, it is even more necessary than food to "feed" a person's sense of well-being.

started her 1st school under a tree w/ a drawing w/a stick in the dirt

13   The Nobel Peace Prize winner Mother Teresa knew this. She often said that more people die from lack of love than from poverty, hunger, or other physical suffering. That's why she actively reached out to society's "untouchables°," often feeding them or tending to their wounds with her own hands. She knew that her caring touch helped restore their sense of dignity°.

14   A San Francisco massage therapist who visited Mother Teresa in India was so inspired by what she saw that she came home with a new sense of purpose. The therapist decided she would make her massage services available to the city's homeless at no charge. She also decided to teach other interested massage therapists how to work with the homeless. She knew that massage was not only a way to help a homeless individual rebuild a sense of self-esteem, but also a way to gain that person's trust, so that he or she might be more willing to take advantage of other available social services. Over ten years ago she opened a Care Through Touch Institute that still provides training and service to the poor.

15   "When you touch another—whether a person, plant, or animal—you make a connection, and they make a connection with you," the therapist explained. "There is an invisible thread of energy that goes back and forth. Who knows who is giving and who is receiving?"

16   Clearly, caring touch is a powerful method for healing. It is of benefit to everyone: rich and poor, young and old,

healthy and ill. Experts say that caring touch has measurable effects. It can lower blood pressure, raise immunity, and decrease depression. It can also—even if given only briefly—influence behavior, as a number of studies show.

17   Something as simple as a firm handshake, for instance, can create an instant good impression of the individual who gives it. In fact, a University of Iowa study suggests that a solid handshake may be more important than a resumé for landing a job. The professor who performed the study says the warm handshake sets the tone for the rest of the interview. Conceivably°, it could set the tone for any important meeting, so it's a good social grace to master.

18   Similarly, studies have shown that waitresses who touch the customer's hand or arm in a light, friendly way when they return the check are likely to get higher tips. An even more fascinating study shows that adults who received a

friendly pat on the back from a female financial adviser were more willing to take a risk with their money than those who were not touched. Researchers guessed that the woman's touch evoked the feelings of security that comes from a mother's touch. As a result, there was a willingness to take greater risks.

19   What gives touch its power? Why is it that a human being can survive without hearing, or sight, but wither without touch? It could be that we human beings were *designed* to touch and be touched. Consider that we have two eyes and two ears, but *five million* nerve endings embedded° in our skin, each ready to be triggered by touch. And we certainly have plenty of touchable skin—roughly 18 square feet if it were laid flat—making skin the body's largest organ.

20   A University of California at Berkeley science professor calls touch "the first language we learn . . . our richest means of emotional expression" throughout life. He is right about touch being the "first language." In fact, our sense of touch develops while we are still in our mother's womb. By the seventh week of life, our lips are sensitive to touch. By the eighth week of life, we have enough sensitivity to touch to recoil° from a pinprick. By the twelfth week, our own hands are fully formed.

21   The ears and eyes, however, take longer to develop. It takes about six months of development in the womb to fully hear and respond to sound. (We won't have the ability to recognize the source of that sound until about four months after birth, however.) And it takes seven months in the womb for all of the working parts in the eyes to develop. After birth, it then takes another four months before we can focus our eyes on a moving object and reach toward where it is. In contrast, full sensitivity to touch is present before, during, and after birth. So touch is what first helps us make full contact with the world outside the womb. No wonder that a lack of touch can make us feel disconnected.

22   For babies, lots of cuddling, holding, and loving contact is essential for healthy development. This contact is just as important to the baby's well-being as making sure the baby is well fed and changing diapers when they are soiled. Studies of babies who were orphaned in Romania bear this out. Although the caretakers were able to feed and change the babies, they did not hold or cuddle them. Researchers found that the children's thinking and social skills were poorer than those of children of the same age who had received plenty of cuddling and holding. The lack of touch had a measurable negative effect on the brain development of those orphans.

23   Even simple touch—such as an arm around the shoulder, a gentle squeeze, or ruffling of the hair, if done often enough—can be very effective in helping a child go from sad to sunny. Phyllis Spangler, a working mother and writer with seven children, found this to be true. She was struggling to help her middle child, six-year-old Debbie, who seemed to need far more time and attention than Phyllis had to give. When

Debbie didn't get the positive attention she longed for, she'd withdraw more and more into her own world. Even her teachers could see how unhappy the little girl was.

24   Phyllis was at a loss to resolve the problem until a family therapist suggested she become more physically affectionate. So Phyllis began to lavish° touch on Debbie and her other children. In a few short weeks, Phyllis saw a big difference. All that touch brought Debbie alive. She smiled and laughed more, as Phyllis explained in an essay she wrote about her parenting experience. Debbie was also more eager to talk and share. It seems that more touch, rather than just more time with Mom, was the answer.

25   Curious, isn't it, how something so simple can make such a big difference? Or maybe it's not—when you consider those five million nerve endings embedded in human skin. They suggest we are literally wired for touch. With this fact in mind, it may be that all the handshakes and hugs that seem to be part of our culture these days are not just for show. They are also serving a good purpose in keeping us connected with one another.

Reading Comprehension Questions

Vocabulary in Context

_A_   1. In the sentence below, the word *evoked* (ĭ-vōkd′) means
   A. brought to mind.
   B. destroyed.
   C. refused.
   D. decided.

What effect might a woman's touch have on a person's feelings of security?

"Researchers guessed that the woman's touch evoked the feelings of security that comes from a mother's touch." (Paragraph 18)

_D_   2. In the excerpt below, the word *wither* (wĭ′thər) means
   A. grow stronger.
   B. continue.
   C. communicate.
   D. become weak.

Antonym clue: *survive.*

"What gives touch its power? Why is it that a human being can survive without hearing, or sight, but wither without touch?" (Paragraph 19)

Central Point and Main Ideas

___C___ 3. Which sentence best expresses the central point of the selection?

Answer A covers only paragraphs 10–11. Answer B covers only paragraphs 20–21. Answer D covers only paragraph 19.

    A. Massage therapists can help people rebuild a sense of self-esteem.

    B. Our sense of touch develops while we are still in our mother's womb.

    C. Touch, the first language we learn, is necessary to all humans' physical and emotional well-being.

    D. Touch is powerful because we have only two eyes and two ears, but there are five million nerve endings embedded in our skin.

___B___ 4. Which sentence best expresses the main idea of paragraphs 17–18?

Answers A and D each cover only part of paragraph 18. Answer C covers only part of paragraph 17.

    A. Some people are more willing to spend money when someone touches them.

    B. Touch can be a positive factor in social and business interactions.

    C. A firm handshake may be more important in getting a job than a resumé.

    D. Some people feel a sense of security from a female financial advisor's touch.

Supporting Details

___B___ 5. According to the selection, Romanian orphans who were not held or cuddled

    A. developed in the same way as any other children.

    B. were found to have poorer thinking and social skills than other children.

                       See paragraph 22.

    C. never learned to talk.

    D. failed to develop physically.

___F___ 6. TRUE OR FALSE? The ears and eyes take less time to develop than the sense of touch.

                                  See paragraph 21.

Transitions

___D___ 7. The relationship expressed in the sentence below is one of

    A. addition.

    B. cause and effect.

                         Illustration signal: *for instance.*

    C. contrast.

    D. illustration.

"It can lower blood pressure, <u>for instance</u>, raise immunity, and decrease depression." (Paragraph 16)

___A___ 8. The relationship between the two sentences below is one of
   A. cause and effect.
   B. comparison.
   C. time.
   D. illustration.

> The words *as a result* signal a cause-effect relationship. *Cause:* feelings of security. *Effect:* willingness to take greater risks.

"Researchers guessed that the woman's touch evoked the feelings of security that comes from a mother's touch. As a result, there was a willingness to take greater risks." (Paragraph 18)

Patterns of Organization

___A___ 9. The pattern of organization of paragraphs 20–21 is mainly
   A. time order.
   B. addition.
   C. illustration.
   D. comparison.

> The paragraphs discuss the development of the senses over time. Note the time signals, such as *by the seventh week* and *it takes six months.*

___B___ 10. In paragraphs 23–24, Grandinetti
   A. defines the term "simple touch."
   B. contrasts what Debbie was like before her mother began to lavish touch on her and what she was like afterward.
   C. compares two similar experiences that Debbie had with her mother.
   D. explains why Debbie needed more attention than her brothers and sisters.

> The last three sentences of paragraph 23 describe what Debbie was like before being touched. Much of paragraph 24 describes how Debbie's behavior changed after "a few short weeks" of being touched more.

Discussion Questions

1. Why do you think Grandinetti begins the selection with the anecdote about the young man who had been badly burned? How does this anecdote relate to her central point?

2. Grandinetti mentions people such as waitresses and financial advisors who make a point of gently touching their clients. How would you feel about being touched in such situations? Do you think it would make you more willing to give a higher tip or take a risk with your money? Or might you react in some other way? Explain.

3. Some families often express affection through touch, while others don't. What was (or is) true of your family? Do you think that their expression of affection through touch (or lack of it) has affected you? Explain.

4. Most people would say that sight and hearing are the most important senses. However, Grandinetti feels differently. Do you agree with Grandinetti's conclusion that we are indeed "wired for touch"? Why or why not?

Note: Writing assignments for this selection appear on page 592.

Check Your Performance   **RELATIONSHIPS II**

Activity	Number Right	Points	Score
Review Test 1 (5 items)	_____	× 2 =	_____
Review Test 2 (10 items)	_____	× 3 =	_____
Review Test 3 (10 items)	_____	× 3 =	_____
Review Test 4 (10 items)	_____	× 3 =	_____
	TOTAL SCORE =		_____%

Enter your total score into the **Reading Performance Chart: Review Tests** on the inside back cover.

RELATIONSHIPS II: Mastery Test 1

A. Fill in each blank with an appropriate transition from the box. Use each transition once. Then, in the space provided, write the letter of the transition you have chosen.

A. as a result	**B.** because	**C.** for example
D. however	**E.** just as	

Hint: Make sure that each word or phrase that you choose fits smoothly into the flow of the sentence. Test your choices by reading each sentence to yourself.

___C___ 1. ¹If you go to a website for medical information, go to one recommended by doctors. ²____For example____, the famous Mayo Clinic offers a one-stop health center: **http://mayoclinic.com**.

The website http://mayoclinic.com is an example of a site recommended by doctors.

___A___ 2. ¹Small feet were admired in ancient China. ²____As a result____, some parents had their female infants' feet tightly bound. ³The feet then grew into a tiny deformed shape. ⁴Some of the women could barely walk.

As a result signals the cause (small feet were admired) and the effect (infants' feet were bound).

___E___ 3. ¹One way to own a book is to take possession by paying for it, ____just as____ you pay for clothes or furniture. ²But full ownership comes only when you have made the book a part of yourself by reading it closely.

Owning a book is being compared to owning clothes or furniture.

___D___ 4. ¹In many European countries, a kiss on the cheek is used as a greeting by men and women, regardless of the sex of the other person, or of how well they know each other. ²In Britain and Germany, ____however____, the cheek-kiss is used only between women, or between men and women who know each other well.

A kiss on the cheek in many European countries is being contrasted with a kiss on the cheek in England and Germany.

___B___ 5. ¹In the search for food, wood mice explore fields that don't contain many landmarks such as large rocks and tall trees. ²When they find new food sources, they build their own signposts out of piles of leaves, twigs, and seed casings. ³This method is safer than leaving scents that could be traced by enemies such as weasels. ⁴____Because____ of these signposts, wood mice are known as the only mammals other than humans that mark their trail.

Cause: Wood mice build signposts to food sources.
Effect: Wood mice are known as the only mammals other than humans that mark their trail with "signposts."

(Continues on next page)

B. Below are the beginnings of five passages. Label each one with the letter of its pattern of organization. (You may find it helpful to underline the transition or transitions in each item.)

    A Definition and example
    B Comparison-contrast
    C Cause and effect

  B 6. ¹The first railroad cars were very <u>similar</u> to horse-drawn carriages. ²<u>Both</u> were called "coaches" and held the same number of passengers—just six people. ³<u>Likewise</u>, train cars and horse carriages also featured the same shape, windows, and decorations. ⁴Even though trains could carry many more people than horses, builders simply followed old plans when they built the first cars for the "iron horse." . . .
      Early railroad cars are being compared to horse–drawn carriages.

  C 7. ¹The depression of the 1930s had powerful <u>effects</u> on families. ²It forced many couples to delay marriage. ³Another <u>effect</u> was a sharp drop in the divorce rate <u>because</u> many couples could not afford to keep up separate households. . . .
      Cause: the depression. *Effects:* delayed marriages, sharp drop in divorce rate.

  A 8. ¹Good listeners can paraphrase well. ²To <u>paraphrase</u> is to state in your own words what someone else has said. ³<u>For instance</u>, after a person has given you directions for getting to a certain place, you might paraphrase, saying, "In other words, what I should do is . . . " ⁴Or if someone tells you a story and you then tell that story to someone else in your own words, you would be paraphrasing the story. . . .

Term being defined: *paraphrase.*

  C 9. ¹Various experiments reveal there are several <u>reasons</u> why people will or will not help others. ²One <u>reason</u> is how deserving the victim is thought to be. ³This was shown in an experiment in which people pretended to be in need of help. ⁴If they carried a cane, they were helped more promptly than if they carried a liquor bottle. . . .

The passage presents a cause (reason) for why people help— or refuse to help— others.

  B 10. ¹<u>In contrast</u> to schools in other countries, the educational system in the United States can be seen as placing limits on teachers. ²Our teachers often cannot choose their own textbooks but must use whatever books are chosen by a local school board or district office. ³<u>On the other hand</u>, teachers in France are free to do their job in almost any way they want. ⁴Teachers are permitted to pick the books for their classes or even not to use any books. . . .
      The passage contrasts the limits on America's teachers with the limits on teachers in other countries.

RELATIONSHIPS II: Mastery Test 2

A. Read the textbook excerpts that follow and fill in each blank with an appropriate transition from the box. Use each transition once. Then, in the spaces provided, write the letter of the transition you have chosen.

A. explanation	**B.** for instance	**C.** however
D. same	**E.** therefore	

___A___ 1. [1]Why is it that about half of America's eligible voters do not take part in national elections? [2]One _____ explanation _____ may be that many of our political leaders do not appeal to voters.

           Explanation signals a *cause* (unappealing leaders) and an *effect* (low voter participation).

___B___ 2. [1]Importing is purchasing products in other nations and bringing them into one's own country. [2]_____ For instance _____, buyers for Target might purchase shirts in India or sneakers in Indonesia or raincoats in England and have them shipped to the United States for sale there.

           For instance signals an example of *importing*.

___E___ 3. [1]Before the 1900s it was widely believed that schoolwork "would make women sick" and would take blood away "from their wombs to their brains," so that they would be less suited to have children.

[2]_____ Therefore _____, women were often denied opportunities for higher education and were kept from entering many colleges and universities.   *Therefore* signals a *cause* (the belief that schoolwork would harm women) and an *effect* (women were denied a higher education).

___C___ 4. [1]For twenty years, Asian Americans were the fastest-growing minority in the United States. [2]They are now about 4 percent of the U.S. population. [3]_____ However _____, they are a much smaller minority than African Americans, who are more than 13 percent, and Latino Americans, who are now nearly 16 percent of the population.

    However signals the contrast between Asian Americans and other minority groups.

___D___ 5. [1]*For example* and *for instance* mean the _____ same _____ thing, just as *therefore* and *as a result* do. [2]Words and phrases with the same meaning allow authors to include more variety in their writing.

        Same signals a comparison between the groups of words.

(Continues on next page)

B. Below are parts of five passages. Label each one with the letter of its pattern of organization. (You may find it helpful to underline the transition or transitions in each item.)

    A Definition and example
    B Comparison-contrast
    C Cause and effect

    __B__ 6. ¹There are notable <u>differences</u> between people with high self-esteem and those with low self-esteem. ²People with good self-concepts tend to be more accepting of others and also more accepting of their own failures. ³<u>In contrast</u>, people with low self-esteem tend to be very critical of others. . . . *This passage contrasts people with high self–esteem and people with low self–esteem.*

Cause: Schools teach students to be passive and quiet. *Effect:* Little discussion in college classrooms.
    __C__ 7. ¹Schools all too often teach students to be passive, viewing instructors as experts who serve up "truth." ²Students are expected to quietly listen and take notes. ³<u>As a result</u>, researchers estimate, just 10 percent of college class time is used for discussion. . . .

    __B__ 8. ¹Stepfamilies and "natural" families have <u>similarities</u> and <u>differences</u>. ²<u>Both</u> types of families have a <u>similar</u> range of everyday values, and <u>both</u> types have backgrounds that tend to be <u>alike</u> as well. ³<u>However</u>, the stepfamily includes more people—ex-husbands, ex-wives, ex-in-laws, and various other relatives on <u>both</u> sides. ⁴Another <u>difference</u> is that the stepfamily has anger, guilt, and conflicts stemming from issues that "natural" families do not face. . . . *This passage compares and contrasts stepfamilies and "natural" families.*

    __C__ 9. ¹"Let's go shopping!" ²These familiar words echo across America like a battle cry. ³Every day, Americans get another fix of their favorite drug: shopping. ⁴There are probably several <u>causes</u> of this shopping madness. ⁵One <u>reason</u> is that we are competitive. ⁶If our neighbors have something, we want it as well, or we feel like losers or feel that we're losing out. . . . *Cause:* competitiveness. *Effect:* shopping madness.

    __A__ 10. ¹Great actors have more than talent. ²They also have a quality known as charisma—a mysterious "x" factor that can't be learned. ³<u>Charisma</u> is that extra something you can't describe but can feel flowing out of them, whether they are on stage or on the screen. ⁴<u>For example</u>, an acting teacher talked about seeing Marlon Brando in a play at the start of his career, before his name was known. ⁵"Suddenly a man came on the stage whom I had never seen or heard of. ⁶Before he even spoke, it was as if a leopard had entered the room." . . . *The passage defines and gives an example of charisma.*

RELATIONSHIPS II: Mastery Test 3

A. (1–4.) Arrange the scrambled sentences below into a logical paragraph by numbering them *1, 2, 3,* and *4* in an order that makes sense. Then, in the space provided, write the letter of the main pattern of organization used.

Note that transitions will help you by making clear the relationships between sentences.

  3   Another <u>result</u> is a higher proportion of male children than normal.

  2   First of all, it has <u>led to</u> a greater number of divorces.

  1   The Chinese policy of allowing only one child per family has had some disturbing <u>effects.</u>

  4   The major <u>reason</u> for this imbalance in the sexes seems to be abortions of female fetuses, <u>because</u> male children are preferred.

  C   5. The primary pattern of organization in the selection is
    A. comparison.
    B. contrast.
    C. cause and effect.
    D. definition and example.

The passage discusses effects of China's policy to allow just one child per family. First of all and another signal the two effects.

B. Read the paragraph and answer the questions that follow.

[1]Have you ever heard the term "<u>sandwich generation</u>"? [2]Some people might guess that it refers to a generation that spends more time eating sandwiches than sitting down to meals. [3]<u>In fact, the term refers to adults who are "caught in the middle," so that they have to care for both their own children and their aging parents at the same time.</u> [4]As people live longer, more and more adults end up taking care of their elderly parents. [5]<u>For instance,</u> a single mother named Rose has to care for her two children, one just six years old, and the other a troubled thirteen-year-old. [6]She must also care for her sixty-six-year-old mother, who has not been able to live independently since suffering a stroke.

  A   6. The main pattern of organization in the selection is
    A. definition-example.
    B. cause-effect.
    C. comparison-contrast.

The paragraph defines and gives an example of the term sandwich generation. For instance signals the example.

     7. A transition that signals the pattern of organization is _For instance_ .

To the Instructor: In the paragraphs in Tests 3–6, the main ideas and transitions relevant to the pattern of organization are underlined in this *Instructor's Edition.*

(Continues on next page)

C. Read the paragraph and answer the questions that follow.

¹In recent years, health-care costs in the United States have skyrocketed. ²The result is that a large number of people—particularly the poor and those in the lower middle class—have not been able to afford health care. ³There are many reasons for the increase in health-care costs. ⁴One cause is the aging of the U.S. population. ⁵Greater numbers of older Americans have created added demand for medical care, leading to higher prices. ⁶Another reason that health-care costs are so high is that medical care is better. ⁷As a result, patients who once died quickly from conditions such as comas and strokes can now live much longer—but need expensive medical care that often goes on for years. ⁸Soaring costs have been caused as well by the way in which health care is used in the United States. ⁹American medicine tends to focus on treating a disease, not preventing it. ¹⁰Therefore, simple steps that could prevent illness and save money—such things as prenatal care and free exams for the elderly—are often ignored. ¹¹When people finally get to a doctor, they are more likely to have advanced problems that cost more money to treat.

_B_ 8. The main pattern of organization in the selection is
  A. definition-example.
  B. cause-effect.
  C. comparison-contrast.

  The paragraph discusses the causes (reasons) for the rapid increase in health-care costs.

9–10. Two transitions that mark the paragraph's pattern of organization are
  Any two of the following: result, reasons, cause, reason,
  As a result, caused, Therefore

RELATIONSHIPS II: Mastery Test 4

A. (1–4.) Arrange the scrambled sentences below into a logical paragraph by numbering them *1, 2, 3,* and *4* in an order that makes sense. Then, in the space provided, write the letter of the main pattern of organization used.

Note that transitions will help you by making clear the relationships between sentences.

___2___ For example, the tailbone is what remains of a tail, something our ancestors once needed to survive.

___3___ Body hairs, too thin to keep us warm or protect our skin, are another example.

___1___ Vestigial organs are those parts of our body that serve little or no purpose to us today but were useful to our pre-human ancestors.

___4___ A final example, the appendix, is believed to have once helped our ancestors digest rough vegetable matter.

___D___ 5. The primary pattern of organization in the selection is
    A. comparison.
    B. contrast.
    C. cause and effect.
    D. definition and example.

The paragraph defines and gives examples of the term vestigial organs.

B. Read the paragraph and answer the questions that follow.

[1]Streetcars had dramatic effects on the character of city life. [2]Before their introduction, cities were limited in size by the distances people could conveniently walk to work. [3]The "walking city" could not easily extend more than two and a half miles from its center. [4]Streetcars increased this radius to six miles or more. [5]As a result, the area of a city expanded enormously. [6]A later effect was a shift in population as those who were better off moved away from the center of the city. [7]In search of air and space, they left the jam-packed older neighborhoods to the poor. [8]This flight of middle-class people from urban centers led to the growth of inner-city ghettos.

___B___ 6. The main pattern of organization of the selection is
    A. definition-example.
    B. cause-effect.
    C. comparison.

The paragraph discusses the effects streetcars had on city life. As a result, effect, and led to signal effects.

7. One transition that signals the paragraph's pattern of organization is

    ___effects or As a result or effect or led to___.

(Continues on next page)

C. Read the paragraph and answer the questions that follow.

> ¹When life brings setbacks and tragedies to optimists, they weather those storms better than pessimists do. ²Optimists look on the bright side. ³They bounce back from defeat, and, with their lives perhaps somewhat poorer, they pick up and start again. ⁴In contrast, pessimists give up and fall into depression. ⁵Optimists take more risks to get what they want, while pessimists are so sure of failure they don't even try. ⁶Optimists also have better health and may even live longer. ⁷However, even when things go well for pessimists, they are haunted by fears of catastrophe.

_C_ 8. The main pattern of organization in the selection is
   A. cause-effect.
   B. comparison.   The paragraph contrasts optimists
   C. contrast.   and pessimists.

  9. One transition that signals this pattern of organization is
     ___In contrast or while or However___.

 10. Another transition that signals the pattern of organization in the selection
     is ___In contrast or while or However___.

RELATIONSHIPS II: Mastery Test 5

A. (1–4.) Arrange the scrambled sentences below into a logical paragraph by numbering them *1, 2, 3,* and *4* in an order that makes sense. Note that transitions will help you by making clear the relationships between sentences.

___4___ Or if you believe that a certain group has a particular talent, you may be disappointed when a member of that group cannot do what you expect.

___3___ For instance, if you believe that a particular group is pushy, you will automatically judge someone belonging to that group as pushy—without waiting to see what that person is really like.

___1___ Stereotyping is holding a set of beliefs about the general nature of a group of people.

___2___ It can greatly interfere with making accurate judgments about others.

___D___ 5. The primary pattern of organization in the selection is
    A. comparison.
    B. contrast.
    C. cause and effect.
    D. definition and example.

The paragraph defines and illustrates the term stereotyping.

B. Read the paragraph and answer the questions that follow.

¹The Industrial Revolution led to dramatic changes in American society. ²At the beginning of the nineteenth century, it could take weeks to produce a single shirt. ³Wool had to be turned into yarn, then dyed, made into fabric, and sewn into patterns—all by hand. ⁴When machines were introduced, this whole process could be done in a fraction of the time. ⁵Many workers' lives were affected by the industrial changes. ⁶Instead of working in their homes or on farms, men, women, and children were soon working twelve- and fourteen-hour days in factories. ⁷Workers such as tailors or carpenters, who previously had their own trade, found themselves employed in the very places that drove them out of business. ⁸Another result was that whole villages started being built around factories, providing families with jobs, houses, schools, churches, and stores—all in one place.

___B___ 6. The main pattern of organization of the selection is
    A. definition-example.
    B. cause-effect.
    C. comparison-contrast.

The paragraph discusses the effects the Industrial Revolution had on American society.

7. One transition that signals this pattern of organization is
    ___led to or affected by or result___.

(Continues on next page)

C. Read the paragraph and answer the questions that follow.

> [1]In a book titled *The Art of Loving*, a psychologist describes the <u>difference</u> between "mother love" and "father love." [2]Mother love says, "I will always love you no matter what. [3]Nothing you ever do or fail to do will make me stop loving you." [4]<u>On the other hand</u>, father love says, "I will love you if you *earn* my love and respect. [5]You must do things like obey me, get good grades, make the team, choose the right friends, get into a good college, and earn a good salary." [6]<u>In contrast</u> to mother love, father love may seem harsh. [7]<u>But</u> sometimes we want to hear that we are loved because we deserve it, not only because the other person cares for us without conditions.

_C_ 8. The main pattern of organization in the selection is
  A. cause-effect.
  B. comparison.   The paragraph contrasts
  C. contrast.   mother love with father love.

9–10. Two word signals that mark the paragraph's pattern of organization are
  Any two of the following: difference, On the other hand,
  _____
           In contrast, But

RELATIONSHIPS II: Mastery Test 6

A. Read the textbook paragraph below. Then answer the question and complete the outline that follows.

> ¹There are some common <u>reasons</u> that small businesses fail. ²<u>One</u> is managers who don't have enough knowledge or experience. ³Some people think that managing a business is just "common sense." ⁴But if managers do not know how to make basic business decisions, they are unlikely to succeed in the long run. ⁵<u>Another</u> reason for failure is neglect. ⁶After the excitement of the grand opening, some business owners fail to focus on business as much as they should. ⁷Small-business owners who are unwilling to work long hours and perform many jobs are likely to fail. ⁸A <u>third</u> common <u>reason</u> small businesses fail is poor record-keeping. ⁹By keeping careful track of sales and costs, a manager can spot serious troubles and make changes before it is too late to do so. ¹⁰<u>Finally</u>, many small businesses fail <u>because of</u> lack of money. ¹¹Here is a well-known rule of thumb: A new business should have enough money to operate at least six months without earning a profit. ¹²Owners of new businesses are almost certain to fail if they expect to pay the second month's rent from the first month's profits.

___B___ 1. The patterns of organization of the paragraph are list of items and
       A. definition-example.
       B. cause-effect.
       C. comparison.
       D. contrast.

The paragraph discusses four causes (reasons) that make small businesses fail. The list words One, Another, third, and Finally signal the causes.

2–5. Complete the outline of the paragraph by writing in the four major supporting details.   *Wording of answers may vary.*

Main idea: There are common reasons that small businesses fail.

1. Managers who lack enough knowledge or experience
2. Neglect
3. Poor record-keeping
4. Lack of money

To the Instructor: In this test, the addition transitions that signal major details are double-underlined.

(Continues on next page)

B. Read the textbook paragraph below. Then answer the question and complete the map that follows.

> [1]When people get sick during the flu season, they are not always sure whether what they have caught is the flu or a cold. [2]It's true that the symptoms of the two overlap. [3]However, there are some distinct <u>differences</u> between cold and flu symptoms. [4]<u>First of all</u>, people rarely get a fever when they have a cold. [5]<u>In contrast</u>, people with the flu typically get a fever of about 100 to 104 degrees Fahrenheit, which lasts three to four days. [6]<u>Also</u>, although a cold is at times accompanied by a headache, headaches are much more likely with the flu. [7]<u>Third</u>, cold victims experience at most a few slight aches and pains. [8]<u>But</u> aches and pains are a usual feature of the flu and can often be quite severe. [9]<u>Finally</u>, even though a cold never exhausts its victims, someone with the flu may suffer extreme fatigue.

___D___ 6. The paragraph lists a series of
     A. definitions.
     B. examples.   The paragraph contrasts cold and flu symptoms.
     C. comparisons.   Four main differences are discussed.
     D. contrasts.

7–10. Complete the map of the paragraph by writing in the missing supporting details. *Wording of answers may vary.*

A cold and the flu often have different symptoms.

Cold

1. Fever is rare.
2. Headaches may or may not occur.
3. Aches and pains, if any, are slight.
4. Victims never suffer exhaustion.

Flu

1. Fever is typical.
2. Headaches are likely.
3. Aches and pains are usual and can be severe.
4. Victims may suffer extreme fatigue.

The pages that follow contain two mastery tests that offer additional practice in the skills covered in Chapters 6 and 7.

- Relationships that involve **addition**
- Relationships that involve **time**
- Relationships that involve **illustration**
- Relationships that involve **comparison and/or contrast**
- Relationships that involve **cause and effect**

For ease in reference, the lists of words that show these relationships have been reprinted on the next page.

Addition Words

one	to begin with	in addition	last
first	another	next	last of all
first of all	second	moreover	final
for one thing	also	furthermore	finally

Time Words

before	next	while	later
previously	soon	during	after
first	often	until	eventually
second	as	now	finally
third	when	then	last

Illustration Words

(for) example	(for) instance	to illustrate
including	such as	once

Comparison Words

(just) as	in like (similar) manner	same
(just) like	similar(ly)	in the same way
alike	similarity	resemble
likewise	both	equally

Contrast Words

but	instead	still	difference
yet	in contrast	as opposed to	different(ly)
however	on the other hand	in spite of	differs from
although	on the contrary	despite	unlike
nevertheless	even though	rather than	while

Cause and Effect Words

therefore	so	because (of)	thus
(as a) result	effect	as a consequence	results in
cause	explanation	consequently	led to
affect	due to	since	reason

RELATIONSHIPS I & II: Mastery Test 1

A. Fill in each blank with an appropriate transition from the box. Use each transition once. Then, in the spaces provided, write the letter of the transition you have chosen.

A. because	**B. for example**	**C. in addition**
D. just like	**E. on the other hand**	

_____A_____ 1. ¹If you have ever eaten spicy food, you may have noticed that drinking water will not calm the fire on your tongue. ²_____*Because*_____ spices are usually oily, water will simply roll right over them. ³To get some relief, you should eat a piece of bread to absorb the oily spices.

The passage explains why water rolls right over spices.

_____C_____ 2. ¹Many prescription drugs are now available in the form of patches, which offer significant advantages over oral drugs. ²Patches generally allow the use of lower doses of a drug, so that there is less risk of side effects. ³_____*In addition*_____, patches can deliver a steady dose of medication for several hours or even several days.

Passage 2 presents a list of items. *In addition* signals the second advantage.

_____B_____ 3. ¹Making people feel old is a poor way to sell products. ²_____*For example*_____, the Heinz company once produced a diet food for seniors that it called Senior Foods. ³The product flopped. ⁴As someone explained, "People didn't want to be seen eating the stuff. ⁵It was labeling them as old—and in our society, that is an embarrassment."

For example signals that sentence 2 is presenting an example of a poor way to sell products.

On the other hand signals the contrast between what would happen to dog owners and what would happen to cat owners.

_____E_____ 4. ¹People who favor dogs over cats make the following argument. ²If you are the owner of a dog and you are suddenly shrunken to the size of a mouse, the dog will still know that you are its owner. ³_____*On the other hand*_____, if you are the owner of a cat and you are suddenly reduced to the size of a mouse, the cat will probably eat you.

_____D_____ 5. ¹According to one eye expert, there is no harm in reading in dim light. ²Reading in dim light is _____*just like*_____ sniffing hard to smell a faint odor. ³You will not injure your eyes any more than you will injure your nose. ⁴The worst thing that will happen is that your eyes will get tired because you're struggling to see instead of reading comfortably.

"Reading in dim light" is being compared to "sniffing hard to smell a faint odor."

(Continues on next page)

B. Fill in each blank with an appropriate transition from the box. Use each transition once. Then, in the spaces provided, write the letter of the transition you have chosen.

A. another	B. before	C. however
D. such as	E. then	

___E___ 6. ¹To recognize whether someone has just had a stroke, ask the person three simple questions. ²First, ask the person to smile. ³_____Then_____ ask him or her to raise both arms. ⁴Finally, ask the person to speak a simple sentence. ⁵The person might say, "It's sunny out today" or "I'm wearing brown pants." ⁶If he or she has trouble with any of these tasks, call 9-1-1 immediately.

The passage presents a sequence of questions to ask in order. *Then* signals the second question in the sequence.

___D___ 7. ¹All of us are subject to social control—attempts by society to regulate people's thoughts and behavior. ²Often, these attempts are informal, _____such as_____ when parents praise or scold in order to control their children. ³Another instance is friends who make fun of someone in their group who studies too much or wears the wrong clothes or is otherwise seen as a threat to their own behavior.

Such as signals the first example of social control.

___B___ 8. ¹Valentine's Day had a romantic, if tragic, beginning. ²When Rome was about to go into battle in the third century, the emperor canceled all marriages so that men would be more willing to join the army. ³However, a priest named Valentine secretly continued to marry couples. ⁴On February 14, he was caught and jailed. ⁵_____Before_____ his execution, Valentine fell in love with the jailer's daughter. ⁶He signed his final note to her, "From your Valentine."

The paragraph narrates a sequence of events in time order. Valentine fell in love *before* he was executed.

___C___ 9. ¹Diamonds are the hardest natural substance on earth. ²_____However_____, they are easier to destroy than you might think. ³If a diamond is baked at a temperature of 1405 degrees Fahrenheit, it will vanish, without leaving any ash.

The passage contrasts a diamond's hardness with the relative ease of destroying a diamond. *However* signals the contrast.

___A___ 10. ¹When you cut an onion, the chemicals in the onion's cells mix together. ²This mixing creates a substance which makes your eyes water. ³If you want to avoid crying when you cut an onion, you should cut it under running water. ⁴The onion's chemicals will dissolve and run into the drain. ⁵_____Another_____ way to avoid tears is to put an onion in the freezer for a few minutes before cutting it. ⁶Cold temperatures will slow down the onion's chemical reactions.

The passage lists two ways to avoid crying when you cut an onion. *Another* introduces the second of these ways.

RELATIONSHIPS I & II: Mastery Test 2

Read each selection and answer the questions that follow.

A. [1]During World War II, a cat named Oscar lived on the *Bismarck*, a German battleship. [2]When the *Bismarck* was torpedoed by a British ship, a sailor rescued Oscar. [3]Five months later, the British ship sank, but another British ship saved Oscar from drowning. [4]Just three weeks after that, Oscar was rescued yet again when a German U-boat destroyed the British ship. [5]Oscar was then returned to land, where he died peacefully in 1955, ten years after the war ended.

   _C_   1. The main pattern of organization of the selection is
- A. list of items.
- B. cause and effect.   The paragraph discusses a series of events
- C. time order.   in time order.

      2. One transition that signals the pattern of organization of this paragraph
is _____ *Any of the following: During, When, later, after, then,* _____.
in 1955, ten years after the war ended

B. [1]In 1996, three-fourths of Americans approved of capital punishment; in 2000, only two-thirds did. [2]Public support for the death penalty continues to decline. [3]There are at least three reasons why. [4]Crime itself has declined over the past decade; when people feel less threatened by crime, they're less likely to favor harsh punishment. [5]Another reason for the loss of support for the death penalty is that the public has become more aware of cases in which people were sentenced to death and later found to be innocent, often as a result of new DNA evidence. [6]A third cause of declining support for the death penalty is a greater mistrust of the entire judicial system, partly due to reports of incompetent or corrupt lawyers, judges, and police officers.

   _B_   3. The main pattern of organization of the selection is
- A. time order.   The paragraph explains three causes (reasons)
- B. cause and effect.   for the decline in support for the death penalty.
- C. definition and example. Sentences 4, 5, and 6 present specific causes.

      4. One transition that signals the pattern of organization of this paragraph
is _____ *Any of the following: reasons, reason, cause* _____.

(Continues on next page)

C. ¹The <u>effects</u> of climate change are visible all over the world. ²In Antarctica, temperatures are rising five times faster than in the rest of the world, and penguins are finding it more and more difficult to survive. ³In Montana, glaciers in Glacier National Park are shrinking at an alarming rate and may be gone by 2020. ⁴Rising temperatures have also <u>led to</u> an 85 percent decline in the ice cap on Africa's tallest mountain. ⁵This ice is expected to disappear completely in less than 20 years.

_A_ 5. The main pattern of organization of the selection is
  A. cause-effect.
  B. comparison and/or contrast.
  C. definition and example.

  The paragraph discusses the effects of climate change. Sentences 2, 3, and 4 present specific effects.

  6. One transition that signals the pattern of organization of this paragraph
  is _____ _Either of the following: effects, led to_ _____.

D. ¹Television advertising is what pays for much of television programming. ²But many people have a number of objections to TV advertising for children. ³<u>First</u>, critics dislike the whole idea of ads for kids. ⁴Young children, they point out, do not understand the self-serving nature of advertising. ⁵They tend to simply accept ads as true. ⁶<u>Another</u> concern is the promotion of war-related toys in a country where kids are already exposed to too much violence. ⁷A <u>third</u> concern is the many ads that promote sugar-coated cereals and other unhealthful "kiddie" foods.

The paragraph lists three objections people have to TV ads for children. Sentences 3, 6, and 7 present specific objections.

_A_ 7. The main pattern of organization of the selection is
  A. list of items.   B. time order.   C. definition and example.

  8. One transition that signals the pattern of organization of this paragraph
  is _____ _Any of the following: First, Another, third_ _____.

E. ¹A stroke is very much <u>like</u> a heart attack. ²In a heart attack, the supply of blood to muscles of the heart is reduced or cut off, so that some of the heart's cells die. ³<u>Similarly</u>, in one common type of stroke, the supply of blood to the brain is hindered, so that some brain cells die. ⁴<u>Just as</u> in a heart attack, how many cells are killed and where they are located—which indicates what their functions were—will determine how severe the stroke is. ⁵In fact, the two events are so <u>alike</u> that a stroke has been called a "brain attack."

_B_ 9. The main pattern of organization of the selection is
  A. time order.
  B. comparison and/or contrast.
  C. definition and example.

  The paragraph compares strokes to heart attacks.

  10. One transition that signals the pattern of organization of this paragraph
  is _____ _Any of the following: like, Similarly, Just as, alike_ _____.

8 Inferences

This Chapter in a Nutshell

- Ideas are often suggested rather than being stated directly. We must **infer**, or figure out, those ideas.

- Discovering ideas that are not stated directly is called **making inferences**.

- We make inferences all the time—in life and in visual and reading materials of all types.

- To make logical inferences, we must look closely at the information available and use our own experience and common sense.

An Introduction to Inferences

Inferences are ideas that are not stated directly. They are conclusions we draw from what we see, hear, and read.

Look at the cartoon below. What conclusions can you draw about it? Check (✓) the **two** inferences that are most logically based on the information suggested by the cartoon. Then read the explanation on the next page.

"It's Junior's report card. The good news is that he's passing his gym class."

_____ 1. The parents have several children in school.

✓ 2. Junior is not doing well in most subjects.

_____ 3. The parents are angry about Junior's grades.

✓ 4. The wife is trying to be positive about a bad situation.

_____ 5. The parents were both good students when they were in school.

Explanation

1. Nothing in the cartoon indicates that the husband and wife have other children. The only child they are talking about is Junior.

2. If "the good news" is that Junior is passing gym, we can infer that there is also bad news: he is not passing some, or even all, of his other classes. You should have checked this item.

3. Nothing suggests that the husband or the wife is angry. They might, for example, be used to Junior's poor performance in academic subjects.

4. By presenting "the good news" about gym class first, the wife is trying to be as positive as possible. You should also have checked this item.

5. There is no evidence that the husband and wife were good students. In fact, they might have had the same kind of academic difficulties as their son, but there's no way to tell.

We make inferences all the time. We hear a sound in the night and infer it is just a squirrel on the roof. We walk into a friend's house for dinner, and the smells coming from the kitchen help us infer that we are about to have a delicious meal. We greet someone and infer from that person's body language or tone of voice that something is troubling him or her. We sense the air suddenly getting cooler and the light changing in the sky and infer that a storm is approaching.

With visual material such as cartoons, book covers, and photographs, we can infer a great deal from all the clues provided. With written material, we can "read between the lines" and pick up ideas the author only suggests, or implies. This chapter will give you practice in making inferences from both visual and reading materials.

Inferences about Visual Materials

Cartoons

How well a cartoon works often depends on the reader's inference skills. Take a moment to look at the *New Yorker* cartoon on the next page. What can you infer about this cartoon? Put a check (✓) by the **two** inferences that are most logically based on the information given in the cartoon.

"He didn't do anything, Gregory. This is a zoo."

© David Sipress/The New Yorker Collection/**www.cartoonbank.com**.

____ 1. The boy doesn't like monkeys.

__✓__ 2. The boy has probably never seen animals in a zoo.

____ 3. The father is angry with the boy.

__✓__ 4. The boy thinks the monkey is being punished.

____ 5. The boy and his father go to the zoo often.

Explanation

1. Nothing the boy says or does suggests he dislikes monkeys. His expression may even suggest that he is concerned about the monkey.

2. The boy would not be so apparently puzzled or upset if he were accustomed to seeing animals behind bars. And the father has to explain to the boy that "This is a zoo." You should have checked this item.

3. Nothing indicates that the father is angry.

4. From what the father is saying, we know that the boy thinks the monkey is in jail. You should have checked this item.

5. The cartoon suggests the boy has not seen an animal in a cage before, so this is not likely.

Check Your Understanding

Now look at the following *Peanuts* cartoon:

Put a check (✓) by the **two** inferences that are most logically based on the information given in the cartoon. Then read the explanation that follows.

  ✓   1. The light-haired girl read *Silas Marner* for a school assignment.

       2. Marcie doesn't like to read.

       3. The light-haired girl very much enjoyed reading *Silas Marner.*

  ✓   4. The cartoonist suggests that reading for true understanding requires real attention.

       5. Marcie and the other girl are sisters.

Explanation

1. Since Marcie says that the light-haired girl should write a report on *Silas Marner*, we can assume that reading the book was a school assignment. This inference is a matter of common sense: Children usually don't write reports on books they read on their own. You should have checked this item.

2. Nothing in the pictures or words suggests that Marcie does not like to read.

3. The light-haired girl says that she "didn't pay any attention" as she read the book. To say the least, this is not the sort of comment one makes about a book one has very much enjoyed.

4. The comment "I didn't pay any attention" suggests that it's possible to read with too little attention. You should have checked this item.

5. The light-haired girl is standing at the door as if she had come to visit Marcie. We must therefore assume that the two girls don't live together and aren't sisters.

Book Covers

Look at the following cover for a book titled *Reading Changed My Life!* by Beth Johnson. Put a check (✓) by the **two** inferences that are most logically based on the information given on the cover.

✓ 1. The "three true stories" are about the three women shown.

___ 2. The women are good friends with one another.

✓ 3. The women's lives have changed in positive ways.

___ 4. All the women had parents who were non-readers.

___ 5. All the women dropped out of school because of reading problems.

Explanation

1. It is logical to assume that people shown on the cover would be the book's subjects. (What other reason would there be for their pictures to be on the cover?) You should have checked this item.

2. There is no evidence given that the women know each other. Also, they are in separate photos, rather than together in one photo.

3. The title of the book and the smiling faces of the women suggest that the changes in their lives have been positive. You should have checked this item.

4. We are not given any information about the women's parents.

5. We are not told that the women dropped out of school.

Check Your Understanding

Now look at the following book cover for the classic story *Gulliver's Travels*, by Jonathan Swift. Put a check (✓) by the **two** inferences that are most logically based on the information given on the cover.

_____ 1. *Gulliver's Travels* is a true story.

_____ 2. The man on the ground is dead.

✓ 3. The book has something to do with a journey.

✓ 4. The man on the ground is probably Gulliver.

_____ 5. The story in the book takes place in modern times.

Explanation

1. The illustration shows either an impossibly huge man or two impossibly tiny men, so the story must be fiction.

2. The fact that the man is being threatened suggests he is alive. If he were dead, he would pose no threat.

3. The word *Travels* in the title and the map in the background suggest that the story indeed is about a journey. You should have checked this item.

4. The title states that the story is about the travels of one man, Gulliver. Therefore, the man shown alone, on the ground, is probably the main character. You should have checked this item.

5. The type of weapons and the clothing shown suggest that the story takes place in another time period.

Poster and Ad

Look at the following poster. Put a check (✓) by the **two** inferences that are most logically based on the information shown.

© GettyImages

____ 1. The woman has been handcuffed by the police.

____ 2. The woman is a former addict.

✓ 3. The woman is addicted to food, cigarettes, and alcohol.

____ 4. Alcohol is more addictive than cigarettes or food.

✓ 5. People who are addicted are not free.

Explanation

1. The picture shows nothing to support the idea that the woman has broken any law or been in contact with the police.

2. The fact that the woman is chained suggests she is still addicted.

3. All three substances are shown with her, so this is a logical inference.

4. Nothing in the poster suggests that one substance is more addictive than the others.

5. Addicts like this woman are "chained" by their addiction. This inference is also logical.

Check Your Understanding

Now look at the following advertisement. Put a check (✓) by the **two** inferences that are most logically based on the information given in the ad. Then read the explanation that follows.

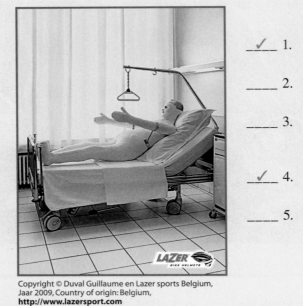

_✓_ 1. The man had a bicycle accident.

_____ 2. It is the man's own fault he is in the hospital.

_____ 3. There should be a law requiring bikers to wear helmets.

_✓_ 4. Wearing a bike helmet protects one's head.

_____ 5. Bicycling is more dangerous than other activities.

Explanation

1. The ad is for Lazer bike helmets. It is clear that the man in the picture has been in some sort of accident. His entire body is in a cast except for the top of his head; this is the part that would be protected by a bicycle helmet. Taken together, these details suggest the man has had a bicycle accident. You should have checked this item.

2. None of the information in the ad indicates who is at fault for the man's accident.

3. The ad suggests that it makes sense to wear a bike helmet. However, nothing indicates that there should be a law requiring bikers to wear helmets.

4. The one part of the man that is not in a cast is a helmet-shaped area at the top of his head. This suggests that wearing a bike helmet protects one's head. You should have checked this item.

5. The ad does not compare the dangers of biking with the dangers of other activities. This is not a logical inference.

A Final Comment about Visual Materials

As the preceding examples—the cartoons, the book covers, the poster and ad—make clear, we live in a world full of images, and we make inferences about such visual materials all the time. In other words, making inferences is a skill all of us already possess.

This chapter will now go on to strengthen your ability to make good inferences when reading.

Inferences about Reading Materials

You have already practiced making inferences while reading an earlier chapter of this book. Do you remember, for example, the following sentence from "Vocabulary in Context"?

In the United States, shaking hands is the *appropriate* way to greet someone; in China, bowing is the right way.

The sentence does not give us a definition of *appropriate*, but it does suggest that *appropriate* is close in meaning to "right." Thus we can infer in this sentence that *appropriate* means "right" or "proper." As you looked at all the sentences in Chapter 2, you inferred the meanings of words by looking closely at the surrounding context.

In all of our everyday reading, we make logical leaps from the information given directly on the page to ideas that are not stated directly. To draw such inferences, we use the clues provided by the writer, and we also apply our own experience, logic, and common sense.

Inferences in Passages

Read the following passage and then check (✓) the **two** inferences that are most firmly based on the given information.

> ¹I once hired a roofer to put a new roof on my home. ²He checked the roof and then quoted me a price of $1,000. ³I agreed. ⁴He tore the old roof off, then came back down. ⁵I noticed a barely hidden smile on his face.
>
> ⁶"Sorry," he said, "it's gonna cost you $1,800. ⁷I didn't know it needed so much work."
>
> ⁸"No way," I said, folding my arms.
>
> ⁹"Whatever you say," the roofer said. ¹⁰He looked up at the sky and commented, "You know, it looks like rain."
>
> ¹¹I sighed, shook my head, and said, "With my luck, it will rain for three days. ¹²Finish the job."

✓ 1. At first, the author did not want to spend the extra $800.

___ 2. The author's old roof would have held up for another year or two.

✓ 3. The roofer may have planned all along to raise the price after the old roof was torn off.

___ 4. The author believes that all roofers are con men.

___ 5. The roofer had been recommended to the author.

Explanation

1. When the roofer first tells the author that the job would cost $1,800, the author says, "No way." Using our common sense, we can conclude that the author of the selection refuses because he doesn't want to spend the extra $800. So you should have checked this item.

2. Nothing in the passage discusses the actual quality of the roof. You should not have checked this item.

3. The roofer says, "I didn't know [the roof] needed so much work." However, in telling us that the roofer had a smile on his face, the author implies that the roofer may have known all along that he planned on charging an extra $800. So you should have checked this item.

4. The passage makes no mention of the author's view of all roofers. We see only his reaction to this roofer. You should not have checked this item.

5. There is no mention in the passage of how the author came to hire the roofer. You should not have checked this item.

Check Your Understanding

Now read the following textbook passage. Then answer the questions about it by writing the letters of the inferences that are most firmly based on the given information. Hints are provided to help you think through the choices for each question.

> [1]A twenty-eight-year-old woman named Catherine Genovese was returning home from work one day. [2]Kitty, as she was called by almost everyone in her Queens neighborhood, had just parked her car. [3]Then a man with a knife grabbed her. [4]She screamed, "Oh my God, he stabbed me! [5]Please help me! [6]Please help me!"
>
> [7]For more than half an hour, thirty-eight neighbors listened to Kitty's screams as the attack continued. [8]The last time he stabbed her, she was slumped on the foot of the stairs to her apartment. [9]Not one person telephoned the police during the fatal attack. [10]Later, the police gathered statements from the witnesses. [11]Among their comments were, "I didn't want to get involved," "We thought it was a lovers' quarrel," and "I was tired. [12]I went back to bed."

  B   1. We can infer that Kitty was attacked
      A. while she was on vacation.
      B. in her own neighborhood.
      C. on her way from work to her car.

      Hint: The passage tells us that Genovese "was returning home from work" and that she "had just parked her car."

  B   2. We can conclude that the man who stabbed Genovese
      A. was someone she knew.
      B. intended to kill her.
      C. was a convicted criminal.

      Hint: Is there evidence that Genovese knew her killer or that he was a convicted criminal? Also, Genovese's killer stabbed her even after he was sure she was wounded and weak.

  A   3. We can infer that the witnesses
      A. might have stopped the attack if they had called the police.
      B. wanted the man to kill Genovese.
      C. would not want someone else to get involved if they themselves were being attacked.

      Hint: The attack continued for at least half an hour.

Explanation

Here is an explanation of each item:

    1. The answer to the first question is B. We have solid evidence to conclude that Genovese was attacked in her neighborhood: she was returning home from work and had parked her car. Since she was returning home from

work, she was not on vacation. Also, we know she had just parked her car after coming home from work. So the attack could not have taken place before she got into the car to go home.

2. The answer to the second question is B. We can conclude that Genovese's attacker wanted to kill her. If his goal was to rob or rape her, he could have done so long before the last time he stabbed her. And no evidence in the passage indicates that Genovese knew her attacker. Finally, although we cannot be sure the attacker was never convicted of a crime, there is absolutely no evidence in the passage to support the conclusion that he was—his past is not referred to at all.

3. The answer to the third question is A. The crime took at least a half hour; thus we can conclude that if the police had been called, there is a chance they would have arrived in time to save Genovese. However, we have no reason to believe the witnesses actually wanted the man to kill Genovese. Most people, in fact, would be horrified to see someone stabbed to death. And on the basis of our knowledge of human nature, we can be pretty sure the witnesses would have wanted others to get involved if they were victims.

Guidelines for Making Inferences

The exercises in this chapter provide practice in making careful inferences when you read. Here are three guidelines to that process:

1   **Never lose sight of the available information.**   As much as possible, base your inferences on the facts. For instance, in the paragraph about Kitty Genovese's attack, we are told that she "was returning home from work." On the basis of that fact, we can readily conclude that she was not on vacation.

It's also important to note when a conclusion lacks support. For instance, the idea that the attacker was a convicted criminal has no support in the selection. We are told of only one instance of his criminal behavior, the attack on Genovese.

2   **Use your background knowledge, experience, and common sense to help you in making inferences.**   Our experience with people, for instance, tells us that witnesses would themselves have wanted help if they had been in Genovese's place.

The more you know about a subject, the better your inferences are likely to be. So keep in mind that if your background in an area is weak, your inferences may be shaky. If you are having study problems, for example, the inferences of a tutor about what you need to do are likely to be more helpful than those of another student.

3   **Consider the alternatives.**   Don't simply accept the first inference that comes to mind. Instead, consider all of the facts of a case and all the possible explanations. For example, the tutor may be aware of many helpful study habits that would work for you.

DO IN CLASS

PRACTICE 1

Read each of the following passages. Then write the letter of the most logical answer to each question, based on the information given in the passage.

A. [1]When Oprah Winfrey was a child, she lived with her mother and two younger half-siblings in a Milwaukee apartment without electricity or running water. [2]One Christmas Eve, her mother told her there would be no celebration that year. [3]There was no money to buy presents. [4]"But what about Santa Claus?" Oprah asked. [5]Her mother answered that there wasn't enough money to pay Santa to come. [6]As she went to bed that night, Oprah dreaded the following day. [7]She knew the neighbor children would be outside playing with their toys and comparing presents. [8]She tried to think of a story she could tell the other kids to explain why she had nothing. [9]Then she heard the doorbell ring. [10]Three nuns had come to the apartment. [11]They brought a turkey, a fruit basket, and toys for the children. [12]"I've never had a stronger feeling of someone lifting me up," she says today. [13]"Their kindness made me feel so much better about myself." [14]Oprah remembers that Christmas as the best she ever had.

_C_ 1. We can infer that before the nuns came, Oprah dreaded the next day because she
   A. would not have any new toys to play with at home.
   B. now knew Santa Claus was not real.
   C. would be shamed in front of her friends.

   Hint: The paragraph tells us Oprah "knew the neighbor children would be outside . . . comparing presents" and that she felt she'd have to "think of a story she could tell the other kids to explain why she had nothing."

_A_ 2. We can conclude this was Oprah's best Christmas because
   A. she was so relieved and grateful for what the nuns had done.
   B. the toys she received were exactly what she had wanted.
   C. she had never received Christmas presents before.

   Hint: The paragraph says that after the nuns arrived, Oprah had the "feeling of someone lifting" her up and felt "so much better" about herself.

_B_ 3. What can we infer Oprah would most likely have done the next day if the nuns had not come?
   A. She would have been angry and hostile toward her mother.
   B. She would have made up a lie about the presents somehow being delayed.
   C. She would have gone out and stolen some toys.

   Hint: The passage states that Oprah knew the next day "the neighbor children would be outside playing with their toys and comparing presents" and that she "tried to think of a story she could tell the other kids to explain why she had nothing."

B. [1]The British prime minister Winston Churchill was a master of the elegant put-down. [2]At one fancy dinner party, he was seated next to a favorite target—a woman whose political views were opposed to his own. [3]The two argued more or less continually throughout the meal. [4]Totally annoyed, the lady said, "Sir Winston, if you were my husband, I'd put poison in your coffee!" [5]"Madam," replied Churchill, "if you were my wife, I'd drink it."

The first sentence suggests that Churchill was known for "the elegant putdown," and the next sentence tells us his "favorite target" was a political opponent.

___B___ 4. We can conclude that Churchill
   A. constantly put people down.
   B. liked to put down his political opponents.
   C. was rarely invited to fancy dinner parties.

Item 5:
Answers A and B are not supported. Answer C can be inferred. Churchill so disliked the woman's company, his joke suggests, that he'd rather die than be married to her.

___C___ 5. When Churchill said, "If you were my wife, I'd drink it," he meant to imply that
   A. he admired the woman so much he would do whatever she said.
   B. he would never insult the woman by refusing her coffee.
   C. if she were his wife, he would prefer to die.

___C___ 6. We can conclude that the author of the passage admires
   A. Churchill's politics.
   B. the woman's politics.
   C. Churchill's wit.

Answers A and B are not supported. Answer C can be inferred. The description of Churchill as "the master of the elegant putdown" reveals the author's admiration for his wit.

Homework

PRACTICE 2

Read the following article, which originally appeared in the newspaper *USA Today*. Then check (✔) the **five** inferences that are most logically based on the information in the article.

In Fall, a Young Man's Fancy Turns to His Teacher

Craig Wilson

[1]Her name was Miss Meinke. [2]Or maybe it was Menke.

[3]What did I know? [4]I was in first grade and she was my teacher. [5]I couldn't even spell my own name at the time, let alone hers.

[6]It didn't matter. [7]I was going to marry her and change her name to mine, and that would take care of that problem once and for all.

[8]I loved her. [9]And I know she loved me. [10]It was obvious, just by the way she winked at me when I came in the room.

[11]She was kind and good and noble—all the things a first-time love should be. [12]She never shouted, never scolded. [13]She praised my every move.

[14]For hours we'd push mahogany-colored chestnuts back and forth across the table. [15]She called it a counting exercise, but I knew it was more than that.

[16]I remember she was tall and willowy. [17]Maybe she was short and dumpy, but in 1954, when I was three feet high, she was tall and willowy. [18]And she had a long and beautiful neck, like a ballerina.

[19]She smelled good too. [20]Nothing racy. [21]Not Miss Meinke. [22]She wasn't that kind of girl.

[23]I was by no means the first student to fall in love with his teacher, and I certainly wasn't going to be the last.

[24]This fall millions of kids will have crushes on their own Miss Meinkes, staying late for special help they don't need, asking questions they already know the answers to. [25]Some will even offer up the proverbial shiny apple to the newest woman in their lives. [26]Could her first name be Eve?

[27]I didn't know Miss Meinke's first name. [28]First-grade teachers didn't have first names back then. [29]Nor did they have personal lives.

[30]I remember seeing her at the supermarket once and thinking how odd that was. [31]She buys food? [32]She cooks? [33]She eats at places other than the teachers' table in the cafeteria?

[34]To me she lived only in that crowded and cluttered pastel-colored classroom. [35]Maybe she slept under her desk. [36]I never asked. [37]But I would be the one to take her away from all that. [38]Who cared if there was a thirty-year age difference? [39]Not me. [40]Why wouldn't she want a younger man? [41]Someone to look after her later on.

⁴²It was a perfect match. . . .

⁴³We've all heard about lovers writing passionate letters to their beloved. ⁴⁴Miss Meinke never wrote me such a letter. ⁴⁵I understand now that she really couldn't, seeing that everything I took home I immediately showed to my mother. ⁴⁶So she did the only thing she could. ⁴⁷She sent messages on my report card.

⁴⁸The first came in October. ⁴⁹On it she wrote that basically I was the ideal young man. ⁵⁰"A delight to have in my classroom," were her exact words. ⁵¹I still have the card. ⁵²Now, if that wasn't a thinly veiled "I'm in love with Craig," I don't know what was.

⁵³But it wasn't meant to be.

⁵⁴She left me. ⁵⁵For another man, I found out later. ⁵⁶Out in California. ⁵⁷She left upstate New York the next fall and never looked back. ⁵⁸Never wrote. ⁵⁹Never called.

⁶⁰In retrospect, I understand it was her way of coping. ⁶¹What else could she do? ⁶²I had already moved on to an older, more mature woman. ⁶³Mrs. Baine, who lived down the hall in a place called second grade.

    ✓   1. Miss Meinke was a kind, caring teacher.

    ____   2. Wilson's mother and Miss Meinke were close friends.

    ____   3. Wilson still feels bitterness toward Miss Meinke for leaving his school.

    ✓   4. Wilson probably also "fell in love" with his second-grade teacher.

    ____   5. Miss Meinke was annoyed by young Wilson's feelings for her.

    ✓   6. Young students often adore their teachers.

    ✓   7. First-graders may find it hard to imagine their teacher anywhere but at school.

    ____   8. Now, Wilson realizes that Miss Meinke was not a very good teacher.

    ____   9. Miss Meinke must have been an extraordinarily beautiful woman.

    ✓   10. Wilson is making lighthearted fun of his childhood crush.

Item 1: See sentences 10–13.

Item 2: No support.

Item 3: Sentences 60–63 show Wilson has no bitterness.

Item 4: Suggested by "moved on" to another woman in sentence 62.

Item 5: Not supported.

Item 6: Suggested by "millions of kids" in sentences 23–24.

Item 7: Suggested by "how odd that was" in sentences 30–33.

Items 8 and 9: Not supported.

Item 10: Wilson's exaggerations (such as "It was a perfect match") show a playful approach.

Do in class

PRACTICE 3

The ability to make inferences will help you in all kinds of reading, including textbook material. Read the following textbook passages. Then, for each passage, check (✔) the **two** inferences that are most logically based on the given facts.

A. [1]A question that interests many is why a woman will remain with a husband who abuses her. [2]Interviews with violent families revealed that the decision is related to three major factors. [3]First, the more severe and more frequent the violence, the more a woman is likely to end her marriage or to seek help from social agencies or the police. [4]The second factor has to do with how much violence she experienced as a child. [5]The more she was struck by her own parents, the more inclined she is to stay with an abusive husband. [6]Third, wives who have not completed high school and those who are unemployed are less likely to leave their husbands. [7]It appears that the fewer resources a woman has, the fewer alternatives she sees and the more trapped in her marriage she becomes.

_____ 1. Abusive husbands tend to be rich.   The passage does not mention the financial status of husbands.

✓ 2. People who were beaten as children learn to tolerate being abused.
                                                       See sentences 4 and 5.
✓ 3. Women who are dependent on their husbands economically are more likely to stay in an abusive marriage.   See sentence 7.

_____ 4. Employed women who are well educated are never abused by their husbands.   The passage does not discuss who is abused; it discusses why women don't leave abusive husbands.

_____ 5. The more abused a woman is, the less likely she is to leave her husband.
                                                       Sentence 3 refutes this statement.

B. [1]It may be important to have a job, but does work make people happy? [2]In many studies during the last two decades, workers have been asked whether they would continue to work if they inherited enough money to live comfortably without working. [3]More than 70 percent replied that they would. [4]Asked how satisfied they were with their jobs, even more—from 80 to 90 percent—replied that they were very or moderately satisfied. [5]But asked whether they would choose the same line of work if they could begin all over again, most said no. [6]Only 43 percent of white-collar and 24 percent of blue-collar workers said yes. [7]And when asked, "Do you enjoy your work so much that you have a hard time putting it aside?" only 34 percent of men and 32 percent of women answered positively.

Items 1 and 2: Since most people would continue working if they had lots of money (sentence 3), work must offer rewards other than pay. Therefore, item 1 is not supported; item 2 is.

Item 3 is not supported.

Item 4: See sentences 4–6.

_____ 1. The only reason people work is to earn money.

✓ 2. Work provides people with rewards other than money.

_____ 3. For most people, work is as enjoyable as a hobby.

✓ 4. Most people like their jobs but are not thrilled by them.

_____ 5. For most people, work is the most important thing in their lives.

Item 5: Sentence 7 states most people easily put work aside, suggesting that work is not the most important thing in their lives.

CHAPTER REVIEW

In this chapter, you learned the following:

- Making inferences is a skill we practice all the time: for example, with cartoons, book covers, ads, other visual images, and everything that we read.

- Many important ideas in reading are not stated directly, but must be inferred.

- To make good inferences, we must look closely at all the information presented and also draw upon our own experience and common sense.

The next chapter—Chapter 9—will also involve making inferences, with the focus on finding main ideas that are implied, rather than stated directly.

On the Web: If you are using this book in class, you can visit our website for additional practice in making inferences. Go to **www.townsendpress.com** and click on "Online Learning Center."

COMPLETE IN CLASS

REVIEW TEST 1

To review what you've learned in this chapter, complete each of the following sentences about inferences.

1. To fully understand a cartoon, book cover, ad, or other visual image, we often must make _____inferences_____.   See page 321.

2. Inferences were part of an earlier chapter in this book when the meaning of vocabulary words was figured out by looking at the _____context_____ in which they appeared.   See page 321.

3. When we read, we often "read between the lines" and pick up ideas that are implied rather than directly _____stated_____.
   See page 314.

4. When making inferences, it is (*a mistake, useful*) _____useful_____ to draw upon our own experience as well as clues provided.

5. When making inferences, it is (*a mistake, useful*) _____useful_____ to draw upon our own common sense as well as clues provided.

Items 4 and 5: See pages 321 and 324.

Homework

REVIEW TEST 2

A. (1–2.) Put a check (✓) by the **two** inferences that are most logically based on the information given in the following cartoon.

___ 1. The dog is afraid of the man.

_✓_ 2. The dog wants to go for a walk.

___ 3. The man doesn't mind leaving his television set.

_✓_ 4. The man has been ignoring the dog.

___ 5. The television set is brand new.

Item 1: The dog shows no evidence of fear.
Item 2: The dog is holding his leash and trying to get the man out of the chair.
Item 3: He must be forced.
Item 4: This is why the dog has had to take matters into his own hands (or paws).
Item 5: There is no evidence for this.

B. Read the following passage. Then, in the space provided, write the letter of the most logical answer to each question, based on the information given in the passage.

> ¹The real heroes of the fight against drugs are the teenagers who resist the ghetto's fast track—those who live at home, stay in school, and juggle their studies and a low-paying job. ²The wonder is that there are so many of them. ³"Most of our youngsters are not involved in crack," says the chief judge of one juvenile court in Michigan. ⁴"Most are not running around with guns. ⁵Most aren't killing people. ⁶Most are doing very well—against great odds." ⁷They are the youngsters who fit these words of Jesse Jackson: "You were born in the slum, but the slum wasn't born in you."

___B___ 3. We can conclude that the author's attitude toward ghetto teenagers who live at home, stay in school, and work is
   A. disapproving.
   B. admiring.
   C. neutral.

   In sentence 1, the author calls them "real heroes."

___A___ 4. We can infer that the author believes resisting crime in the ghetto
   A. is a challenge.
   B. requires no effort at all.
   C. is impossible.

   The words great odds *in sentence 6 suggest the author believes resisting crime is a challenge.*

___B___ 5. When Jackson says, ". . . but the slum wasn't born in you," he implies that
   A. being born in the slums is good.
   B. people can rise above their slum environment.
   C. people can never overcome the problems of the slums.

   By pointing out that "the slum" isn't inside a person, Jackson suggests a person can rise above the problems of the ghetto. If the problem were inside a person, there would be no escape.

DO IN CLASS

REVIEW TEST 3

A. (1.) Read the following passage and check (✓) the **one** inference that is most firmly based on the given information.

> ¹At a White House dinner during the Civil War, an elderly guest waved his hat and cried out, "Mr. President, I'm from New York State, where we believe that God Almighty and Abraham Lincoln will save this country."
>
> ²Lincoln—a modest man whose political thought was guided and shaped by his religious faith—smiled and nodded. ³"My friend," he said, "you're half right."

Item 1:
Lincoln's religious faith and modesty (sentence 2) suggest he would agree that God—not himself—would save the country.

✓ 1. Lincoln believed the guest was right in saying God would save the country.

___ 2. Lincoln believed the guest was right in saying that he, Lincoln, would save the country.   Lincoln said the guest was only "half right" (sentence 3).

___ 3. Lincoln believed that the man was supporting the wrong political party.   The political party of the man is not mentioned.

B. (2–3.) Put a check (✓) by the **two** inferences that are most logically based on the information given in the following passage:

> ¹When I look back at myself in high school, I am amazed by two things: how smart I thought I was, and how much I didn't know. ²It seems to me now that I learned few, if any, important lessons in high school. ³For example, I learned a good deal about "romance." ⁴That is, I learned about fighting, jealousy, spreading rumors, breaking up, gossip, and using other people. ⁵I don't think I learned anything about genuine love and concern for a partner. ⁶I learned about "fun." ⁷That meant partying, drinking, smoking, putting off work, and lying to my parents. ⁸I learned very little about the satisfaction of doing a job well or the rewards of discipline. ⁹Finally, I learned all about fitting in and going along with the crowd and being one of the cool people. ¹⁰I didn't learn anything about standing up for what I believed, or even figuring out what that was. ¹¹I learned almost nothing about being me.

___ 1. The author had low self-esteem in high school.   Not mentioned.

___ 2. The author was not popular in high school.   Refuted by sentence 9.

✓ 3. Schoolwork was not a priority for the author during high school.

___ 4. The author is proud of his or her behavior in high school.

✓ 5. If the author could go to high school again, he or she would do things differently.

Part B
Item 3: The author does not mention schoolwork.
Item 4: The tone of the passage is one of shame, not pride.
Item 5: Because the author missed so many important lessons in high school, it can be inferred that he or she would do things differently a second time.

C. (4–5.) Read the following textbook passage and check (✓) the **two** inferences that are most firmly based on the given information.

> [1]In America during the 1700s, the typical woman gave birth to her children at home. [2]Female relatives and neighbors would gather at her bedside to offer support and encouragement. [3]Records show that the daughter of a Puritan official gave birth to her first child on the last day of January 1701. [4]At least eight other women were present at her bedside, including her mother and four or more other neighbors. [5]Most women were assisted in childbirth not by a doctor, but by a midwife. [6]Skilled midwives were highly valued. [7]Communities tried to attract experienced midwives by offering a salary or a house rent-free. [8]In addition to assisting in childbirth, midwives helped farm animals give birth and attended the baptisms and burials of infants. [9]During labor, midwives gave no painkillers except alcohol. [10]Pain in childbirth was considered God's punishment for Eve's sin of eating the forbidden fruit in the Garden of Eden. [11]After delivery, new mothers were often treated to a banquet. [12]Women from well-to-do families were then expected to spend three to four weeks in bed recovering. [13]Women from poorer families were generally back at work in one or two days.

Item 1: The passage does not say there were no doctors, just that they did not assist with childbirth (sentence 5).

Item 2: See sentence 2.

Item 3: See sentence 8.

Item 4: Today pain is treated with medication and not viewed as God's punishment.

Item 5: The passage does not mention how long the women took to recover—just how long they were "out of work." (Since the poor women returned to work in a day or two, they might have actually been forced to recover faster than the rich women, who, by contrast, were encouraged to stay in bed "recovering" for weeks.)

____ 1. In colonial America, there were no doctors.

____ 2. Giving birth in colonial America was typically a lonely experience.

✓ 3. In colonial America, midwives filled several community roles.

✓ 4. Society's view of pain in childbirth has changed since the 1700s.

____ 5. Poor women recovered more slowly from childbirth than rich women.

REVIEW TEST 4

Here is a chance to apply your understanding of inferences to a longer reading selection. Jean Sutton grew up in West Oak Lane, a mostly African American community in northwest Philadelphia, and attended Franklin & Marshall College in rural Lancaster, Pennsylvania. There, she met her future husband. Jean's essay offers valuable suggestions about preparing for adult life, choosing a mate, and building a strong marriage.

Following the reading are questions on inferences. There are also questions on the skills taught in previous chapters.

Words to Watch

Below are some words in the reading that do not have strong context support. Each word is followed by the number of the paragraph in which it appears and its meaning there. These words are indicated in the selection by a small circle (°).

> *vulnerable* (5): not protected
> *mentor* (9): someone older and more experienced who provides advice and
> support
> *savvy* (10): well-informed
> *potential* (11): the possibility of becoming something in the future
> *acknowledged* (12): accepted
> *monks* (14): priests
> *advocate* (22): supporter
> *despair* (27): a feeling of hopelessness

A PATH TO MARRIAGE

Jean Sutton

1   "If I died, you'd have nothing. I have nothing to leave you."

2   Those are harsh words to hear when you're only 11, but I knew my mother was only telling me the truth.

3   "Don't make the same mistake I did," she said. "Educate yourself. Don't grow up expecting that a man will always provide for you. Anything can happen."

4   She knew what she was talking about. She had learned that lesson the hard way. With only an eighth-grade education, she had few job opportunities available to her. She provided childcare out of our home, a row house in a working-class neighborhood of Philadelphia. My father was a high-school graduate who had joined the military, and had then gone to work in a steel plant.

5   Then my father died suddenly. My mother and I were forced onto the emotional roller coaster that follows the death of a loved one. Our sorrow was compounded by the financial impact of my father's loss. My mother struggled to make ends meet. We had to give up our car, and we very nearly lost our house. At a very early age, I realized how vulnerable° an uneducated woman is.

6   I think that was my first lesson in selecting a mate and in preparing myself for adulthood. I learned that I wanted to be a financial equal in a marriage. I didn't want to have to marry in order to survive. I didn't want to be unable to support myself if my man was no longer around. I set about the task of becoming self-sufficient. I completed my formal education and am now an assistant vice president at an insurance company. I am

happily married, but I have also prepared myself for life's unexpected events.

7   From my elementary years on, I was a good student. I enjoyed school, but beyond that, I never forgot that education would provide me with the opportunities my mother hadn't had. When it was time for college, Franklin & Marshall College in Lancaster, Pennsylvania, offered me a scholarship. F&M is a very good school with a small minority enrollment. When I attended, there were 1,500 students, of whom about 50 were African American. I had gone to a Catholic high school with white students, so being with white people was not that big a deal. For me, the adjustment was more about class than about race. In high school, we'd all worn uniforms, so it wasn't so obvious who had money and who didn't.

8   But at F&M I really saw the difference. Now that I was living around people who had always had money, I felt poor in a way I never had before. My classmates were surprised that I took my work-study job in the cafeteria so seriously. If they had jobs, it was just to earn pocket money. But I needed my job so that I could buy a winter coat. In the summers I worked full-time in order to buy textbooks for the next year. Although I tried hard to find affordable used books, one year I ran out of money before the second semester began. That term I developed a new schedule. I would sleep in the evening while my dorm mates studied. Then I would borrow the books I needed and study through the night. I took special satisfaction in making the dean's list that term!

Because F&M didn't have a large enrollment of Black students, the Black Student Union made special efforts to help us get to know each other. The BSU assigned each of us incoming students a mentor°, and early in my freshman year they hosted a dance. My mentor noticed me sitting on the sidelines and asked one of the older students to invite me to dance. That student was Rod Sutton, the man I would later marry. I told Rod that I didn't feel like dancing. He said, "Okay, but then I'm going to sit and talk with you."   9

What I first noticed about Rod was the same thing most people notice— that he's *big*: a big, tall man with a big voice. And being from inner-city Newark, New Jersey, he's very street savvy°. As we sat and talked, however, I sensed that this big, loud guy was also kind and gentle. I felt a bond with him, as we had both grown up in the city without much money.   10

For a full year after that first meeting, Rod and I were just friends. Yes, for real, *friends*. And since I was just his friend, he wasn't trying to impress me. He was   11 just being himself. During that year, we had long talks about how we wanted our lives to turn out. He talked about his plan to teach and to attend graduate school. He told me that he wanted to complete his education before he got married. He talked about the girls he'd known in his old neighborhood who had become teenage mothers, and how sad he was that those smart, talented girls would be unlikely to ever realize their full potential°. He said he didn't want to bring a child into this world before he was ready to be a devoted, responsible parent.

12   Wow, I thought. Even as he was criticizing teenage pregnancy, he did it in a way that didn't trash the girls involved. He acknowledged° that they were smart and talented. He respected them. That impressed me.

13   Other things impressed me as well. During our friendship, I had the chance to hang out with Rod and his friends. Many of those friends were good-looking guys, attractive and smart. But some were disrespectful of their own girlfriends or were involved in relationships built on guilt or control. Once I heard one of these guys call his girlfriend the "b" word right to her face. She shrugged it off as if it were nothing. Can you believe that the next day she was walking across the campus with him, arm in arm? When Rod heard such things, he always spoke up to the guy. He would criticize the disrespectful attitude toward "the young lady," as he always carefully referred to the girl.

14   As Rod and I exchanged our life stories, I came to respect him even more.

I learned that this gentle, kind man had been an angry, troubled kid who had been repeatedly kicked out of school for fighting. He'd finally been sent to a kind of last-chance school, one run by monks°. There, gradually, he had turned around. As I heard him talk about how his attitude had changed and as I watched him in his daily life, I could see he was for real. He was consistent in his actions as well as his words. He wasn't saying things because he thought they were what I wanted to hear. He didn't just talk the talk—he walked the walk.

15   We began to date, and my good opinion of Rod kept growing. After we graduated from F&M, he got a job teaching elementary school. He lived in Philly but commuted to Camden, New Jersey, every day. That first winter, the temperature fell to zero after a storm that dropped seven inches of snow. The schools in Philly and Camden were closed, but Rod left for work so early in the morning that he missed the announcement and drove all the way to Camden anyway. Here was a single guy, no wife or children to support, and yet he had such a strong work ethic he always showed up at work, often earlier than anyone else.

16   Watching him, I thought, He's hardworking, considerate, respectful, and a communicator. What more could a girl ask for?

17   Then I saw him interact with an elderly woman. When we were in a department store, Rod noticed her carrying a heavy shopping bag and struggling to open the door. "Let me help you with that, ma'am," he said. He

took her bag and opened the door for her. "Thank you!" she said with a smile. He stood and watched her go until he was sure she was okay.

18   That sealed the deal for me. On top of everything else, he cared about our elderly! To this day, he respects the senior women in our church. He visits the sick and shut-ins. He goes beyond simply opening the door or helping with a bag. He engages them in a way that makes each one feel like the most important person in the world. I tease him about how he flatters the seniors, but I admire the care and respect that he shows. Given all the wonderful things I'd observed in Rod over the years, there was no question in my mind about what to say when he asked me to marry him.

19   My appreciation for his good qualities has only continued to grow since our wedding many years ago. Before my mother passed away, she was seriously ill for many months, and I was her sole caregiver. When I came down with the flu, Rod stepped in without hesitation. He visited her every single day, making sure she had a good meal and fresh water by her bedside. Some days he sat with her for hours, just to keep her company.

20   In parenthood, as well as elsewhere in our lives, Rod and I are true partners. We agreed that we wanted to wait to start our family until we felt really ready. I know that during the years before we had a child, Rod took some criticism from men he knew. They'd pressure him, saying things like "Don't you know how to make a baby?" They'd say it in a joking way, but you know a lot of guys would have been bothered by that. They were implying he wasn't a "real man" until he had fathered a child. But Rod never let such things get to him. He made it clear that *we* were going to make that decision; that we were a team, and that no outside pressure was going to influence us. I am so grateful that Rod felt the same way I did—that bringing a new human being into the world is a very serious decision, and not something to be done lightly.

21   We did make that decision in our own time, and our family now includes Paige, who is 13; Justin, 11; and Abu, an 8-year-old we're in the process of adopting. Abu has gone through a lot in his short life, and we are all excited about his move from the foster-care system to his forever home. In Rod's career as a teacher and now as an assistant principal, he has seen so many angry, scared, neglected children. He's worked very hard to help them, but as a teacher you can do only so much. We feel we've been very blessed in our own lives, and we've always wanted to share our good fortune with another child.

22   So by now you know that I'm a big fan of my husband and an advocate° of marriage. But rest assured that marriage is not easy. It takes a lot of negotiating° and hard work. That's why it is so important to have patience in selecting and getting to know your mate. You cannot get to know someone in a day, a week, or even a month. It takes time. A good rule of thumb is to know your mate through at least four seasons before you get married. Don't rush!

23   And don't just listen to what a

guy *says*. Words are easy. Observe his *actions*. Observe how he treats his family and close friends. That will be a good indication of how he'll treat you.

24   I see so many of the girls I grew up with settle for, in my opinion, far less than they deserve. We African American women face some special challenges. To begin with, we simply outnumber our marriageable men. So many of our men are in prison. And there is a widespread belief that high-achieving Black men don't marry Black women, that they go outside the race. I don't know how true that is, but many women believe it.

25   So I think a lot of women end up saying, "Well, this guy is halfway decent and not in prison," and they settle. And the result is so much divorce and so many children growing up without fathers. I understand why it happens. When your friends are getting married and having babies, it's easy to get swept up in the excitement of that. You don't want to be left behind. But marriage and parenthood are too important to go into for less than the right reasons.

26   I am convinced that good men, loving men, dependable men who hold themselves to high standards, are out there. Hold out! Give it time. Look in the right places—places like school, church, and work. I'll tell you where *not* to look—in bars and clubs. Sure, a good guy could be at a club. But in general, guys hanging out in clubs are looking for someone for a while, not for a lifetime.

27   Ladies, love yourself enough to, first, be the best person that you can be. Then love yourself enough to demand of your partner all that is rightfully yours. Take the time to be certain that the love you have is a love that will always be there. I'm not talking about the sexy love of your youth. I'm talking about a love that will be there at the end of your life, holding your hand when you take your last breath—a love that lasts not only through joy and fun, but also through sickness and despair° and whatever life may bring. Do not settle for less. Love yourself enough to hold out for all that you deserve.

Reading Comprehension Questions

Vocabulary in Context

___C___ 1. In the excerpt below, the word *compounded* (kŏm-pound′əd) means
A. hidden.
B. weakened.
C. increased.
D. explained.

What would financial troubles do to the sorrow of a family already suffering from the emotional blow of the father's death?

"Then my father died suddenly. My mother and I were forced onto the emotional roller coaster that follows the death of a loved one. Our sorrow was compounded by the financial impact of my father's loss." (Paragraph 5)

     D   2. In the excerpt below, the words *self-sufficient* (sĕlf'sə-fĭsh'ənt) mean
        A. attractive.
        B. important.
        C. interesting.
        D. independent.

> If she didn't want to have to marry and wanted to be able to support herself, what must she have decided to become?

> "I didn't want to have to marry in order to survive. I didn't want to be unable to support myself if my man was no longer around. I set about the task of becoming self-sufficient." (Paragraph 6)

Central Point and Main Ideas

     C   3. Which of the following sentences best expresses the central point of the selection?
        A. Sutton's father died when she was still a girl, leaving herself and her mother without much money.
        B. Sutton met her future husband when both were students at Franklin & Marshall College.
        C. Sutton believes that young Black women should not rush into marriage, but should first become self-sufficient and wait for a respectful, considerate partner.
        D. Sutton noticed that Rod Sutton was a hard worker, respectful of women, and kind to elderly people.

Answer A covers only paragraph 5. Answer B covers only paragraph 9. Answer D covers only paragraphs 11–18.

     A   4. Which sentence best expresses the main idea of paragraph 8?
        A. Despite not having as much money as her classmates at F&M, Sutton succeeded academically.
        B. Sutton needed her work-study job so that she could buy a winter coat.
        C. One year, Sutton ran out of money before the second semester began.
        D. Sutton took special satisfaction in making the dean's list at F&M.

Answers B, C, and D each cover only one sentence of paragraph 8.

Supporting Details

     C   5. What "sealed the deal" for Jean about marrying Rod Sutton was that he
        A. spoke up to guys who called their girlfriends the "b" word.
        B. traveled through a snowstorm to get to his teaching job in Camden, New Jersey.
        C. helped an elderly woman carrying a shopping bag.
        D. helped to care for Jean's elderly mother when she became seriously ill.

See paragraph 18.

Transitions

__B__   6. The sentence below begins with a word that signals
    A. time order.
    B. cause and effect.
    C. a contrast.
    D. a comparison.

> *Cause:* F&M didn't have many black students.
> *Effect:* The Black Student Union made special efforts to help blacks get to know one another.

"Because F&M didn't have a large enrollment of Black students, the Black Student Union made special efforts to help us get to know each other." (Paragraph 9)

Patterns of Organization

__A__   7. In paragraph 24, Sutton mainly
    A. lists some special challenges African American women face.
    B. gives reasons why so many African American men are in prison.
    C. contrasts the attitudes of Black men with the attitudes of Black women.
    D. compares attitudes toward marriage within the African American community.

> List words: *some special challenges.*
> Addition words: *To begin with.*

Inferences

__C__   8. From paragraph 13, we can infer that
    A. Jean liked some of Rod's friends more than she liked him.
    B. Rod sometimes called Jean the "b" word.
    C. Jean would never tolerate a boyfriend calling her the "b" word.
    D. Jean forced Rod to speak to his friends about the way they treated women.

> Answers A, B, and D are not supported. The third sentence from the end of paragraph 13 supports answer C.

__B__   9. Paragraph 15 suggests that

> Answers A, C, and D are not supported. The last sentence of paragraph 15 supports answer B.

    A. Jean Sutton thought Rod was crazy for going to work in seven inches of snow.
    B. Jean Sutton admires people who have a strong work ethic.
    C. Jean Sutton had never met a hard-working man before she met Rod.
    D. Rod Sutton nearly had an accident on his way to work.

__A__   10. On the basis of "A Path to Marriage," we can infer that

> Answers B, C, and D are not supported. Answer A is supported by paragraphs 10–19.

    A. Rod Sutton's respectful attitude toward women earned Jean's love and admiration.
    B. Rod Sutton hadn't always had a respectful attitude toward women.
    C. finding a good, dependable man to love is impossible for most African American women.
    D. physical attraction is the most important factor in selecting a mate.

Discussion Questions

1. After reading what Jean Sutton has to say about relationships, do you think she believes in "love at first sight?" Why or why not?

2. Sutton says several times that it's more important to pay attention to what a romantic partner *does* than what he *says*. Do you think her advice is worthwhile? Why or why not?

3. Sutton mentions that her husband, Rod, was teased by some male friends for not having a child sooner. Why do you think men would put pressure on each other that way? What did you think of Rod's response?

4. Jean Sutton describes her husband Rod as a true partner. Based on her description, what qualities must a mate have to be considered a true partner? Are those qualities ones that are important to you? Are there others you would add?

Note: Writing assignments for this selection appear on pages 592–593.

Check Your Performance   **INFERENCES**

Activity	Number Right	Points	Score
Review Test 1 (5 items)	_____	× 2 =	_____
Review Test 2 (5 items)	_____	× 6 =	_____
Review Test 3 (5 items)	_____	× 6 =	_____
Review Test 4 (10 items)	_____	× 3 =	_____
		TOTAL SCORE =	_____ %

Enter your total score into the **Reading Performance Chart: Review Tests** on the inside back cover.

INFERENCES: Mastery Test 1

A. (1–4.) Shown below is a note that was actually found on a car windshield in Chicago. Put a check (✓) by the **four** inferences that are most logically based on the information given in the note.

> Mario—
> You said you had to work then whys your car here at HER place? I hate you, you slime.
> P.S. text me later

  ✓ 1. The note was written by Mario's girlfriend.

  ___ 2. The car was not really Mario's.

  ___ 3. Mario had gotten out of work early.

  ✓ 4. Mario's car was parked at another woman's house.

  ✓ 5. Mario had lied to his girlfriend.

  ___ 6. The author of the note will never speak to Mario again.

  ✓ 7. The author of the note thinks Mario is cheating on her.

  ___ 8. Mario and the author of the note are married.

Logical inferences:
Item 1: Who else but a girlfriend would say things such as were written in the note?
Item 4: "HER place" suggests that Mario's car was parked at another woman's house.
Item 5: The note says, "You said you had to work then whys your car . . . ."
Item 7: Clues: "HER place" and "I hate you, you slime."

Items that are not logical inferences:
Item 2: There is no way to know who owns the car.
Item 3: There is no way to know what Mario's work hours are or when he works.
Item 6: The note indicates the opposite: "text me later."
Item 8: Nothing indicates the marital status of either.

(Continues on next page)

B. After reading each short passage, check (✓) the **two** inferences that are most logically based on the given information.

5–6. ¹There's an old story about a certain state legislator who had spent some time in a mental institution. ²For years after, when debate in the legislature got heated, he would wave his release papers and declare, "I've got papers that prove I'm sane! ³What about the rest of you?"

____ A. The legislator was ashamed of having been in a mental institution.
For years he had been telling everyone.

✓ B. When he left the institution, the legislator was considered sane.
Sentence 2: "I've got papers that prove I'm sane!"

✓ C. The legislator had been reelected despite his mental problems.
He was in the legislature "for years after."

____ D. The legislator should never have been released from the mental institution.
Nothing in the passage indicates that the legislator is still mentally ill.

7–8. ¹"Most people don't believe me when I tell them that reading aloud is the single most important factor in reading success," author Jim Trelease says as he prepares to speak to an audience of parents and teachers. ²"They don't believe me for three reasons: One, it's simple. ³Two, it's free. ⁴And three, the child enjoys it. ⁵But if reading required a $149 machine, we'd have it in half the homes of America. ⁶And if kids hated it, we'd have it in every classroom."

Statement C: Sentence 1 identifies Trelease as an author speaking to parents and teachers. We can assume his book is about children and reading.

____ A. The use of a machine is the best way to teach a child to read.
Not supported. Sentence 1 states that reading aloud is the best way.

✓ B. If something is simple, free, and enjoyable, people believe it's too good to be true.
See sentences 2–4.

✓ C. Jim Trelease has probably written a book about children and reading.

____ D. Learning to read is a complex and difficult challenge for any child.
Not mentioned.

9–10. ¹A well-known prayer goes as follows: "Oh, God, grant me the courage to change what I must change, the patience to bear what I must bear, and the wisdom to know the difference."

✓ A. It sometimes takes courage to change one's life.
The fact that the prayer asks for courage suggests that courage is needed for change.

____ B. Courage is more important than patience.
Neither courage nor patience is evaluated in the passage.

____ C. Courage and patience are much the same.

✓ D. We sometimes aren't wise enough to know when we must simply accept a situation.
The fact that the prayer asks for wisdom suggests that people sometimes don't have enough wisdom to know when to accept a situation.

INFERENCES: Mastery Test 2

A. (1–4.) Put a check (✓) by the **four** inferences that are most logically based on the information given in the following cartoon.

Items 1–2: The figure on the left is muscular, suggesting he works out regularly.

Item 3: The different shapes of the two figures suggest they do different things.

Item 4: Not supported.

Item 5: The figure's large head suggests that his time at the library caused his mind to grow—an important effect.

___ 1. The figure on the left does not work out at all.

✓ 2. The figure on the left probably spends lots of time working out.

✓ 3. The two figures do very different things when they work out.

___ 4. The two figures do not like each other.

___ 5. Spending time at the library has had no effect on the figure on the right.

✓ 6. Spending time at the library has made the figure on the right mentally strong.

___ 7. Working out at the library has the same effect as working out at the gym.

✓ 8. Working out at the library involves mental—not physical—effort.

Item 6: The right figure's large head suggests he has a strong mind, just as the left figure's large muscles suggest he has a strong body.

Item 7: The differences in the two figures show that their "workouts" have different effects.

Item 8: The size of the right figure's large head and small body suggest his work is mental, not physical.

(Continues on next page)

345

B. After reading each short passage, check (✓) the **two** inferences that are most logically based on the given information.

5–6. ¹A doctor calls a patient into his office to reveal the results of some recent tests. ²"I have some bad news and some worse news," says the doctor. ³"The bad news is that you only have 24 hours to live."

⁴"Oh no," says the patient. ⁵"What could be worse than that?"

⁶The doctor answers, "I've been trying to reach you since yesterday."

_____ A. The patient learns he has cancer.   The doctor does not tell the patient what his medical problem is.

✓ B. The patient learns he will die that very day.   See sentences 3 and 6.

_____ C. The patient learns he will die a painless death.   Not mentioned.

✓ D. The patient at first cannot believe anything is worse than having only one day to live.   See sentence 5.

7–8. ¹Americans tend to see old age negatively, as a time of physical and mental decline. ²In Japan, the situation is very different. ³For instance, elderly guests arriving at a hotel in Japan are asked their age—a tradition meant to ensure that they will receive the proper respect. ⁴Japanese grandmothers wear red to show their high status. ⁵And to celebrate reaching age sixty, a Japanese man wears a red vest. ⁶This, too, is a sign of great honor.

✓ A. The Japanese tend to view old age more positively than Americans do.   See sentences 1 and 2.

_____ B. Old people in Japan do not experience as much physical or mental decline as old people in the United States.   The passage does not discuss people's decline in old age.

_____ C. Guests at a Japanese hotel would probably be embarrassed to state their age.   See sentences 4–5. In Japan, people don't hide old age; they show it off.

✓ D. The color red apparently has a special meaning in Japan.   See sentences 4–6.

9–10. ¹"I hate war," said U.S. General Dwight Eisenhower, "as only a soldier who has lived it can, as one who has seen its brutality, its futility, its stupidity. ²Every gun that is made, every warship launched, every rocket fired, signifies in the final sense a theft from those who hunger and are not fed, those who are cold and not clothed."

_____ A. Eisenhower did not like the military.   Not supported. He speaks of war, not the military.

✓ B. Eisenhower's involvement in war made him hate war.   See the last part of sentence 1.

✓ C. Eisenhower believed that the money spent on war could be put to better use.   See sentence 2.

_____ D. Eisenhower believed the military was directly responsible for poverty and hunger.   Not supported. He says war steals from the poor and the hungry, not that the military is responsible for hunger and poverty.

INFERENCES: Mastery Test 3

A. (1–4.) After reading each short passage, check (✓) the **two** inferences that are most firmly based on the given information.

1–2. ¹For centuries, coca leaves have been chewed by South American Indians to combat fatigue, hunger, and thirst. ²When processed into cocaine, coca becomes much more powerful. ³Cocaine was once believed to be a safe painkiller and was prescribed by doctors. ⁴In fact, Coca-Cola originally contained a small amount of cocaine. ⁵In recent times, cocaine has been recognized as a dangerous addictive drug.

_____ A. Cocaine is not an effective painkiller. The fact that cocaine was once prescribed by doctors suggests it was effective.

✓ B. Coca grows naturally in South America. Since coca has been chewed in South America for centuries, it must grow there naturally.

_____ C. Coca leaves are more dangerous than processed cocaine. Cocaine is more powerful (sentence 2); it is probably more dangerous.

✓ D. Cocaine was once legal in the United States. Since cocaine was prescribed by doctors and used in Coca-Cola, it must have once been legal in the U.S.

3–4. ¹A small private plane developed engine trouble while still many miles from a suitable landing strip. ²The pilot, realizing there was nothing he could do to keep the plane in the air, rushed back to where his three passengers sat and explained the situation. ³He added, "I am a married man with two small children. ⁴I regret to tell you there are only three parachutes aboard." ⁵And with that, he grabbed one of the parachutes and bailed out.

⁶One of the passengers reacted quickly to the pilot's exit. ⁷"I am a brilliant scientist!" he announced. ⁸"I am the world's smartest man! ⁹The world cannot do without me!" ¹⁰And with that, he too bailed out.

¹¹The other two passengers, an elderly priest and a Boy Scout, were quiet for a moment. ¹²"Son," the priest said finally, "I am old and have lived a full life. ¹³I am ready to meet my Maker."

¹⁴"You'll have to cancel the meeting, Father," the Boy Scout answered, smiling. ¹⁵"The world's smartest man just bailed out with my backpack!"

_____ A. Scientists tend to think highly of themselves. One scientist's self-assessment cannot be applied to all scientists.

✓ B. The "world's smartest man" wasn't as smart as he thought. He wasn't smart enough to grab the parachute.

_____ C. Scientists are more important to the world than priests and Boy Scouts. The passage doesn't make judgments about people's importance.

✓ D. No matter how smart someone is, he or she needs to examine the facts closely before acting. The "brilliant scientist" should have looked—to make sure he had a parachute—before he leaped.

(Continues on next page)

B. After reading each short passage, check (✓) the **three** inferences that are most firmly based on the given information.

5–7. [1]A disk jockey in Dallas asked his listeners to send him money, and they did. [2]One day, Ron Chapman of station KVIL simply told his listeners, "Go to your checkbooks. [3]Write a check payable to KVIL Fun and Games. [4]Make it in the amount of $20 and mail it to this address." [5]He never stated why listeners should send the money, only that they should. [6]Chapman expected that about three or four hundred listeners would respond. [7]He intended to return their checks and send them a bag of goodies from his sponsors. [8]However, instead of four hundred checks, over twelve thousand were received, amounting to $244,240. [9]The station donated the money to charity.

Statement C:
The fact that Chapman had planned to return the money with "goodies" suggests his announcement was meant to be a trick on listeners.

✓   A. People will sometimes do what they're told without knowing exactly why.   Many people sent money (sentence 8) even though they were not told why (sentence 5) they should.

___ B. The station gave the money to the homeless.   Not mentioned.

✓   C. Chapman made his announcement to play a trick on his listeners.

___ D. Chapman's sponsors were furious about the stunt.   Not mentioned.

✓   E. Chapman assumed that a small percentage of his listeners would send money without knowing why.   See sentence 6.

8–10. [1]At Wellness Community meetings, cancer patients give each other various types of support, including the opportunity to laugh. [2]They laugh with each other about things that would make outsiders uneasy. [3]One joke told by patients is about a man with cancer who has just learned that he has only one more night to live. [4]He asks his wife to come to the bedroom with him for one last sexual encounter. [5]His wife says, "Gosh, Hugo, I'd love to, but I'm too tired." [6]Hugo says, "Oh, come on." [7]And his wife says, "That's easy for you to say. [8]You don't have to get up in the morning."

___ A. In real life, cancer patients cannot participate in sex.

✓   B. Cancer patients can laugh about their problems.   See sentence 2.

✓   C. The author feels that healthy people may be uncomfortable over jokes about death.   See sentence 2.

✓   D. The wife in the joke is aware that Hugo will die the next morning.

___ E. All cancer patients in the Wellness Community meeting will die from their illness.

Statement A: Whether cancer patients can or cannot participate in sex is not mentioned.

Statement D: See sentence 8. The wife's words "you don't have to get up" suggests she knows Hugo will die.

Statement E: The passage does not comment about the death of the patients. It just tells a joke about the death of one man.

INFERENCES: Mastery Test 4

A. Read each passage and check (✓) the **two** inferences that are most firmly based on the given information.

1–2. ¹"You're just like an ostrich, burying your head in the sand!" ²We say this about a person who foolishly pretends not to notice danger approaching. ³Actually, the ostrich does not do anything quite so silly. ⁴When threatened, an ostrich may sit down and stretch its long neck against the ground. ⁵In that position, the bird resembles a grassy mound of earth. ⁶This is also the ostrich's position while guarding its nest. ⁷During the day, the dull-brown-colored female stretches out across the nest. ⁸At night, the black male takes over.

Statement A: We can infer this is true since the female ostrich—which can blend into its environment—is brown. If it did not match its surroundings, it would not be able to hide (sentence 7).

✓ A. During the day, the natural environment of the ostrich probably is a dull brown color.

___ B. Ostriches are among the most intelligent of animals.   The passage does not address the intelligence of ostriches.

✓ C. If they mistake the ostrich for a mound of earth, unfriendly animals will ignore it.   We can infer this is true since most animals have no reason to bother "a mound of earth."

___ D. People should feel complimented when they are compared to ostriches.   The passage does not suggest that it's good or bad for humans to be compared to ostriches.

3–4. ¹Trial lawyers point out that eyewitness accounts of crimes—often used to build a case against a suspect—are not always reliable. ²Experiments back up their claim. ³In one experiment, for example, a group of students was shown a film of a car accident. ⁴Then the students were questioned about the film. ⁵Some were asked, "How fast was the white sports car going when it passed the barn?" ⁶A week later, all the students were asked whether there had been a barn in the film. ⁷Nearly 20 percent of the students who had been asked the initial question "remembered" the barn. ⁸In fact, there was no barn in the film.

✓ A. Experiments support trial lawyers' claim that eyewitness testimony is not always reliable.   The entire passage describes an experiment showing that eyewitnesses were unreliable.

___ B. Students are obviously less reliable than many firsthand witnesses in trials.   The passage does not compare types of eyewitnesses.

___ C. Eyewitnesses are the least reliable sources of evidence.   The passage does not address other sources of evidence.

✓ D. Eyewitnesses can be influenced into giving untrue testimony without realizing it.   See sentences 6 and 7. The experimenter planted the barn in the minds of the students, although it did not appear in the film.

(Continues on next page)

B. Read each passage and check (✓) the **three** inferences that are most firmly based on the given information.

5–7. ¹In Brazil, life moves slowly, and personal relationships are more important than financial success. ²Social life revolves around friends, relatives, and special occasions, like weddings or communions. ³People greet each other with a peck on each cheek or a hearty embrace, and being too much on one's own is seen as abnormal. ⁴Businesspeople in the cities go home to nearby apartments for lunch. ⁵Shops close from noon to 2:00 p.m. so the family can be together. ⁶No one feels a need to always be "on time," and people get there when they get there. ⁷The important thing is to enjoy life.

Item A:
Difficulty is not discussed, but it would seem that a slower life might be easier, not harder.

____ A. Life in Brazil is more difficult than life in the United States.

✓ B. Brazilians are less concerned with financial success than Americans.
See sentence 1.

✓ C. Brazilians are a warm, social people.
See sentence 3.

____ D. Brazilians place a high value on promptness.
See sentence 6.

✓ E. Brazilians place a high value on family life.
See sentences 2 and 5.

8–10. ¹There are two strong influences on the content of dreams. ²One influence is the time of your dream. ³When you are closest to waking, your dreams are apt to be about recent events. ⁴Those are the dreams you are most likely to remember because you tend to remember dreams you have had just before waking up. ⁵In the middle of the night, however, your dreams are more likely to involve childhood or past events. ⁶The other influence on the content of dreams is presleep conditions. ⁷In one study, subjects who had six hours of active exercise before sleep tended to have dreams with little physical activity. ⁸The researcher concluded that dream content may offset waking experiences to some extent. ⁹Other research supports that conclusion. ¹⁰For instance, subjects who had experienced a day of social isolation had dreams with a great amount of social interaction. ¹¹Also, subjects who had been water-deprived dreamed of drinking.

____ A. Some people rarely dream.
The passage does not address whether we dream or not or how often.

✓ B. The researchers sometimes woke people up to ask what they were dreaming about.
To learn what people were dreaming during the night, researchers must have wakened sleepers.

✓ C. If you dream about your tenth birthday, the dream is likely to occur in the middle of the night.
See sentence 5.

____ D. A student studying for finals will probably dream about studying.

✓ E. People who go to bed hungry probably tend to dream of eating.
See sentence 11.

Statement D:
Sentences 6–10 suggest the opposite— a person who studies is not likely to dream of studying.

INFERENCES: Mastery Test 5

A. Read the passage and then write, in each space provided, the letter of the inference most logically supported by the information given.

¹Beware! ²Right now, a movie filled with blood, gore, and severed body parts is on its way to a theater near you. ³The movie's title doesn't matter. ⁴It will follow the same plot as the countless other "slash and gore" movies that have come before it. ⁵These movies are easy to spot. ⁶All involve young, attractive teens having sex and then getting sliced and diced. ⁷The chopping is usually done by an evil villain with bad teeth and a deep, threatening laugh. ⁸And if one of these movies does well at the box office, a sequel will be made—usually with an even larger dose of gore and butchery. ⁹Such movies manage to draw large audiences because they offer date-night appeal. ¹⁰People tend to hold, squeeze, and grab each other when they're scared. ¹¹These movies also offer some privacy to teens intent on making out. ¹²Any sensible adult wouldn't be caught dead at one of these movies.

_C_ 1. We can conclude that the movies to which the author refers
   A. attract only adults.
   B. are uninteresting to teens.
   C. attract teens.

   Sentence 11 suggests that teens are present at these movies.

_A_ 2. We can infer that the author of the passage feels that the audience of horror movies
   A. likes to be scared at the movies.
   B. does not like to be scared at those movies.
   C. is never scared at the movies.

   See sentence 9 ("date-night appeal") and sentence 10 ("hold, squeeze, and grab each other when they're scared").

_C_ 3. We can infer that the author of the paragraph feels the "slash and gore" plots are generally
   A. harmful to audiences.
   B. surprising.
   C. not very creative.

   Sentence 4 mentions the "countless other 'slash and gore' movies that have come before it" and that "follow the same plot."

B. (4–8.) Read the following passage from *Homecoming*, an autobiography by Floyd Dell (1887–1969). Then check (✓) the **five** statements that are most logically supported by the information given.

¹That fall, before it was discovered that the soles of both my shoes were worn clear through, I still went to Sunday school. ²And one time the Sunday school superintendent made a speech to all the classes. ³He said that these were hard times, and that many poor children weren't getting enough to eat. ⁴It was the first

(Continues on next page)

Logical inferences:

Item 1:
See sentence 6.

Item 3:
Most people don't eat the same thing every day because they like the taste that much. Potatoes were cheap.

Item 6:
See sentence 26.

Item 7:
See sentence 16.

Item 8:
See sentence 1.

Items that are not logical inferences:

Item 2:
Even if something is good, we don't usually eat it every day—unless we have to.

Item 4:
See sentence 14. The father was a joker and pretended to be surprised. His comment was not serious.

Item 5:
The entire narrative suggests that the author wanted very much to help the poor.

that I had heard about it. [5]He asked everybody to bring some food for the poor children next Sunday. [6]I felt very sorry for the poor children.

[7]Also, little envelopes were distributed to all the classes. [8]Each little boy and girl was to bring money for the poor, next Sunday. [9]The pretty Sunday school teacher explained that we were to write our names, or have our parents write them, up in the left-hand corner of the little envelopes. . . . [10]I told my mother all about it when I came home. [11]And my mother gave me, the next Sunday, a small bag of potatoes to carry to Sunday school. [12]I supposed the poor children's mothers would make potato soup out of them. . . . [13]Potato soup was good. [14]My father, who was quite a joker, would always say, as if he were surprised, "Ah! I see we have some nourishing potato soup today!" [15]It was so good that we had it every day. [16]My father was at home all day long and every day, now; and I liked that, even if he was grumpy. . . .

[17]Taking my small bag of potatoes to Sunday school, I looked around for the poor children; I was disappointed not to see them. [18]I had heard about poor children in stories. [19]But I was told just to put my contribution with the others on the big table in the side room.

[20]I had brought with me the little yellow envelope with some money in it for the poor children. [21]My mother had put the money in it and sealed it up. [22]She wouldn't tell me how much money she had put in it, but it felt like several dimes. [23]Only she wouldn't let me write my name on the envelope. [24]I had learned to write my name, and I was proud of being able to do it. [25]But my mother said firmly, no, I must not write my name on the envelope; she didn't tell me why. [26]On the way to Sunday school I had pressed the envelope against the coins until I could tell what they were; they weren't dimes but pennies.

✓ 1. At the time, the author did not realize he was a poor child himself.

___ 2. The family had potato soup every day because it was so good.

✓ 3. The family had potato soup every day because it was so inexpensive.

___ 4. The father's comment on potato soup showed his interest in nutrition.

___ 5. The author feels that it is a bad idea to try to help the poor.

✓ 6. The author's mother didn't want his name on the envelope because she was ashamed of their small donation.

✓ 7. The author's father had probably lost his job.

✓ 8. The author soon stopped going to Sunday school.

INFERENCES: Mastery Test 6

A. (1–4.) Read the following textbook passage. Then check (✓) the **four** statements that are most logically supported by the information given.

[1]Sitting alone in a dining room where bank officers had lunch, a researcher listened to what they were talking about at nearby tables. [2]When no woman was present, the men talked mostly about business. [3]They rarely spoke about people. [4]The next most popular topics were food, sports, and recreation. [5]When women talked alone, their most frequent topic was people, especially friends, children, and partners in personal relationships. [6]Business was next, and then health, including weight control. [7]Together, women and men tended to avoid the topic that each group liked best. [8]Instead, they settled on topics of interest to both, but they followed the style of the men-only conversations. [9]They talked about food the way men did, focusing on the food and restaurant rather than diet and health. [10]They talked about recreation the way men did, concentrating on sports figures and athletic events rather than on exercising for weight control. [11]And they talked about housing the way men did, dealing mostly with location, property values, and commuting time. [12]They did not talk about whether a house is suitable for the family, how safe the neighborhood is for the children, or what kinds of people live next door.

Logical inferences:

Item 1: Sentences 2–5 support this inference.

Item 4: See sentence 3.

Item 6: Sentences 8–11 support this inference.

Item 7: See sentences 6–9. Women talk about diets and health; men don't.

✓ 1. Men and women prefer different topics and styles of conversation.

___ 2. Women never change their style of conversation.

___ 3. Women have fewer personal relationships than men do.

✓ 4. Men tend not to talk about their personal relationships.

___ 5. Women care more about food than men do.

✓ 6. Women speak differently when speaking to each other than they do when speaking with men.

✓ 7. Women are more interested in dieting than men are.

___ 8. There's really very little difference between men's and women's conversations.

Items that are not logical inferences:

Item 2: Sentences 8–11 disprove this inference. Women do change their conversation style.

Item 3: Not supported.

Item 5: Not supported. Both genders talk about food.

Item 8: Sentences 2–6 disprove this inference.

(Continues on next page)

B. (5–8.) Read the following textbook passage. Then check (✓) the **four** statements that are most logically supported by the information given.

¹The cause of cholera was not discovered until 1883. ²That's when Robert Koch, the famous scientist, led a group to Egypt that found the guilty germ. ³The deadly bacteria settle in the intestines of their victims. ⁴Dirty hands or raw fruits and vegetables often transmit the disease. ⁵But most cholera epidemics are spread by drinking water that has been polluted with raw sewage.

⁶Unfortunately, America's cities in 1832 had more than enough filth to encourage an epidemic. ⁷New York City was especially dirty. ⁸Residents were required by law to pile their garbage in the gutter in front of their homes for removal by the city. ⁹However, it seldom got collected. ¹⁰The only effective "sanitary engineers" in New York were the thousands of pigs that roamed the streets, eating the refuse.

¹¹Thanks to this filth, there was a great plague of death when cholera reached New York. ¹²Thousands died in the epidemic. ¹³There were so many bodies that the undertakers could not keep up with the volume. ¹⁴They had to stack corpses in warehouses and public buildings to await burial.

¹⁵In the midst of their suffering, New Yorkers could not help wondering why some people got the disease while others escaped it. ¹⁶Some of America's doctors thought they had an answer. ¹⁷People who kept God's laws, they explained, had nothing to fear.

Logical inferences:

Item 3: The fact that garbage was allowed to pile in front of homes—without being removed—suggests New Yorkers did not know of its dangers.

Item 4: Sentences 1 and 6 support this inference. Cholera hit New York in 1832; the cause of the disease was not discovered until 1883.

Item 5: See sentences 16–17.

Item 8: Today we have clean drinking water and do not expose ourselves to the pollution mentioned in sentence 5.

____ 1. New York was the only American city to suffer from cholera.

____ 2. Cholera is more likely to spread in the countryside than in the city.

✓ 3. In the early 1800s, the dangers of polluting water with garbage were not clear to New Yorkers.

✓ 4. At the time of the plague in New York, doctors did not really know what caused cholera.

✓ 5. Some doctors turned to religion to explain what they did not understand.

____ 6. Many victims of the New York cholera epidemic never got buried.

____ 7. In the 1800s, cholera was, in fact, easily cured.

✓ 8. A cholera epidemic is unlikely to occur in the United States today.

Items that are not logical inferences:

Item 1: Sentence 6 ("America's cities") suggests that New York was not the only one.

Item 2: Not supported. The issue of cholera in the countryside is not discussed.

Item 6: Sentences 13 and 14 imply that they would be buried but had to "await burial."

Item 7: Since the cause of the cholera was not discovered until 1883, it is unlikely the disease would have been easy to cure before then.

9 Implied Main Ideas

This Chapter in a Nutshell

- Main ideas may be clearly suggested, or **implied**, rather than stated directly.

- In such cases, look closely at the supporting details. Then decide what general idea includes or summarizes those details.

- A general idea must "fit" the details; it must not be either too narrow or too broad for those details.

What Are Implied Main Ideas?

Main ideas are not always stated directly. Sometimes you must infer them from the evidence presented. For instance, what is the main idea of the poster below?

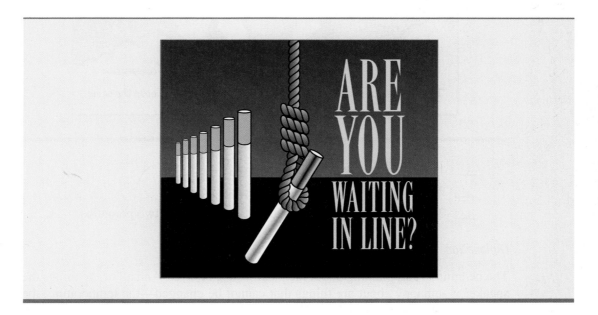

Write here what you think is the implied main idea: _____

_____ Smoking kills. (Or: If you smoke, you are waiting in line to die.) _____

Explanation

Let's consider the details: There's a hangman's noose around one cigarette, and the other cigarettes are waiting in line for the noose. These details vividly express the idea that smoking kills, so anyone who smokes is waiting in line to die.

Check Your Understanding

Look at the following cartoon. Put a check (✓) by the implied main idea.

what sentence is left out?

____ 1. The speaker will not be happy anywhere.

✓ 2. The speaker wants to live somewhere else.

____ 3. The speaker does not get along with the other two penguins.

Explanation

The penguin is complaining about the place where he lives. And all of the things the speaker is unhappy about are things that cannot be changed—the temperature, the snow, and what others look like. These details all imply that the penguin wants to live somewhere else.

Finding Implied Main Ideas in Reading

In reading as well as in visual materials, the main idea is often not directly stated, but clearly implied. Such is the case with the paragraph below. See if you can infer its main idea. Check (✓) the letter of the statement that best summarizes all the supporting details.

> ¹I was in an alley dressed in light summer clothing. ²Coming out of the darkness at the end of the alley were hundreds of large gray rats. ³Their razor-sharp teeth glistened with saliva, and their eyes glowed red with a cold fury. ⁴I turned to run away, but attacking in the other direction were a dozen angry dogs—pit bulls! ⁵And these particular pit bulls were foaming at the mouth; they all had rabies. ⁶"Just my luck," I muttered and did my best to wake up as quickly as possible.

_____ A. The writer is losing his mind.

_____ B. Gray rats and pit bulls are scary animals.

_____ C. Everyone has nightmares.

__✓__ D. The writer had a really bad dream.

Explanation

A. You may at first have thought the writer was indeed going mad. But the last sentence makes clear that the disturbing details of the paragraph were in a nightmare.

B. The statement that the rats and pit bulls are scary doesn't account for the last line of the paragraph, in which the writer reveals that all the details up to that point were in a nightmare.

C. The scary details of the paragraph are in one person's dream, but there's no support for the statement that everyone has nightmares.

D. The words "I . . . did my best to wake up as quickly as possible" plus all the scary details make clear that item D is the implied main idea.

As the above paragraph shows, a paragraph may lack a main idea *sentence*, but that doesn't mean it lacks a main idea. In this chapter, you will practice finding implied main ideas.

Following is a four-step process that will develop your skill at finding implied main ideas.

Step 1: Recognizing Implied General Ideas

Learning how to find unstated general ideas or subjects is a helpful step in finding unstated main ideas. Read the following list of specific items, and then write the letter of the general idea that best covers them. The answer will be the group to which all of the specific ideas belong.

　_C_　*Specific ideas:* baseball cap, football helmet, Easter bonnet

　　The general idea is
　　A.　sports hats.
　　B.　clothing.
　　C.　hats.

Since an Easter bonnet is not a sports hat, answer A is wrong—it is too narrow to cover all the specific ideas. It is true that all the specific ideas are items of clothing, but they have more in common than that—they are only items of clothing worn on the head. Thus answer B is much broader than necessary, and answer C is the correct choice.

When you are looking for the general idea, remember these points:

1　The general idea must cover all of the specific ideas. (*Hats* covers *baseball cap, football helmet,* and *Easter bonnet.*)

2　The general idea must not be so narrow that it excludes any of the specific ideas. (*Sports hats* is too narrow—it does not cover *Easter bonnet.*)

3　A general idea that covers many kinds of specific ideas in addition to the ones in the list is too broad. (*Clothing* is too broad—it covers specific ideas in addition to *hats,* such as *shoes* and *pajamas.*)

Check Your Understanding

Read the following list of specific items, and then write the letter of the general idea.

　_B_　*Specific ideas:*

　　"I couldn't take the final because my grandmother died."
　　"I couldn't come in to work because I had a migraine headache."
　　"I couldn't study because I forgot to bring my book home."

　　The general idea is
　　A.　common remarks.
　　B.　common excuses.
　　C.　common student excuses.

Explanation

The specific ideas are common remarks. Yet *common remarks* covers various types of remarks—common compliments, common greetings, common excuses, and so on. But all of the specific ideas on the previous page are one type of common remark—common excuses. Thus answer A is too broad, and answer B is the correct answer. Answer C is too narrow because only two of the three specific ideas are student excuses; one is a worker excuse.

> *Hint:* When you are trying to discover a general idea, ask yourself these questions:
>
> 1) Does a general idea cover **all** of the specific ideas listed? If not, it is **too narrow**.
>
> 2) Does a general idea cover **more** ideas than the specific ideas listed? If so, it is **too broad**.

PRACTICE 1

Read each group of specific ideas. Then, in the space provided, write the letter of the general idea that tells what the specific ideas have in common. Keep in mind that the correct general idea will not be too narrow or too broad.

__B__ 1. *Specific ideas:* blueberries, strawberries, cranberries, cherries, peaches

The general idea is
A. foods.
B. fruits.
C. berries.

Answer A is too broad.
Answer C is too narrow.

__A__ 2. *Specific ideas:* worn brakes, body rust, weak battery, cracked windshield

The general idea is
A. car problems.
B. external car problems.
C. transportation problems.

Answer B is too narrow.
Answer C is too broad.

__A__ 3. *Specific ideas:* penny, nickel, dime, dollar bill

The general idea is
A. money.
B. coins.
C. folding money.

Answers B and C are too narrow.

___B___ 4. *Specific ideas:* church, synagogue, temple, mosque

The general idea is

A. institutions.

Answer A is too broad.
Answer C is too narrow.

B. religious institutions.

C. Christian institutions.

___A___ 5. *Specific ideas:* combs, brushes, razors

The general idea is

A. items for grooming.

Answers B and C are too narrow.

B. women's items for grooming.

C. men's items for grooming.

___C___ 6. *Specific ideas:* eyeglasses, telescope, microscope, magnifying glass

The general idea is

A. inventions.

Answer A is too broad.
Answer B is too narrow.

B. very recent inventions.

C. inventions for seeing.

___A___ 7. *Specific ideas:* letter, e-mail, telephone, smoke signal

The general idea is

A. forms of communication.

Answers B and C are too narrow.

B. forms of electronic communication.

C. forms of written communication.

___C___ 8. *Specific ideas:* nose, pupil of an eye, bull's-eye, doughnut hole

The general idea is

A. objects.

Answer A is too broad.
Answer B is incorrect.

B. body parts.

C. things in the middle.

___C___ 9. *Specific ideas:* "Mayor Reelected by Wide Margin." "Stocks Fall." "Stocks Rise." "Body Found in Trunk." "Storm Paralyzes City."

The general idea is

A. titles.

Answer A is too broad.
Answer B is incorrect.

B. titles of books.

C. headlines in news articles.

___C__ 10. *Specific ideas:* syllable divisions, pronunciation, plural forms, meanings

The general idea is

A. information.

Answers A and B are too broad.

B. useful information.

C. information found in a dictionary entry.

Step 2: Putting Implied General Ideas into Your Own Words

Now that you have practiced recognizing general ideas, you are ready to practice stating such ideas on your own. Below is an example. Consider the four specific ideas, and then decide on a general idea that is neither too broad nor too narrow.

General idea: Liquids

Specific ideas: orange juice
water
milk
blood

At first glance it might seem that the general idea of these specific ideas is *beverages*. But blood does not fall into that category (except for Dracula). So you must use a broader general idea to include *blood*. Thus the general idea here is *liquids*.

DO IN CLASS

PRACTICE 2

In the following lists, the specific ideas are given, but the general ideas are unstated. Fill in the blanks with the unstated general ideas. Parts of some answers are provided for you.   *Wording of answers may vary.*

1. *General idea:*   Directions

   Specific ideas: up
   down
   northwest
   south

2. *General idea:*   Seafood

   Specific ideas: salmon
   lobster
   shrimp
   flounder

3. *General idea:*   Tests (or Test questions)

   Specific ideas: multiple choice
   essay
   true-false
   fill in the blank

4. *General idea:* _____Noises (or Sounds)_____

   Specific ideas: squeak
   whistle
   shout
   buzz

5. *General idea:* Parts of a_____book_____

   Specific ideas: cover
   table of contents
   chapters
   index

6. *General idea:* Jobs in a _____restaurant_____

   Specific ideas: chef
   waitress
   cashier
   bus boy

7. *General idea:* Things that are _____white_____

   Specific ideas: snow
   wedding dress
   milk
   the President's house

8. *General idea:* _____Baby_____ animals

   Specific ideas: kitten
   puppy
   chick
   lamb

9. *General idea:* _____Signs_____

   Specific ideas: DO NOT ENTER
   REST ROOMS
   FIRE EXIT
   RIGHT TURN ONLY

10. *General idea:* _____Opposites (or Words with opposite meanings)_____

    Specific ideas: *sick* and *well*
    good and *evil*
    cheap and *expensive*
    left and *right*

Step 3: Recognizing Implied Main Ideas I

Just as with the unstated general ideas above, your choice of an unstated main idea must not be too broad or too narrow. You must select a general statement that includes all or most of the specific ideas in a paragraph. The following practice will help you find unstated main ideas.

Check Your Understanding

Begin by reading the supporting statements below. Then put a check (✓) by the idea that you think is the unstated point.

Support

● Men accuse women of not trusting them.

● Men complain that women have little interest in sports.

● Men say that women change the subject when they're losing an argument.

Point: The unstated main idea is:

____ A. Men think women don't trust them.

____ B. Men accuse women of talking too much.

_✓_ C. Men have various complaints about women.

____ D. Men have strong positive and negative views about women.

Explanation

1. Item A is too narrow to be the unstated main idea. It applies to only one of the statements, the first one.

2. Item B is too narrow to be the main idea. It is a specific complaint, like each of the three supporting details above.

3. Item C is the main idea—it covers all three of the supporting statements (each of which is a specific complaint about women).

4. Item D is incorrect because it is too broad. It refers to positive views about women as well as negative ones.

Homework

PRACTICE 3

Read each group of three supporting details. Then, in the space provided, write the letter of the answer that best states the implied main idea of those details.

Group 1

Support

- The average part-timer earns three dollars an hour less than the average full-time worker.
- Part-time workers are easily laid off.
- Most part-time workers get no fringe benefits.   Each of the three statements presents a disadvantage

___A___ 1. The **implied main idea** is: of being a part-time worker.
   - A. Part-time workers have second-class status.   Answer B is too narrow.
   - B. Part-timers get paid lower salaries.   Answer C is too broad.
   - C. Workers have numerous problems.   Answer D is not supported.
   - D. Part-timers make up a significant part of our working population.

Group 2

Support

- Parents identified honesty, judgment, and obedience as the top three traits they value in their children.
- The second most desirable trait for children was "good sense and sound judgment."
- Obedience to parents came in third.

___A___ 2. The **implied main idea** is:
   - A. For a survey, parents chose the traits they felt were most important for children.
   - B. Parents feel it is more important for children to be honest than obedient.
   - C. The trait most parents agree children should have is honesty.
   - D. A survey shows that most people feel honesty is the most important human trait.   Answers B and C are too narrow.
                     Answer D is unsupported because it refers to "most people,"
Group 3   but the four statements are about only the traits chosen by parents.

Support

- An octopus can escape its enemies by shooting out a jet of water that gives it a burst of speed.
- The octopus can avoid being discovered by changing its body color so that it blends into the environment.

● The octopus can also avoid attack by releasing its ink, which dulls an attacker's sense of smell, making it harder to find the octopus.

_B__ 3. The **implied main idea** is: The three statements list some of the octopus's
       A. An octopus must protect itself from enemies.   means of defense.
       B. An octopus has several means of defense.   Answers A and C
       C. An octopus has an interesting lifestyle.   are not supported.
       D. An octopus can change its coloring and blend into the environment.   Answer D is too narrow.

Step 4: Recognizing Implied Main Ideas II

You have practiced finding implied main ideas for a group of supporting statements. The final step is to work at finding implied main ideas in paragraphs.

Check Your Understanding

Read the following paragraph and see if you can choose the statement that best expresses its main idea.

[1]If people stop to think about the plots in children's stories, they may be surprised. [2]Hansel and Gretel, for example, were abandoned by their father and stepmother and left to wander in a dark forest. [3]In another well-known story, Cinderella was treated like a slave by her stepmother and stepsisters. [4]Then there is the case of Little Red Riding Hood, who was eaten by a wild animal. [5]Finally, consider the example of the three blind mice. [6]As if being blind were not bad enough, they also had to deal with the horror of having their tails cut off by the farmer's wife.

_D_ The unstated main idea is:
       A. Children's stories are about stepfamilies.
       B. Cinderella was treated like a slave.
       C. Animals and children are important characters in children's stories.
       D. Children's stories often deal with evil and violence.

Explanation

An important clue to the main idea of this paragraph is the first sentence: "If people stop to think about the plots in children's stories, they may be surprised." From this we see that, in addition to having to cover most or all of the details, the main idea must be about something surprising in children's stories.

With these ideas in mind, let's examine the four answer options:

A. **Children's stories are about stepfamilies.**
   Only two of the details of the paragraph are about stepfamilies, so answer A is too narrow to be the main idea. Also, it is not surprising.

B. **Cinderella was treated like a slave.**
   Only one of the details in the paragraph is about Cinderella, so answer B is much too narrow to be the main idea.

C. **Animals and children are important characters in children's stories.**
   The detail about Cinderella has nothing to do with animals and children. Also, this answer is not surprising—most people would expect animals and children to be common characters in children's stories.

D. **Children's stories often deal with evil and violence.**
   The fact that children's stories deal with very mean and violent behavior could surprise people, since many think such themes are not suited to children. And all of the examples in the paragraph are about children's stories that include evil and violence. Thus statement D expresses the implied main idea of the paragraph.

Homework

PRACTICE 4

The following paragraphs have implied main ideas, and each is followed by four sentences. In the space provided, write the letter of the sentence that best expresses the implied main idea.

Paragraph 1

¹Personality plays a big role in who is chosen to be a TV game-show contestant. ²Producers of *The Price Is Right*, for instance, like contestants who almost jump onto the stage. ³Of course, another major factor is that contestants must be good game players. ⁴Appeal and energy are not enough if a person does not have skill at the game. ⁵Game-show producers find out just how good candidates are through tryouts. ⁶A third important factor, then, is that would-be contestants should live in the Los Angeles area. ⁷Except for a few shows that sponsor auditions around the country, most tryouts take place in Los Angeles.

The passage presents the factors involved in choosing contestants. Answers A and B are too narrow. Answer D is too broad.

_C_ 1. The implied main idea is:
   A. Producers of *The Price Is Right* like very energetic contestants.
   B. Game-show contestants must have the right type of personality.
   C. There are several factors involved in selecting TV game-show contestants.
   D. Producing television shows is a very complicated process.

Paragraph 2

[1]Jasmin was having trouble in her American Government class. [2]Although she read her textbook carefully, she never got better than a C on an exam. [3]She went to the study skills center to get help and discovered from her tutor that she was not taking good lecture notes in class. [4]Because she listened rather than took notes, she did not get down a written record of what ideas her teacher considered most important for her to learn. [5]The tutor made Jasmin realize that there was no way she could possibly remember everything the teacher said in class. [6]As a result, it was very important for her to start taking plenty of notes in class and to rely heavily on those notes when preparing for a test. [7]When Jasmin followed her tutor's advice, she soon began getting better grades.

___C___ 2. The implied main idea is:

    A. Textbook notes are more important than class notes in doing well in a course.

    B. Jasmin worked hard in her American Government class, but she was not successful.

    C. Thanks to a tutor, Jasmin learned to take detailed notes and improved her grades.

    D. All too often, students neglect to benefit from the helpful services at their school's study skills center.

                                                Answer A is incorrect.
Answer B is too narrow. Answer C is a good summary of the paragraph.
Answer D is too broad, since the paragraph is about only one student.

Paragraph 3

[1]The former talk show host Dick Cavett tells a story about his interview with a TV host named Raymond. [2]Raymond wore a loud green jacket and matching tie. [3]He also wore a cheap wig that said "bargain basement." [4]Cavett had to work to keep his eyes off it. [5]As the interview got underway, Raymond began to ask rude personal questions. [6]For example, he asked Cavett, who is 5'6" tall, "Why does it bother you so much that you're so short?" [7]And since Cavett had gone to Yale, Raymond asked, "Why do you think going to Yale has made you smarter than other people?" [8]Cavett put up with these questions for a while but finally had had enough. [9]"Raymond," he said, "'Why' seems to be your favorite word. [10]May I ask you a 'Why' question?" [11]When Raymond nodded, Cavett asked, "Why do you wear a rug that looks like a wedge of blueberry pie sitting on top of your head?"

___D___ 3. The implied main idea is:

    A. Raymond was not a college graduate.

    B. Cavett was criticized by the TV network for his insulting remark.

    C. People who ask rude questions should not be given rude answers.

    D. Sometimes rude behavior calls for a rude response.

Answers A and B are incorrect because no information is given about Raymond's education or the reaction to Cavett's remark. Answer C is not supported. Answer D is implied by the details of Cavett's story.

CHAPTER REVIEW

In this chapter, you learned the following:

- At times authors imply, or suggest, a main idea without stating it directly in one sentence.
- You can figure out an implied main idea by looking closely at the supporting details.
- To find the main idea, look for a general idea that exactly covers the details in question, rather than one that is too broad or too narrow.

The final chapter in Part One—Chapter 10—will deepen your ability to think in a clear and logical way.

On the Web: If you are using this book in class, you can visit our website for additional practice in recognizing implied main ideas. Go to **www.townsendpress.com** and click on "Online Learning Center."

IN CLASS

REVIEW TEST 1

To review what you've learned in this chapter, answer each of the following questions.

1. A selection may have an _____implied_____ main idea rather than a directly stated one.

   See page 355.

2. When a main idea is not directly stated, you can often figure it out by considering carefully the _____supporting details_____.

   See page 355.

3. A general idea that is too (*narrow, broad*) _____narrow_____ is one that fails to cover some of the specific details in the passage.

   See pages 358–359.

4. A general idea that is too (*narrow, broad*) _____broad_____ is one that covers more kinds of specific ideas than the ones in the passage.

   See pages 358–359.

5. If a person talks about a movie and says that the acting is poor, the plot makes no sense, and the characters are boring, the implied main idea is that the movie _____is bad (or is not worth seeing)_____.

   Item 5: Wording of answer may vary.

IN CLASS

REVIEW TEST 2

A. (1.) Look at the following photograph of a highway sign in a Philadelphia suburb.

Item 1: Wording of answer may vary.

Write here what you think is the implied main idea: _____

Come to a complete stop at the stop sign, or you'll get a ticket.

B. Read each group of specific ideas. Then write the letter of the general idea that tells what the specific ideas have in common. Keep in mind that the correct general idea will not be too narrow or too broad.

___A___ 2. *Specific ideas:* Persian cats, cocker spaniels, elephants, canaries

The general idea is
A. animals.
B. household pets.   Answers B and C are too narrow.
C. jungle animals.

___B___ 3. *Specific ideas:* a smile, a wave, a frown, a push

The general idea is
A. communication.   Answer A is too broad.
B. nonspoken communication.   Answer C is incorrect.
C. friendly communication.

C. In the following lists, the specific ideas are given but the general ideas are unstated. Fill in the blanks with the unstated general ideas.   *Wording of answers may vary.*

4. *General idea:* _____ Books (or Novels or Movies) _____

    Specific ideas: *Dracula*   These items are all
                  The Call of the Wild   famous novels.
                  The Adventures of Tom Sawyer   (They have also been
                  A Tale of Two Cities   made into movies.)

5. *General idea:* _____ Definitions _____

    Specific ideas: *Exploit* means "take advantage of."
                  Patron means "a regular customer." Each item in the list is
                  Obstinate means "stubborn."   a term and its meaning.
                  Recipient means "one that receives."

REVIEW TEST 3 *IN CLASS*

A. Read each group of three sentences. Then, in the space provided, write the letter of the sentence that best states the implied main idea.

Group 1

Support

- In 1800, there was no "election day"; voting stretched from March to December.

- Less than ten percent of the population had the right to vote.

- No paper ballots were provided; the voter had to bring his own ballot or vote by voice.

  _D_   1. The **implied main idea** of these sentences is:
       A. The election process was unfair in 1800.
       B. It was easier to win an election in 1800 than it is today.
       C. Elections are less honest today than they were in 1800.
       D. Voting in the election of 1800 was very different from voting today.
          All three statements state facts about voting in 1800 that show it was
          very different from voting today. Answers A, B, and C are not supported.

Group 2

Support

- In order to be able to go to work, single parents need daycare.

- The rise in divorce has increased the number of single-parent households.

- Families with two working parents also need daycare.

___C___ 2. The **implied main idea** of these sentences is:
   A. The divorce rate has grown.
   B. The number of single-parent households continues to increase.
   C. There is a great need for daycare.
   D. Most mothers work outside the home.

Answers A and B are too narrow. Answer D is not supported. The statements provide reasons daycare is needed.

Group 3

Support

- Children sometimes imitate the violent acts they see in TV cartoons.
- Television viewers may become less sensitive to violence.
- Potential lawbreakers sometimes get ideas for crimes from television shows.

___B___ 3. The **implied main idea** of these sentences is:
   A. Cartoons can be bad for children.
   B. Television may be contributing to aggression and violence in society.
   C. Television can make viewers less concerned about violence in real life.
   D. It is not unusual for television to show violent acts such as murder and rape.

Answers A, C, and D are too narrow.

B. Write the letter of the answer that best states the implied main idea in each paragraph.

___D___ 4. ¹Many of the "witches" executed in Salem, Massachusetts, in the 1690s were actually mentally ill. ²Their odd behavior made people believe they were in league with the devil. ³In other times and places, mentally ill people have been punished. ⁴Often they were beaten or chained up. ⁵It was thought that their illness was the result of an evil nature or lack of willpower. ⁶Only recently have people accepted the idea that mental illness can be a medical problem.

   A. Mentally ill people were once thought to be witches and were thus executed for being in league with the devil.
   B. Mental illness has become more common since the 1690s.
   C. The mentally ill are still treated badly today.
   D. Throughout history, there have been different views about the nature of mental illness.

Answer A is too narrow. Answers B and C are unsupported.

___B___ 5. ¹The novel *Lord of the Flies* begins with a group of schoolboys who are left alone on an island after a plane crash. ²At first the boys are cooperative, helping one another to find food and shelter. ³Then they divide into two camps. ⁴One is led by a peaceful boy named Ralph; the other, by a violent boy named Jack. ⁵Jack's group then grows bigger and more powerful until Ralph is the only "civilized" person left on the island. ⁶He is nearly killed by the other boys before a rescue ship finally arrives.

The unstated main idea is:
A. *Lord of the Flies* is a fictional view of how young people interact with each other in various circumstances.
B. *Lord of the Flies* is a fictional view of what can happen when young people are alone and removed from civilization.
C. The author of *Lord of the Flies* feels that boys are basically more uncivilized than girls.
D. *Lord of the Flies* is a story about a rescue ship.

The paragraph discusses *Lord of the Flies*, a novel that tells about what happens to a group of young people cut off from civilization. Answer A is too broad. Answer C is unsupported. Answer D is too narrow.

REVIEW TEST 4

Here is a chance to apply your understanding of implied main ideas to an essay that was written on the topic "Taking Charge of My Life." The author tells how, alone with three children and far from her native home, she managed to get past her despair and create a meaningful life for herself.

The selection is followed by questions on implied main ideas as well as on the reading skills you have practiced in earlier chapters.

Words to Watch

Below are some words in the reading that do not have strong context support. Each word is followed by the number of the paragraph in which it appears and its meaning there. These words are indicated in the selection by a small circle (°).

regal (2): royal
haze (3): confused state of mind
intervened (7): came in to change a situation
bleak (8): gloomy
bleary-eyed (18): with blurred vision
preoccupation (18): extreme concern with something
Morpheus (20): the god of dreams in Greek mythology
preemies (29): babies born prematurely

LIGHTING A MATCH

Regina Ruiz

1   I feel funny. So very funny, telling you about my life, my feelings, my secrets. I do not know how to welcome you into my heart and soul. You see, nobody ever asked me what I thought or how I felt about life's challenges. Or, maybe, they never really cared about what I thought.

2   My journey to Burlington County College began many years ago in Caracas, Venezuela, where I was born and grew to a young lady full of energy and life. My parents called me Regina because there was something regal° about the sound. They had high hopes of my marrying a local boy from a good, wealthy family. You know the kind— slick, black hair, long sideburns, driving a sports car. The kind who brings you flowers on every date and swears his undying love for you three days a week, and the other days he is sleeping with Maria, the local social worker.

3   To get even, or because I was in a romantic haze°, I met and married a U.S. Marine from Des Moines, Iowa, who was stationed at our local Embassy, where I also worked.

4   Marriage, a home in America, and three beautiful children occupied twenty-five years of my life.

5   Where did my life go? It went somewhere. But there is no lost-and-found department for a life lost in the years.

6   The marriage was bad. It was so bad that I cried every night for all those years. I would tell myself, "You are in a strange country—maybe the customs are different. The children need you, and you cannot admit failure to your parents back in Venezuela."

7   As luck would have it, fate intervened°. My ex-Marine husband found someone new and left me and the children with no money, very hurt and depressed.

8   I quickly took an inventory— foreign-born, with not a great command of the English language, no money, no job training, and two kids in college. The future looked bleak°.

9   But it did not stop. My father died. I loved him so much, and he was always my source of strength in need. Mother became ill.

10   I felt very hurt, lonely, angry, and very sorry for myself.

11   However, I remembered a saying my Dad would quote to me when things were going wrong and the future looked black. He may have gotten this quote from the Spanish edition of *Reader's Digest*. He would say, "My dear, it is always the darkest when you are fresh out of matches."

12   "Dad, I am out of matches." Or so I thought.

13   I decided to make my life something worthwhile by helping people. I wanted to help and heal and maybe, at the same time, heal myself.

14   I appeared before the college doors with my knees shaking and full of doubt. I said that I wanted to be a nurse.

15   I enrolled in college. I was proud of

sounds familiar? →

myself for not falling into the garbage pit waiting so close by.

16   Then the fun began—subjects that were very hard for me.

17   In order to survive, I managed to get two jobs to keep up with house payments and food. The kids found college money by working and by appealing to their father. I met my challenges on a daily basis.

18   Now, my days are very active and long. Before the sun makes its appearance, I stumble bleary-eyed° to the shower and afterwards select the day's outfit. After a quick check in the mirror, I make my way downstairs to prepare a quick breakfast along with my lunch, feed the cat (who happens to be my alarm clock), and do what seem like a million other small chores. Then I drive for forty-five minutes to the Pemberton Campus, while studying my chemistry notes on index cards before a test. I would do this with tears in my eyes. You see, at the same time I am worrying about the situation with my water heater that slowly but surely is leaking and may not last until the new one can be installed. In addition, I am anxious to schedule my exterminator's visit to treat the termites discovered in my basement. My preoccupation° with such household woes is due to a canceled appointment to have my furnace cleaned, which resulted in a periodic spray of soot.

19   After a hectic morning of classes, I rush to my car for a hurried thirty-minute ride to the office, where a desk piled high with import documents is waiting for me, along with innumerable phone calls from the brokers, custom officials,

and suppliers. Meanwhile, an impatient boss wants to know the precise location of one of the fifty containers traveling between eastern Europe and Burlington, New Jersey.

20   As the clock winds toward 5:00 p.m., I get ready to travel back to the Cinnaminson Campus for another round of classes. As I arrive on campus, I waste another thirty minutes searching for that nonexistent parking spot. My class continues until ten o'clock in the evening, and I praise the Lord it doesn't last longer. By that time, I am beginning to see double. I slowly make my way to the car and begin the long commute home, counting in my mind how many customers I will see as a result of my second job—hairdressing. On evenings when I have no classes scheduled, I take appointments to cut hair or give permanents. As I arrive home, I find a hungry son and starving cat, both waiting to be fed. I usually

cook something simple for us, then proceed to do the few dishes because I hate the thought of adding one more chore to my early morning schedule. By the time I finish getting ready for bed, it is midnight; I look up and see the stairway leading to the bedroom, which by then seems longer than the one outside the Philadelphia Museum of Art, and proceed to crawl in bed and into the arms of Morpheus°.

21   People question the wisdom of my studying to be a nurse. It may take four or five years.

22   "You will never last," they tell me.

23   "You will be too old to lift a bedpan," they mock.

24   But I am not discouraged. There are twenty more courses ahead of me before I get into the nursing area. While all these things challenge me, the greatest of all is to be able to hold my head high.

25   Somehow, just somehow, I think it might be all worth it—if I can hold the hand of someone dying all alone in a cold hospital ward and whisper in their ear, "You are not alone. I am here. I am here. I will never leave you."

26   Maybe, just maybe, I will find that life that was lost. It is out there somewhere.

27   But I know one thing—I am in charge, and I will never let go again. Never.

Update

28   Regina Ruiz successfully completed her registered nurse degree and is only a few credits away from earning her bachelor's degree at Jefferson University in Philadelphia. She is a nurse at Voorhees Pediatric Rehabilitation Hospital in New Jersey.

29   At the hospital, Regina's patients range in age from newborns to eighteen-year-olds. As she grows attached to particular patients, she requests that they be assigned to her daily shift, giving "extra love" to children battling illness, fear, and loneliness. "To see tiny preemies° and children who are so sick grow and get better and be released to their families—it is wonderful to be part of that. School was very difficult, and nursing is a demanding profession, but when I am at work, I am in heaven."

30   When she is not working, Regina takes pride in keeping her home beautiful. "After my divorce and through all those long, difficult years, I worried so much about not being able to keep up with things," she said. "The roof leaked so badly at one point I had trash cans sitting in the living room. So I had to learn to budget my money as well as my time. When I had three jobs, one was for tuition and food, and the others were for repairs—a roof, siding, new windows, everything. Now I can look at the house and feel so good. A little neighbor boy told me the other day, 'Mrs. Ruiz, you have the nicest house on the street.'"

31   Regina still does hair for a handful of longtime clients. "They were my friends for so many years," she said. "When I'd come home from a test crying because I was sure I'd failed, they'd be the ones to say, 'No, Regina! You're going to make it.' Now, maybe I don't have to cut hair anymore to earn a living," she says with a chuckle, "but how can I tell them to go jump in the lake?"

Reading Comprehension Questions

Vocabulary in Context

_D_ 1. In the sentence below, the word *appealing* (ə-pēl′ĭng) means
  A. paying.
  B. saying no.
  C. hiding their need.
  D. making a request.

  To get money from their father, what did the children do?

  "The kids found college money by working and by appealing to their father." (Paragraph 17)

Central Point

_C_ 2. Which sentence best expresses the central idea of the selection?
  A. Ruiz got married to an American Marine and left her native land of Venezuela.
  B. Ruiz should not have married the Marine and moved so far from home.
  C. After a bad marriage, Ruiz learned to take charge of her life and build a worthwhile future.
  D. Ruiz is often exhausted by her schedule of school and two jobs.

  Answers A, B, and D are too narrow.

Main Ideas

_A_ 3. A main idea may cover more than one paragraph. Which sentence best expresses the implied main idea of paragraphs 2–3?
  A. Born in Venezuela and betrayed by a boyfriend, Ruiz married an American Marine for mixed reasons.
  B. Ruiz wasn't particularly happy with the type of future her parents had in mind for her.
  C. Ruiz grew up in a wealthy family.
  D. Ruiz met the Marine she would marry at the Embassy in Caracas, where they both worked.

  Answers B, C, and D are too narrow.

_B_ 4. Which sentence best expresses the implied main idea of paragraphs 10–13?
  A. Ruiz remembered a saying her father used to say.
  B. Ruiz at first saw no way out of a bad situation, but then thought of a worthwhile path.
  C. Ruiz's father may have gotten inspiration from the Spanish edition of *Reader's Digest*.
  D. Ruiz thought helping people was a worthwhile goal.

  Paragraphs 10–13 discuss Ruiz's thoughts about her situation and her plans to make her life worthwhile. Answers A, C, and D are too narrow.

___A___ 5. Which sentence best expresses the main idea of paragraphs 18–20?
    A. "Now, my days are very active and long."
    B. "Before the sun makes its appearance. I stumble bleary-eyed to the shower and afterwards select the day's outfit."
    C. "I drive for forty-five minutes. . . . I would do this with tears in my eyes."
    D. "By the time I finish getting ready for bed, it is midnight. . . . "

    Answers B, C, and D are too narrow.

___C___ 6. Which sentence best expresses the implied main idea of paragraphs 21–24?
    A. Others feel that Ruiz should not become a nurse.
    B. It may take Ruiz four or five years to become a nurse.
    C. Despite discouragement, Ruiz is determined to become a nurse.
    D. Ruiz still has twenty more courses ahead of her before she gets into nursing.

    Answers A, B, and D are too narrow.

Supporting Details

___C___ 7. Ruiz's marriage ended when
    A. her father died.
    B. she enrolled in college and her husband divorced her.
    C. her husband left her for another woman.
    D. Ruiz's parents demanded that she come back to Venezuela.

    See paragraph 7.

Transitions

___C___ 8. The sentence below begins with a transition that shows
    A. addition.
    B. contrast.
    C. time.
    D. cause and effect.

    After is a time transition.

    "After a hectic morning of classes, I rush to my car for a hurried thirty-minute ride to the office . . . " (Paragraph 19)

Patterns of Organization

___B___ 9. The main pattern of organization of the selection is
    A. list of items.
    B. time order.
    C. contrast.
    D. comparison.

    This selection narrates events in Ruiz's journey to a better life, which "began many years ago" (paragraph 2).

Inferences

_____ B _____ 10. We can infer that Ruiz
   A. wishes she had married "a local boy from a good, wealthy family."
   B. believes she married the U.S. Marine too quickly.
   C. regrets having three children.
   D. believes enrolling in the nursing program was not wise.

> Answers A, C, and D are incorrect. Paragraphs 3–6 indicate that
> Ruiz regretted her decision to marry so quickly.

Discussion Questions

1. During the years of her unhappy marriage, Ruiz told herself, "The children need you, and you cannot admit failure to your parents back in Venezuela." Do these seem to you like understandable reasons for remaining in an unhappy relationship? Are they *good* reasons?

2. Ruiz writes that after she enrolled in college, she was proud of herself "for not falling into the garbage pit waiting so close by." What do you think she means by the words "the garbage pit waiting so close by"? Have you ever made a choice that you feel either saved you from or dropped you into "a garbage pit"?

3. Like Ruiz, adults who return to college often have a difficult time balancing the demands of their work, family, and classes. What challenges do you face as a student? What ways have you found to deal with them?

4. Ruiz briefly explains her decision to become a nurse. Why have you chosen your own course of study? What about it interests you? What do you hope it will offer to you after college?

Note: Writing assignments for this selection appear on page 593.

Check Your Performance			**IMPLIED MAIN IDEAS**
Activity	*Number Right*	*Points*	*Score*
Review Test 1 (5 items)	_____	× 2 =	_____
Review Test 2 (5 items)	_____	× 6 =	_____
Review Test 3 (5 items)	_____	× 6 =	_____
Review Test 4 (10 items)	_____	× 3 =	_____
		TOTAL SCORE =	_____ %

Enter your total score into the **Reading Performance Chart: Review Tests** on the inside back cover.

IMPLIED MAIN IDEAS: Mastery Test 1

A. (1.) Look at the following cover for a book titled *Up from Slavery: An Autobiography* by Booker T. Washington. Put a check (✓) by the main idea that is implied by the information given on the cover.

____ A. The book is about many people who were former slaves; the man pictured is the author.

____ B. The book is about people such as Booker T. Washington who attempted to rise up from slavery but failed to succeed.

_✓_ C. Booker T. Washington, the man pictured, rose up from slavery and became an educated man.
The title refers to the man pictured, whose autobiography (self-written) tells how he rose up from slavery. Only an educated man would (in all likelihood) have written such a book.

B. Read each group of specific ideas. Then, in the space provided, write the letter of the general idea that tells what the specific ideas have in common. Keep in mind that the correct general idea will not be too narrow or too broad.

_B_ 2. *Specific ideas:* toaster, microwave oven, dishwasher, coffeemaker

The general idea is
A. household appliances.
B. kitchen appliances.
C. cooking appliances.

Answer A is too broad.
Answer C is too narrow.

_B_ 3. *Specific ideas:* sailboat, canoe, ship, raft

The general idea is
A. means of transportation.
B. means of water transportation.
C. military means of water transportation.

Answer A is too broad.
Answer C is too narrow.

(Continues on next page)

___C___ 4. *Specific ideas:* rose, scarlet, pink, maroon

The general idea is
A. flowers.
B. colors.
C. shades of red.

Answer A is incorrect.
Answer B is too broad.

___A___ 5. *Specific ideas:* New York City, Philadelphia, Los Angeles, London

The general idea is
A. cities.
B. eastern American cities.
C. American cities.

Answers B and C are too narrow.

___B___ 6. *Specific ideas:* "Yes," "No," "Maybe," "Not now"

The general idea is
A. words.
B. answers.
C. answers to test questions.

Answer A is too broad.
Answer C is too narrow.

___C___ 7. *Specific ideas:* cars, bikes, wheelchairs, supermarket carts

The general idea is
A. things to drive.
B. things to push.
C. things with wheels.

Answers A and B are too narrow.

___C___ 8. *Specific ideas:* blossoms, apples, oranges, leaves

The general idea is
A. fruit.
B. things that grow.
C. things that grow on trees.

Answer A is too narrow.
Answer B is too broad.

___B___ 9. *Specific ideas:* a cold, a baseball, a thief, a bus

The general idea is
A. things to avoid.
B. things to catch.
C. things to find.

Answer A is too narrow.
Answer C is incorrect.

___A___ 10. *Specific ideas:* Chapter 1, an appetizer, January, the letter A

The general idea is
A. beginnings.
B. parts of a book.
C. months.

Answers B and C are too narrow.

IMPLIED MAIN IDEAS: Mastery Test 2

In the following items, the specific ideas are given, but the general ideas are unstated. Fill in the blanks with the unstated general ideas.

Wording of answers may vary.

1. *General idea:*   Tools

   Specific ideas: saw
   hammer
   screwdriver
   drill

2. *General idea:*   Sports (or Team sports or Professional sports)

   Specific ideas: football
   baseball
   basketball
   soccer

3. *General idea:*   Cookies

   Specific ideas: chocolate chip
   oatmeal-raisin
   Oreo
   sugar

4. *General idea:*   Jobs

   Specific ideas: salesperson
   nurse
   auto mechanic
   computer programmer

5. *General idea:*   Crimes

   Specific ideas: robbery
   murder
   rape
   illegal drug possession

6. *General idea:*   Music (or Types of music)

   Specific ideas: pop
   country
   classical
   rock

(Continues on next page)

7. *General idea:* _____Breakfast foods_____

Specific ideas: oatmeal
cereal
bacon and eggs
pancakes

8. *General idea:* _____Good working conditions_____

Specific ideas: short travel time to work
fair boss
good pay
friendly coworkers

9. *General idea:* _____Wedding preparations_____

Specific ideas: Decide on whom to invite.
Send out invitations.
Order the bride's gown.
Hire a photographer.

10. *General idea:* _____Ways to fail a course_____

Specific ideas: Don't go to class much.
Never take notes when you do go to class.
Don't hand in assignments.
Never study for quizzes or exams.

IMPLIED MAIN IDEAS: Mastery Test 3

Read each group of three supporting details. Then, in the space provided, write the letter of the answer that best states the implied main idea of those details.

Group 1

Support

- Young mothers tend to have fewer problems during pregnancy and childbirth.
- Young parents are likely to have more energy to cope with the demands of childcare.
- Young parents tend to be more in tune with their child when he or she reaches adolescence.

__C__ 1. The implied main idea of the above sentences is:
   A. Young parents never have problems with child rearing.
   B. Postponing parenthood is always a mistake.
   C. Having children early in life has certain advantages.
   D. Americans, on average, are having children earlier and earlier.

   > Answer A is incorrect. (The first statement says they have *fewer* problems, indicating they do have *some* problems.) Answers B and D are also incorrect because nothing is said about when people should (or do) have children.

Group 2

Support

- In most fad diets, the dramatic initial weight loss is mostly just a loss of water from the body.
- Fad diets suggest unrealistic foods to eat and avoid, causing dieters to soon give up.
- Fad diets tend to ignore exercise, which is a crucial element of any good weight-loss program.

__B__ 2. The implied main idea of the above sentences is:
   A. Fad diets have become increasingly popular.
   B. Fad diets typically fail for several reasons.
   C. Dieters who lack willpower cannot succeed.
   D. Exercise is important not only for weight loss but also for preventing heart disease.

   > Answers A, C, and D are incorrect because the support statements do not mention popularity of fad diets, willpower in relation to dieters in general, or heart disease.

(Continues on next page)

Group 3

Support

- An unpopular child may be a child with a "chip on the shoulder," always looking for a fight.
- An unpopular child may be one who acts silly or seems babyish.
- An unpopular child may be a showoff or, at the other extreme, may be very shy and withdrawn.

___C___ 3. The implied main idea of the above sentences is:
  A. Unpopular children usually will "grow out of it."
  B. Unpopular children usually will not "grow out of it."
  C. Children become unpopular for several common reasons.
  D. Why some children are unpopular is a mystery to psychologists.

   Answers A and B are unsupported because the statements do not mention outgrowing unpopularity. Answer D is incorrect, since the statements do explain why certain types of children are unpopular.

Group 4

Support

- The colon [:] is used to introduce a list.
- The colon is also used to introduce a long quotation.
- In addition, a colon can introduce an explanation.

___A___ 4. The implied main idea of the above sentences is:
  A. The colon is a punctuation mark with several specific uses.
  B. Some writers avoid using the colon.
  C. Student writers often make mistakes in using the colon.
  D. Correct punctuation is an important part of writing well.

   The supporting statements discuss three specific ways the colon is used. Answers B, C, and D are not supported.

IMPLIED MAIN IDEAS: Mastery Test 4

In the space provided, write the letter of the sentence that best expresses the implied main idea of each of the following paragraphs.

A 1. ¹Some workers skip breakfast and try to make up for it by eating a big lunch. ²Studies show that workers who do this lose as much efficiency at work as people who've missed a whole night's sleep. ³Workers who eat a high-protein breakfast and a light lunch, on the other hand, tend to be energetic and efficient throughout the day. ⁴Furthermore, a separate study proved that teens who eat breakfast do far better in school than their classmates who don't.

    A. Eating a good breakfast increases one's energy, efficiency, and performance all day.
    B. Skipping lunch probably does not make one less efficient.
    C. Teens who want to do well in school should eat a good breakfast.
    D. A glass of milk, whole wheat bread, and cheese make a good breakfast.   Answer B is unsupported. Answers C and D are too narrow.

D 2. ¹One benefit of owning a pet is that an animal can make a person feel less lonely. ²According to the National Heart Association, owning a pet is also good for the heart. ³Studies show that stroking an animal can lower blood pressure and slow the heart rate. ⁴In addition, studies show that pet owners are more likely to survive during the first year after a heart attack than people who don't own pets. ⁵The elderly also benefit from pet ownership. ⁶Older people who own dogs are more likely to get daily exercise than those who don't. ⁷Moreover, feeding a pet encourages older people to pay better attention to their own diet.

    A. Pet ownership is more widespread than ever.
    B. People who have suffered a heart attack should consider getting a pet.
    C. Pets should be made available in elementary classrooms.
    D. Owning a pet has a number of advantages.   Answers A and C are not supported. Answer B is too narrow.

(Continues on next page)

B   3. ¹To make your clothes last longer, avoid using the dryer. ²Over time, the heat will fade colors and weaken fabrics. ³Instead, in cold weather, hang your clothing to dry inside the house. ⁴When the weather is warm, hang it outside—but away from direct sunlight, which can also fade colors. ⁵Also, don't use bleach more than is absolutely necessary. ⁶Bleach contains strong chemicals that can weaken fibers. ⁷In addition, never store knitted clothes on hangers—they can stretch out of shape. ⁸Instead, keep them folded in a drawer. ⁹Finally, get rid of stains promptly—if you let them set, they are much harder, if not impossible, to remove.

A. Most people don't know how to make their clothes last longer.
B. You can make your clothes last longer by following some simple guidelines.
C. Dryers and bleach are bad for your clothes.
D. There are several reasons to avoid using your dryer.   Answers A and D are not supported. Answer C is too narrow.

B   4. ¹Women who are poorly nourished before or during pregnancy are at risk for complications during pregnancy and delivery. ²They are more likely to bear low-birthweight babies or stillborn babies. ³Also, their babies are more likely to die soon after birth. ⁴The same is true for women who gain too much weight during pregnancy, or who were obese when they became pregnant. ⁵Their babies run a greater risk of medical problems than babies of mothers with normal weight.

A. The babies of poorly nourished women are more likely to die soon after birth.
B. A woman's diet and weight affect her and her baby's health during and after pregnancy.
C. Pregnant women tend to be poorly nourished or overweight before and during pregnancy.
D. Obesity is the cause of various medical problems for women and their children.   Answer A is too narrow. Answer C is incorrect. Answer D is too broad.

IMPLIED MAIN IDEAS: Mastery Test 5

In the space provided, write the letter of the sentence that best expresses the implied main idea of each of the following paragraphs.

___C___ 1. ¹Most cases of baldness are caused by heredity. ²People with hereditary baldness gradually lose the bulbs from which new hair would grow. ³This type of hair loss is called male-pattern baldness, and it is the most common type of hair loss affecting men. ⁴This hair loss is permanent. ⁵Some types of hair loss, however, are not permanent. ⁶Their causes include high fevers and certain types of drugs, including drugs that are used to treat cancer. ⁷The hair may fall out as long as three or four months after the illness or treatment. ⁸Such hair loss is almost always temporary.

    A. Male-pattern baldness is permanent.
    B. Various factors may lead to temporary hair loss.
    C. Baldness may be either permanent or temporary.
    D. Hair loss, whether temporary or permanent, is much more common in men than in women. *The passage discusses permanent and temporary hair loss. Answers A and B are too narrow. Answer D is not supported.*

___A___ 2. ¹One way that pigs show their intelligence is through curiosity. ²If you put something in their pens, such as a key chain, they'll sniff and poke at it to find out what it is. ³Also, hog farmers have noted that if a pig finds an escape hole in the pasture fence one summer and then is put in the barn for the winter, he'll head right over to the hole when he's back in the pasture next spring. ⁴One farmer said that he had a terrible time with one sow that learned how to use her snout to open the gate latch when it wasn't completely fastened. ⁵"She'd be checking it out every half hour to see if we'd slipped up, which we sometimes did," he said. ⁶More evidence that pigs are intelligent is the fact that they are more subject to psychological stress than other farm animals. ⁷They get bored and distressed when they're confined and there's nothing to do. ⁸In fact, like people, they can develop ulcers from an unfriendly environment.

    A. Pigs show their intelligence in many ways.
    B. Pigs have more curiosity than any other animal.
    C. Pigs react as strongly as people to stressful situations.
    D. Once pigs learn something, they are not likely to forget it.

        The passage discusses the various ways pigs show their intelligence. Answer B is not supported. Answers C and D are too narrow.

(Continues on next page)

_B_   3. [1]A team of researchers surveyed patients who had suffered serious illnesses. [2]Sixty of the patients had suffered a heart attack. [3]Another thirty were breast cancer patients. [4]All had completed therapy for their medical conditions at the time of the survey. [5]Subjects were asked what positive changes had happened to them after their illness. [6]About half reported healthy lifestyle changes. [7]And over a quarter reported a greater appreciation of life and health as well as improved close relationships. [8]Other common positive changes included feeling lucky to be given a second chance and an improved understanding of others.

    A. A survey of patients was conducted to discover the changes that had happened to people with serious illnesses.

    B. A survey of patients shows that serious illness can have positive effects.

    C. Serious illness can result in better relationships with other people.

    D. Recovering from serious illness can give a sense of gratitude and good fortune.   Answers A, C, and D are too narrow.

_C_   4. [1]If a child is having trouble seeing the difference between squares, circles, and triangles, that's one sign that he or she may have dyslexia, a common learning disorder. [2]A second sign is seeing or writing scrambled or reversed messages. [3]For instance, a dyslexic child may confuse "was" and "saw," "dog" and "bog," or even "hot" and "cold." [4]The number 517 could be interpreted as 751. [5]Also, a dyslexic child may have trouble distinguishing between right and left.

    A. Reversing letters is a sure sign of dyslexia.

    B. Dyslexia is one of the most common learning disorders.

    C. There are several signs that a child has dyslexia.

    D. A child who has trouble distinguishing between right and left is likely to be dyslexic.   Answers A and D are too narrow.
                                           Answer B is too broad.

IMPLIED MAIN IDEAS: Mastery Test 6

In the space provided, write the letter of the sentence that best expresses the implied main idea of each of the following textbook paragraphs.

___A___ 1. ¹Newspapers are usually thrown out after a day. ²Magazines, however, may stay around the house or office for weeks or months. ³In addition, they may be passed from person to person. ⁴Therefore the ads in magazines have a better chance of being read and remembered. ⁵Magazines also allow for more colorful photography and artwork on quality paper. ⁶So they provide a way for advertisers to create a high-quality image with ads. ⁷Furthermore, many magazines now publish a range of editions aimed at specific areas and groups, instead of a single national edition. ⁸For example, *Time* magazine publishes 357 different editions worldwide. ⁹They include special editions for doctors, educators, and college students. ¹⁰Such editions make it possible for ads to be aimed at very specific audiences.

    A. Magazines have some important advantages for advertisers.
    B. Magazine ads are remembered longer than newspaper ads.
    C. Television ads reach more people than magazine ads.
    D. Magazines allow advertisers to reach specific market segments.

                   Answers B and D are too narrow. Answer C is not supported.

___D___ 2. ¹Thomas H. Holmes, a psychiatrist, developed a scale to rate the amount of stress brought on by what he calls Life-Changing Units (LCUs). ²Some LCUs are obviously negative. ³They include the death of a spouse (rated at 100 points) or a jail term (63 points). ⁴Others may be positive: pregnancy (40 points) or an increase in responsibility at work (29 points). ⁵Holmes interviewed more than five thousand hospital patients as part of his study. ⁶He found that half the people who had scored between 150 and 300 LCUs in a year had become ill. ⁷About 70 percent of those scoring more than 300 LCUs in a year had gotten sick.

    A. Life-changing events include jail or death.
    B. A psychiatrist interviewed more than 5,000 hospital patients.
    C. Even positive life-changing units can cause stress.
    D. According to a psychiatrist's study, the stress of life-changing events makes people more likely to become sick.

                         Answers A, B, and C are too narrow.

(Continues on next page)

_B_   3. ¹It is widely believed that the institutions of marriage and the family are less stable today than ever before. ²It is true that divorce is very common these days. ³However, the divorce rate has been rising and falling for years. ⁴It was nearly as high during the 1920s as it is now. ⁵In addition, while divorce creates many single-parent households today, the same was true about death in earlier times. ⁶So many parents died early during the eighteenth and nineteenth centuries that most children spent at least part of their early lives growing up in single-parent households.

   A. The institutions of marriage and the family are unstable today.
   B. The institutions of marriage and family are no less stable today than at other times.
   C. Divorce is very common now; it was also common in the 1920s.
   D. Divorce and death have been responsible for creating many single-parent households.   Answers A, C, and D are too narrow.

_C_   4. ¹Mothers touch their little girls more than they touch their boys; they speak to their infant daughters more frequently and longer than they do to their sons. ²By age 2, girls generally prefer to play closer to their mothers than boys do. ³Little boys are more likely to be tossed, swung, and chased. ⁴In most cultures, they are also more likely than girls to be aggressive and to get into conflicts. ⁵The parents of boys are also more concerned with discipline and with pushing their child toward achievement than the parents of girls are. ⁶Fathers are more likely to reward their daughters for playing with other girls but punish their sons for playing with girls.

   A. Boys in most cultures are likely to be more aggressive than girls.
   B. By age 2, children are already beginning to show the effects of the way they are brought up.
   C. Some of the differences between boys and girls may be the result of being brought up differently.
   D. Fathers and mothers often disagree about how to raise children.
          Answers A and B are too narrow. Answer D is not supported.

10 The Basics of Argument

This Chapter in a Nutshell

- A good thinker understands what it means to *make* a point.
- A good thinker understands what it means to *support* a point.

Look at the following cartoon and see if you can answer the questions that follow.

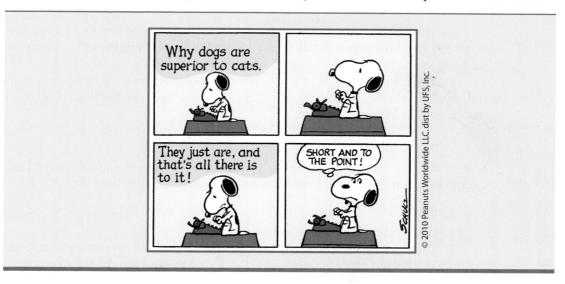

- What is Snoopy's argument here? In other words, what is his point?

  Your answer: His point is that _____dogs are superior to cats._____

- What is his support for his point?

  Your answer: _____There is no support._____

Explanation

Snoopy's point is that dogs are superior to cats. But he offers no support whatsoever to back up his argument! There are two jokes here. First, he is a dog, and so naturally he believes that dogs are superior. The other joke is that his evidence ("they just are, and that's all there is to it!") is a lot of empty words. His somewhat guilty look in the last panel suggests that he knows he has not proved his point. To make a good argument and prove a point, you must offer real support.

Evaluating Arguments

A **critical thinker** is one who can look at an **argument**—a point and its support—and decide whether the support is solid or not. Look at the following point:

Point: You should not put your hand into that box.

Now, is there solid support for this point? In other words, is the person who made it thinking clearly and logically? Let's say the person goes on to provide these details:

Support
1. A flesh-eating spider the size of a large crab just crawled in there.
2. Inside the box are freshly cut leaves of poison ivy.
3. A loaded mousetrap is inside, ready to spring.

As you can see, the details do provide solid support for the point. They give us a basis for understanding and agreeing with the point. In light of the details, we probably won't be putting a hand anywhere near that box.

This is a small example of what critical thinking is about: recognizing a point and deciding whether there is support that effectively backs up the point. Let's look now at another example:

Point: Our meal in that new restaurant was unpleasant.

Is there support for this point? Is the person thinking clearly and logically? Let's say the person then goes on to provide the following details:

Support
1. Our meal took forty-five minutes to arrive.
2. The chicken we ordered was tough, and the rice and vegetables were cold.
3. The dessert choices were limited to stale cake and watery Jell-O.

Again, the details provide solid support for the point. They give us a basis for understanding and agreeing with the point. Having heard these details, we would not be eager to eat at that restaurant.

But what if the person had provided the reasons below for saying the meal at the restaurant was unpleasant?

Support
1. We had to wait fifteen minutes for the food to arrive.
2. The chicken we ordered was too juicy, and the vegetables were buttery.
3. The dozen dessert choices did not include my favorite, carrot cake.

We might question these reasons for not liking the restaurant. Waiting fifteen minutes is not so bad. Many people like juicy chicken and buttery vegetables, and many people would welcome a dozen dessert choices.

When evidence is provided, we can judge for ourselves whether or not there is enough logical support for a point. If the reasons above were the only ones given, we might decide to try the restaurant ourselves.

Argument in Everyday Life

In everyday life, people are constantly arguing all kinds of points and trying to provide convincing support. Here are some examples:

- A lawyer states, "So and so is guilty," and then tries to provide evidence to support his point. Another lawyer says, "So and so is not guilty," and attempts to back up her statement with different evidence.

- An advertiser tries to convince us that something is "a great product."

- A political candidate offers reasons why he or she is the person to vote for.

- Textbook authors or instructors advance and support all kinds of theories.

- Reviewers offer their thoughts about why a given book, movie, TV show, or restaurant is good or bad.

- Editorial writers, magazine columnists, and sportswriters argue their opinions on one issue or another.

- In everyday conversation, people make points, such as "Everyone likes the boss," "I hate my job," "She is a good friend," "You should help that person," "That child is troubled," and "She is the best teacher in the school." They then offer reasons to support their points.

In sum, all around us is a mix of points and support. If the points were always logically supported, the world would be in pretty fine shape. Unfortunately, many people are not skillful thinkers. The ideas they advance often lack reasonable support.

Chances are that you, like most people, will benefit greatly from sharpening your thinking skills. By learning to constantly ask, "What is the point?" "What is its support?" and "How logical is the support?" you can become an effective one-person jury. Such questions may seem simple, but learning to use them will not happen overnight. You must train your mind to become a critical thinker.

You have already learned a lot about critical thinking in this book as you have studied main ideas, supporting details, relationships, and inferences. In the pages that follow, you will have a chance to build on what you already know. The skill that you develop in thinking clearly and logically will prove of enormous value in all your college work.

Practice in Evaluating Arguments

1   Recognizing Point and Support

This first activity will review and sharpen your sense of the difference between a point and its support. As you learned earlier in the book, a **point** is a general idea; **support** is the specific information that backs up the point.

Check Your Understanding

Look at the following group of items. It is made up of a point and three statements that logically support the point. See if you can put a **P** in front of the point and an **S** in front of the three supporting statements.

____S____   A. The children argue and fight constantly.

____S____   B. The mother looks as if she's scared to say anything.

____P____   C. Our neighbors do not seem like a happy family.

____S____   D. When I hear the father speak to the children, he's usually shouting.

Explanation

Statement A presents a specific fact about the neighbors. Statements B and D also contain specific facts about them. Statement C, on the other hand, is a general statement and expresses a point about the neighbors—that they are not happy. Therefore statement C is the point. The other statements support that point with specific examples.

PRACTICE 1   *Homework*

In each of the following groups, one statement is the point, and the other statements are support for the point. Identify each point with a **P** and each statement of support with an **S**.

Group 1

____S____   A. People would look at me and ask, "Cat got your tongue?"

____S____   B. I used to hide in my bedroom when visitors came.

____S____   C. I cried on the first day of kingergarten.

____P____   D. As a child, I was very quiet and shy.   Statements A, B, and C are
examples which support the point that the writer "was very quiet and shy."

Group 2

___S___ A. Many jobs require you to apply online.

___S___ B. Some teachers keep in touch with parents by e-mail.

___P___ c. It's helpful to have regular Internet access nowadays.

___S___ D. It's quick and easy to pay bills electronically.

Statements A, B, and D are reasons it is "helpful to have regular Internet access."

Group 3

___P___ A. It's not a good idea to buy bottled water.

___S___ B. Bottled water costs about 5 cents an ounce, while tap water costs only about 1 cent per gallon.

___S___ c. In most places, bottled water is no healthier than tap water.

___S___ D. Bottled water produces up to 1.5 million tons of plastic waste every year.

Statements B, C, and D explain why buying bottled water is "not a good idea."

Group 4

___S___ A. Uniforms cost less than store-bought clothes.

___S___ B. Studies show that students work better when they are dressed in uniforms.

___P___ c. Requiring kids to wear uniforms to school is a good idea.

___S___ D. Uniforms stop kids from teasing each other about the clothes they wear.

Statements A, B, and D explain why "requiring kids to wear uniforms" is a good idea.

2 Identifying Logical Support I

Once you identify a point and its support, you need to decide if the support really applies to the point. The critical thinker will ask, "Is this support logical and relevant? Or is it beside the point?" In their enthusiasm to advance a point, people often bring up support that does not apply.

For example, say that a student claims her English instructor is a poor teacher. To support that point, the student may say, "He speaks so softly I can hardly hear him. In addition, he wears ridiculous clothes." A critical thinker will realize that although a soft voice may in fact interfere with an instructor's effectiveness, what the instructor wears has nothing to do with how well he teaches. The first reason for disliking the English teacher is relevant support, but the second reason is beside the point.

The following activity will sharpen your ability to decide whether evidence truly supports a point.

Check Your Understanding

Read the following point and the three items of "support" that follow. Then check (✓) the letter of the **one** item that provides logical support for the point.

Point: That woman on the news was courageous.

Support

_____ A. [1]She collected bags of canned and boxed food for months and then brought it to the Golden Door Soup Kitchen to be used for Thanksgiving. [2]Thanks to her efforts, the soup kitchen was able to feed five hundred more people this year than last year. [3]That number includes over a hundred children.

_____ B. [1]She had at hand all the facts and figures to back up her statements, citing three different studies by experts in the field. [2]She handled the reporter's questions with ease and confidence.

__✓__ C. [1]When she saw the child being attacked, she went to his aid without a moment's hesitation. [2]She ran up, shouting "Let him go!" and then kicked the ferocious pit bull as hard as she could. [3]When the dog released the child, she grabbed the boy and pushed him to safety, even as the dog turned on her.

Explanation

A. The information here tells us that the woman on the news was kind and generous with her time. However, nothing she did required her to face danger, so no courage was required. You should not have chosen this item. It is about generosity, not courage.

B. The woman described here showed mastery of her subject and skill in being interviewed, but neither demands great courage. You should not have chosen this item either.

C. The woman referred to here put herself in danger to help a child. Clearly, to do so, she had to be courageous. If you checked the letter of this item, you were correct.

PRACTICE 2

Each item on the next page contains a point followed by three items of information. Put a check (✓) next to the **one** item that logically supports the point.

1. **Point: That child is very curious.**

Item A supports the point "That child is very bright."
Item B supports the point "That child is uncooperative."

_____ A.   [1]He was reciting the alphabet when he was only three years old. [2]By age seven, he was doing math at a fourth-grade level. [3]He skipped third and fifth grades.

_____ B.   [1]His favorite word is "NO!" [2]He doesn't start picking up his toys until the fifth or sixth time he is told. [3]Mealtime is a battle to get him to eat properly.

✓ C.   [1]He has taken apart all the clocks in the house to see how they work. [2]He borrowed his father's hammer to break rocks because he "wanted to see what they looked like inside." [3]He is forever asking questions that start with "How" and "Why."

2. **Point: Aunt Isabel is my least favorite relative.**

Item B supports the point "Aunt Isabel is someone I admire."
Item C is about Isabel's physical appearance, not about why the speaker does not like her.

✓ A.   [1]When we meet, she always has something critical to say, such as "What have you done with your hair?" or "You look terrible in that color." [2]She calls my sister "the smart sister" and me "the dumb one." [3]On my birthday, she said, "I didn't think you wanted a present."

_____ B.   [1]She works as a billing clerk at a hospital. [2]She dropped out of high school, but earned her GED and then attended community college. [3]She's held the job for more than 15 years and has been the hospital's "Employee of the Month" a number of times.

_____ C.   [1]Isabel is about five foot seven and is a little on the heavy side. [2]She wears her hair very short and always has on long dangly earrings. [3]She's almost 50 but looks younger. [4]She wears very little makeup—just some mascara and sometimes lip gloss.

3. **Point: The teenage boys at the dance were much more shy than the girls.**

_____ A.   [1]They yelled and laughed out loud, drawing attention to themselves. [2]One of them complained, "This sounds like music my grandmother would dance to!" [3]Many leaned against the wall or sat at tables and made fun of the way girls were dancing. [4]Then, many left with their friends to go to a nearby party.

Item A supports "rude."
Item C supports "very friendly."

✓ B.   [1]They all gathered at one end of the room, away from the girls. [2]They looked nervously at the girls who were dancing. [3]When a group of girls approached them, they got quiet and pretended not to notice. [4]Several girls had to drag them out in order for them to dance.

_____ C.   [1]They walked right up to a group of girls and introduced themselves. [2]They smiled broadly and asked the girls to dance. [3]Before they left at the end of the night, they asked the girls for their phone numbers.

4. **Point: Our biology teacher is lazy.**

____✓____   A.   ¹He has his top students present the lessons to the class so he doesn't have to do anything. ²If someone is having trouble in class, he tells him or her to get help from one of the other students. ³So he doesn't have to grade papers, he allows us to grade each other's homework and test papers, even midterm and final exams.

_____   B.   ¹His favorite saying is, "There is no such thing as partial credit. ²Either the answer is right or it isn't." ³We can expect at least two hours of biology homework every night, and more on weekends and holidays. ⁴Even the best students in class have trouble finishing his tests before the end of the period, and the average grade for his class is a C.

_____   C.   ¹He always arrives exactly on time for class; you could set your watch by him. ²He predictably begins with two or three questions, then lectures for most of the period, and with five minutes to go, writes on the board exactly what he wants us to read before the next class.

Item B supports "tough."
Item C supports "organized, professional, and prompt."

3   Identifying Logical Support II

Check Your Understanding

Below is a point followed by five statements. Three of the statements logically support the point; two of the statements do not. In the spaces provided, write the letters of the **three** logical statements of support.

Point: English 102 was an extremely hard course.

A.   The course included a research paper, five essays, three oral reports, and two major exams.

B.   The course was required for my major.

C.   The teacher called on students without warning and deducted points when they didn't know an answer.

D.   The teacher has been at the school for over twenty years.

E.   I had to do at least three hours of homework for every hour in class.

Items that logically support the point: ___A___   ___C___   ___E___

Explanation

The fact that a course is required doesn't make it more difficult, so item B does not support the point. Item D does not support the point either—how long a teacher has been at a school has nothing to do with how hard the course is. So you should have chosen items A, C, and E. Each one tells about a different difficulty experienced in taking the course.

PRACTICE 3

Each point is followed by three statements that provide logical support and two that do not. In the spaces, write the letters of the **three** logical statements of support.

1. **Point: I'm a perfect example of someone who has "math anxiety."**
    A. Fear of math is almost as widespread as fear of public speaking.
    B. I feel dread every time I sit down to take our Friday math quiz.
    C. During the math midterm, I "froze" and didn't even try to answer most of the questions.
    D. I also have a great deal of anxiety when I sit down to write a paper.
    E. I turned down a job as a salesclerk because I would have had to figure out how much change customers should get back.

    Items that logically support the point: ___B___ ___C___ ___E___

    Statements A and D are about speaking and writing papers, not about the speaker's math anxiety.

2. **Point: My kids are getting into the spirit of Halloween.**
    A. Today I found a plastic spider in my soup.
    B. Last night there was a bloody rubber hand on my pillow.
    C. Today a cardboard tombstone with my name on it appeared in the backyard.
    D. My kids also like to decorate the house on Thanksgiving.
    E. The other day, my oldest daughter said she was too old to go trick-or-treating.

    Items that logically support the point: ___A___ ___B___ ___C___

    Statement D is not about Halloween.
    Statement E is about *not* getting into the Halloween spirit.

3. **Point:** **Packing your lunch to take to work saves time and money.**

   A. In many large cities, there are fast-food restaurants on nearly every block.
   B. Those who bring their lunch to work don't have to spend time getting their food.
   C. Packing a lunch allows you to keep reusing your containers and utensils.
   D. Those who consume a lot of calories at lunch tend to eat even more calories at dinner.
   E. People who pack a lunch often bring leftovers, allowing them to stretch their food budget.

   Items that logically support the point: ___B___   ___C___   ___E___

   Statement A is about the number of fast food restaurants in cities.
   Statement D is about how much one eats, not about saving time or money.

4. **Point:** **People should be careful when buying used cars.**

   A. Many used cars do not come with a guarantee, so you will have to pay if something breaks.
   B. Used cars are much cheaper than brand-new ones.
   C. A used car may have serious mechanical problems and still look fine on the outside.
   D. Some used cars come with a guarantee and are nearly as reliable as new cars.
   E. Used cars whose past owners did not take care of them are more likely to develop problems.

   Items that logically support the point: ___A___   ___C___   ___E___

   Statements B and D are about advantages of used cars,
   not about reasons to be careful when buying one.

5. **Point:** **Schools should eliminate the summer vacation.**

   A. It costs too much money for school buildings to remain empty in the summer months.
   B. Children have more energy than adults.
   C. Year-round school can better prepare students for year-round work in the adult world.
   D. During summer classes, schools should be air-conditioned.
   E. Recent studies show that children remember more and forget less if they attend school during the summer.

   Items that logically support the point: ___A___   ___C___   ___E___

   Statement B is not about summer vacation.
   Statement D is not a reason for keeping schools open in the summer.

4   Determining a Logical Point

This activity will develop your ability to come to a logical conclusion. You will look closely at supporting evidence and then decide what point is well supported by that evidence. The skill of making a reasonable judgment based upon the information presented is a significant part of critical thinking.

Check Your Understanding

Look at the following three items of support:

Support

- Before underground plumbing, city people dumped raw sewage out of their windows and into the streets.

- In the days when city vehicles were horse-drawn, manure was piled high in the roadways.

- Before trash collection was available, pigs were set loose in city streets to eat the garbage thrown there.

Now check (✓) the **point** that is logically supported by the above evidence. Then read the explanation that follows.

_____   A. Cities of the past were probably pleasant places to live.

_____   B. Cities of the past were not all that different from today's cities.

_____   C. Cities of the past were troubled with crime.

___✓___   D. Cities of the past were very dirty.

Explanation

A. Obviously, none of the details suggest that cities of the past were pleasant places to live. So you should not have chosen this point.

B. The support clearly states that cities of the past were dramatically different places to live, with pigs in the streets, among other details. You should not have chosen this point.

C. The supporting statements make no mention of crime, so you shouldn't have chosen this point.

D. If the city streets were filled with raw sewage, manure, and garbage, they would certainly have been very dirty. This point is adequately supported. It is the one you should have chosen as the point.

Homework

PRACTICE 4

For each group, read the three items of supporting evidence. Then check (✓) the point that is most logically supported by that evidence.

Group 1

Support

- Dozens of angry bees attacked people sitting at the picnic table.
- A rain shower made all the food soggy and wet.
- Nearby kids threw a football onto the table, spilling all the drinks.

Point: Which of the following conclusions is best supported by all the evidence above?

_____ A. Picnics can be a fun way to spend an afternoon.

__✓__ B. The picnic was a disaster.

_____ C. Kids should be careful when they play outdoors.

_____ D. Everyone loves picnics.

> Items A and D are incorrect; the support does not discuss why picnics are fun or why people love picnics.
> Item C is too narrow.

Group 2

Support

- During the supposedly sad scenes in the movie, many people in the audience giggled.
- At least a third of the audience members left before the movie was over.
- As he left, one audience member said to people standing in line to buy tickets, "Don't waste your money!"

Point: Which of the following conclusions is best supported by all the evidence above?

__✓__ A. The movie was terrible.

_____ B. Today's movie audiences are difficult to please.

_____ C. Movie tickets cost too much.

_____ D. The movie was a comedy.

> Items B and C are incorrect; audiences in general and ticket prices are not discussed.
> Item D is not supported because nothing suggests the movie was supposed to be a comedy.

Group 3

Support

- A shrub brought into this country to stop soil from washing away eventually became a harmful weed that choked and killed countless other plants.

- Rabbits released in Australia for hunting quickly multiplied and destroyed much of the country's farmland.

- Caterpillars brought to the United States to start a silk industry broke free and destroyed large tracts of forest land.

Point: **Which of the following conclusions is best supported by all the evidence above?**

_____ A. Plants are difficult to grow properly.

___✓___ B. Great damage has been caused by bringing foreign plants and animals to new lands.

_____ C. Farmers should never use chemicals on their farms.

_____ D. There is no good way to stop soil from washing away.

> Items A, C, and D are incorrect. The support presents examples of damage caused by bringing foreign plants and animals to new lands.

Group 4

Support

- A study showed that regular churchgoers had lower blood pressure than non-churchgoers.

- Researchers have found lower rates of depression among religious people.

- A study found that patients who have strong faith have a much greater chance of surviving heart surgery than those who do not.

Point: **Which of the following conclusions is best supported by all the evidence above?**

___✓___ A. Scientists have some evidence that religious faith is good for one's health.

_____ B. Studies show that religious people are more intelligent than others.

_____ C. Medical science rejects the idea that religion can help people.

_____ D. Today, many hospitals encourage people to express their religious feelings openly.

> Items B and D are incorrect; intelligence and the expression of religious views are not discussed. Item C is not supported by the evidence; the support does not mention medical science's opinion of religion.

CHAPTER REVIEW

In this chapter, you learned the following:

- A good argument is made up of a point, or a conclusion, and evidence to back it up.
- To think through an argument, you need to decide if each bit of evidence is relevant and logical.
- Critical thinking also includes looking at evidence and deciding what logical point, or conclusion, can be drawn from that evidence.

On the Web: If you are using this book in class, you can visit our website for additional practice in the basics of argument. Go to **www.townsendpress.com** and click on "Online Learning Center."

In class

 REVIEW TEST 1

To review what you learned in this chapter, fill in the blanks.

1. A point is the (*general idea, evidence, logic*) _____*general idea*_____ that a speaker or writer advances.
See page 394.

2. A critical thinker is one who can look at an argument—a point and its support—and decide whether the _____*support*_____ is solid or not.
See page 392.

3–5. To become an effective one-person jury, learn to constantly ask three questions:

   a. What is the _____*point*_____?

   b. What is its _____*support*_____?

   c. How logical is the _____*support*_____?
See page 393.

REVIEW TEST 2 ~~IN CLASS~~

A. Here is another cartoon about Snoopy as a writer. Look at the cartoon, and then answer the question that follows.

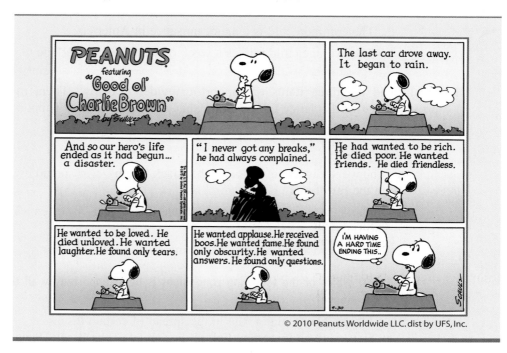

___D___ 1. This time Snoopy *does* support his point. What is his well-supported point?
- A. From the beginning, the hero pursued wealth, love, and fame.
- B. The hero wanted answers but found only questions.
- C. The "last car [that] drove away" must have been at the hero's funeral.
- D. The hero's life had been a disaster.   All the details given in the cartoon show that the hero's life was a disaster. Answers A, B, and C are too narrow.

B. (2–9.) In each of the following groups, one statement is the point, and the other statements are support for the point. Identify the point with a **P** and each statement of support with an **S**.

Group 1

___P___ A. It is good for people to limit the amount of time they watch TV.

___S___ B. When people spend less time watching TV, they pursue healthier activities, including exercise.

___S___ C. Studies show that when the TV is turned off, families talk and share more with each other.

___S___ D. Watching less TV means that kids will be exposed to less violence.

   Statements B, C, and D are reasons it's good for people to watch less TV.

Group 2

_____S_____ A. Each year, Americans spend billions of dollars buying cold medications.

_____S_____ B. Colds cause American business to lose millions of hours of work every year.

_____P_____ C. The common cold is a major nuisance in America.

_____S_____ D. The average child misses a week of school each year due to colds.

> Statements A, B, and D explain why the common cold is "a major nuisance."

C. (10.) Read the three items of supporting evidence below. Then, in the space provided, write the letter of the point that is most logically supported by that evidence.

Support

- The worst disease in history—the Black Death—was spread by fleas living in the fur of rats.

- Malaria, a disease affecting millions each year, is often carried by a mosquito.

- Roaches are a major cause of the increase in asthma cases.

_____A_____ **Point: Which of the following conclusions is best supported by all the evidence above?**

    A. Insects play a major role in the spread of certain diseases.
    B. Rats were an important link in the spread of the Black Death.
    C. Rats are the biggest threat to human health today.
    D. Asthma rates will continue to rise if the number of roaches increases.

> Statements B and D are incorrect because they focus on just one disease. Statement C is wrong because the "biggest threat" is not discussed. Each supporting item is an example of how insects have played a role in the spread of certain diseases.

REVIEW TEST 3

A. (1–4.) In the following group, one statement is the point, and the other statements are support for the point. Identify the point with a **P** and each statement of support with an **S**.

_____S_____ A. Cell phones make it possible for people to talk to or text-message their friends and family almost anywhere at any time.

_____S_____ B. Through e-mail, people can quickly exchange letters, no matter how far apart they are.

_____P_____ C. Modern technology has helped connect people and strengthen relationships.

_____S_____ D. Digital cameras allow people to instantly take and share special photos with each other.
> Statements A, B, and D are examples of items in modern technology that help connect people and make relationships stronger.

B. Each point is followed by three statements that provide logical support and two that do not. In the spaces, write the letters of the **three** logical statements of support.

5–7. **Point: The bus service on this route is unreliable.**

Statement B is about the age of the buses. Statement C is about a replacement for the buses. Neither is support for the point that the existing bus service is unreliable.

A. Several times each week, the bus on this route arrives more than a half hour late.

B. The buses on this route are at least twenty years old.

C. The transit authority is building a rail line to replace the bus route.

D. The bus schedule often gets changed without an announcement.

E. At least once per month, a bus on this route breaks down, causing long delays.

Items that logically support the point: ____A____   ____D____   ____E____

8–10. **Point: People should get rid of their credit cards.**

Statement B supports having only one credit card. Statement D explains why some people do not have credit cards in the first place. Neither statement supports getting rid of all one's credit cards.

A. Many credit-card companies charge high yearly fees—even if the card is never used.

B. Having only one credit card keeps people from charging too much.

C. Having credit cards encourages people to spend more money than they have, resulting in high debts.

D. Not everyone is approved to get a credit card.

E. The interest rate on many credit cards is so high that people end up paying a lot more than the purchase price for what they buy.

Items that logically support the point: ____A____   ____C____   ____E____

REVIEW TEST 4

Here is a chance to apply all your reading skills to a full-length selection. In his book *Think Big*, Dr. Ben Carson tells us about the time he was in fifth grade and believed he was "the dumbest kid in the class." Read the excerpt to see how Carson turned his life around from a path that was leading to failure. Then go on to answer the questions covering all of the reading skills you've worked on since beginning this book.

Words to Watch

Below are some words in the reading that do not have strong context support. Each word is followed by the number of the paragraph in which it appears and its meaning there. These words are indicated in the selection by a small circle (°).

inasmuch as (13): because
potential (18): capacity for development and progress

solely (20): alone
rebellious (46): resisting authority
indifferent (58): uninterested
acknowledged (67): recognized
startled (75): surprised
astonished (81): surprised

DO IT BETTER!

Ben Carson, M.D., with Cecil Murphey

1   "Benjamin, is this your report card?" my mother asked as she picked up the folded white card from the table.

2   "Uh, yeah," I said, trying to sound casual. Too ashamed to hand it to her, I had dropped it on the table, hoping that she wouldn't notice until after I went to bed.

3   It was the first report card I had received from Higgins Elementary School since we had moved back from Boston to Detroit, only a few months earlier.

4   I had been in the fifth grade not even two weeks before everyone considered me the dumbest kid in the class and frequently made jokes about me. Before long I too began to feel as though I really was the most stupid kid in fifth grade. Despite Mother's frequently saying, "You're smart, Bennie. You can do anything you want to do," I did not believe her.

5   No one else in school thought I was smart, either.

6   Now, as Mother examined my report card, she asked, "What's this grade in reading?" (Her tone of voice told me that I was in trouble.) Although I was embarrassed, I did not think too much about it. Mother knew that I wasn't doing well in math, but she did not know I was doing so poorly in every subject.

7   While she slowly read my report card, reading everything one word at a time, I hurried into my room and started to get ready for bed. A few minutes later, Mother came into my bedroom.

8   "Benjamin," she said, "are these your grades?" She held the card in front of me as if I hadn't seen it before.

9   "Oh, yeah, but you know, it doesn't mean much."

10   "No, that's not true, Bennie. It means a lot."

11   "Just a report card."

12   "But it's more than that."

13   Knowing I was in for it now, I prepared to listen, yet I was not all that interested. I did not like school very much and there was no reason why I should. Inasmuch as° I was the dumbest kid in the class, what did I have to look forward to? The others laughed at me and made jokes about me every day.

14   "Education is the only way you're ever going to escape poverty," she said. "It's the only way you're ever going to get ahead in life and be successful. Do you understand that?"

15   "Yes, Mother," I mumbled.

16   "If you keep on getting these kinds of grades, you're going to spend the rest of your life on skid row, or at best sweeping floors in a factory. That's not the kind of life that I want for you. That's not the kind of life that God wants for you."

17   I hung my head, genuinely ashamed. My mother had been raising me and my older brother, Curtis, by herself. Having only a third-grade education herself, she knew the value of what she did not have. Daily she drummed into Curtis and me that we had to do our best in school.

18   "You're just not living up to your potential°," she said. "I've got two mighty smart boys and I know they can do better."

19   I had done my best—at least I had when I first started at Higgins Elementary School. How could I do much when I did not understand anything going on in our class?

20   In Boston we had attended a parochial school, but I hadn't learned much because of a teacher who seemed more interested in talking to another female teacher than in teaching us. Possibly, this teacher was not solely° to blame—perhaps I wasn't emotionally able to learn much. My parents had separated just before we went to Boston, when I was eight years old. I loved both my mother and father and went through considerable trauma over their separating. For months afterward, I kept thinking that my parents would get back together, that my daddy would come home again the way he used to, and that we could be the same old family again—but he never came back. Consequently, we moved to Boston and lived with Aunt Jean and Uncle William

Dr. Ben Carson today

Avery in a tenement building for two years until Mother had saved enough money to bring us back to Detroit.

21   Mother kept shaking the report card at me as she sat on the side of my bed. "You have to work harder. You have to use that good brain that God gave you, Bennie. Do you understand that?"

22   "Yes, Mother." Each time she paused, I would dutifully say those words.

23   "I work among rich people, people who are educated," she said. "I watch how they act, and I know they can do anything they want to do. And so can you." She put her arm on my shoulder. "Bennie, you can do anything they can do—only you can do it better!"

24   Mother had said those words before. Often. At the time, they did not mean much to me. Why should they? I really believed that I was the dumbest kid in fifth grade, but of course, I never told her that.

25   "I just don't know what to do about you boys," she said. "I'm going to talk to God about you and Curtis." She paused, stared into space, then said (more to herself than to me), "I need the Lord's guidance on what to do. You just can't bring in any more report cards like this."

26   As far as I was concerned, the report card matter was over.

27   The next day was like the previous ones—just another bad day in school, another day of being laughed at because I did not get a single problem right in arithmetic and couldn't get any words right on the spelling test. As soon as I came home from school, I changed into play clothes and ran outside. Most of the boys my age played softball, or the game I liked best, "Tip the Top."

28   We played Tip the Top by placing a bottle cap on one of the sidewalk cracks. Then taking a ball—any kind that bounced—we'd stand on a line and take turns throwing the ball at the bottle top, trying to flip it over. Whoever succeeded got two points. If anyone actually moved the cap more than a few inches, he won five points. Ten points came if he flipped it into the air and it landed on the other side.

29   When it grew dark or we got tired, Curtis and I would finally go inside and watch TV. The set stayed on until we went to bed. Because Mother worked long hours, she was never home until just before we went to bed. Sometimes I would awaken when I heard her unlocking the door.

30   Two evenings after the incident with the report card, Mother came home about an hour before our bedtime. Curtis and I were sprawled out, watching TV. She walked across the room, snapped off the set, and faced both of us. "Boys," she said, "you're wasting too much of your time in front of that television. You don't get an education from staring at television all the time."

31   Before either of us could make a protest, she told us that she had been praying for wisdom. "The Lord's told me what to do," she said. "So from now on, you will not watch television, except for two preselected programs each week."

32   "Just *two* programs?" I could hardly believe she would say such a terrible thing. "That's not—"

33   "And *only* after you've done your homework. Furthermore, you don't play outside after school, either, until you've done all your homework."

34   "Everybody else plays outside right after school," I said, unable to think of anything except how bad it would be if I couldn't play with my friends. "I won't have any friends if I stay in the house all the time—"

35   "That may be," Mother said, "but everybody else is not going to be as successful as you are—"

36   "But, Mother—"

37   "This is what we're going to do. I asked God for wisdom, and this is the answer I got."

38   I tried to offer several other arguments, but Mother was firm. I glanced at Curtis, expecting him to speak up, but he did not say anything. He lay on the floor, staring at his feet.

39   "Don't worry about everybody else. The whole world is full of 'everybody else,' you know that? But only a few

make a significant achievement."

40   The loss of TV and playtime was bad enough. I got up off the floor, feeling as if everything was against me. Mother wasn't going to let me play with my friends, and there would be no more television—almost none, anyway. She was stopping me from having any fun in life.

41   "And that isn't all," she said. "Come back, Bennie."

42   I turned around, wondering what else there could be.

43   "In addition," she said, "to doing your homework, you have to read two books from the library each week. Every single week."

44   "Two books? Two?" Even though I was in fifth grade, I had never read a whole book in my life.

45   "Yes, two. When you finish reading them, you must write me a book report just like you do at school. You're not living up to your potential, so I'm going to see that you do."

46   Usually Curtis, who was two years older, was the more rebellious°. But this time he seemed to grasp the wisdom of what Mother said. He did not say one word.

47   She stared at Curtis. "You understand?"

48   He nodded.

49   "Bennie, is it clear?"

50   "Yes, Mother." I agreed to do what Mother told me—it wouldn't have occurred to me not to obey—but I did not like it. Mother was being unfair and demanding more of us than other parents did.

51   The following day was Thursday. After school, Curtis and I walked to the local branch of the library. I did not like it much, but then I had not spent that much time in any library.

52   We both wandered around a little in the children's section, not having any idea about how to select books or which books we wanted to check out.

53   The librarian came over to us and asked if she could help. We explained that both of us wanted to check out two books.

54   "What kind of books would you like to read?" the librarian asked.

55   "Animals," I said after thinking about it. "Something about animals."

56   "I'm sure we have several that you'd like." She led me over to a section of books. She left me and guided Curtis to another section of the room. I flipped through the row of books until I found two that looked easy enough for me to read. One of them, *Chip, the Dam Builder*—about a beaver—was the first one I had ever checked out. As soon as I got home, I started to read it. It was the first book I ever read all the way through even though it took me two nights. Reluctantly I admitted afterward to Mother that I really had liked reading about Chip.

57   Within a month I could find my way around the children's section like someone who had gone there all his life. By then the library staff knew Curtis and me and the kind of books we chose. They often made suggestions. "Here's a delightful book about a squirrel," I remember one of them telling me.

58   As she told me part of the story, I tried to appear indifferent°, but as soon

as she handed it to me, I opened the book and started to read.

59   Best of all, we became favorites of the librarians. When new books came in that they thought either of us would enjoy, they held them for us. Soon I became fascinated as I realized that the library had so many books—and about so many different subjects.

60   After the book about the beaver, I chose others about animals—all types of animals. I read every animal story I could get my hands on. I read books about wolves, wild dogs, several about squirrels, and a variety of animals that lived in other countries. Once I had gone through the animal books, I started reading about plants, then minerals, and finally rocks.

61   My reading books about rocks was the first time the information ever became practical to me. We lived near the railroad tracks, and when Curtis and I took the route to school that crossed by the tracks, I began paying attention to the crushed rock that I noticed between the ties.

62   As I continued to read more about rocks, I would walk along the tracks, searching for different kinds of stones, and then see if I could identify them.

63   Often I would take a book with me to make sure that I had labeled each stone correctly.

64   "Agate," I said as I threw the stone. Curtis got tired of my picking up stones and identifying them, but I did not care because I kept finding new stones all the time. Soon it became my favorite game to walk along the tracks and identify the varieties of stones. Although I did not realize it, within a very short period of time, I was actually becoming an expert on rocks.

65   Two things happened in the second half of fifth grade that convinced me of the importance of reading books.

66   First, our teacher, Mrs. Williamson, had a spelling bee every Friday afternoon. We'd go through all the words we'd had so far that year. Sometimes she also called out words that we were supposed to have learned in fourth grade. Without fail, I always went down on the first word.

67   One Friday, though, Bobby Farmer, whom everyone acknowledged° as the smartest kid in our class, had to spell "agriculture" as his final word. As soon as the teacher pronounced his word, I thought, *I can spell that word.* Just the day before, I had learned it from reading one of my library books. I spelled it under my breath, and it was just the way Bobby spelled it.

68   *If I can spell "agriculture," I'll bet I can learn to spell any other word in the world. I'll bet I can learn to spell better than Bobby Farmer.*

69   Just that single word, "agriculture," was enough to give me hope.

70   The following week, a second thing happened that forever changed my life. When Mr. Jaeck, the science teacher, was teaching us about volcanoes, he held up an object that looked like a piece of black, glass-like rock. "Does anybody know what this is? What does it have to do with volcanoes?"

71   Immediately, because of my reading, I recognized the stone. I waited, but none of my classmates raised their

hands. I thought, *This is strange. Not even the smart kids are raising their hands.* I raised my hand.

72   "Yes, Benjamin," he said.

73   I heard snickers around me. The other kids probably thought it was a joke, or that I was going to say something stupid.

74   "Obsidian," I said.

75   "That's right!" He tried not to look startled°, but it was obvious he hadn't expected me to give the correct answer.

76   "That's obsidian," I said, "and it's formed by the supercooling of lava when it hits the water." Once I had their attention and realized I knew information no other student had learned, I began to tell them everything I knew about the subject of obsidian, lava, lava flow, supercooling, and compacting of the elements.

77   When I finally paused, a voice behind me whispered, "Is that Bennie Carson?"

78   "You're absolutely correct," Mr. Jaeck said, and he smiled at me. If he had announced that I'd won a million-dollar lottery, I couldn't have been more pleased and excited.

79   "Benjamin, that's absolutely, absolutely right," he repeated with enthusiasm in his voice. He turned to the others and said, "That is wonderful! Class, this is a tremendous piece of information Benjamin has just given us. I'm very proud to hear him say this."

80   For a few moments, I tasted the thrill of achievement. I recall thinking, *Wow, look at them. They're all looking at me with admiration. Me, the dummy! The one everybody thinks is stupid. They're looking at me to see if this is really me speaking.*

81   Maybe, though, it was I who was the most astonished° one in the class. Although I had been reading two books a week because Mother told me to, I had not realized how much knowledge I was accumulating. True, I had learned to enjoy reading, but until then I hadn't realized how it connected with my schoolwork. That day—for the first time—I realized that Mother had been right. Reading is the way out of ignorance, and the road to achievement. I did not have to be the class dummy anymore.

82   For the next few days, I felt like a hero at school. The jokes about me stopped. The kids started to listen to me. *I'm starting to have fun with this stuff.*

83   As my grades improved in every subject, I asked myself, "Ben, is there any reason you can't be the smartest kid in the class? If you can learn about obsidian, you can learn about social studies and geography and math and science and everything."

84   That single moment of triumph pushed me to want to read more. From then on, it was as though I could not read enough books. Whenever anyone looked for me after school, they could usually find me in my bedroom—curled up, reading a library book—for a long time, the only thing I wanted to do. I had stopped caring about the TV programs I was missing; I no longer cared about playing Tip the Top or baseball anymore. I just wanted to read.

85   In a year and a half—by the middle of sixth grade—I had moved to the top of the class.

Reading Comprehension Questions

Vocabulary in Context

___D___ 1. In the excerpt below, the word *trauma* (trou′mə) means
   A. love.
   B. knowledge.   What did the author experience when his
   C. distance.   parents separated?
   D. suffering.

> "I loved both my mother and father and went through considerable trauma over their separating. For months afterward, I kept thinking that my parents would get back together, . . . but he never came back." (Paragraph 20)

Central Point and Main Ideas

___B___ 2. Which sentence best expresses the central point of the selection?
   A. Children who grow up in single-parent homes may spend large amounts of time home alone.
   B. Because of parental guidance that led to a love of reading, the author was able to go from academic failure to success.
   C. Most children do not take school very seriously, and they suffer as a
      result.   The selection is about the author's childhood,
   D. Today's young people watch too much television.   not children
                                  in general. Answers A, C, and D are too broad.

___A___ 3. Which sentence best expresses the main idea of paragraph 56?
   A. Bennie's first experience with a library book was positive.
   B. The first book that Bennie ever checked out at a library was about a beaver.
   C. The librarian was very helpful to Bennie and Curtis.
   D. At first, Bennie could not read most of the animal books at the
      library.   Answers B, C, and D are too narrow.

Supporting Details

___D___ 4. To get her sons to do better in school, Mrs. Carson insisted that they
   A. watch less TV.
   B. finish their homework before playing.
   C. read two books every week.   See paragraphs 31, 33,
   D. all of the above.   and 43.

__D__   5. The major details in paragraphs 65–82 are
        A. books that Bennie Carson read.
        B. new skills Bennie Carson had gained.
        C. various people in Bennie Carson's elementary school class.
        D. two events that convinced Bennie Carson of the importance of reading books.
        See paragraph 65.

Transitions

__D__   6. The sentence below contains a transition that shows
        A. addition.
        B. contrast.   *Cause:* The teacher was more interested in talking.
        C. an example.   *Effect:* The author hadn't learned much.
        D. cause and effect.

        "... I hadn't learned much <u>because of</u> a teacher who seemed more interested in talking to another female teacher than in teaching us." (Paragraph 20)

__D__   7. The major details in paragraphs 65–82 are signaled by the addition words
        A. *Two, other.*
        B. *Two, One.*   See the first sentence in paragraph 66
        C. *One, other, finally, next.*   and the first sentence in paragraph 70.
        D. *First, second.*

Patterns of Organization

__B__   8. The main pattern of organization of the selection is
        A. list of items.
        B. time order.   Events are presented in the
        C. contrast.   order in which they happened.
        D. definition and example.

Inferences

__D__   9. We can conclude that the author's mother believed
        A. education leads to success.
        B. her sons needed to be forced to live up to their potential.
        C. socializing was less important for her sons than a good education.
        D. all of the above.   The mother's words in paragraphs 14, 30, and 34–35 support answer D.

Argument

____C____ 10. Write the letter of the statement that is the point of paragraphs 70–80.
   A. Bennie knew that the name of the rock held by the teacher was obsidian.
   B. Bennie knew how to spell *agriculture*.
   C. Reading was the reason that Bennie became a better student.
   D. Bobby Farmer was the smartest kid in the class.

Paragraphs 70–80 discuss an event that shows how reading made Bennie a better student.

Discussion Questions

1. Why did Bennie consider himself "the dumbest kid in the class"? How did his image of himself affect his schoolwork?

2. The author recalls his failure in the classroom as an eight-year-old child by writing, "Perhaps I wasn't emotionally able to learn much." Why does he make this statement? What things in a child's home or social life might interfere with his or her education?

3. Part of Carson's mother's plan for helping her sons to improve their schoolwork was limiting their television watching to two programs a week. How much of a role do you think this limit played in the success of her plan? Do you agree with her that unrestricted television watching can be harmful to children?

4. Reading on a regular basis helped turn Carson's life around. Think about your daily schedule. If you were to do regular reading, where in your day could you find time to relax for half an hour and just read? What do you think would be the benefits of becoming a regular reader?

Note: Writing assignments for this selection appear on page 594.

Check Your Performance   THE BASICS OF ARGUMENT

Activity	Number Right	Points	Score
Review Test 1 (5 items)	_____	× 2 =	_____
Review Test 2 (10 items)	_____	× 3 =	_____
Review Test 3 (10 items)	_____	× 3 =	_____
Review Test 4 (10 items)	_____	× 3 =	_____
		TOTAL SCORE =	_____ %

Enter your total score into the **Reading Performance Chart: Review Tests** on the inside back cover.

THE BASICS OF ARGUMENT: Mastery Test 1

A. (1–8.) In each of the following groups, one statement is the point, and the other statements are support for the point. Identify each point with a **P** and each statement of support with an **S**.

Group 1

___S___ A. My husband is a vegetarian.

___S___ B. My mother, who lives with us, can't digest certain vegetables.

___S___ C. One of my children is allergic to milk, wheat, and eggs.

___P___ D. My family is difficult to cook for.   Statements A, B, and C are specific reasons it is difficult to cook for the family.

Group 2

___S___ A. Hungry fans can buy anything from hot dogs to barbecued sandwiches to vegetarian food.

___S___ B. The restrooms are large, plentiful, and well maintained.

___S___ C. No matter where you sit, you always have a good view of the action.

___P___ D. The new stadium is a great place to enjoy a game.
   Statements A, B, and C are specific examples of why the new stadium is a great place to enjoy a game.

B. (9.) Below is a point followed by three items of information. Put a check (✓) next to the **one** item that logically supports the point.

Point: Margo is a very rude worker.

_____ A. ¹She can barely stay awake while at work. ²Almost every day, she arrives at the store a few minutes late, having slept till the last minute. ³She works in slow motion, and it takes her so long to do any one thing that people never ask for her help. ⁴If she didn't spend the day pumping herself full of caffeine, she probably would not be able to move at all.

___✓___ B. ¹She keeps customers waiting while she talks with a coworker. ²When someone asks her about a sale item, she snaps, "If it isn't on the shelf, we don't have it!" ³When her boss isn't watching her, she answers the telephone by saying, "Yeah, what do you want?"

_____ C. ¹She can answer the phone, ring up a customer's purchases, and count large amounts of money all at the same time. ²She often volunteers to help customers bring their bags to their cars. ³She does not mind taking time to answer a customer's question or help someone stock a shelf.

   Item A supports "slow and unreliable." Item C supports "very good worker."

(Continues on next page)

C. (10.) Read the three items of supporting evidence below. Then, in the space provided, write the letter of the point that is most logically supported by that evidence.

> *Support*
>
> ● Cats are relatively quiet, while dogs bark all the time.
>
> ● Unlike dogs, cats can be left on their own for a few days if their owner is traveling.
>
> ● Cats will use a litter box, rather than requiring several trips outside a day, as dogs do.

___A___ **Point: Which of the following conclusions is best supported by all the evidence above?**

    A. Cats make better pets than dogs.
    B. Cats are quieter than dogs.
    C. Everyone should own a cat.
    D. Cats and dogs do not get along very well with each other.

      Answer B is too narrow because it focuses only on the first item of support.
      Answers C and D are not supported.

THE BASICS OF ARGUMENT: Mastery Test 2

A. Each point is followed by three statements that provide logical support and two that do not. In the spaces, write the letters of the **three** logical statements of support.

1–3. Point: Mel's new restaurant has a good chance of succeeding.

Statement A is an indication that Mel's will not *succeed. Statement E has nothing to do with the restaurant's success.*

A. Another restaurant at the same location did not do well.
B. The menu offers delicious dishes at reasonable prices.
C. The restaurant itself is bright, clean, and attractive.
D. Mel is a good host who makes customers feel welcome and special.
E. The weekly specials at the restaurant change every Thursday.

Items that logically support the point: ___B___   ___C___   ___D___

4–6. Point: I do not trust my sister's new boyfriend.

Statements A and D tell us what music the boyfriend likes and how he met the writer's sister. They are not reasons to distrust him.

A. He likes one of my favorite bands very much and has seen it in concert three times.
B. He gets calls on his cell phone at odd hours and then leaves without an explanation.
C. He borrows money from my sister but has yet to pay her back any of it.
D. My sister met him at the video store where she works.
E. When I saw him in a restaurant with another girl, he acted very embarrassed and left before I could say hello.

Items that logically support the point: ___B___   ___C___   ___E___

7–9. Point: Planting a garden in that vacant lot might benefit the neighborhood.

Statements A and E are general statements about farming and planting. They have nothing to do with the specific benefits of planting a garden in the vacant lot.

A. Farming was one of the earliest activities of civilization.
B. Flowers would make the neighborhood look better and attract customers for local businesses.
C. A garden could improve residents' diet by providing fresh produce to the neighborhood.
D. Planting a garden might bring young and old people together, making the community stronger.
E. There are many types of plants that could be planted in this climate.

Items that logically support the point: ___B___   ___C___   ___D___

(Continues on next page)

B. (10.) Below is a point followed by three items of information. Put a check (✓) next to the **one** item that logically supports the point.

Point: Greg is irresponsible.

_____ A. ¹He gives up his bus seat to elderly commuters. ²When he sees people carrying heavy packages or struggling with squirming children, he rushes to open doors to help them out.

_____ B. ¹No matter how much trouble I'm having with my English assignment, he refuses to do any of it for me. ²He says that between his own homework and his job, he doesn't have time. ³But he always gets B's, and I have trouble getting C's. ⁴Furthermore, when I need someone to cover for me at work so that I can see my girlfriend, he's always too busy with something else to help me out.

__✓__ C. ¹He never pays his bills on time. ²When he borrows things, he returns them damaged, or not at all. ³He is usually late for appointments, if he even remembers them at all.

Item C supports the point—that Greg is irresponsible. Item A suggests Greg is polite. Item B suggests Greg is busy with his own life.

THE BASICS OF ARGUMENT: Mastery Test 3

A. (1–8.) In each of the following groups, one statement is the point, and the other statements are support for the point. Identify each point with a **P** and each statement of support with an **S**.

Group 1

<u>S</u> A. The fans loudly boo the visiting team as soon as it appears.

<u>S</u> B. Recently, a man wearing a jacket from the opposing team was beaten up in the stands.

<u>P</u> C. Fans of our city's football team do not display good sportsmanship.

<u>S</u> D. Paper cups, beer cans, and even rocks are thrown onto the playing field during the game.　　　　*Statements A, B, and D support the point that the fans do not display good sportsmanship.*

Group 2

<u>P</u> A. Play is an important part of a child's development.

<u>S</u> B. During physical play, kids strengthen muscles and improve coordination.

<u>S</u> C. When children "pretend," they develop imagination and creativity.

<u>S</u> D. By acting out stories, they learn to understand emotions and feelings.

Statements B, C, and D list three examples of the importance of play to a child's development.

B. (9.) Below is a point followed by three items of information. Put a check (✓) next to the **one** item that logically supports the point.

Point: That roller coaster is dangerous.

_____ A. ¹It is slower than any other roller coaster in the state. ²The curves of its track are so wide and the hills are so shallow that a ride on this roller coaster seems like a drive in the country. ³People don't scream when they ride it. ⁴Instead, they enjoy the view from above the park.

_____ B. ¹It is known as one of the best roller coasters in the country. ²People will wait in lines for hours just to try it. ³At certain points it reaches the same speeds as cars do on highways. ⁴The track is so tall and long that you can see it miles away.

<u>✓</u> C. ¹Last year, it broke down several times, leaving people stranded in their cars sixty feet off the ground. ²In most cars, the seatbelts are torn and don't always buckle properly. ³One area of the track shakes and makes a strange grinding sound whenever a car passes over it.

Item A supports "isn't scary." Item B supports "great."

(Continues on next page)

C. (10.) Read the three items of supporting evidence below. Then, in the space provided, write the letter of the point that is most logically supported by that evidence.

Support

- In ancient times, "doctors" sometimes bored holes in the skulls of mentally ill people.
- In many parts of the world, mentally ill people were tortured to drive out their "evil spirits."
- Some societies in the past forced mentally ill people to live in colonies on deserted islands.

___B___ **Point: Which of the following conclusions is best supported by all the evidence above?**

A. Mentally ill people should be treated with kindness, not cruelty.
B. In the past, mental illness was often treated harshly.
C. Not all ancient societies treated mentally ill people with cruelty.
D. Mentally ill people should never be held responsible for their actions.

Each supporting statement presents an example of harsh treatment of mentally ill people. Answers A, C, and D are not supported.

THE BASICS OF ARGUMENT: Mastery Test 4

A. Each point is followed by three statements that provide logical support and two that do not. In the spaces, write the letters of the **three** logical statements of support.

Statement C presents an advantage of raising the speed limit. Statement E restricts the higher speed limit to open highways. Neither statement presents a disadvantage of a higher speed limit.

1–3. Point: Raising the speed limit on America's highways is a bad idea.

A. Raising the speed limit will make traffic accidents more severe, since cars will be hitting each other at higher speeds.

B. Cars traveling at higher speeds produce more pollution.

C. By traveling faster, people can get where they are going in less time.

D. Cars get poorer gas mileage at higher speeds than at lower speeds.

E. The higher speed limit will apply only to open highways, not to roads that are heavily crowded.

Items that logically support the point: ____A____ ____B____ ____D____

4–6. Point: There are some simple ways to save money at the supermarket.

A. Avoid products that charge extra for packaging, such as cheese wrapped individually by slice.

Statement C is about how to organize a shopping list, not about ways to save money. Statement E is about saving time, not money.

B. Buy store brands of basic items instead of expensive name-brand products.

C. Some people organize a shopping list alphabetically; others group items by categories.

D. Shop when you are not hungry, so that you won't be tempted to buy pricey treats.

E. Go to the store at odd hours or on weekdays to reduce the time you spend in lines.

Items that logically support the point: ____A____ ____B____ ____D____

7–9. Point: Mayor Stump is the most dishonest politician I've ever seen.

Statements B and E present positive facts about Stump. Statements A, C, and D present information that show Stump is dishonest.

A. He used taxpayer money to buy expensive gifts for his family and friends.

B. Before becoming mayor, Stump was a successful trial lawyer.

C. Stump gave his daughter-in-law a "no-show" job that pays a salary of $80,000 a year.

D. Our local newspaper says that Stump accepted bribes in exchange for government contracts.

E. Stump is proud of the fact that several new businesses have opened in our town.

Items that logically support the point: ____A____ ____C____ ____D____

(Continues on next page)

B. (10.) Below is a point followed by three items of information. Put a check (✓) next to the **one** item that logically supports the point.

Point: The meal I cooked for my girlfriend was horrible.

_____ A. ¹The chicken took an hour to prepare and two hours to cook. ²I had to travel for twenty miles to find a produce store that sold the vegetables I wanted. ³In order to make all this food, I had to buy a whole new set of pots and pans. ⁴Afterward, it took me hours to clean the kitchen and wash the dishes.

_____ B. ¹My girlfriend's car would not start when she wanted to come over. ²By the time she arrived, she was two hours late and very angry. ³As we sat down to eat, all she could talk about was how much it would cost to have her car fixed. ⁴When I tried to change the subject, she said I never listen to her, so I apologized. ⁵Then she accused me of apologizing too much. ⁶We both got so mad that we hardly touched dinner.

___✓___ C. ¹The chicken came out so tough and dry that I could barely cut it with a steak knife. ²I overcooked the fresh vegetables so much that they changed from a bright green color to the color of an army jeep. ³The cake I tried to bake collapsed into itself, turning into a shapeless chewy mass that resembled a giant cookie.

Item C supports the point—that the meal was horrible.
Item A suggests the meal was lots of work. Item B does not discuss the meal.

THE BASICS OF ARGUMENT: Mastery Test 5

A. (1–4.) In the following group, one statement is the point, and the other statements are support for the point. Identify the point with a **P** and each statement of support with an **S**.

___P___ A. Hearing can be damaged by a number of common sounds.

___S___ B. Loud music at a concert or in headphones can cause significant hearing loss.

___S___ C. Machinery such as lawn mowers and leaf blowers can contribute to deafness.

___S___ D. The noise level of many buses and trucks is high enough to damage hearing permanently.

Statements B, C, and D give examples of common sounds that can damage hearing.

B. The point below is followed by three statements that provide logical support and two that do not. In the spaces, write the letters of the **three** logical statements of support.

5–7. **Point: High-school proms should be banned.**

Statements D and E present matter-of-fact details about proms, not reasons proms should be banned.

A. Proms pressure students to spend a ridiculous amount of money on gowns, tuxes, flowers, and even limos.

B. The social pressure to get a date for the prom makes many people miserable.

C. Prom preparations distract students for many weeks from the real business of school, which is education.

D. Proms usually feature a theme, and the room the prom is held in is decorated according to that theme.

E. At most schools, proms are chaperoned by teachers and administrators.

Items that logically support the point: ___A___   ___B___   ___C___

C. Each point below is followed by three items of information. Put a check (✓) next to the **one** item that logically supports each point.

8. **Point: Susan is a generous person.**

_____ A. [1]She bows her head and gives thanks before every meal, even when eating out. [2]She spends most of every Sunday in church. [3]She votes for political candidates who she feels have a strong connection to God.

(Continues on next page)

_____ ✓ _____ B. ¹If I admire an outfit she's wearing, she'll offer to lend it to me. ²She often treats when the gang goes out for pizza. ³She can't pass a homeless person without giving away her loose change. ⁴And she donates two evenings a week to Big Sisters and an adult literacy program.

_____ _____ C. ¹When her cousin failed to repay a loan, she said, "He told me he just can't get his life together," but this same cousin takes expensive vacations. ²She believed a salesman's story that the used car she bought had been owned by a little old lady who drove it only to church on Sundays.   Item A supports "religious and active in her church." Item C supports "will believe anything."

9. **Point: Neil is a hypocrite—he usually does the opposite of what he says.**

   _____ ✓ _____ A. ¹He spent a half hour talking and laughing with someone yesterday, then later confided to me, "I can't stand that man!" ²He lectures his daughters about the dangers of drug addiction, but he is a heavy drinker and smoker.

   _____ _____ B. ¹He waits until December to put in winter storm windows, and his Christmas tree is often still up in March. ²He usually pays his bills a few days after they are due, and he never gets around to dental or medical checkups until real problems develop.

   _____ _____ C. ¹After thirty-seven years of marriage, he still writes love letters to his wife. ²He took early retirement so he could stay home and care for her when an illness left her bedridden. ³He never leaves the house without bringing her back something special.
   Item B supports "lazy." Item C supports "loving, caring husband."

10. **Point: My boss is considerate.**

    _____ _____ A. ¹She greets employees and customers alike with a warm smile and a hearty, "Hi! How are you today?" ²She is forever telling us, "A stranger is just a friend you haven't met yet."

    _____ ✓ _____ B. ¹Instead of giving us orders, she asks us to do things. ²She always thanks an employee for completing a task. ³She often helps out when she sees that things are getting stressful.

    _____ _____ C. ¹Getting a raise out of her is impossible—even for long-term employees. ²Her secretary is still using an old typewriter because the boss won't buy anything new. ³We had to have the retirement party for the office manager during our lunch hour, and the boss was waiting by the time clock when we got back—to make sure we weren't a minute late.
    Item A supports "very friendly." Item C supports "not generous."

THE BASICS OF ARGUMENT: Mastery Test 6

A. (1–4.) In the following group, one statement is the point, and the other statements are support for the point. Identify the point with a **P** and each statement of support with an **S**.

   _S_   A. The authors do not define the new terms they use in each chapter.

   _P_   B. That sociology textbook is not very helpful.

   _S_   C. The sentences are long and hard to understand, and the material does not seem well organized.

   _S_   D. The book has few illustrations and no index.

                     Statements A, C, and D describe ways that the textbook is not helpful.

B. The point below is followed by three statements that provide logical support and two that do not. In the spaces, write the letters of the **three** logical statements of support.

5–7. Point: Early automobiles were uncomfortable and difficult to operate.

Statement A is about the price of cars. Statement D is about building vehicles for military use. Neither supports the idea that early cars were uncomfortable or difficult to operate.

A. The start of the factory assembly line made the price of the Model T drop from $440 in 1915 to $290 in 1925.

B. Hard, high-pressure tires on early cars made for very bumpy rides.

C. Early cars were open on top, and drivers choked on dust and dirt.

D. During World War II, many cars and trucks were made for military use.

E. A driver had to start the car's engine by cranking it by hand, and the crank sometimes sprang back and broke the driver's thumb.

Items that logically support the point: _B_   _C_   _E_

C. (8–10.) For each group on the next page, read the three items of supporting evidence. Then, in the space provided, write the letter of the point that is most logically supported by that evidence.

(Continues on next page)

Group 1

Support

- It feels good to help people who are in need.
- You can meet a lot of interesting, friendly people while volunteering.
- You can learn new skills—some of which may help you land a paying job.

__B__ **Point: Which of the following conclusions is best supported by all the evidence above?**

    A. Doing volunteer work is the best way to find a paying job.
    B. Doing volunteer work can be a rewarding experience.
    C. If you're looking for reliable friends, doing volunteer work is better than social networking on the Internet.
    D. These days, too many people lack food, clothing, and a decent place to live.

Each supporting item presents an example of how volunteer work can be rewarding.

Group 2

Support

- Pigeons enjoy living in populated areas, especially big cities.
- Coyotes are increasing their numbers in populated suburban areas.
- Cities and suburbs are packed with an increasing number of squirrels.

__B__ **Point: Which of the following conclusions is best supported by all the evidence above?**

    A. Coyotes may soon be a health problem for many suburban communities.
    B. Some wild animals are able to live near human beings.
    C. Big cities are dangerous places for all forms of wildlife.
    D. Many urban residents enjoy feeding and caring for pigeons.

Each supporting item presents an example of a wild animal that is able to live near humans.

Group 3

Support

- Buses and trains reduce air pollution.
- Traffic problems lessen where people take buses or trains to work.
- When more people take public transportation, fuel is saved.

Each supporting item presents a reason people should use public transportation more often.

__C__ **Point: Which of the following conclusions is best supported by all the evidence above?**

    A. One answer to pollution is the use of public transportation.
    B. City streets would be safer if fewer people drove their cars to work.
    C. People should use public transportation more often.
    D. Highways should be built wider to reduce traffic accidents.

Part Two

Ten Reading Selections

1 Winners, Losers, or Just Kids?
Dan Wightman

Preview

Did a high-school teacher ever suggest that you'd never amount to anything? And when you were in high school, did you sometimes feel that happiness and success were going to happen to other people, but not to you? If so, like the author of this selection, you should realize that "A" students sometimes earn D's in life, and high-school losers sometimes turn out to be winners.

Words to Watch

coyly (1): with pretended shyness
flaunted (1): showed off
blotto (2): very drunk
swank (3): ritzy
metamorphoses (4): great changes
morose (7): gloomy
fare (8): make out
endeared (9): made dear
sheepish (11): shamefaced
presumptuous (11): taking too much for granted
regressed (13): gone backward
quick (15): the sensitive flesh under the fingernails
stride (17): pace

1   If I envied anyone in high school, it was the winners. You know who I mean. The ones who earned straight A's and scored high on their Scholastic Aptitude Tests. The attractive ones who smiled coyly°, drove their own sport cars, and flaunted° those hard, smooth bodies that they kept tan the year round.

2   By contrast, my high-school friends were mostly losers. We spent a lot of time tuning cars and drinking beer. Our girlfriends were pale and frumpy, and we had more D's than B's on our report cards. After graduation, many of us went into the Army instead of to a university; two of us came back from Vietnam in coffins, three more on stretchers. On weekends, when we drank Colt 45 together in my father's battered Ford, we'd laughingly refer to ourselves as the "out crowd." But, unless we were thoroughly blotto°, we never laughed

hard when we said it. And I, for one, rarely got blotto when I was 16.

3   The reason I mention this is that last month 183 winners and losers from my Northern California high-school graduating class got together at a swank° country club for a revealing fifteen-year reunion.

4   Predictably, only happy and successful people attended. The strange thing, though, was that the people I once pegged as losers outnumbered the winners at this reunion by a visible margin. And, during a long session at the bar with my informative friend Paula, I got an earful about the messy lives of people I'd once envied, and the remarkable metamorphoses° of people I'd once pitied.

5   Paula reported that Len, a former class officer, was now a lost soul in Colorado, hopelessly estranged from his charming wife. Tim, one of the sorriest students I'd ever known, was a successful sportswriter, at ease with himself.

6   Estelle, who was modestly attractive in her teens, was now a part-time stripper in the Midwest, working to support her young son. Connie, a former car-club "kitten," had become a sophisticated international flight attendant.

7   Paula told me that Gary, a college scholarship winner, was overweight, underemployed, and morose°. Ron, who had shown little flair for music, had become a symphony violinist.

8   Sipping a piña colada, I thought to myself how terribly mistaken my senior counselor had been when she told me that high-school performance indicates how one will fare° later.

9   I looked at Paula, a high-school troublemaker with a naughty smile, whose outgoing personality and rebellious spirit had endeared° her to me so long ago. Together, we once stole a teacher's grade book, changed some of our low marks, then dropped the book in the lost-and-found box. The savvy teacher never said a word about the incident, but at the end of the year, when report cards were issued, gave us the D's we deserved.

10   Now Paula was a housewife, a volunteer worker, and the mother of two sons. She wore a marriage-encounter pin on her modest dress, and sat at the bar tippling Perrier on ice.

11   She shook her head when I reminded her of the grade-book escapade, and the sheepish° look on her face reminded me how presumptuous° it is to predict the lives of others.

12   It also got me thinking about my own life since high school—how I'd gradually shaken my loser's image,

gotten through college, found a decent job, married wisely, and finally realized a speck of my potential.

13   I thought about numerous situations where I could have despaired, regressed°, given up—and how I hadn't, though others had—and I wondered why I was different, and had more luck, less guilt.

14   "The past is fiction," wrote William Burroughs. And, although I don't subscribe to that philosophy entirely, the people I admire most today are those who overcome their mistakes, seize second chances, and fight to pull themselves together, day after day.

15   Often they're the sort of people who leave high school with blotchy complexions, crummy work habits, fingernails bitten down to the quick°. And of course they're bitterly unsure of themselves, and slow to make friends.

16   But they're also the ones who show up transformed at fifteen-year reunions, and the inference I draw is that the distinction between winners and losers is often slight and seldom crucial—and frequently overrated.

17   In high school especially, many people are slow getting started. But, finding their stride°, they quickly catch up, and in their prime often return to surprise and delight us—their lives so much richer than we'd ever imagined.

Vocabulary Questions

A. Use context clues to help you decide on the best definition for each italicized word. Then, in the space provided, write the letter of your choice.

___B___ 1. In the excerpt below, the word *pegged* (pĕgd) means
    A. feared.
    B. labeled.
    C. admired.
    D. envied.

    In this sentence, what had the author once done to losers?

    ". . . the people I once pegged as losers outnumbered the winners." (Paragraph 4)

___C___ 2. In the excerpt below, the word *estranged* (ĭ-strānjd′) means
    A. enriched.
    B. free.
    C. separated.
    D. rich.

    A person who is a "lost soul" is likely to be separated from loved ones.

    ". . . a lost soul . . . hopelessly estranged from his charming wife." (Paragraph 5)

_C_   3. In the sentence below, the word *flair* (flâr) means
　　　A. dislike.
　　　B. inability.
　　　C. talent.　　　*What had Ron not shown for music?*
　　　D. money.

　　　"Ron, who had shown little flair for music, had become a symphony violinist." (Paragraph 7)

_D_   4. In the excerpt below, the word *savvy* (săv′ē) means
　　　A. foolish.
　　　B. cruel.　　　*The teacher had to be "knowing" to give the students the grade they deserved.*
　　　C. misled.
　　　D. knowing.

　　　"The savvy teacher . . . gave us the D's we deserved." (Paragraph 9)

_A_   5. In the excerpt below, the words *subscribe to* (səb-skrīb′ tōō) mean
　　　A. agree with.
　　　B. disagree with.　　*The author agrees with Burroughs's statement but suggests it does not hold true for everyone—*
　　　C. understand.　　*not everyone can overcome past mistakes.*
　　　D. pay for.

　　　"'The past is fiction,' wrote William Burroughs. And although I don't subscribe to that philosophy entirely, the people I admire . . . are those who overcome their mistakes . . . ." (Paragraph 14)

B. Below are words, or forms of words, from "Words to Watch." Write in the one that best completes each sentence. Then write the letter of that word in the space provided.

| A. endeared | B. flaunted | C. metamorphosis |
| D. morose | E. sheepish | |

_B_   6. For the first week after her engagement, Janice _____flaunted_____ her diamond ring at the office.　　*Janice showed off her engagement ring.*

_D_   7. After his pet cat died, Lee felt _____morose_____ for days.
　　　The cat's death would make Lee feel gloomy.

_A_   8. The boss's gentle manner _____endeared_____ him to the workers.
　　　A gentle manner makes the boss dear to the workers.

_E_   9. When the teacher said, "I see you've forgotten your homework again,"
　　　Richie looked _____sheepish_____.　　*The teacher's comment made Rich shamefaced.*

_C_   10. Having to work for a living brings about a _____metamorphosis_____ in young people's attitude toward money.　　*Earning a living brings about a great change in young people's attitude.*

Reading Comprehension Questions

Central Point and Main Ideas

_D_   1. Which sentence best expresses the central point of the selection?
   A. High-school winners get good grades and are attractive.
   B. High-school losers drink beer and fix cars.
   C. The author attended his fifteen-year reunion.
   D. High-school performance doesn't show how well a student will do
      later in life.   Answers A, B, and C are too narrow.
                    Each relates to only one detail in the selection.

_A_   2. The main idea of paragraph 2 is best expressed in the
   A. first sentence.
   B. second sentence.   The first sentence states that the author's friends
   C. third sentence.   were losers. The rest of the paragraph goes on to
   D. last sentence.   explain how his friends fit into this category.

Supporting Details

_B_   3. The author's old friend Paula, a troublemaker in high school,
   A. became a part-time stripper.
   B. became a housewife, mother, and volunteer worker.
   C. remained a troublemaker.
   D. told the author nothing about their classmates' lives.
                    See the first sentence of paragraph 10.

_C_   4. According to the author, high-school losers
   A. are less interesting than other people.
   B. have little potential for success.
   C. have a lot of potential for success.
   D. should try to become friends with winners.   See paragraph 17.
                    (This idea is also supported by the descriptions of
                        high-school losers who later succeeded.)

Transitions

_B_   5. The relationship of paragraph 2 to paragraph 1 is one of
   A. comparison.
   B. contrast.   The second paragraph contrasts the author's "loser"
   C. an example.   friends with the high-school "winners" in the first
   D. time.   paragraph. Note the transition *by contrast.*

_D_   6. In paragraph 17, the relationship of the second sentence to the first
      sentence is one of   The second sentence contrasts people's high-school
   A. addition.   performance with
   B. illustration.   C. comparison.   their success later in life.
                           D. contrast.   The contrast transition is *but.*

Patterns of Organization

_B_   7. The details in paragraphs 5–7 are organized in a pattern of
- A. time order.
- B. a list of items.
- C. cause and effect.
- D. definition and example.

The paragraphs list names and descriptions of people who had gone to high school with the author.

Inferences

_D_   8. From the article, we can conclude that in high school, the author
- A. thought the winners would not always be winners.
- B. thought the winners did not deserve their grades.
- C. felt the winners did not know they were winners.
- D. might have wanted to trade places with the winners.

_A_   9. The author implies that
- A. people often think that high-school losers will remain losers.
- B. the difference between winners and losers in high school is usually very important to their futures.
- C. fifteen-year reunions change losers to winners.
- D. everyone knows that high-school losers often become winners.

_C_ 10. The author implies that
- A. being a winner in high school is a poor start in life.
- B. being a high-school winner is more important to one's future than determination.
- C. determination and hope change people's lives.
- D. people's abilities are fully developed by high school.

Item 8:   In paragraphs 1 and 4, the author suggests he "envied" the winners when he was in high school. There is no evidence for answers A, B, or C.

Item 9:   In paragraph 4, the author says it is strange or surprising that the former losers outnumber the winners at the reunion. In paragraph 8, he says that his senior counselor had suggested that high-school losers were likely to remain losers. In paragraph 17, he says that the losers often surprise us with their success. All of these details imply the author's assumption that people often think high-school losers will remain losers.

Item 10: In paragraphs 13–14, the author writes about qualities such as overcoming mistakes, fighting to pull oneself together, not despairing, and not giving up. These sorts of qualities demonstrate determination and hope.

Summarizing

Note: A **summary** is the reduction of a large amount of information to its most important points. The length and kind of summary will depend upon one's purpose as well as the material in question. Often, a summary will consist of a central point and its major supporting details. As a general guideline, a paragraph might be reduced to a sentence or two, an article (such as the one you have just read) might be reduced to a paragraph, and a textbook chapter might be reduced to about three or so pages of notes.

_C_   1. Write the letter of the statement that best summarizes the central point of "Winners, Losers, or Just Kids?" as expressed in the first four paragraphs.
   A. In high school, the author was a loser who envied the winners.
   B. High-school reunions can teach us important lessons about life in general.
   C. The reunion showed that many high-school winners and losers had not turned out as the author had expected.

_C_   2. Write the letter of the statement that best summarizes the first set of supporting details for the central point (paragraphs 5–12).
   A. At his reunion, the author found out what had happened to his classmates.
   B. The author's friend Paula had turned her life around and was now happily married and a contributor to society.
   C. The author realized that some losers in his high-school class, including himself, had done more with their lives than some of the winners he had once envied.

_A_   3. Write the letter of the statement that best summarizes the second set of supporting details for the central point (paragraphs 13–17).
   A. The winners in life include those who overcome early mistakes and problems and persist in building good lives for themselves.
   B. The winners in life are the ones who leave high school as attractive people with impressive records.
   C. The author began life as a loser but ended up as a winner.

Item 1: Answer A is too narrow. Answer B is not supported. The last sentence of paragraph 4 sums up the idea expressed in answer C.

Item 2: Answer A is true, but too vague to be a useful summary. Answer B is too narrow, covering only one of the details in paragraphs 5–12. Answer C gives a specific and accurate summary of paragraphs 5–12.

Item 3: Answer B is incorrect because, in paragraphs 13–17, the author describes the losers who succeed. Answer C is too narrow because he does not describe only himself. Answer A gives a useful summary of paragraphs 13–17.

Discussion Questions

1. What does Wightman really mean by "winners" and "losers"? Why does the title also say, "or Just Kids"?

2. Were you surprised that Wightman's classmates turned out as they did? Why or why not?

3. What is the meaning of the sentence "The past is fiction"? To what extent do you think it's true, if at all? In what ways *isn't* it true?

4. Wightman writes that he "wondered why he was different, and had more luck, less guilt" than others. What factors do you suppose are involved in determining whether or not people shake their "loser's image"? What factors does Wightman name?

Note: Writing assignments for this selection appear on page 594.

Check Your Performance	WINNERS, LOSERS, OR JUST KIDS?		
Activity	Number Right	Points	Total
Vocabulary			
A. Vocabulary in Context (5 items)	_____	× 10 =	_____
B. Words to Watch (5 items)	_____	× 10 =	_____
		SCORE =	_____%
Comprehension			
Central Point and Main Ideas (2 items)	_____	× 8.5 =	_____
Supporting Details (2 items)	_____	× 8.5 =	_____
Transitions (2 items)	_____	× 8.5 =	_____
Patterns of Organization (1 item)	_____	× 8.5 =	_____
Inferences (3 items)	_____	× 8.5 =	_____
Summarizing (3 items)	_____	× 5 =	_____
		SCORE =	_____%

FINAL SCORES: Vocabulary _____% Comprehension _____%

Enter your total score into the **Reading Performance Chart: Ten Reading Selections** on the inside back cover.

2 Owen, the Stray Cat
Emily Carlin

Preview

Hundreds of people rushed along a busy city street, not noticing the small, terrified kitten hiding in the shadows. Then someone did notice it—and naturally, it was a man who didn't even like cats. At least that's what he kept telling anyone who would listen . . .

Words to Watch

twist (3): an unexpected turn of events
goner (7): dead body
sarcastically (8): meaning the opposite of what is said
macho (9 and 29): having a strong sense of masculinity
glint (12): a brief flash of light
gruel (16): a thin, watery cereal
vigorously (22): energetically
estimated (27): made an educated guess

1   Well, we have another cat.

2   This fact should not come as a great surprise to anyone who knows me. I have a reputation as a pet magnet. You know those high-pitched whistles that only dogs can hear? I sometimes think that I have a sign hanging around my neck that only animals can read. It says, "SOFT TOUCH." My ability to Just Say No to a needy animal is seriously underdeveloped. That is why, in a nutshell, we are now the owners of two dogs, three cats, a cockatiel, and a parakeet, and have seen a succession of gerbils, lizards, and other creatures come and go over the years.

3   But like all good stories, this one has a twist°. I am not responsible for this latest pet. The orange-striped kitten now sitting at the foot of my bed owes its existence to my husband, Bob.

4   As he would be the first to tell you, Bob is not a cat person. He's a dog guy and is fond of Logan, our terrier, and Alex the retriever mix. He particularly likes to go on long walks by the creek with Alex, who plunges with insane abandon into the water and retrieves sticks until he is

limp with exhaustion. Cats, by contrast, seem like relatively useless creatures to Bob. Left to his own devices, Bob would live in a cat-free zone.

5   And yet, a few weeks ago, I had this phone call . . .

6   To set the scene, you need to know that Bob works in center city Philadelphia. Traffic is heavy; people hurry by, especially at rush hour. The sidewalks are wide and bare, completely without hiding places.   Offices and stores line the street. There is no place, logically, for a tiny kitten to come from.

7   But there was Bob on his cell phone, staring at a filthy ball of fur pressed close to the side of his building. "There's this *cat*," he told me. "It's a goner° if it stays here. Should I try to catch it and bring it home?"

8   "Nah, I don't think so," I said sarcastically°. "Leave it on Market Street so it'll get squished by a car."

9   After eight years of marriage, he knew how to interpret that. "Yeah, yeah, OK. I'll try," he said. He returned his cell phone to his pocket, but he forgot to turn it off. And so for the next twelve minutes, I was able to listen in as Bob and, eventually, two homeless guys he persuaded to help him, tried to corral the kitten. "HERE LITTLE GUY! C'MON, HERE YA GO!" they kept saying. It was evident from the "Oofs!" and "Darn its!" that the panicked cat was not making the job easy. Curious passersby stopped to watch the drama, and each time I heard my macho° husband explain, "This isn't my idea. I don't even LIKE

Owen today

cats. It's my wife . . ." In the kitchen thirty miles away, I rolled my eyes.

10   Eventually the phone went dead, and I was left in the dark as to the outcome of the rescue mission. Just in case, I put food and water and a litter box in the bathroom, where I figured I could quiet a frightened animal.

11   Finally Bob's car pulled in. He walked into the house carrying a paper bag, which he handed over to me as if it contained a live grenade. "I think it might be dead," he cautioned me.

12   The bag did indeed seem to contain a small lifeless body. I took it into the bathroom, sat down, and opened it. An unmoving ball of fur lay there, but I could see the glint° of two gray-green eyes. I scooped the kitten out and put

it on the floor. It made one sad attempt to scramble away, then fell down, obviously exhausted beyond measure. I stroked its fur briefly and spoke gently to the tiny creature. Assuming it was half-dead with terror, I set it down near its food and water and left it alone in the quiet room for an hour.

13   When I returned to the bathroom, the kitten was not looking good. It had moved itself behind the toilet and was lying there limply, its eyes dull and half-closed, its breathing shallow. It had not touched its food.

14   I searched the kitchen for the most irresistible cat treat available. At the back of a cabinet, I found a forgotten container of sardines. I broke off a crumb of sardine, took the cat in my lap, gently opened its tiny jaws, and deposited the fish in its mouth. There was no response. The cat didn't chew, didn't swallow, didn't shake its head in disgust, didn't try to get away. It just lay there passively with the bit of food in its mouth.

15   "I don't think it's going to make it," I told Bob, who was by then peering through the bathroom door. "It's too weak to eat."

16   Sadly, we looked at the dirty, doomed little creature before us. I returned to the kitchen, this time finding a dropper from a bottle of medicine I had gotten for one of my other cats. I cut off its tip to widen the opening, and I mashed the sardine up with a bit of water to make a sort of sardine soup. Taking the cat onto my lap once again,

I gently squirted a tiny bit of the gruel°-like mixture into its mouth.

17   Nothing. Then the little creature stirred. Its nose twitched, and it swallowed weakly. I waited a few minutes, then tried another squirt. Another swallow. A few more squirts, and the kitten began licking its chops after swallowing. Then licking the dropper. Then weakly biting the dropper with the unmistakable message, "More!!"

18   Afraid of overloading its starved little belly, I gave the kitten only a little food at a time during that first night. But with every passing hour it became more alert and more eager to greet the dropper. By morning it was eating the mashed sardines off my fingers; by noon it was standing at the bowl of sardine soup and was helping itself. After every feeding the kitten fell into a deep, deep sleep, but it was a healthful, healing sleep, not the near-coma of the previous night. I was covered with sardine juice and smelled like a cat food factory, but I couldn't have been happier. The new pet was going to make it.

19   Three days later, I took our round-bellied kitten to the vet for its first checkup. As I sat in the waiting room, it purred loudly in my lap, just as it had purred throughout its first bath, its first ear-cleaning, and, today, its first drive to the vet. A three-year-old boy sitting with his mother nearby came over to inspect it.

20   "Nice kitty," he said, staring into the kitten's enormous gray-green eyes.

21   "It *is* a nice kitty, isn't it?" I answered.

22   He nodded vigorously°. "What's its name?"

23   I hadn't even thought about that. "It doesn't have a name yet. We just got it. Do you have any ideas?"

24   He thought very hard, then said, "Owen."

25   "Owen!" I said. "That's an unusual ... Wait a minute. Is YOUR name Owen?"

26   More vigorous nodding.

27   Three weeks into his life with us, Owen (who, the vet estimated°, was about ten weeks old) is as funny and frisky as any kitten ever born. He lurks under the bed and leaps out to slap Logan the terrier, who regards him with enormous amusement. He scrambles over Alex the quiet retriever, who just looks with good will at him. White Cat and Felix, our two adult cats, treat him like the youngster he is, occasionally swatting his nose to remind him to mind his manners. And when there is a human lap to snuggle into, he does so, purring so loudly it's hard to believe such a huge sound is coming from such a tiny body.

28   At night, as we are going to sleep, we have more than once been wakened by the sound of Owen clawing his way up the side of the bed. He's still too little to make the leap. Falling back on old habits, Bob will say, "Your cat isn't letting me sleep."

29   "That isn't *my* cat, macho man. I never would have known that cat EXISTED if it weren't for you."

30   "Well you're the one who SAID I should bring it home ..."

31   Owen listens to us argue. And he just purrs and purrs and purrs.

Vocabulary Questions

A. Use context clues to help you decide on the best definition for each italicized word. Then, in the space provided, write the letter of your choice.

_____D_____ 1. In the following excerpt, the word *succession* (sək-sĕsh′ən) means
A. victory.
B. surprise.
C. lack.
D. series.

> If the creatures have come and gone over the years, there has been a series of them.

"My ability to Just Say No to a needy animal is seriously underdeveloped. That is why, in a nutshell, we are now the owners of two dogs, three cats, a cockatiel and a parakeet, and have seen a succession of gerbils, lizards, and other creatures come and go over the years." (Paragraph 2)

___B___ 2. In the following sentence, the word *abandon* (ə-băn′dən) means
    A. being left behind.
    B. lack of self-control.
    C. fear.
    D. power.

> The words *plunges* and *insane* suggest that *abandon* means "lack of self-control."

> "He particularly likes to go on long walks by the creek with Alex, who plunges with insane abandon into the water and retrieves sticks until he is limp with exhaustion." (Paragraph 4)

___D___ 3. In the following excerpt, the word *corral* (kə-răl′) means
    A. color.
    B. drive away.
    C. frighten.
    D. capture.

> The words "*HERE . . . C'MON, HERE YA GO*" suggest they are trying to get the kitten to come over to them so they can capture it.

> "I was able to listen in as Bob and, eventually, two homeless guys he persuaded to help him, tried to corral the kitten. 'HERE LITTLE GUY! C'MON, HERE YA GO!' they kept saying." (Paragraph 9)

___A___ 4. In the following excerpt, the word *passively* (păs′ĭv-lē) means
    A. quietly.
    B. sweetly.
    C. carefully.
    D. angrily.

> If the cat didn't chew, swallow, shake its head, or try to get away, how was it lying there?

> "The cat didn't chew, didn't swallow, didn't shake its head in disgust, didn't try to get away. It just lay there passively with the bit of food in its mouth." (Paragraph 14)

___C___ 5. In the following excerpt, the word *lurks* (lûrks) means
    A. searches.
    B. eats.
    C. hides.
    D. falls asleep.

> Leaping out "to slap Logan" suggests that Owen hides under the bed, waiting to jump out at Logan.

> "Owen . . . is as funny and frisky as any kitten ever born. He lurks under the bed and leaps out to slap Logan the terrier, who regards him with enormous amusement." (Paragraph 27)

B. Below are words, or forms of words, from "Words to Watch." Write in the one that best completes each sentence. Then write the letter of that word in the space provided.

A. estimate	B. glints	C. sarcastically
D. twist	E. vigorously	

___C___ 6. Marcy's mom stated _____sarcastically_____, "I just love it when people track mud across the new carpet."
Clearly, Marcy's mom means the opposite of what she says.

___E___ 7. To prepare for his fight, the boxer trained _____vigorously_____.
A boxer who is preparing for a fight would train energetically.

___B___ 8. I like the way my new silver bracelet _____glints_____ in the sun.
A silver bracelet gives off bright flashes of light in the sun.

___A___ 9. Scientists _____estimate_____ that the sun has enough fuel to go on for another five billion years.
Scientists can only make an educated guess about how much fuel the sun has.

___D___ 10. The children's book *The Paper Bag Princess* contains an unusual _____twist_____: this time, the princess defeats the dragon and rescues the prince from danger.
A princess rescuing a prince is an unexpected turn of events.

Reading Comprehension Questions

Central Point and Main Ideas

___D___ 1. Which sentence best expresses the main idea of the selection?

Answers A, B, and C are too narrow. A covers only paragraph 2 and the first sentence of paragraph 9. B covers only paragraphs 16–18. C covers only paragraphs 22–24.

A. During their eight-year marriage, Carlin and her husband have adopted a number of animals.
B. Carlin saved a stray kitten by feeding it sardine soup.
C. A kitten got its unusual name when a boy at the vet's suggested that the kitten be named Owen.
D. The kitten that Carlin's husband rescued—despite his not being a "cat person"—is now a happy, healthy pet.

___C___ 2. Which sentence best expresses the main idea of paragraph 27?

Answers A, B, and D each cover only one detail of the paragraph. Those three details give examples of how Owen has made himself at home, answer C.

A. Owen likes to lurk under the bed and then jump out to attack Logan the terrier.
B. The household's other two cats sometimes swat Owen to remind him to behave nicely.
C. Owen has made himself at home in Carlin and Bob's house.
D. Owen purrs loudly when he sleeps in a human lap.

Supporting Details

___C___ 3. Bob discovers the stray kitten
- A. in a cat-free zone.
- B. in the middle of a city street.
- C. huddled against the side of his building.
- D. in an alley.

See paragraph 7.

___B___ 4. Carlin rolls her eyes when
- A. Bob hands her a paper bag with a half-dead kitten inside.
- B. she hears Bob explain to passersby why he is trying to catch a stray kitten.
- C. the kitten begins to weakly bite the medicine dropper.
- D. the little boy at the vet's office suggests that she name the kitten Owen.

See paragraph 9.

___F___ 5. TRUE OR FALSE? Carlin gives Owen a lot of food during the first night he stays with her.

See paragraph 18.

Transitions

___D___ 6. The relationship between the two sentences below is one of
- A. addition.
- B. time.
- C. comparison.
- D. cause and effect.

Cause: Carlin's inability to say no to a needy animal.
Effect: They have taken in many animals over the years.
The words *That is why* are similar to the cause-effect transition *as a result.*

"My ability to Just Say No to a needy animal is seriously underdeveloped. That is why, in a nutshell, we are now the owners of two dogs, three cats, a cockatiel and a parakeet, and have seen a succession of gerbils, lizards, and other creatures come and go over the years." (Paragraph 2)

Patterns of Organization

___D___ 7. Paragraph 4 mainly
- A. compares Bob's attitude toward Logan with his attitude toward Alex.
- B. lists things Bob likes to do with Alex the retriever.
- C. explains in time order what Bob and Alex do at the creek.
- D. contrasts Bob's attitude toward dogs with his attitude toward cats.

Contrast transition: *by contrast.*

___C___ 8. The main pattern of organization of the entire selection is
  A. definition and example.
  B. list of items.
  C. time order.
  D. comparison and contrast.

The selection tells the story of Owen in the order in which the events occurred.

Inferences

___B___ 9. On the basis of the selection, we can infer that Carlin
  A. prefers cats to dogs.
  B. has probably rescued stray animals before.
  C. would like to adopt many more animals.
  D. once thought about becoming a veterinarian.

See paragraph 2. Answers A, C, and D are not supported.

___B___ 10. In paragraph 9, when Carlin's husband explains to passersby that "This isn't my idea. I don't even LIKE cats. It's my wife . . . ," we can infer that
  A. he is angry with his wife.
  B. he is embarrassed to be seen trying to catch a kitten.
  C. he is not trying very hard to catch the kitten.
  D. the passersby are trying to prevent Bob from catching the kitten.

The fact that Bob pretends he is trying to rescue the kitten only because his wife has asked him to suggests that he is embarrassed to be seen trying to catch the kitten. Answers A and D are not supported. Answer C is contradicted by what the wife hears on the phone.

Outlining

Prepare an outline of "Owen, The Stray Cat" by filling in the missing details, which are scrambled in the list below.

● Three days later, Carlin takes the kitten to the vet for its first checkup.

● When Owen disturbs Bob's sleep, Carlin and Bob argue over who is really responsible for the kitten being there.

● A small boy at the vet's office names the stray kitten Owen.

● When Carlin puts the kitten on the bathroom floor with food and water, the kitten is too weak to eat.

Central point: Although Carlin's husband Bob is not a cat person, he rescues a starving kitten from a city sidewalk.

1. Carlin gets a call from her husband Bob, asking her if he should rescue a stray kitten that he sees huddled against a building in center city Philadelphia.

2. After Carlin replies sarcastically that Bob should leave the cat to get run over by a car, Bob catches it and brings it home.

3. When Carlin puts the kitten on the bathroom floor with food and

water, the kitten is too weak to eat.   See paragraphs 12–15.

4. Carlin makes "sardine soup" and feeds it to the kitten through a medicine dropper.

5. By noon of the next day, the kitten is eating sardine soup from a bowl.

6. Three days later, Carlin takes the kitten to the vet for its first

checkup.   See paragraph 19.

7. A small boy at the vet's office names the stray kitten Owen.

See paragraphs 20–26.

8. When Owen disturbs Bob's sleep, Carlin and Bob argue over who is

really responsible for the kitten being there.   See paragraphs 28–31.

Discussion Questions

1. Carlin rolls her eyes when she hears Bob explaining to passersby why he's trying to catch the stray kitten. Do you believe Bob when he tells passersby that he's doing it because his wife told him to? Why or why not?

2. Carlin mentions that she and her husband have owned a number of pets over the years. Why do you think people like Carlin and Bob like owning animals? Do you? If you do, do you prefer cats, dogs, or some other kind of pet? Explain.

3. Even though he's not a "cat person," Bob goes to a lot of trouble to catch the kitten and bring it home. Carlin then stays up all night trying to get the kitten to eat. Have you ever had a similar experience involving rescuing and caring for an animal in distress? How far did (or would) you go to save a hurt or lost creature?

4. Every year, overcrowded animal shelters are forced to "put to sleep" three to four million unwanted cats and dogs. If you were planning to adopt a cat or a dog, where would you look for one—at a breeding kennel, a pet shop, or a shelter for animals that, like Owen, have been rescued? Why would this be your choice?

Note: Writing assignments for this selection appear on page 595.

Check Your Performance   OWEN, THE STRAY CAT

Activity	Number Right	Points		Total	
Vocabulary					
A. Vocabulary in Context (5 items)	_____	×	10	=	_____
B. Words to Watch (5 items)	_____	×	10	=	_____
		SCORE		=	_____%
Comprehension					
Central Point and Main Ideas (2 items)	_____	×	8	=	_____
Supporting Details (3 items)	_____	×	8	=	_____
Transitions (1 item)	_____	×	8	=	_____
Patterns of Organization (2 items)	_____	×	8	=	_____
Inferences (2 items)	_____	×	8	=	_____
Outlining (4 items)	_____	×	5	=	_____
		SCORE		=	_____%

FINAL SCORES: Vocabulary _____% Comprehension _____%

Enter your total score into the **Reading Performance Chart: Ten Reading Selections** on the inside back cover.

3 Eye Contact
Ron Clark

Preview

In his book *The Essential 55*, Ron Clark, winner of the 2001 Disney Teacher of the Year Award, presents 55 rules that he thinks are essential for every classroom. Some of those rules are ones you'd probably expect, such as "Do your homework every day." But others are surprising, like the "rule" you are about to read.

Words to Watch

proposal (1): offer
emphasis (2): importance
torture (5): suffering
various (6): many different
custodians (6): people responsible for cleaning and general upkeep of a building
appreciated (6): valued
obvious (6): clear

1   Keeping eye contact is something that many people find hard to do, but it is important when you are trying to get your point across to people and show them you are serious about what you are saying. For example, if you go in to talk to your boss and ask for a raise, he is going to be far more likely to take you seriously if you are looking him in the eyes rather than glancing downward. If you are making a business proposal°, people will be more likely to trust you and believe in your ideas if they see that you are confident, sure of yourself, and making eye contact with them.

2   I spend a lot of time encouraging my students to make eye contact. In order to give them practice, I put the kids in groups of two. I then tell them that making eye contact when you make a statement gives what you are saying more emphasis° and emotion. When you look away or down at the floor, it shows you aren't sure of what you are saying and that you possibly aren't telling the truth. I also tell them that I have heard that repeated glances to the upper left-hand side mean you are being dishonest. Once they are in their groups, I have them practice talking to

3   each other, taking note of how effective they are at maintaining eye contact with their partners.

Making eye contact is not only a way to show confidence, but it is also an important way to show respect. In class, when a student is expressing an opinion, I make sure all of the other students turn and are focused on that individual. I don't allow them to raise their hands to make additional comments until that person is finished, because, if they do, it looks as if they are more concerned with what they want to say than with the opinions of the speaker. I tell them to imagine what it would be like if they were trying to express a thought and everyone around them kept waving their hands. It would make them feel like their opinions had no value, and so therefore, we don't do it.

4   I can remember when I was in school that it was awfully hard to daydream while staring at the teacher. If I could focus on the head in front of me or on my pencil, I was good to go, but watching the teacher just took something out of it. Therefore, I make sure to have all eyes on me at all times. That way, as I'm teaching, I can see the looks on the students' faces and can tell if they are confused and lost or entertained and attentive. Also, since I am a very visual learner and teacher, I am constantly making motions with my hands and on the board, and I want the kids to follow along with me and know exactly where I'm coming from.

5   I have worked many a day in fast food. I've spent countless hours making the doughnuts at Dunkin' Donuts and

waiting tables at various restaurants. Serving the public can be a thrill, but it can also be torture° when you have to deal with difficult customers. I can remember how I always liked it when people would look me in the eyes to give their order. It is far more respectful to look a person in the face. As they were leaving, I always expected them to say thank you; but many didn't, and it baffled me. What were they thinking? Many who did say thank you just said it as they turned away and drove off. Why not take one second to look the person in the eyes and say thank you as if you mean it?

6   I try to get my students to practice doing this with various° adults in the school who aren't teachers. Often the custodians°, cafeteria workers, secretaries, and teacher's aides aren't considered worthy of the respect teachers get, and I work hard to change

that image in the minds of my students. I explain to the students the role of each person at the school and how his or her job makes it possible for kids to get a great education. I then tell them that people work harder and with more effort if they feel appreciated° and that they are making a difference. I make sure to model the type of behavior I expect, as I interact with all members of the staff in a friendly and respectful manner. It doesn't take much effort before the students are following my lead, and the results are always obvious°. When we go to the lunchroom, the students aren't allowed to talk in the line, and when they get their food, they must look the cafeteria workers in the eyes and say "May I" when asking for anything. In turn, they always thank the lunchroom workers and tell them to have a good day. The workers always comment on how wonderful the class is and how much they appreciate the respect.

No matter how we are interacting with others around us and regardless of what we are saying, we will be taken more seriously and our actions will be much more appreciated if they come with eye contact. 7

Vocabulary Questions

A. Use context clues to help you decide on the best definition for each italicized word. Then, in the space provided, write the letter of your choice.

_A_   1. In the sentence below, the word *maintaining* (mān-tān′ĭng) means
    A. continuing.
    B. asking for.
    C. stopping.
    D. risking.

> Throughout the reading, Clark emphasizes the importance of continuing eye contact when speaking with people.

"Once they are in their groups, I have them practice talking to each other, taking note of how effective they are at maintaining eye contact with their partners." (Paragraph 2)

_B_   2. In the sentence below, the words *focused on* (fō′kəst ŏn) mean
    A. taking a picture of.
    B. looking directly at.
    C. frightened by.
    D. wondering about.

> The students turn in order to look directly at the student who is speaking.

"In class, when a student is expressing an opinion, I make sure all of the other students turn and are focused on that individual." (Paragraph 3)

_B_ 3. In the sentence below, the word *visual* (vĭzh′o͞o-əl) means
   A. relating to the sense of hearing.
   B. relating to the sense of sight.   Making hand motions and using the
   C. boring.   board are actions that are meant to be seen.
   D. slow-moving.

   "Also, since I am a very visual learner and teacher, I am constantly making motions with my hands and on the board, and I want the kids to follow along with me and know exactly where I'm coming from." (Paragraph 4)

_D_ 4. In the excerpt below, the word *baffled* (băf′əld) means
   A. angered.
   B. shocked.   The question "What were they thinking?"
   C. amused.   suggests that *baffled* means "puzzled."
   D. puzzled.

   "As they were leaving, I always expected them to say thank you, but many didn't, and it baffled me. What were they thinking?" (Paragraph 5)

_C_ 5. In the excerpt below, the word *model* (mŏd′l) means
   A. correct.
   B. see.   By interacting in a friendly and respectful
   C. be an example of.   manner, Clark is being an example of the
   D. wear.   behavior he expects.

   "I then tell them that people work harder and with more effort if they feel appreciated and that they are making a difference. I make sure to model the type of behavior I expect, as I interact with all members of the staff in a friendly and respectful manner." (Paragraph 6)

B. Below are words, or forms of words, from "Words to Watch." Write in the one that best completes each sentence. Then write the letter of that word in the space provided.

A. emphasis	B. obvious	C. proposal
D. torture	E. various	

_D_ 6. The last few school days before summer vacation always seem like
        Someone eager for vacation to begin would experience
   _____torture_____ to me; they seem to pass so slowly.   *suffering*
                                                    if the days pass slowly.

_B_ 7. It is _____obvious_____ that Tatiana loves clothes; she wears a
   different outfit every day.   If Tatiana wears a different outfit every day,
                                  it's *clear* that she loves clothes.

_C_ 8. My neighbor had a _____proposal_____ for me: he told me he
   would pay me $20 for mowing his lawn.   The neighbor makes an *offer*
                                            to pay to have his lawn mowed.

_E_ 9. The kindergartners were told to sort the _____various_____ beads according to color.

If the beads need to be sorted, there must be many different beads.

_A_ 10. From the _____emphasis_____ our teacher places on the words "Do your own work," I can tell that he really means what he says.

If it is clear the teacher means what he says, he must be placing importance on his words.

Reading Comprehension Questions

Central Point and Main Ideas

_B_ 1. Which sentence best expresses the central point of the selection?
   A. Clark treats all school staff members in a friendly and respectful way.
   B. Clark encourages his students to make eye contact because he knows that doing so will help them seem confident and earn respect.
   C. Although he is now a teacher, Clark spent a good deal of time working in fast food and waiting on tables in restaurants.
   D. Clark has students practice making eye contact with the adults in the school who are not teachers.

Answers A, C, and D are too narrow. Answers A and D cover only paragraph 6; answer C covers only paragraph 5.

_D_ 2. Which sentence best expresses the main idea of paragraph 4?
   A. When he was a student, Clark avoided daydreaming by focusing on the head in front of him or on his pencil.
   B. While teaching, Clark looks at his students' faces to make sure they aren't confused.
   C. Clark is a visual learner and teacher who always uses hand movements and writes on the board.
   D. Since he wants the students' full attention, Clark makes sure that his students keep their eyes on him.

Answer A contradicts a detail in the paragraph. Answers B and C are too narrow. Each covers only a part of the paragraph.

Supporting Details

_C_ 3. Clark tells his students that repeated glances to the upper left side mean that a person
   A. is left-handed.
   B. lacks confidence.
   C. is dishonest.
   D. is nervous.

See paragraph 2.

_C_ 4. Clark describes himself as
   A. an excellent teacher.
   B. a strict teacher.
   C. a visual learner and teacher.
   D. all of the above.

See paragraph 4.

Transitions

_____D_____ 5. The relationship between the two sentences below is one of
A. addition.
B. illustration.   *Cause*: Looking at the teacher prevents daydreaming.
C. contrast.   *Effect*: Clark makes sure his students look at him at all times.
D. cause and effect.

> "If I could focus on the head in front of me or on my pencil, I was good to go, but watching the teacher just took something out of it. Therefore, I make sure to have all eyes on me at all times." (Paragraph 4)

_____B_____ 6. The relationship of the second part of the sentence below (after the semicolon) to the first part is one of
A. illustration.
B. contrast.   In contrast to Clark's always expecting
C. addition.   them to say thank you, many did not.
D. cause and effect.

> "As they were leaving, I always expected them to say thank you; but many didn't, and it baffled me." (Paragraph 5)

Patterns of Organization

_____C_____ 7. The selection mainly
A. narrates important events in the author's life.
B. contrasts those who make eye contact with those who don't.
C. illustrates the importance of making eye contact.
D. compares working in fast food with being a teacher.
   Every paragraph discusses the importance of eye contact.

Item 8:
Answer A is contradicted by paragraph 6.
Answer B is contradicted in paragraph 1.
Answer C is incorrect because Clark says nothing about students avoiding such work. (See paragraph 5.)

Item 9:
See paragraph 6.
Answer A is incorrect because the reading suggests the opposite is true.
Answers B and D are not supported because there is no indication of how long Clark has been a teacher.

Inferences

_____D_____ 8. Which of the following statements would Clark probably agree with?
A. "Because teachers are better educated than custodians and cafeteria workers, they should receive more respect."
B. "If you look your boss in the eye when asking for a raise, he or she will probably become angry with you."
C. "Working in fast food is something students should avoid."
D. "Employees tend to work harder for bosses who treat them with respect than for those who don't."

_____C_____ 9. We can infer from the selection that Clark
A. is an easygoing teacher.
B. has only been teaching a few years.
C. believes that teachers should practice what they preach.
D. has been a teacher for over twenty-five years.

_A_   10. The selection suggests that Clark
    A. is appreciated by the adults in his school who are not teachers.
    B. is too easygoing to be an effective teacher.
    C. once worked in a school cafeteria.
    D. looks down on people who work in the fast-food industry.

See paragraph 6.
Answers B, C, and D are not supported.

Summarizing

Complete the following summary of "Eye Contact" by filling in the blanks.

Wording of answers may vary.

Because Ron Clark believes that making eye contact shows confidence and respect, he spends a lot of time encouraging his students to do so. One thing he has them do is practice talking to each other, while he _takes note of how effective they are at maintaining eye contact with their partners._ In class, when a student is expressing an opinion, he makes sure all of the other students are focused on that individual. He doesn't allow them to _raise their hands to make additional comments until the speaker is finished._

When he's teaching, he makes sure to have all eyes on him at all times. The many hours he spent working in fast food taught him that it is a sign of respect to look a person in the face. As a result, he _tries to get his students to practice making eye contact with various adults in the school who aren't teachers._

When his students go to the lunchroom, they aren't allowed to talk in the line, and when they get their food, they must _look the cafeteria workers in the eye and say "May I" when asking for anything._ In turn, they always thank the lunchroom workers and tell them to have a good day. The workers say _that the class is wonderful and that they appreciate the respect._

Clark concludes that we will be taken more seriously, and our actions will be much more appreciated, if we also make eye contact with the people we speak to.

Item 1: See paragraph 2.
Item 2: See paragraph 3.
Items 3–5: See paragraph 6.

Discussion Questions

1. Clark writes that he worked in fast food for "many a day." How do you think that working in the fast-food industry and in restaurants has affected his teaching?

2. Think of a person you know who is good at making eye contact. How does that person make you feel when she or he looks you in the eye? On the other hand, do you know anyone who is bad at making eye contact? What effect does his or her inability to make eye contact have on you?

3. Do you think you're good at making eye contact? In what situations might it be difficult for you to make eye contact? If you had the chance, would you sign up for Clark's class? Why or why not?

4. Eye contact is one form of nonverbal communication—in other words, communicating to others without using words. What are some other kinds of nonverbal communication? Under what circumstances might these alternate forms of communication be even more effective than spoken words? (For one response to this question, read "Wired for Touch," page 288.)

Note: Writing assignments for this selection appear on page 595.

Check Your Performance   EYE CONTACT

Activity	Number Right	Points		Total
Vocabulary				
A. Vocabulary in Context (5 items)	_____	× 10 =		_____
B. Words to Watch (5 items)	_____	× 10 =		_____
		SCORE =		_____ %
Comprehension				
Central Point and Main Ideas (2 items)	_____	× 8 =		_____
Supporting Details (2 items)	_____	× 8 =		_____
Transitions (2 items)	_____	× 8 =		_____
Patterns of Organization (1 item)	_____	× 8 =		_____
Inferences (3 items)	_____	× 8 =		_____
Summarizing (5 items)	_____	× 4 =		_____
		SCORE =		_____ %

FINAL SCORES: Vocabulary _____ % Comprehension _____ %

Enter your total score into the **Reading Performance Chart: Ten Reading Selections** on the inside back cover.

4 Disaster and Friendship
Chuck Wilson

Preview

Some situations are especially good for showing what people are really like. During a trip south, Chuck Wilson lived through such a situation, one he was not prepared for. He was also not prepared for what the people he met were really like. This selection is his account of that experience.

Words to Watch

relate (1): tell
bearing (3): advancing
stereotyped (4): oversimplified and prejudiced
stocky (4): solidly built
severe (5): harsh
intensified (5): increased
mocking (6): scornful
trusty (7): a convict who has been given special privileges

1   I shall relate° to you as accurately as possible what happened when I, a black man, had a car accident in North Carolina during a trip to Florida. I am by profession a golf caddy. I usually caddy in the Philadelphia area during the spring, summer, and fall, and find some other type of work during the winter months. One particular winter was a poor one in the area for work, so I decided to go to Florida and caddy until spring. I packed my clothes in my car, made my goodbyes to my wife and three children, and left for Florida on a Saturday around noon.

2   The trip was very long and boring, especially since I was traveling alone. I drove straight through Delaware and Virginia until about 3:00 a.m., when I noticed a cafe open in a small town in North Carolina. I stopped with the intention of getting a cup of coffee and perhaps a sandwich. However, it just so happened that the cafe sold not only coffee but also beer and bootleg liquor. Not realizing how tired I really

was or how a drink or two would affect me, I had a hamburger, two beers, and, worse, a drink of North Carolina's special "white lightning."

3   When I got back on the road, it was almost 5 a.m. I didn't think the drinks would have an adverse effect on my driving, but I was wrong. About 5:30, soon after I passed a sign informing me I was passing through the town of Warrendale, I went to sleep behind the wheel and missed a curve around an island in the center of the road. When I suddenly awoke, I could see that I was bearing° onto the island, and I was too late in snatching the wheel quickly to the right. The front wheels hit the curb, causing my car to flip over on its top and slide across the grass of the island. After the car stopped, I must have spent a minute in total darkness, upside down and having no clear idea of what had happened to me. Eventually I realized that I was physically all right, and I rolled down the driver's window and managed to climb through it and out of the car. A passing motorist, a white man, stopped to see if I needed help. After convincing me and himself that I was all right, he said he would contact the local sheriff and drove off.

4   Because of the chilly weather, and the fact that I had only a light golf jacket on, I climbed back into my car through the open window. I was lying there with my feet hanging out the window when the sheriff arrived. I heard him exclaim, "My God, not another one!" and I then crawled out from the car. The sheriff explained to me that another accident had happened at the same spot just a week before, but the driver had been killed. My first reaction on seeing the sheriff was apprehension, for he looked like the stereotyped° image of the white Southern country sheriff—short, stocky°, and red-necked.

5   But he turned out to be just the opposite of what I feared. He called for a wrecker to take away my car and took me to his office. He listened sympathetically to my account of how the accident happened and of my intention of traveling to Florida to make a living for myself and my family. He searched his violation book for the violation that carried the least severe° fine and finally decided that I had "failed to yield right of way." He told me that I would have to accompany him to Chester, North Carolina, which was the county seat, and appear before the magistrate there. We then drove the eighteen miles to Chester, and that was where my troubles really intensified°.

6   I was brought before a white magistrate who, to put it mildly, was very peeved at having been awakened at 6:00 a.m. to hear a case. The magistrate read the charges and swore at the sheriff for writing out a ticket that wasn't consistent with what actually happened. The sheriff explained that I had limited money and that I was going to Florida to try to make a living for my family. The magistrate then turned to me and said, "Boy, how much money have you got?" His eyes were filled with

a hard, mocking° look; calling me "Boy" clearly gave him great pleasure. I was very angry, but knowing where I was, I tried to control myself. I told him that I had $24.50, just enough money to get to Florida. He then said, "The fine's $24.50." I paid the fine with my last money and then requested that I be given lodging for the rest of the night, since I had no money and no place to go. He said all right and turned me over to the jailer, who took me upstairs to the county jail and put me in one of the cells.

7   I fell asleep very quickly, exhausted by everything that had happened. I was awakened about 7:30 that morning by a black trusty° bringing breakfast. There was a small tray with a cup of cold coffee, two hard biscuits, and a small helping of grits. When I said I didn't want anything to eat, the fellow in the next cell asked me for mine, which I readily gave to him. I went back to sleep and woke up at about 3:00 p.m. Thinking that I was free to go, I asked the trusty to get the jailer for me. When he came, my spirits, which were low anyway, really got a jolt. The jailer looked at me with amusement through the bars and said that I owed an additional $2.50 for lodging and breakfast. I really felt that the bottom had fallen out of things now, and had visions of working on a chain gang somewhere. I wondered if this was the reason the magistrate had been so ready to let me stay in the jail to sleep.

8   My salvation was that the trusty took a liking to me and offered me the $2.50 that I needed. I was taken downstairs, and when I paid the magistrate, his final words were, "Now, boy, git out of my town." I found out the name of the small town where I had the accident and which direction it was. I also learned that it was eighteen miles away. I began walking the dusty, lonesome road to Warrendale in the chilly evening air. As I did, a police car with two white officers who had been in the magistrate's office sped by me. I had heard that they were going on a patrol to the city's limits, but certainly wasn't surprised that they declined to offer me a ride. I did notice the officer in the passenger's seat looking out at me as the car went by, and I expected to get an obscene finger gesture or a mocking smile. I was surprised, then, to see that his face showed an expression more like that of regret.

9   The first person to see me as I completed my eighteen-mile marathon at 11:30 p.m. was the white sheriff. He picked me up and asked me what I was doing on the road at this hour. After I explained what had happened in Chester, he told me that he would find me a place to stay for the night. He stopped at about three houses before he finally found a young black couple who agreed to take me in for the night. I don't think I could have accepted a complete stranger in my house the way they did. They may have been intimidated by the presence of the white sheriff. But beyond that, they were simply a very good and friendly couple. They gave me a clean bed to sleep in and the next morning, which was Monday, gave me breakfast and left to take their children to a babysitter and to go to work themselves. They told me to leave whenever I wanted and just be sure to lock the door.

10   I left their home at about 9:00 a.m. and walked over to the garage where my car was being held. The owner of the garage was white and hostile, and told me that there was a thirty-five-dollar towing charge even though the accident had occurred approximately seventy-five yards from his garage. I tried to explain my situation to him, but he made it clear by quickly walking away that the only thing he would listen to was the money. He even refused to let me open the trunk of my car to get out the clothes and things I thought I would need if I had to stay in the area until I earned the money. After looking around the town of Warrendale for a while, I realized I would have to go back to Chester to try to find work.

11   I started hitchhiking, and who but the friendly sheriff picked me up. I told him my situation, and he agreed to take me to Chester. In Chester, I went to the chamber of commerce and asked the lady in charge to help me find a job. When she understood my situation, she got in touch with the minister heading the local church federation and the president of the local bank. Within an hour they had gotten money for the release of my car and another twenty-five dollars to help me reach Florida. The minister drove me back to Warrendale, got my car for me, and sent me on my way. The remainder of the trip proceeded without incident, giving me plenty of time to think about all the good and bad things that had happened to me.

Vocabulary Questions

A. Use context clues to help you decide on the best definition for each italicized word. Then, in the space provided, write the letter of your choice.

___B___ 1. In the excerpt below, the word *adverse* (ăd-vûrs′) means
   A. positive.
   B. unfavorable.
   C. humorous.
   D. impossible.

   Going to sleep behind the wheel is an example of something unfavorable.

   "I didn't think the drinks would have an adverse effect on my driving, but I was wrong. . . . I went to sleep behind the wheel." (Paragraph 3)

___C___ 2 In the sentence below, the word *apprehension* (ăp′rĭ-hĕn′shən) means
   A. joy.
   B. confusion.
   C. fear.
   D. romance.

   A "red-necked" sheriff would tend to inspire fear in a black man who had just caused an accident.

   "My first reaction on seeing the sheriff was apprehension, for he looked like the stereotyped image of the white Southern country sheriff—short, stocky, and red-necked." (Paragraph 4)

___C___ 3. In the sentence below, the word *peeved* (pēvd) means
   A. pleased.
   B. flattered.
   C. annoyed.
   D. fearful.

   Someone awakened so early is likely to be annoyed.

   "I was brought before a white magistrate who, to put it mildly, was very peeved at having been awakened at 6:00 a.m." (Paragraph 6)

___A___ 4. In the excerpt below, the word *jolt* (jōlt) means
   A. sudden shock.
   B. encouragement.
   C. inspiration.
   D. something expected.

   A surprise charge would have been a sudden shock.

   "Thinking that I was free to go, I asked the trusty to get the jailer for me. When he came, my spirits . . . really got a jolt. The jailer . . . said that I owed an additional $2.50 for lodging and breakfast." (Paragraph 7)

___C___ 5. In the excerpt below, the word *intimidated* (ĭn-tĭm′ĭ-dāt′ĭd) means
  A. pleased.
  B. angered.
  C. frightened.
  D. discouraged.

> How might a white sheriff make a young black couple feel?

> "a young black couple . . . agreed to take me in for the night. . . . They may have been intimidated by the presence of the white sheriff. But beyond that, they were simply a very good and friendly couple." (Paragraph 9)

B. Below are words, or forms of words, from "Words to Watch." Write in the one that best completes each sentence. Then write the letter of that word in the space provided.

A. bearing	B. intensified	C. related
D. severely	E. stereotyped	

___E___ 6. Dora does not fit the _____ stereotyped _____ image of a grandmother—she jogs fifteen miles a week and manages her own catering company.
> A grandmother who jogs and runs her own company does not fit the *oversimplified* and *prejudiced* image of a grandmother.

___B___ 7. Once the flames ate into the logs, the heat from the fireplace _____ intensified _____.
> The flames eating into the logs would *increase* the heat.

___C___ 8. Elvin sat down next to his son, who had just lost his job, and _____ related _____ the story of how he too had lost his very first job.
> Elvin *told* his son the story of losing his first job.

___A___ 9. When he saw three tacklers _____ bearing _____ toward him, the quarterback quickly stepped back and passed the football.

___D___ 10. If you punish your child too _____ severely _____, he or she may resent you rather than learn from the experience.

> **Item 9:** The quarterback would pass the football if he saw three tacklers *advancing* toward him.
> **Item 10:** Punishing a child too *harshly* can make the child resentful.

Reading Comprehension Questions

Central Point and Main Ideas

___B___ 1. Which sentence best expresses the central point of this selection?
  A. Drinking and driving can be disastrous.
  B. Sometimes kindness is found where it is least expected.
  C. Always carry extra money for emergencies when you travel.
  D. Small-town people are unlikely to help a stranger in trouble.

> Answers A and C are too narrow. Answer D is an untrue generalization.

___A___ 2. Which sentence best expresses the main idea of paragraph 9?

      A. Once again, good people helped Wilson, this time with a ride and a place to stay.

      B. Wilson had to walk the eighteen miles.

      C. The sheriff had a little trouble finding a place for Wilson to stay.

      D. A young black couple let Wilson stay overnight.

Answers B, C, and D are too narrow. Each presents only one detail of the paragraph.

Supporting Details

___D___ 3. Wilson

      A. usually had to go to Florida to find work in the winter.

      B. knew that he was too tired to drive after drinking.

      C. couldn't remember why he lost control of his car.

      D. was not hurt in the accident.

See the last three sentences of paragraph 3.

___B___ 4. The white magistrate fined Wilson

      A. $2.50.

      B. all the money Wilson had.

      C. $50.00.

      D. $25.00.

See paragraph 6.

___C___ 5. The owner of the garage

      A. was located far from the accident.

      B. was willing to forget the towing charge.

      C. refused to let Wilson open his car trunk.

      D. offered Wilson work so he could work off his debt.

See the next-to-last sentence of paragraph 10.

Transitions

6. Narratives naturally benefit from time transitions. Write here two of the time transitions Wilson uses in paragraph 3.

      Any two of the following: When, after, eventually

___C___ 7. The sentence below begins with a transition that shows

      A. time.

      B. addition.

      C. cause and effect.

      D. comparison.

Causes: the cold weather and light jacket.
Effect: Wilson gets back into his car.

      "Because of the chilly weather, and the fact that I had only a light golf jacket on, I climbed back into my car through the open window." (Paragraph 4)

Patterns of Organization

___A___ 8. Like paragraphs, longer selections use patterns of organization. The
pattern of organization of this selection, like all narratives, is mainly
   A. time order.
   B. a list of items.
   C. cause and effect.
   D. definition and example.

Wilson's essay narrates a series of events in the order in which they happened.

Inferences

___B___ 9. From the story, we can conclude that Wilson never expected
   A. to find a job in Florida.
   B. to pay for staying in jail.
   C. to see his car again.
   D. any trouble with the local sheriff.

See paragraph 7. Wilson thought he was free to leave jail and was shocked by the news that he owed money, so we can infer that he had not known he would have to pay for staying in jail.

___D___ 10. From the story, we can conclude that
   A. Wilson preferred working in Florida to working in the Philadelphia area.
   B. the white magistrate treated everyone equally, regardless of color.
   C. people rarely go out of their way to help others.
   D. not all Southern law officers are racists.

The white sheriff was very helpful to Wilson (paragraphs 5, 9, and 11), and a police officer had an expression of regret when passing Wilson on the road (paragraph 8).

Mapping

Following is a map of "Disaster and Friendship." Complete the map by filling in
the letters of the missing major supporting details, which are listed below in random
order. (Two of the items have already been filled in for you.)

Main idea: Trouble can be an opportunity to experience unexpected kindness.

B → F → E → D → C → A

Major Supporting Details Missing from the Map

   A. Help in finding a place to sleep after jail   See paragraph 9.
   B. The reason for Wilson's trip to Florida   See paragraph 1.
   C. A racist magistrate's treatment and a day in jail   See paragraph 6.
   D. The sheriff's efforts to help Wilson get off easily   See paragraph 5.
   E. A passing driver's help   See paragraph 3.
   F. Wilson's stop at the cafe and the resulting accident   See paragraphs 2–3.

Discussion Questions

1. Wilson was worried that the sheriff would be just "like the stereotyped image of the white Southern country sheriff." What is that image?

2. Wilson asked the woman in charge at the Chester Chamber of Commerce to help him find a job. Instead, she arranged for him to get some money and his car so he could go on to Florida. Why might she have done that?

3. Wilson's experience was notable partly because it showed how wrong stereotypes can be. What experiences have you had in which people did not fit their stereotypes?

4. How do stereotypes influence our treatment of other people? What can we do to make sure we treat people as individuals, not as stereotypes?

Note: Writing assignments for this selection appear on page 596.

Check Your Performance	DISASTER AND FRIENDSHIP		
Activity	*Number Right*	*Points*	*Total*
Vocabulary			
A. Vocabulary in Context (5 items)	_____	× 10 =	_____
B. Words to Watch (5 items)	_____	× 10 =	_____
		SCORE =	_____%
Comprehension			
Central Point and Main Ideas (2 items)	_____	× 8 =	_____
Supporting Details (3 items)	_____	× 8 =	_____
Transitions (2 items)	_____	× 8 =	_____
Patterns of Organization (1 item)	_____	× 8 =	_____
Inferences (2 items)	_____	× 8 =	_____
Mapping (4 items)	_____	× 5 =	_____
		SCORE =	_____%

FINAL SCORES: Vocabulary _____% Comprehension _____%

Enter your total score into the **Reading Performance Chart: Ten Reading Selections** on the inside back cover.

5 Read All About It
Fran DeBlasio

Preview

When are people too old to turn their lives around? Ten? Twenty? Twenty-five? Here is the story of someone who made her life very different—and better— beginning at the age of thirty-five.

Words to Watch

decipher (1): read or make sense of something
unique (2): unusual
pass the buck (4): pass the responsibility on to someone else
chaos (5): disorder
landmarks (8): objects or structures that help people find their way
stunned (10): shocked

1   For most of her life, Fran DeBlasio, 36, tried to conceal her shame. Unable to read the street signs or subway maps in her native Manhattan, let alone decipher° warning labels on medicine bottles, she lived, like many illiterates, in constant fear of the unknown. An even greater terror was that friends would discover her secret. "I was embarrassed," DeBlasio says. "I thought there must be something wrong with me."

2   DeBlasio's case is not unique°. Studies suggest that perhaps one in ten adult Americans is unable to read well enough to complete this article. The costs to society— in terms of welfare and unemployment payments and underproductivity—are enormous. With a growing awareness of the literacy crisis, a lucky few are getting help. DeBlasio enrolled last year in a program sponsored by Literacy Volunteers of New York City, a nonprofit organization, and can now read and write at a junior-high-school level. She described her personal triumph to reporter Jane Sugden.

3   By the time I reached junior high school, I could read a little, but not very much. Whenever I was asked to read aloud in class, I felt terrible. I was afraid and nervous. I tried to tell myself, "Fran, you're smart. You have something up there." But I was confused and didn't know where to turn. My parents had separated when I was young, and my mother supported me and my two brothers by working as a cleaning lady.

She was a traditional Italian woman who always told us how important it was to get a good education. But even after she went to my school to try to find out why I was having problems, nothing changed.

4   I was going to public school in a working-class neighborhood in Manhattan. When I had to take written tests, I scribbled down some answers. I almost always flunked, but they still passed me on to the next grade anyway. When I told my teachers I was scared I wouldn't be able to keep up, they all gave me the same story: "Go home this summer and study hard on your vacation. If you work hard, you'll do better next year." But the impression I really had was they thought I was just too stupid to learn and would drop out sooner or later anyway. It's as if everyone just wanted to pass the buck° and get rid of me as quickly as possible. No one ever tried to give me any special help with my reading, and there weren't any experts at the school who knew how to teach people who didn't catch on right away. They just made me feel it was all my fault—that I didn't try hard enough. Meanwhile, I felt rejected and alone. Very alone. I get so angry when I think about that now.

5   Even though I had never been a discipline problem, in the seventh grade they put me in a class for kids who were troublemakers or wise guys. It was total chaos°. All day, the teacher yelled at the students, and they yelled back. It was no good for learning.

6   High school was worse. I went

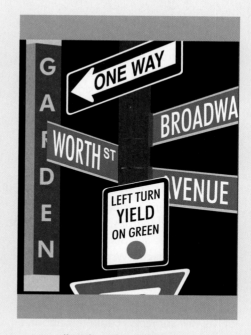

to an all-girls school where a lot of the kids were tough. Fights broke out almost every day. I was too frightened to use the john because girls had been attacked there, sometimes sexually attacked by other girls. When I turned 17, I couldn't take it any more and quit. I figured, "What's the difference? I'm not learning anything anyway."

7   After quitting school, I didn't know what to do. Baby-sitting was one of the few jobs I could handle. I also worked at an amusement park in New Jersey, taking tickets for kiddie rides. Once I went to apply for a city job. I didn't understand most of the application, so I asked to take it home. But she said I had to fill it out there. I said, "Never mind. I don't want this job anyway," and ran out. I didn't want to be a bum, but I was very afraid of being rejected.

8   Trying to get a driver's license was impossible because I knew I couldn't pass the written test. Even simple street directions were a problem because I was not able to read signs. At the same time, I was ashamed to tell my friends I couldn't read, so I bluffed a lot. I memorized landmarks° in order to get around. Since I couldn't understand the menus at restaurants, I learned to be a good actress. I asked my friends, "What are you having? What looks good?" Sometimes at parties, people wanted to play games like Scrabble, and I had to fake a headache. When people talked about the books they were reading— maybe a best-seller—I'd say, "I read sports books," because sports was one of the few subjects I could talk about.

9   By the time I was 25, my reading had improved slightly from studying the sports pages of the newspaper. Then a friend helped me fill out an application to work in the mail distribution department of a bank and—I couldn't believe it—I got the job. I had a tough time at first, learning to tell the difference between hundreds of different names. But my boss was very helpful. I learned to do the job well and began to feel much better about myself.

10   In June 1985, after ten years on the job, I was offered a promotion to assistant supervisor, but I was terrified because the new position involved a lot of paperwork. Luckily, a friend told me about Literacy Volunteers and arranged for me to meet with Barbara Greenfield, one of the coordinators of the program. When I told Barbara about my fear of taking on the new position, she volunteered to tutor me during her own free time. I was stunned° that someone would go out of her way to help me like that. When I walked out of her office, I felt born again.

11   Within a few months, I joined a small reading group which meets for two-hour sessions three times a week. When I first began, I would read a passage twenty-five times and not know what it meant. Or I would get hung up on one word for a half hour without getting the sense of a whole sentence. But during one session a few weeks later, one of my tutors asked me questions about something I read, and I suddenly realized I was giving her the answers. She said, "Fran, you understand!" I said, "Holy Christ! This is me. I can read."

12   The tutors also encouraged me to write. At first I had trouble putting down a single sentence, but before long I was writing stories and even poetry. I particularly like to write about my family. At a special meeting of my reading group one night, I recited a story I had written on my birthday about my mother, who died three years ago. When I finished, the whole group had tears in their eyes. I've written other pieces about my grandfather, who is ninety years old and lives with me. When he was in the hospital for a stroke three months ago, I sat with him every day and wrote about my feelings.

13   Things that once seemed impossible are now fun. I've read books about

George Washington and Babe Ruth. I'm studying for my high-school equivalency exam and my driver's license test. I recently went to see an opera and was able to read an English translation of the story that they projected above the stage. Wow, that made me feel good! Even watching TV is different. Now I can read the ads. I understand street signs, menus, all those things. It's as if a great burden has been lifted off my back.

14   Recently, I've confessed to my friends about the problem I always had reading. One very close friend I used to play softball with moved to Florida several years ago and kept writing to me. She didn't know I couldn't write back, so she called me one time to ask why she hadn't received any letters from me. I said, "Oh, I'm just not very good about writing." I was ashamed to tell her the whole truth, so I had a friend write a letter for me. A few months ago, I wrote her a letter in my own handwriting and explained my problem. I told her how much I was learning and how exciting it was to finally be able to read. She wrote back and said, "I'm very proud of you. Very proud. I'm glad you told me." She understood.

Vocabulary Questions

A. Use context clues to help you decide on the best definition for each italicized word. Then, in the space provided, write the letter of your choice.

_____A_____ 1. In the excerpt below, the word *rejected* (rĭ-jĕktʹĭd) means
    A. refused.
    B. hired.
    C. honored.
    D. forgotten.

> DeBlasio was afraid she would be refused the job and would end up as a bum.

"I said, 'Never mind. I don't want this job anyway,' and ran out. I didn't want to be a bum, but I was very afraid of being rejected." (Paragraph 7)

_____D_____ 2. In the excerpt below, the word *bluffed* (blŭft) means
    A. coughed.
    B. talked.
    C. questioned.
    D. pretended.

> A person who has "learned to be a good actress" with friends is probably one who often pretends about something.

". . . I was ashamed to tell my friends I couldn't read, so I bluffed a lot. I memorized landmarks. . . . I learned to be a good actress." (Paragraph 8)

_____C_____ 3. In the excerpt below, the word *recited* (rĭ-sīt′ĭd) means
    A. thought about.
    B. sang.   Since the group members
    C. read aloud.   responded to her story,
    D. examined.   she must have read it to them.

    "At a special meeting of my reading group one night, I recited a story I
    had written. . . . When I finished, the whole group had tears in their eyes."
    (Paragraph 12)

_____B_____ 4. In the excerpt below, the word *projected* (prə-jĕkt′ĭd) means
    A. read out loud.
    B. made appear.   If she read the translation above the
    C. erased.   stage, it must have appeared there.
    D. forgot.

    "I . . . was able to read an English translation of the story that they
    projected above the stage." (Paragraph 13)

_____B_____ 5. In the excerpt below, the word *burden* (bûr′dn) means
    A. shirt.
    B. load.   Being able to read things she once did
    C. bump.   not understand is like having a weight,
    D. pleasure.   or load, taken off her back.

    "I understand street signs, menus, all those things. It's as if a great burden
    has been lifted off my back." (Paragraph 13)

B. Below are words, or forms of words, from "Words to Watch." Write in the one
that best completes each sentence. Then write the letter of that word in the space
provided.

A. chaos	B. decipher	C. landmark
D. stunned	E. unique	

_____A_____ 6. The birthday party for my three-year-old daughter created such

    _____*chaos*_____ in the living room that it took me all

    afternoon to clean up.   If it took all afternoon to clean up,
                                              the party created *disorder*.

_____D_____ 7. Norm and I have been going together for two years now, but my parents

    were still _____*stunned*_____ to learn that we plan to get married.

        If the couple had been together for two years, wedding plans should not
        have come as a surprise. However, the parents reacted differently: they were
        shocked to learn of the plan to get married. (Note the contrast signal: *but*.)

_C_ 8. Because the statue of President Grant is in the middle of town, everyone

uses it as a _____landmark_____.

_E_ 9. The little dolls on top of the wedding cake had a _____unique_____ touch—the bride wore a maternity wedding dress.

_B_ 10. Pharmacists always manage somehow to _____decipher_____ doctors' prescriptions.

> **Item 8:** A statue in the middle of town would be an *object that would help people find their way.*
>
> **Item 9:** A doll in a maternity wedding dress is an *unusual* wedding cake decoration.
>
> **Item 10:** Doctors are notorious for poor handwriting; therefore, pharmacists must *make sense of* doctors' prescriptions.

Reading Comprehension Questions

Central Point and Main Ideas

_B_ 1. Which sentence best expresses the central point of the selection?
   A. DeBlasio could not read.
   B. Learning to read has changed DeBlasio's life.
   C. DeBlasio felt ashamed that she couldn't read.
   D. DeBlasio didn't learn to read in school.

> Answers A, C, and D are too narrow. Each states only one detail of the selection.

_D_ 2. Which sentence best expresses the main idea of paragraph 7?
   A. DeBlasio could handle baby-sitting.
   B. DeBlasio once worked at an amusement park taking tickets for children's rides.
   C. DeBlasio couldn't fill out the application form for a city job.
   D. DeBlasio's inability to read limited her job opportunities and made applying for jobs difficult.

> Answers A, B, and C are too narrow. Each covers only one detail of the paragraph.

_A_ 3. Which sentence best expresses the main idea of paragraph 13?
   A. DeBlasio is enjoying activities she thought she would never be able to do.
   B. DeBlasio can now read books.
   C. DeBlasio is studying for a high-school equivalency exam and a driver's license test.
   D. DeBlasio can even read the English translation of an opera.

> Answers B, C, and D are too narrow. Each covers only one detail of the paragraph.

Supporting Details

_C_ 4. Before she was tutored by a Literacy Volunteers coordinator, DeBlasio
   A. could not read at all.
   B. never even wished she could read.
   C. could read a little.
   D. could read enough to feel very capable at work.

> See the first sentences of paragraphs 3 and 9.

Transitions

___B___ 5. Paragraph 7 begins with a transition that shows
    A. addition.
    B. time.
    C. an example.
    D. cause and effect.

After is used to tell the reader when the author "didn't know what to do."

___B___ 6. The relationship expressed in the sentence below is one of
    A. contrast.
    B. cause and effect.
    C. time.
    D. addition.

Cause: DeBlasio knew she couldn't pass the written test. *Effect:* Trying to get a driver's license was impossible.

Trying to get a driver's license was impossible <u>because</u> I knew I couldn't pass the written test. (Paragraph 8)

Patterns of Organization

___B___ 7. The pattern of organization of paragraph 13 is
    A. time order.
    B. list of items.
    C. definition and example.
    D. contrast.

DeBlasio lists things she does now that had once been impossible for her.

Inferences

___C___ 8. DeBlasio implies that
    A. she was too stupid to learn to read in public school.
    B. her teachers did the best they could for her.
    C. the schools she went to were not good places for her to learn in.
    D. in school she managed to keep her self-image strong despite the fact that she couldn't read.

See paragraphs 4–6.

___T___ 9. TRUE OR FALSE? DeBlasio implies that she should not have been put in a class for students who were discipline problems.

See paragraph 5.

Item 10:
In paragraph 8, DeBlasio says she was ashamed of not being able to read. She then describes some of the ways she hid the fact. It is logical to conclude that other people would react the same way in that situation. In addition, there is no evidence in the article to support answers A, C, or D.

___B___ 10. From this article we can conclude that
    A. people can get along very well without reading.
    B. those who can't read may find ways of hiding that fact.
    C. when people don't learn to read in school, it is all their own fault.
    D. once people reach their thirties, it is almost impossible for them to learn new skills.

Summarizing

Complete the following summary of "Read All About It" by filling in the blanks.

Wording of answers may vary.

DeBlasio didn't learn to read in her schools, which did a poor job of teaching her. After she quit high school, there were few jobs she could tackle, and her everyday activities were restricted because she couldn't read. Ashamed of her inability to read, DeBlasio hid it from her friends. By the time she was 25, however, her reading had improved a little, and she got a job _____*distributing mail in a bank*_____.

See the second sentence in paragraph 9.

After working at the bank for ten years, _____*DeBlasio was offered*_____ _____*a promotion*_____. She wasn't sure, however, that she could handle the paperwork of the new job. Luckily, a friend told her about Literacy Volunteers, and she began to learn to read with the help of a tutor. Later she also joined _____*a reading group*_____ and began to write. DeBlasio is now able to enjoy many activities she once thought impossible for her. She feels much happier with herself and has even told _____*her friends about*_____ _____*the problem she had with reading*_____.

See the first sentence in paragraph 10.

See the first sentence in paragraph 11.

See paragraph 14.

Discussion Questions

1. Do you know anybody who has trouble reading? How does that trouble affect his or her life?

2. Just how difficult is it to live in our society without being able to read? To get an idea of the answer to this question, think about your activities at home, at work or school, when shopping, in restaurants, and while driving. How much of what you do involves reading?

3. DeBlasio gives a bleak picture of the schools she attended. In what ways were your own schools like, or unlike, hers? Why do you think her teachers behaved as they did?

4. We tend to think that people don't learn important new skills as they get older, but DeBlasio's story contradicts that idea. Describe a person or persons you know who have been able to learn new skills as they get older. What skills have these people mastered, and what character traits might be responsible for their continued progress?

Note: Writing assignments for this selection appear on pages 596–597.

Check Your Performance   READ ALL ABOUT IT

Activity	Number Right	Points			Total	
Vocabulary						
A. Vocabulary in Context (5 items)	_____	×	10	=	_____	
B. Words to Watch (5 items)	_____	×	10	=	_____	
		SCORE		=	_____	%
Comprehension						
Central Point and Main Ideas (3 items)	_____	×	8	=	_____	
Supporting Details (1 item)	_____	×	8	=	_____	
Transitions (2 items)	_____	×	8	=	_____	
Patterns of Organization (1 item)	_____	×	8	=	_____	
Inferences (3 items)	_____	×	8	=	_____	
Summarizing (4 items)	_____	×	5	=	_____	
		SCORE		=	_____	%

FINAL SCORES: Vocabulary _____ % Comprehension _____ %

Enter your total score into the **Reading Performance Chart: Ten Reading Selections** on the inside back cover.

6 Adult Children at Home
Marilyn Mack

Preview

Parents used to expect their children to leave home not long after high school or college. Nowadays, however, children leave home later than ever, and even then they may not be gone for good. Marilyn Mack explains this new pattern and its ups and downs.

Words to Watch

ruefully (2): with regret
phenomenon (10): noteworthy situation or event
cope (12): manage
fixed (13): unchanging
precautions (18): actions taken in advance to protect against possible problems
consent (22): agreement

1   Ruth Patterson remembers the day the last of her children left home. "Dan was 18 and headed off to the state university," said the Pennsylvania housewife. "I cried awhile, and then told myself, 'Cheer up! At last you and Dave have the house to yourselves!'"

2   Six years later, Mrs. Patterson laughs a little ruefully° at that memory. Since her youngest son left for college, three of her four children—one with a three-year-old daughter—have moved back to the family home for at least six months at a time.

3   "The 'empty nest' hasn't been quite as empty as we expected," says Mrs. Patterson.

4   The Pattersons' situation is becoming less unusual all the time. Adult children have been "nesting," or moving back to the family home, in increasing numbers in recent years. In 1970, according to the U.S. Census Bureau, 54 percent of men and 41 percent of women between the ages of 18 and 24 depended on their parents for housing. Lately, those figures have risen much higher. One survey in 2010 found that as many as 85 percent of students graduating from college in the spring planned to move back home.

5   Why are adult children coming home? The case of the Pattersons provides some typical reasons.

6   Their oldest daughter, Suzanne, 35, a bank teller, returned home with her toddler after a painful divorce. Two years later, she is still there, with her mother caring for her little girl. "She needed a place to lick her wounds," said her mother. "We thought it would be for just a few months, but when we realized what it would cost her to keep Jenny in day care while she worked, it didn't make sense for them to move out again."

7   Five years after high school, their son Peter, now 28, moved back in. The plan was for him to spend a year working on a painting crew while he and his fiancée saved money for the down payment on a house. One year turned into three; long stretches between jobs made it impossible for Peter to make the kind of money he needed. Eventually he and his fiancée married and moved into a tiny apartment. They still hope to buy a house someday, but fear that "someday" may never come.

8   Their daughter Lesley, 30, has moved in and out of the house so many times "we've lost count," says her mother. A legal secretary, Lesley "earns enough to have her own place, if she'd learn to live within her means. But she wants to live like the lawyers she works with." That translates into an expensive car, lots of evenings out, and a wardrobe that bursts the limits of her modest salary.

9   Only the Pattersons' youngest child, Dan, now 24, has followed the route his parents expected. He graduated from college, found a job teaching high-school social studies, and lives on his own in a city apartment.

10   Many factors have contributed to the phenomenon° of nesting. First and foremost is the general slump in the economy. As many commentators have noted, "The rich are getting richer; the poor are getting poorer; and the middle class is disappearing." Even for college graduates, the prospect of easily finding employment and starting on the path toward home ownership is doubtful. Other contributing factors include the rise in the divorce rate, increased housing costs, college debts, and the trend to delay marriage. Once out on their own, many young people are finding it unexpectedly difficult to maintain the standard of living they hoped for. Apartment rentals, particularly in major cities, can make living alone an impossible option. Even for those fortunate enough to have found steady employment, buying a house can seem unlikely—a first-time home-buyer can expect to pay over 40 percent more today than twenty years ago.

11   Returning home can be a financial lifesaver for struggling young people. Some credit counselors recommend nesting as a solution for people who've gotten in over their heads with credit cards and utility bills. "I was really in a mess financially when I moved back in with Mom and Dad," said Tony Woelk, a 28-year-old stereo equipment salesman. "I don't know what I would have done if

they hadn't helped me pay off my bills and make a fresh start." Today, after two years of living with his parents, Tony is on his own again and determined to keep his spending under control.

12   Another advantage mentioned by some nesters is the emotional support they were shown by their parents in a time of need. Judy Loewen, 22, moved back in with her family for a month after breaking up with her long-time boyfriend. "I quit my job and left the city where he was," she remembers today. "I really felt that I couldn't cope° unless I got away immediately, and where could I go with no money and no job except to my folks? And bless them, they said, 'Just take it easy here for a while and don't rush into anything.' After a few weeks, I was ready to take a lot more realistic view of the situation and make some good decisions."

13   Parents, too, can find some practical and emotional benefits when their adult children return home. A child's contribution to room and board can help out with household expenses, particularly if the parents are living on a fixed° income. In addition, parents may enjoy having a younger person around to help out with household repairs and other chores. "As I get older, taking care of the house and yard has become more of a burden for me," said Bill Robinson, a widower whose 35-year-old son has been sharing the house for the last two years. "Joseph pays some rent, but his real contribution has been to take a lot of those worries off my shoulders."

But the nesting phenomenon 14 has its gloomy side as well. Parents and children report the number-one problem as the lack of space and privacy experienced by everyone involved.

"Never, never, never again," vowed 15 Vicki Langella, 23, who lived with her parents for six months after losing her job in a township clerk's office. "We get along fine when we visit, but within ten minutes of moving back in, I felt like a twelve-year-old. It was constantly, 'Where are you going? When will you be back? Who are you going to be with?' And I found myself reacting to them as if I really were 12. The worst part of it was knowing that it was my own fault—I'd chosen to move back in with them."

"Believe it or not, sixty-year-olds 16 enjoy some privacy too," said Ella Purcell, whose two adult daughters have both returned home for brief periods. "Coming into my own living room to find my daughter and a date smooching on the couch made me feel like an intruder. I finally had to say, 'I love you—but out already!'"

17   Finances can be another difficult area for parents and returned children. Parents often struggle with the decision of whether to ask their children for rent. "When you're letting them stay with you in order to save money, it seems silly to charge rent. But when we saw the way Ed was throwing money around, we began to feel taken advantage of," said the mother of one adult nester.

18   Despite its possible pitfalls, psychologists, family counselors, and others believe that nesting can succeed for many families if some precautions° are taken. They offer the following tips on maintaining a happy "nest."

19   • Regardless of their financial situation, adult children should pay some room and board. Monica O'Kane, the author of *Living with Adult Children,* admits that this can be difficult. "It's hard to squeeze blood from a turnip, especially when it's your own turnip. But paying for room and board helps children grow in financial independence."

20   • Establish clear expectations about household duties. "I remembered all too well being treated like the family servant when the kids were teenagers," said one experienced mother of a nester. "So when Rob moved back in, I said, 'Fine. Here is your share of the laundry, grocery-shopping, and cleaning duties.' Once it was clear that I was serious, he pitched right in."

21   • Respect one another. Children should not expect to be treated as guests or to use the parental home as a hotel, coming and going at all hours with no explanations. Parents, on the other hand, should recognize that the nester is no longer a youngster whose activities need constant supervision.

22   • And, most importantly: Don't let it go on forever. "When a child returns home, everyone should agree on a tentative date for him to move out again," said one family therapist. "If that date is changed later by the mutual consent° of everyone concerned, that's OK, but everyone should understand that this isn't a permanent arrangement."

Vocabulary Questions

A. Use context clues to help you decide on the best definition for each italicized word. Then, in the space provided, write the letter of your choice.

___C___ 1. In the excerpt below, the word *modest* (mŏd′ĭst) means
   A. noble.
   B. strange.
   C. small.
   D. large.

   A salary with limits that can be burst by wardrobe purchases is likely to be small.

   "But she wants . . . a wardrobe that bursts the limits of her modest salary." (Paragraph 8)

___B___ 2. In the excerpt below, the word *maintain* (mān-tān′) means
   A. avoid.
   B. keep up.
   C. remember.
   D. sum up.

   What would one want to do to a hoped-for standard of living?

   ". . . many young people are finding it unexpectedly difficult to maintain the standard of living they hoped for." (Paragraph 10)

___A___ 3. In the excerpt below, the word *option* (ŏp′shən) means
   A. choice.
   B. discovery.
   C. failure.
   D. limit.

   High apartment rentals make it impossible to choose to live alone.

   "Apartment rentals . . . can make living alone an impossible option." (Paragraph 10)

___D___ 4. In the excerpt below, the word *tentative* (tĕn′tə-tĭv) means
   A. unchangeable.
   B. public.
   C. according to law.
   D. agreed upon for the time being.

   A date that can be "changed later" is one "agreed upon for the time being."

   "'When a child returns home, everyone should agree on a tentative date for him to move out again,' said one family therapist. 'If that date is changed later . . . that's OK. . . .'" (Paragraph 22)

_____A_____ 5. In the excerpt below, the word *mutual* (my$\overline{oo}$′ch$\overline{oo}$-əl) means
    A. shared.
    B. mistaken.
    C. spoken.
    D. divided.

> An agreement come to by "everyone concerned" is a shared agreement.

> "'If that date is changed later by the mutual consent of everyone concerned, that's OK. . . .'" (Paragraph 22)

B. Below are words, or forms of words, from "Words to Watch." Write in the one that best completes each sentence. Then write the letter of that word in the space provided.

A. consent	B. fixed	C. phenomenon
D. precautions	E. ruefully	

_____C_____ 6. The disappearance of the dinosaurs is a _____phenomenon_____ that scientists are still trying to figure out.   The disappearance of the dinosaurs (at that time, the dominant land-dwelling animals on Earth) is a *noteworthy event.*

_____B_____ 7. My brother's opinions are _____fixed_____; he never changes his mind about anything, even when he is clearly wrong.   If he never changes his mind, his opinions are *unchanging.*

_____E_____ 8. Nathan looked _____ruefully_____ at the clock; he wished he had started his paper earlier.   If he wishes he had started earlier, he is looking at the clock *with regret.*

_____D_____ 9. Sexually active teenagers must learn to take _____precautions_____ against pregnancy.   A sexually active teenager must learn to take *actions in advance to protect against* pregnancy.

_____A_____ 10. In order to go on the field trip, students must first get the _____consent_____ of their parents.   Students must get the *agreement* of their parents before going on the trip.

Reading Comprehension Questions

Central Point and Main Ideas

_____C_____ 1. Which sentence best expresses the central point of the selection?
    A. Parents are not sure if they should ask for rent money from their grown children who live at home.
    B. The Pattersons are a good example of nesting.
    C. Nesting, which has increased, has advantages and disadvantages, but it can succeed if families take precautions.
    D. Between 1970 and 2010, nesting has greatly increased among adult children.   Answers A, B, and D are too narrow. Each covers only one detail of the selection.

_A_ 2. The main idea of paragraph 10 is expressed in its
   A. first sentence.
   B. second sentence.
   C. third sentence.
   D. last sentence.

The first sentence has a list signal: *many factors*. The rest of the paragraph lists factors that contribute to nesting.

_A_ 3. The main idea of paragraph 13 is
   A. in the first sentence.
   B. in the second sentence.
   C. in the last sentence.
   D. implied.

The first sentence has a list signal: *some practical and emotional benefits*. The rest of the paragraph details some of the benefits.

Supporting Details

_D_ 4. Adult children return home
   A. after divorces.
   B. when it's hard to find a job.
   C. so that they can pay their bills.
   D. for all of the above reasons.

See paragraph 10.

_F_ 5. TRUE OR FALSE? There are no disadvantages to having adult children return home to live.   See paragraphs 14–17.

_D_ 6. According to the article, when adult children return home, they
   A. gain privacy.
   B. should be allowed to stay indefinitely.
   C. should be treated like guests.
   D. should help out with finances and household chores.

See paragraphs 19–22.

Item 7:
The "gloomy side" of nesting is contrasted with the benefits presented in the previous paragraphs.

Transitions

_A_ 7. The sentence below begins with a transition that shows
   A. contrast.   C. addition.
   B. time.   D. an example.

   "But the nesting phenomenon has its gloomy side as well." (Paragraph 14)

Item 8:
The sentences contrast children's responsibilities with adults' responsibilities.

_C_ 8. The relationship between the two sentences below is one of
   A. addition.   C. contrast.
   B. illustration.   D. time.

   "Children should not expect to be treated as guests or to use the parental home as a hotel, coming and going at all hours with no explanations. Parents, on the other hand, should recognize that the nester is no longer a youngster whose activities need constant supervision." (Paragraph 21)

Patterns of Organization

<u>C</u>   9. The pattern of organization of paragraph 10 is
   A. comparison.
   B. contrast.
   C. list of items.
   D. time order.

The list signal many factors *in the first sentence is helpful in identifying the pattern of organization.*

Inferences

<u>T</u>   10. TRUE OR FALSE? The author implies that money problems are the main reason that adult children return home to live.   See paragraph 10.

Most of the factors contributing to nesting are related to financial problems, suggesting that money is the key reason for the increase in nesting.

Outlining

Complete the following outline of the article by filling in the letters of the missing major details, listed below.

Central point: **The growing phenomenon of nesting, which has advantages and disadvantages, can work well for families if precautions are taken.**

1. Introductory anecdote (paragraphs 1–3)
2. Increase in nesting (paragraph 4)
3. <u>B</u>   (paragraphs 5–10)
4. <u>A</u>   (paragraphs 11–13)
5. <u>D</u>   (paragraphs 14–17)
6. <u>C</u>   (paragraphs 18–22)

Major Details Missing from the Outline

   A. Advantages of nesting
   B. Reasons for increased nesting
   C. Precautions for successful nesting
   D. Disadvantages of nesting

Item 3: Paragraph 5 contains a list signal: *some typical reasons.* Paragraphs 6–10 then list examples.

Item 4: Paragraph 11 discusses one advantage. Paragraph 12 uses an addition word (*Another*) to signal a second advantage. Paragraph 13 states a third advantage.

Item 5: Paragraph 14 contains a contrast transition *(But)* to signal the shift from advantages to disadvantages. Paragraphs 15–17 list disadvantages.

Item 6: Paragraph 18 contains list signals: *some precautions* and *following tips.* Paragraphs 19–22 then list four precautions.

Discussion Questions

1. Do you know any cases of nesting? Why did the children return home? How did it work out?

2. Do you think today's young adults are having a harder time financially than their parents' generation? Or is the "standard of living they hoped for" higher? Or both?

3. Mack mentions the "people who've gotten in over their heads with credit cards and utility bills." Why do you think people get into this situation? What advice would you give them?

4. Do you agree that adult children who return home, "regardless of their financial situation," should pay some room and board? If not, what financial situations should excuse adult children from paying room and board?

Note: Writing assignments for this selection appear on page 597.

Note: Writing assignments for this selection appear on page 597.

Check Your Performance   ADULT CHILDREN AT HOME

Activity	Number Right	Points		Total
Vocabulary				
A. Vocabulary in Context (5 items)	_____	× 10	=	_____
B. Words to Watch (5 items)	_____	× 10	=	_____
		SCORE	=	_____ %
Comprehension				
Central Point and Main Ideas (3 items)	_____	× 8	=	_____
Supporting Details (3 items)	_____	× 8	=	_____
Transitions (2 items)	_____	× 8	=	_____
Patterns of Organization (1 item)	_____	× 8	=	_____
Inferences (1 item)	_____	× 8	=	_____
Outlining (4 items)	_____	× 5	=	_____
		SCORE	=	_____ %

FINAL SCORES: Vocabulary _____ %   Comprehension _____ %

Enter your total score into the **Reading Performance Chart: Ten Reading Selections** on the inside back cover.

7 How to Make It in College, Now That You're Here

Brian O'Keeney

Preview

Give yourself some credit—you're now a college student! But getting into college is only the first step. It's time to plan not only how to deal with the academic demands of college, but also how to cope with the additional demands of family, friends, and work. Based on interviews with college students, this article offers you practical, realistic steps to college success.

Words to Watch

hurdle (1): difficulty
coping with (2): dealing with
queasy (3): sick
distracted (4): sidetracked
relatively (4): compared with something else
plod (7): walk slowly and heavily
maintain (13): keep
hermit (13): one who lives alone, apart from others
simmer down (21): calm down

1   Today is your first day on campus. You were a high-school senior three months ago. Or maybe you've been at home with your children for the last ten years. Or maybe you work full-time, and you're coming to school to start the process that leads to a better job. Whatever your background is, you're probably not too concerned today with staying in college. After all, you just got over the hurdle° (and the paperwork) of applying to this place and organizing your life so that you could attend. And today, you're confused and tired. Everything is a hassle, from finding the classrooms to standing in line at the bookstore. But read my advice anyway. And if you don't read it today, save this article. You might want to look at it a little further down the road.

2   By the way, if this isn't your first day, don't skip this article. Maybe you haven't been doing as well in your studies as you'd hoped. Or perhaps you've had problems juggling your work schedule, your class schedule, and your social life. If so, read on. You're about to get the inside story on making it in college. On the basis of my own experience as a final-year student, and on dozens of interviews with successful students, I've worked out a no-fail system for coping with° college. These are the inside tips every student needs to do well in school. I've put myself in your place, and I'm going to answer the questions that will cross (or have already crossed) your mind during your stay here.

What's the Secret to Getting Good Grades?

3   It all comes down to getting those grades, doesn't it? After all, you came here for some reason, and you're going to need passing grades to get the credits or degree you want. Many of us never did much studying in high school; most of the learning we did took place in the classroom. College, however, is a lot different. You're really on your own when it comes to passing courses. In fact, sometimes you'll feel as if nobody cares if you make it or not. Therefore, you've got to figure out a study system that gets results. Sooner or later, you'll be alone with those books. After that, you'll be sitting in a classroom with an exam sheet on your desk. Whether you stare at that exam with a queasy° stomach,

or whip through it fairly confidently, depends on your study techniques. Most of the successful students I talked to agreed that the following eight study tips deliver solid results:

1. Set up a study place. Those students   4
you see "studying" in the cafeteria or game room aren't learning much. You just can't learn when you're distracted° by people and noise. Even the library can be a bad place to study if you constantly find yourself watching the clouds outside or the students walking through the stacks. It takes guts to sit, alone, in a quiet place in order to study. But you have to do it. Find a room at home or a spot in the library that's relatively° quiet—and boring. When you sit there, you won't have much to do except study.

5   **2. Get into a study frame of mind.** When you sit down, do it with the attitude that you're really going to get this studying done. You're not going to doodle on your notebook or make a list for the supermarket. Decide that you're going to study and learn now, so that you can move on to more interesting things as soon as possible.

6   **3. Give yourself rewards.** If you sweat out a block of study time, and do a good job on it, treat yourself. You deserve it. You can "psych" yourself up for studying by promising to reward yourself afterward. A present for yourself can be anything from a favorite TV show to a relaxing bath to a dish of double-chocolate ice cream.

7   **4. Skim the textbook first.** Lots of students sit down with an assignment like "read chapter 5, pages 125–150" and do just that. They turn to page 125 and start to read. After a while, they find that they have no idea what they just read. For the last ten minutes, they've been thinking about their five-year-old or what they're going to eat for dinner. Eventually, they plod° through all the pages but don't remember much afterward.

8   In order to prevent this problem, skim the textbook chapter first. This means the following: look at the title, the subtitles, the headings, the pictures, and the first and last paragraphs. Try to find out what the person who wrote the book had in mind when he or she organized the chapter. What was important enough to set off as a title or in bold type? After skimming, you should be able to explain to yourself what the main topics of the chapter are and even some of the main points. Unless you're the kind of person who would step into an empty elevator shaft without looking first, you'll soon discover the value of skimming.

9   **5. Take notes on what you're studying.** This sounds like a hassle, but it works. Go back over the material after you've read it, and jot down key words and phrases in the margins. When you review the chapter for a test, you'll have handy little things like "definition of rationalization" or "example of regression" in the margins. If the material is especially tough, organize a separate sheet of notes. Write down definitions, examples, lists, and main ideas. The idea is to have a single sheet or two that boil the entire chapter down to a digestible lump.

10   **6. Review after you've read and taken notes.** Some people swear that talking to yourself works. Tell yourself about the most important points in the chapter. Once you've said them out loud, they seem to stick better in your mind. If you can't talk to yourself about the material after reading it, that's a sure sign you don't really know it.

11   **7. Take a break when you're tired.** It's all right to let up for a bit when you've had enough. You should try to make it through at least an hour, though. Ten minutes here and there are useless.

When your head starts to pound and your eyes develop spidery red lines, quit. Rest for a bit with a short nap, and go back later.

12   **8. Take the college skills course if you need it.** Don't hesitate or feel embarrassed about enrolling in a study skills course. Many students say they wouldn't have made it without one.

How Can I Keep Up with All My Responsibilities without Going Crazy?

13   You've got a class schedule. You're supposed to study. You've got a family. You've got a husband, wife, boyfriend, child. You've got a job. How are you possibly going to cover all the bases in your life and maintain° your sanity? This is one of the toughest problems students face. Even if they start the semester with the best of intentions, they eventually find themselves tearing their hair out trying to do everything they're supposed to do. Believe it or not, though, it is possible to meet all your responsibilities. And you don't have to turn into a hermit° or give up your loved ones to do it.

14   The secret here is to organize your time. But don't just sit around half the semester planning to get everything together soon. Before you know it, you'll be confronted with midterms, papers, family, and work all at once. Don't let yourself reach that breaking point. Instead, try these three tactics:

1. Prepare a monthly calendar. Get   15 one of those calendars with big blocks around the dates. Give yourself an overview of the whole term by marking down the due dates for papers and projects. Circle test and exam days. This way those days don't sneak up on you unexpectedly.

2. Make up a study schedule. Sit   16 down during the first few days of this semester and make up a sheet listing the days and hours of the week. Fill in your work and class hours first. Then try to block out some study hours. It's better to study a little every day than to create a huge once-or-twice-a-week marathon session. Schedule study hours for your hardest classes for the times when you feel most energetic. For example, I battled my tax law textbook in the mornings; when I looked at it after 7:00 p.m., I might as well have been reading Chinese. The usual proportion, by the way, is one hour of study time for every class hour.

In case you're one of those people   17 who get carried away, remember to leave blocks of free time, too. You won't be any good to yourself or anyone else if you don't relax and pack in the studying once in a while.

3. Use "to-do" lists. This is the secret   18 that singlehandedly got me through college. Once a week (or every day if you want to), make a list of what you have to do. Write down everything from "write English paper" to "buy cold cuts for lunch." The best thing about a "to-do" list is that it seems to tame all those stray "I have to" thoughts that nag at your mind. After you finish something on the list, cross it off. Don't be compulsive about finishing everything; you're not Superman or Wonder Woman. Get the important things done first. The secondary things you don't finish can simply be moved to your next "to-do" list.

What Can I Do If Personal Problems Get in the Way of My Studies?

19   One student, Roger, told me this story:

> Everything was going okay for me until the middle of the spring semester. I went through a terrible time when I broke up with my girlfriend and started seeing her best friend. I was trying to deal with my ex-girlfriend's hurt and anger, my new girlfriend's guilt, and my own worries and anxieties at the same time. In addition to this, my mother was sick and on a medication that made her really irritable. I hated to go home because the atmosphere was so uncomfortable. Soon, I started missing classes because I couldn't deal with the academic pressures as well as my own personal problems. It seemed easier to hang around my girlfriend's apartment than to face all my problems at home and at school.

And here's what another student, Marian, told me: 20

> I'd been married for eight years, and the relationship wasn't going too well. I saw the handwriting on the wall, and I decided to prepare for the future. I enrolled in college because I knew I'd need a decent job to support myself. Well, my husband had a fit because I was going to school. We were arguing a lot anyway, and he made it almost impossible for me to study at home. I think he was angry and almost jealous because I was drawing away from him. It got so bad that I thought about quitting college for a while. I wasn't getting any support at home, and it was just too hard to go on.

Personal troubles like these are   21 overwhelming when you're going through them. School seems like the least important thing in your life. The two students above are perfect examples of this situation. But if you think about it, quitting or failing school would be the worst thing for these two students. Roger's problems, at least with his girlfriends, would simmer down° eventually, and then he'd regret having left school. Marian had to finish college if she wanted to be able to live independently. Sometimes, you've just got to hang tough.

But what do you do while you're   22 trying to live through a lousy time? First of all, do something difficult. Ask yourself, honestly, if you're exaggerating small problems as an excuse to avoid classes and studying. It takes strength to admit this, but there's no sense in kidding yourself. You need to know if your problems are really bad in themselves or if you are perhaps making them worse than they are.

23   Second, if your problems are serious, and real, try to make some human contacts at school. Lots of students hide inside a miserable shell made of their own troubles and feel isolated and lonely. Believe me, there are plenty of students with problems. Not everyone is getting A's and having a fabulous social and home life at the same time. As you go through the term, you'll pick up some vibrations about the students in your classes. Perhaps someone strikes you as a compatible person. Why not speak to that person after class? Share a cup of coffee in the cafeteria, or walk to the parking lot together. You're not looking for a best friend or the love of your life. You just want to build a little network of support for yourself. Sharing your difficulties, questions, and complaints with a friendly person on campus can make a world of difference in how you feel.

24   Finally, if your problems are overwhelming, get some professional help. Why do you think colleges spend countless dollars on counseling departments and campus psychiatric services? More than ever, students all over the country are taking advantage of the help offered by support groups

and therapy sessions. There's no shame attached to asking for help, either. In fact, almost 40 percent of college students (according to one survey) will use counseling services during their time in school. Just walk into a student center or counseling office and ask for an appointment. You wouldn't think twice about asking a dentist to help you get rid of your toothache. Counselors are paid—and want—to help you with your problems.

Why Do Some People Make It and Some People Drop Out?

Anyone who spends at least one   25 semester in college notices that some students give up on their classes. The person who sits behind you in accounting, for example, begins to miss a lot of class meetings and eventually vanishes. Or another student comes to class without the assignment, doodles in his notebook during the lecture, and leaves during the break. What's the difference between students like this and the ones who succeed in school? My survey may be unscientific, but everyone I asked said the same thing: attitude. A positive attitude is the key to everything else—good study habits, smart time scheduling, and coping with personal difficulties.

What does "a positive attitude"   26 mean? Well, for one thing, it means not acting like a zombie. It means not only showing up for your classes, but also doing something while you're there.

Really listen. Take notes. Ask a question if you want to. Don't just walk into a class, put your mind in neutral, and drift away to never-never land.

27   Having a positive attitude goes deeper than this, though. It means being mature about college as an institution. Too many students approach college classes like six-year-olds who expect first grade to be as much fun as *Sesame Street*. First grade, as we all know, isn't as much fun as *Sesame Street*. And college classes can sometimes be downright dull and boring. If you let a boring class discourage you so much that you want to leave school, you'll lose in the long run. Look at your priorities. You want a degree, or a certificate, or a career. If you have to, you can make it through a less-than-interesting class in order to achieve what you want. Get whatever you can out of every class. But if you simply can't stand a certain class, be determined to fulfill its requirements and be done with it once and for all.

28   After the initial high of starting school, you have to settle in for the long haul. If you follow the advice here, you'll be prepared to face the academic crunch. You'll also live through the semester without giving up your family, your job, or *Monday Night Football*. Finally, going to college can be an exciting time. As you learn things, the world truly becomes a more interesting place.

Vocabulary Questions

A. Use context clues to help you decide on the best definition for each italicized word. Then, in the space provided, write the letter of your choice.

____B____ 1. In the excerpt below, the word *confronted* (kən-frŭnt′ĭd) means
   A. delighted.
   B. faced.
   C. finished.
   D. forgotten.

   What will you have to do, sooner or later, about midterms, papers, family, and the like?

   "But don't just sit around half the semester planning to get everything together soon. Before you know it, you'll be confronted with midterms, papers, family, and work all at once." (Paragraph 14)

_A_ 2. In the excerpt below, the word *tactics* (tăk′tĭks) means
   A. methods.
   B. reasons.
   C. requirements.
   D. scenes.

   Example clues for tactics:
   "Prepare a monthly calendar. . . .
   Make up a study schedule . . . .
   Use 'to-do' lists."

   "The secret here is to organize your time. . . . try these three tactics: 1. Prepare a monthly calendar. . . . 2. Make up a study schedule. . . . 3. Use 'to-do' lists. . . ." (Paragraphs 14–18)

_A_ 3. In the sentence below, the word *compulsive* (kəm-pŭl′sĭv) means
   A. overly concerned.
   B. careless.
   C. interested.
   D. honest.

   If you're not superhuman and are trying to finish everything, you might be overly concerned about finishing everything on your list.

   "Don't be compulsive about finishing everything; you're not Superman or Wonder Woman." (Paragraph 18)

_C_ 4. In the excerpt below, the word *overwhelming* (ō′vər-hwĕl′mĭng) means
   A. silly.
   B. boring.
   C. overpowering.
   D. enjoyable.

   Antonym-like clue: *least important.*
   Personal troubles such as those mentioned in paragraph 21 can seem too powerful to overcome.

   "Personal troubles like these are overwhelming when you're going through them. School seems like the least important thing in life." (Paragraph 21)

_B_ 5. In the excerpt below, the word *compatible* (kəm-păt′ə-bəl) means
   A. unfriendly.
   B. easy to get along with.
   C. highly intelligent.
   D. concerned only about himself or herself.

   What kind of person would you want to talk to and walk with?

   "Perhaps someone strikes you as a compatible person. Why not speak to that person after class? Share a cup of coffee in the cafeteria or walk to the parking lot together." (Paragraph 23)

B. Below are words, or forms of words, from "Words to Watch." Write in the one that best completes each sentence. Then write the letter of that word in the space provided.

A. distracted	**B. hermit**	**C. hurdle**
D. maintain	**E. relatively**	

Item 7:
Fear of
water is a
difficulty
for someone
trying to
learn to
swim.

___E___ 6. My Spanish class was _____*relatively*_____ easy, but I found general math really difficult. *Compared with* general math, the Spanish class was easy.

___C___ 7. Jasmin's fear of water was a major _____*hurdle*_____ she had to overcome before learning to swim.

___A___ 8. During the play, the actors were obviously _____*distracted*_____ by something going on offstage. Something going on offstage would *sidetrack* the actors.

___D___ 9. The couple tried to _____*maintain*_____ a long-distance relationship, but it came apart. The couple was unable to *keep* the relationship.

___B___ 10. The man who lives in the corner house is such a _____*hermit*_____ that even his next-door neighbors have never met him. If the neighbors have never met the man, he *lives apart from others*.

Reading Comprehension Questions

Central Point and Main Ideas

___B___ 1. Which sentence best expresses the central point of the selection?
   A. Going to college is exciting.
   B. There are ways to succeed in college and stay in control of your life.
   C. Most students are not concerned about staying in college.
   D. College can be confusing and tiring. Answers A and D are too narrow. Answer C is incorrect.

___C___ 2. Which sentence best expresses the main idea of paragraph 27?
   A. First grade is less fun than kindergarten.
   B. College classes are sometimes quite boring.
   C. Students should be mature enough to tackle a class even when it's boring.
   D. A boring class encourages some students to leave school.
   Answers A and B are too narrow because each covers only one detail of the paragraph. Answer D is not supported.

Supporting Details

___C___ 3. The method of time control that was most helpful for the author was
A. a monthly calendar.
B. a study schedule.   See the second sentence of paragraph 18.
C. "to-do" lists.

Transitions

___C___ 4. The sentence below expresses a relationship of
A. illustration.   C. contrast.
B. comparison.   D. cause and effect.

"Don't let yourself reach that breaking point. Instead, try these three
tactics." (Paragraph 14)   Allowing yourself to reach a breaking point is
                                  being contrasted with using tactics to keep from
___D___ 5. The sentence below expresses a relationship of   reaching a breaking point.
A. illustration.   C. contrast.
B. comparison.   D. cause and effect.

"Soon, I started missing classes because I couldn't deal with the academic
pressures as well as my own personal problems." (Paragraph 19)
                              Cause: not being able to deal with pressures and problems.
                                  Effect: started missing classes.

Item 6:
The last
sentence of
paragraph 3 ___A___ 6. Just as paragraphs are organized according to patterns, so are groups
has a list signal: of paragraphs. What is the main pattern of organization of paragraphs
the following eight   3–12?
study tips. Because
they are boldfaced,   A. List of items   C. Definition and example
the eight study tips   B. Time order   D. Comparison-contrast
can be seen
at a glance. ___B___ 7. Paragraph 19 combines the patterns of   The story of Roger's personal
                                          problems is told in time order.
A. list of items and contrast.   The words *until, when,* and *soon* indicate
B. time order and cause-effect.   time order. The relationship between the
C. definition/example and time order.   personal problems (the cause) and
D. definition/example and comparison.   the missed classes (the effect) is
                                          signaled by the word *because.*

___T___ 8. TRUE OR FALSE? Paragraphs 26–27 contrast a positive attitude with a
poor one.   By telling what a positive attitude is *not,*
                              the paragraphs draw a contrast.

Item 9:
See the
first five
sentences ___D___ 9. You can conclude that this article was written for
of paragraph 1.   A. incoming college students who have just completed high school.
Answers A   B. older students returning to college years after high-school graduation.
and B are too narrow.   C. high-school students considering college.
Answer C   D. students of any age who are beginning college.
is not supported.

Patterns of Organization

Inferences

___A___ 10. The author suggests that many students who drop out of college
A. have only themselves to blame.
B. tried their best to do the work, but failed.
C. were good students in high school.
D. spent too much time making friends with classmates.

Paragraphs 25–28 strongly suggest that making different choices and having a different attitude will prevent many students from dropping out of college.

Outlining

Complete the following outline of the selection by filling in the five missing details.

Central point: There are practical steps you can take to make yourself successful in college.   *Wording of answers may vary.*

A. Eight study tips will help:

1. Set up a quiet place to study.

2. *Get into a study frame of mind.*

3. Reward yourself for good studying.

4. Learn to skim a textbook.

5. Take notes on what you're reading.

6. *Review your textbook and your notes.*

7. Take a break when you're tired.

8. Take a study skills course if necessary.

B. Three tactics will help organize time:

1. Prepare a monthly calendar.

2. *Make up a study schedule.*

3. *Use "to-do" lists.*

C. Three approaches to personal problems can help:

1. Ask yourself if you're exaggerating your problems.

2. Make friends with other classmates so you feel less alone.

3. *If your problems are overwhelming, see a counselor.*

D. A positive attitude can help.

Item A2: See paragraph 5. The eight tips are listed by number in paragraphs 4–12.
Item A6: See paragraph 10. The eight tips are listed by number in paragraphs 4–12.
Item B2: See paragraph 16. The three tactics are listed by number in paragraphs 15–18.
Item B3: See paragraph 18. The three tactics are listed by number in paragraphs 15–18.
Item C3: See paragraph 24. The three approaches are discussed in paragraphs 22–24.

Discussion Questions

1. What would you say is the single biggest obstacle between you and better grades? Do you need to get organized? Do you exaggerate your personal problems? How might O'Keeney's article help you overcome this obstacle?

2. Do you make "to-do" lists? If not, do you think you should? What are three items that you would put on your "to-do" list for today?

3. "Sometimes, you've just got to hang tough," O'Keeney tells us (paragraph 21). What does he mean? What are some techniques for hanging tough, instead of giving in, that have worked for you or for people you know?

4. O'Keeney writes in paragraph 27, "Look at your priorities. You want a degree, or a certificate, or a career." What are *your* priorities? Explain the kind of life you hope to have and how college fits into these plans.

Note: Writing assignments for this selection appear on page 598.

Check Your Performance   HOW TO MAKE IT IN COLLEGE

Activity	Number Right	Points		Total
Vocabulary				
A. Vocabulary in Context (5 items)	_____	× 10 =		_____
B. Words to Watch (5 items)	_____	× 10 =		_____
		SCORE =		_____ %
Comprehension				
Central Point and Main Ideas (2 items)	_____	× 8 =		_____
Supporting Details (1 item)	_____	× 8 =		_____
Transitions (2 items)	_____	× 8 =		_____
Patterns of Organization (3 items)	_____	× 8 =		_____
Inferences (2 items)	_____	× 8 =		_____
Summarizing (5 items)	_____	× 4 =		_____
		SCORE =		_____ %

FINAL SCORES: Vocabulary _____ % Comprehension _____ %

Enter your total score into the **Reading Performance Chart: Ten Reading Selections** on the inside back cover.

8 False Ideas about Reading
Robert and Pam Winkler

Preview

Some people see reading as a chore. They try to make reading part of their lives, but doing so seems impossible. Such people may be the victims of certain false ideas about reading. This selection explains three such false notions and how they may keep people from becoming everyday readers.

Words to Watch

sound (3): logical
dry (5): dull, lifeless
commentary (5): explanations or interpretations
plow through (5): to complete a difficult task
assert (6): claim
imprinted (7): clearly impressed
passively (9): inactively
resources (10): knowledge and skills that can be beneficial

1   There are a few false ideas, or myths, that people have about the reading process. These myths prevent them from becoming better readers.

MYTH 1:
You Must Read Every Word

2   Perhaps the most common such myth is that whenever you read a book, you have to read every word. Victims of this myth may not feel it's their duty to read every word in a newspaper or magazine story; but put a book in their hands, and their attitude changes. They treat the book like sacred Scripture and regard every word as a holy thing. Because they think that every word must be carefully read, they are not likely to read anything.

3   In contrast to popular belief, there are two sound° reasons why you need not read every word. First of all, your purpose in reading may not require it. Perhaps you are reading a textbook chapter, and all you need to cover are main ideas. You know this from past tests the teacher has given or because

the teacher has said directly, "All you have to know are the high points of the chapter." In such cases, there may be no need to read many of the supporting details that may occupy 75 percent or more of the space in the chapter. Instead, you might skim the chapter quickly, skipping secondary information and reading only main points and enough details to help you understand those main points. You then have more time to study, learn, and remember those main ideas.

4   Or perhaps you are using the textbook only to supplement class notes, which will be the real basis for a test. All you may need, then, are certain key points from the text to round off ideas in your notes. In that case, you can just scan the text—that is, look it over quickly with the goal of finding the few points you need.

5   The second reason not to read every word is simply that certain material may not interest you. It may bore you because of your personal interests or because the material is dull, or both. If the material is in a class textbook and is important, you have no choice. But if it is in personal reading, you do have a choice—you can simply skip the uninteresting material. Some people, for instance, often skip passages of nature description or dry° commentary°. But many others feel it is their duty to plow through° long, dull passages they could not care less about. In fact, they are so unwilling to skip anything that they are more likely to quit reading altogether.

6   Here is a story that will help you feel less guilty about omitting words. One British writer recalls in her autobiography how shocked she was when her professor at Oxford University said to her, "You will never be a reader unless you learn the art of skipping." She explains how from her earliest years she had been taught that skipping a word in reading was like cheating at cards. Her professor pointed to the books jamming the shelves in his office and said, "Do you mean to assert° that every word in all these volumes is worth reading? You must choose in life what is worth and what is not worth your attention." After this talk with her professor, the woman was able to skip, without guilt, sections of many of the books she read.

MYTH 2:
Reading Once Is Enough

7   Students who believe they must read every word are often victims of a related myth—the idea that reading something once is enough. Such students think that since they forced themselves to read every word, they've done all the work that is necessary. Whatever is important in the book should be imprinted° by then in their brain, ready for them to transfer to a test paper upon command. If there's something they don't know, or don't remember, they think, "It's a lost cause. I'm not going to waste any time trying any further." Or they think, "If one reading isn't enough, it's because I'm

stupid. There's no point in my trying to read any more." Students with such a crazy attitude are good candidates for failure, since one reading is seldom enough for study purposes. Instead, it is often the first step in the mastery of material. Any person with normal intelligence will have to go back, reread the material, and then take notes on the material if he or she hopes to master and remember it.

MYTH 3:
Reading Has to Be Work

8   A final myth about reading, perhaps the worst one of all, is that reading has to be work. It is true that reading is at times a most demanding (and rewarding) effort. But reading doesn't always require hard work. It can be simply for fun, for relaxing pleasure.

9   Unfortunately, students are unlikely to read for fun for two reasons. First, most or all of the reading in school is associated with work. One must do it and then be tested and graded on it. The result of such school experience is that reading is seldom connected with pleasure. Second, students, and people in general, are unlikely to read for entertainment because it is easier to turn on the television. The fact that many people watch television is understandable. Some shows are good, and while many others are trash, even trash can be fun to watch, at least once in a while. After a long, hard day of work, it is relaxing to sit passively° and

unthinkingly, soaking up the bright images that flash across the screen. The danger is that one will sit night after night, for many hours on end, doing nothing but watching television. Then it truly becomes an "idiot box."

10   What many people need to do, in order to widen their experience and resources°, is to learn how to read for pleasure. Unfortunately, people are likely to have the false idea that reading is a chore, not entertainment. The fact is that such people haven't given reading a chance. They should expect to do a bit of work at first, until they become accustomed to the reading process. But if they persist, and if they give a book time to gain their interest, they will almost certainly experience a pleasant surprise. And if one book does not gain their interest, there are many more that

will. They will soon find a whole new source of enjoyment open up to them. It is helpful to remember, too, that reading for pleasure will provide bonuses that other forms of recreation cannot. It will develop word power, improve spelling, increase reading speed, and help people discover and explore parts of themselves that they may not know existed.

11   A simple way to learn pleasure reading is to set aside some time for a book each day. It might be a half hour ordinarily spent watching television or time before going to bed. What is important is that it be a realistic time slot that you can use for reading more or less regularly. What is important, too, is that you persist—that you give a book a chance to catch on, and yourself a chance to get into a book.

To review, then, there are three   12 damaging myths that interfere with good reading. They are that every word must be read, that reading something once should be enough, and that all reading must be work. Be aware of these myths and how they may affect your own attitudes about reading. Don't let any of them prevent you from developing into a better reader.

Vocabulary Questions

A. Use context clues to help you decide on the best definition for each italicized word. Then, in the space provided, write the letter of your choice.

___B___ 1. In the excerpt below, the word *skim* (skĭm) means
   A. read slowly.
   B. glance through.
   C. stare.
   D. labor.

   The sentence shows that to skim is to read "quickly," "skipping" parts—in other words, to glance through the chapter.

   "Instead, you might skim the chapter quickly, skipping secondary information and reading only main points and enough details. . . ." (Paragraph 3)

___C___ 2. In the sentence below, the word *supplement* (sŭp′lə-mənt) means
   A. skip.
   B. avoid.
   C. add to.
   D. decrease.

   If the class notes are the main focus of the test, the text would be used only to add to the notes.

   "Or perhaps you are using the textbook only to supplement class notes, which will be the real basis for a test." (Paragraph 4)

___A___ 3. In the sentence below, the word *jamming* (jăm'ĭng) means
  A. crowding.
  B. lying flat on.
  C. coloring.
  D. absent from.

Since the shelf contains "all these volumes," we can infer that they may be crowding the shelves.

"Her professor pointed to the books jamming the shelves in his office and said, 'Do you mean to assert that every word in all these volumes is worth reading?'" (Paragraph 6)

___B___ 4. In the excerpt below, the word *seldom* (sĕl'dəm) means
  A. usually.
  B. rarely.
  C. always.
  D. luckily.

Antonym clue: *often.*

". . . one reading is seldom enough for study purposes. Instead, it is often the first step in the mastery of material." (Paragraph 7)

___D___ 5. In the excerpt below, the word *persist* (pər-sĭst') means
  A. quit.
  B. forget.
  C. run.
  D. stick with it.

One must stick with it in order to "become accustomed to the reading process" and enjoy "a pleasant surprise."

"They should expect to do a bit of work at first, until they become accustomed to the reading process. But if they persist, . . . they will almost certainly experience a pleasant surprise." (Paragraph 10)

B. Below are words, or forms of words, from "Words to Watch." Write in the one that best completes each sentence. Then write the letter of that word in the space provided.

A. asserted	B. dry	C. passive
D. resources	E. sound	

___B___ 6. Our history teacher's lectures are so _____dry_____ that half the students never listen.

If the students don't listen, the lectures are probably dull.

___C___ 7. After a busy day of work, Keisha likes to spend part of her evening doing something _____passive_____, like listening to music or going on Facebook.

Listening to music and going on Facebook can be inactive pastimes.

___E___ 8. A good argument must include _____sound_____ reasoning.

A good argument must include logical reasoning.

____D____ 9. Part-time jobs that students work at during high school provide them

with _____*resources*_____ that they can use to succeed in full-

time jobs later.   Students can gain *knowledge and skills* that will help

them later succeed in full-time jobs.

____A____ 10. "Wrinkles," _____*asserted*_____ Mark Twain, "should merely

indicate where smiles have been."   Mark Twain *claimed* this about wrinkles.

Reading Comprehension Questions

Central Point and Main Ideas

____B____ 1. Which sentence best expresses the central point of the selection?
  A. Reading requires effort.
  B. Certain myths prevent people from becoming better readers.
  C. It is a myth that you must always read every word.   Answer A is not
  D. Reading once is often not enough.   always correct; answers C and D
    are too narrow because each covers only one detail of the selection.

____D____ 2. Which sentence best expresses the main idea of paragraph 7?
  A. Some students believe one reading is enough for study purposes.
  B. Some students believe that reading more than once is a lost cause.
  C. Some students think only a stupid person needs to read something more than once.
  D. It is a myth that reading once is enough for study purposes.
    Answers A, B, and C are too narrow.

____B____ 3. Which sentence best expresses the main idea of paragraph 11?
  A. Pleasure reading can be learned by reading regularly.
  B. Pleasure reading can be learned by reading regularly and giving a book a chance to catch your interest.
  C. One good time for pleasure reading is a half hour that is usually spent watching television.
  D. You must give a book a chance to catch your interest.
    Answers A, C, and D are too narrow.
    Each covers only one detail of the paragraph.

Supporting Details

____B____ 4. According to the authors, one reason for not reading every word is
  A. you don't have the book.
  B. certain material may not interest you.
  C. the vocabulary may be too difficult.
  D. grades are of secondary importance in a learning experience.
    See the first sentence of paragraph 5.

_D_ 5. For study purposes,
    A. one reading is enough.
    B. read every word.   See the last sentence of paragraph 7.
    C. use only class notes.
    D. reread material and take notes.

Transitions

_C_ 6. The relationship between the two parts of the sentence below is one of
    A. contrast.   *Cause:* people thinking that
    B. time.   every word must be carefully read.
    C. cause and effect.   *Effect:* those people being
    D. addition.   unlikely to read anything.

      "<u>Because</u> they think that every word must be carefully read, they are not likely to read anything." (Paragraph 2)

_B_ 7. The relationship of the second sentence below to the first sentence is one of
    A. addition.   The fact that reading can be demanding is
    B. contrast.   contrasted with the idea that reading
    C. illustration.   does not always require hard work.
    D. time.

      "It is true that reading is at times a most demanding (and rewarding) effort. <u>But</u> reading doesn't always require hard work." (Paragraph 8)

Patterns of Organization

_D_ 8. Just as paragraphs are organized in patterns, so are longer selections. The main pattern of organization of this selection is
    A. time order.   This selection lists and discusses three
    B. definition and example.   myths about reading. Paragraph 12
    C. comparison.   summarizes the selection and contains a
    D. list of items.   list signal: *three damaging myths.*

Inferences

_D_ 9. The authors imply that
    A. schoolwork makes people interested in reading for pleasure.
    B. all television shows are trash.
    C. you should stop reading a book if you don't like the first page.
    D. too few people read purely for enjoyment.
        The statement that "many people need . . . to learn how to read for pleasure" (paragraph 10) implies that too few people are doing so.

_T___ 10. TRUE OR FALSE? The authors imply that reading for pleasure takes some
will power.   Since the authors say that reading for pleasure can
require "a bit of work at first" (paragraph 10),
we can infer that some will power is needed.

Outlining

Prepare an outline of "False Ideas about Reading" by filling in the central point and
the three major supporting details.   *Wording of answers may vary.*

See paragraphs   **Central point:** Three myths about reading keep people from becoming
1 and 12.
better readers.

See paragraphs
2–6.   1. The first myth is that every word must be read.

See paragraph 7.   2. The second myth is that reading once is enough.

See paragraphs   3. The third myth is that reading has to be work.
8–11.

Discussion Questions

1. Which one of the myths about reading is most helpful for you to know about?
    How has this myth affected your reading and study habits?

2. Give an example of someone you know who has been influenced by one of the
    myths about reading. What could you tell this person that might change his or
    her attitude?

3. What do you think are the benefits of not reading every word? What are the
    dangers?

4. The Winklers write that books can "help people discover and explore parts of
    themselves that they may not know existed." What do you mean by this? What
    parts of yourself have books helped you discover and explore? Give examples
    from one or more books you have read.

Note: Writing assignments for this selection appear on pages 598–599.

Check Your Performance   FALSE IDEAS ABOUT READING

Activity	Number Right	Points	Total

Vocabulary

A. Vocabulary in Context (5 items)	_____	× 10 =	_____
B. Words to Watch (5 items)	_____	× 10 =	_____
		SCORE =	_____%

Comprehension

Central Point and Main Ideas (3 items)	_____	× 8 =	_____
Supporting Details (2 items)	_____	× 8 =	_____
Transitions (2 items)	_____	× 8 =	_____
Patterns of Organization (1 item)	_____	× 8 =	_____
Inferences (2 items)	_____	× 8 =	_____
Outlining (4 items)	_____	× 5 =	_____
		SCORE =	_____%

FINAL SCORES: Vocabulary _____% Comprehension _____%

Enter your total score into the **Reading Performance Chart: Ten Reading Selections** on the inside back cover.

9 Dealing with Feelings
Rudolph F. Verderber

Preview

Is it sometimes useful to conceal your feelings when you're hurt? Or when you're angry, is it usually best to simply yell out and let your anger loose? Finally, is it risky to tell others how you really feel? Think of your answers to these questions. Then read the following excerpt from the college textbook *Communicate!*, Sixth Edition, to see what the author says.

Words to Watch

self-disclosure (1): revealing
decipher (2): interpret
seethe (2): boil with emotion
perceived (3): seen
undemonstrative (3): tending not to express feelings
inconsequential (4): unimportant
interpersonally (7): involving relations between people
potential (12): possible
net (14): final
triggered (16): set off
elated (17): very happy

1   An extremely important aspect of self-disclosure° is the sharing of feelings. We all experience feelings such as happiness at receiving an unexpected gift, sadness about the breakup of a relationship, or anger when we believe we have been taken advantage of. The question is whether to disclose such feelings, and if so, how. Self-disclosure of feelings usually will be most successful not when feelings are withheld or displayed but when they are described. Let's consider each of these forms of dealing with feelings.

Withholding Feelings

2   Withholding feelings—that is, keeping them inside and not giving any verbal or nonverbal cues to

their existence—is generally an inappropriate means of dealing with feelings. Withholding feelings is best exemplified by the good poker player who develops a "poker face," a neutral look that is impossible to decipher°. The look is the same whether the player's cards are good or bad. Unfortunately, many people use poker faces in their interpersonal relationships, so that no one knows whether they hurt inside, are extremely excited, and so on. For instance, Doris feels very nervous when Candy stands over her while Doris is working on her report. And when Candy says, "That first paragraph isn't very well written," Doris begins to seethe°, yet she says nothing—she withholds her feelings.

3   Psychologists believe that when people withhold feelings, they can develop physical problems such as ulcers, high blood pressure, and heart disease, as well as psychological problems such as stress-related neuroses and psychoses. Moreover,

people who withhold feelings are often perceived° as cold, undemonstrative°, and not much fun to be around.

4   Is withholding ever appropriate? When a situation is inconsequential°, you may well choose to withhold your feelings. For instance, a stranger's inconsiderate behavior at a party may bother you, but because you can move to another part of the room, withholding may not be detrimental. In the example of Doris seething at Candy's behavior, however, withholding could be costly to Doris.

Displaying Feelings

5   Displaying feelings means expressing those feelings through a facial reaction, body response, and/or spoken reaction. Cheering over a great play at a sporting event, booing the umpire at a perceived bad call, patting a person on the back when the person does something well, or saying, "What are you doing?" in a nasty tone of voice are all displays of feelings.

6   Displays are especially appropriate when the feelings you are experiencing are positive. For instance, when Gloria does something nice for you, and you experience a feeling of joy, giving her a big hug is appropriate; when Don gives you something you've wanted, and you experience a feeling of appreciation, a big smile or an "Oh, thank you, Don" is appropriate. In fact, many people need to be even more demonstrative of good feelings. You've probably seen the

bumper sticker "Have you hugged your kid today?" It reinforces the point that you need to display love and affection constantly to show another person that you really care.

7   Displays become detrimental to communication when the feelings you are experiencing are negative—especially when the display of a negative feeling appears to be an overreaction. For instance, when Candy stands over Doris while she is working on her report and says, "That first paragraph isn't very well written," Doris may well experience resentment. If Doris lashes out at Candy by screaming, "Who the hell asked you for your opinion?" Doris's display no doubt will hurt Candy's feelings and short-circuit their communication. Although displays of negative feelings may be good for you psychologically, they are likely to be bad for you interpersonally°.

Describing Feelings

8   Describing feelings—putting your feelings into words in a calm, nonjudgmental way—tends to be the best method of disclosing feelings. Describing feelings not only increases chances for positive communication and decreases chances for short-circuiting lines of communication; it also teaches people how to treat you. When you describe your feelings, people are made aware of the effect of their behavior. This knowledge gives them the information needed to determine whether they should continue or repeat that behavior. If you tell Paul that you really feel flattered when he visits you, such a statement should encourage Paul to visit you again; likewise, when you tell Cliff that you feel very angry when he borrows your jacket without asking, he is more likely to ask the next time he borrows a jacket. Describing your feelings allows you to exercise a measure of control over others' behavior toward you.

9   Describing and displaying feelings are not the same. Many times people think they are describing when in fact they are displaying feelings or evaluating.

10   If describing feelings is so important to communicating effectively, why don't more people do it regularly? There seem to be at least four reasons why many people don't describe feelings.

11   1.   *Many people have a poor vocabulary of words for describing the various feelings they are experiencing.* People can sense that they are angry; however, they may not know whether what they are feeling might best be described as annoyed, betrayed, cheated, crushed, disturbed, furious, outraged, or shocked. Each of these words describes a slightly different aspect of what many people lump together as anger.

12   2.   *Many people believe that describing their true feelings reveals too much about themselves.* If you tell people

when their behavior hurts you, you risk their using the information against you when they want to hurt you on purpose. Even so, the potential° benefits of describing your feelings far outweigh the risks. For instance, if Pete has a nickname for you that you don't like, and you tell Pete that calling you by that nickname really makes you nervous and tense, Pete may use the nickname when he wants to hurt you, but he is more likely to stop calling you by that name. If, on the other hand, you don't describe your feelings to Pete, he is probably going to call you by that name all the time because he doesn't know any better. When you say nothing, you reinforce his behavior. The level of risk varies with each situation, but you will more often improve a relationship than be hurt by describing feelings.

13   3.   *Many people believe that if they describe feelings, others will make them feel guilty about having such feelings.* At a very tender age, we all learned about "tactful" behavior. Under the premise that "the truth sometimes hurts," we learned to avoid the truth by not saying anything or by telling "little" lies. Perhaps, when you were young, your mother said, "Don't forget to give Grandma a great big kiss." At that time you may have blurted out, "Ugh—it makes me feel yucky to kiss Grandma. She's

got a mustache." If your mother responded, "That's terrible—your grandma loves you. Now you give her a kiss, and never let me hear you talk like that again!" then you probably felt guilty for having this "wrong" feeling. But the point is that the thought of kissing your grandma made you feel "yucky" whether it should have or not. In this case, what was at issue was the way you talked about the feelings—not your having the feelings.

4.   *Many people believe that describing*   14 *feelings causes harm to others or to a relationship.* If it really bothers Max when his girlfriend, Dora, bites her fingernails, Max may believe that describing his feelings to Dora will hurt her so much that the knowledge will drive a wedge into their relationship. So it's better for Max to say nothing, right? Wrong! If Max says nothing, he's still going to be bothered by Dora's behavior. In fact, as time goes on, Max will probably lash out at Dora for other things because he can't bring himself to talk about the behavior that really bothers him. The net° result is that not only will Dora be hurt by Max's behavior, but she won't understand the true source of his feelings. By not describing his feelings, Max may well drive a wedge into their relationship anyway.

5.   If Max does describe his feelings to   15 Dora, she might quit or at least try

to quit biting her nails; they might get into a discussion in which he finds out that she doesn't want to bite them but just can't seem to stop, and he can help her in her efforts to stop; or they might discuss the problem and Max may see that it is really a small thing and not let it bother him as much. The point is that in describing feelings, the chances of a successful outcome are greater than they are in not describing them.

16   To describe your feelings, first put the emotion you are feeling into words. Be specific. Second, state what triggered° the feeling. Finally, make sure you indicate that the feeling is yours. For example, suppose your roommate borrows your jacket without asking. When he returns, you describe your feelings by saying, "Cliff, I [indication that the feeling is yours] get really angry [the feeling] when you borrow my jacket

without asking [trigger]." Or suppose that Carl has just reminded you of the very first time he brought you a rose. You describe your feelings by saying, "Carl, I [indication that the feeling is yours] get really tickled [the feeling] when you remind me about that first time you brought me a rose [trigger]."

You may find it easiest to begin by   17 describing positive feelings: "I really feel elated° knowing that you were the one who nominated me for the position" or "I'm delighted that you offered to help me with the housework." As you gain success with positive descriptions, you can try negative feelings attributable to environmental factors: "It's so cloudy; I feel gloomy" or "When the wind howls through the cracks, I really get jumpy." Finally, you can move to negative descriptions resulting from what people have said or done: "Your stepping in front of me like that really annoys me" or "The tone of your voice confuses me."

Vocabulary Questions

A. Use context clues to help you decide on the best definition for each italicized word. Then, in the space provided, write the letter of your choice.

___B___ 1. In the excerpt below, the word *exemplified* (ĭg-zĕm′plə-fīd′) means
      A. challenged.
      B. illustrated.   The poker player is an example (illustration)
      C. surprised.   of withholding feelings.
      D. stolen.

"Withholding feelings is best exemplified by the good poker player who develops a 'poker face,' a neutral look. . . ." (Paragraph 2)

___D___ 2. In the sentence below, the word *detrimental* (dĕt′rə-mĕn′tl) means
      A. useful.
      B. private.   In the example given, withholding
      C. helpless.   may not be harmful.
      D. harmful.

"For instance, a stranger's inconsiderate behavior at a party may bother you, but because you can move to another part of the room, withholding may not be detrimental." (Paragraph 4)

___C___ 3. In the sentence below, the word *premise* (prĕm′ĭs) means
      A. question.
      B. choice.   "The truth sometimes hurts" is a belief.
      C. belief.   It is not a question, a choice, or a disagreement.
      D. disagreement.

"Under the premise that 'the truth sometimes hurts,' we learned to avoid the truth by not saying anything or by telling 'little' lies." (Paragraph 13)

___A___ 4. In the sentence below, the word *wedge* (wĕj) means
      A. something that divides.
      B. loyalty.   What does Max believe describing his
      C. friendship.   feelings will do to the relationship?
      D. many years.

"Max may believe that describing his feelings to Dora will hurt her so much that the knowledge will drive a wedge into their relationship." (Paragraph 14)

_B_   5. In the excerpt below, the words *attributable to* (ə-trĭb′yoō-tə-bəl toō) mean
   A. that cannot be explained by.
   B. that can be explained by.
   C. unrelated to.
   D. confused by.

> The negative feelings are due to and explained by environmental factors.

> "As you gain success with positive descriptions [of feelings], you can try negative feelings attributable to environmental factors: 'It's so cloudy; I feel gloomy. . . .'" (Paragraph 17)

B. Below are words, or forms of words, from "Words to Watch." Write in the one that best completes each sentence. Then write the letter of that word in the space provided.

A. decipher	B. elated	C. inconsequential
D. perceived	E. seethe	

_D_   6. Charlene was _____*perceived*_____ as being cold, but in reality she was just very shy.

> Charlene was *seen* as being cold.

_E_   7. Reading about all the tax breaks that the rich get makes me _____*seethe*_____.

> The tax breaks for the rich make the person *boil with emotion.*

_A_   8. Ellie recognized her baby's various cries so well that she could _____*decipher*_____ the meaning of each one.

> If Ellie recognized the various cries, she could *interpret* each one.

_C_   9. By the time people have several years of success in a career, their school records usually become _____*inconsequential*_____.

> Several years of success in a career tend to make school records *unimportant.*

_B_   10. Howard was _____*elated*_____ to learn he got an A in biology.

> The A in biology made Howard *very happy.*

Reading Comprehension Questions

Central Point and Main Ideas

___B___ 1. Which sentence best expresses the central point of the selection?
   A. Everyone has feelings.
   B. There are three ways to deal with feelings; describing them is most useful for educating others about how you want to be treated.
   C. Withholding feelings means not giving verbal or nonverbal clues that might reveal those feelings to others.
   D. Expressing feelings often leads to problems with others.
   Answer A is too broad. Answers C and D are too narrow.

___D___ 2. Which sentence best expresses the main idea of paragraph 3?
   A. Withholding negative feelings may lead to physical problems.
   B. Withholding negative feelings may lead to psychological problems.
   C. Withholding positive feelings can make one seem cold.
   D. Withholding feelings has several disadvantages.   Answers A, B, and C are too narrow. Each describes only one disadvantage.

___A___ 3. Which sentence best expresses the main idea of paragraph 8?
   A. Describing your feelings can influence others' behavior toward you.
   B. It is possible to encourage friends to visit you again.
   C. It is possible to encourage friends to ask before they borrow things from you.   Answers B and C are too narrow;
   D. It is possible to encourage friends.   answer D is too broad.

Supporting Details

___A___ 4. According to the author, you are more likely to create physical problems for yourself by
   A. withholding your feelings.   See the first sentence in paragraph 3.
   B. displaying your positive feelings.
   C. describing your positive feelings.
   D. describing your negative feelings.

___C___ 5. Describing your feelings means
   A. keeping your feelings inside.   See the first sentence in paragraph 8.
   B. giving a nonverbal response to feelings.
   C. putting your feelings into words.
   D. telling "little" lies.

Transitions

___C___ 6. The two parts of the sentence below express a relationship of
    A. time.
    B. addition.   The sentence contrasts the good psychological
    C. contrast.   effect with the bad interpersonal effect.
    D. comparison.

    "<u>Although</u> displays of negative feelings may be good for you psychologically, they are more likely to be bad for you interpersonally." (Paragraph 7)

7. The two illustration words in paragraph 4 are _____*For instance*_____
   and _____*example*_____.

Patterns of Organization

___C___ 8. The author develops paragraph 5 with
    A. a contrast.
    B. a comparison.   The paragraph defines and provides
    C. a definition and examples.   examples of the concept of
    D. time order.   describing feelings.

Inferences

___B___ 9. From the reading, we can conclude that describing feelings
    A. is usually easy for people.   In paragraph 8, the author
    B. is often a good way to solve problems.   states that describing feelings
    C. should be done only for positive feelings.   "allows you to exercise a measure of control
    D. should make you feel guilty.   over others' behavior toward you," thereby correcting some situations.

___C___ 10. Which sentence can we conclude is an example of displaying a feeling?
    A. Sonia refused to tell Tom that she hated his haircut.
    B. Betty told her son, "I enjoy reading your letters so much."
    C. The father clapped joyfully when the baby said, "Dada."
    D. Hakim avoided Jackie because he had forgotten her birthday.
      By clapping, the father displayed happiness when the baby called his "name."

Mapping

Below is a map of "Dealing with Feelings." Complete the map by filling in the central point (which Verderber presents in the first paragraph of the passage) and the three major supporting details.

Wording of answers may vary.

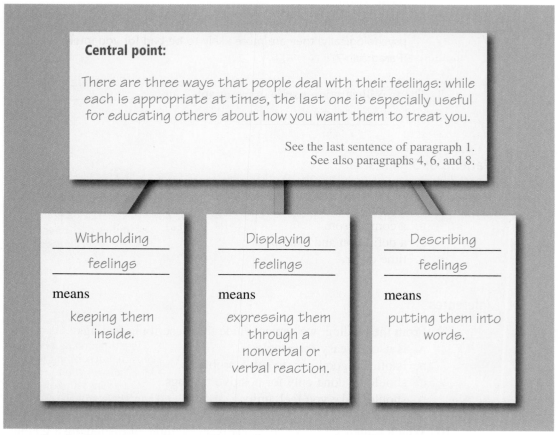

Central point:

There are three ways that people deal with their feelings: while each is appropriate at times, the last one is especially useful for educating others about how you want them to treat you.

See the last sentence of paragraph 1.
See also paragraphs 4, 6, and 8.

<u>Withholding</u>
<u>feelings</u>

means

keeping them inside.

<u>Displaying</u>
<u>feelings</u>

means

expressing them through a nonverbal or verbal reaction.

<u>Describing</u>
<u>feelings</u>

means

putting them into words.

See the first sentence of paragraph 2.

See the first sentence of paragraph 5.

See the first sentence of paragraph 8.

Discussion Questions

1. What is the difference between describing feelings and displaying them? How might Doris describe her feelings to Candy after Candy says, "That first paragraph isn't very well written" (paragraph 2)?

2. What do you think would be Verderber's advice on "little lies"? (See paragraph 13.)

3. Why do you think Verderber emphasizes describing feelings over the other two methods of dealing with feelings?

4. What are some examples from your own experience of withholding, expressing or displaying, and describing feelings? How useful was each method?

Note: Writing assignments for this selection appear on page 599.

Check Your Performance   **DEALING WITH FEELINGS**

Activity	Number Right	Points	Total
Vocabulary			
A. Vocabulary in Context (5 items)	_____	× 10 =	_____
B. Words to Watch (5 items)	_____	× 10 =	_____
		SCORE =	_____ %
Comprehension			
Central Point and Main Ideas (3 items)	_____	× 8 =	_____
Supporting Details (2 items)	_____	× 8 =	_____
Transitions (2 items)	_____	× 8 =	_____
Patterns of Organization (1 item)	_____	× 8 =	_____
Inferences (2 items)	_____	× 8 =	_____
Mapping (4 items)	_____	× 5 =	_____
		SCORE =	_____ %

FINAL SCORES: Vocabulary _____ % Comprehension _____ %

Enter your total score into the **Reading Performance Chart: Ten Reading Selections** on the inside back cover.

10 Childhood Stress and Resilience
Diana E. Papalia and Sally Wendkos Olds

Preview

Have you ever met people who, despite misfortunes, seem to be able to recover unharmed? Have you ever wondered why those people could successfully deal with problems that would have stopped others? In the following selection from the college psychology textbook *A Child's World*, Sixth Edition, the authors search for answers to these questions. They explore factors that enable some children to bounce back from hardship, and they note that any person may find the strength to rise above difficult circumstances.

Words to Watch

resilience (title): ability to recover strength or good spirits quickly
sibling (1): brother or sister
subject to (4): to cause to experience
resourceful (6): able to deal well with new situations and problems
hereditary (8): passed down genetically from generation to generation
adaptable (9): able to adjust well
consoles (9): comforts
adverse (12): unfavorable, harmful
compensate (13): make up for

1   Stressful events are part of every childhood. Illness, the birth of a sibling°, frustration, and parents' temporary absence are common sources of stress. Other nonroutine stresses are all too likely to occur in a child's world. Divorce or death of parents, hospitalization, and the day-in, day-out grind of poverty affect many children. Some children survive wars and earthquakes. The increase in the number of homeless families in the United States has brought severe psychological difficulties to children. Violent events like kidnappings and playground sniper attacks make children realize that their world is not always safe and that parents cannot always protect them. This realization is stressful to children in the short run and may affect them in the long run as well.

What Children Are Afraid Of

Adults have become increasingly concerned about the number of dangers facing children and worry about children's own fears of personal or global catastrophe. Children do have anxieties about homelessness, AIDS, drug abuse, crime, and nuclear war, but most childhood fears are about things much closer to youngsters' daily lives. According to research in six countries—Australia, Canada, Egypt, Japan, the Philippines, and the United States—children from many different cultures are remarkably alike in what they are afraid of.

When third- through ninth-grade children were asked to rank a list of twenty events in order of how upsetting they would be, the primary fear among children in each country was the same: fear of losing a parent. Close in importance to this were events that would embarrass children—being kept back in school, wetting their pants in public, or being sent to the principal.

Surprisingly, children of every country rated the birth of a new sibling least upsetting of all (perhaps, at this age, children are so busy outside the home that they are less affected by a new arrival—or at age 8 and older, few were dealing with the birth of a new baby). Boys and girls rated events about the same; by and large, so did children of different ages.

For most children, school is a source of insecurity—partly because it is so important in their lives and partly because so many belittling practices (like accusing children of lying, or ridiculing them in class) flourish there. Adults can stem fears by respecting children, encouraging them to talk about their worries, and not expecting fears to simply disappear.

Most childhood fears are normal, and overcoming them helps children grow, achieve identity, and master their world.

Children's fears reflect their awareness of many modern stresses, as seen in the box above.

2   Children today have new pressures to cope with. Because families move around more than they used to, children are more likely to change schools and friends and less likely to know many adults well. They know more than children of previous generations did about technology, sex, and violence; and when they live in single-parent homes or have to consider parents' work schedules, they are likely to shoulder adult responsibilities.

The child psychologist David Elkind   3 has called today's child the "hurried child." Like some other thoughtful observers, he is concerned that the pressures of life today are making children grow up too soon and are making their shortened childhood too stressful. Today's children are pressured to succeed in school, to compete in sports, and to meet parents' emotional needs. Children are exposed to many adult problems on television and in real life before they have mastered the problems of childhood. Yet children are not small adults. They feel and think like children, and they need these years of childhood for healthy development.

4   Sometimes a child's healthy development is thwarted by the very people expected to help it—the parents, who subject° their children to physical abuse or psychological maltreatment. Some children, however, known as "resilient" children, are able to overcome enormous life stress.

Coping with Stress: The Resilient Child

5   The effects of stress are unpredictable because people are unpredictable. Children's reactions to stressful events may depend on such factors as the event itself (children respond differently to a parent's death and to divorce), the child's age (preschoolers and adolescents react differently), and the child's sex (boys are more vulnerable than girls). Yet of two children of the same age and sex who are exposed to the same stressful experience, one may crumble while the other remains whole and healthy. Why is this so?

6   **Resilient children** are those who bounce back from circumstances that would blight the emotional development of most children. They are the children of the ghetto who go on to distinguish themselves in the professions. They are the neglected or abused children who go on to form intimate relationships, be good parents to their own children, and lead fulfilling lives. In spite of the bad cards they have been dealt, these children are winners. They are creative, resourceful°, independent, and enjoyable to be with. What is special about them?

7   Several studies have identified "protective factors" that may operate to reduce the effects of such stressors as kidnapping or poor parenting. Several of these factors may also protect children who have been psychologically abused.

8   Are some children born with stress-proof personalities? Or can children develop resilience? There has been little research on hereditary° factors

in handling stress or on the effect of differences in temperament, which seems to be partly hereditary. Factors like the following seem to contribute to children's resilience:

9   • *Personality*. Resilient children tend to be adaptable°. They are usually positive thinkers, friendly, sensitive to other people, and independent. They feel competent and have high self-esteem. Intelligence, too, may be a factor: good students seem to cope better. These children are often able to diminish the importance of their problems by the way they look at them—as does the child hero of the movie *My Life As a Dog*, who consoles° himself by thinking, "It could always be worse."

10   • *Family*. Resilient children are likely to have good relationships with parents who are emotionally supportive of them and each other, or, failing that, to have a close relationship with at least one parent. If they lack even this, they are likely to be close to at least one other adult who shows interest in them and obviously cares for them, and whom they trust. Resilient abused children are likely to have been abused by only one parent rather than both and to have had a loving, supportive relationship with one parent or a foster parent when growing up.

11   • *Learning experiences*. Resilient children are likely to have had experience solving social problems.

They have seen parents, older siblings, or others dealing with frustration and making the best of a bad situation. They have faced challenges themselves, worked out solutions, and learned that they can exert some control over their lives.

12   • *Reduced risk*. Children who have been exposed to only one of a number of factors strongly related to psychiatric disorder (such as discord between the parents, low social status, overcrowding at home, a disturbed mother, a criminal father, and experience in foster care or an institution) are often able to overcome the stress. But when two or more of these factors are present, children's risk of developing an emotional disturbance increases fourfold or more. When children are not besieged on all sides, they can often cope with adverse° circumstances.

13   • *Compensating experiences*. A supportive school environment and successful experiences in sports, in music, or with other children or interested adults can help make up for a dismal home life. In adulthood, a good marriage can compensate° for poor relationships earlier in life.

14   All this research, of course, does not mean that what happens in a child's life does not matter. In general, children with an unfavorable background have more problems in adjustment than children with a favorable background. What is

heartening about these findings is the recognition that childhood experiences do not necessarily determine the outcome of a person's life, that many people do have the strength to rise above the most difficult circumstances, and that we are constantly rewriting the stories of our lives as long as we live.

Vocabulary Questions

A. Use context clues to help you decide on the best definition for each italicized word. Then, in the space provided, write the letter of your choice.

___B___ 1. In the excerpt below, the word *shoulder* (shōl′dər) means
    A. resent.
    B. take on.
    C. desire.
    D. remember.

> What are the children likely to do with adult responsibilities in single-parent homes?

". . . when [children] live in single-parent homes or have to consider parents' work schedules, they are likely to shoulder adult responsibilities." (Paragraph 2)

___D___ 2. In the sentence below, the word *thwarted* (thwôr′tĭd) means
    A. encouraged.
    B. taken care of.
    C. known.
    D. prevented.

> Physical abuse or psychological maltreatment would tend to prevent a child's healthy development.

"Sometimes a child's healthy development is thwarted by the very people expected to help it—the parents, who subject their children to physical abuse or psychological maltreatment." (Paragraph 4)

___C___ 3. In the sentence below, the word *blight* (blīt) means
    A. satisfy.
    B. have no effect on.
    C. greatly harm.
    D. encourage.

> Children who can recover quickly will "bounce back" from something that would greatly harm most children.

"Resilient children are those who bounce back from circumstances that would blight the emotional development of most children." (Paragraph 6)

_D_   4. In the excerpt below, the word *discord* (dĭs′kôrd′) means
   A. agreement.
   B. conversation.
   C. closeness.
   D. conflict.

> *What would exist between parents that could contribute to a psychiatric disorder?*

"Children who have been exposed to only one of a number of factors strongly related to psychiatric disorder (such as discord between the parents, low social status . . .) are often able to overcome the stress." (Paragraph 12)

_C_   5. In the sentence below, the word *besieged* (bĭ-sējd′) means
   A. behind.
   B. agreeable.
   C. surrounded by unfriendly forces.
   D. encouraged to do better.

> *The words on all sides suggest being surrounded; adverse circumstances suggests the presence of something negative.*

"When children are not besieged on all sides, they can often cope with adverse circumstances." (Paragraph 12)

B. Below are words, or forms of words, from "Words to Watch." Write in the one that best completes each sentence. Then write the letter of that word in the space provided.

A. adverse	**B.** compensate	**C.** console
D. resilience	**E.** subject	

_A_   6. Gina decided to cancel her trip and stay at home when she heard about the _____adverse_____ weather conditions.   *Unfavorable weather conditions would cause Gina to cancel her trip.*

Item 8:
Being a superior student could *make up for* Jill's poor athletic skills.

_C_   7. One of the duties of a camp counselor is to _____console_____ young campers who are homesick.   *A homesick young camper needs to be comforted.*

_B_   8. To _____compensate_____ for her poor athletic skills, Jill decided that she would make herself a superior student.

Item 9:
Weeds that return after being sprayed have the *ability to recover strength quickly.*

_D_   9. Fred was impressed by the _____resilience_____ of the weeds in his garden; they returned even after he sprayed them with weed killer.

_E_   10. The concerned mother left the movie theater because she didn't want to _____subject_____ her child to the obscene language in the film.   *If the mother left the theater, she didn't want to cause her child to experience the obscene language.*

Reading Comprehension Questions

Central Point and Main Ideas

__C__   1. Which sentence best expresses the central point of the selection?
   A. Children today experience much more stress than children did in the past.
   B. A supportive school environment and successful experiences in activities such as sports or music can help make up for a troubled home life.
   C. Although nearly all children experience stress that may affect them negatively later in life, much can be learned by studying resilient children.
   D. The increase in the number of homeless families in the United States has brought severe psychological difficulties to children.

   Answers A, B, and D are too narrow.

__A__   2. The main idea of paragraph 1 is best expressed in its
   A. first sentence.
   B. second sentence.
   C. next-to-last sentence.
   D. last sentence.

   The paragraph lists examples of the idea stated in the first sentence—that stress is part of childhood.

__A__   3. The main idea of paragraph 2 is best expressed in its
   A. first sentence.
   B. second sentence.
   C. last sentence.
   D. none of the above.

   Sentence 1 contains a list signal: *new pressures.* The rest of the paragraph presents examples of the new pressures mentioned in the first sentence.

__B__   4. Which sentence best expresses the main idea of paragraph 3?
   A. Today's children are pressured to succeed in school and compete in sports.
   B. The pressures of life today force children to grow up quickly and often make their shortened childhood too stressful.
   C. Children are exposed to many adult problems on television.
   D. There are many pressures on today's children.

   Answers A and C are too narrow; each states only one detail of the paragraph. Answer D is also too narrow; it does not mention the negative results of the pressures.

Supporting Details

__C__   5. Resilient children tend to have
   A. low self-esteem.
   B. little experience in solving social problems.
   C. a close relationship with at least one parent or other adult.
   D. foster parents.

   See paragraph 10.

Transitions

_B_   6. The relationship of the second sentence to the first is one of
     A. an example.
     B. contrast.
     C. addition.
     D. time.

> The fact that children must deal with adult problems is contrasted with the fact that children are not adults.

> "Children are exposed to many adult problems on television and in real life before they have mastered the problems of childhood. Yet children are not small adults." (Paragraph 3)

_D_   7. The sentence below expresses a relationship of
     A. time.
     B. illustration.
     C. contrast.
     D. cause and effect.

> *Cause:* Families move around more.
> *Effect:* Children change schools more and know fewer adults well.

> "Because families move around more than they used to, children are more likely to change schools and friends and less likely to know many adults well." (Paragraph 2)

Patterns of Organization

_A_   8. The main pattern of organization of paragraph 6 is
     A. definition and example.
     B. comparison.
     C. list of items.
     D. time order.

> The first sentence defines "resilient children"; the rest of the paragraph provides examples of them.

Inferences

Item 9:
Much childhood fear centered on school experiences suggests that educators cause the fear; examples are being accused of lying or being ridiculed.

_D_   9. From the information in the box on page 517, we can conclude that
     A. childhood fears have remained the same throughout the centuries.
     B. boys and girls have remarkably different fears.
     C. parents are less important to third- to ninth-graders than people think.
     D. educators add to children's fears.

_B_   10. We can conclude that compensating experiences
     A. always occur alone.
     B. provide a sense of support and achievement.
     C. can occur only during childhood.
     D. can harm the development of children who have a lot of stress at home.

> See paragraph 13, which lists experiences that provide support and achievement.

Summarizing

Complete the following summary of "Childhood Stress and Resilience" by filling in the blanks.   *Wording of answers may vary.*

Stressful events are part of every childhood. However, children today have new pressures to deal with. These pressures, such as _____

See paragraph 1.

divorce or death of parents, hospitalization, poverty, wars, _____

earthquake, homelessness, and violence _____,

See paragraph 4.

result in more stress for children. In addition to the stresses of the modern world, some children experience physical or _____*psychological*_____ maltreatment from the very people who are supposed to support their healthy development: their parents. The effects of these stresses on children are unpredictable because children are unpredictable. However, it is known that some children seem to be able to bounce back from unfortunate circumstances that other children would not have been able to overcome. These children are known as

See paragraph 4.

_____*resilient children*_____. Factors which researchers feel contribute to

See paragraphs 10–13.

childhood resilience cover the following areas: personality, _*family, learning*_

experiences, reduced risk, and compensating experiences. _____.

Such findings are encouraging because they show we are able to overcome even very difficult circumstances and make positive changes in our lives.

Discussion Questions

1. How has childhood changed since you were young? How was your own childhood different from that of your parents? What was better about your childhood as compared with childhood today? As compared with your parents' childhood? What was worse?

2. Do you recall any experiences that you found particularly stressful as a child? If so, how did you deal with them?

3. The author states that children today are forced to grow up too quickly. What are some of the things that you believe children need time to learn and experience as children?

4. Sometimes a child's healthy development is hindered by the very people who are supposed to encourage it—the child's parents, relatives, or friends. What do you believe could be done to prevent child abuse (both physical and mental)? Why do you think child abuse is so common in the United States?

Note: Writing assignments for this selection appear on pages 599–600.

Check Your Performance   **CHILDHOOD STRESS AND RESILIENCE**

Activity	Number Right	Points	Total
Vocabulary			
A. Vocabulary in Context (5 items)	_____	× 10 =	_____
B. Words to Watch (5 items)	_____	× 10 =	_____
		SCORE =	_____ %
Comprehension			
Central Point and Main Ideas (4 items)	_____	× 8 =	_____
Supporting Details (1 item)	_____	× 8 =	_____
Transitions (2 items)	_____	× 8 =	_____
Patterns of Organization (1 item)	_____	× 8 =	_____
Inferences (2 items)	_____	× 8 =	_____
Summarizing (4 items)	_____	× 5 =	_____
		SCORE =	_____ %

FINAL SCORES: Vocabulary _____ %   Comprehension _____ %

Enter your total score into the **Reading Performance Chart: Ten Reading Selections** on the inside back cover.

Part Three

Active Reading and Combined-Skills Tests

1 An Introduction to Active Reading

Two Kinds of Readers

Many people are passive rather than active readers. Read the following description of passive and active readers and check (✓) the kind of reader that more fairly describes you. (It's OK to be honest.)

____ **Passive readers** read word after word without thinking much. Their attention may wander because they don't become interested in what they're reading. And since they aren't thinking about the material, they are likely to miss the main ideas and important details.

____ **Active readers** interest themselves by becoming involved in what they're reading. They think about what they read and ask themselves questions. Such active reading helps them to concentrate on what the author has to say. As a result, they are more likely than passive readers to understand and remember what they have read.

If you checked the first description, don't worry. You have already taken steps to break the habit of passive reading. With most chapters in this book, you have practiced an active reading skill:

- Guessing at the meaning of unfamiliar words
- Finding main ideas
- Recognizing key supporting details
- Understanding transitional words
- Identifying patterns of organization
- Making inferences
- Recognizing point and support

The goal of Part Three is to make you an active reader who is able to apply all of the skills, as needed. While you will practice here on short passages like those in standardized tests, the skills apply to material of any length.

Becoming an Active Reader

The following tips will help you read actively:

 TIP 1   When you read a passage for the first time, try to read it straight through. Frequent stops along the way will interfere with your getting the big picture. Don't feel you have to understand everything the first time through. Instead, focus on steady, active reading. After you have a good overall sense of the material, you can then go back to reread parts that were not clear at first.

 TIP 2   As you read, think about the main idea. Look for the main idea in the opening sentence or two. Ask yourself, "Is the main idea in one of these sentences? If not, where is it?" Just by asking this question, you'll get a head start on finding the main idea.

 TIP 3   As you read, think about the supporting details. As you continue reading the passage, actively ask yourself, "What is the main idea, and what is the support for that idea?" Again, asking questions helps you look for the answers. And if the main idea is unstated, the supporting details will help you figure out what the main idea is.

 TIP 4   As you read, look for relationships. Are there transitions that tell you, for example, that a list is being presented, or that two things are being contrasted, or that causes are being explained? Finding relationships is an important aid in understanding what you read.

 TIP 5   Along the way, make reasonable guesses. See if you can guess the meaning of any unknown words by looking at their context. And try to "read between the lines," guessing at some of the author's unstated meanings, when that seems to makes sense.

 TIP 6   Reread as needed. Almost no one reads something just once and comes away with full comprehension. Instead, a careful first reading is often the first stage of understanding. Plan to go back and reread parts of the material as needed to gradually deepen your comprehension.

Most of all, the active reader is always trying to get to the heart of a passage: its main idea and the major details that support that idea. The two parts always go together; you cannot fully understand one without the other.

By now you may be saying to yourself, "Good grief. Active reading is asking a lot. I'm supposed to read a passage quickly but carefully, trying to understand it as best I can. I'm also supposed to be thinking about the main idea and its support as well as about relationships and implied ideas. Isn't this too much to do all at once?" The answer is definitely "No!" If you have the desire and if you practice, you will become a more effective reader.

A Model Passage

Read the passage below as quickly as you can with understanding. Look for the main idea in the opening sentence or two, and look for supporting details for the main idea. Then answer the questions and read the explanations that follow.

[1]Elephants attracted to the odor of brewing beer have brought terror to some Indian villages. [2]The beer is made from rice and is brewed after the rice harvest. [3]The smell of the brew in one remote village attracted thirteen elephants, who drank the town's beer. [4]Then they marched drunkenly through town, searching for more. [5]In the process, they killed five people and injured twelve. [6]Two thousand residents were forced to flee. [7]Recently, similar disturbances by elephants have taken place in many villages, devastating more than fifteen thousand acres of rice paddies in one month.

____A____ 1. In sentence 7, the word *devastating* means
   A. destroying.
   B. avoiding.
   C. planting.
   D. burning.

____A____ 2. Which sentence expresses the main idea of the passage?
   A. "Elephants attracted to the odor of brewing beer have brought terror to some Indian villages."
   B. "The smell of the brew in one remote village attracted thirteen elephants, who drank the town's beer."
   C. "Two thousand residents were forced to flee."
   D. "Recently, similar disturbances by elephants have taken place in many villages, devastating more than fifteen thousand acres of rice paddies in one month."

____T____ 3. TRUE OR FALSE? The elephants get drunk from rice beer.

_C_   4. The answer to question 3 can be found in sentence
      A. 1.
      B. 3.
      C. 4.
      D. 7.

_C_   5. The idea below is
      A. true according to the paragraph.
      B. false according to the paragraph.
      C. not mentioned in the paragraph.

      Elephants have been causing destruction in Indian villages for years.

_C_   6. Rice beer is brewed
      A. all year.
      B. before the rice harvest.
      C. after the rice harvest.
      D. every other year.

_B_   7. The relationship between sentences 3 and 4 is one of
      A. definition and example.
      B. time.
      C. contrast.
      D. comparison.

_C_   8. The passage implies that
      A. rice beer is no longer being made in India.
      B. the beer was brewed for the elephants.
      C. rice is an important crop in India.
      D. in India, rice is grown to feed the elephants.

Explanation

1. To find out the meaning of *devastating*, you could have asked, "What would drunken elephants do to acres of rice paddies that would be considered 'disturbances'?" Then you would have guessed the correct meaning of *devastating*: "destroying." So the answer to this question is A.

2. If you read the first sentence actively, you would have thought, "Is this sentence supported by the rest of the paragraph? Will I get details about terror in Indian villages?" In fact, you do, and the first sentence is the main idea. So the answer to this question is A.

3. Careful reading reveals that the answer to question 3 is *true*.

    > *Hint:* When questioned on a detail that you're not sure about, pick out key words in the question and look for those words in the passage. The key words in the question are *drunk* and *rice beer*. As you look for these key words in the passage, you quickly see that the elephants drank the beer and "marched drunkenly" through the town.

4. The answer is C—the answer to the third question can be found in sentence 4 in the words *they marched drunkenly*. Those words make it clear that elephants do, in fact, get drunk from the beer.

5. The answer is C, for the paragraph does not mention how long elephants have been causing the destruction. If you weren't sure of the answer to this question, a quick rereading would have given you the answer.

6. The answer to this question is C because sentence 2 tells us that the beer "is brewed after the rice harvest."

7. The answer is B. The transition *then* at the beginning of sentence 4 signals a time relationship: First, the elephants drank the town's beer; and after that, they marched through town, searching for more.

8. The correct answer is C. Sentence 7 tells us that many villages grow thousands of acres of rice. Nothing in the passage hints at answers A, B, or D.

Check Your Understanding

Again, read the paragraph below as quickly as you can with understanding. Look for the main idea in the opening sentences, and look for supporting details for this idea. Then answer the questions and read the explanations that follow.

> [1]Officials often try to move homeless people to city shelters, where they can get a hot meal and a bed for the night. [2]But for a variety of reasons, the homeless resist being helped. [3]One reason is simple pride. [4]If they remain on the street, they are their own bosses and do not feel humiliated by having to accept charity. [5]In addition, many of the homeless are former mental patients who have difficulty getting along in society. [6]For them, it is next to impossible to follow shelter rules and become part of a group of other homeless people. [7]Finally, conditions in the shelters are not always pleasant. [8]There may be noise and smells and disturbing sights, and drug use and petty theft are common.

___B___ 1. In sentence 4, the word *humiliated* means
     A. hungry.
     B. shamed.
     C. the joy of being helped.
     D. a great deal richer.

___B___ 2. Which would be the best title for this paragraph?
     A. Shelters for the Homeless
     B. Why the Homeless Avoid City Shelters
     C. Former Mental Patients
     D. Unpleasant Conditions in City Shelters

___B___ 3. Which sentence expresses the main idea of the passage?
     A. Many homeless people are mental patients.
     B. Homeless people resist going to shelters for several reasons.
     C. Shelters can be unpleasant in various ways.
     D. City services often do not reach the people they are meant to help.

___C___ 4. According to the passage, mental patients find it difficult to
     A. remain on the street.
     B. leave homeless shelters.
     C. follow shelter rules.
     D. all of the above.

___C___ 5. The answer to question 4 can be found in sentence(s)
     A. 2.
     B. 3–4.
     C. 5–6.
     D. 7–8.

_C_   6. The relationship between sentences 1 and 2 is one of
      A. time.
      B. addition.
      C. contrast.
      D. comparison.

_B_   7. The paragraph is organized as
      A. a series of events.
      B. a list of reasons.
      C. a contrast between two things.
      D. a definition and examples.

_D_   8. From the passage we can infer that
      A. shelters actually have no rules to follow.
      B. city officials don't care about the pride of the homeless.
      C. the former mental patients eventually get better.
      D. homeless people face difficulties both on the street and in shelters.

Explanation

1. You could have guessed the correct meaning of *humiliated* from sentences 3 and 4: "One reason is simple pride. If they remain on the street, they are their own bosses and do not feel humiliated by having to accept charity." These sentences suggest that a person who feels humiliated experiences the opposite of pride—in other words, shame. So the correct answer is B, "shamed."

2. A selection titled "Shelters for the Homeless" would tell us more about shelters—perhaps how they are run, what they do throughout a day, and so on. This paragraph tells us only one thing about the shelters—reasons the homeless resist going to them. So answer A is incorrect, and answer B is correct. Answer C could not be correct—it is too narrow. It mentions only former mental patients, but the paragraph is about all homeless people. Answer D is also too narrow—it refers to only one of the reasons the homeless avoid shelters.

3. Answers A and C are both too narrow—each is about only one part of the paragraph. Answer D is too broad—it refers to city services in general, but the paragraph is about only one specific service, city shelters. Answer B expresses the main idea of the passage, which is about the reasons the homeless resist going to shelters. (*A variety of reasons* is an example of list words, as explained on page 128.)

4–5. To find the answer to question 4, you had to remember (or go back and see) that only sentences 5–6 deal with mental patients. Those sentences say that "it is next to impossible" for mental patients "to follow shelter rules and become part of a group." So the correct answer for question 4 is C ("follow shelter rules"), and the correct answer for question 5 is also C ("sentences 5–6").

6. The first word of sentence 2, *but*, signals a contrast, so the answer to this question is C. The author is contrasting the effort of city officials with the opposing response of the homeless.

7. The supporting details are three reasons that explain why "the homeless resist being helped": 1) pride; 2) for mental patients, it is difficult to follow shelter rules and be part of a group of homeless people; and 3) shelters have unpleasant conditions. So the answer to this question is B, "a list of reasons." (The words *One, In additon,* and *Finally* are examples of addition words, as explained on page 129.)

8. The passage suggests that people living out on the street have trouble getting a hot meal and a bed for the night. The paragraph also suggests that being in a shelter can be unpleasant. Thus answer D is correct. Answer A isn't correct. Sentence 6 says that shelters *do* have rules. Answer B is also incorrect. There is no evidence in the paragraph to tell us whether or not city officials care about the pride of the homeless. Nor is there evidence to support answer C— that former mental patients eventually get better. The paragraph states only that they have problems in shelters.

The combined-skills tests in the chapter that follows will help you develop your active reading skills.

2 Practice in Active Reading: Combined-Skills Tests

Following are eighteen tests that cover the skills taught in Part One and reinforced in Part Two of this book. Each test consists of a short reading passage followed by questions on any of the following: vocabulary in context, main ideas, supporting details, transitions, patterns of organization, and inferences.

Notes:

1. The combined-skills tests are on facing pages so that students can easily see the full text and all the questions on a single spread. In addition, having everything on one page or spread is the same format used in standardized tests.

2. Because of this format, you may not want students to remove any of the test pages from the book. One alternative is to ask students to put their test answers on a piece of notebook paper, which you can then collect. Or you can have them use copies of the model answer sheet on page 574.

COMBINED SKILLS: Test 1

Read the passage below. Then write the letter of the best answer to each question that follows.

¹A girl who had been late every day so far came up after class to inform me that she was probably going to be late a lot, and didn't want me marking her late. ²(Being late counts for one-third an absence.)

³"Why are you going to be late?" I asked. ⁴She explained that the traffic is heavy between her house and the school, and the drive takes longer than it should. ⁵"Doesn't that mean you need to leave your house earlier?" I asked. ⁶She looked exasperated and said, "No! I LEAVE at 7. ⁷I only live 30 miles away. ⁸It shouldn't take more than an hour to get here."

⁹There was a brief silence as I waited for her to say something that made sense. ¹⁰Nothing was forthcoming. ¹¹I finally said, "But apparently it does take more than an hour, so . . . I think the only solution is for you to leave earlier." ¹²She wailed, "But that would mean leaving home at SIX-THIRTY. ¹³Can't I do some extra credit work or something?"

¹⁴Again, we just looked at each other as I shook my head. ¹⁵Did she expect me to say to her, "Oh, of course, YOU don't have to be on time. ¹⁶Just the other students."

_____C____ 1. In sentence 6, the word *exasperated* means
   A. tired.
   B. frightened.
   C. frustrated.
   D. pleased.

   How would she look if the drive was taking longer than she thought it should and the instructor didn't seem to understand her problem?

_____A____ 2. In sentence 11, the word *apparently* means
   A. evidently.
   B. unfairly.
   C. not very often.
   D. strangely.

   The fact that she has been late every day makes it evident that the trip takes more than an hour.

_____D____ 3. Which sentence best states the main idea of the selection?
   A. A student must get up at 6:30 a.m. to arrive on time for her class.
   B. A student asks her teacher for extra credit work because she knows she will often be late for class.
   C. A teacher gives a student some good advice about getting to class on time.
   D. A teacher is amazed that a student wants the rules about lateness bent just for her.

   Answer D is supported by sentences 9 and 15–16. Answer A is incorrect because the problem concerns what time the student leaves her house, not what time she gets up. Answers B and C are too narrow; each gives only one detail of the passage.

_B_ 4. According to the passage, the student
  A. lives an hour away from her school.
  B. does not want to leave home before 7 a.m.
  C. drives to school at a time when there is little traffic.
  D. is a very cautious driver.

_D_ 5. The main pattern of organization used in this passage is
  A. list of items.
  B. comparison.
  C. definition and example.
  D. time order.

_C_ 6. We can infer from the passage that the writer
  A. has had many students ask for favors.
  B. knows the student has a good reason for being late.
  C. is a teacher.
  D. is a parent whose children are college students.

_B_ 7. We can infer from the passage that the teacher
  A. will no longer mark the student late for class.
  B. will continue to mark the student late for class.
  C. will probably give the student extra credit work.
  D. will tell the student that she is acting like a spoiled brat.

_C_ 8. The passage suggests that
  A. teachers need to be more flexible about classroom rules.
  B. it is not a good idea to schedule classes in the morning.
  C. some students are unwilling to do what it takes to succeed in school.
  D. the student will probably drop out of school.

Item 4: See sentences 6 and 12–13. Answers A and C are contradicted in the passage. Answer D is not supported.

Item 5: The passage presents a sequence of events in the order in which they happened.

Item 6: The fact that the writer is concerned about being late to class and the fact that the student asks if she can do extra credit work both suggest this. Answers A, B, and D are not supported.

Item 7: The teacher's reactions to the student's arguments suggest that the teacher will continue to mark the student late.

Item 8: The student's refusal to leave home a little earlier to get to class on time demonstrates that she is unwilling to do what it takes to succeed in school.

COMBINED SKILLS: Test 2

Read the passage below. Then write the letter of the best answer to each question that follows.

¹If you saw students sitting quietly in a lecture hall, you might think they were all involved in the lecture. ²However, if you shot off a gun at sporadic points during a lecture and asked the students to reveal their thoughts at each of those moments, you would find that very few of them were actively listening to the lecturer. ³During a typical lecture, about 20 percent of the students are thinking sexual thoughts. ⁴Another 20 percent are reminiscing about past events in their lives. ⁵Only 20 percent are actually paying attention to the lecture. ⁶And only 12 percent are actively listening. ⁷The others are worrying, daydreaming, or thinking about lunch or—surprise!—religion.

_D_ 1. In sentence 2, the word *sporadic* means
   A. zero.
   B. expected.   "Each of those moments" suggests that the gun is
   C. high.   shot off at occasional points during the lecture.
   D. occasional.

_C_ 2. In sentence 4, the words *reminiscing about* mean
   A. forgetting about.
   B. talking about.   During a quiet lecture, what might you
   C. looking back on.   be doing about past events in your life?
   D. not thinking of.

_A_ 3. The sentence that best expresses the main idea of the passage is sentence
   A. 2.   Answers B, C, and D are too narrow. Each is a
   B. 3.   supporting detail that describes what (besides
   C. 4.   the lecture) the students may be thinking about.
   D. 7.

_B_ 4. The relationship of sentence 4 to the sentence before it is one of
   A. time.
   B. addition.   The relationship is signaled by the
   C. an example.   addition transition *Another.*
   D. cause.

_D_ 5. The main pattern of organization of this paragraph is
   A. time order.
   B. definition and example.   The items listed are the different topics
   C. cause and effect.   students think about during a lecture.
   D. list of items.

___B___ 6. We can conclude that a researcher must have
   A. guessed about what students were thinking at various points during school lectures.
   B. asked students what they were thinking at various points during school lectures.
   C. asked lecturers what they thought students were thinking at various points during school lectures.
   D. been in the lecture hall every day.   This would be the only way to be sure what students were thinking.

___B___ 7. We can conclude that a lecturer might improve student attention by
   A. changing the beginning of a lecture.
   B. having students participate in class.
   C. shooting a gun at various times during the lecture.
   D. lecturing for a longer period of time.   If the students were directly participating, they could not think about other things.

___A___ 8. We can conclude from this passage that
   A. there is a difference between paying attention to something and actively listening to it.
   B. only very few people have the ability to listen actively.
   C. active listening is easy.
   D. most lectures are not very important.   See sentences 5 and 6.

COMBINED SKILLS: Test 3

Read the passage below. Then write the letter of the best answer to each question that follows.

[1]One day, a man walked into a bank as if he was ready for war. [2]He was carrying an ax, a stun gun, a smoke grenade, and a can of Mace. [3]He demanded a lot of money in small bills right away. [4]The tellers quickly loaded up a big bag with small bills. [5]The problem was the robber was holding so many weapons he didn't have any hands left to carry the bag. [6]Holding the bag as best he could, he took off out the door but then tripped. [7]Another man passing by on the street jumped on him and held him down until the police arrived.

[8]Another incredible but true story is about the man in the Elvis mask who held up a store. [9]He got the money and turned so fast to run that the mask didn't turn with him. [10]It was now on backwards. [11]He sprinted toward the door anyway but then hit the doorframe so hard that he knocked himself out. [12]He learned—the hard way—that a robber's mask might look good on TV, but it can be a problem in real life.

[13]And there was another would-be thief who tried the old paper-bag trick. [14]Cutting two holes in the bag for his eyes, he tried to rob a convenience store. [15]But he didn't cut out a hole for his mouth. [16]As a result, the clerk couldn't understand what he was saying. [17]"What?" the clerk kept asking. [18]The robber flew into a rage. [19]He tried to tear a hole for his mouth, but ended up tearing the bag right off his head. [20]The clerk looked at him and said, "*Jerry?*" [21]Sure enough, the robber was another clerk who worked at the store.

___B___ 1. In sentence 11, the word *sprinted* means
   A. walked.
   B. ran.
   C. looked.   *How would the thief be moving if he*
   D. yelled.   *knocked himself out on the doorframe?*

___D___ 2. Which sentence best states the main idea of the selection?

The passage gives   A. It's not a good idea to wear a mask while robbing a bank or store.
three examples   B. Some robberies are more successful than others.
of really stupid   C. Robbing banks or stores is not really a serious crime.
would-be criminals. D. Some would-be criminals are really stupid.

___B___ 3. The bank robber failed because
   A. he hit the door frame so hard that he knocked himself out.
   B. he was thrown off balance by all the stuff he was carrying.
   C. the can of Mace he was carrying went off in his face.
   D. he couldn't breathe through his mask.   *See sentence 6.*

___D___ 4. One robber became angry when
      A. his Elvis mask got turned around.
      B. the clerk in the store he was robbing recognized him as a coworker.
      C. he couldn't breathe through the mask he was wearing.
      D. a clerk couldn't understand what he was saying. See sentences 16–18.

___A___ 5. The relationship of sentence 8 to the sentences that come before it is one of
      A. addition.   Addition word: *Another.*
      B. time.
      C. contrast.
      D. cause and effect.

___C___ 6. The relationship of sentence 16 to sentence 15 is one of
      A. time.   *Cause:* The thief didn't cut a hole for his mouth.
      B. addition.   *Effect:* The clerk couldn't understand what he was
      C. cause and effect.   saying. Cause and effect words: *As a result.*
      D. an example.

___B___ 7. The first paragraph suggests that the bank robber
      A. was prepared to kill someone.
      B. felt he needed to carry as many weapons as possible.
      C. had robbed other banks.
      D. was angry at the way the bank had treated him in the past.
                     See sentence 2. Answers A, C, and D are not supported.

___B___ 8. We can infer from the passage that
      A. each of the would-be robbers had robbed other places.
      B. all of the criminals were caught.
      C. each of the robberies had been carefully planned.
      D. most robberies are unsuccessful.   See sentences 7, 11, and 20–21.
                              Answers A and D are not supported.
                         Answer C is contradicted by the passage.

COMBINED SKILLS: Test 4

Read the passage below. Then write the letter of the best answer to each question that follows.

> ¹Constant everyday fatigue and lack of energy can be due to various causes. ²One common cause, not surprisingly, is insufficient sleep. ³Many people simply do not allow themselves enough hours to sleep; and others have sleep disturbances, such as insomnia, that prevent them from getting the sleep they need. ⁴Another cause of fatigue is anemia—a low level of hemoglobin in the blood—which usually requires a better diet or nutritional supplements. ⁵Lack of exercise can also be a cause of fatigue. ⁶You might think that exercise will make you tired, but on the contrary, it tends to prevent fatigue. ⁷Low thyroid function can cause fatigue, too, unless remedied with hormone supplementation. ⁸Clinical depression, a serious but very treatable condition, is still another possible cause of fatigue. ⁹So, if you "feel tired all the time," could it be for one of these reasons?

___A___ 1. In sentence 7, the word *remedied* means
     A. corrected.
     B. caused.
     C. damaged.
     D. invented.

Each specific detail in the passage describes a problem that can cause fatigue. Each also suggests or implies a way to fix the problem. It's logical to conclude that hormone supplements could fix, or correct, the problem of low thyroid function.

___A___ 2. The main idea of this passage is found in sentence
     A. 1.
     B. 2.
     C. 3.
     D. 4.

The main idea contains a list signal: *various causes.* Sentences 2, 3, and 4 each describe causes of fatigue.

___C___ 3. How many possible reasons for fatigue does the passage provide in support of the main idea?
     A. 3
     B. 4
     C. 5
     D. 6

The five reasons are signaled by these addition words: *One, Another, also, too, another.*

___B___ 4. A possible treatment for anemia is
     A. more exercise.
     B. a better diet.
     C. hormone supplements.
     D. more sleep.

See sentence 4.

___D___ 5. One possible cause of fatigue is

    A. an overactive thyroid.

    B. extreme exercise.   See sentence 7.

    C. too much hemoglobin in the blood.

    D. an underactive thyroid.

___A___ 6. The main pattern of organization used in this passage is

    A. cause and effect.

    B. time order.   The passage lists the causes of being tired.

    C. contrast.   The list signal in sentence 1 *(various causes)*

    D. definition and examples.   indicates the pattern of organization.

Item 7:
Answers B and D
are not   ___A___ 7. The passage implies that
supported.
Answer C is   A. most causes of everyday fatigue can be successfully treated.
incorrect because
the passage does   B. constant everyday fatigue is an increasingly common problem.
not indicate which   C. lack of exercise is the most common reason for fatigue.
reason is most
important.   ___D___ D. people should be able to just "snap out" of being depressed.

___D___ 8. We might conclude from the passage that

    A. it is natural to feel more fatigued as one grows older.

    B. most cases of constant fatigue are caused by serious medical problems.

    C. fatigue is usually a mental problem, not a physical one.

    D. if getting more sleep and exercise doesn't relieve fatigue, it's time to see a doctor.   Anemia, low thyroid function, and clinical depression would need to be treated by a medical doctor.

COMBINED SKILLS: Test 5

Read the passage below. Then write the letter of the best answer to each question that follows.

¹Feelings come and go within minutes. ²A mood, on the other hand, is a more sustained emotional state that colors our view of the world for hours or days. ³One researcher found that bad moods descend upon us an average of three out of every ten days.

⁴There are gender differences in dealing with moods. ⁵Men typically try to distract themselves (a partially successful strategy) or use alcohol or drugs (an ineffective tactic). ⁶Women are more likely to talk to someone (which can help) or to spend a long time thinking about why they feel bad (which doesn't help).

⁷The most effective way to banish a sad or bad mood is by changing what caused it in the first place. ⁸Keep in mind that most bad moods are caused by loss or failure—in school, in work, or in intimate relationships. ⁹If you can do anything to fix the loss or failure, take action and solve it. ¹⁰For example, ask to take a makeup exam. ¹¹Or tell your friend you feel bad about the argument you had with her.

¹²If there's nothing you can do, accept what happened and focus on doing things differently next time. ¹³Studies show that resolving to try harder actually can be as effective in improving a mood as taking action in the present.

¹⁴Another good option is to get moving. ¹⁵Studies have shown that exercise ranks as the single most effective way to banish bad feelings. ¹⁶Exercise can boost spirits, improve sleep and appetite, and reduce anxiety and anger.

_____C_____ 1. In sentence 2, the word *sustained* means
   A. organized.
   B. negative.
   C. long-lasting.
   D. confusing.

   If moods last for hours or days, rather than just a few minutes, how should moods be described?

_____D_____ 2. In sentences 7 and 15, the word *banish* means
   A. understand.
   B. encourage.
   C. remember.
   D. drive away.

   The passage describes ways to get out of a sad or bad mood. That context suggests that *banish* means "drive away."

Item 3:
Answers A, B, and C are too narrow.
Answer A covers only sentences 1–2.
Answer B covers only the second paragraph. Answer C covers only the third paragraph.

_____D_____ 3. Which sentence best states the main idea of the selection?
   A. Moods last much longer than feelings.
   B. Men and women differ in the way they deal with bad moods.
   C. The most effective way to banish a sad or bad mood is by changing what caused it in the first place.
   D. There are several effective ways to banish a sad or bad mood.

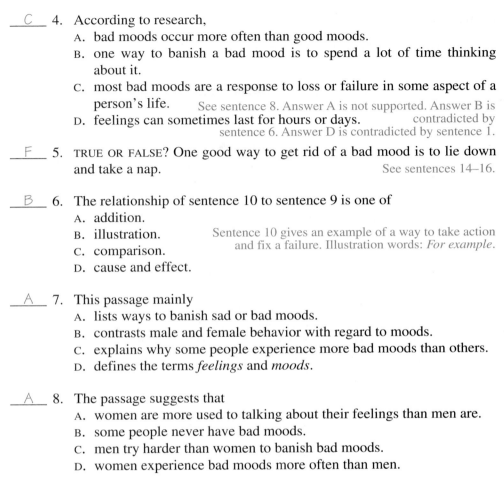

____C____ 4. According to research,
  A. bad moods occur more often than good moods.
  B. one way to banish a bad mood is to spend a lot of time thinking about it.
  C. most bad moods are a response to loss or failure in some aspect of a person's life.   See sentence 8. Answer A is not supported. Answer B is
  D. feelings can sometimes last for hours or days.   contradicted by
            sentence 6. Answer D is contradicted by sentence 1.

____F____ 5. TRUE OR FALSE? One good way to get rid of a bad mood is to lie down and take a nap.   See sentences 14–16.

____B____ 6. The relationship of sentence 10 to sentence 9 is one of
  A. addition.
  B. illustration.   Sentence 10 gives an example of a way to take action
  C. comparison.   and fix a failure. Illustration words: *For example.*
  D. cause and effect.

____A____ 7. This passage mainly
  A. lists ways to banish sad or bad moods.
  B. contrasts male and female behavior with regard to moods.
  C. explains why some people experience more bad moods than others.
  D. defines the terms *feelings* and *moods*.

____A____ 8. The passage suggests that
  A. women are more used to talking about their feelings than men are.
  B. some people never have bad moods.
  C. men try harder than women to banish bad moods.
  D. women experience bad moods more often than men.

Item 7:   Answer B covers only the second paragraph. Answer C is not mentioned. Answer D is incorrect; sentences 1 and 2 note how long feelings and moods last but do not define the terms.

Item 8:   See sentence 6. Answers B, C, and D are not supported.

COMBINED SKILLS: Test 6

Read the passage below. Then write the letter of the best answer to each question that follows.

[1]Jury duty can be a stressful experience. [2]To begin with, a trial may involve disturbing and even frightening details. [3]In a trial involving a violent crime, jurors may have to see photographs of, and hear testimony about, death and bloodshed. [4]The jury's decision-making can also be stressful. [5]Disputes among the jurors can sometimes lead to angry words and feelings, and many people are unprepared for this kind of conflict. [6]In addition, jurors who feel strongly about their own conclusions—or who may simply want to reach a verdict so that they can go home—may put too much pressure on others to give in. [7]Fourth, a case that goes on for a long time creates a disruption in a juror's life. [8]For instance, the jurors must be away from their work and perhaps even from their families, and must spend each day away from their usual surroundings. [9]Finally, there is the stress of dealing with an unusual responsibility. [10]Most jurors are conscientious, and so they worry about making the wrong decision—about convicting an innocent defendant or letting a guilty one walk free.

___A___ 1. In sentence 7, the word *disruption* means
  A. unwelcome interruption.
  B. pleasant break from the routine.
  C. high point.
  D. emergency.

  See sentence 8 for an example clue.

___D___ 2. In sentence 10, the word *conscientious* means
  A. overly self-confident.
  B. careless.
  C. ignorant of the law.
  D. concerned with doing the right thing.

  See the synonym-like clue in sentence 10, "worry about making the wrong decision."

___A___ 3. The main idea of the passage is found in sentence
  A. 1.
  B. 2.
  C. 3.
  D. 9.

  The main idea contains words that provide focus for the topic: stressful experience. The supporting details show how being a juror is stressful.

___D___ 4. According to the passage, jurors who feel strongly about a case might
  A. refuse to serve on the jury.
  B. want to go home quickly.
  C. feel frightened.
  D. put too much pressure on other jurors.

  See sentence 6.

___B___   5. The main pattern of organization used for this passage is
    A. time order.
    B. list of items.   *Addition words are used to signal the major supporting*
                              details: To begin with, also, In addition, Fourth, Finally.
    C. contrast.
    D. comparison.

___B___   6. The relationship of sentence 7 to sentence 6 is one of
    A. comparison.
    B. addition.   *Sentence 6 has the addition words In addition;*
                        sentence 7 has the addition word Fourth.
    C. illustration.
    D. time.

___D___   7. The relationship of sentence 8 to sentence 7 is one of
    A. addition.
    B. time.   *An illustration transition is used:*
                         For instance.
    C. contrast.
    D. illustration.

___B___   8. The passage implies that
    A. most jury trials involve violent crimes.
    B. jurors may be surprised by how stressful being on a jury is.
    C. a trial by jury is not a fair way to judge a person's guilt or innocence.
    D. the people who take jury duty least seriously are the ones who find the experience most stressful.   *Answers A, C, and D are not supported*
                        in the passage, which details stresses of being on a jury.
                      Words such as unprepared (sentence 5) and unusual
                      responsibility (sentence 9) support answer B
                      by suggesting that jurors may not be expecting
                      the stressful situations they encounter.

COMBINED SKILLS: Test 7

Read the passage below. Then write the letter of the best answer to each question that follows.

¹Touching is vital to human development. ²During the nineteenth and early twentieth centuries, a large percentage of children died from a disease then called *marasmus*. ³In Greek, this word means "wasting away." ⁴In some orphanages, the mortality rate was nearly 100 percent. ⁵However, even children in the most "advanced" homes and institutions died regularly from the disease. ⁶Researchers finally found that the infants suffered from lack of physical contact with parents or nurses. ⁷The children hadn't been touched enough, and as a result, they died. ⁸From this knowledge came the practice in institutions of picking a baby up, carrying it around, and handling it several times each day. ⁹At one hospital that began this practice, the death rate for infants fell from between 30 and 35 percent to below 10 percent.

_____A_____ 1. In sentence 1, the word *vital* means
   A. necessary.
   B. beside the point.   Sentences 2–7 describe why touch is
   C. superior.   necessary, or vital.
   D. an added bonus.

_____B_____ 2. In sentence 4, the word *mortality* means
   A. health.
   B. death.   Synonym-like clue: Sentence 5 says
   C. Greek.   the children "died regularly."
   D. touching.

_____A_____ 3. The main idea of the paragraph is stated in sentence
   A. 1.   Sentences 2–7 tell how it was discovered that touching
   B. 2.   is vital to human development and why. Sentences 8–9
   C. 8.   explain what institutions are now doing and the results.
   D. 9.

_____C_____ 4. *Marasmus* is
   A. an illness that struck people of all ages.
   B. mainly a Greek illness.
   C. an illness that killed children in orphanages and elsewhere.
   D. all of the above.   See sentences 2–5.

___C___   5. The relationship between the first and second parts of sentence 7 is one
of

    A. comparison.

    B. contrast.

    C. cause and effect.

    D. time.

Cause-effect transition: as a result.
The cause: children not being touched enough.
The effect: children dying.

___A___   6. Within the context of the passage, touch is

    A. a cause.

    B. an effect.

    C. something compared.

    D. an example.

Lack of enough touching is cited
as a cause of death.

___B___   7. From this passage, we can assume that in the nineteenth and early
twentieth centuries, children tended to get less attention

    A. at home, from their parents.

    B. in orphanages.

    C. in Greece.

    D. at hospitals where *marasmus* was understood.

See sentence 4.

___B___   8. From the passage, we can infer that touching is one advantage of

    A. giving birth to a child.

    B. breast-feeding a child.

    C. putting a child in a hospital.

    D. giving a child vitamins.

Breast-feeding requires holding and
touching an infant for a sustained
period of time.

COMBINED SKILLS: Test 8

Read the passage below. Then write the letter of the best answer to each question that follows.

[1]Water has no vitamins, no protein, and no carbohydrates. [2]However, even though water itself has little nutritional value, it is an essential part of our diet. [3]A major reason that water is essential is that it transports nutrients to the cells of our body. [4]It also removes waste products from cells. [5]In addition, water aids in food digestion and regulates the body's temperature. [6]It cushions vital organs and lubricates the joints. [7]The cells of our body are partially made up of water. [8]In fact, our body weight consists of between 60 and 80 percent water. [9]The body can survive long periods without food, but it can exist for only a few days without water.

_D_ 1. In sentence 3, the word *transports* means
    A. adds.
    B. creates.
    C. subtracts.
    D. carries.

> Sentence 4 says that waste products are removed or carried away by water. It is logical to conclude, then, that nutrients would be carried to the cells by water.

_B_ 2. The topic of the passage is
    A. health.
    B. water.
    C. food.
    D. digestion.

> The word *water* is mentioned seven times in the passage—in every sentence except sentences 4 and 6, which use the pronoun *it* to refer to water.

_B_ 3. The main idea of the passage is sentence
    A. 1.
    B. 2.
    C. 3.
    D. 9.

> Sentence 1 introduces the topic of water. Sentences 3 and 9 give two specific details about the body's need for water. Sentence 2 presents the overview that water is essential.

_D_ 4. Water is important to the body's cells because
    A. it removes waste matter from cells.
    B. the cells are partially made of water.
    C. it brings nutrients to the cells.
    D. of all of the above.

> See sentences 3, 4, and 7.

_B_ 5. According to the passage,
    A. water itself contains many essential nutrients needed by the body.
    B. water has various functions within the human body.
    C. everyone's body contains exactly the same amount of water.
    D. because the human body stores so much water, it can exist for longer periods without water than it can without food.

> Sentences 3–6 describe six functions of water in the body. Answer A is contradicted by sentence 2. Answer C is contradicted by sentence 8. Answer D is contradicted by sentence 9.

___D___ 6. The relationship between the two parts of sentence 9 is one of
   A. time.
   B. addition.
   C. cause and effect.
   D. contrast.

Contrast transition: but. The sentence contrasts survival time without food with survival time without water.

___B___ 7. The passage suggests that the cells of our body
   A. are few.
   B. need to be fed nutrients.
   C. need to be lubricated.
   D. need to be replaced.

See sentence 3.

___C___ 8. We can conclude that
   A. a very small part of the human body is water.
   B. just about all of the human body is water.
   C. most of the human body is water.
   D. almost half of the human body is water.

See sentence 8.

COMBINED SKILLS: Test 9

Read the passage below. Then write the letter of the best answer to each question that follows.

[1]Turn on your TV on a weekday afternoon or a Saturday, and you'll probably see cute cartoon characters urging kids to try the latest candy-coated cereal or rush out the door for some tasty fast food. [2]For years, people have debated whether ads like these, which target young children, should be allowed on the air. [3]The idea of banning children's ads is supported by many parents, teachers, and doctors. [4]These people quote studies showing that young children often can't tell the difference between a TV program and a TV commercial. [5]Because they don't understand the real purpose of ads, they think everything an ad says is true. [6]But cereal companies, television networks, and major advertising agencies strongly disagree—and with good reason. [7]They earn a lot of money producing these ads, broadcasting these ads, or selling products with these ads.

[8]The average American child now spends about 25 hours a week in front of a TV. [9]This means that in one year, that child watches more than 20,000 TV commercials. [10]Two-thirds of those ads are for junk food: soda, candy, sugary cereals, and burgers and fries. [11]As a result, children now see almost two hours of junk-food ads every week. [12]Sadly, American kids aren't learning the truth about food, either in the classroom or on the Internet. [13]Instead, they're being told what to eat by junk-food ads that they see over and over.

_____D_____ 1. In sentence 3, the word *banning* means
  A. correcting.
  B. inventing.
  C. recognizing.
  D. doing away with.

What would parents, teachers, and doctors want to do about children's ads on TV?

Item 2: Answer A states the main idea, emphasized in the second paragraph. Answers B and C might be inferred from the passage, but neither of them is the main idea. Answer D is too narrow; it covers only part of the first paragraph.

_____A_____ 2. Which sentence best states the main idea of the selection?
  A. The eating habits of American kids are shaped by watching TV commercials for junk food.
  B. American kids watch too much TV.
  C. American kids eat too much junk food.
  D. Banning ads targeted at children is opposed by some groups and supported by others.

_____C_____ 3. The average American child
  A. watches 10,000 TV commercials a year.
  B. sees about 5 hours of junk-food ads a week.
  C. spends about 25 hours a week watching TV.
  D. sees about one hour of junk-food ads every day.

See sentence 8. Answers A, B, and C contradict details given in sentences 9 and 11.

___D___ 4. According to the passage, young children
    A. watch more TV than older children do.
    B. like to watch ads for junk food more than other types of ads.
    C. often learn about healthy eating before they start school.
    D. believe that what ads say is true. See sentence 5.

___D___ 5. The relationship of sentence 6 to the sentences before it is one of
    A. addition.   Sentence 6 contrasts the opinion held by cereal
    B. cause and effect.   companies, television networks, and advertising
    C. illustration.   agencies with the opinion of parents, teachers,
    D. contrast.   and doctors stated in sentences 3–5.
                                            Contrast transition: *But.*

___A___ 6. We can conclude from the passage that
    A. many breakfast cereals are not good for children's health.
    B. schools are doing a fine job of educating kids about healthy eating.
    C. cereal companies, television networks, and ad agencies put the
       health of American children above making money.
    D. all of the above.

___B___ 7. The passage suggests that
    A. if parents, teachers, and doctors join together, they can ban TV
       advertising aimed at kids.
    B. cereal companies, television networks, and major ad agencies are
       more powerful than parents, teachers, and doctors.
    C. the people who work for cereal companies, television networks, and
       ad agencies do not have children.
    D. ads targeting kids will soon begin to show up on the Internet.

___D___ 8. The author clearly implies that
    A. people have only recently begun to debate ads targeting kids.
    B. parents should not permit their children to watch more than a couple
       of hours of TV a week.
    C. in the next few years, TV stations will not be permitted to broadcast
       commercials aimed at kids.
    D. it would be a good idea to ban TV advertising aimed at kids.

Item 6:   Answer A is suggested by sentences 10, 12, and 13. Answer B is contradicted by
          sentence 12. Answer C is contradicted by sentences 7–8. Answer D is incorrect
          because answers B and C are incorrect.

Item 7:   The fact that the ads are still on TV—in spite of the opinion of parents, teachers,
          and doctors—supports answer B. Answers A, C, and D are not supported.

Item 8:   Words such as *junk-food ads, Sadly,* and *kids aren't learning the truth* support
          answer D. Answers A, B, and C are not supported.

COMBINED SKILLS: Test 10

Read the passage below. Then write the letter of the best answer to each question that follows.

[1]On a Saturday morning in February, 1851, Shadrach Minkins was working as a waiter at a Boston coffeehouse. [2]Suddenly, two men pretending to be customers grabbed him and announced that he was under arrest. [3]Minkins, an escaped slave from Virginia, had thought he was safe in the "free state" of Massachusetts. [4]But the Fugitive Slave Law of 1850 had changed that. [5]Under this law, residents of free states had to cooperate with authorities capturing runaway slaves. [6]If they didn't, they could be jailed and fined. [7]Many residents of Boston were opposed to slavery, and the news of Minkins's capture made them furious. [8]A crowd of black and white citizens quickly gathered at the courthouse where Minkins was being held. [9]They forced their way past armed guards and carried Minkins away. [10]After hiding him briefly in an attic, they smuggled him to safety in Canada. [11]Nine of the people who rescued Minkins were arrested, although charges against them were eventually dropped. [12]The citizens of Boston had made their point: they would not cooperate with the Fugitive Slave Law.

_B_ 1. In sentence 4, the word *fugitive* means
      A. dangerous.
      B. escaped.   Sentence 3 has a synonym clue: *escaped.*
      C. legal.   Sentence 5 has a synonym clue: *runaway.*
      D. pardoned.

_D_ 2. In sentence 10, the word *smuggled* means
      A. kept from.
      B. accepted.   If they first hid him in the attic, it is
      C. chased.   logical to conclude that they would
      D. secretly took.   take him to Canada secretly.

_D_ 3. The main idea of the passage—a summary of the events described—is
      found in sentence
      A. 1.   Sentences 1–11 narrate the tale of how some citizens
      B. 2.   of Boston took part in the escape of Minkins to Canada
      C. 3.   because they did not accept the Fugitive Slave Law.
      D. 12.

_C_ 4. Under the Fugitive Slave Law of 1850,
      A. slavery was made illegal.
      B. it became illegal to hire a former slave.
      C. people in free states had to help authorities catch runaway slaves.
      D. Shadrach Minkins won his freedom.   See sentence 5.
              Answers A and B are contradicted by sentences 5–6.
          Answer D is incorrect because Minkins escaped slavery only
             by being smuggled to Canada; he did not win his freedom.

_A_ 5. Some of the people who helped Shadrach Minkins escape
     A. were arrested, but charges were later dropped.
     B. were fined and imprisoned.   See sentence 11.
     C. had to escape to Canada.
     D. chose to live in Canada.

_D_ 6. The main pattern of organization used in this passage is
     A. comparison and/or contrast.
     B. list of items.   The events of the escape are detailed
     C. definition and example.   in the order in which they happened.
     D. time order.

_A_ 7. The relationship of sentence 4 to sentence 3 is one of
     A. contrast.   Contrast transition: *But*. The two sentences contrast the
     B. illustration.   fact that Minkins was not safe in Massachusetts with
     C. comparison.   Minkins's belief that he was safe there.
     D. time.

_A_ 8. The passage implies that
     A. in 1851, slavery was still legal in Virginia.
     B. Shadrach Minkins was a well-known activist.
     C. only African-American people were concerned about slavery.
     D. Minkins was the first person arrested in Massachusetts under the
          Fugitive Slave Law.   See sentences 3–5. Answers B and D are not
                      supported. Answer C is untrue because Minkins
                      had the help of black and white citizens.

COMBINED SKILLS: Test 11

Read the passage below. Then write the letter of the best answer to each question that follows.

[1]Behavior is contagious. [2]One person giggles, coughs, or yawns, and others in the group are soon doing the same. [3]A cluster of people stands gazing upward, and passersby pause to do likewise. [4]Laughter, even canned laughter, can be catching. [5]Bartenders and street musicians know enough to "seed" their tip cups with money to suggest that others have given.

[6]Sometimes the effects of suggestibility are more serious. [7]Sociologists have found that suicides increase following a well-known suicide. [8]So do fatal auto accidents and private airplane crashes (some of which disguise suicides)—and they do so only in areas where the suicide is publicized. [9]Following the film star Marilyn Monroe's suicide on August 6, 1961, the number of August suicides in the United States exceeded the usual count by two hundred. [10]In Germany and the United States, increases in suicide have also followed fictional suicides in TV dramas. [11]Such copycat suicides help explain the clusters of teenage suicides that now and then occur in some communities.

(handwritten, left margin: Attitude / Behavior is / contagious)

_A_ 1. In sentence 6, the word *suggestibility* means the tendency to
    A. follow other people's lead.
    B. commit suicide.
    C. drive poorly.
    D. giggle.

> Example clues are given in sentences 7–10. In sentence 11, *copycat* is a synonym-like clue.

_C_ 2. In sentence 9, the word *exceeded* means
    A. missed.
    B. equaled.
    C. was greater than.
    D. exaggerated.

> Sentences 7, 8, and 10 describe circumstances under which suicides increase. It is logical to conclude that in the author's specific example in sentence 9, the number of suicides is greater than usual.

_A_ 3. The main idea of the first paragraph is stated in sentence
    A. 1.
    B. 2.
    C. 3.
    D. 5.

> Sentences 2–5 illustrate the general point made in sentence 1.

_A_ 4. The main idea of the second paragraph is stated in sentence
    A. 6.
    B. 7.
    C. 8.
    D. 11.

> Sentences 7–11 provide specific support for the general point in sentence 6.

___B___ 5. The paragraphs explain
    A. events in time order.
    B. a cause and effect relationship.   One act causes or
    C. definitions and examples.   influences another.
    D. certain contrasts.

___C___ 6. We can conclude that bartenders and street musicians "seed" their tip cups mainly to
    A. make it look as if they are rich.   Suggesting that others had
    B. offer money to others.   left tips would encourage
    C. encourage people to tip them.   people to do the same.
    D. all of the above.

___B___ 7. The passage suggests that a person is more likely to laugh at a movie
    A. when he or she is one of a few people in the audience.
    B. when there are many others laughing at the movie too.
    C. after he or she has seen the movie several times.
    D. if he or she is watching it at home on a DVD player.
        See sentences 2 and 4.

___D___ 8. We can infer from the passage that
    A. our decisions are not really affected by what others are doing.
    B. it is always a bad idea to copy what others are doing.
    C. most of our behavior is copycat behavior.
    D. people can be greatly influenced by what they see on television.
        See sentence 10.

COMBINED SKILLS: Test 12

Read the passage below. Then write the letter of the best answer to each question that follows.

¹People have a number of reasons for taking up smoking. ²It may be their response to stress or depression. ³It may be because their friends smoke or their parents do. ⁴It may be because cigarette companies spend billions of dollars each year on ads that falsely connect smoking to health, happiness, fitness, and sexual appeal.

⁵But whatever the reasons for lighting up that first cigarette, a very different factor keeps cigarettes burning pack after pack, year after year. ⁶In national polls, 7 out of 10 smokers say that they want to quit but can't. ⁷It's not simply because of a lack of willpower. ⁸Nicotine—the addictive ingredient in tobacco—is the reason.

⁹Nicotine has a much more powerful hold on smokers than alcohol does on drinkers. ¹⁰About 10 percent of alcohol users lose control of their intake of alcohol and become alcoholics. ¹¹On the other hand, as many as 80 percent of all heavy smokers have tried to cut down or quit smoking but cannot overcome their dependence.

¹²Nicotine causes dependence by at least three means. ¹³First, it acts on brain chemicals to provide a strong sensation of pleasure. ¹⁴In addition, it leads to fairly severe discomfort during withdrawal. ¹⁵Last, it creates cravings long after obvious withdrawal symptoms have passed. ¹⁶Few drugs act as quickly on the brain as nicotine does. ¹⁷It travels through the bloodstream to the brain in seven seconds—half the time it takes for heroin injected into a blood vessel to reach the brain. ¹⁸And a pack-a-day smoker gets 200 hits of nicotine a day—73,000 a year.

_____D_____ 1. Which sentence best states the main idea of the passage?
  A. People start smoking for a number of reasons.
  B. Nicotine has a much more powerful hold on smokers than alcohol does on drinkers.
  C. Cigarette companies spend billions of dollars each year on ads that connect smoking to health, happiness, fitness, and sexual appeal.
  D. Whatever a person's reason for taking up smoking, the nicotine in cigarettes makes it extremely difficult to stop.

_____A_____ 2. After it has been inhaled through smoking, how long does it take for nicotine to reach the brain?
  A. 7 seconds
  B. 10 seconds
  C. 14 seconds
  D. one minute

Item 1: See sentence 8. Sentences 9–18 give details supporting this idea. Answer A covers only the first paragraph. Answer B covers only the third paragraph. Answer C covers only sentence 4.

Item 2: See sentence 17.

___C___ 3. The percentage of people who drink and become alcoholics is
- A. 70%.
- B. 20%.
- C. 10%.
- D. 1%.

See sentence 10.

___D___ 4. The relationship of sentence 11 to sentence 10 is one of
- A. comparison.
- B. cause and effect.
- C. illustration.
- D. contrast.

The two sentences contrast the relatively small percent of drinkers who become alcoholics with the large percent of smokers dependent on cigarettes. Contrast transition: *On the other hand.*

___B___ 5. The main patterns of organization of paragraph 4 are list of items and
- A. time order.
- B. cause and effect.
- C. comparison.
- D. contrast.

Cause: Nicotine.
Effects: Sensation of pleasure, severe discomfort during withdrawal, and long-term cravings.
Cause-effect transitions: *causes, leads to.*

Item 6:
By stating nicotine reaches the brain twice as fast as heroin and by describing how highly addictive nicotine is, the author suggests it is a dangerous drug. Answers A, C, and D are not supported.

___B___ 6. By comparing the amount of time it takes nicotine and heroin to pass through the bloodstream to the brain, the author is suggesting that
- A. nicotine is a far less harmful drug than heroin.
- B. nicotine, like heroin, is a dangerous drug.
- C. people who inject heroin would be better off injecting nicotine instead.
- D. it is better to inhale heroin than to inject it.

___A___ 7. We can conclude that
- A. most heavy smokers are aware that smoking is bad for their health.
- B. many heavy smokers are also alcoholics.
- C. most people start smoking to relieve depression.
- D. all of the above.

See sentence 6. If 7 out of 10 want to quit, it is logical to conclude that they believe smoking is not good for them.

___B___ 8. The passage suggests that
- A. cigarette companies do not realize that nicotine is addictive.
- B. cigarette companies hope that people will become addicted to the nicotine in cigarettes.
- C. people would still find smoking pleasurable if cigarettes did not contain nicotine.
- D. being an alcoholic or heroin addict is less dangerous than being a heavy smoker.

If cigarette companies spend billions of dollars each year to get people to smoke and they do nothing to remove the addictive nicotine from cigarettes, the companies must want smokers to become hooked and keep buying their product.

COMBINED SKILLS: Test 13

Read the passage below. Then write the letter of the best answer to each question that follows.

> [1]Until about the 1940s, infectious diseases—those caused by "germs" or viruses—were the leading cause of illness and death in the developed countries of the world. [2]That situation has now changed. [3]Today, most leading diseases in developed countries are noninfectious. [4]The most important of these is noninfectious heart disease, the leading cause of death in developed nations, including the United States. [5]Closely related is stroke, a disease of the blood vessels that is also not infectious. [6]Cancer, the second leading cause of death, is another noninfectious disease. [7](The possibility that some cancers may be caused by viruses has been suggested but has not been proved.) [8]Diabetes, a dangerous disease that is increasingly common, is noninfectious as well. [9]Two other significant noninfectious diseases are arthritis and allergies. [10]However, there is one exception to the generalization that today's leading diseases are noninfectious: AIDS is an infectious disease caused by a virus.

___D___ 1. In sentence 10, the word *generalization* means a
- A. mistaken belief.
- B. traditional saying.
- C. lie.
- D. broad statement.

"Today's leading diseases are noninfectious" is a broad statement that covers all the specific examples of noninfectious diseases given in sentences 4–9.

___C___ 2. The main idea of the passage is found in sentence
- A. 1.
- B. 2.
- C. 3.
- D. 10.

Sentences 1 and 2 are introductory details. Sentence 3, the main idea, has a list signal: *leading diseases*. Sentences 4–9 give examples.

___C___ 3. Two diseases considered closely related by the author of the passage are
- A. diabetes and heart disease.
- B. AIDS and cancer.
- C. stroke and heart disease.
- D. stroke and arthritis.

See sentences 4 and 5.

___B___ 4. The leading cause of death in developed countries is
- A. stroke.
- B. heart disease.
- C. AIDS.
- D. cancer.

See sentence 4.

___D___ 5. Before the 1940s in developed nations, most deaths were caused by
A. accidents.
B. noninfectious diseases.   See sentence 1.
C. heart disease.
D. infectious diseases.

___C___ 6. The main pattern of organization used in this passage is
A. time order.
B. definition and example.   The passage lists the main noninfectious
C. list of items.   diseases in developed countries.
D. comparison.

___B___ 7. The relationship of sentence 10 to sentence 9 is one of
A. comparison.   Contrast transition: *However.*
B. contrast.   The sentences contrast an infectious disease
C. addition.   (AIDS) with noninfectious diseases.
D. time.

___A___ 8. We can infer from the passage that
A. infectious diseases are still a common cause of death in undeveloped countries.
B. noninfectious diseases are killing people in developed countries at a faster rate than infectious diseases ever did.
C. cures for heart disease and stroke are expected to be discovered soon.
D. no one knows why diabetes is becoming more common.

Answer B is incorrect because the passage does not make comparisons.
Answers C and D are not mentioned in the passage.
Answer A is supported by the fact that the word *developed* is used three times in the passage. This would lead us to infer that the statements are not true for undeveloped countries.

COMBINED SKILLS: Test 14

Read the passage below. Then write the letter of the best answer to each question that follows.

¹Research shows that we make assumptions about people on the basis of what they are wearing. ²In one study, a man and woman were stationed in a hallway so that anyone who wished to go by had to respond to them in some way. ³They could either politely excuse themselves or rudely ignore them. ⁴Sometimes the conversationalists wore "formal daytime dress." ⁵At other times, they wore "casual attire." ⁶Passers-by behaved differently toward the couple, depending on the style of clothing being worn. ⁷They responded positively to the well-dressed couple and negatively when the same people were casually dressed. ⁸Similar results in other situations show the influence of clothing. ⁹Pedestrians were more likely to return lost coins to well-dressed people than to those dressed in low-status clothing. ¹⁰We are also more likely to follow the lead of high-status dressers, even when it comes to violating social rules. ¹¹For example, 83 percent of the pedestrians in one study followed a well-dressed jaywalker who crossed when a traffic light flashed "wait." ¹²But only 48 percent followed a jaywalker dressed in lower-status clothing.

___D___ 1. In sentence 2, the word *stationed* means
   A. imagined.
   B. avoided.
   C. forced.
   D. placed.

   Because this is part of a research study, we can conclude that the couple was intentionally placed in the hall so that the reactions of others could be observed.

___A___ 2. In sentence 10, the word *violating* means
   A. breaking.
   B. understanding.
   C. following.
   D. learning.

   In the example in sentence 11, we are told about people breaking the law by jaywalking. Therefore, "violating the rules" must mean "breaking the rules."

___B___ 3. Which sentence best states the main idea of the selection?
   A. In one experiment, people who passed a casually dressed couple responded negatively to them.
   B. The way people dress affects the way we view them and the level of influence they have over us.
   C. To get ahead in a career, dress in a high-status manner.
   D. Pedestrians were more likely to return coins to well-dressed people than to those dressed in low-status clothing.

   Answer B gives an overview of the material in the paragraph. Answers A and D are too narrow; each gives only one detail of the paragraph. Answer C is not supported.

___C___ 4. According to the experiment, we are more likely to return lost coins to
A. men.
B. women.
C. people in high-status clothing.   See sentence 9.
D. people in low-status clothing.

___C___ 5. People tend to react more positively toward
A. men who are casually dressed.
B. women.
C. people who are dressed formally or in a high-status manner.
D. couples who are dressed alike.   See sentences 7, 9, and 10.

___C___ 6. The relationship of sentence 8 to sentence 7 is one of
A. time.   Comparison transition: *Similar*. The responses to
B. illustration.   clothing in the hallway situation are being compared
C. comparison.   to the responses to clothing in other situations.
D. contrast.

___B___ 7. The relationship of sentences 11 and 12 to sentence 10 is one of
A. time.
B. illustration.   Illustration transition: *For example*.
C. contrast.
D. comparison.

___D___ 8. We can infer from this passage that our reactions are sometimes
A. not thought out.
B. based on appearances.   The entire passage suggests answer D.
C. illogical.
D. all of the above.

COMBINED SKILLS: Test 15

Read the passage below. Then write the letter of the best answer to each question that follows.

¹As one sociologist points out, adolescents and old people, as groups in our culture, are strikingly similar in certain ways. ²First, they are both often segregated from the rest of society. ³Young people are in schools, and old people are in retirement communities, assisted-living facilities, and nursing homes. ⁴Second, they both tend to be poorer than young adults or middle-aged people. ⁵Adolescents have less money because they do not yet have the education or experience to command high salaries, and old people have lower incomes because they are retired and living on their savings and social security. ⁶Third, independence is important for both groups—they are conscious of wanting it, while young adults and middle-aged people take it for granted. ⁷Adolescents want to become independent of their parents; old people want to keep their independence and not have to rely on their children or on institutions. ⁸Fourth, they both tend to have a relatively large amount of leisure time or, at least, time that they can choose or not choose to fill with study, work, or hobbies. ⁹However, young and middle-aged adults typically spend most of their time at their jobs or taking care of home duties such as child-rearing.

_C_ 1. In sentence 5, the word *command* means
   A. pay.
   B. desire.
   C. deserve.
   D. avoid.

   Education and experience make a worker more valuable and, therefore, more deserving of a high salary.

_C_ 2. In sentence 6, the word *conscious* means
   A. bored.
   B. pleased.
   C. aware.
   D. tired.

   Antonym-like clue in sentence 6: *take it for granted.* If you take something for granted, you do not notice it or are not aware of it.

_A_ 3. The main idea of this passage is stated in sentence
   A. 1.
   B. 2.
   C. 5.
   D. 9.

   Main idea signal: *similar in certain ways.* The rest of the passage points out four similarities between adolescents and old people.

_B_ 4. One thing old people and adolescents tend to have a lot of is
   A. money.
   B. leisure time.
   C. independence.
   D. education.

   See sentence 8.

___B___ 5. This selection is mainly organized as
   A. events in the lives of adolescents and the elderly, in a time order.
   B. a list of comparisons between adolescents and old people.
   C. definitions of adolescence and old age, with examples of each.
   D. causes of problems in adolescence and old age.   Addition words
              used with the list of items pattern: *First, Second, Third, Fourth.*

___D___ 6. The paragraph contrasts adolescents and old people with
   A. unemployed people.
   B. children and teenagers.   See sentences 4, 6, and 9.
   C. poor people.
   D. middle-aged people and young adults.

___A___ 7. The relationship between sentences 8 and 9 is one of
   A. contrast.   Contrast transition: *However.*
   B. comparison.   Adolescents and old people are contrasted
   C. addition.   with young and middle-aged adults.
   D. time.

___C___ 8. The paragraph implies that people of all ages value
   A. employment.
   B. social security.   See sentence 6.
   C. independence.
   D. intellectual challenge.

COMBINED SKILLS: Test 16

Read the passage below. Then write the letter of the best answer to each question that follows.

¹Driving has always been dangerous, but a new epidemic stretching across America's highways is making it even more risky. ²Researchers call this problem "road rage"—an intense anger that makes drivers become violent. ³Road rage is usually triggered by a minor traffic incident, such as someone honking a horn at another driver, or one person cutting in front of another. ⁴But once it strikes, this rage instantly turns ordinary people into possible killers. ⁵For example, recently one motorist on his way to work got angry when a car zipped in front of him, forcing him to slow down. ⁶The driver was so enraged that he pulled out a gun, drove up to the side of the other car, and tried to shoot the driver. ⁷Instead, he hit and killed the passenger—the driver's pregnant wife. ⁸Sadly, stories like this have been reported all over the country, particularly in crowded urban areas.

⁹Psychologists think that road rage is caused by a buildup of stress that acts like a time bomb waiting to explode. ¹⁰Once an event triggers the release of the tension, road rage strikes. ¹¹Since anyone on the road can be one of these "time bombs," police suggest that you drive carefully. ¹²They also say to call them if someone looks particularly angry and is driving in an inconsistent way.

_____C_____ 1. In sentence 3, the word *triggered* means
   A. imitated.
   B. shot.   Sentence 5 gives the example of a driver who got
   C. started.   angry because another driver cut him off. This
   D. ended.   minor traffic incident started, or triggered, his rage.

_____C_____ 2. Which sentence best expresses the main idea of the first paragraph?
   A. Road rage is an intense anger felt by drivers.
   B. A motorist became so angry when another car cut in front of him that he tried to shoot the other driver, but shot the driver's passenger instead.
   C. Driving is more dangerous than ever because many drivers are becoming violently angry.
   D. People are more likely to become angry and violent in crowded urban areas than in other areas.

   Answers A, B, and D are too narrow. Each gives only one detail from the paragraph.
   Answer C gives an overview of the idea illustrated by the details in the paragraph.

___B___ 3. According to the passage, drivers with road rage often
   A. are angered by dangerous driving.
   B. become violent over minor events.   *See sentence 3.*
   C. are poor drivers.
   D. are excellent drivers.

___A___ 4. Road rage is more likely to occur
   A. in crowded urban areas.
   B. on country roads.   *See sentence 8.*
   C. in parking lots.
   D. on suburban roads.

___C___ 5. The idea below is
   A. true according to the passage.   *Drinking is not mentioned*
   B. false according to the passage.   *or suggested.*
   C. not mentioned in the passage.

      People who drink are more likely to have road rage.

___B___ 6. Sentences 9 and 10 explain
   A. a time relationship.   *Cause:* Buildup of stress.
   B. a cause-effect relationship.   *Effect:* Tensions released and road rage
   C. contrasting situations.   strikes. Cause-effect transition: *caused.*
   D. a comparison.

___D___ 7. The author suggests that people with road rage often
   A. are young.
   B. are unemployed.   *See sentence 9.*
   C. drive very carefully.
   D. experience a lot of stress.

___D___ 8. We might infer from the passage that
   A. we are very unlikely to bump into a person with road rage.
   B. drivers are less likely to become angry at female drivers.
   C. most drivers experience road rage.
   D. it is best to keep one's distance from aggressive drivers.

      Answer A is the opposite of the message in the passage.
      Answers B and C are not supported.
      Sentences 11–12 suggest that it is best to try to prevent
      getting involved in road rage.

COMBINED SKILLS: Test 17

Read the passage below. Then write the letter of the best answer to each question that follows.

[1]Whether a surgeon tells someone that 10 percent of patients die during a particular surgery or that 90 percent survive, the information is the same. [2]But the effect is not. [3]The risk seems greater to people who hear that 10 percent will die. [4]The way we pose an issue is called framing.

[5]Similarly, consumers respond more positively to ground beef described as "75 percent lean" rather than "25 percent fat." [6]A new medical treatment strikes people as more successful and recommendable if framed as having a "50 percent success rate" rather than a "50 percent failure rate." [7]People are more bothered by an incident of student cheating if told that 65 percent of students had cheated than if told that 35 percent had not cheated. [8]And 9 in 10 college students rate a condom as effective if it supposedly has a "95 percent success rate" in stopping the AIDS virus; only 4 in 10 think it successful when given a "5 percent failure rate." [9]Merchants may mark up their "regular prices" to appear to offer huge savings on "sale prices." [10]A $100 coat marked down from $150 by store X can seem like a better deal than the same coat priced regularly at $100 by store Y.

___B___ 1. In sentence 4, the word *pose* means
  A. hide.
  B. state.
  C. research.
  D. remember.

  Sentence 1 describes two ways that a surgeon can tell patients about the survival rate. We can conclude that the passage will discuss how we state an issue.

___D___ 2. In sentence 5, the word *positively* means
  A. angrily.
  B. hungrily.
  C. fearfully.
  D. approvingly.

  Experience tells us that most people respond more approvingly to ground beef described as "lean" than to ground beef described as "fat."

___C___ 3. Which sentence best expresses the main idea of the passage?
  A. Statistics are often not accurate.
  B. Consumers prefer to think they are buying a bargain.
  C. How a point is worded influences its effect on people.
  D. Too often, the public is told lies.

  The passage concerns the different effects of different wordings of the same fact. Answers A and D are not supported. Answer B is too narrow.

___B___ 4. The passage explains the term
  A. *information.*
  B. *framing.*   See sentence 4.
  C. *response.*
  D. *percent.*

___B___ 5. The passage shows that
  A. it is sometimes OK to stretch the truth.
  B. a point can be stated in more than one way.
  C. there are very few true sales in stores.
  D. framing happens rarely.   The passage gives six examples of points
                                     being stated in two different ways.

___A___ 6. The passage is organized as a list of
  A. examples.
  B. reasons.   The examples illustrate *framing.*
  C. questions.
  D. facts.

___B___ 7. The passage implies that
  A. a 95 percent success rate is better than a 5 percent failure rate.
  B. framing can be used to influence reactions to information.
  C. framing and lying are exactly the same thing.
  D. most merchants are dishonest.   Examples show that people
                                          get results with framing.

___C___ 8. From the passage, we can conclude that
  A. statistics are usually incorrect.
  B. surgeons and businesses are alike in one way—neither can be trusted.
  C. knowing about framing can help us better evaluate information.
  D. there is no such thing as a bargain.

  If we know about framing, we are less likely to be influenced by it—
                            and thus more likely to be objective.

COMBINED SKILLS: Test 18

Read the passage below. Then write the letter of the best answer to each question that follows.

[1]Money appears to be very much on the minds of college freshmen, according to a recent survey of nearly 220,000 full-time freshmen at 300 colleges. [2]Colleges were advised to prepare for students who are "increasingly anxious" about the economy.

[3]The report states that students today are more likely to need loans than they were in the past. [4]More students than before are saying that an offer of financial aid is "very important" in choosing a college. [5]Moreover, a record 78 percent identified "being well-off financially" as a top objective. [6]That's higher than "raising a family" (74 percent) or "helping others in difficulty" (69 percent). [7]Forty years ago, the primary goal of most students was "to develop a meaningful philosophy of life." [8]Today, however, the main goal is to have financial security.

[9]There are other signs that financial concerns are intensifying. [10]Over 40 percent of students surveyed said that cost was a large factor in their choice of a school. [11]More students than in past surveys have an unemployed father and/or mother. [12]And more students than ever said a very important factor in selecting a college was whether its "graduates get good jobs."

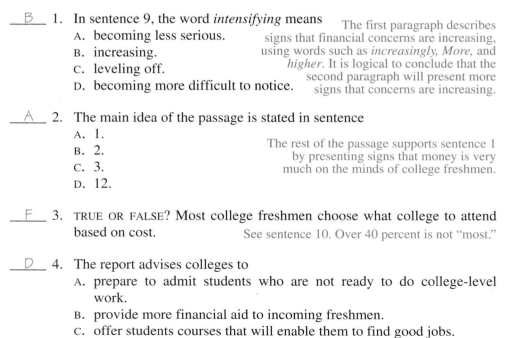

____B____ 1. In sentence 9, the word *intensifying* means
    A. becoming less serious.
    B. increasing.
    C. leveling off.
    D. becoming more difficult to notice.

The first paragraph describes signs that financial concerns are increasing, using words such as *increasingly, More,* and *higher.* It is logical to conclude that the second paragraph will present more signs that concerns are increasing.

____A____ 2. The main idea of the passage is stated in sentence
    A. 1.
    B. 2.
    C. 3.
    D. 12.

The rest of the passage supports sentence 1 by presenting signs that money is very much on the minds of college freshmen.

____F____ 3. TRUE OR FALSE? Most college freshmen choose what college to attend based on cost.

See sentence 10. Over 40 percent is not "most."

____D____ 4. The report advises colleges to
    A. prepare to admit students who are not ready to do college-level work.
    B. provide more financial aid to incoming freshmen.
    C. offer students courses that will enable them to find good jobs.
    D. prepare for students who are anxious about the economy.

See sentence 2.

___D___ 5. The relationship of sentence 5 to sentences 3 and 4 is one of
   A. time order.
   B. contrast.
   C. definition and example.
   D. addition.

> Sentence 5 adds another sign of financial concern to the concerns mentioned in sentences 3 and 4. Addition transition: *Moreover*.

___C___ 6. The selection mainly
   A. compares male and female college freshmen.
   B. explains why so many of today's college students are applying for scholarships.
   C. provides facts and statistics that support the idea that today's college students are very concerned about money.
   D. provides examples of typical freshman behavior.

> Answers A and D are not mentioned. Answer B covers only sentences 4 and 10.

___A___ 7. The passage suggests that a college freshman today would be less likely to
   A. take courses simply because he or she enjoys them.
   B. seek financial aid.
   C. work at a part-time job while going to school.
   D. come from families who are struggling to pay their bills.

___B___ 8. The passage suggests that
   A. there are fewer college freshmen today than there were forty years ago.
   B. today's college freshmen fear that they may not be able to find jobs after they graduate.
   C. most college freshmen enroll in the least expensive college they can find.
   D. college students no longer major in impractical subjects such as art and music.

Item 7:   Answer B is contradicted by sentences 3, 4, 10, and 11. Answer C is incorrect; it can be inferred from the long list of financial concerns that students would be more likely to work, not less likely. Answer D is contradicted by sentence 11.

Item 8:   See sentence 12. Answer A is not mentioned. Answer C is incorrect; sentence 10 says only that cost is "a large factor" for "over 40 percent" of students. Answer D is not supported because the passage says nothing about what students major in.

Sample Answer Sheet

Use the form below as a model answer sheet for the eighteen combined-skills tests on the preceding pages.

Name _____ Date _____

Section _____ SCORE: (Number correct) _____ x 12.5 = _____ %

COMBINED SKILLS: Test _____

1. _____

2. _____

3. _____

4. _____

5. _____

6. _____

7. _____

8. _____

Appendixes

Separating Fact from Opinion

Fact

A **fact** is information that can be proved true through objective evidence. This evidence may be physical proof or the spoken or written testimony of witnesses. For instance, there are some foods at McDonalds that cost only one dollar. One can visit a McDonalds and confirm this statement is true.

Following are some more facts—they can be checked for accuracy and thus proved true.

Fact: **The Quad Tower is the tallest building in this city.**

(A researcher could go out and, through inspection, confirm that the building is the tallest.)

Fact: **Albert Einstein willed his violin to his grandson.**

(This statement can be checked in historical publications or with Einstein's estate.)

Fact: **On September 11, 2001, terrorists destroyed the New York World Trade Center, killing thousands.**

(This event was witnessed in person or on television by millions, and it's in records worldwide.)

Opinion

An **opinion** is a belief, judgment, or conclusion that cannot be objectively proved true. As a result, it is open to question. For example, "McDonalds is a terrible place to eat" is an opinion. While some people might argue that fast food in general is harmful to one's health, other people enjoy the convenience and taste of fast food.

Or consider this example: After watching a movie, someone might state that the film was boring. The statement is an opinion because it cannot be objectively proved. Another person might see the same movie and find it exciting. Neither statement can be proved; both are opinions.

Here are some more opinions:

Opinion: **The Quad Tower is the ugliest building in the city.**

(There's no way to prove this statement because two people can look at the same building and come to different conclusions about its beauty. *Ugly* is a **value word**, a word we use to express a value judgment. Value, or judgment, words are signals that an opinion is being expressed. By their very nature, these words represent opinions, not facts.)

Opinion: **Einstein should have willed his violin to a museum.**

(Who says? Not his grandson. This is an opinion.)

Opinion: **The attack on the World Trade Center was the worst act of terrorism in the history of humankind.**

(Whether something is "worst" is always debatable. *Worst* is another value word.)

Points about Fact and Opinion

There are several points to keep in mind when considering fact and opinion.

1 **Value words** (ones that contain a judgment) often represent opinions. Here are examples of these words:

best	worse	lovely	bad
worst	great	disgusting	good
better	terrible	beautiful	wonderful

Value words often express judgments—they are generally subjective, not objective. While factual statements *report on* observed reality, subjective statements *interpret* reality. For example, the observation that it is raining outside is an objective one. The statement that the weather is bad, however, is subjective, an evaluation of reality. (Some people—for example, farmers whose crops need water—consider rain to be good weather.)

2 The words *should* and *ought to* often signal opinions. Those words introduce what people think should, or ought to, be done. Other people will disagree.

Couples should definitely not live together before marriage.

Couples ought to live together before getting married to be sure they are compatible.

3 Don't mistake widely held opinions for facts. Much information that sounds factual is really opinion. A real estate agent, for example, might say, "At the price listed, this rancher is a great buy." Buyers would be wise to wonder what the value word *great* means to the agent. Or an ad may claim that a particular automobile is "the most economical car on the road today," a statement that at first seems factual. But what is meant by *economical*? If the car offers the most miles per gallon but the worst record for expensive repairs, you might not agree that it's economical.

4 Finally, remember that much of what we read and hear is a mixture of fact and opinion. The reality is that most of what matters in life is very complex and cannot be separated into simple fact and opinion. Our challenge always is to arrive at the best possible informed opinion, and even then there will be people who disagree with us.

Fact and Opinion in Reading

In general, textbook authors try to be as factual as possible. Most textbook material is based on scientific observation and study, and textbook authors do their best to present us with all the facts and objective informed opinion. On the other hand, many essays, editorials, political speeches, and advertisements may contain facts, but those facts are often carefully selected to back up the authors' opinions.

 PRACTICE 1

To sharpen your understanding of fact and opinion, read the following statements and decide whether each is fact or opinion. Put an **F** (for "fact") or an **O** (for "opinion") beside each statement. Put **F+O** beside the **two** statements that are a mixture of fact *and* opinion.

> *Hint:* Remember that opinions are signaled by value words—words such as *great* or *hard* or *beautiful* or *terrible* that express a value judgment. Take care to note such words in your reading.

  F   1. Last night, a tree outside our house was struck by lightning.

  O   2. The waiters at that restaurant are <u>rude</u>, and the food costs <u>twice as much as it's worth</u>.

  F   3. Ostriches do not hide their heads in the sand.

  O   4. George Clooney and Halle Berry are the <u>most gorgeous</u> movie stars in Hollywood today.

 F+O 5. Low-flow showerheads save water, so all homeowners <u>should</u> be required to buy and install them in their showers.

To the Instructor: Words indicating opinions are underlined in this *Instructor's Edition.*

___O___ 6. *Watchers*, by Dean R. Koontz, is a <u>terrifying</u> story that is <u>bound to keep you awake at night</u>.

___F___ 7. The Grimm brothers collected their fairy tales from other storytellers.

___O___ 8. There is <u>nothing like</u> a bottle of Coca-Cola to satisfy thirst.

___F___ 9. In the late 1890s, when Coke was first sold, it included a small amount of cocaine, which was then legal.

_F+O_ 10. One of the <u>most delicious</u> of soft drinks, Coca-Cola was first intended to cure various ills, including headaches.

PRACTICE 2

Some of the statements below are facts, and some are opinions; in addition, **two** include fact and opinion. Label facts with an **F**, opinions with an **O**, and statements of fact *and* opinion with an **F+O**.

___O___ 1. German shepherds are the <u>scariest</u> dogs alive.
The word *scariest* is a value word.

___F___ 2. The dog that bites people the most often, according to one twenty-seven-
year study, is the German shepherd.
This fact can be checked by looking at the study.

The fact that German shepherds are used in police work and as guide dogs can be confirmed by research. Whether or not they make poor pets is an opinion.

_F+O_ 3. German shepherds, <u>which always make poor pets</u>, are used in police work and as guide dogs for the blind.

___F___ 4. Smoking has been found to be one cause of lung cancer. Confirmed by information from the American Cancer Society and in medical literature.

___O___ 5. Executives of corporations that pollute the environment <u>should be jailed</u>.
The word *should* signals this opinion.

___F___ 6. According to scientists, all the water on Earth has been recycled for millions of years, and we drink the same water as the dinosaurs did.
This fact can be confirmed by looking up scientific information on water.

_F+O_ 7. Because many studies have concluded that smoking is a health hazard, <u>cigarettes should be banned</u>. The fact that smoking is a health hazard can be confirmed by looking at the studies. The word *should* signals an opinion.

___F___ 8. Scientists predict that one-third of people who begin smoking under the age of 18 will die prematurely because of their habit. This prediction can be confirmed by research in scientific journals.

___O___ 9. <u>There's no illness harder to cope with than depression</u>. Some people might feel that other illnesses (for example, cancer) are harder to cope with.

___F___ 10. Depression is most common among persons between the ages of 25 and 44. This fact can be confirmed by researching the age group among which depression is most common.

On the Web: If you are using this book in class, you can visit our website for additional practice in separating fact from opinion. Go to **www.townsendpress.com** and click on "Online Exercises."

Identifying an Author's Purpose and Tone

Purpose

Authors write with a reason in mind, and you can better evaluate their ideas by determining what that reason is. The author's reason for writing is also called the **purpose** of a selection. Three common purposes are as follows:

- To **inform**—to give information about a subject. Authors with this purpose wish to provide facts that will explain or teach something to readers.

  For example, the author of an informative paragraph about sandwiches might begin, "Eating food between two slices of bread—a sandwich—is a practice that has its origins in eighteenth-century England."

- To **persuade**—to convince the reader to agree with the author's point of view on a subject. Authors with this purpose may give facts, but their main goal is to argue or prove a point to readers.

  The author of a persuasive paragraph about sandwiches might begin, "There are good reasons why every sandwich should be made with whole-grain bread."

- To **entertain**—to amuse and delight; to appeal to the reader's senses and imagination. Authors with this purpose entertain in various ways, through fiction and nonfiction.

  The author of an entertaining paragraph about sandwiches might begin, "What I wanted was a midnight snack, but what I got was better—the biggest, most magical sandwich in the entire world."

While the cover and title of anything you read—books, articles, and so on—don't necessarily suggest the author's main purpose, often they do. On the next page are the covers of three books. See if you can guess the primary purpose of each of these books.

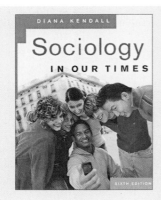

As you probably concluded, the main purpose of the textbook is to inform; the main purpose of *The Overspent American* is to persuade; and the main purpose of *Dave Barry's Money Secrets*—whose humorous subtitle reads, "Like Why Is There a Giant Eyeball on the Dollar?"—is to entertain.

PRACTICE 1

Read each of the three paragraphs below and decide whether the author's purpose is to inform, to persuade, or to entertain.

1. Each Saturday morning, TV commercials advertise fast foods and high-calorie cereals directly to children. These ads teach children unhealthy eating habits and have been linked to childhood obesity. Parents must realize how harmful such commercials are and should pressure companies to stop marketing unhealthy products to children.   Persuasive clues: *must* and *should*.

   Purpose: _____ To persuade _____

2. About 113 billion people have lived and died in the history of our planet, according to scientific estimates. Of all these people, the names of about 7 billion, or approximately 6 percent, are recorded in some way—on monuments or in books, manuscripts, and public records. The other 106 billion people are gone without a trace.   Factual details.

   Purpose: _____ To inform _____

3. Because of the war between his medium-size shirts and pants and his extra-large-size body, my brother has made a commitment to only three meals a day. His definition of a meal, however, is as broad as his belly. If we spot a pretzel salesman or a hot-dog stand on our way to a restaurant, for example, he is not beyond suggesting that we stop. "It'll make a good appetizer," he says.

   Purpose: _____ To entertain _____

                                        Playful and exaggerated details.

PRACTICE 2

Label each item according to its main purpose: to inform (**I**), to persuade (**P**), or to entertain (**E**).

___P___ 1. Professional athletes do not deserve their inflated salaries, nor does their behavior merit so much media attention.   Persuasive clue: *do not deserve.*

___I___ 2. The career of a professional athlete is usually quite short.
                                                    Direct statement of fact.

___P___ 3. Nurses assigned to intensive-care units should be given shorter shifts and higher pay because the work is unusually demanding and stressful.
                                                    Persuasive clue: *should.*

___I___ 4. On average, women dream more than men, and children dream more than adults.   Objective information.

___E___ 5. The best approach to take when you feel the urge to exercise is to lie down quickly in a darkened room until the feeling goes away.
                                    Humorous advice for avoiding exercise.

___E___ 6. It's easy to quit smoking; I've done it hundreds of times.
                                    Humorous twist on what it means to "quit smoking."

___P___ 7. More women should get involved in local politics and support the growing number of female candidates for public office.
                                                    Persuasive clue: *should.*

___I___ 8. An artificial odor is added to natural gas so that people can tell whether or not gas is leaking.   Straightforward fact.

___E___ 9. Once football season begins, Matt starts jogging every night—to the refrigerator during commercial breaks.   The humor comes from
                                                    Matt's jogging habits.

___I___10. The first person to die of radiation poisoning was a co-discoverer of radium, Marie Curie.   Straightforward information.

Tone

A writer's **tone** reveals the attitude that he or she has toward a subject. Tone is expressed through the words and details the writer selects. Just as a speaker's voice can project a range of feelings, a writer's voice can project one or more tones, or feelings: anger, sympathy, hopefulness, sadness, respect, dislike, and so on. Understanding tone is, then, an important part of understanding what an author has written.

To appreciate the differences in tone that writers can employ, look at the following versions of a murder confession. Then read them aloud—in the tone of voice appropriate in each case.

"I just shot my husband five times in the chest with this .357 Magnum." (*Tone:* matter-of-fact, objective.)

"How could I *ever* have killed him? I just can't *believe* I did that!" (*Tone:* shocked, disbelieving.)

"Oh, my God. I've murdered my husband. How can I *ever* be forgiven for this dreadful deed?" (*Tone:* guilty, regretful.)

"That dirty rat. He's had it coming for years. I'm glad I finally had the nerve to do it." (*Tone:* revengeful, self-satisfied.)

Words That Describe Tone

Here are some words often used to describe tone. Except for *matter-of-fact* and *objective*, the words reflect a feeling or judgment.

admiring	concerned	grateful	self-pitying
affectionate	critical	humorous	serious
amused	cruel	insulting	sorrowful
angry	curious	joyous	sympathetic
apologetic	defensive	loving	threatening
ashamed	doubtful	matter-of-fact	tragic
calming	encouraging	objective	warm
caring	excited	playful	worried
cheerful	forgiving	praising	
conceited	frightened	respectful	

PRACTICE 3

Below are five statements expressing different attitudes about a boss. Five different tones are used:

admiring	critical	objective	sympathetic	worried

For each statement, write the tone that you think is present. Use each tone once.

_____admiring_____   1. Tony is an <u>excellent</u> manager—the <u>best</u> one I've ever had.

_____sympathetic_____ 2. I know Tony's daughter has been sick. Naturally it's hard for him to concentrate on work right now.

_____critical_____ 3. Tony's too ambitious for his own good. That ambition may destroy both him and the company.

_____objective_____ 4. Since Tony Roberts became manager, sales in the appliance division have increased 30 percent.
The lack of emotion demonstrates an objective tone.

_____worried_____ 5. I'm afraid there's something wrong with Tony. For the last month or so, he's seemed distracted. Sometimes he repeats himself. And I've seen him taking pills several times a day.

PRACTICE 4

Following are five reactions to a fender-bender accident (in which one car hits and slightly damages the rear fender of another car). Label each statement with the tone of voice that you think is present. Choose each tone from the following box, and use each tone only once.

A. angry	B. apologetic	C. calm
D. concerned	E. defensive	

_D_ 1. "Are you hurt? Are you sure you're okay? Don't move too quickly. Take your time getting out of the car."   Both questions and both statements show the speaker's concern for the other person.

_B_ 2. "I am really sorry. I was daydreaming a bit, which is no excuse. I should have been more careful."   Statements of apology.

_A_ 3. "You idiot! If you hadn't stopped short, I would never have hit you. You should be tossed in jail. You could have gotten us both killed."
Angry statements.

_C_ 4. "It's no big deal. Neither of us was hurt, which is all that counts. The damage is slight. Don't worry about it."   Signs of calm.

_E_ 5. "Hey, this wasn't my fault. Don't even think about blaming me. You're the one that stopped too quickly, not me. I did nothing wrong here."
Defensive statements.

To the Instructor: Words that indicate tone are underlined in this *Instructor's Edition.*

On the Web: If you are using this book in class, you can visit our website for additional practice in identifying an author's purpose and tone. Go to **www.townsendpress.com** and click on "Online Exercises."

Writing Assignments

A Brief Guide to Effective Writing

Here in a nutshell is what you need to do to write effectively.

Step 1: Explore Your Topic through Informal Writing

To begin with, explore the topic that you want to write about or that you have been assigned to write about. You can examine your topic through **informal writing**, which usually means one of three things.

First, you can **freewrite** about your topic for at least ten minutes. In other words, for ten minutes, write whatever comes into your head about your subject. Write without stopping and without worrying at all about spelling or grammar or the like. Simply get down on paper all the information about the topic that occurs to you.

A second thing you can do is to **make a list of ideas and details** that could go into your paper. Simply pile these items up, one after another, like a shopping list, without worrying about putting them in any special order. Try to accumulate as many details as you can think of.

A third way to explore your topic is to **write down a series of questions and answers** about it. Your questions can start with words like *what, why, how, when,* and *where.*

Getting your thoughts and ideas down on paper will help you think more about your topic. With some raw material to look at, you are now in a better position to decide on just how to proceed.

Step 2: Plan Your Paper with an Informal Outline

After exploring your topic, plan your paper, using an informal outline. Do two things:

- **Decide on and write out the point of your paper.** It is often a good idea to begin your paragraph with this point, which is known as the **topic sentence**. If you are writing an essay of several paragraphs, you will probably want to include your main point somewhere in your first paragraph. In a paper of several paragraphs, the main point is called the **central point**, or **thesis**.

- **List the supporting reasons, examples, or other details that back up your point.** In many cases, you should have at least two or three items of support.

Step 3: Use Transitions

Once your outline is worked out, you will have a clear "road map" for writing your paper. As you write the early drafts of your paper, use **transitions** to introduce each of the separate supporting items (reasons, examples, or other details) you present to back up your point. For instance, you might introduce your first supporting item with the transitional words *first of all*. You might begin your second supporting item with words such as *another reason* or *another example*. And you might indicate your final supporting detail with such words as *last of all* or *a final reason.*

Step 4: Edit and Proofread Your Paper

After you have a solid draft, edit and proofread the paper. Ask yourself several questions to evaluate your paper:

1. Is the paper **unified**? Does all the material in the paper truly support the opening point?

2. Is the paper **well supported**? Is there plenty of specific evidence to back up the opening point?

3. Is the paper **clearly organized**? Does the material proceed in a way that makes sense? Do transitions help connect ideas?

4. Is the paper **well written**? When the paper is read aloud, do the sentences flow smoothly and clearly? Has the paper been checked carefully for grammar, punctuation, and spelling mistakes?

Writing Assignments for the Twenty Readings

Note: Your instructor may also permit you to write a paper that is based upon one of the discussion questions that follow each reading.

Part One Readings

Responsibility

1. Peck writes about the great lengths people will go to "avoid assuming responsibility for personal problems." Think of times you have observed people blaming someone else or circumstances for their own problem. Then write a paper that begins with the following topic sentence:

   4 things

   > Just like M. Scott Peck, I have seen someone refuse to take responsibility for his (*or* her) own problem.

   Then go on to develop your paper by explaining who the person is, what the person's problem was, how he or she helped to create it, and how he or she blamed others or circumstances rather than accept responsibility.

2. Peck explains that the only way to solve a problem is to solve it—in other words, to take responsibility for the problem and find a solution. Write a paper about a time in your own life when you had to accept responsibility for a problem and figure out a solution for it. In choosing a topic for this assignment, it can be helpful to list areas in which you have experienced problems. Following, for example, is one such list:

   - Getting along with parents
   - Balancing a budget
   - Use of alcohol
   - Obeying the law
   - Holding a job

   When you have your list, ask yourself which of those problems you have accepted responsibility for and solved or improved. Once you have decided on a topic to write about, you might begin with a statement like this:

   > After years of scraping together just enough money to get from one week to the next, I've taken steps to deal with my money problems.

   Support your opening statement with the following: 1) one or more examples of the problem, 2) an explanation of how and when you began to understand the problem, and 3) a detailing of the steps you have taken to deal with the problem.

All the Good Things

1. In life, we often forget to let others know how much they have helped us. Sister Helen learned of the value of her work with her students only after one of them died. Write about someone to whom you are grateful, and explain what that person has done for you. Begin by introducing the person and the relationship he or she has to you. For example:

   My brother Roy has been an important part of my life.

   My best friend Ginger helped me through a major crisis.

   Mrs. Morrison, my seventh-grade English teacher, taught me a lesson for which I will always be grateful.

   Then provide detailed examples that show what the person did for you and how important that person has been for you.

2. Early in her essay, Sister Helen describes how a "teacher's mistake" forced her to punish a student in front of the class. Write about a time when you were pressured to do something because others around you expected it. Explain what the situation was, just what happened, and how you felt afterward. Here are two sample opening sentences:

   Even though I knew it was wrong, I went along with some friends who shoplifted at the mall.

   Just because my friends did, I made fun of a kid in my study hall who was a slow learner.

Group Pressure

1. Have you had the following experience? From conversation with a friend, you believe you know his or her opinion on some matter. But when the two of you are with a larger group, you hear the friend agree with the general group opinion, even though it is different from the one he or she held before. The opinion might be about something unimportant, such as the quality of a new movie or TV show. Or it may be on something more important, such as whether or not someone is likable. Write a description of that experience. An opening statement for this paper might be something like this one:

   I believe that group pressure caused _____ to change his (*or* her) opinion about someone new at school.

2. The "lines on the card" experiment gives just a hint of the kind of pressure group opinion can bring to bear on an individual. What bigger, more important examples of group pressure can you think of? They might be ones occurring in your family, in your town, in your school, in your city, in the country, or in the world. Write a paper in which you describe one or more examples that you believe show group pressure on individual behavior. Here are a few topics to consider writing about:

    ● Making fun of a particular student   ● Being part of a gang
    ● Racial problems in a school or city   ● Being a fan of a sports team
    ● The use of drugs or alcohol within a group of friends

    As you describe someone's behavior, be sure to include details that help show group pressure.

A Door Swings Open

1. When Roxanne found out she had lupus, she had to learn, very quickly, a great deal about the disease. Like Roxanne, people are often forced to learn new things rapidly when they are put into an unfamiliar situation. Write about a time that you had to become informed quickly about a new situation that affected you. You might consider writing about what you had to learn:

    ● when you moved to a new town
    ● when you entered a new school
    ● when a loved one developed an illness
    ● when you started a new job

    As you write, be specific about *what* sort of things you had to learn and *how* you found the information you needed.

2. When little Michelle died, Roxanne learned a painful lesson: life is not fair. What experience in *your* life made you think, "Life isn't fair"? Write a description of that experience, explaining in what way you think its outcome was unfair. Here are some sample first lines from papers like the one you might write:

    It wasn't fair that my grandmother had to suffer so much at the end of her life.

    It wasn't fair that my hard-working parents lost their house.

    It wasn't fair that my mean neighbor won the lottery.

Body Language

1. This essay describes body language in two settings: a job interview and a singles' bar. In what other setting have you observed body language at work? Write a paper that describes where and how you have seen people communicating without words. You can write about any setting, including any of the following:

- A family dinner
- A date
- An office or other workplace
- A classroom

In the opening of your paper, explain the setting, the participants, and the general mood that was being communicated by the nonverbal behavior. For example, here are some opening sentences:

> The body language in our math class shows students are bored and confused.

> Anyone who watches my parents together can tell that they are still in love.

Go on to describe in detail the body language you observe and what you believe it means and why.

2. Johnson states in her essay that some body language comes from our roots in the animal world. Think of behavior you've observed in an animal—a pet dog or cat, for example. What body language have you observed? Can the animal communicate its needs or desires through its actions? Describe all the ways you can think of that a pet communicates through body language. Here's a sample of a sentence that expresses the main point for this paper:

> My dog, Red, has a large "vocabulary" of body language.

Behind Closed Doors: Violence in the Family

1. Have you ever been aware that someone was being abused in the home of a neighbor, friend, or relative? Write a paper about the situation. (You may use made-up names if you feel uncomfortable using the people's real identities.) Explain who you believe was being hurt and why you believe it. Then explain what, if any, action you took and what (if anything) happened to change the situation.

2. The essay makes this statement: "In effect, parenthood confers a 'license for hitting' in our society." Do you believe that parents are justified in sometimes hitting a child? Write a paper that supports one of the following statements:

> I think there are times when a parent has the right to hit a child.

> It is a bad idea, under any circumstances, for parents to hit their children.

Support your main point with reasons that back up your opinion. If you take the first point of view, describe specific times when you think hitting would be justified. If you take the second point of view, write about circumstances when hitting a child would be tempting, and explain why you think it would be the wrong thing to do. Suggest alternate ways of dealing with the situation.

Wired for Touch

1. Grandinetti states that "all the handshakes and hugs that seem to be part of our culture these days … are also serving a good purpose." Write a paper in which you compare or contrast how much physical affection your family showed, when you were younger, with how much *you* now show. You might begin with a sentence like this:

   Like my family, I show a lot of physical affection to my friends.

   Although my family was very "huggy," I don't show affection that way.

   My family doesn't do a lot of hugging, but I do.

   Continue with examples that illustrate your family's way of showing affection and your own way of showing affection.

2. In her essay, Grandinetti points out that our sense of touch develops even before our ability to see or hear. Which of those senses do you think is most important to your own happiness? If you had to give up one of those three senses—hearing, sight, or touch—which would it be, and why? Begin with a topic sentence like this:

   If I had to give up one of my senses, it would be my ability to see.

   Then continue by explaining why you chose that sense and how you think you would make up for its loss.

A Path to Marriage

1. It is apparent that Jean and Rod Sutton have a good marriage. Among the couples you know, who do you think has the best marriage? Write about that couple and their relationship. Include details about their words and actions that reveal why you admire their marriage.

2. As she grew to know Rod, Jean noticed some very specific characteristics she admired in him—for instance, his work ethic, his ability to communicate, and his respectful attitude towards older people. What are two or three characteristics that *you* would like to see in a potential mate? Write about those characteristics and why they are important to you. As Jean does, give examples of how those characteristics can be expressed.

Lighting a Match

1. Ruiz and her parents had very different ideas about whom she should marry. How well have your plans for your life fit your parents' hopes for you? Write a paper about a decision in your life on which you and your parents have either clashed or agreed. Tell exactly what your parents had in mind and how they communicated their hopes to you. Also explain clearly your decision and the reasons for it. You may wish to conclude by telling how you feel now about your decision. Here are some sample openings for this assignment:

   > Although my parents urged me to become a teacher, I am studying to be a veterinary assistant.

   > My parents did not want me to marry my high-school girlfriend, and I surprised them—and myself—by doing what they wanted.

2. Ruiz writes about her typical morning, from stumbling out of bed to getting to and through school. She tells in detail about getting ready in the morning, studying for a test while driving to school, and thinking about her "household woes" at the same time. Write a paper describing your typical morning. To make sure you have plenty of interesting specific details, do some freewriting or list making, or both. Then think of a sentence that will cover all of the details you will write about. Here, for instance, is one possible statement of the main point:

   > Though a typical morning in my life starts slowly, it develops into some very productive—but hectic—hours.

   Before writing your final draft, double-check your opening point to see if it still covers the details in your paper or if it needs adjusting. (Perhaps you realized your morning doesn't start so slowly after all.) Also, use a few time transitions to make the sequence of events clear to your reader. You could write, for example, "*First* I hear my alarm go off at 6 a.m. *Then* I take a shower, ending with a few seconds of ice-cold water to wake up my body and my brain."

Do It Better!

1. "Do It Better!" suggests that television can interfere with children's academic progress. Write a paper on what you believe is another unfortunate effect that television has on children. To find a topic and then to gather colorful details, you may find it helpful to spend a few sessions in front of the TV with a notebook. Below are sample points you might choose to write about:

   ● TV advertising encourages children to want to buy too much.
   ● TV situation comedies promote poor family values.
   ● Television keeps children from more useful recreational activities.

   Support your paper's main point with specific details and examples.

2. Reading helped Bennie, and it can do a lot for adults too. Most of us, however, don't have someone around to insist that we do a certain amount of personal reading every week. In addition, many of us don't have the amount of free time that Bennie and Curtis had. How can adults find time to read more? Write a paper listing several ways adults can add more reading to their lives.

   A good prewriting strategy for this assignment is list making. Simply write out as many ways as you can think of. Don't worry about putting them in any special order. You will select and organize the methods you wish to include in your paper after accumulating as many ideas as you can.

Part Two Readings

Winners, Losers, or Just Kids?

1. No matter what we we're like in high school, we change in important ways as we get older. Write about some good changes in your life since high school and perhaps about changes you would like to make in the future. Your main point for this paper might be similar to this: "My life has changed in important ways since high school, and I'm hoping for even more and better changes in the future."

2. Write about someone you know who has changed a great deal since high school. The change could be for the good—or not so good. Describe what that person was like in high school, how he or she is today, and what you think might have caused the changes. You might, for instance, write about one of the following:

   ● A person who was once a successful student who is now having problems in life
   ● A person you thought would never achieve anything who is now doing well
   ● A person who once was mean or unfriendly but is now pleasant

Owen, the Stray Cat

1. Are you a cat and/or dog lover? Or can you do without cats and/or dogs in your life? Write a paper in which you try to persuade the rest of the world to share your feelings about these animals. Strengthen your argument by providing three reasons for feeling the way you do. You may write about cats *and* dogs, or you may focus on either cats *or* dogs. Begin with a sentence something like one of these:

   "I don't want cats or dogs in my life for the following reasons: They smell bad, they're expensive to feed, and they make a mess of a house."

   "I love having dogs in my life because they're great company, they provide protection, and they give me a reason to get out and exercise."

   Then develop your paper by providing support for each of your three reasons.

2. Bob rescued the kitten even though he wasn't a cat person. When has someone you know done something that seemed surprisingly out of character? Perhaps a timid friend went skydiving, or a kind person lashed out at a friend in a cruel way. Write about that event, making it clear not only what the person did but also why it seemed out of character for him or her. Your topic sentence might be something like this:

   I was surprised when I heard my usually very honest friend tell a lie.

   My stingy uncle was amazingly generous when I needed help recently.

Eye Contact

1. "Making eye contact" is not something that is talked about in many classrooms, but Ron Clark makes it part of his students' education. Do you think that it's appropriate to talk in school about topics like making eye contact, showing respect to school employees, and the other kinds of behavior that Clark refers to? Or should teachers discuss only the particular subject they are teaching? Write a paragraph that supports one of these two topic sentences:

   I think Ron Clark is right to talk to his students about eye contact and showing respect.

   I don't think it's a teacher's job to talk to students about things like eye contact and showing respect.

   Explain why you chose the topic sentence you did and how you see a teacher's role in his or her students' lives.

2. In his classroom, Ron Clark insists on some rules such as "make eye contact," "do not interrupt a student who is speaking," and "keep your eyes on the teacher." If you were a teacher, what are some rules you would make for your students? Write about two or three rules you would put in place and why they are important to you.

Disaster and Friendship

1. Wilson felt his experience was worth writing about because it had some surprising twists—things didn't happen quite the way he expected. Write a paper in which you tell about a similarly surprising experience—one that didn't quite turn out as you expected. For example, you might write about a person who surprised you with his or her behavior. In that case, your main point might be "I thought I knew what _____ was like, but he (*or* she) revealed himself (*or* herself) to be quite different." Here are three other possible main points to start with:

   > Going to college has turned out to be a different experience than I expected.
   >
   > Working in a department store was a pleasant surprise for me.
   >
   > As I've grown older, I've realized that my parents are wiser than I thought.

2. Wilson's trip south was his solution to a work problem he faced as a caddy. Write about a time you faced a problem with your work life and what you did to try to solve that problem. For example, you could write about any of the following:

   ● Having trouble finding a job
   ● Working overly long hours
   ● Having a troublesome boss
   ● Having to work with someone you really disliked
   ● Being laid off

Read All About It

1. Write about someone (even yourself) who, like DeBlasio, changed his or her life as an adult. Discuss what the person's life was before, what he or she did in order to change, and what that person's life is like now. Below are some of the many topics you might write about:

   ● Someone who married or had a child late in life
   ● Someone who changed careers
   ● Someone who got divorced
   ● An adult who learned to read (or drive, or type, or perform any other important skill)

   Begin with a sentence telling who and what you are writing about. For instance:

   > Chris has changed dramatically since he was in trouble with the law.
   >
   > I am no longer the shy person I used to be in high school.

   Then provide details that show what the person used to be like and what he or she is like today.

2. If you could improve any of the schools you attended, what would you do? Write about two or three changes you would make. Provide specific details to show precisely what you would change and why you would change it. In your opening sentence, state the things you would change so that readers will know exactly what your paper is about. For example:

> If I were in charge of my college, I would change the cafeteria food and the cost of tuition.
>
> If I were in charge of my high school, there are three things I would change: the athletic facilities, the way tests are graded, and the books that are used.

Then go on to explain exactly what the changes would be and why you would make these changes.

Adult Children at Home

1. The typical household used to be thought of as Dad and Mom and the kids. But these days, a great many people live in other types of arrangements. Write a paper about the advantages and disadvantages of one of these other arrangements. Here are some possible topics:

   ● Living alone
   ● Living with a person with whom you are involved romantically
   ● Living with a group of friends of both sexes
   ● Living with a person of the opposite sex with whom you are not involved romantically
   ● Older parents living with grown children

   Or you may write a paper that compares two types of living conditions—living alone as opposed to living with a friend, for example.

2. Mack ends her article with a list of "tips on maintaining a happy 'nest.'" Write a paper in which you offer a list of suggestions for getting along in a particular situation. Begin by explaining why it is important for the situation to go well. Then go on to list your suggestions. (To see how to develop a series of tips, reread paragraphs 19–22 of the selection.) Some possible topics for this paper are how to keep up a

   ● close friendship.   ● good relationship with a boss.
   ● good marriage.   ● positive relationship with a landlord.

   Here's an example of an opening sentence for this paper:

   > There are four guidelines a person should follow in order to have a good relationship with a boss.

How To Make It in College, Now That You're Here

1. What particular pressures do you deal with as you go to school? Write a paper that describes some of the biggest problems that stand in the way of your doing your best job as a student. Describe how each of them affects you, and briefly state how you try to overcome them. Here are some typical problems many students might mention:

   ● Roommate problems   ● Money worries
   ● Personal difficulties   ● Distractions (parties, etc.)

2. Drawing upon your own experience as a student, write about "making it" at your particular school. Come up with three or four "secrets of success" that you believe would benefit other students. They may be serious or lighthearted—anything from "avoid the first floor of the library—it's too noisy to study there" to "stay away from the cheese fries at the snack shop." You may use the following or something similar for your main point: "There are a few things new students at this school would benefit from knowing." Then discuss each of your three or four suggestions, choosing colorful details to explain your points.

False Ideas about Reading

1. The Winklers write about how people can be affected by myths—ideas that many people believe but that are not always true. Write a paper about how your life has been affected by a myth. Describe the myth and tell how it affected your life. Your paper can be serious or lighthearted. You might write about a myth concerning any of the following:

   ● A big city
   ● Television
   ● Teachers
   ● Children
   ● The differences between men and women

   Here is a sample opening sentence for this paper:

   > A powerful myth that affected my childhood was the idea that children should be seen but not heard.

2. Write a paper about how one of the three "False Ideas about Reading" has affected you. Tell how that idea has influenced how you study and how you read (or don't read) for pleasure. If you feel the selection may change your approach to reading, discuss that too. Here's one possible opening sentence for this assignment:

The myth that reading once is enough has affected both my studying and my view of my own abilities.

Dealing with Feelings

1. Can you think of times that you (or someone else) *withheld* or *displayed* feelings—when *describing* them would have been more useful? Write about one such time. You might begin with something like this statement of the main point:

   > An experience I had recently showed that describing is often the best strategy for dealing with feelings.

   Then narrate the event, showing how feelings were withheld or displayed and what the result was. Finally, contrast the outcome of the event with what might have happened if feelings had been described.

2. "Dealing With Feelings" lists and discusses several ways to deal with feelings. Write a paper in which you present three ways to do something else. Your tone may be serious or humorous. You might write about three ways to

   - cut expenses.
   - meet people.
   - criticize in a helpful manner.
   - ruin a meal.
   - embarrass your friends.
   - hurt a relationship.

   Here is a possible opening sentence for this assignment:

   > In order to ruin a meal, you must follow three simple steps.

Childhood Stress and Resilience

1. "Stressful events are part of every childhood," write Papalia and Olds. Write a paper about a stressful experience of your childhood and how you dealt with it. You might also discuss how that stressful situation still affects you today. Here's one possible opening sentence for this assignment:

   > There was one especially stressful situation in my childhood that I had to struggle to overcome.

   The rest of your paper can describe the situation and how you coped with it.

2. Whatever the stresses of your childhood, you are likely to have had several "compensating experiences"—that is, positive experiences that helped you to become stronger and to overcome some of the stresses of your childhood. Write a paper in which you list and discuss several of these compensating experiences. Your opening sentence might be something like this one:

> My relationship with my grandparents and being part of the school football team helped me deal with the stresses of my childhood.

Reread paragraph 13 of the selection to see the compensating experiences listed by the authors. You may write about any of them or any others you can think of.

Limited Answer Key

An important note: To strengthen your reading skills, you must do more than simply find out which of your answers are right and which are wrong. You also need to figure out (with the help of this book, the teacher, or other students) *why* you missed the questions you did. By using each of your wrong answers as a learning opportunity, you will strengthen your understanding of the skills. You will also prepare yourself for the review and mastery tests in Part One, the reading comprehension questions in Part Two, and the combined-skills tests in Part Three, for which answers are not given here.

Answers to the Practices in Part One

1 Dictionary Use

Practice 1

1. pelican, Peking, penalty kick
2. exact, evil, ewe
3. kindergarten, killing, kilowatt
4. during, duplicate, dunk
5. stumble, subcompact, style

Practice 2

1. occasion
2. duty
3. decided
4. accident
5. neighbor
6. autumn
7. remember
8. attention
9. experiment
10. photocopy

Practice 3

2. dis•close, 2
3. hur•ri•cane, 3
4. un•der•tak•er, 4
5. in•hu•man•i•ty, 5

Practice 4

1. A
2. A
3. B
4. A
5. A
6. B
7. B
8. B
9. B
10. B

Practice 5

A. 2. majority, 1
   3. isolate, 1
   4. artificial, 2
   5. natural, 2

B. 7. ăd′və-kāt′
   8. ŏp′tə-mĭst
   9. är′ə-gənt
   10. hī-pŏth′ĭ-sĭs

Practice 6

1. 4; second
2. 4; second
3. 3; first
4. 5; second
5. 3; second

Practice 7

1. noun, verb
2. noun, verb
3. noun, verb, adjective
4. preposition, adverb
5. noun, verb, adjective, adverb

Practice 8

1. verb
   wrote; written; writing
2. adjective
   craziest
3. noun
   qualities

Practice 9

1. Definition 1
2. Definition 2
3. Definition 2

2 Vocabulary in Context

Practice 1: Examples

1. Examples: *numerous paper cups, ticket stubs, sandwich wrappings, cigarette butts;* C
2. Examples: *white bread, rice, mashed potatoes;* C
3. Examples: *New York, Boston, Philadelphia;* B
4. Example: *extra calcium, large doses of vitamin C;* A
5. Examples: *backing his car into the side of his boss's Cadillac, trying to walk through a glass door;* B
6. Examples: *the death of a child, the death of a spouse;* B
7. Examples: *buying or selling a product;* C
8. Examples: *baptisms, church weddings, funeral services;* B
9. Examples: *"adware," "clickthrough rate," "spambot";* A
10. Examples: *car dealerships, department stores, frozen-yogurt stands, online drugstores;* B

Practice 2: Synonyms

1. self-important
2. powerful
3. cloudy
4. secret
5. believable
6. discussion
7. force
8. rich
9. prove
10. variety

Practice 3: Antonyms

1. Antonym: *in-depth;* A
2. Antonym: *temporary;* A
3. Antonym: *allowed;* C
4. Antonym: *old;* A
5. Antonym: *order;* B
6. Antonym: *planned;* B
7. Antonym: *expert;* C
8. Antonym: *making progress;* C
9. Antonym: *concerned;* C
10. Antonym: *carefully thought-out;* B

Practice 4: General Sense

1. C
2. A
3. A
4. C
5. A
6. B
7. C
8. B
9. A
10. C

3 Main Ideas

Practice 1

1. S, S, G, S
2. S, S, S, G
3. S, G, S, S
4. G, S, S, S
5. S, S, S, G
6. S, S, S, G
7. S, G, S, S
8. G, S, S, S
9. S, S, G, S
10. S, S, S, G

Practice 2

Answers will vary. Here are some possibilities:

1. milk, coffee
2. football, basketball
3. father, nephew
4. tuna, egg salad
5. newspaper, magazine
6. shrimp, crabmeat
7. angry, pleading
8. selfishness, dishonesty
9. loyalty, honesty
10. "Hi there," "Good morning"

Practice 3

1. S, S, P, S
2. S, S, S, P
3. S, S, S, P
4. P, S, S, S

Practice 4

1.	S	3.	S
	S		P
	S		S
	P		S
2.	S	4.	P
	S		S
	P		S
	S		S

Practice 5

Group 2		Group 4	
A.	SD	A.	SD
B.	MI	B.	SD
C.	T	C.	MI
D.	SD	D.	T

Group 3

A. MI
B. T
C. SD
D. SD

Practice 6

Paragraph 1
1. *Topic:* B
2. *Main idea:* Sentence 1

Paragraph 2
1. *Topic:* A
2. *Main idea:* Sentence 1

Paragraph 3
1. *Topic:* C
2. *Main idea:* Sentence 1

Paragraph 4
1. *Topic:* A
2. *Main idea:* Sentence 2

Practice 7

1. a number of advantages
2. several ways
3. three major inventions
4. A series of mistakes
5. two important steps
6. some alarming facts
7. First of all
8. In addition
9. Also
10. Finally

4   Supporting Details

Practice 1 *(Wording of answers may vary.)*

Passage 1
1. Serious money problems
   a. Checks that bounce
   b. Minimal monthly payment on credit card cannot be made
2. Distinct mood pattern
   a. Tension before shopping
3. Shoplifting
4. Other addictive behaviors

Words that introduce a list: signs of addiction to shopping

Words that introduce:
   First major detail: One
   Second major detail: second
   Third major detail: Another
   Fourth major detail: Last of all

Passage 2
1. Cheaper
   b. Another $30 for drinks and snacks
2. More comfortable
   a. No bumper-to-bumper traffic
3. More informative
   a. Close-ups and instant replays
   b. Detailed explanations by commentators

Words that introduce a list: several advantages

Words that introduce:
   First major detail: One
   Second major detail: Morover
   Third major detail: Finally

Practice 2 *(Wording of answers may vary.)*

Passage 1

Be specific.   Stick to the present.
Don't use insults.   Complain privately.

Words that introduce a list:
   several sensible guidelines

Words that introduce:
   First major detail: First
   Second major detail: Second
   Third major detail: In addition
   Fourth major detail: last

Passage 2
Chest discomfort
Pain or discomfort in upper body
Shortness of breath
Lightheadedness, nausea, or cold sweat

> *Words that introduce a list:*
> *various signs*

> *Words that introduce:*
> *First major detail:* For one thing
> *Second major detail:* Next
> *Third major detail:* Also
> *Fourth major detail:* Finally

5   Locations of Main Ideas

Practice 1

1. *Main idea:* Sentence 1
2. *Main idea:* Sentence 2
3. *Main idea:* Sentence 9
4. *Main idea:* Sentence 5

Practice 2

1. *Main idea:* Sentence 8
2. *Main idea:* Sentence 1
3. *Main idea:* Sentence 2
4. *Main idea:* Sentence 3

Practice 3

1. *Main idea:* Sentence 2
2. *Main idea:* Sentence 1
3. *Main idea:* Sentence 7
4. *Main idea:* Sentence 2

6   Relationships I

Practice 1

1. B Another
2. A also
3. D In addition
4. C For one thing
5. E second

Practice 2 *(Answers may vary.)*

1. A After
2. E When
3. D Then
4. B Before
5. C during

Practice 3 *(Wording of answers may vary.)*

A. Main idea: Research has revealed three different types of kindness.
1. Natural
2. Rule-guided
3. Imitative

B. Main idea: Opossums cope with danger by using a few defense methods.

| Play dead | Scare off enemies |

Practice 4 *(Wording of answers may vary.)*

Main idea: All of us have certain fears at different points in our lives.
1. Young children worry about something bad happening to their parents.
2. Teenagers fear social rejection.
3. Parents fear that their children will be harmed.
4. Elderly people are afraid of poor health and death.

Practice 5 *(Wording of answers may vary.)*

Main idea: To study a textbook effectively, follow a few helpful steps.
Read and mark the selection.
Write study notes.
Study the notes.

Practice 6

1. B
2. A
3. A
4. B
5. A
6. B
7. A
8. B
9. A
10. B

7 Relationships II

Practice 1 *(Answers may vary.)*

1. For example
2. Once
3. such as
4. for instance
5. example

Practice 2

A. Term being defined: *stimulant*; definition—3; *example 1*—4; *example 2*—5

B. Term being defined: *jargon*; definition—1; *example 1*—3; *example 2*—4

Practice 3 *(Answers may vary.)*

1. just as
2. Similarly
3. as
4. similar
5. just like

Practice 4 *(Answers may vary.)*

1. but
2. Although
3. on the other hand
4. Despite
5. however

Practice 5 *(Wording of answers may vary.)*

A. Comparison: Abraham Lincoln and John F. Kennedy
B. Contrast: high school and college

Practice 6 *(Answers may vary.)*

1. Because
2. Therefore
3. resulted in
4. As a result
5. reason

Practice 7 *(Wording of answers may vary.)*

A. *Main idea (the effect): Two reasons explain weight gain among the Japanese.*
   Cause 1: Less active lifestyles
   Cause 2: High-fat diet

B. **Main idea** *(the cause):* Increases in the numbers of elderly people will have a major impact in Europe, Canada, and the United States.
   Major supporting details (the effects):
   1. Fewer people available to fill jobs
   2. Bigger demand on pension systems
   3. Great strain on national medical services

Practice 8

1. B	6. A
2. A	7. C
3. C	8. B
4. B	9. A
5. C	10. C

8 Inferences

Practice 1

A. 1. C
   2. A
   3. B

B. 4. B
   5. C
   6. C

Practice 2

1, 4, 6, 7, 10

Practice 3

A. 2, 3
B. 2, 4

9 Implied Main Ideas

Practice 1

1.	B	6.	C
2.	A	7.	A
3.	A	8.	C
4.	B	9.	C
5.	A	10.	C

Practice 2 *(Wording of answers may vary.)*

1. Directions
2. Seafood
3. Tests (*or* Test questions)
4. Noises (*or* Sounds)
5. book
6. restaurant
7. white
8. Baby
9. Signs
10. Opposites (*or* Words with opposite meanings)

Practice 3

1. A
2. A
3. B

Practice 4

1. C
2. C
3. D

10 The Basics of Argument

Practice 1

Group 1		Group 3	
A.	S	A.	P
B.	S	B.	S
C.	S	C.	S
D.	P	D.	S

Group 2		Group 4	
A.	S	A.	S
B.	S	B.	S
C.	P	C.	P
D.	S	D.	S

Practice 2

1.	C	3.	B
2.	A	4.	A

Practice 3

1. B, C, E
2. A, B, C
3. B, C, E
4. A, C, E
5. A, C, E

Practice 4

Group 1: B
Group 2: A
Group 3: B
Group 4: A

Answers to the Practices in the Appendixes

Separating Fact from Opinion

Practice 1

1. F
2. O
3. F
4. O
5. F+O
6. O
7. F
8. O
9. F
10. F+O

Practice 2

1. O
2. F
3. F+O
4. F
5. O
6. F
7. F+O
8. F
9. O
10. F

Identifying an Author's Purpose and Tone

Practice 1

1. To persuade
2. To inform
3. To entertain

Practice 2

1. P
2. I
3. P
4. I
5. E
6. E
7. P
8. I
9. E
10. I

Practice 3

1. admiring
2. sympathetic
3. critical
4. objective
5. worried

Practice 4

1. D
2. B
3. A
4. C
5. E

Acknowledgments

Bassis, Michael S., Richard J. Gelles, and Ann Levine. "Behind Closed Doors: Violence in the Family." From *Sociology: An Introduction*, 3rd ed. Copyright © 1998 by McGraw-Hill, Inc. Reprinted by permission.

Black, Roxanne. "A Door Swings Open." Originally published as "In the Beginning." From *Unexpected Blessings* by Roxanne Black, copyright © 2008 by Roxanne Black. Used by permission of Avery Publishing, an imprint of Penguin Group (USA) Inc.

Blauvelt, Bill. Photo on page 369. Reprinted by permission.

Carlin, Emily. "Owen, the Stray Cat." Reprinted by permission.

Carson, Ben, M.D., with Cecil Murphey. "Do It Better!" Taken from *Think Big* by Dr. Benjamin Carson; Cecil Murphey. Copyright © 1992 by Benjamin Carson, M.D. Used by permission of Zondervan. **www.Zondervan.com.**

Clark, Ron. "Eye Contact." From *The Essential 55* by Ron Clark. Copyright © 2003 Ron Clark. Reprinted by permission of Hyperion. All Rights Reserved.

DeBlasio, Fran. "Read All About It." From *People Weekly*, © 1986 by *Time*, Inc.

Grandinetti, Deborah. "Wired for Touch." Reprinted by permission.

Johns Hopkins Children's Center. Photo of Dr. Ben Carson on page 409. Reprinted by permission.

Johnson, Beth. "Body Language" and photos on page 6 and 440. Reprinted by permission.

Langan, Paul. "One Reader's Story." Reprinted by permission.

Mack, Marilyn. "Adult Children at Home." Reprinted by permission.

Mrosla, Sister Helen P. "All the Good Things." Originally published in *Proteus*, Spring 1991. Reprinted by permission as edited and published by *Reader's Digest*.

O'Keeney, Brian. "How To Make It in College, Now That You're Here." Reprinted by permission.

Papalia, Diane E., and Sally Wendkos Olds. "Childhood Stress and Resilience." From *A Child's World*, 6th ed. Copyright © 1993 by McGraw-Hill, Inc. Reprinted by permission of The McGraw-Hill Companies.

Peck, M. Scott. "Responsibility." Reprinted with the permission of Simon & Schuster, Inc., from *The Road Less Traveled*, by M. Scott Peck, M.D. Copyright © 1978 M. Scott Peck.

Ruiz, Regina. "Lighting a Match." Reprinted by permission.

Stark, Rodney. "Group Pressure." From *Sociology*, 3rd ed. Copyright © 1989 Wadsworth, a part of Cengage Learning, Inc. Reproduced by permission. **www.cengage.com/permissions**

Sutton, Jean. "A Path to Marriage." Originally published as "Jean Sutton Speaks" in *Sister to Sister: Black Women Speak to Young Black Women*, ed. by Beth Johnson. Copyright © 2010 by Townsend Press, Inc. Reprinted by permission of the author.

Taylor, Hal. Cover and illustrations on pages 3, 58, 97, 115, 137, 156, 174, 191, 204, 221, 222, 245, 261, 289, 336, 355, 374, 432, 450, 459, 467, 204, 477, 485, 498, 506, and 518. Reproduced by permission.

Verderber, Rudolph F. "Dealing with Feelings." From *Communicate!*, 6th ed. Copyright © 1990 Wadsworth, a part of Cengage Learning, Inc. Reproduced by permission. **www.cengage.com/permissions**

Wightman, Dan. "Winners, Losers, or Just Kids?" Originally published in *Los Angeles Times*, July 25, 1979. Reprinted with permission of the author.

Wilson, Chuck. "Disaster and Friendship." Reprinted by permission.

Wilson, Craig. "In Fall, a Young Man's Fancy Turns to His Teacher." Copyright © September 23, 1997, *USA Today*. Reprinted by permission.

Winkler, Robert, and Pam Winkler. "False Ideas about Reading." Reprinted by permission.

Index